PORTRAITS OF WOMEN IN INTERNATIONAL LAW

Portraits of Women in International Law

New Names and Forgotten Faces?

Edited by
IMMI TALLGREN

OXFORD
UNIVERSITY PRESS

OXFORD
UNIVERSITY PRESS

Great Clarendon Street, Oxford, OX2 6DP,
United Kingdom

Oxford University Press is a department of the University of Oxford.
It furthers the University's objective of excellence in research, scholarship,
and education by publishing worldwide. Oxford is a registered trade mark of
Oxford University Press in the UK and in certain other countries

First Edition published in 2023

Published in the United States of America by Oxford University Press
198 Madison Avenue, New York, NY 10016, United States of America

British Library Cataloguing in Publication Data
Data available

Library of Congress Control Number: 2023934681

ISBN 978–0–19–886846–0 (pbk.)
ISBN 978–0–19–886845–3 (hbk.)

DOI: 10.1093/oso/9780198868453.001.0001

Printed and bound by
CPI Group (UK) Ltd, Croydon, CR0 4YY

To the memory of Karen Knop (1960–2022)
and all unknown daughters of international law

Foreword
Looking at Portraits

*Karen Knop**

Decades ago, feminist art historians could confidently write: 'It is no longer necessary to assert that there have been women artists.'[1] In international law—where 'the teachings of the most highly qualified publicists of the various nations' are a means of determining the law itself[2]—the same cannot be said. Feminism arrived later and began with a different question. 'Why has gender not been an issue in this discipline?' Hilary Charlesworth, Christine Chinkin, and Shelley Wright asked in a revolutionary article in 1991.[3] A wealth of feminist approaches to international law followed but left relatively untouched the 'where are the women?' question that had been a wedge in the door in the humanities. This volume changes that in compellingly rich and varied fashion.

However, *Portraits of Women in International Law: New Names and Forgotten Faces?* confronts the challenge of adding faces of women across the history of international law and recognizing their contributions at a time when even the most revelatory of portrait galleries, such as this one, is simultaneously desired and suspect.[4] On the one hand, universities, like other spaces, are increasingly recognized as 'occupied', in Sara Ahmed's term: 'This occupation leaves traces on walls; portraits of past leaders can surround you ... [U]se leaves traces in places'.[5] *Portraits of Women in International Law* thus brings much-awaited change to the mental, and potentially physical, hallways of international law. Its forty-two portraits begin as early as the fourteenth century and span the globe. In them, gender intersects with race, colonialism, class, sexuality,

* This Foreword has benefitted from discussions in the contributors' workshops for this volume and from comments by Sarah Riley Case, Christopher Gevers, Fleur Johns, and Martti Koskenniemi. I also acknowledge with gratitude the support of the Helsinki Collegium for Advanced Studies, where I worked on the Foreword while in residence as the 2020–21 Jane and Aatos Erkko Visiting Professor in Studies on Contemporary Society.

1 Rozsika Parker and Griselda Pollock, *Old Mistresses: Women, Art and Ideology* (rev edn, IB Tauris 2013) (1981) xxix.

2 International Court of Justice Statute, art 38(1)(d).

3 Hilary Charlesworth, Christine Chinkin, and Shelley Wright, 'Feminist Approaches to International Law' (1991) 85 AJIL 613, 614.

4 See Griselda Pollock, *Differencing the Canon: Feminist Desire and the Writing of Art's Histories* (Routledge 1999) 8.

5 Sara Ahmed, *What's the Use?* (Duke University Press 2019) 165. As I write, a statue of Egerton Ryerson has been toppled at the university named for him in Toronto, the city where I live. Rosa Saba, 'Protesters Behead Toppled Statue of Edgerton Ryerson Following Rally Honouring Residential School Victims' *Toronto Star* (6 June 2021) <https://www.thestar.com/news/gta/2021/06/06/statue-of-egerton-ryerson-toppled-at-university-after-rally-for-residential-school-victims.html> accessed 17 July 2021.

and other forms of difference. The subjects are groups as well as individuals, material as well as ideational contributions to international law, forgotten names as well as familiar faces (in the title's phrase). On the other hand, the idea of a canon as a collection of revered masters or valued texts has become suspect. Whereas some feminists argue that the problem with the literary canon is that it is unrepresentative of female tradition, for others the problem is that a canon exists at all: a female canon would be no less oppressive because it would necessarily represent only a particular socio-demographic group of women. 'Canon building is empire building. Canon defense is national defense', wrote the novelist Toni Morrison bluntly.[6] And, in international law, Gerry Simpson wrote: 'Monuments, as we know, do not simply fail to remember: they actively "un-remember" that which is not commemorated.'[7] Can the canon be rehabilitated by recognizing the contributions of 'old mistresses' as well as masters (as feminist art historians archly put it) or is the idea itself unsalvageable?[8]

In international law, there has been little focus on the notion of a canon.[9] The category of 'woman' as a subject has been problematized extensively, as have approaches to the history of international law. There have also been important initiatives to expand the canon, particularly by recognizing thinkers from the global South. As an idea, however, the canon in international law has not been intensely debated as it has been in the humanities. Nonetheless, the lines of how the debate might run are visible in a recent exchange between Henri de Waele and Janne Nijman. In an article titled 'A New League of Extraordinary Gentlemen? The Professionalization of International Law Scholarship in the Netherlands, 1919–1940', de Waele sets out to remedy the absence of the Dutch international law tradition in histories of this period.[10] Although he refers to 'learned gentlemen'[11] and his title alludes to a 2003 film featuring well-known male fictional characters as Victorian-era superheroes, de Waele does not pursue the significance of the maleness or masculinity of the Dutch international lawyers he discusses.[12] In response, Nijman argues that expanding or correcting international law historiography should also correct the neglect of women and colonialism in these accounts.[13] Her piece models how to go about finding women's contributions to Dutch inter-war international law scholarship by employing a broader understanding

[6] Toni Morrison, 'Unspeakable Things Unspoken: The Afro-American Presence in American Literature' (1990) 11 Tanner Lecture on Human Values 123, 132.

[7] Gerry Simpson, 'Unprecedents' in Immi Tallgren and Thomas Skouteris (eds), *The New Histories of International Criminal Law: Retrials* (OUP 2019) 12, 24.

[8] Parker and Pollock (n 1). See also, eg, Jan Gorak, *The Making of the Modern Canon: Genesis and Crisis of a Literary Idea* (Athlone 1991).

[9] Paolo Amorosa, *Rewriting the History of the Law of Nations: How James Brown Scott Made Francisco de Vitoria the Founder of International Law* (OUP 2019) 9. But see Paulo Amorosa and Claire Vergerio, 'Historicizing the Canon in International Law and International Relations' Leiden Journal of International Law (forthcoming 2022).

[10] Henri de Waele, 'A New League of Extraordinary Gentlemen? The Professionalization of International Law Scholarship in the Netherlands, 1919–1940' (2020) 31 EJIL 1005.

[11] ibid 1015, 1022.

[12] cf Benjamin Allen Coates, *Legalist Empire: International Law and American Foreign Relations in the Early Twentieth Century* (OUP 2016) 60, 62–63, 74 (relevance of Victorian-era codes of masculinity in the history of United States international legal thought).

[13] Janne E Nijman, 'Marked Absences: Locating Gender and Race in International Legal Histories' (2020) 31 EJIL 1025.

Figure 0.1 Oil painting 'Vitoria' detail in stairway of Great Hall, Department of Justice, Washington, D.C. United States, 2007. October. Photograph. https://www.loc.gov/item/2010720245/.

Source: Photograph in the Carol M. Highsmith Archive, Library of Congress, Prints and Photographs Division.

of the process of professionalization and by bringing what she terms 'imagination' to research and use of sources. She also explores the obstacles, legal and other, that point to why there were no women among Dutch international law professors between the wars.[14]

Nijman uses an analogy with art history to focus her disagreement with de Waele on the canon, and his reply can be read as typical of canon debates.[15] Transposed to women in international law, the sequence of attitudes that Morrison identifies as defending the canon against incursions would be: (1) there were no women international lawyers, following which the arguments would be (2) there were, but they were inferior, (3) there were and they were superior when they measured up according to the existing 'universal' standards of professional excellence, or (4) their contribution was not so much 'international law' as raw material to be processed by international lawyers.[16] Whereas work on women in the history of international law to date has not been organized around these debates, *Portraits of Women in International Law* equips international lawyers for an assault on the canon. That said, it does not prescribe it. Indeed, some might even oppose such a deployment. Musing on the aptness of the pun 'canon fodder', Morrison is reminded of 'a kind of trained muscular response that appears to be on display in some areas of the recent canon debate' and the feeding of 'readily available people/texts of little value' into the argument machine.[17]

My plan in this Foreword is to take up not a set of questions about candidates for inclusion, but the problem of active 'un-remembering', in Simpson's phrase. Specifically, I will show how the volume's organizing imagery, perhaps despite first appearances, can be understood as addressing this problem of exclusion. The impression that I pursue is as follows. At first glance, its tropes of the portrait and the portrait gallery might appear old-fashioned—think 'portrait of a lady'—or worse than quaint, oblivious. The portrait gallery metaphor seems to play into canon building as nation building, the imperial pleasure in collecting, European high culture with postcards. What makes these two tropes daringly, rather than simply, old-fashioned, I will suggest, is that *Portraits of Women in International Law* takes them literally. Literalization can turn both into critical tools. In addition, although I only gesture to them here, literalization enables connections to be drawn with a number of approaches to history that have recently made an appearance in international law, including an interest in the visual, new materialist thinking, life-writing, and theories of the archive.

By literalization, I mean first that 'portrait' in *Portraits of Women in International Law* refers not only to the biographical nature of the texts. Actual portraits matter. Contributors were asked to choose a painting or photograph representing their subject and invited to think beyond the sort of professional headshots found in the frontispieces of the Hague Academy of International Law's series of collected courses, for example (although that format here could be a considered choice). Some contributors

[14] ibid 1033–34. On the role of imagination in researching the forgotten in history, see, eg, Ashley D Farmer, 'In Search of the Black Women's History Archive' (2018) 1 Modern American History 289.

[15] Nijman (n 13) 1026; Henri de Waele, 'Betwixt and Between: What We Write About When We Write About International Legal History' (EJIL: Talk! 12 February 2021) <https://www.ejiltalk.org/betwixt-and-between-what-we-write-about-when-we-write-about-international-law-history/> accessed 17 July 2021.

[16] Morrison (n 6) 129–30. See also Pollock (n 4) 23–29.

[17] Morrison (n 6) 123.

even discuss the image they selected, using it as an object of contemplation, a keyhole onto their subject or a clue. In Part II, I extend this method. Starting with an actual portrait of a famous male international lawyer without any women at all, I show how this portrait can generate a series of critical perspectives on the making of the international law canon and illuminate the role of women, including in that very portrait.

Literalization also refers to the metaphor of the portrait gallery. Editor Immi Tallgren uses 'portrait gallery' as more than a synonym for a collection of biographical essays. She conceives of the book as if an actual building were being renovated: for example, she names its parts as if they were new wings of an existing institution such as the National Portrait Gallery in London.[18] As with the portrait, this metaphor may seem dated if not Eurocentric. There is almost an air of the Grand Tour: the eighteenth- and nineteenth-century coming-of-age trip undertaken typically by upper-class young Western men and women to acquire cultural polish by viewing antiquities and art at Europe's great galleries. To the contrary, I suggest in Part III how the literalization of the portrait gallery metaphor can be interpreted as parodic, a critical commentary on the canon and its vulgarization in institutional spaces, and also as pointing to the inevitable absences of women and ways to engage them.

Finding Doris Stevens

A concern with adding 'new names and forgotten faces' to the international law canon is that the diversification of the canon alone will leave its 'already sacred texts' uninterrogated. In literary studies, therefore, another focus has been to find the ghost in the machine: the ways in which the presence of the forgotten 'has shaped the choices, the language, the structure—the meaning' of so much canonical work.[19] Toni Morrison makes this argument as regards the African-American presence in American literature, and it also finds some reflection in *Portraits of Women in International Law*. In this part, I illustrate how the volume's integration of actual portraits can become a way of finding the ghost in the machine.

Portrait as Image and Object

In the Department of Justice Building in Washington, DC, built in 1934, the famous sixteenth-century Spanish international lawyer Francisco de Vitoria is depicted as one of the 'Great Codifiers of the Law' in a mural of eighteen larger-than-life panels in the Ceremonial Entrance. The other panels show Sir Edward Coke, the Magna Carta, Sir William Blackstone, John Marshall, the Constitution, James Kent, Aemilius Papinianus, Solon, Justinian I, Thomas Aquinas, Oliver Wendell Holmes, Hugo

[18] cf Karen Knop and Susan Marks, 'The War Against Cliché: Dispatches from the International Legal Front' in Christine Chinkin and Freya Baetens (eds), *Sovereignty, Statehood and State Responsibility: Essays in Honour of James Crawford* (Cambridge University Press 2015) 3, 13–17 (on literalization in international law scholarship).

[19] Morrison, 'Unspeakable Things Unspoken' (n 6) 135–36.

Grotius, Jesus, Socrates, Menes, Moses, Hammurabi—and the even more famous international lawyer, seventeenth-century Dutch Protestant Hugo Grotius, often dubbed the 'father of international law'.[20]

Similar to the portrait-lined hallways that have come under scrutiny in university faculties or the hallway's virtual counterpart—the 'about' or 'history' tab on a professional organization's home page that links to pictures of important figures in its past[21]—the Great Codifiers mural reminds us that the history of the profession is also visual. Indeed, international legal scholars are becoming interested in the representation of their discipline in art and architecture and, conversely, in their discipline's own recruitment of imagery for purposes such as book covers.[22] These developments chime with a turn in international law towards how knowledge is materially produced, focusing, for example, on the role of an 'archive' and, recently, international law's 'objects'.[23] How do we know what, or whom, we know? In the case of the Great Codifiers of the Law, a first answer is that the painter, Boardman Robinson, was advised by the United States Supreme Court Justice Harlan Fiske Stone and Harvard Law School Dean Roscoe Pound.[24]

Portrait and the Canon as Project

We can take the story of the Vitoria portrait further. Robinson slyly modelled a farm servant in the Magna Carta panel on himself, while for the likeness of Vitoria, he used a sketch of James Brown Scott, a United States international lawyer, translator of Vitoria's works and Secretary of the Carnegie Endowment for International Peace.[25]

The story as told by Scott's protégé George Finch is that Scott was unable to find a likeness of Vitoria for the artist and therefore became a substitute. For Finch, this tribute was 'Poetic Justice'.[26] Scott, a widely influential figure in his day, campaigned

[20] 'The Robert F. Kennedy Building: Celebrating Art and Architecture on the 75th Anniversary' (US Department of Justice, undated) <https://www.justice.gov/file/1431931/download> accessed 4 July 2021, 71.

[21] See, eg, 'History' tab (*Institute of International Law*) <https://www.idi-iil.org/en/> accessed 4 July 2021; 'Galerie des Internationalistes Francophones' (*Société française pour le droit international*) <https://www.sfdi.org/galerie_internationalistes/ > accessed 4 July 2021.

[22] See, eg, Symposium on Art, Aesthetics and International Justice (2020) 114 AJIL Unbound 103; Jean d'Aspremont and Eric De Brabandere, 'Paintings of International Law' in Jessie Hohmann and Daniel Joyce (eds), *International Law's Objects* (OUP 2019) 330; Hilary Charlesworth, 'The Travels of Human Rights: The UNESCO Human Rights Exhibition 1950–53' (Essex Public International Law Lecture 15 March 2021) <https://www.youtube.com/watch?v=EppodE7akCU> accessed 4 July 2021; Daniel Litwin, 'Stained Glass Windows, the Great Hall of Justice of the Peace Palace' in Jessie Hohmann and Daniel Joyce (eds), *International Law's Objects* (OUP 2019) 463; Kate Miles, 'Painting International Law as Universal: Imperialism and the Co-opting of Art and Image' (2020) 8 London Review of International Law 367.

[23] See, eg, Madelaine Chiam, Luis Eslava, Genevieve Renard Painter, Rose Sydney Parfitt, Charlotte Peevers, 'History, Anthropology and the Archive of International Law' (2017) 5(1) London Review of International Law (symposium); Hohmann and Joyce (n 22); Daniel R Quiroga-Villamarín, 'Domains of Objects, Rituals of Truth: Mapping Intersections between International Legal History and the New Materialisms' (2020) 8 International Politics Reviews 129.

[24] 'The Robert F. Kennedy Building' (n 20) 71.

[25] ibid.

[26] George A Finch, 'James Brown Scott, 1866–1943' (1944) 38 AJIL 183, 199. The discussion of this portrait draws on Karen Knop, Review of Paolo Amorosa, *The American Project and the Politics of History: James Brown Scott and the Origins of International Law* (2015) 25 Finnish Yearbook of International Law 257.

to change the conventional story of the origins of international law so that it began not with Grotius, but earlier, with Vitoria.[27] As Antony Anghie has powerfully demonstrated, the identity of the first international law figure matters greatly to the discipline's historical self-understanding. Beginning with Grotius locates its origins in Europe whereas starting with Vitoria makes its origins in colonization inescapable.[28]

Scott's project to make Vitoria and the later Spanish scholastic Francisco Suárez part of the canon of international law was so successfully absorbed into the discipline that most international lawyers have no idea that it was ever anyone's project—even as Vitoria is hotly debated as a critic of the Spanish conquests in America or an apologist for them.[29] Yet any international lawyer who has taken a volume of the *Carnegie Classics of International Law* off a library shelf has unknowingly laid hands on Scott's canon, which he popularized through this series of English translations funded by the Carnegie Endowment for International Peace.

Building on Anghie, Anne Orford reinterprets Finch's vignette of the Scott-as-Vitoria portrait to emphasize the material production of historical knowledge. Scott's position as the Endowment's Secretary and Director of its Division of International Law from its establishment by United States industrialist Andrew Carnegie in 1910 until Scott's retirement in 1940 made him 'arguably the best-funded international lawyer the world had ever seen'.[30] In addition to the *Classics of International Law*, the professionalization (and ready record) of international law that we inherit from this period is largely of Scott's making, including the founding of the American Society of International Law and its *American Journal of International Law*, the American Institute of International Law, and the Hague Academy of International Law. For Orford,

> Vitoria who was reclaimed for twentieth century international law arrived between the covers of a book emblazoned with the name of one of the richest industrialists of the nineteenth century, in a series edited by one of the most influential American international lawyers and moralists of the early twentieth.[31]

Portrait as Style of Argument

To what present uses can an addition to the canon be put? Here the story of the Scott-as-Vitoria portrait takes another turn and arrives at the 'where are the women?' question. The explanation for what might seem like the artist's wink to Scott or Scott's own act of vanity actually lies in one of the purposes to which Scott put Vitoria, namely,

27 Amorosa, *Rewriting the History of the Law of Nations* (n 9).

28 Antony Anghie, *Imperialism, Sovereignty and the Making of International Law* (Cambridge University Press 2005).

29 See, eg, Andrew Fitzmaurice, 'The Problem of Eurocentrism in the Thought of Francisco de Vitoria' in José María Beneyto and Justo Corti Varela (eds), *At the Origins of Modernity: Francisco de Vitoria and the Discovery of International Law* (Springer 2017) 77.

30 Paolo Amorosa, *The American Project and the Politics of History: James Brown Scott and the Origins of International Law* (doctoral dissertation, University of Helsinki 2018) <http://urn.fi/URN:ISBN:978-951-51-4133-0> accessed 17 July 2021, 40.

31 Anne Orford, 'The Past as Law or History? The Relevance of Imperialism for Modern International Law' IILJ Working Paper 2012/2 (June 2012) <http://ssrn.com/abstract=2090434> accessed 4 July 2021, 17.

women's equality. The official account is that it was Justice Stone and Dean Pound who advised Boardman on the list of Great Codifiers of the Law. However, recent research on Scott by Paolo Amorosa uncovers that it was Doris Stevens, a mutual friend, who proposed the addition of Vitoria to the mural in the first place (as well as Scott as a fitting stand-in).[32] Stevens and another prominent United States feminist activist Alice Paul sought to achieve two inter-American treaties on women's equality. As encapsulated in this rather improbable 1932 telegram from Scott to Spain's permanent delegate to the League of Nations, the place that Scott had carved out for Vitoria in the history of international law was central to Scott's strategy in support: 'I URGE YOUR SUPPORT ... ALICE PAUL'S RESOLUTION ... WE HOPE SPANISH LEADERSHIP HUMAN RELATIONSHIPS IN ACCORDANCE VITORIA'S PROGRESSIVE LAW NATIONS'.[33]

Portraits of Women in International Law is self-conscious about the idea that portraying a figure in the past can also be a style of argument in the present or a way of writing about oneself. The latter is reminiscent of the relational thinking that openly characterizes some feminist biography and history,[34] while the former recalls the notion of 'life-writing' that Susan Marks and Andrew Lang have used to interpret historical scholarship in international law. Adopting a literary explanation of life-writing as including a 'deliberate blurring of the distinction between biography and autobiography', Marks and Lang characterize Martti Koskenniemi's work in intellectual history as life-writing because, they argue, it performs as well as advances his critique of international law.[35]

Accordingly, we might ask what adding Vitoria to the Great Codifiers of Law mural meant for Doris Stevens? A glimpse can be seen in the first United States meeting of the all-male *Institut de droit international* in 1929, in which Scott included Stevens as the Secretary of Sessions. During the meeting, Stevens used a Columbus Day banquet to toast a woman, Isabella of Castile, as the ruler who had sent Christopher Columbus west and therefore without whom Vitoria would not have founded the modern law of nations.[36] Stevens thus tried to leverage Vitoria to argue for women's political leadership in keeping with the equal-rights feminism of her time.

Equality and Inequality

This brings us to the end of the story of the Scott-as-Vitoria portrait as already told. While approaching the portrait as an image uncovered, Scott, treating it as an object being produced revealed Stevens as its *sine qua non*. Indeed, Stevens is a striking example of women being invested in the male canon for their own purposes. Adding

[32] Amorosa, *Rewriting the History of the Law of Nations* (n 9) 306–08.
[33] ibid 297 (emphasis in original).
[34] See, eg, Blanche Wiesen Cook, 'Biographer and Subject: A Critical Connection' in Carol Ascher, Louise DeSalvo, and Sara Ruddick (eds), *Between Women: Biographers, Novelists, Critics, Teachers and Artists Write About Their Work* (Beacon Press 1984) 397.
[35] Andrew Lang and Susan Marks, 'People with Projects: Writing the Lives of International Lawyers' (2013) 27 Temple International & Comparative Law Journal 437, 439.
[36] Amorosa, *Rewriting the History of the Law of Nations* (n 9) 288–90.

more men to the gallery of men in the Justice Building was a way to further women's equality—one, however, that also participated in un-remembering the inequality to which Vitoria contributed by justifying Spain's colonization of the Americas.

We can read Stevens's Columbus Day toast to Isabella similarly. Much as Scott was busy naturalizing a canon of international lawyers, a succession of different groups in different places for different reasons had transformed 12 October 1492—the date for which Columbus did not even make a separate log entry—into the day that he discovered the New World. In the United States, groups appropriating Columbus ranged from the Tammany Society (Columbian Order) of the late eighteenth century through Italian and Irish-American organizations (such as the Knights of Columbus) in the first half of the nineteenth century to the United States business interests behind the 1893 World Fair known as the World's Columbian Exposition of Chicago.[37] In the process, Michel-Rolph Trouillot argues, 'Columbus had to become whiter' and '[a]s Columbus became whiter he also contributed to the whitening of the people who claimed him as part of their past'.[38] Thus, in crediting Isabella for Vitoria through Columbus, Stevens again made use of portrayals of great men being actively promoted and again highlighted women's equality at the expense of the equality of peoples.

In *Portraits of Women in International Law*, we find Doris Stevens, in effect, called out on this sort of approach in the portrait of Uruguayan feminist activist Paulina Luisi.[39] In the early years of the Inter-American Commission of Women, when she was its leader, Stevens had even praised Cuban dictator Rafael Trujillo Machado as a 'feminist president'.[40] Citing the 1933 Montevideo Equal Rights Treaty as an example—one of the two treaties that Scott dubbed the 'Stevens treaties'[41]—Luisi argued that authoritarian states used Pan-American conferences to publicize ostentatiously their support for women's rights without ever implementing those treaties they had ratified and without ever incurring opprobrium for their hypocrisy. The Inter-American Commission of Women was 'especially unconcerned' about this situation and had even 'helped to legitimate many of the most reactionary and undemocratic states in the Americas', Luisi underscored in a public speech contrasting the state-led Pan-American conferences with her own grassroots conference.

The trail from Vitoria to Scott to Stevens to Luisi illustrates the potential of the portrait's literalization to cast a critical light on the making of the canon as well as to help answer the question 'where are the women?' It is not Vitoria who encountered Luisi, which would of course have been historically impossible. Rather, it is his portrait, traced as different projects in different male and female hands, that is confronted aggressively by her portrait. At the same time, Doris Stevens has no portrait of her own in this volume and appears only through the portraits of others, Luisi, as well as Vitoria. Shifting from portrait to portrait gallery, the next part of the Foreword takes up these themes of the relationship between portraits and their relationship with the un-portrayed.

[37] Michel-Rolph Trouillot, *Silencing the Past: Power and the Production of History* (Beacon Press 1995) 119–36, 140. I thank Christopher Gevers for this connection.
[38] ibid 133–34.
[39] Andrei Mamolea, 'The Role of International Law in Paulina Luisi's Activism' (ch 38, in this volume).
[40] ibid.
[41] Amorosa, *Rewriting the History of the Law of Nations* (n 9) 303.

In the Portrait Gallery

Different from literalizing the portrait, *Portraits of Women in International Law* also literalizes the metaphor of the book as a portrait gallery. Chapters are organized into such architectural wings as the Vestibule of the Legendary Ancients; the Hall of Woman for Social and Economic Development; the Winter Garden of Abolition and Resistance: Women Against Slavery, Racism, and Imperialism; and the Roof-Top Garden of Diplomacy and International Relations. In this part, I suggest that rather than being an unconscious exercise in European high culture, this literalization can be read in several ways as critical, constructive, or both.

In the first place, it can be read as a parody of a parody. As well as a reminder of the visual in the telling of the law's history, the 'Great Codifiers of the Law' mural (including Moses, the Magna Carta, and Oliver Wendall Holmes) is a reminder of the jumble that often represents tradition in institutional settings.[42] For example, Annelise Riles as a young professor at Northwestern School of Law in Chicago describes the unavoidable and baffling aesthetic legacy of its early twentieth-century dean, noted legal scholar John Wigmore, which she seeks to decipher methodologically:

> Cartoon-like coats of arms in the moldings display the names of the great legal scholars of Wigmore's day.... Like an idiosyncratic treasure box, the building is cluttered with a parade of oddities: lithographs from English periodicals that lampoon the courtroom, the barrister, or the judge; portraits of famous legal figures; facsimiles of the American Declaration of Independence and other assorted documents; even an eight-foot-tall copy of the stone bearing the Hammurabi Code.[43]

Portraits of Women in International Law does not pretend to add, in one go, all of the female figures missing from the history of international law. Parody is a way of implicitly acknowledging that impossibility while at the same time pointing out the ridiculous self-assurance of efforts such as the 'Great Codifiers' or Wigmore's treasure box.

A second way in which the architectural blueprint in *Portraits of Women in International Law* can be read as a critical device is via the resonance of building metaphors in feminist, postcolonial, and critical race studies. A feminist classic on the history of women writers, for instance, takes its title from the 'madwoman in the attic' in Charlotte Brontë's novel *Jane Eyre*, a tormented character whose Creole background Jean Rhys later imagines in her prequel *Wide Sargasso Sea*.[44] More to the point, Audre Lorde famously used a building metaphor to warn against merely adding differences among women to an existing frame of knowledge: 'the master's tools will never dismantle the master's house'.[45] It is perhaps a play on the master's house that

[42] I am grateful to Fleur Johns for pressing me further on this point.

[43] Annelise Riles, 'Wigmore's Treasure Box: Comparative Law in the Era of Information' (1999) 40 Harv ILJ 221, 258.

[44] Sandra M Gilbert and Susan Gubar, *The Madwoman in the Attic: Women Writers and the Nineteenth-Century Literary Imagination* (2nd edn, Yale University Press 2000).

[45] Audre Lorde, 'The Master's Tools Will Never Dismantle the Master's House' in Reina Lewis and Sara Mills (eds), *Feminist Postcolonial Theory: A Reader* (Edinburgh University Press 2003) 25, 26–27.

Portraits of Women in International Law adds women's portraits to the gallery's liminal spaces: lobby, indoor garden, roof, and so on. That is, the blueprint might work to remind us that the canon, like the portrait gallery, permits only so much renovation. Then again, Hortense Spillers uses the architectural image of the vestibule more transformatively.[46] For Spillers, 'vestibularity' refers to the shaping of 'black culture' in the United States by its enforced distance from, yet relation to, the dominant culture that profited from slavery and its afterlives. She argues that because of this vestibularity, black culture 'could, by virtue of the very act of discrimination, *become* culture, insofar as, historically speaking, it was forced to turn its resources of spirit toward negation and critique',[47] that is, towards alternatives that might bear both on its own 'projects of liberation' and on reimagining modernity and futurity.[48] This potential for a dynamic relationship between parts of a building brings me to my final reading of the literalized portrait gallery metaphor.

The preceding part of this Foreword engaged Toni Morrison's anti-empire-building search for ways 'to enhance canon readings without enshrining them'.[49] In closing, I want to come back to Gerry Simpson's observation in international law that monuments 'do not simply fail to remember: they actively "un-remember" that which is not commemorated'.[50] In contrast to monuments, exhibitions imply the un-exhibited. They signal their selectiveness and therefore also a residue: what is not selected. Starting in the mid-1990s, the word 'curate' began to be used beyond museums and galleries, becoming 'a fashionable code word among the aesthetically minded, who seem to paste it onto any activity that involves culling and selecting'.[51] Hotel libraries, parties, menus, news, even the future began to be described as 'curated'. 'Curated content' is now everywhere in digital media.

Thus, a third way to understand the literalness of the new exhibition wings in *Portraits of Women in International Law* critically is as implying the portrait gallery's storage areas—its backrooms or basement housing the permanent collection not on display—and, beyond the building, the altogether un-portrayed. In addition to the deliberateness of absence, this mental image can mark the constructive potential, in Aleida Assman's words, 'for mutual influx and reshuffling'. Assman argues that the selecting and collecting reflected in the gallery's exhibitions or 'canon' (active memory) exist against the accumulating associated with, and retrievable from, the storehouse or 'archive' (passive memory).[52] Metaphorically, *Portraits of Women in International Law* anticipates re-curation.

[46] See Hortense J Spillers, 'Mama's Baby, Papa's Maybe: An American Grammar Book' (1987) 17 Diacritics 64, 67, 74; Hortense J Spillers, 'The Idea of Black Culture' (2006) 6(3) New Centennial Review 7, 25; Louiza Odysseos, 'Stolen Life's Poetic Revolt' (2019) 47 Millennium: Journal of International Studies 341, 366–71.

[47] Spillers, 'The Idea of Black Culture' (n 46) 26.

[48] Odysseos, 'Stolen Life's Poetic Revolt' (n 46) 368.

[49] Morrison, 'Unspeakable Things Unspoken' (n 6) 128.

[50] Simpson, 'Unprecedents' (n 7) 24.

[51] Alex Williams, 'On the Tip of Creative Tongues' *New York Times* (2 October 2009) <https://www.nytimes.com/2009/10/04/fashion/04curate.html> accessed 17 July 2021; *Curating the Curators* <https://curatingthecurators.tumblr.com/> accessed 17 July 2021.

[52] Aleida Assman, 'Canon and Archive' in Astrid Erll and Ansgar Nünning (eds) with Sara B Young, *Cultural Memory Studies: An International and Interdisciplinary Handbook* (Walter de Gruyter 2008) 97, 99, 106.

Most radically, the image of the portrait gallery is generative because it can even open the door to what has been conceived of as an imaginary archive. The accumulation that fills the archive is also selective. Its gaps are not merely random or accidental, as is conspicuous from the case of colonial archives. The archive has therefore been described as a 'full-fledged historical actor'.[53] Many portraits in this collection, including that of Paulina Luisi, register the lives that were the object of their subjects' activism. The chapter on Luisi, for instance, describes her attraction to eugenics, which originated partly in her experience delivering children who were 'irretrievably condemned to a slow agonizing death' but which she strongly distanced from its use by Nazi Germany.[54] But it is often impossible to trace the lives affected by those portrayed in this volume. In the case of those engaged in social work, for example, records may be confidential or simply non-existent.[55]

Among historians of the forgotten, a search for missing sources is increasingly complemented by approaches to reading the gaps and faint traces of evidence speculatively[56] or, further still, creatively. To the subjective archive of the figure's own writings, the critical archive of writings about her, and the author's archive of theoretical presumptions and practices can be added an 'imaginative archive', an archive that 'seeks to tell the unsayable and imagine what cannot be retrieved'.[57] 'Speculative' histories have emerged particularly in postcolonial theory and fiction and feminism.[58] Known for her method of 'critical fabulation',[59] Saidiya Hartman, for example, 'elaborates, augments, transposes, and breaks open archival documents'.[60] The power of *Portraits of Women in International Law* is thus both in the brilliance of the volume's portraits and in the openings created by its use of the portrait and portrait gallery as organizing ideas.

[53] Antoinette Burton, 'Introduction: Archive Fever, Archive Stories' in Antoinette Burton (ed), *Archive Stories: Facts, Fictions and the Writing of History* (Duke University Press 2005) 1, 7.

[54] Luisi ch 38, in this volume.

[55] The classic reference is Gayatri Chakravorty Spivak, *Can the Subaltern Speak?: Reflections on the History of an Idea* (Columbia University Press 2010).

[56] In legal history, see eg, Christopher Tomlins, *In the Matter of Nat Turner: A Speculative History* (Princeton University Press 2020) xvi–xvii (equating 'speculative' with the need for 'conjecture and the imaginative use of the historian's tools').

[57] Clare Hemmings, *Considering Emma Goldman: Feminist Political Ambivalence and the Imaginative Archive* (Duke University Press 2018) 6–8, 33.

[58] ibid 33–35.

[59] Saidiya Hartman, 'Venus in Two Acts' (2008) 12(2) Small Axe: A Caribbean Journal of Criticism 1, 11–12.

[60] Saidiya Hartman, *Wayward Lives, Beautiful Experiments: Intimate Histories of Riotous Black Girls, Troublesome Women, and Queer Radicals* (Norton 2019) xiv.

Acknowledgements

The best party often takes place in the kitchen. People come and go, bottles are opened, salads washed, and the chatting is easy. Expectations of good time together bubble in the air, mixing with the scents from the oven. For this publication project, I had great plans for academic 'parties': conferences, encounters, exchanges here and there. The mood, however, changed brutally in early 2020. Universities, libraries, and archives got closed. Travelling became impossible. Meeting colleagues was told to be risky. Many of us saw our care obligations grow increasingly complex. The rapid turn to teleworking and distant teaching had to be managed. The illness reached us or our families. All the events I had planned had to be, one by one, cancelled.

If one had to find a fancy (customarily in international law: French) word to describe what COVID-19 meant for our 'methodology', it would be *débrouillardise*: astute resourcefulness and inventive self-efficacy in the lack of appropriate means, typically what women have had to be good at in modest households. This time, *débrouillardise* was not about mending clothes and reinventing recipes with fewer ingredients but about building up a collective project on six continents, addressing past figures and topics on which there was little or no primary research, and managing a broad and long project without the happy glue of future or past conferences, research visits, coffee breaks, and dinners together. For several of us, at various periods, *débrouillardise* also meant bare-handed distant working: we had to try to do decent research without proper access to archives, literature, previous files and with little opportunity to present early thoughts.

Excuse me, an impatient reader interrupts, *but who is this 'we', and this 'I'?* Thank you for a good question. The 'we' here refers to the diverse, global, multitalented group of fifty contributors to this publication project, the list of whom is available below. They were invited personally and introduced to the background, format and key interrogations of the project—the errors and failings remaining, however, the sole responsibility of its editor, the 'I' on these two pages of acknowledgements.

The 'I' in the chapter entitled 'Opening' that follows, in contrast, is not exactly the same subject. For writing out the 'I' can have diverse purposes. Authorship in various types of feminism has since long experimented with writing out the 'I'. At times for authenticity and intimacy, at others for more audacious dynamics of representation, such as searching a rupture with dominant tones and traditions. That 'I' here performs disquietudes of a sketched plural subject, 'women in international law', who search for signs of their own past, place, and value in the spaces and institutional cultures hegemonized by another sketched subject, 'men'.

The performance is polemical, at times extravagantly ironical, at others dramatic—and always without any claim for universality or coherence, of the 'we' in this publication or beyond. There are no universal plural subjects, no exclusive binary of 'women' and 'men', nor a universal theater of 'international law', as is amply discussed in what follows. There are no clear-cut generations, either. Women who became professionally active before the mid-1990s, when men only occupied the bench of the International Court of Justice, the International Law Commission and most other visible posts, may recognize the disquietudes more intimately than some other women seeking to enter international law professions today. Yet others, elsewhere, such as international human rights law experts in Afghanistan and Russia in the 2020s, have been brutally excluded from such temporal progress narratives.

Having entered the turbulence of COVID-19, we invented surrogate ways of socializing and collaborating. In an authors' workshop online, we presented drafts and commented each other's work, invited guests, collected and exchanged readings, discussed methodology, visioned images together and chatted, getting closer to each other from far. In 2020–21, we met fourteen times for sessions up to four hours. I am much indebted to all the portraitists for their commitment and generosity with their ideas and time. I am very grateful to our precious guests: Paulo Amorosa (Helsinki University), David Armitage (Harvard University), Matilda Arvidsson (University of Gothenburg), Karen Engle (University of Texas), Martti Koskenniemi (Helsinki University), Benjamin Lahusen (Humboldt University), Marja Lehto (Member of the ILC, MFA Finland), Samuel Moyn (Yale University), Liliana Obregon (Universidad de los Andes), Ilse Paakkinen (Felm and Helsinki University), Outi Penttilä (Helsinki University), Myriam Piguet (Université de Genève), and Gerry Simpson (London School of Economics).

There are so many others I would like to thank for their support, expertise, and helping hand in my challenging task of editing such a broad range of contributions. I can only mention a few names here. Hilary Charlesworth (International Court of Justice) is the rock on which this project builds. Her intellectual sensibility, feminist tact, and unfailing support are exemplary of academic mentorship—and friendship. Karen Knop (University of Toronto) was such an enthusiastic and joyful companion in research and in everyday life, sharing her sparkling wit and versatile knowledge without ever counting. While mourning her tragic absence when we finally will get to party in person, I know we will fondly reminisce the moments together in the author's workshop, grateful for so much. Anna van der Velde (Erik Castrén Institute) has been an astute contributor at several fronts, an unflappable support in matters big and small. As many other portraitists, Roxana Banu, Christopher Gevers, Alexandra Kemmerer, Frédéric Mégret, Parvathi Menon, Vasuki Nesiah, Sarah Nouwen, Anne Orford, Di Otto, Reut Yael Paz and Sergey Vasiliev encouraged and assisted me in innumerous ways. Fleur Johns (University of NSW) kindly took care of the proofs of Karen Knop's foreword. At diverse phases, Shanna Constantinescu, Katariina Flinck, Sonja Hukkanen, Eleni Ilia, and Benedetta Pigiani assisted the project diligently. Thank you!

This project has commonalities and shared interests with research in disciplines and contexts beyond international law. I owe to a great number scholars to whom I introduced the project early on and discussed epistemological and methodological questions, but I can only mention a few. I am grateful for the Leverhulme project on Women and the History of International Thought (Sussex University, Oxford University) by Patricia Owens, Katharina Rietzler, Kim Hutchings, Sarah Dunstan, and Jo Wood. Patricia has always been available for fruitful exchanges. Sarah and Jo invited me as a keynote to their seminar at the EISA Conference in Bucharest. Glenda Sluga (European University Institute) is a constant inspiration, thank you for the exchanges online and in Florence, where Sarah Nouwen kindly hosted me. Doreen Lustig (Tel Aviv University) invited me to the Law and History Workshop at Tel Aviv University, the participants of which made interesting comments. Finally, Anne-Charlotte Martineau (CNRS, Paris) and Franck Latty (Université Paris Nanterre) organized a wonderful seminar to address my project's key ideas in Nanterre: *merci encore!*

This publication is part of my research project *The End of International Law (As We Know it)?'Women' and the Construction of Another International Order* 2019–2023, funded by the KONE Foundation and hosted at the Erik Castrén Institute of International Law, University of Helsinki and the Centre for Women, Peace and Security, London School of Economics. I am grateful for everyone involved at KONE Foundation and all dear friends and colleagues at my institutional homes. I also wish to thank the staff of Oxford University Press and New Generation. Finally, warm food and chilled wine, loving care, and encouragement were abundant in several family kitchens in Finland and France. Dear seniors and juniors, my dearest chief cook, the furry therapists Kamu and Kelly—kiitos, *merci!*

Table of Contents

List of Figures

List of Abbreviations

AAPSO	Afro-Asian People's Solidarity Organization
ACWC	All Ceylon Women's Association
AIWC	All India Women's Conference
ASG	United Nations Assistant Secretary General
ATS	Auxiliary Territorial Service
BBNJ	Global Treaty on Marine Biodiversity in Areas Beyond National Jurisdiction
BME	British Methodist Episcopal
CBE	Commander of the Order of the British Empire
CEDAW	Committee on the Elimination of Discrimination Against Women
CERD	Committee on the Elimination of Racial Discrimination
CHM	common heritage of mankind (
CHR	Commission on Human Rights
CICC	Coalition for an International Criminal Court
CMG	Companion Order of St Michael and St George
CNFF	Conseil National des Femmes Françaises
CNR	*Conseil national de resistance française*
CSCE	Conference on Security and Cooperation in Europe
CSDHA	Centre for Social Development and Humanitarian Affairs
CWS	UN Commission on the Status of Women
DALTO	Department of Aid to the Less Technically Oriented
DEDAW	Declaration on the Elimination of Discrimination Against Women
ECE	UN Economic Commission for Europe
ECOSOC	United Nations Economic and Social Council
EEC	European Economic Community
FCO	UK Foreign & Commonwealth Office
FO	UK Foreign Office
FYROM	Former Yugoslav Republic of Macedonia
GMD	Guomindang also referred to as Kuomintang (KMT)
IACW	The Inter-American Commission of Women
ICC	International Criminal Court
ICJ	International Court of Justice
ICRC	International Committee of the Red Cross
ICTR	International Criminal Tribunal for Rwanda Tribunals
ICTY	International Criminal Tribunal for the Former Yugoslavia
ICW	International Council of Women
IDI	*Institut de droit international*
IIASL	International Institute of Air and Space Law
IISL	International Institute of Space Law
ILA	International Law Association
ILC	International Law Commission
ILO	International Labour Organization

IMTFE	*International Military Tribunal for the Far East*, also known as the Tokyo Tribunal
IOI	International Ocean Institute
IPPF	International Planned Parenthood Federation
ISS	International Social Service
ISSAB	International Social Service American Branch
IWCO	Independent World Commission for the Oceans
IWSA	International Alliance for Women's Suffrage
JD	law degree
JFH	Egypt chapter of the International Federation of Independent Revolutionary Art
JSIL	Japanese Society of International Law
KPD	Communist Party of Germany
k.u.K	*kaiserlich und königlich* (imperial state institutions from Austro-Hungarian Empire)
LLB	Bachelor of Laws
LLM	Master of Laws
LONSEA	League of Nations Search Engine'
MPIeR	Max Planck Institute for European Legal History in Frankfurt
NAACP	National Association for the Advancement of Colored People
NAM	Non-Aligned Movement
NATO	North Atlantic Treaty Organization
NGO	Non-governmental organization
NIEO	New International Economic Order
NKVD	People's Commissariat for Internal Affairs/Soviet secret police
ODA	Official Development Assistance (Japan)
POW	prisoner of war
PrIL	public and private international law
SFDI	*Société française pour le droit international*
SG	UN Secretary General
SPD	German Socialist Democratic Party
SWA	Stiftung Warburg Archiv/Warburg Archive Foundation
UDHR	Universal Declaration of Human Rights
UN	United Nations
UNAT	United Nations Administrative Tribunal
UNCIO	United Nations Conference on International Organization
UNCLOS	UN Convention on the Law of the Sea
UNCSW	UN Commission on the Status of Women
UNESCO	United Nations Educational, Scientific, and Cultural Organization
UNFPA	United Nations Family Planning/Population Fund
UNGA	General Assembly of the United Nations
UNRRA	United Nations Relief and Rehabilitation Administration
WAM	Women's Active Museum on War and Peace (Japan)
WCGJ	Women's Caucus for Gender Justice
WHO	World Health Organization
WID	Women in Development
WIDF	Women's International Democratic Federation
WILPF	Women's International League for Peace and Freedom
WPA	World Plan of Action

List of Contributors

Michael Addaney is a Lecturer at the Department of Planning and Sustainability of the University of Energy and Natural Resources, Sunyani, Ghana.

Benjamin Auberer (LMU Munich) is a global historian who studies the Secretariat of the League of Nations to investigate the social history of international relations.

Roxana Banu is a Lecturer in Private International Law at Queen Mary University of London Faculty of Law and researches on the history and theory of private international law with a particular focus on gender.

Antoine Buchet is a Legal Adviser to the European Commission who currently serves as the Chairman of the Board of Appeal of the European Chemicals Agency.

Sarah Riley Case is an incoming Assistant Professor at the McGill University Faculty of Law, where her research and teaching focus on colonialism, slavery and the law, critical race theory, Black life, Third World approaches to international law, arts, and the natural world.

Hilary Charlesworth is a Judge at the International Court of Justice.

Boyd van Dijk is a McKenzie Fellow at the Melbourne Law School.

Serena Forlati is Professor of International Law and Head of the Department of Law at the University of Ferrara, Italy.

Ana Caldeira Fouto is Auxiliar Professor at the Faculty of Law of Universidade de Lisboa, Legal History Department, with research interests in the history of legal thought and the history of international law.

Pedro Caridade de Freitas is Associate Professor at the Faculty of Law of Universidade de Lisboa, Legal History Department, with research interests in the history of international relations and history of public international law.

Christopher Gevers teaches international law and legal theory at the School of Law, University of KwaZulu-Natal.

Kate Grady is a Senior Lecturer in Law at SOAS, University of London.

Gina Heathcote is Professor of Gender Studies and International Law at SOAS, University of London.

António Pedro Barbas Homem is Full Professor at the Faculty of Law of Universidade de Lisboa, Legal History Department, with research interests in the history of legal thought, theory of law, and history of international relations.

Alexandra Kemmerer is a Senior Research Fellow and academic coordinator at the Max Planck Institute for Comparative Public Law and International Law, and head of the Institute's Berlin Office.

Jan Klabbers is Professor of International Law at the University of Helsinki.

Karen Knop was Professor of Law and Cecil A Wright Chair at the University of Toronto and a Max Planck Law Fellow.

Outi Korhonen is Professor of International Law at the University of Turku, Finland.

Margareth Kuo is Professor of History at the California State University, Long Beach. She writes about gender and law in Chinese history.

Anne Lagerwall is Professor at the Center of International Law, Université libre de Bruxelles.

Franck Latty is Professor at Université Paris Nanterre, a Member and former Director of the Centre de Droit International de Nanterre (CEDIN), and President of the French Branch of the International Law Association.

Raimo Lintonen is a retired former researcher at the Department of Political Science, University of Helsinki, Department of Strategic Studies of the National Defence University, and the Finnish Institute of International Affairs (FIIA).

Miriam Bak Mackenna is Associate Professor of Law, Roskilde University, Department of Social Science and Business. She researches law, gender, and political economy, and more generally, the relationship between international law and social (in)justice.

Andrei Mamolea is an Assistant Professor at Boston University's Pardee School of Global Studies.

Frédéric Mégret is a Full Professor, Dawson Scholar, and co-Director of the Centre for Human Rights and Legal Pluralism at the Faculty of Law, McGill University.

Parvathi Menon is a researcher at the Erik Castrén Institute of International Law and Human Rights and an adjunct lecturer at the University of Helsinki.

Shinya Murase is Professor Emeritus of Sophia University, Tokyo, and Member of the UN International Law Commission.

Henk Nellen is guest researcher of the Huygens Institute for the History of the Netherlands (Amsterdam).

Vasuki Nesiah is Professor of Human Rights and International Law at the Gallatin School at NYU.

Janne E Nijman is Professor of History and Theory of International Law, University of Amsterdam, and Professor of International Law, the Graduate Institute of International and Development Studies, Geneva. Nijman is also chairperson of the executive board and Academic Director of the TMC Asser Instituut, The Hague.

Sarah Nouwen is a Chair and Professor of Public International Law at the European University Institute, on leave from the University of Cambridge where she is a Professor of International Law and Fellow of Pembroke College.**Anne Orford** is Melbourne Laureate Professor and Michael D Kirby Chair of International Law at Melbourne Law School.

Dianne Otto is Professorial Fellow at Melbourne Law School and her research examines the role that gender, sexuality, and race hierarchies play in international law.

Marilena Papadaki is a postdoctoral researcher at the University of Athens and Research Fellow at the Kalliopi Koufa Foundation for the Promotion of International and Human Rights' Law.

Reut Yael Paz is a Visiting Fellow at Queens College, Cambridge and senior researcher who specializes in international law, EU law, international relations, and legal history at the Justus Liebig University of Giessen, Germany.

Luiza Leão Soares Pereira is a Lecturer in International Law at the University of Sheffield and PhD Candidate at the University of Cambridge.

Imogen Saunders is Associate Professor at the Australian National University College of Law, where she researches and teaches public international law.

Bérénice K Schramm is Assistant Professor of Law at Bahçeşehir University (BAU), Director of the BAU Gender Law Clinic, and co-Director of the OLYMPE research network on Francophone Feminist Approaches to International Law.

Sara Seck is an Associate Professor and Yogis and Keddy Chair in Human Rights Law with the Schulich School of Law and Marine & Environmental Law Institute at Dalhousie University, Halifax, Canada.

Ksenia Shestakova is Associate Professor of International Law and Academic Director of the Public International Law Masters' Programme at Saint Petersburg University, Russia.

Hatsue Shinohara is Professor at the Graduate School of Asia-Pacific Studies, Waseda University.**Mai Taha** is an Assistant Professor of Human Rights at the Department of Sociology, London School of Economics.**Immi Tallgren** is a Research Fellow at the Erik Castrén Institute of International Law, Adjunct Professor at the University of Helsinki, and a Visiting Fellow at the Centre for Women, Peace and Security, London School of Economics.

Sergey Vasiliev is an Associate Professor of Criminal Law at the University of Amsterdam.

Anna van der Velde is a former project planner at the Erik Castrén Institute of International Law who works at the Finnish Ministry for Foreign Affairs.

Agatha Verdebout is a Researcher at the *Groupe de Recherche et d'Information sur la Paix et la Sécurité* (GRIP) in Brussels.

Christiaan Verwer is a retired civil servant specializing in transport and mining law.

Wouter Werner is Professor of International Law at the Vrije Universiteit Amsterdam as well as the University of Curacao.

Deborah Whitehall is a Visiting Scholar at the Institute for International Law and the Humanities, University of Melbourne.

Dr **Keina Yoshida** is a human rights barrister, associate member of Doughty Street Chambers, visiting fellow at the Center for Women, Peace and Security, and currently legal adviser at the Center for Reproductive Rights.

PART I
OPENING THE EXHIBITION

1
Re-curating the Portrait Gallery of International Law
The Objectives, Process, and Floorplan of the Exhibition

*Immi Tallgren**

Possessing the Past?

'Faces are facts', declared an English visitor to St Peter's Basilica in the Vatican in 1925, 'the countenances of the princes, prelates, priests, and monks of the Church. For these faces do not change. There is not one... that one has not seen before, in this picture or that'.[1] This volume tells a story to the contrary. The collection of portraits you are holding—or eyeing on a screen—present countenances that few have seen before. Most do not automatically evoke a thematic context, a well-known event, or a temporality. Some faces have lost the connection to an identity, a name, such as 'the unnamed woman back row, left' in the group photograph of the League of Nations Legal Secretariat.[2]

The idea for this project did not see the light in Rome, the centre of the Catholic Church eminent in the histories of international law, but rather in London, one of the key imperial centres. Visiting the National Portrait Gallery in early 2019, I was pacing past the endless gilded frames and the precious figures in hats and gowns, many of them truly exquisite artworks, revered examples of this Western originated genre of cultural production. Strolling ahead, the gendered, raced, and classed patterning of societal roles and hierarchies in Britain and the British Empire were not hard to decipher on the walls. Suddenly a different kind of gallery of portraits appeared—as if flashed before my eyes—of a history of international law as a profession and a social practice, an intellectual orientation, and a political endeavour, lined up as a huge collection exhibiting the human habitus behind the ideas, norms, institutions, and the familiar chains of great events in international law.

I saw the intellectuals and professionals of the international law textbooks and academic journals appearing as figures in frames, spread over the walls of a labyrinth

* I am grateful to Anna van der Velde for her unwavering support and assistance. I thank Hilary Charlesworth, Christopher Gevers, Alexandra Kemmerer, Karen Knop, Martti Koskenniemi, Susan Marks, Parvathi Menon, and Patricia Owens for discussing with me earlier versions of the manuscript, and Eleni Ilia and Katariina Flinck for research assistance. My research project *The End of International Law (As We Know it)?'Women' and the Construction of Another International Order* 2019–2023 is funded by the KONE Foundation and hosted by the Faculty of Law, University of Helsinki and the Centre for Women, Peace and Security, London School of Economics.

[1] Edward Verrall Lucas, *A Wanderer in Rome* (George H Doran 1926) 40.

[2] Benjamin Auberer, 'Female Staff in the Legal Section of the League of Nations', Ch. 23 in this volume.

Immi Tallgren, *Re-curating the Portrait Gallery of International Law* In: *Portraits of Women in International Law.*
Edited by: Immi Tallgren, Oxford University Press. © Immi Tallgren 2023. DOI: 10.1093/oso/9780198868453.003.0001

Figure 1.1 Floorplan—the making-of.
Source: Immi Tallgren.

of corridors and halls, with squeaking oak floors. In one painting, I recognized the scholastics solemnly gathered in a long aula; and in another, a ballroom filled with tens of portraits of Hugo Grotius—oil on canvas, carvings, and etchings on medals.[3] The famous 'men of 1873' were gathered in the *Salle d'Arsenal* in Ghent,[4] not far from the imperial experts in white linen busy administering their colonial subjects.[5] Further on the left, hope was gleaming from the eyes of a crowd gathered in Geneva in the 1920s, busy codifying international norms.[6] Hope had turned to anxiety in late 1930s, as Hersch Lauterpacht was sitting in deep thoughts in his Cambridge study, staring at portraits of Hugo Grotius, Hans Kelsen, and Arnold McNair on the wall.[7] The frames kept spinning around, in the back of my mind, as the famous judges, negotiators, and scholars searched for a spot to hang in the countless rooms, halls, corridors, on stuffed floors of the protruding wings. After a few crashes and scratches, they got neatly

[3] Hugo Grotius' portraits were numerous, and frequently copied and reproduced. See Eltjo Aldegondus van Beresteyn, *Iconographie van Hugo Grotius* (Martinus Nijhoff 1929); Anita Jansen, *De portretfabriek van Michiel van Mierevelt* (Wbooks 2011).

[4] See Martti Koskenniemi, *The Gentle Civilizer of Nations: The Rise and Fall of International Law 1870–1960* (Cambridge University Press 2001) 48, hereafter Koskenniemi, *The Gentle*.

[5] For a notable example, see Frederick Lugard, *The Dual Mandate in British Tropical Africa* (Routledge 1926).

[6] See, eg, Haakon A Ikonomou and Karen Gram-Skjoldager (eds), *The League of Nations: Perspective from the Present* (Aarhus University Press 2019).

[7] Martti Koskenniemi, 'Lauterpacht: the Victorian Tradition in International Law' (1997) 8 EJIL 215–63, 217–18.

lined up as noble families, schools, and congregations, from the demanding great-grandfather to the youngest prodigy.

Why should any images, faces, or names of the intellectuals and professionals of international law matter? Because international law is not just any kind of law, as its current histories teach their readers. International law consists of ideas aiming at a universality by definition but built by and on 'the international lawyer', the identity through which its histories are narrated. A leading author of international law, Martti Koskenniemi writes how international law is not just 'a set of ideas … nor of practices, but a sensibility' that 'also involves broader aspects of the political faith, image of self and society, as well as the structural constraints within which international law professionals live and work'.[8] International law 'invites everyone to participate in the imagining of humankind's collective telos';[9] and it offers a 'set of rules, institutions, and practices through which the forms of collective life are constantly imagined, debated, criticised, and reformed, over and again'.[10] In short, international law at its best is imagined as gathering all humans together to care for humanity, led by the international lawyer as the mediating figure.

From a socio-historical point of view, nevertheless, international law may come across as a narrow, privileged, and interest-bound set of 'images of self and society'.[11] The tradition of the polyvalent academic-practitioner-expert that until recently dominated in Europe, in particular, has sent mixed messages of the 'public' role of the mediating figures, international lawyers, pious in scholarship but available for purchase to serve any causes. Not to forget the critical international law scholars' unmasking of the indeterminate nature of international legal structures through attention to actors, power, and assemblages, desacralizing international lawyers as 'people with projects'. What people, what projects? Andrew Lang and Susan Marks underline the continuity of the assumptions, intellectual inspirations, and dispositions through which the professional sensibilities of international lawyers surface, get entrenched, transmitted, and propagated. This brings international lawyers 'face to face' with the processes through which they are themselves 'enrolled in, and shaped by, the collectively produced disciplinary structures (they) inhabit'.[12]

Students of international law may not enrol to study 'history'. Yet they enter an academic discipline and a social, professional field rich with tales of past moral struggles, births, failures, and rebirths where hope is suspended at constant trials of faith. In these curricula, the 'founders' emanate from intellectual genealogies of political philosophy, religious pacifism, and the early practices of diplomacy. Historical time advancing, the growth in complexity of human societies, transnational commerce and migrations accelerate international law's evolution. Carried by pioneers and savants, progressing in encounters with political sciences, sociology, and international relations… this is the

[8] Koskenniemi, *The Gentle* (n 4) 2.

[9] Martti Koskenniemi, 'Law, Teleology and International Relations: An Essay in Counterdisciplinarity' (2011) 26 International Relations 3–34, 25.

[10] Martti Koskenniemi, 'What Use of Sovereignty Today?' (2010) 1 Asian Journal of International Law 61–70, 69.

[11] Koskenniemi, *The Gentle* (n 4) 8.

[12] Andrew Lang and Susan Marks, 'People with Projects: Writing the Lives of International Lawyers' (2013) 27 Temple International and Comparative Law Journal 437–53.

familiar path that histories, here primarily referring to intellectual and professional histories authored by insiders of international law, also referred to in what follows as 'disciplinary history', take to bring international law and its agents to present times.

The process by which 'the history of international law' is, in the stereotyped self-understanding of international lawyers, 'cyclically handed to incoming generations of international lawyers for them to become intellectually socialised within the tradition of the field' gets trusted with diverse objectives, such as setting 'the ground for them to continue contributing to the development of the contemporary dimensions of the international legal order in the future of the theory and practice of the discipline'.[13] In the packages handed on, the norm-creating events, codification efforts and births of institutions are typically organized thematically and chronologically. The genesis of ideas and doctrines, in contrast, often takes the form of lineages, transmissions, and legacies of individual invention and authorship. Even if biological ancestry remains rare, the inheritance of international law's intellectual, political, social, cultural, and financial capital tend to descend in a dynastic manner.[14]

In any genealogical narratives of family lineage, progeny and property typically interact with gendered constellations of power, interpreted and entrenched in visual representations, most times in portraiture. Familiar aesthetics of affiliation and reminiscence crystallize the ideas of a shared consciousness, a community, its origins and telos, a desire to belong. Students visiting international law's family estates, the most prestigious being the Peace Palace hosting the International Court of Justice, may ask themselves, 'at the intersection of the self and history': 'Where does (my) biography end and history begin? How do (my) own memories and experiences relate to what is written in history books?'[15] Some students may welcome the familiarity. The precious frames contain faces not dissimilar from their own and the portraits decorating their home universities, artworks acquired by previous generations with funds collected by pupils and peers of the portrayed, the descendants 'humbled and honoured' in a process of extolling their mutual professional value, community, and profession.

Other students struggle to recognize themselves among the ancestors. It is not that their textbook histories would not describe a universal passage of the torch of international law through peace and war, time and space, without specific mentions of sex and gender, racial and ethnic identities, religions, class, sexual orientation, or (dis)ability. In these matters, 'silence and evasion have historically ruled' also the discourse of international law.[16] That lack of precision may appear to embrace universality and equality, ideals growing from the seeds planted by the family elders as international human rights. At closer inspection, nevertheless, the student visioning the family tree of international law may find it as curiously lopsided—'unisexual' and pale. The most prominent histories envelop their readers in a Sunday atmosphere of pleasant antiquarian bookstores

[13] Ignacio de la Rasilla, *International Law and History* (Cambridge University Press 2021) 7.

[14] Pierre Bourdieu, 'The Forms of Capital' in John Richardson (ed), *Handbook of Theory and Research for the Sociology of Education* (Greenwood 1986).

[15] Linda Nochlin, *Representing Women* (Thames & Hudson 1999) 33.

[16] Toni Morrison, *Playing in the Dark: Whiteness and the Literary Tradition* (Harvard University Press 1992) 9. On colour-blindness as the default mode in international legal scholarship, see James Thuo Gathii, 'Studying Race in International Law Scholarship using a Social Science Approach' (2021) 22 Chicago Journal of International Law 71.

or wealthy dwellings. They display an archetype of an intellectual-professional-expert, the 'international lawyer', the habitus and consciousness of whom equals in most cases that of the socio-political elite, not dissimilar from the illustrious fathers.

The image of 'international lawyers' as individuals, sensible and sensitive human persons is thus essential to the positive self-understanding inside the profession, to qualify as thinking, choosing, moral agents—in contrast to parts of a 'managerial' machine, with no ethics or politics of the collective good. At the same time, that image has remained strikingly male, white, and elitist. It is that curious still-life of international law that this volume reacts to, in the 2020s, where students are made to study histories of international law where academics, legal experts, diplomats, judges, administrators, intellectuals, politicians, notables, journalists, factory owners—in short anyone with any intellectual, political, or economic agency—are assigned as 'men' and 'white'. The life-world 'international law' is understood here in the broadest of terms, as an intellectual tradition and social practice, a professional and ideological vocation, an academic discipline and a field of political struggles, where a large number of heterogeneous agents adhere and operate today but nevertheless sustain curiously homogenous and reductive collective images of 'their' history.

The focus here is on how images of the history of international law are gendered, ie both affected by and maintaining the cultural meanings associated with perceived sexual and gendered differences, until recently understood as binary (in the West) and the diverse ways in which the differences are held as a basis for social, political, cultural, and economic inequalities.[17] The exhibition underlines both how complex and intersecting such inequalities and their histories are and how repressed they still remain in international law.[18] Intersections are striking between gender, wealth, and social class, for example, as both economic resources and education are crucial elements for an existence as an agent of knowledge production in international law.[19] Racialized and ethnic identities have determined such an existence in ways international law histories are only beginning to grasp.[20] To quote Anna Julia Cooper's address to the World Congress of Representative Women in 1893: while 'white woman could at least plead for her own emancipation; the black women, *doubly enslaved*, could not but suffer and struggle and be silent'.[21]

This opening chapter introduces the experimental setting of the new exhibition in the *Portrait Gallery of International Law*. It analyses how international law histories

[17] There is no lack of literature on gender and international law, to start with the ground-breaking work by Hilary Charlesworth and Christine Chinkin, such as, *The Boundaries of International Law* (Manchester University Press 2000), hereafter Charlesworth and Chinkin, *Boundaries*. See Dianne Otto, 'Feminist Approaches to International Law', in Anne Orford and Florian Hoffmann (eds) with Martin Clarke, *Oxford Handbook of the Theory of International Law* (OUP 2016).

[18] See Saidiya Hartman, calling for 'attending to the articulation of various modes of power, without simply resorting to additive models of domination or interlocking oppressions that analytically maintain the distinctiveness and separation of these modes and their effects, as if they were isolated elements that could be easily enumerated', *Scenes of Subjection* (OUP 1997), 118–19.

[19] See Andrea Bianchi, 'Knowledge Production in International Law: Forces and Processess' in International Law's Invisible Frames, ed. by Andrea Bianchi and Moshe Hirsh (Oxford University Press, 2021) 155.

[20] See UCLA Law Review Symposium, 'Transnational Legal Discourse on Race and Empire' (2021) 67 UCLA Law Review.

[21] See Christopher Gevers, 'Anna Julia Cooper: A Voice from the (Global) South', Ch. 8, in this volume.

have addressed 'women' and their contributions and introduces women's, feminist, and gendered histories and their emergence in international law. It addresses portraiture both as visual culture—the power of image to manage perceptions, to organize politics, and to (re)produce stereotypes and hierarchies—and as an element of discourse in the field of historiographical, biographical, and literary creation and representation. It describes, furthermore, the volume's 'making of' and tentatively situates that process as an authorship of history. It provides a floorplan of the exhibition, detailing the rooms, the portraits and the portraitists. It concludes by looking into the future, for avenues of understanding the past and present without obscuring power relations and naturalizing social hierarchies.

The Portrait Gallery of International Law

Portrait galleries, those prestigious edifices with an air of imperial or nationalistic nostalgia, are only the tip of the iceberg. Everyday international law resides in numerous spatial arrangements and social processes where individual accomplishments and ideas face repetitive processes of recognition or oblivion. Physical, symbolic, diverse, spaces and visual memorabilia play a role in representing imaginaries of power, constructing hierarchies, and assuring their transmission. The material processes of affecting the consciousness of an intellectual and professional community and its ways of recognizing merit are, for sure, not restricted to exhibiting objects in institutional spaces. Universities, philanthropic foundations, professional associations, courts, diverse institutional and governmental entities express their ownership and preferences also in many other, often more discrete ways. Social events are venues where ritualistic affiliation and reminiscence are practised, from celebrations of prizes or honoris causa degrees, Festschrifts, to keynotes and seating arrangements at conference dinners. Affiliation at its simplest, but perhaps at its most effective takes place in peer review evaluations of expertise, curriculums, and footnotes—at times connoting adherence to an explicit idea, at others as if an implicit flagging of esteem.[22]

The Portrait Gallery of International Law is introduced here to serve as a metaphor for international law's collective self-portrait with ancestors. The Gallery exhibits *Geschichtsbilder*, images of history, not oil colours on canvas but images in the immaterial sense of understandings, collective rather than individual, of a thematic context or a temporality in the past and its significance in the present. The impressions of the past and its meanings for today affect the ways in which an individual or a collective relates to their past, as well as their present and future, identifying themselves and forming an opinion of their roles, responsibilities, or entitlements. Images of history possess persuasive power, experienced as intuitive and ahistorical. In social sciences, they are understood to emerge and evolve in multi-layered processes of representation

[22] See Liane Boer, '"The Greater Part of Jurisconsults": On Consensus Claims and Their Footnotes in Legal Scholarship' (2016) 28 Leiden Journal of International Law 1021; Hilary Charlesworth, 'Talking to Ourselves? Feminist Scholarship in International Law,' in Sari Kouvo and Zoe Pearson (eds), *Feminist Perspectives on Contemporary International Law: Between Resistance and Compliance?* (Hart 2014).

and interpretation, not only by remembering and reminiscing, but also by forgetting and obscuring.

Images of history appear fixed but are in a continuous flux, as new interpretations take form, on sediments of past images. In that sense, images of history reflect not the past but the present, contemporary *mélanges* of cultural products and exchanges, in education, media, professional historiography, and popular histories. Of particular importance for the current volume is the difference between remembering and reminiscing in those processes of consciousness: in ruthlessly simplified terms here, a person remembers what she happens to remember but reminisces about what she wishes to be reminisced.[23] In contrast to memory, reminiscence therefore also correlates with the offer and demand in temporal and spatial contexts: whose lives, accomplishments, and events continue to matter, are worth reminiscing and why, by whom, and when? Which histories are to be silenced?[24]

Since I started studying law, I have been puzzled by the representation of legal scholars at my alma mater, the Faculty of Law at the University of Helsinki, created in 1640. In the Nordic modernist building of 1957, portraits in their heavy frames fill the walls of the corridors of the law faculty, its lecture halls, and the faculty board meeting room. From the office I occupy in the *Erik Castrén Institute of International Law and Human Rights*, it is impossible to reach the coffee machine or the elevators without those silent faces, including Erik Castrén, professor of international law, staring at passers-by. Some faces are stern and sulky, others with an expression more inclined towards accepting a woman's presence. The frames are engraved with names that sound Scandinavian (the older portraits, in particular) or Finnish in the case of more recent portraits. The skin of the portrayed is brushed in white, grey, or beige tones. One tiny bronze head with female features sits on a window ledge in the faculty room.[25] Professor Inkeri Anttila, the first and only woman reminisced, is looking out of the window into the lively crowd of students, as if searching for peers.

The spatial arrangements of many other law faculties or institutions with diverse staff, students, and constituencies, prominently display the 'dominant gendered visual order in law'.[26] Nikki Golden-Rasul writes how men are typically represented 'in positions of power and authority, with formal poses and attire', conveying the message that they are 'best positioned' to represent and uphold the values of their profession and university.[27] The rare portraits of women are less traditional and formal in style. Few

[23] Remembering is considered primarily an individual cognitive process, whereas reminiscing is a collective, social, and cultural phenomenon, a controversial component of history in its popular, public, and academic forms. The relationships between individual and collective memory, reminiscence, history, and historiography have been widely researched. See, eg, Maurice Halbwachs, *Les cadres sociaux de la mémoire* (Librairie Félix Alcan 1925); Paul Ricoeur, *Temps et recit* (Le Seuil 1983); Jacques Le Goff, *Histoire et mémoire* (Gallimard 1988); Pierre Nora, *Les lieux mémoire* (Gallimard 1992); Dominic LaCapra, *History in Transit. Experience, Identity, Critical Theory* (Cornell University Press 2004).

[24] See, eg, Michel-Rolph Trouillot, *Silencing the Past: Power and the Production of History* (2nd edn, Beacon Press 2015).

[25] See Harriet Silius, 'Inkeri Anttila, the First Woman Law Professor in Finland (1916–2013)' in Ulrike Schultz, Gisela Shaw, and Rosemary Auchmuty (eds), *Gender and Careers in the Legal Academy* (Hart 2021).

[26] Nikki Godden-Rasul, 'Portraits of Women in the Law: Re-envisioning Gender, Law and the Legal Profession in Law Schools' (2019) 39 Legal Studies 415.

[27] ibid.

faculties, mainly in the UK and Northern America, have paid attention to increasing 'public knowledge of women who have been influential in law'.[28]

Leisurely pacing along the corridors of galleries or law faculties in Europe seems a classed and antiquated manner of appreciating power and hierarchy or projecting fame and recognition. The life-worlds and deeds that matter in international law, to its intellectuals and professionals, are told to situate elsewhere today, on the notorious 'fields of pain and death'. In contrast to being some unitary and stable body of norms, agents, institutions, and practices, international law today exists and evolves in the most varied and conflictual contexts, international, global, local, national, and regional.[29] Portrait galleries, however, have also travelled, exiting palaces with an air of imperial nostalgia to reside in public parks and university campuses, tagged on buses or corridors of dormitories. The cultural practices of exhibiting representations to communicate values, power, and hierarchy continue to exist and excite public controversies, as *Rhodes Must Fall* and *Black Lives Matter* movements illustrate.[30] Earlier, the end of the Cold War set in motion a violent de-sacralization of past idols and the previous politics of memory.[31] Today's transitional justice initiatives finance the erection of memorials and museums, in revisionist history-writing projects chaperoned by international criminal courts.[32]

With the digitalization of media, portraits are in a fast process of turning from physical objects to pixels that circulate at a higher speed, drawing the lines between inclusion and exclusion, remembrance and obscurity. As digital media travels light and cheaply, foregrounding visual rather than textual transmission of ideas, the new 'portraits' reach a more global audience and diverse sociological contexts. Despite the fragmentation of the socio-economic frames of identification, faces and names remain 'facts'[33] and represent value: turning to signs, symbols, if not trademarks, they serve as tools in orientating ideas, fame, and the flows of various types of capital. Today almost every book launch, colloquium, or keynote of international law is broadcasted and archived online with images. Academic publications are marketed less at exposition tables of academic conferences and campus bookstores than in social media. Events in

[28] ibid. See also, eg, Rosemary Auchmuty and Erika Rackley 'The Women's Legal Landmarks Project: Celebrating 100 Years of Women in the Law in the UK and Ireland' (2016) 16 Legal Information Management 30; Leslie J Moran, 'Judicial Bodies as Sexual Bodies: A Tale of Two Portraits' (2008) 29 Australian Feminist Law Journal 91.

[29] See Anthea Roberts, *Is International Law International?* (OUP 2017); Onuma Yasuaki, 'When Was the Law of International Society Born? —An Inquiry of the History of International Law an Intercivilization Perspective' (2000) 2 Journal of the History of International Law 1; Lauri Mälksoo, 'International Law between Universality and Regional Fragmentation: The Historical Case of Russia' in Alexander Orakelashvili (ed), *Research Handbook on the Theory and History of International Law* (Edward Elgar 2011).

[30] The desire and practice of contestation by destroying memorabilia are not new: ancient Greeks mutilated monuments, Egyptians used to carve out the noses and eyes of statutes, and Romans used the complementary punishment of *damnatio memoriae* to erase the memory of public figures fallen from grace. Alex Zhang, 'Damnatio Memoriae and Black Lives Matter' (2020) 73 Stanford Law Review 77.

[31] Memorabilia from the Soviet Union and Eastern Europe is today exhibited as abandoned monuments, see, eg, in Spandau, Berlin <https://www.zitadelle-berlin.de/en/museums/unveiled/> accessed 31 October 2022.

[32] See, eg, Maria Elander, 'Education and Photography at Tuol Sleng Genocide Museum' in Peter Rush and Olivera Simic (eds), *The Arts of Transitional Justice* (Springer 2014).

[33] Lucas (n 1).

the institutional core, such as rendering a decision at the International Criminal Court in The Hague, have become a photo opportunity, also for international lawyers.[34]

The Missing Images

As the media coverage from 'the international law capital of the world' brings to view, a major transition is taking place in international law. Individuals with a different habitus have surfaced and increasingly act as capable of knowledge production in international law. A century after the League of Nations Statute stated that '(a)ll positions under or in connection with the League, including the Secretariat, shall be open equally to men and women',[35] women are no longer explicitly excluded from any field or role in international institutions. In most countries, they are no longer prohibited from studying law, entering the bar, teaching and researching law, being elected as judges, or entering diplomatic services.[36]

The transition did not start uniformly across thematic contexts and professional roles. Just as in national contexts, much earlier than in international law in most cases, women entered law in gendered themes and sectors of activity. Criminal accountability for sexual and gendered violence in armed conflicts and the legal rights of those victimized were women's most consensual and visible entry points into the international legal imagination.[37] Those norms and institutional roles were advanced by gendered identifications, biological or social, of women trained in international or national law expected to excel in 'women's causes', representing victims subjected to harm by men.[38] Thirty years later, women are increasingly accessing positions of

[34] See the special issue Barbora Hola and Olivera Simic, 'ICTY Celebrities: War Criminals Coming Home' (2008) 28 International Criminal Justice Review 285.

[35] League of Nations, *The Covenant of the League of Nations* (28 April 1919), art 7. See Aoife O'Donoghue, 'Article 7 of the Covenant of the League of Nations, 1919', Erika Rackley and Rosemary Auchmuty (eds), *Women's Legal Landmarks—Celebrating the History of Women and Law in the UK and Ireland* (Bloomsbury Publishing 2018) 125); Carol Ann Miller, *Lobbying the League: Women's International Organizations and the League of Nations* (DPhil, Oxford University 1992); Myriam Piguet, 'Gender Distribution in the League of Nations: The Start of a Revolution?' in Gram-Skjoldager and Ikonomou (eds), (n 6) 60.

[36] For personal accounts of the change, see, eg, Navanethem Pillay, 'Equal Justice for Women: A Personal Journey' (2008) 50 Arizona Law Review 657; Liesbeth Lijnzaad, 'The Smurfette Principle: Reflections about Gender and the Nomination of Women to the International Bench' in Freya Baetens (ed), *Identity and Diversity on the International Bench* (OUP 2020); Patricia Wald, 'Six Not-So-Easy Pieces: One Woman's Journey to the Bench and Beyond' (2005) 36 University of Toledo Law Review 979; Sue Boyd, *Not Always Diplomatic: An Australian Woman's Journey Through International Affairs* (UWA Press 2021).

[37] See, eg, Nienke Grossman, 'Achieving Sex-Representative International Court Benches' (2016) 110 AJIL 82; Kimi Lynn King and Megan Greening, 'Gender Justice or Just Gender? The Role of Gender in Sexual Assault Decisions at the International Criminal Tribunal for Former Yugoslavia' (2007) 88 Social Science Quarterly 1049; Kimi Lynn King, James D Meernik, and Eliza G Kelly, 'Deborah's Voice: The Role of Women in Sexual Assault Cases at the International Criminal Tribunal for the Former Yugoslavia' (2007) 98 Social Science Quarterly 548.

[38] For discussion and critique, see, eg, Janet Halley, 'Rape in Rome: Feminist Interventions in the Criminalization of Sex-Related Violence in Positive International Criminal Law' (2008) 30 Michigan Journal of International Law 1; Kiran Kaur Grewal, 'International Criminal Law as a Site for Enhancing Women's Rights? Challenges, Possibilities, Strategies' (2015) 23 Feminist Legal Studies 149; Doris Buss, 'Performing Legal Order: Some Feminist Thoughts on International Criminal Law' (2011) 11 International Criminal Law Review 409; Heidi Matthews, 'Redeeming Rape: Berlin 1945 and the Making of Modern International Criminal Law' in Immi Tallgren and Thomas Skouteris (eds), *The New Histories*

professional and intellectual authority more broadly, excelling in diverse subfields of international law.[39]

Where do today's 'women in international law' come from, whom did they follow, and why? Where to find answers? The indexes of the most-read history books have male names only, just as the footnotes of prominent textbooks reflect primarily scholarship by men. Was agency by women really that non-existent in international law's past? Or has it been rendered invisible amidst the wealth of inherited images continuously reminisced and the gendered appreciation of the limits of horizon? Was the discrimination merely a consequence of the general socio-economic context or could one identify particular continuities of agency and policy of discrimination—and ruptures? How did the discriminatory institutional structures and processes in international law compare to other intellectual disciplines and professional fields? How, where, and why did changes in the intellectual and professional community (start to) take place?

Little of this is known. Research on 'the history of international law' focuses either on telling 'the ma(i)nstream narrative' or retelling it from a critical perspective, deepening or reproducing analyses of the often-times same intellectual and professional identities. Research on what is called the 'margins', ie 'women and non-Europeans',[40] lacks in intellectual investment and resources, perhaps audiences, too. There is no palpable corpus of pertinent research to represent 'competing visions of the international lawyer and the institutional and social arenas in which he or she operates'.[41] This gendered blind spot, a lacuna of research, its breadth, causes, and consequences are not considered inside the scope of international law history, as such,[42] but further qualified—kept apart—as women's, feminist, gender, or 'socio-legal' history. As a result, women and their eventual agency remain marked by their gendered deviance. No matter how integrated, conforming, and thriving in intellectual and professional arenas, 'women in international law' emerge from the shadows of the monumental male genesis. They are typically represented as if they just now 'entered history', without ownership of the intellectual estate of international law. In images of history, 'women in international law' are born to unknown parents, lacking a pedigree, whereas their colleagues are protected under the wings of their 'fathers and grandfathers in the profession'.[43]

of International Criminal Law (OUP 2019); Karen Engle, *The Grip of Sexual Violence in Conflict: Feminist Interventions in International Law* (Stanford University Press 2020).

39 See, eg, Hilary Charlesworth, 'L'IDI dans le monde d'aujourd'hui', *Livre du Sesquicentenaire de l'Institut de Droit International 1873–2023* (forthcoming).

40 Koskenniemi, *The Gentle* (n 4) 9.

41 Doreen Lustig, 'Governance Histories of International Law' in Markus D Dubber and Christopher Tomlins (eds), *The Oxford Handbook of Legal History* (OUP 2018) 860.

42 See Bardo Fassbender and Anne Peters (eds), *The Oxford Handbook of the History of International Law* (OUP 2012) 11; Alexander Orakelashvili (ed), *Research Handbook on the Theory and History of International Law* (Edward Elgar Publishing 2011); Valentina Vadi, 'International Law and its Histories: Methodological Risks and Opportunities' (2017) 58 Harvard International Law Journal 311; Ingo J Hueck, 'The Discipline of the History of International Law: New Trends and Methods on the History of International Law' (2001) 3 Journal of the History of International Law; Anthony Carty, 'Anthology of the History of International Law' in *Oxford Bibliographies in International Law*, <www.oxfordbibliographies.com/ page/international-law> accessed 8 June 2022, hereafter *Oxford Bibliographies*.

43 Koskenniemi, *The Gentle* (n 4) 5. Koskenniemi does not 'exclude the possibility—indeed, the likelihood—that in the margins [. . .] there have been women and non-Europeans whose stories would

This volume questions such broad, non-historicized categories of 'women and non-Europeans' and the absoluteness of their marginalization. In doing so, it is inspired by diverse social sciences where the forms of knowledge and social identities authored and authorized have been re-thought and reconsidered in the past thirty years, resulting in moves beyond clear-cut narratives indulging reductive interpretations. Various dislocations of identity and selfhood of the colonizers and the colonized, for example, are currently maintained to have taken place early on, in diverse works in post-colonial studies, anthropology, and global history. Explorations of fractured subjectivities are starting to capture disjuncture, blending, and assimilations between those 'white men' and the othered, no longer featured as powerless and voiceless victims only. The exhibition that follows makes such granularities visible via portraits of 'women in international law'.

The past cannot be changed, but the questions asked in its research can evolve, affecting the understandings of the past. To take the example of the *Royal Museum for Africa* in Tervuren, the (in)famous monument for Leopold II's colonial exploitation. In the former Colonial Palace were exhibited 'naturalised animals, geographic samples, commodities, Congolese ethnographic and artistic objects and art objects'.[44] The museum completed a full revision of its purpose in 2020. To borrow the language of art curators and museum professionals, this volume would like to launch a 're-curation' of the Portrait Gallery of International Law. The experiment rests on the intuition that products today understood as 'intellectual history' of international law and biographies of 'international lawyers' are closely related to each other, and furthermore, both of them are intertwined with the exercise of portraying through the centrality of the act of interpretation they entail. As Marcia Pointon writes, 'paintings of people, and, in particular, portraits of individuals known to have lived in the past, appear to invite us to understand them as visual biographies'.[45] They share 'the symbolic function of representation and the structural relationship between objects and their environments, between artefacts and their precursors, and between usage and aspiration'.[46] In what follows, the concept and vocabulary of the portrait (an object, typically a framed image), the portrayed individual (sitter), and the portraitist (artist) are, however, used not only in the concrete sense—of canvases, poses in an attic atelier, the artist with a beret—but in a broader and more abstract sense, referring to written portraits and, in a metaphorical sense, to 'the act of portraying' as the act of representing for view or attention an individual, or a group, or a profession in a particular context.

desperately require telling so as to provide a more complete image of the profession's political heritage', ibid 9.

[44] <www.africamuseum.be/en/discover/history> accessed 10 November 2020. In the park of the museum was exposed an 'African village', serving as 'home to Congolese individuals during the day'—seven died during their time in the village. On the re-curation, see Hilary Charlesworth, *Art and Law*, Lectures of The Hague Academy, General Course, (forthcoming); Christophe Boltanski, King Kasaï (Stock, 2023).

[45] Marcia Pointon, *Hanging the Head: Portraiture and Social Formation in Eighteenth-Century England* (Yale University Press 1993) 5, hereafter Pointon, *Hanging the Head*.

[46] ibid 141.

Who Is 'That Name'?

'Women in international law', in the title, may raise eyebrows in the 2020s. Rightly so, for the intention is to call for attention: the exhibition is a manifesto, albeit belated. Attention to sex and gender used to be absent from intellectual, professional, and institutional histories not only in international law but on any field of activity beyond household work or midwifery. In most fields or disciplines, however, a transformation and re-writing has taken place since the 1970s.[47] Decades after the post-structuralist questionings of identity, agency, power, and the situatedness of knowledge, flagging the 'women question' with regard to how international law's past(s) are imagined may therefore seem outdated.

This exhibition argues, however, that the waves of critical questioning and eventual revision did not reach international law histories yet. At least they have left curiously few traces. The avant-garde in women's, feminist, and gender history has moved ahead from the mere rehabilitation of agents invisible in 'the traditionally received historical analyses that excluded women',[48] intrigued by questions no longer positioned solely in the male coordinates which constituted the standards of 'reality'.[49] International law's collective images of history remain, in contrast, steadily anchored in those coordinates.[50] Exclusions and discriminations for sex and gender, and their structural embeddedness in and by both international law and its histories, are hidden or analysed with remarkable parsimony and delay even compared to histories of European law and institutions or international relations, hardly forerunners in the matter.[51]

The status quo did not crumble by the 1990s 'turn to history', nor by the subsequent moves to focus on global, transnational, imperial, or micro-history.[52] Post-colonial

[47] ibid 9. Laurel Thatcher Ulrich, *Well-Behaved Women Seldom Make History* (Vintage Books 2007); Bonnie G Smith (ed), *The Oxford Encyclopaedia of Women in World History* (OUP 2008). Kathleen Canning, *Gender History in Practice: Historical Perspectives on Bodies, Class and Citizenship* (Cornell University Press 2006). See also, Denise Riley, *'Am I That Name?' Feminism and the Category of Woman in History* (Macmillan Press 1988).

[48] See Gerda Lerner, 'Placing Women in History: Definitions and Challenges' (1975) 3 Feminist Studies 5; Mary Kay Thompson Tetrault, 'Rethinking Women, Gender, and the Social Studies' (1987) 51 Social Education 170.

[49] See, eg, Amia Srinivasan, 'Genealogy, Epistemology and Worldmaking' (2019) 119 Proceedings of the Aristotelian Society 127.

[50] See, eg, Gina Heathcote, *Feminist Dialogues on International Law: Successes, Tensions, Futures* (OUP 2019) 37; Aoife O'Donoghue, 'The Admixture of Feminine Weakness and Susceptibility: Gendered Personifications of the State in International Law' (2018) 19 Melbourne Journal of International Law 227.

[51] See Rosemary Foot, 'Where Are the Women? The Gender Dimension in the Study of International Relations' (1990) 14 Diplomatic History 615; Glenda Sluga and Carolyn James (eds), *Women, Diplomacy and International Politics Since 1500* (Routledge 2016), hereafter Sluga and James, *Women*; Karen Garner, *Women and Gender in International History: Theory and Practice* (Bloomsbury Academic 2018). For the recent changes, see Patricia Owens, 'Women and the History of International Thought' (2018) 63 International Studies Quarterly, hereafter Owens, *Women and History*; Patricia Owens and Katharina Rietzler (eds), *Women's International Thought: A New History* (Cambridge University Press 2021), hereafter Owens and Rietzler, *Women's International Thought*; Sarah Dunstan, Kimberly Hutchings, Patricia Owens, and Katharina Rietzler (eds), *Women's International Thought: Towards A New Canon* (Cambridge University Press 2022); Rebecca Adami and Dan Plesch (eds), *Women and the UN: A New History of Women's International Human Rights* (Routledge 2021).

[52] See Thomas Skouteris, 'The Turn to History in International Law', in *Oxford Bibliographies* (n 42); Lauren Benton and Lisa Ford, *Rage for Order* (Harvard University Press 2016); Jennifer Pitts, *Boundaries of the International: Law and Empire* (Harvard University Press 2019); Andrew Fitzmaurice, *Sovereignty,*

histories or critical race studies also most times tacitly share the gendered blind spot of the narratives they otherwise resist or criticize.[53] Even if theoretical critiques of international law's gendered structures and doctrinal work with a feminist reformist agenda excel in quality since the early 1990s, the foundational statement of how '(w)omen form over half the world's population, but their voices, in all their variety, have been thoroughly obscured by and within the international legal order'[54] is most times met with silence. Considering the ambitions often attached to international law as an instrument of (universal) justice, serving diverse emancipatory agendas of progress, that silence inside the intellectual and professional community detonates.

The exhibition may also appear to signal a curious adherence to the binary categories (men-women) as foundational and exclusive—ignoring or dismissing the rich research and controversies in gender, queer, feminist, and masculinity studies and the racialized situatedness of the discourse. That is a false impression, for the re-curation project contests essentialism and all reductionist generalizations. The universal 'woman', 'a cultural and ideological composite Other', does not exist.[55] International law in force today is, nevertheless, understood to comprise also 'women's rights' even if there is no clear concept of 'woman' and 'women'.[56] The lack did not bother international lawyers much in the past, as women were in any case considered outside international law, excluded from both all the public and the political spheres—as discussed in what follows.

Academic discourses today, in contrast, struggle to express the infinite diversity of understandings and descriptions of sex and gender. The exhibition had to cope with languages and idioms of diverse societal and professional contexts in an open temporality. In what follows, 'woman', 'women' and 'man', 'men', are used for individuals who are/were either self-identifying or identified as such in their social context, in the sources available. Instead of a universalistic and neutral conceptualization, the exhibition advances its contrary: how sex and gender interact with other characteristics and circumstances in the diverse contexts of the portrayed.[57] Nor does the vocabulary

Property, and Empire, 1500–2000 (Cambridge University Press 2014); Philippe Sands, *East West Street* (Weidenfeld & Nicolson 2017).

[53] See, eg, James Thuo Gathii, 'Studying Race in International Law Scholarship Using a Social Science Approach James' (2021) 22 Chicago Journal of International Law; Adom Getachew, *Worldmaking after Empire: The Rise and Fall of Self-Determination* (Princeton University Press 2019); Ali Hammoudi, 'Reconstituting the Hegemony of Western Law in the Third World: A Postcolonial Critique of Twining's "General Jurisprudence"' (2013) 4 Transnational Legal Theory 527.

[54] Charlesworth and Chinkin, *Boundaries* (n 17). For the beginning, see Hilary Charlesworth, Christine Chinkin, and Shelley Wright, 'Feminist Approaches to International Law' (1991) 85 AJIL 613, and Ratna Kapur (ed), *Feminist Terrains in Legal Domains: Interdisciplinary Essays on Women and Law* (Kali for Women 1996). For an overview, see Dianne Otto, 'Feminist Approaches to International Law' in Orford and Hoffmann (n 17). See also Heathcote (n 50); Susan Harris Rimmer and Kate Ogg (eds), *Research Handbook on Feminist Engagement with International Law* (Edward Elgar 2019); Loveday Hodson and Troy Lavers, *Feminist Judgments in International Law* (Hart Publishing 2019).

[55] Chandra Talpade Mohanty, 'Under Western Eyes: Feminist Scholarship and Colonial Discourse' (1984) 12 Feminist Review 61, 62.

[56] The most recent analysis is by Christine Chinkin, in the thematic context of the Women, Peace, and Security Agenda, see Christine Chinkin, *Women, Peace and Security and International Law* (Cambridge University Press 2021) 31–36, hereafter Chinkin, *Women, Peace and Security*.

[57] See, eg, Kimberlé Crenshaw, 'Demarginalizing the Intersection of Race and Sex: A Black Feminist Critique of Antidiscrimination Doctrine, Feminist Theory and Antiracist Politics' (1989) 8 University of Chicago Legal Forum 139; Bell Hooks, *Yearning: Race, Gender, and Cultural Politics* (South End Press 1990)

stand for a patriarchal, heteronormative oblivion, dismissal, or exclusion of the social and legal realities of transgender, non-binary, or non-determinate genders, or the diversity of sexualities.[58]

Such is the landscape in which the exhibition is situated: disparate speeds of inter- or multidisciplinary, a hesitant consideration of research on sex and gender—causes and effects on (international) law and politics, international lawyers, and histories of them—and fragmented frames of historical inquiry. The re-curation tried to turn the delay to some advantage, to learn from the struggles and stigmas of early revisionist histories. The desire to make visible and to 'render agency' entails challenging moves, for the sense of equilibria ideally required. The monumental tales of male heroes are at best not replaced with new hagiographies of heroic women, by those glorifying accounts of 'trailblazers' excelling in the criteria of merit established in the absence of women.[59] Similarly, a heteronormative framing of sex and gender and a 'naturalist' celebration of maternity[60] may reduce and hierarchize the scope of women's experiences. A further question of whether one should aim at containing the (often rightful) resentment of (past and present) exclusion or 'to write out women's anger'[61] remains open.

The title of the volume does not refer to 'women international lawyers' but to 'women in international law'. That is because the exhibition wants to flag the following questions: what was/is international law and, as a result, who were/are 'international lawyers'? What did 'international lawyers' do in 'the past' to be called by that name today? What did 'women' do at that time? Any research effort to include previously unknown figures, potentially excluded or marginalized, presumes a frame where the presence and absence are debated. As several authors underline, recently Anne Orford: 'Each historical project that takes international law as an object is part of the contemporary struggle over how international law should be understood and represented.'[62] To portrait 'women' in an open-ended geographical and chronological setting of 'international law', what ideas, intellectual streams, scholarly products, professional practices, and institutional initiatives matter? Which ways of engagement, languages, and traditions (of law, or of something else) to look into? And, perhaps the thorniest question, does exhibiting 'women in international law' together suggest that

Ch 3; Kathy Davis, 'Intersectionality as Buzzword: A Sociology of Science Perspective on what Makes a Feminist Theory Successful' (2008) 9 Feminist Theory 67.

[58] See Dianne Otto, *Queering International Law* (Routledge 2018); Shinya Murase, 'Thomas Baty and International Law Beyond Sex and Gender', Ch. 34, in this volume; and Outi Korhonen, 'Simone Weil: Otherwise than Human Rights, Human Roots', Ch. 40 in this volume.

[59] For discussion, see Rosemary Auchmuty and Erika Rackley, 'Feminist Legal Biography: A Model for All Legal Life Stories' (2020) 41 The Journal of Legal History 186.

[60] For an insightful example that has influenced much of the feminist thinking on ethics of care, violence, and peace, see Sara Ruddick, *Maternal Thinking: Towards a Politics of Peace* (Beacon Press 1995); for analysis, see Fiona Robinson and Catia Confortini (eds), 'Symposium: Maternal Thinking for International Relations?' (2014) 10(1) Journal of International Political Theory 38.

[61] See, eg, Heathcote (n 50) 15; Angela McRobbie, *The Aftermath of Feminism: Gender, Culture and Social Change* (Sage 2009) 13–23; Wendy Brown, *States of Injury* (Princeton University Press 1995) on 'the wounded attachments' and ressentiment.

[62] Anne Orford, *The Politics of History of International Law* (Cambridge University Press 2021) 257.

the individuals or groups portrayed necessarily had more in common with each other than being thus identified in their particular social and professional contexts?

Not necessarily, the exhibition tentatively answers to the last question. Such a response does not denigrate the shared agendas, struggles, and mutual solidarity of women, also in international law, of which there is ample empirical evidence—as there is of differences of view.[63] The starting point here was not to analyse whether a particular woman was 'a feminist' and in which manner. The project is interested in how the persistent othering of 'women' in international law has forced upon them an identity, meaning—to twist a classic quote—that 'man is defined' as an international lawyer 'and woman as a female'. Whenever a woman has performed as an international lawyer, there has been a likelihood 'she is said to imitate the male'.[64] Whatever may have united women, creating affinities and collective political dynamics in their social and ideological contexts as intellectuals and professionals, the exhibition suggests that 'one is not born, but rather becomes'[65] a 'woman in international law'.

There currently exists no temporally, thematically, or geographically comprehensive efforts in international law to map intellectual and professional history in terms of sex and gender, nor of the transmission of women's ideas, expertise, or prestige. This is certainly not to claim that the current project started on a tabula rasa. To the contrary, an interesting, even if fragmented, corpus of previous research exists and can roughly be divided in two groups: 'women-specific' or 'general'. The first features, for example, anthologies on early activists for women's rights, mainly in Europe or North America, and their transnational, regional, or global collaborations;[66] on international dimensions of women's civil and political rights, with emphasis on suffrage and women's status in (what is today known as) private international law;[67] entry into legal professions;[68] protection of women (and children) from 'white slavery' and pornography, and, more recently, in armed conflict.[69] The second features research on intellectual

[63] See, eg, Vasuki Nesiah, 'Toward a Feminist Internationality: A Critique of US Feminist Legal Scholarship' (1993) 16 Harvard Women's Law Journal 189; Janet Halley and others *Governance Feminism* (University of Minnesota Press 2018).

[64] Simone de Beauvoir, *The Second Sex* (Penguin 1972). For examples of this, see, David P Forsythe, *The Humanitarians: The International Committee of the Red Cross* (Cambridge University Press 2005) 204, on Denise Bindschedler-Robert; and Immi Tallgren, 'Absent or Invisible? Women Intellectuals and Professionals at the Dawn of a Discipline' in Immi Tallgren and Frédéric Mégret (eds), *The Dawn of a Discipline: International Criminal Justice and Its Early Exponents* (Cambridge University Press 2020).

[65] de Beauvoir (n 64).

[66] See, eg, Britta Waldschmidt-Nelson and Anja Schüler (eds), *Forging Bonds Across Borders: Transatlantic Collaborations for Women's Rights and Social Justice in the Long Nineteenth Century* (Supplement 13, Bulletin of the German Historical Institute 2017); Laura Beers, 'Advocating for a Feminist Internationalism Between the Wars' in Sluga and James, *Women* (n 51) 202; Leila J Rupp, *Worlds of Women: The Making of an International Women's Movement* (Princeton University Press 1997).

[67] See Karen Knop, 'Gender and the Lost Private Side of International Law' in Annabel Brett, Megan Donaldson, and Martti Koskenniemi (eds), *History, Politics, Law* (Cambridge University Press 2021); Roxana Banu, 'Forgotten Female Figures in Private International Law: The International Social Service', in this volume; Christine Chinkin and Karen Knop, 'Remembering Chrystal MacMillan: Women's Equality and Nationality in International Law' (2001) 22 Michigan Journal of International Law 523; Paolo Amorosa, *Rewriting the History of the Law of Nations: How James Brown Scott Made Francisco de Vitoria the Founder of International Law* (OUP 2019).

[68] See, eg, Sara L Kimble and Marion Röwekamp (eds), *New Perspectives on European Women's Legal History* (Routledge 2016).

[69] See Judith Gail Gardam, 'The Law of Armed Conflict: A Gendered Regime?' in Dorinda Dallmeyer (ed), *Reconceiving Reality; Women and International Law* (American Society of International Law 1993) 171.

outputs and collective activism in causes of public international law, in the thematic areas of pacifism, abolition of slavery, and humanitarian law, for example, as well as engagements in diplomacy and international relations, social justice and economic development by women, in specific temporalities and diverse approaches, with a comparative transnational focus or a specific thematic, disciplinary, regional, linguistic, or cultural frame.[70]

This diverse scholarship is most times ignored in disciplinary international law history, as if by a tacit consensus that whatever 'international law' is considered to have been in the past, it is not what women were doing. When not ignored, the multidisciplinary and pluralist research where women, sex, or gender appear, no matter how, by whom and with which intention, are amalgamated under 'the feminist method' or 'feminist approaches'. Histories of new ideas or doctrinal analysis of international law advanced by women, normative reform initiatives by collectives of women, social policies or practices developed by women, and so on, are lumped together with biographies of individuals of the female sex working or at least present in international law and institutions and further connected to any authors on women's rights (including the rare men). All the parts of the bulk are suggested to be 'identified by their common *animus historiandi*', that of redressing the 'invisibility of women'.[71] In contrast, the histories omitting women, sex, and gender in all respects, continue to represent the neutral, ie general, uninterested, non-biased 'history of international law'. No general label appears to exist for the *animus historiandi* of all the research which chooses not to consider the legalized physical oppression, social and political discrimination, and economical exploitation of half of the human population globally.

Women's absence in histories of international law is rarely commented upon—perhaps genuinely not noticed. In recent works, it may get deplored in passing, but swiftly declared unavoidable. Such scholarship introduces the academic community and students with the only possible history to write, one claims: such was the discipline's sociological reality, was it not?[72] One part of reality, not more. Without doubt, anyone searching only for carbon-copies of James Brown Scott, Georges Scelle, or Johann Kaspar Bluntschli finds 'women's history' disappointing. Such versatile academics-experts-bureaucrats are the superheroes of international law, accumulating roles of professor of international law, expert for the government or international judge, chairman of professional associations, creator of academic journals. These institutional positions and professional roles were since the nineteenth century

[70] See, eg, Freya Baetens, 'The Forgotten Peace Conference: The 1915 Congress of Women' in Rüdiger Wolfrum (ed), *Max Planck Encyclopedia of Public International Law* (OUP 2010); Lela B Costin, 'Feminism, Pacifism, Internationalism and the 1915 International Congress of Women' (1982) 5 Women's Studies International Forum 301; Owens and Rietzler, *Women's International Thought* (n 51); Diane Marie Amann's work on international criminal justice, see the IntLawGrrls blog <https://ilg2.org/author/dianemarieamann> accessed 8 June 2022; Rasilla, (n 13) Ch 6.

[71] Rasilla (n 13) 183.

[72] See Henri de Waele, 'A New League of Extraordinary Gentlemen? The Professionalization of International Law Scholarship in the Netherlands, 1919–1940' (2020) 31 EJIL 105; Janne E Nijman, 'Marked Absences: Locating Gender and Race in International Legal Histories' (2020) 31 EJIL 1025; Henri de Waele, 'Betwixt and Between: What We Write About When We Write About International Legal History' (EJIL: Talk! 12 February 2021) <www.ejiltalk.org/betwixt-and-between-what-we-write-about-when-we-write-about-international-law-history> accessed 17 July 2021.

often held by a circle of like-minded, moving from one role to another or accumulating them.[73] To find a woman, one must scroll the disciplinary narrative past the Second World War to find Suzanne Bastid who exercised all those roles and more, in her native France and internationally.[74]

Such notable figures launched the establishment of the two leading scientific and professional associations of international law in the 1870s, *Institut de droit international (IDI)* and *International Law Association (ILA)*, followed later by the *Carnegie Endowment* and many other associations and entities.[75] These events mark a key milestone in how the emergence of a distinct discipline is today understood.[76] In those moments of constructing an intellectual and professional identity, women were either totally absent or a tiny minority—a detail that rarely figures in those histories. In the interwar period, for example, five of the 1,000 or so members of the International Law Association can be identified as women and 660 as men.[77] Such numbers do not adequately reflect the level of interest women—individually and in a wealth of diverse associations—took in questions of international law and international thought, as the exhibition demonstrates.

Does this mean that women's efforts to invest themselves in the process of professionalization and 'scientification' of international law and international relations at the late nineteenth and early twentiethth centuries were on purpose rejected or downplayed? Again, disciplinary international law history fails to answer the question, as that process has not been approached in terms of critically inquiring about whom the men leading the efforts wanted to position their projects against. Fragments are known. In the context of the International Committee of the Red Cross, for example, Gustave Moynier saw no role for women, other than nursing the wounded in wartime.[78] The minutes of the early board meetings of the Carnegie Endowment give an indication of who the directors and board members saw as the non-professional and non-scientific 'other': on the one hand, the ultra-nationalist and monarchist reactionaries, and on the other hand, the 'professional pacifists' and radical reformers, which for them included organizations such as WILPF and the League of Women Voters.[79]

To continue the super-hero history after Suzanne Bastid, one finds Dame Rosalyn Higgins who got elected judge at the International Court of Justice in 1995—the year of the Fourth World Conference of Women in Beijing. She was the first to preside over the court from 2006 to 2009. The United Nations *International Law Commission*, established in 1947 for 'the promotion of the progressive development of international

[73] For the British context, see Luíza Leão Soares Pereira and Niccolò Ridi, 'Mapping The 'Invisible College of International Lawyers' through Obituaries' (2021) 34 Leiden Journal of International Law 67.

[74] Immi Tallgren and Antoine Buchet, 'Suzanne Bastid: The First of the "Firsts"', Ch.17, in this volume.

[75] Such as, the American Society of International Law; the International Peace Bureau; La Paix par la Droit; Royal Institute of International Studies; the League of Nations Union; Grotius Society; National World Court Committee.

[76] Koskenniemi, *The Gentle* (n 4); Arnulf Becker Lorca, *Mestizo International Law* (Cambridge University Press 2015).

[77] The rest are listed with first name initials and could contain more women.

[78] See Boyd van Dijk, 'Marguerite Frick-Cramer: A Life Shaping the Geneva Conventions', in this volume, referring to Silvia Cadei, 'Le Comité du CICR: Une Affaire d'Hommes?' (2017) Histoire & Genre 74, 76.

[79] I thank Jens Wegener for this preliminary lead, to be followed. (The Covid-19 restrictions hindered my travel to access the Carnegie collection at the Columbia University.)

law and its codification' and consisting of 'of 34 members who shall be persons of recognised competence in international law',[80] has until 2021 had 229 members of which seven have been women: seven in seventy years.[81] The first two, Paula Escarameia and Xue Hanqin, entered in 2002. Since then, other male-only bastions have nominated their 'first women', such as Christine Chinkin as the chair of the ILA in 2021. Should these names and dates be considered the happy ending of a history of 'women in international law'?

The re-curation regards them as a beginning. Asking what else falls under that title, for whom, why, and why not, amounts to a vast research agenda. How to study the signs and traces of the culturally determined and internalized inferiority of other genders than the dominant male in international law? What has the persistent inferiority of other than male ideas and behaviour meant for its jurisprudence? Which agendas, ideas, practices, characters to foreground (or not); whether to highlight international law's emancipatory potential in fighting against (national) discrimination and violence based on sex and gender or focus on international law as an instrument of imperialism, colonialism, and patriarchy? Should one pay attention to intellectuals and professionals most representative or most unknown to the canon; what 'canon'?[82] How did early 'women in international law' themselves conceptualize their work, with regard to the 'international legal order' and 'international society'? Who, where, and how has set the borders between histories of domestic, transnational, international, and global law that obscure women's legal thinking and practices, pluri-contextual and ever-changing as their appear, with transplants and borrowed influences?

This re-curation process has no ambition and no pretension to answer all these questions. The exhibition serves appetisers of a vast research agenda, while contouring some of the above-mentioned challenges by its playful excursion in inquiries into law and visual culture.[83] By explicitly framing the interrogation of collective historical images in terms of 'representation, not accept(ing) it as mimesis',[84] the exhibition contrasts with mainstream histories which at times continue to obscure their own artifice, as if aiming at a reality effect. The metaphor of Portrait Gallery underlines the contrary: portraits are, by definition, artificial. Their contributors are not writing as if they were observing the sitters acting in their professional lives and uttering ideas on

[80] Statute of the International Law Commission, adopted by the General Assembly in resolution 174 (II) of 21 November 1947.

[81] See The United Nations, *Seventy Years of the International Law Commission: Drawing a Balance for the Future* (Brill 2021); Miguel de Serpa Soares, 'Seven Women in Seventy Years: A Roundtable Discussion on Achieving Gender Parity at the International Law Commission' (New York 24 May 2018) <https://legal.un.org/ola/media/info_from_lc/mss/speeches/MSS_ILC70_gender_side_event-24-May-2018.pdf>accessed 30 August 2022. Elections for after 2021 took place in November 2021.

[82] See Karen Knop, 'Foreword', in this volume. On the many meanings of 'canon', see Jan Gorak, *The Making of the Modern Canon* (Bloomsbury Academic 2013). See also Clare Hemmings, *Considering Emma Goldman: Feminist Political Ambivalence and the Imaginative Archive* (Duke University Press 2018).

[83] An area of research has developed in the past twenty years, see Anne Wagner and Richard K Sherwin (eds), *Law, Culture and Visual Studies* (Springer 2014); Oren Ben-Dor (ed), *Law and Art: Justice, Ethics and Aesthetics* (Routledge 2011); Ana Laura Nettel, 'The Power of Image and the Image of Power: The Case of Law' (2005) 21 Word & Image 136; see also Hilary Charlesworth, *Art and Law*, Lectures of The Hague Academy, General Course, forthcoming. On visual media, Daniel Joyce, *Informed Publics, Media and International Law* (Hart Publishing 2020).

[84] Pointon, *Hanging the Head* (n 45) 9.

'international law' in their particular contexts. Nor were the contributors able to construct a replica of that past, relying on publications, manuscripts, photographs, maps, letters, and other relics that archives and libraries may contain—so much less for women than men, as discussed below. Instead, they painted portraits, not by brushes on canvas but with words and visual images.

Portrait: An Object, an Event, and a Symbol of Power

A visual portrait is 'a painting, drawing, photograph, or engraving of a person, especially one depicting only the face or head and shoulders'.[85] A portrait can be 'concerned with likeness as contained in a person's physical features' but it also represents 'the subject's social position or "inner life", such as their character or virtues'.[86] Portraiture typically evokes distinction, an 'inscription of social identity'.[87] Even if the idea of likeness with the sitter remains crucial in defining portraiture, the expectations and criteria have evolved through various periods of time, as much as the means, intentions, and conventions of representation.[88] The contexts of production, display, and reception of portraits have been as diverse as its forms and functions. In this volume, portraiture is not engaged with as an attempt to discover the 'real' people behind the representations. The interest lies in portraiture understood 'as processes whereby subjects are—through a relatively mundane act of sitting for a portrait—woven into a complex web of discourses'.[89]

The genre of portraiture in visual arts grew on an emphasis on individual identity as a historical and social construction, geographically and culturally situated in the West. The National Portrait Gallery in London was established in 1856, the first of its kind in the world. Created to construct history through the representations of those who held power, the great men of a great nation, it rendered national and imperial mythologies individual and visual. For long, it was a massive monument of how colonialism shaped and funded the creation of the portrait collections and how deeply imperialism underpins British art.[90] Paradoxically, it is exactly this entanglement which makes portraiture ever more befitting as a mirror for the images of history of *international* law: its professionalization and 'scientification' were notoriously marked by its stark Eurocentrism and its readiness to condone the violence of imperial history. This shared destiny of the visual art of portraiture and international law may appear to continue today, now that either ailment or fast approaching death are regularly diagnosed for both.

[85] The Oxford English Dictionary, <www.oed.com> accessed 8 June 2022.

[86] Shearer West, *Portraiture* (OUP 2004) 21.

[87] John Tagg, *The Burden of Representation: Essays on Photographies and Histories* (Palgrave MacMillan 1988) 37.

[88] Hans Belting, *An Anthropology of Images* (Princeton University Press 2011), 66–67; Richard Brilliant, *Portraiture* (Reaction Books Ltd 1991), 23–25; Joanna Woodall, *Portraiture, Facing the Subject* (Manchester University Press 1997).

[89] Marcia Pointon, *Strategies for Showing: Women, Possession and Representation in English Visual Culture 1665–1800* (OUP 1997) 12.

[90] The National Portrait Gallery is undergoing renovation, see <www.npg.org.uk> accessed 8 June 2022. See also, eg, *Uncomfortable Art Tour* <www.theexhibitionist.org> accessed 8 June 2022.

Portraiture became central to noble culture during the sixteenth century in Britain, when naturalistic portraits were understood as direct substitutes, personifying the kingdom or the bravery of the military. To quote Joanna Woodall, portraiture 'also articulated the patriarchal principle of genealogy upon which aristocratic ideology was built. The authorising relationship between the living model and its imaged likeness was analogous to that between father and son, and processes of emulation presumed identity to be produced through resemblance to a potent prototype.'[91] Understanding a portrait as a direct substitute for the one represented meant that 'the circulation of portraits could mirror and expand the system of personal patronage whereby power, privilege and wealth were distributed.'[92] The portraits of men in their professional or military attire, as part of the tradition of *viri illustres*, represented social status, standing, and the attributes of power.[93] For Woodall, 'the *raison d'être* of these images was actually to represent sitters as worthy of love, honour, respect, and authority. It was not just that the real was confused with the ideal, but that divine virtue was the ultimate, permanent reality.'[94]

Women's portraits have typically been of the private kind, made visible in homes, in their private spaces. As Felicity Edholm observes:

> Behind many portraits... is an assumption of a biography, a known or knowable story, for men in particular a story of potential when young and achievement when middle-aged. Women's lives and faces cannot tell the same story... in terms of representation, it is beauty—or if not that, due modesty and gracefulness—when young, and the loss of beauty when old.[95]

Early private portraits of women were followed from the seventeenth century by portraits of famous women and later children, couples, and families. Bourgeois and meritocratic figures, scientists, doctors, and other notables of culture became represented in nineteenth century Europe. Similarly with families and civic bodies invested in portraiture for 'marking continuity in a world of discontinuities', also professional groups, such as lawyers, started to accumulate portraits 'in a continual train of historical objectification at one and the same time archival and commemorative'.[96]

The art form of representative portraiture aiming at visual likeliness started its decline a century ago. The same has gradually happened to the social practice of commanding, acquiring, exposing, and viewing portraiture, including the related rituals of recognition of value. The decline has no doubt many reasons, one being the technology of photography and another the change of paradigm in the modernist

[91] Woodall (n 88) 3.
[92] ibid.
[93] Marianna Jenkins, *The State Portrait: Its Origin and Evolution* (College Art Association of America in conjunction with the Art Bulletin 1947) 1.
[94] ibid.
[95] Felicity Edholm, 'Beyond the Mirror: Women's Self-Portraits' in Frances Bonner, Lizbeth Goodman, and Richard Allen (eds), *Imagining Women: Cultural Representations and Gender* (Cambridge University Press 1995) 159.
[96] Pointon, *Hanging the Head* (n 45) 27; Godden-Rasul (n 26) 7–8. See also, Simon Schama, *The Face of Britain; The Nation through its Portraits* (Viking 2015) 43–57.

aesthetics' rejection of the necessity or appropriateness of the mimesis, the portrait's visual resemblance to represent identity.[97] The individuality, globalization, and mediatization are transforming the social functions of portraiture. In the *Gallery of Portraits of International Law*, few future acquisitions shall be objects made of canvas, pigments, and gilded wooden frames. Instead, the curricula, gradings of doctrine, nominations, funding decisions, and the intellectual and professional histories taught in law schools construct hierarchies in continuous exhibition of names and faces, surfacing on screens. Portraiture immaterializes into more ephemeral forms of face and name recognition, attribution of professional worth and intellectual value. Diverse approaches to researching, remembering, and reminiscing intellectuals and professionals, their roles and trajectories interact and partly integrate.

The exhibition that follows combines intellectual history with 'biography, and its sister art of portraiture',[98] so that its portraits are both *textual* biographies which focus on the intellectual and professional pathways of those portrayed and *visual* images. The textual and visual components are at times intersecting, at others complementary, resembling how 'the exemplary and genealogical principles of traditional portrait collections were combined with textual authority to support a powerful history of "great men"'.[99] That successful combination is here recycled for new purposes, to tell different histories.

Next to portraiture, other genres of visual art could have been chosen. A promising option was pointillism, à la Georges Seurat. Each point of colour (or a particular texture of a material) would stand for a temporality, agency, origin, gender, or carry other coded meanings on a canvas representing 'the history of international law'. Such an approach would resemble the astute methods of inquiry chosen by Patricia Owens to calculate the percentages of female names in international relations curriculums and textbook references, presenting the (meagre) result in detailed tables.[100] Similarly, a handwoven carpet could be designed to present a visual image of history, each thread of textile representing with its colour, texture, and volume a role in the knowledge production in its past.[101] Portraiture seemed, however, the most adapted to the context. Its multiple cultural frames of existence in visual art and literature and its pursuit of both likeness and lasting value in representation and authorship echoed the interrogations at hand.

Visual portraiture in public spaces is the most limpid way of communication on merit and reminiscence of experiences and accomplishments that are valued and rendered authoritative. No matter the form and place their exhibition takes, however, portraits are part of a symbolic structure. Following Pointon's invitation 'not only to look closely at individual portraits but also to excavate portraiture as a system, as a shaping and defining mechanism in terms of class, rank and gender',[102] previous images of history demonstrate the gendered, raced, and classed entry into merit in

[97] See West (n 86) and Woodall (n 88) 6–7.
[98] Pointon, *Hanging the Head* (n 45) 85.
[99] Woodall (n 88) 4.
[100] Owens, *Women and History* (n 51).
[101] See, eg, Maria Kapajeva's artwork *Golden Age* (2020) at <https://digigiid.ee/en/exhibitions/maria-kapajeva-when-the-world-blows-up-i-hope-to-go-down-dancing/golden-age> accessed 8 June 2022.
[102] Pointon, *Hanging the Head* (n 45) 4.

international law. If and when other than white male European originated individuals figure, they appear as exceptions. The eventual conformity of the sitter notwithstanding, their portraits stand for difference, a disruption. The colonial, imperial, and European biases of international law, lawyers, and historiography and the restricted knowledge-production have been critically questioned before.[103] By framing the disciplinary history in terms of visual representation, a gallery of portraits, the exhibition captures the conformities of those images, as well as the vast blank spaces. The aim is to render visible also the alienation the biases entail and the experiences of intellectual solitude and stigma, otherness in the profession, that they produce. The exhibition hopes, however, to share also the delights of discovery and encounters that the experiment accorded to its contributors, wishing similar joys for its visitors.

Portraits as (Intellectual) Biographies

The act of portraying has, of course, various other understandings and dimensions beyond visual arts: in literature, historiography, psychology, criminology, to mention a few. 'Intellectual portraits' is a name given today to a particular genre of biographical historiography that became popular in histories of international law in the 1990s, culminating at Koskenniemi's *The Gentle Civilizer of Nations*. Notwithstanding the intended critical edge of the influential book,[104] it launched a genre the best-known examples of which are marked by their focus on a particular kind of portrayed individual of European background and by their style and tone, most times detached of the socio-economic conditions in which their work was produced and of its consequences.[105] A complementary wave of portraits on sitters from different geographical and political frames has followed.[106]

What such intellectual portraits have in common is to represent men only, to exclude any consideration of sex and gender and to accord a great importance to the individual and collective agency of international lawyers. International lawyers' intellectual assumptions, personal ambitions, political agendas and their perceptions of themselves are typically presented as if in an artificial studio decor. In portraiture of the centre and of its imagined peripheries alike, the personal virtue of the protagonists is positioned as the decisive element of history, if not as the ultimate guarantor of

103 The classic being Tony Anghie, *Imperialism, Sovereignty and the Making of International Law* (Cambridge University Press 1987). For a recent analysis and a bibliography, see James Thuo Gathii, 'The Promise of International Law: A Third World View' (2021) 36 The American University International Law Review. See also, Anne Orford (ed), *The Others of International Law* (Cambridge University Press 2006).

104 See Koskenniemi's 'Introduction', *The Gentle* (n 4) 1–10.

105 For a series of portraits of Europeans, including Hubert Thierry, 'The Thought of Georges Scelle' (1990) 1 EJIL (1990) 193; Martti Koskenniemi, 'Hersch Lauterpacht' (1990) 8 EJIL; J Verhoeven, 'Charles de Visscher: Living and Thinking International Law' (2000) 11 EJIL.

106 For examples, see Fleur Johns, Thomas Skouteris, and Wouter Werner, 'Editors' Introduction: Alejandro Alvarez and the Launch of the Periphery Series' (2006) 19 Leiden Journal of International Law 875; Fleur Johns, Thomas Skouteris, and Wouter Werner, 'Editors' Introduction: Taslim Olawe Elias in the Periphery Series' *(2008)* 21 Leiden Journal of International Law 289; and Fleur Johns, Thomas Skouteris, and Wouter Werner, 'Editors' Introduction: India and International Law in the Periphery Series' (2010) 23 Leiden Journal of International Law 1.

the international rule of law—the latter imagined in different shapes.[107] International lawyers, before and after the much-critiqued language of 'the civilised conscience of the mankind',[108] appear to have rarely perceived a contradiction in their particular social identities being asserted as the universally sensitive 'self'. No tradition appears to guide them to accompany their role as the mouthpiece of universal law by self-doubts about their ability or legitimacy to imagine 'everybody's vital interests'.[109] The most explicit 'self' one can grasp in international law scholarship still belongs to generations that asked few questions radical enough to affect the edifice supporting the privileged access to (their) power and knowledge.

Meanwhile elsewhere, the genres of biography and autobiography, often depreciated in mainstream historiographical analysis, have grown into a favoured form of expressing marginalization and exclusion for sex and gender, racialized or ethnic identity, and/or social class.[110] Intellectuals and authors unable to identify in conventional role models have escaped their objectification and the delays in their recognized access to literary and academic agency into live-writing, encompassing biography, memoirs, autobiography.[111] Autobiography qualifies as a feminist mode of expression, in particular, associated with the emancipatory ideal of being grounded on real-life experiences and bridging the private and the public in the life-world of the author. Biography has a broader frame, from general public products to sophisticated academic inquiries. As a genre of intellectual history, biographies are shadowed by doubts on the relationship one can assume between the individual's life circumstances and the work produced.

Whereas the 'intellectual portraits' of international law have remained Victorian on the biological, cultural, and social identities and the social life-worlds of their sitters, the playful experiment with portraits in this exhibition combines text and image in the search for more transparency on the diversity on which the politics of differences are nominally based.[112] Neither a glossy tea table catalogue nor a compilation of orthodox intellectual history, the exhibition wishes to incite new imagenaries of history in international law. The habitus, morphologies, vestimentary styles, coiffures, facial and bodily expressions of the portrayed and their visible background tell stories of their own, through the multiple layers of aesthetics which separate today on-lookers from the particular contexts of representation. Echoing the feminist tradition by questioning the notions of private and public, the portraits situate the sitters both in their professional environments and their everyday contexts. Thereby the exhibition flags news questions, such as, what international lawyers did when they were not busy with

[107] Andrew Lang and Susan Marks, 'Even the Dead Will Not Be Safe: International Law and the Struggle over Tradition' in Wouter Werner, Marieke De Hoon, and Alexis Galán (eds), *The Law of International Lawyers: Reading Martti Koskenniemi* (Cambridge University Press 2017).

[108] Statute of the International Court of Justice <www.icj-cij.org/en/statute> accessed 8 June 2022.

[109] As famously by suggested Hersch Lauterpacht. *The Function of Law in International Community* (Oxford University Press 1933) 202–41.

[110] Francoise Lionnet, *Autobiographical Voices: Race, Gender, Self-Portraiture* (Cornell University Press 1989).

[111] Malin Lidström Brock, *Writing Feminist Lives: The Biographical Battles over Betty Friedan, Germaine Greer, Gloria Steinem, and Simone De Beauvoir* (Palgrave Macmillan 2016); Birgitte Possing, *Understanding Biographies: On Biographies in History & Stories in Biography* (University Press of Southern Denmark 2022).

[112] Rebecca Mae Salokar and Mary L Volcansek (eds), *Women in Law, A Bio-bibliographical Source Book* (Greenwood Press 1996).

international law. In the most-read histories, an international lawyer typically appears travelling for an important meeting, observing, reflecting, perhaps cherishing the memory of his intellectual peers. In this exhibition, in contrast, the portrayed are also taking care of household work, giving birth, struggling with their basic income, and caring for their everyday surroundings.

In the diversity of portraiture as representation, what is the relationship of the visual content and the text, and does the hybridity produce additional meaning? In the portraits that follow, there is no established balance of power so that, for example, the text with its power of detail would always frame the picture and tame it. The narrative potential of visual images is not necessarily tethered to the text that introduces them or comments them a posteriori nor can it be simply 'translated'. Diverse visitors are likely to differ in what they see in the portraits. The ambition of 'demonstrating the need to reimagine and reinvent a new moralised self-image for international lawyers, responsive to the conditions and concerns of the contemporary world'[113] is here experimented with in methodological and intellectual heterodoxy.

The Process of Portraying and Exhibiting Portraits as Authorship of History

Since Christine de Pizan's birth around 1365 to the current day—the stretch of the sitters' lives—stances to history, law, and art as well as ideas, norms, and practices referred to as 'international law' in present times lack any immutable meaning or reference. The same concerns 'sex', 'gender', 'agency', and other words or concepts in this volume. What sense can attention to sex and gender of 'international lawyers' make? The key interrogations in historiographical philosophy and methodology, such as the standing of individuals in history, must here be contended with in the simplest terms, by letting the process situate the experiment, as follows. Curating and exhibiting a portrait is here—tentatively—assimilated with intellectual and professional histories, primarily authored by insiders of international law. Those histories have a role in imprinting the names and faces that matter in the collective images of history and in the 'canon of international law'. Portraiture is here considered also as an event, and as such, a visible result of a process. Its critical potential lies in who portrays whom, and how the event unfolds. The current re-curation process—from the idea to the selection of sitters, contributors, workshop sessions, visual images—is tentatively employed as a mirror to examine the gendered ideological, intellectual, and social contexts of production and transmission of international law histories.

The contributors feature scholars of international law and its history, professionals of international law, historians, international relations scholars, collaborators or students of the sitters. Their geographical location, language, education, profession, sex and gender, age, career stage, and research interests differ. Overcoming Eurocentrism and the exclusivity of the English language guided the selection, yet it had to face the reality of publishing in English only. Gender balance was a central criterion, in order

[113] Martti Koskenniemi, 'International Law: Constitutionalism, Managerialism and the Ethos of Legal Education' (2007) 1 European Journal of Legal Studies 1.

to avoid once again remaining amongst women to discuss 'women's history'—not that the doors would in other cases have been closed from the inside either.[114]

The selections were constrained by the size of the volume, and portraits were therefore allocated diverse roles in the exhibition. Some flag landmark characters, signposts for a transition or a line of thought. Others tease out the stereotypical roles or statuses: mother, wife, daughter, loyal assistant, unnamed secretary, 'the first woman'. Doubling of efforts was avoided when excellent recent work already existed.[115] The networks, affiliations, knowledge, linguistic competences and other circumstances of the contributors and the curator affected the selection. All visitors to the exhibition are likely to come up with women who were, again, excluded or feel that a particular portrait should rather hang in another hall, a higher floor, a different corridor. The exhibition does not complete any of its objectives fully, it only marks a start of a general, systematic mapping and analysis of 'women in international law'. The temporary exhibition's aim of bringing under the benevolent presumption of professional and intellectual value a broader, more heterodox imagery of 'international lawyers' is, however, permanent: it wishes to bestow recognition and authority not only to those portrayed, but others who should have been included. All visitors are therefore issued an invitation for a continuous re-curation: please join the workshop of hands-on-activities and produce a portrait of your ancestor(s) in international law or those of your next-door intellectual neighbour.

Whereas the terminology of portraiture and gallery may suggest a static and polished representation of solemn figures, posing in an atelier in Sunday outfits, the contrary is the aim here. A key intention in the process was to counter the expectation that a portrait needs to flatter. As Martin Gayford writes: 'the sitter's vanity is a wild card in the history of portraiture, often—in fact, almost always—a factor when the subject is paying for the result'.[116] Beyond the eventual vanity of the sitter, the re-curation had to confront the temptation of ideological vanity, selecting only sitters who are flattering either to feminism, women, or international law. Were there women in international law's past one would rather not 'find' and expose to view?

The women portrayed in the exhibition are not represented as exemplary in all regards, either as women, feminists, or lawyers. Some have been accused of racial prejudice, co-optation with white supremacy, colonialism, exploitation, or cowardice.[117]

[114] See Hilary Charlesworth, 'Talking to Ourselves? Feminist Scholarship in International Law' in Sari Kouvo and Zoe Pearson (eds), *Feminist Perspectives on Contemporary International Law: Between Resistance and Compliance?* (Hart Publishing 2014).

[115] See, eg, Josephine Jarpa Dawuni (ed), *International Courts and the African Woman Judge Unveiled Narratives* (Routledge 2019); Diane Marie Amman, 'Glimpses of Women at the Tokyo Tribunal' in Viviane E Dittrich and others (eds), *The Tokyo Tribunal: Perspectives on Law, History and Memory* (Torkel Opsahl 2020) 103–29; Ignacio de la Rasilla, 'Concepción Arenal and the Place of Women in Modern International Law' (2020) 88 The Legal History Review 211. Natalia Wheatley, 'What Can We (She) Know about Sovereignty?: Krystyna Marek and the Worldedness of International Law', in Owens and Rietzler, *Women's International Thought* (n 51).

[116] Martin Gayford, *Man with a Blue Scarf: On Sitting for a Portrait by Lucian Freud* (Thames and Hudson 2012).

[117] See, eg, Serena Forlati, 'Lea Meriggi: A Fighter—For the Wrong Cause', Ch. 28, in this volume. See also Susan Pedersen, 'Metaphors of the Schoolroom: Women Working the Mandates System of the League of Nations' (2008) 66(1) History Workshop Journal 188; Immi Tallgren, '"Voglio una donna!": Of Contributing to History of International Criminal Law with the Help of Women Who Perpetrated International Crimes'

They appear in the dynamics of their lives and professional choices, sometimes erring, at others failing, and often criss-crossing the paths of other protagonists. The ambition was not to get some extra-ordinary women framed on the wall but to push all 'women in international law' out the cabinet of curiosities of international law history, to normalize the sight of them—not to sacralize and idolize them. The differences in the political and legal standpoints are laid out in open. Several of the portrayed confronted each other in the spaces of international law, not always seeing eye to eye on themes they were active on. One prominent example of this is the context of family planning/population control.[118]

The re-curation had to face the same epistemological challenges all (intellectual) histories and biographies of marginalized figures typically face: the struggle to gather sources to prove a veracity and verifiability is arduous, due to the exact circumstances of marginalization or erasure one aims at alleviating. Research in history is governed by rules of methodological best practices. Intellectual histories in law typically focus on written sources.[119] The practices of documenting and archiving in the intellectual and professional communities have been, however, as gendered as the conceptions of merit and value. As Rosemary Auchmuty writes, women face 'double marginalisation',[120] an inferior position both in their life contexts and in the sources that remain.[121] Because most early women in international law occupied adjunct functions, and their works appeared in lower-class publications, if at all, they left no or less individual traces. Many ideas can be found only in speeches, oral interviews, letters, meeting minutes, newspaper articles, or unpublished manuscripts.[122] Even Sarah Wambaugh, who worked as a recognized expert with a firm status in her field in the United States, has not had her archive organized and made available.[123]

Ownership of women's ideas is cumbersome to discern with clarity also because women do not necessarily appear as signatories of their ideas. In the practice of collective authorship, their role used to get diluted, if not directly appropriated by men, as

in Immi Tallgren and Thomas Skouteris (eds), *The New Histories of International Criminal Law: Retrials: The History and Theory of International Law* (OUP 2019).

118 Vasuki Nesiah, 'Avabai Wadia—The Gentle Rebel of (Other) Nations?', Ch. 10, in this volume; Raimo Lintonen, 'Helvi Sipilä: Advocating Women's Rights at the UN', Ch. 16, in this volume; Anne Orford, 'Alva Myrdal: The Rise and Fall of Social Democratic Internationalism', in this volume; Michael Addaney, 'Canonizing the Memory of Annie Ruth Jiagge in the Global Efforts Towards Gender Equality', Ch. 13, in this volume; Parvathi Menon 'Vijayalakshmi Pandit: Gendering and Racing against the Postcolonial Predicament', Ch. 19', in this volume.

119 For recent arguments for renewal, see Daniel Ricardo Quiroga-Villamarín, 'Beyond Texts? Towards a Material Turn in the Theory and History of International Law' (2020) 1 Journal of the History of International Law; Jessie Hohmann and Daniel Joyce (eds), *International Law's Objects* (OUP 2018).

120 Rosemary Auchmuty, 'Recovering Lost Lives: Researching Women in Legal History' in Linda Mulcahy and David Sugarman (eds), *Legal Life Writing: Marginalized Subjects and Sources* (Wiley Blackwell 2015).

121 In national contexts, see Ulrike Schultz, 'Introduction: Gender and Careers in the Legal Academy: Overview and Synthesis' in Ulrike Schultz and others (eds), *Gender and Careers in the Legal Academy* (Hart Publishing 2021) 151.

122 Liz Stanley, 'The Epistolarium: On Theorizing Letters and Correspondences' Auto/Biography (2004) 127, 201–35; Sarah Dunstan, 'Women's International Thought in the Twentieth-Century Anglo-American Academy: Autobiographical Reflection, Oral History and Scholarly Habitus' (2021) 33 Gender & Histories 487.

123 Saunders, 'Sarah Wambaugh: Life at the Frontiers of International Law', Ch. 26, in this volume.

Reut Yael Paz explains.[124] Women's written works are, furthermore, often out of print and not digitalized, and no longer accessible.[125] The Covid-19 epidemy coinciding in time with the work on the portraits aggravated the epistemological struggles. The portraitists coped the best they could, at times with disparate and 'subaltern' sources.

As the process advanced, many portraitists increasingly saw their role—in the curator's subjective impression—less as aiming at the customary tone of intellectual history as 'objective' judgements of the achievements and intellectual value of their sitter but building on personal interpretations. The stratagem of portraiture may have become, in several cases, a playful way of unsettling the discourse, questioning the choices of themes and agents worthy of attention. The contributors were invited to explain their personal choice of the sitter and to spell out their sitter's relation to international law. Here the experiment may have accomplished other kind of work: it created the portraitist, an openly subjective intervening self in a mutual relationship, the triangle formed by the portraitist, the sitter and the public/viewers. As Jean-Luc Nancy discussed, the relationship between the portraitist and the sitter is not one-dimensional, but an exchange.[126] The following are examples of how the contributors make visible parts of the multidimensional relationships in their personal choices of whom to represent as 'women in international law', why, and how:

Imogen Saunders had one day found, by chance, Sarah Wambaugh's *A Monograph on Plebiscites* (1920): 'I realised that in the entire time I had been researching international law works from the early 20th century, I had never come across one obviously written by a woman.'[127] Reut Yael Paz, a scholar of international law in Germany, portrays legal historian Marie Therese Fögen, spelling out 'the rotten deal that objectifies and enslaves women'.[128] She appears to situate not only Fögen but herself in the misogyny of that academic context, yet to follow a more optimistic continuity: 'at least now women can also be creative, brilliant and extraordinary jurists'.[129] Keina Yoshida, a barrister and feminist scholar based in the UK, travelled to Tokyo to portray Yaori Matsui, a Japanese journalist and civil society activist who was instrumental in bringing international law on sexual and gendered violence visible in Japan. Through her 'conversations with feminist activists and Japanese international lawyers', Yoshida 'discovered that Yaori Matsui had been both an inspirational and controversial figure in Japan'.[130] In the process of seeking to satisfy her 'own curiosity to know why she had advocated for the Tribunal'[131] Yoshida's personal and professional worlds appear to meet and integrate.

Sara Seck is a professor at Dalhousie University in Halifax, as Elisabeth Mann Borgese was. Seck recounts how Mann Borgese's 'approach and vision to overcome narratives of western individualism intrigue me because it coincides with some of my own work'. As a legal scholar who started her career as a professional musician, Seck

[124] Reut Yael Paz, 'Marie Theres Fögen: The Universalization of a Rotten Deal', Ch. 32, in this volume.
[125] Jan Klabbers, 'The Timing of Felice Morgenstern', in this volume, Ch. 20, on Morgenstern's book.
[126] See Jean-Luc Nancy, *Le regard du portrait* (Galilée 2000).
[127] Saunders (n 123).
[128] Paz (n 124).
[129] ibid 12.
[130] Keina Yoshida, 'Yayori Matsui: Challenging the Silences of International Law Through Pan Asian Feminist Solidarity', Ch. 12, in this volume.
[131] ibid.

was 'curious to learn that Mann Borgese observed that her only academic training was in music'.[132] For Serena Forlati, professor at the university of Ferrara, there was no joy in portraying her predecessor. Forlati 'felt bound to shed light on the choices made in 1943 by the institution' she now works for.[133] She exposes her 'feeling of shame' about a figure of the past of her own university whom many would rather forget: Lea Meriggi, 'the first—for several decades the only—woman to hold a chair of International law in Italy' but also 'one of the few staunch supporters of the fascist regime among the international law academic community'.[134]

Sarah Riley Case starts her portrait of Mary Ann Shadd by relating how 'my grandfather was raised by family members who were enslaved in British Guiana'. Riley Case 'wished to trace the paths' Shadd 'took because of our shared history of slavery and migration'[135] but struggled to find a sense in situating Shadd in international law, instead of the Black radical tradition: Shadd's 'life reveals conditions of Black life that exist alongside an international order that has not alleviated global anti-Black violence through borders, policing, labour, health, education and climate change'.[136] Anne Orford writes how studying Alva Myrdal 'left me with a feeling of sadness about what happened to her optimistic dreams for the future of Sweden and social democracy globally'. Orford 'was going over the details of her life and work, trying to find the moment where she made the wrong choice' until she found solace for 'those standing in the ruins of social democracy' in Myrdal's 'perseverance, her fighting spirit, and her commitment to "labouring, planning, and dreaming"'.[137]

Finally, the re-curation process also sheds light on the frequently obscured aspect of patronage, not necessarily dissimilar in art and in academic research. Artists and researchers alike need an income to live, to acquire materials, canvases or computers, a place of work, and a community of peers. Whether understood as individuals, charismatic creators or determined by their social circumstances, they most times must exchange their products for an income and/or institutional support, explicitly or implicitly.[138] Portraiture symbolizes the socio-economic relationships and institutional hierarchies of cultural production. Portraits of international lawyers (here meaning visual objects) are commissioned by national and international institutions, associations, universities, at times initiated by private personalities, and organizations. Are the sitters portrayed because they have a particular authority, importance, and excellence in their field of activity in society? For Ernst van Alphen, the intuitive acceptance of the 'real' authority of the sitter is 'the most innocent reading of portraits' but

> from the perspective of the viewer this innocent reading is a case of analepsis, of chronological reversal. It is because we see a portrait of somebody that we presume

132 Sara Seck, 'Elisabeth Mann Borgese: Ecology, Relationality, and Law of the Sea', Ch. 31, in this volume.
133 Serena Forlati, 'Lea Meriggi: A Fighter—For the Wrong Cause', Ch. 28, in this volume.
134 ibid.
135 Sarah Riley Case, 'Homelands of Mary Ann Shadd', Ch. 9, in this volume.
136 ibid.
137 Orford (n 118).
138 See, eg, Pierre Bourdieu, *The Field of Cultural Production* (Polity Press 1993).

> that the portrayed person was important and the portrayed becomes the embodiment of authority in whatever way.[139]

The act of commissioning a portrait launches the investment—not only financial but intellectual, emotional, and social—in the authority of the portrayed. Portraits, framed by their institutional exhibition places, expect viewers 'to stand in awe, not so much of the portrait, but of the portrayed'.[140] The identity of the sitter intertwining with that of the portraitist, a portrait represents the portraitist and the patrons, in addition to the sitter.[141] Portraiture makes visible not only the agency of the portraitist and her belonging in a history and a tradition, but the agency of those who command, finance, and expose portraits—their interventions in the reproduction or transformation of a professional culture, its past and present. The re-curation of the International Law Portrait Gallery brings that question on the table with regard to history-writing and academic production in international law.

Floorplan

The exhibition consists of forty-two portraits of 'women in international law' in ten rooms. The re-curation opened up the mythological pair of words, 'international lawyers'. It here includes individuals or groups who imagined, developed, or contested international law; who gained their lives in and by it and its institutions; or who, even if active in other endeavours, changed its course in their particular manner either contemporaneously or later. International 'law' encompasses here also ideas, causes, behaviour, norms, and social practices before they had legal relevance in a positivist sense in the temporal contexts in question, such as agendas and arguments concerning morals, social justice, or equity before the international legal discourse emerged. Little attention is paid to formal education or professional titles as 'lawyers' as women were not, until the last century, allowed to get educated, adhere to a profession, or exercise salaried activities outside the household. For similar structural reasons, the understanding of 'authorship' with a potential of relevance for international law is widened, comprising, for example, journalists, artists, legal librarians, civil society activists, and various assistants.[142]

Before visitors jump to conclusions, two clarifications must be made. First, the current exhibition seeks to complement, not replace, the vast Portrait Gallery of International Law. It does not argue for a separate history of 'women in international law', but the contrary: a multivocal, inclusive, shared narrative. In most cases, the women portrayed developed their ideas or acted for a cause together with those

139 Ernst van Alphen, 'The Portrait's Dispersal: Concepts of Representation and Subjectivity in Contemporary Portraiture', in Woodall (n 88) 240.

140 ibid.

141 See, eg, Michael Baxandall, *Painting and Experience in Fifteenth Century Italy: A Primer in the Social History of Pictorial Style* (OUP 1972); Michael Baxandall, *Patterns of Intention: On the Historical Explanation of Pictures* (Yale University Press 1985).

142 For similar choices, see Patricia Owens and Kimberley Hutchings, 'Women Thinkers and the Canon of International Thought: Recovery, Rejection, and Reconstitution' (2021) 115 American Political Science Review 347.

otherwise gendered. That was how this exhibition was created, too. Second, exhibiting these portraits together does not claim that 'all women' shared the same lived experiences in international law, shadowed by gendered marginalization or invisibility. As the diverse and nuanced portraits show, identifications are multiple and intersecting, and (professional) lives escape simplifications. The suggestion is, instead, that the agency of women remains absent or obscure in the representations of chains of generations engendering, creating, and developing international law to such an extent that women are erased from the collective imagination of its history.

Preceded by Karen Knop's astute foreword which situates the experiment in various contexts of inquiry,[143] the exhibition starts in the *Vestibule of the Legendary Ancients*. The name of the first hall flags a complex open issue. The order in which artworks are organized in an exhibition is typically understood as a narrative, a direction the curator tries to impose. Is it a juxtaposition of origins, or an alignment of similarities in ideological and intellectual currents? Is it thematic or temporal? Situating the women sitters of this exhibition in the male centred periodization of international law histories is cumbersome, even awkward.[144] In general, the word 'legendary' refers to famous, appreciated figures not necessarily historicized in a detailed manner. The word 'ancients' carries the meaning of representing an ancestry. Transposing that logic to international law histories where hardly any women are historicized and all women appear to lack ancestry, would it not mean that every sitter active before the 1990s belongs in the Vestibule? I am, however, trying to tease out five potential understandings of legendary ancients of 'women in international law'.

The first consists of women in diplomacy and international politics as reigning or consort queens, princesses, mistresses or the various categories of 'ladies' serving in the European courts. As there exists remarkable recent scholarship, most notably by Glenda Sluga, highlighting how women exercised influence by way of their access to the intimacy of rulers, politicians, notables, diplomats, and the spaces of power, such as negotiations of transnational legal instruments, no example was needed in this exhibition.[145] The second option is to include an early author of philosophy, theology or arts and humanities, whose works also dealt with themes today understood as 'international law'.[146] The *Vestibule* includes one prominent example, Christine de Pizan

[143] Karen Knop, 'Foreword: Looking at Portraits', in this volume.

[144] On periodization in the history of international law, see Oliver Diggelmann, 'The Periodization of the History of International Law', in Fassbender and Peters (eds), *The Oxford Handbook* (2012) 997–1011; and William Butler, 'Periodization and International Law' in Alexander Orakhelashvili (ed), *Research Handbook on the Theory and History of International Law* (Edward Elgar 2011) 379–93.

[145] See Sluga and James, *Women* (n 51); Glenda Sluga, 'Madame de Stael and the Transformation of European Politics 1812–1817' (2015) 37 International History Review 142; Glenda Sluga, 'On the Historical Significance of the Presence, and Absence, of Women at the Congress of Vienna 1814–1815' (2014) 25 L'homme 49; Mark Bryant, 'Partner, Matriarch, and Minister: Madame de Maintenon of France, Clandestine Consort, 1680–1715' in Campbell Orr (ed), *Queenship in Europe 1660–1815: the Role of the Consort* (Cambridge University Press 2004) 77–107; and on regencies, André Corvisier, *Les régences en Europe. Essai sur les délegations de pouvoirs souverains* (Persée 2002).

[146] Carol Pal, *Republic of Women: Rethinking the Republic of Letters* (Cambridge University Press 2012), especially ch 3, Marie de Gournay, Marie du Moulin, and Anna Maria van Schurman, 'Constructing intellectual kinship' 78; Jeanie R Brink, *Female Scholars: A Tradition of Learned Women Before 1800* (Eden Press Women's Publications 1980).

(*c*1365–*c*1430), portrayed by Franck Latty.[147] Pizan, who has been referred to as 'the mother of international law',[148] wrote on a broad array of topics, including the laws of war. She has been cited as 'the mother' of other disciplines, too.

The third option is to focus on the earliest proponents of the cause of women, women's right to life and physical inviolability, and their political, civic, and social and economic rights. As the perhaps best-known symbolic figure for the cause, Olympe de Gouges (1748–1793) is portrayed by Anne Lagerwall and Agatha Verdebout, professors of international law. For them, de Gouges belongs amongst 'the famous figures associated with the French Revolution of 1789'.[149] She remains, nevertheless, absent in the disciplinary history of international law.[150] What could explain dismissing de Gouges's virulent contestation of the gendered legal and political imagination of the revolutionaries, the *Declaration of the Rights of Woman and of the Female Citizen* (1791), as well as Mary Wollstonecraft's *A Vindication of the Rights of Woman* (1792)[151]? Excluding both the oppression of women and its contestation at the time can hardly be argued to result from epistemic impossibility, for there were indeed women who 'produced books that have survived'.[152]

Men at the time wrote about women, too. D'Alembert may have been the first in 1774 to compare women's position in France, as well as in most other states, to slavery and maltreatment of slaves:

> L'esclavage et l'espèce d'avilissement où nous avons mis les femmes; les entraves que nous donnons à leur esprit et à leur âme... Si la plupart des nations ont agi comme nous à leur égard, c'est que partout les hommes ont été les plus forts, et que partout le plus fort est l'oppresseur et le tyran du plus faible.[153]

Also other Encyclopedists and public figures of the Enlightenment, such as Marquis de Condorcet[154] and Paul Henri Thiry d'Holbach[155] trespassed the divide of public-private by critically questioning the scope of the equality and liberty of citizenship and promoting women's education and emancipation in society.

[147] Franck Latty, 'Christine de Pizan: The Law of Warfare as Seen by a Medieval Woman', Ch. 1, in this volume.

[148] Maria T Guerra Medici, 'The Mother of International Law: Christine de Pisan' (1999) 19 Parliaments, Estates and Representation 15.

[149] See Anne Lagerwall and Agatha Verdebout, 'Olympe de Gouges: Beyond the Myth', Ch. 3, in this volume.

[150] For a recent but not rare example, see, Martti Koskenniemi, *To the Uttermost Parts of the Earth: Legal Imagination and International Power 1300–1870* (Cambridge University Press 2021), hereafter Koskenniemi, *To the Uttermost*.

[151] Mary Wollstonecraft, *A Vindication of the Rights of Woman* (J Johnson 1792); Mary Wollstonecraft, *An Historical and Moral View of the Origin and Progress of the French Revolution and the Effect It Has Produced in Europe* (J Johnson 1794).

[152] Koskenniemi, *To the Uttermost* (n 150) 13.

[153] D'Alembert, *Des Femmes*, 1774, see also John Pappas, 'Condorcet, "le seul" et "le premier" féministe du 18ème siècle?' (1991) 23 Dix-Huitième Siècle 441–43. Wollstonecraft in her *A Vindication of the Rights of Woman* (1792) develops the comparisons of the positions of women and slaves.

[154] Marquis de Condorcet, *Sur l'Admission des Femmes au Droit de Cité* (1790).

[155] Paul Henri Thiry d'Holbach, *Système social*, Tome 3, Chapitre X "des femmes" (London 1773); Pierre Guyomar, *Le Partisan de l'Egalité Politique des Individus, ou Problème Très Important de l'Egalité en Droits et de l'Inégalité en Faits*, 29 April 1793. Other examples are, Denis Diderot, Charles Louis de Montesquieu, and Francois Pouillan de La Barre. See also Karen Offen, *The Woman Question in France, 1400–1870* (Cambridge University Press 2017).

The fourth type of legendary ancients flags how some sitters are already famous intellectuals but not historicized as such in international law. Rosa Luxemburg (1871–1919), a 'bourgeois woman and a Jewish Pole',[156] is portrayed by Deborah Whitehall as a political intellectual with multiple facets and agendas, including an engagement with anti-capitalist international law, for an 'alternative vision of global order' that 'resists the unitary tale of one internationalism'. Luxemburg stands here for the radical urge to approach the 'distant guiding star', 'the ultimate goal'[157]of revolution which requires no less than the transformation of the whole world. That reaching world peace, self-determination, and environmental protection requires much more than international legal reform by capitalist states, Luxemburg was early to underline.

Fifth, legendary ancient women in international law can be searched for in the vicinity of its great men. Henk Nellen portrays an alternative 'mother of international law', the wife of its father.[158] Hugo Grotius is the most written on intellectual in international law up to present times[159]—even if his paternity gets disputed.[160] Maria van Reigersberch (1589–1653) married, at the age of nineteen, Hugo Grotius. Nellen hesitated to portray van Reigersberch for this exhibition. 'She did not even speak Latin', he worried: 'it will be (practically) impossible for me to connect Grotius' importance for international law and natural law with Maria'. Nellen finally took up the challenge and succeeded, because 'as a biographer of Grotius I fully recognise Maria's essential role in Grotius' life'.[161]

Van Reigersberch's inclusion in the *Vestibule* flags her role as a key member, the managing director, of the 'household academy' of children and other family members contributing to the production of Grotius' works, translating and editing his books and ensuring his legacy.[162] Van Reigersberch and her helpful maids belong to seldom historicized categories of subaltern agency at the margins of the dominant narratives of international law. By including her and a group of women in diverse assisting roles,[163] the exhibition suggests that the locations dominated by the male intellectuals—libraries, tobacco rooms, and auditoriums—as well as the benches of

[156] Deborah Whitehall, 'The Reign of Order and the Rights of Siege According to Rosa Luxemburg', Ch. 4, in this volume.

[157] Rosa Luxemburg, quoted by Whitehall (n 156).

[158] Henk Nellen, 'Maria van Reigersberch: Wife of Hugo Grotius', Ch. 5, in this volume.

[159] See, eg, Arnoldus Lysen (ed), *Hugo Grotius: Essays on His Life and Works Selected for the Occasion of the Tercentenary of His De jure belli ac pacis, 1625–1925* (A W Sythoff's Publishing Co 1925).

[160] See Peter Haggenmacher, 'La place de Francisco de Vitoria parmi les fondateurs du droit international' in Antonio Truyol Serra and others (eds), *Actualité de la pensée juridique de Francisco de Vitoria* (Bruylant 1988) 27–80 at 29. Thomas Erskine Holland, 'Alberico Gentili' in *Studies in International Law* (Clarendon Press 1898) 1–39. Randall Lesaffer and Janne Nijman (eds), *The Cambridge Companion to Hugo Grotius* (forthcoming); Charles Leben, 'Grotius: serait le père du droit international' in Hervé Ascensio and others, *Dictionnaire des idées reçues en droit international* (Pedone 2017) 279–85.

[161] Correspondence, on file with the author.

[162] See Martine J van Ittersum, 'Knowledge Production in the Dutch Republic: The Household Academy of Hugo Grotius' (2011) 72 Journal of the History of Ideas 523; on household academy in a broader understanding, see Sarah Ross, *The Birth of Feminism: Women as Intellect in Renaissance Italy and England* (Harvard University Press 2009); Margaret JM Ezell, *The Patriarch's Wife: Literary Evidence and the History of the Family* (University of North California Press 1987).

[163] Auberer(n 2); Diane Otto, 'Fearless Speech: A Portrait of UN Typist Shirley Hazzard, Ch. 43, in this volume.

international courts and treaty negotiation halls incorporated varied unrecognized inputs.[164] The intellectual, psychological, clerical, and physical support and care for 'important men' was often unremunerated, at the heart of the public/private divide marking early feminist scholarship.[165] In the context of the faculty wives and spouses of men in diplomatic careers the private was at times planned also as public at the outset.[166] The roles that marriage has been understood to accord to women, from everyday material servitude up to romantic ambitions of a symbiosis of minds and bodies to procreate cover a wide range in diverse temporalities.[167] The opacity of a wife's role and the gendered appreciation of her achievements is addressed also in Anne Orford's portrait of Alva Myrdal.[168]

After the legendary ancients but before the gender transformation of the 1990s, whom to call 'women in international law' and expose in the exhibition? In the disciplinary history of international law, one finds next-to-nobody. Beyond that frame, women, individually and often in collaboration in various associations, were participating in or leading diverse agendas of legal reform and global societal progress, in contexts of analysis and practices exceeding the national states. Typically led by European characters who were brandishing international or universal ambitions—similarly to initiatives by men in other cities of Europe in the same temporal context. For Marion Röwekamp, women in the late nineteenth and early twentieth centuries 'had in fact instituted a parallel network in trying to formulate international legal solutions',[169] they engaged in intellectual activities and practices centred around (transnational, international) normativity. The subsequent four halls of the exhibition, adjoining the gallery garden, present portraits of 'women in international law' organized by themes of involvement of the sitters—not necessarily in a temporal chronology. Use of force (or not), humanitarian law, international criminal justice, social justice, abolition of slavery, elimination of racial discrimination and discrimination of women, reproductive rights and population control, anti-imperialism, trafficking of women and children, equal rights to economic development were the main causes the following eleven women portrayed worked on.

Works in international thought have analysed how the ethical commitment to the abolition of war and the activism for peace through law have a gendered connotation

[164] See, eg, Hilary Callan and Shirley Ardener (eds), *The Incorporated Wife* (Routledge 1984).

[165] See, eg, Silvia Federici, *Wages Against Housework* (Power of Women Collective 1975); Margaret Thornton (ed), *Public and Private: Feminist Legal Debates* (OUP 1995).

[166] Hilary Callan and Shirley Ardener (eds), *The Incorporated Wife* (Croom Helm 1984); Cynthia H Enloe, *Bananas, Beaches and Bases* (Pandora Press 1989).

[167] See, eg, on seventeenth-century England, Margaret J M Ezell, The Patriarch's Wife (The University of North Carolina Press 1987).

[168] See Orford (n 118).

[169] Marion Röwenkamp, 'A Dilemma of Law and Morality: Helen Silving and International Law' in Leora Bilsky and Annette Weinke (eds), *Jewish-European Émigré Lawyers: Twentieth Century International Humanitarian Law as Idea and Profession* (Wallstein 2021). See also Marion Röwekamp, A Parallel Legal World. Women formulating international law (1878–1914) <https://www.canal-u.tv/107757> (accessed 15 September 2022); Sara L Kimble, 'Transatlantic Networks for Legal Feminism, 1888–1912' in Britta Waldschmidt-Nelson and Anja Schüler (eds), *Forging Bonds Across Borders* (n 69); Oliver Janz and Daniel Schönpflug (eds), *Gender History in a Transnational Perspective: Networks, Biographies, Gender Orders* (Berghahn 2014).

as female, and often also as marginal.[170] The law on the use of force, the rules of military intervention and the conduct of armed hostilities are gendered male, and in the core of international law. The hall of *Figureheads of Fighting for Peace* questions that gendered order by two sitters who both received the Nobel Prize. Janne Nijman portrays Bertha von Suttner (1843–1914), the author of a bestselling novel *Die Waffen Nieder!* (1889) and a *salonière* hosting networking on the scenes of international negotiations. Despite the atypical modes of activity, Von Suttner played an active role 'at the foundations of the international legal institutions in The Hague' and her ideas on international law therefore 'deserve serious discussion', Nijman writes.[171] Kate Grady and Gina Heathcote chose for entry in the exhibition Jane Addams (1860–1935), a thinker and activist for whom 'international peace was not merely about regulating interactions between states, but connected to social justice, anti-nationalism and anti-militarism'.[172] Whereas Von Suttner was active in The Hague during the 1899 and 1907 Peace Conferences, Addams played a central role in the International Congress of Women Peace Conference in The Hague in 1915.[173]

Winter Garden of Abolition and Resistance features women engaged against slavery, racism, and imperialism in diverse ways that had relevance for international law—it is argued here. The activism for women's rights, most notably suffrage, and the societal movements over slavery and abolition were intertwined in transatlantic political cultures. In those contexts, Kathryn Kish Sklar and James Brewer Stewart argue, diverse women 'created and encountered unprecedented opportunities for self-discovery, intellectual exploration, and political engagement on behalf of the enslaved, and on their own behalf as well'.[174] In how far racial identities defined the boundaries of women's activism, and in which form did the ideas of abolitionism and emancipation become transnational or international, are the crucial questions here.

Christopher Gevers deepens the analysis of Anna Julia Cooper (1858–1964) intellectual oeuvre by focusing on her powerful critique of international law that introduced or anticipated current concepts of 'intersectionality' and 'racial capitalism'.[175] Sarah Riley Case portrays Mary Ann Shadd (1823–1893), a schoolteacher, an activist of abolitionism, author, and a lawyer, in Canada and the United States. Situating Shadd in the Black radical tradition, moving between opposition and dialogue with international law of the current international order, Case brings to view not only one Black woman lawyer but a dispossessed and displaced people with a dream. Vasuki Nesiah brings to view Avabai Wadia (1913–2005) from Sri Lanka as a pioneering professional and academic in the transnational struggle for reproductive rights and sexual self-determination. One of the founders of the International Planned Parenthood

[170] See, eg, Ann Tickner, *Gender in International Relations: Feminist Perspectives in Achieving Global Security* (Columbia University Press 1992).

[171] Janne E Nijman, 'Bertha von Suttner: Locating International Law in Novel and *Salon*', Ch.6, in this volume.

[172] Kate Grady and Gina Heathcote, 'Jane Addams: Positive Peace from the Everyday to the International', Ch. 7, in this volume.

[173] Freya Baetens, 'International Congress of Women (1915)' in Max Planck Encyclopedia of Public International Law (2011) 1–11.

[174] Kathryn Kish Sklar and James Brewer Stewart (eds), *Women's Rights and Transatlantic Antislavery in the Era of Emancipation* (Yale University Press 2007).

[175] Gevers (n 21).

Federation (IPPF), solidary and charismatic, Wadia has features of a feminist anti-imperialist hero. As Nesiah concludes, however, Wadia faced difficult choices, such as building 'strategic alliances with activists and policy makers... whose family planning politics were infused with racial, caste and class prejudice'.[176]

Hall of Diversity of Feminist Activism in International Law starts with Frédéric Mégret's portrait of Ghénia Avril de Sainte-Croix (1855–1939) in the context of activism for the suppression of White Slave Trade, 'la traite des blanches' at the League of Nations.[177] Keina Yoshida presents Yayori Matsui (1934–2002), a Japanese journalist and civil society activist who was a key figure in mobilizing the Women's International War Crimes Tribunal on Japan's Military Sexual Slavery held in Tokyo. The women's tribunal flagged the omission of the Allied and subsequently the state of Japan to address the responsibility for large-scale, organized sexual violence during the Second World War in Asia.[178] Michael Addaney sets himself the objective to contributing towards 'canonising the memory of Annie Ruth Jiagge' (1918–1996), a high court judge and a long-term representative of Ghana in the UNCSW. As the most important role she exercised, Addaney selects Jiagge's role in authoring the first draft of the UN Declaration on the Elimination of Discrimination against Women in 1967.[179]

The Hall of Women for Social and Economic Development by International Law presents women who defended ideas of human well-being, gender equality, and socio-economic development by means of international law and institutions. Anne Orford portrays Alva Myrdal (1902–1986), a Swedish intellectual, international civil servant, diplomat, later in her career a negotiator and activist for disarmament, Nobel Prize winner—as well as life-long wife and intellectual peer of economist Gunnar Myrdal. Orford situates Alva Myrdal at the centre of the 'social laboratory and modernist utopia' Sweden became after the Second World War, in the eyes of the outside world, shedding light but also shadows on an eventful career.[180] Miriam Bak Mackenna presents the Danish economist Ester Boserup (1910–1999), author of the influential *Woman's Role in Economic Development*[181] as a key figure in early international economic law. Boserup was, in particular, an astute analyst of the interrelationships between development and women's subordination, poverty, and economic 'invisibility'.[182]

Helvi Sipilä (1915–2009), portrayed by Raimo Lintonen, was a Finnish attorney and a long-term member and chair of the *Commission on the Status of Women* (CWS) who became the first women Assistant Secretary-General of the UN.[183] International welfare feminism, 'international women alliances on welfare rights that disrupted patriarchal and colonial interests relative to women's labour' was clearly never Nordic

[176] Nesiah (n 118).

[177] Frédéric Mégret, 'Ghénia Avril de Sainte-Croix: Abolitionism and the League of Nations', Ch. 11, in this volume.

[178] Yoshida (n 130).

[179] Michael Addaney, 'Canonizing the Memory of Annie Ruth Jiagge in the Global efforts towards Gender Equality', Ch. 13, in this volume.

[180] Orford (n 118).

[181] Ester Boserup, *Woman's Role in Economic Development* (George Allen and Unwin 1970).

[182] Miriam Bak Mackenna, 'Ester Boserup: Women and Development on the Margins', Ch. 15, in this volume.

[183] Lintonen (n 118).

only.[184] The temporal and thematic context presented in the hall was tingling with agents, agendas, and political, gendered, and racialized tensions: the Cold War battles for influence in the decolonialized states, the mediatized alarmism of a 'population bomb' and the controversial efforts to control it. The context in which the portrayed women tried to import 'the Nordic model' of a social democratic welfare state with public policies of gender equality, free education, health care, and social inclusion to the international level was also a swan song of that model.

Turning from these thematically organized halls to address international law in general terms, the exhibition continues in the hall of *Breakers of the Glass Ceiling: the 'First and Only' in International Institutions.* In women's and feminist histories, attention is often given to women who entered an institutional context or excelled in a professional category occupied exclusively by men, in a particular temporal and spatial context.[185] Why is 'the firstness' interesting? For Susan Carle, the firsts are 'part of our cultural history, of the story of the development of law, education and the professions. They are the ones who broke the ice and opened the barriers ... even if they were not always the role models and feminist forerunners we would like them to have been.'[186] Gerda Lerner calls this type of historical characters 'notable women', 'women worthies',[187] adapting closest to the male criteria of value, talent, or excellence. Their opening of the barriers has not been a stable, gradually ascending progress story. There are contextual peeks and lows, such as when women replaced men in diverse sectors during a world war but must make space for men thereafter.[188]

By the entrance of the hall figures Immi Tallgren and Antoine Buchet's portrait analysing representations of Suzanne Bastid (1906–1995), a French international lawyer with a striking career as 'the first' both in her country and in international institutions and professional associations.[189] Boyd van Dijk introduces Marguerite Frick-Cramer (1887–1963), the first woman in many roles in the traditional milieu of humanitarian law, also appointed as 'the first' to the Committee of the International Red Cross in 1918. Boyjd van Dijk, 'Marguerite Frick-Cramer: A Life Spent Shaping the Geneva Conventions, Ch. 18, in this volume. Parvathi Menon's portrait of Vijayalakshmi Pandit (1900–1990) critically navigates between apparent contradictions. Pandit became the first woman to chair the UN General Assembly in 1953, but for many she was and remains 'just' a sister of Jawaharlal Nehru, India's first Prime Minister. Pandit's positions were nationalist and at times radically anti-colonial, yet she was shunned for her elitism and British-oriented education.[190] Jan Klabbers portrays Felice Morgenstern, a legal adviser of the ILO and an

[184] Rebecca Adami, 'International Welfare Feminism: CSW Navigating Cold War Tensions' in Adami and Plesch, *Women (n 51)* 55, also mentioning, eg, Bertha Lux, active both in the UN and ILO. In the Socialist countries, comparable ideas were developed at that time in a Marxist framework.

[185] Mary Jane Mossmann, *The First Women Lawyers: A Comparative Study of Gender, Law and the Legal Professions* (Hart Publishing 2006). See also Sara Kimble and Marion Röwekamp (eds), *New Perspectives on European Women's Legal History* (Routledge 2016).

[186] Ulrike Schultz, 'Introduction: Gender and Careers in the Legal Academy: Overview and Synthesis' in Ulrike Schultz Gisela Shaw, Margaret Thornton, and Rosemary Auchmuty (eds), *Gender and Careers* (Hart 2021) at 15; Susan Carle, 'The Way to Barbara Armstrong, First Tenure-Track Law Professor in an Accredited US Law School', in the same volume.

[187] Lerner (n 46).

[188] See, eg, Susan R Grayzel, *Women and the First World War* (Routledge 2002) 106–09.

[189] Tallgren and Buchet (n. 74).

[190] Menon (n 118).

productive scholar. Klabbers finds merit in her work, even if she was not 'a leading theorist by any standards', as well as 'spikiness', such as, Morgenstern's 'sneering comparison between the status of international organizations in international law, and women in domestic law'.[191] Ana Fouto, António Pedro Barbas Homem, and Pedro De Freitas portray Paula Escarameia (1960–2010), a professor of international law and one of the first two women to enter the International Law Commission of the UN.[192]

The following hall turns from individual portraits to group pictures. Much of the disciplinary history in international law builds upon intellectual and professional collectives such as The *Institut de droit international*, the *International Law Association*, the *Carnegie Foundation*, The *Hague Academy of International Law*, and *Advisory Committee of Jurists of the League of Nations*. They got organized and formed their agendas with no or few women members.[193] That situation evolved rapidly in the twentieth century, so that amongst the women portrayed in the exhibition, there is one whose membership at the American Society of International Law got rejected in 1915, Jane Addams, the 'first' to be elected as Vice-President (in 1962) and receive the Manley O Hudson medal, Marjorie M Whiteman, and the 'first' as an Honorary Member, Suzanne Bastid (in 1972).[194] It would, in any case, be mistaken to imagine women had no associative activities, collective agendas, and comradeship in international law before late twentieth century. A few are well-known today, such as the WILPF.[195] Examples of less-known and fragmented groups are represented in the hall of *The Other Group Pictures in International Law*. Roxana Banu portrays a group of social workers and volunteers after the First World War paying attention to socio-legal problems of women and children in the context of transatlantic migration. The network developed into the International Social Service, a large organization offering both pragmatic assistance and legal advice in international private law, such as, transnational marriage, adoption, maintenance obligations, inheritance.[196]

Benjamin Auberer brings to view women working at the Legal Section of the League of Nations as a group of hierarchically low positioned, often short-term members of the service. Despite the promise of its Statute (see above at p. 11), women never occupied positions in the Legal Section of the League at the level of the qualified civil servants. Few exceptions can be found amongst the League's civil servants, in general.[197]

[191] Klabbers (n 125), pp. 254–255.

[192] Ana Caldeira Fouto, Antonio Pedro BarbasHomen, and Pedro Caridabe de Freitas, Paula Escarameia: Envisioning the Human Face of International Law in the Twenty-First Century, Ch. 21, in this volume.

[193] Adami and Plesch (eds), *The League of Nations and the Development of International Law* (Routledge 2021). The American Society of International Law was reserved to 'any man of good moral character' until 1921, see Alona E Evans and Carol Per Lee Plumb, 'Women and the American Society of International Law' (1974) 68 (2)AJIL 290, 293.

[194] See Hatsue Shinohara, 'Marjorie M. Whiteman—Not Flowers but a Medal', Ch. 36, in this volume, p. 430; Evans and Plumb, 'Women and the American' (2017), at 291, 293.

[195] Gertrude C Bussey and Margaret Tims, *Pioneers for Peace: Women's International League for Peace and Freedom 1915–1965* (WILPF British Section 1980); Jo Vellacot, 'A Place for Pacifism and Transnationalism in Feminist Theory: The Early Work of the Women's International League for Peace and Freedom' (1993) 2 Women's History Review 23.

[196] Roxana Banu, 'Forgotten Female Actors in Private International Law: The International Social Service', Ch. 22, in this volume.

[197] Auberer (n 2). On questioning the changes the League of Nations brought, see Michel Marbeau, 'Les femmes et la Société des Nations (1919–1945): Genève, la clé de l'egalité?' in Jean-Marc Delaunay and Yves Denéchère (eds), *Femmes et les relations internationales au XX siècle* (Sorbonne PSN 2007) 173; Myriam

Bérénice K Schramm portrays a famous context of international law, the Conference for Women in Beijing in 1995, but with unknown characters. 'Indigenous women' were meeting in a shadow conference and negotiated a Declaration which suggests an alternative kind of international law.[198] Anna van der Velde brings to view another context which is both known and unknown. The negotiations of the Rome Statute of the International Criminal Court are famously profiled as a feminist victory, but little is known of the primary motor on the NGO side, The Women's Caucus for Gender Justice.[199]

Women make out a growing number of law students in the last decades globally, outnumbering male students in many countries. Nevertheless, women in higher hierarchical positions of the legal academia remain clearly in a minority position.[200] Women carry a growing share of work but lack a pedigree, invisible or othered in curriculums, public rituals, social codes of conduct, and attire, etc. A law school, Godden-Rasul writes, 'where students begin to formally learn about law provides a space in which to intervene in the gendered visual codes and dimensions of law. Students come to law school primed with portrayals of (male) lawyering, and stereotypes of the good man lawyer.'[201] *The Missing Faces of the Faculty Corridors* present eight scholars, teachers, informaticians, experts of international law. Sarah Wambaugh (1882–1955), portrayed by Imogen Saunders, was a leading specialist of plebiscites in the United States.[202] Lilly Melchior Roberts (1903–1966) had to emigrate from Germany and converted to a profession of information management in European and international law, as Alexandra Kemmerer presents.[203] Lea Meriggi (1902–1944) was amongst the first as a professor of international law in Europe, writes Serena Forlati from the same university. Her memory is tarnished by her open support to National-Socialism.[204] Isabella Diederiks-Verschoor (1915–2017) was an expert in aviation and space law, and a motor of international exchanges and collaboration, Christiaan Verwer and Anna van der Velde write.[205] Gezina van der Molen (1892–1978) academic and activist, is not literally 'missing in the corridors': the Free University of Amsterdam holds her portrait and named a scholarship after her. Sarah Nouwen and Wouter Werner narrate, however, how controversial decisions in the wake of World War II made

Piguet, 'Gender Distribution in the League of Nations: The Start of a Revolution?' in Gram-Skjoldager and Ikonomou, *The League* (n 6) 60.

198 Bérénice K Scramm, 'The "Indigenous women" behind the "Other" Beijing Declaration', Ch. 24, in this volume.

199 Anna van der Velde, 'The Womens Caucus for Gender Justice: Writing Gender into International Criminal Law', Ch. 25, in this volume.

200 See Ulrike Schultz, 'Introduction: Gender and Careers in the Legal Academy: Overview and Synthesis', in Schultz (n 24).

201 Godden-Rasul (n 26) 12.

202 Saunders (n 127).

203 Alexandra Kemmerer, 'Exile and Access: Lilly Melchior Roberts and the Infrastructures of International Law', Ch. 27, in this volume. Another early legal librarian is Florence Wilson (1884–1977) at the library of the League of Nations, Michel Marbeau, 'Les femmes et la Société des Nations (1919–1945)' Jean-Marc Delaunay and Yves Denéchère (eds), *Femmes et relations internationals au XXe siècle* (Sorbonne PSN 2007) 170.

204 Forlati(n 133).

205 Christiaan Verwer and Anna van der Velde, 'Isabella Diederiks-Verschoor: (A Life) Creating Spaces', Ch. 29, in this volume.

her 'a recognized international lawyer who cannot be celebrated'.[206] Elisabeth Mann Borgese (1918–2002), a predecessor and inspiration for the portraitist Sara Seck, was an interdisciplinary talent with an intimate take on her area of research, the protection of the seas and maritime environments.[207] Marie Theres Fögen's (1946–2008) research in the history of international law was creative and feminist, but shadowed by the traditionalist academic context and her untimely death, Reut Yael Paz's portrait deplores.[208] Marilena Papadaki features Kalliopi Koufa (born 1936), the first woman as an international law professor in Greece and a renowned expert at the UN and other institutional contexts.[209]

The Roof-Top Gallery of Diplomacy and International Relations exhibits sitters who engaged with international law from diverse institutional positions in the context of foreign policy and the emerging international institutionalization. The approach is not that of the genres of diplomatic history or history of international relations, with focus on the most visible acts by the most notable actors, but rather on biographical and ethnographical history of everyday actors.[210] The first is a British international lawyer, Thomas Baty (1869–1954), known for having served the Foreign Ministry of the imperial Japanese government.[211] Shinya Murase presents another view of Baty, the anonymous creator of the transgender journal, *Urania*, arguing for a society without the divisive importance given to sex and gender.[212] Margaret Kuo features Zheng Yuxiu (1896–1956) as an activist nationalist and feminist, in diverse professional roles as a diplomate, judge, legislator, law professor, and legal practitioner. Zheng's main interest in international law was to overturn the unequal treaties imposed on China and to protect its sovereignty.[213] Marjorie M Whiteman had a long and rich career at the United States State Department. She published enormously, including the Digest of International Law and a treatise on damages but, as her portraitist Hatsue Shinohara regrets, gets 'often overlooked and ... forgotten in scholarship'.[214]

Sergey Vasiliev portrays Alexandra Kollontai's (1872–1952) many faces, from a venerable Soviet delegate to the League of Nations, ambassador, and foreign trade technocrat, to an intellectual with avant-gardist ideas of women's sexual and economic autonomy without the restraints of marriage, erased by the regime.[215] Paulina Luisi (1875–1950), a medical doctor from Uruguay, is portrayed by Andrei Mamolea as passionate for international feminist activism, advancement of domestic social

[206] Sarah Nouwen and Wouter Werner, 'Gezina van der Molen', Ch. 30, in this volume.
[207] Seck (n 132).
[208] Paz (n 124).
[209] Marilena Papadaki, 'Kalliopi Koufa: First Greek Female Academic of Public International Law', Ch. 33, in this volume.
[210] See, eg, Ulrike Niedner-Kalthoff (eds), *Ständige Vertretung*: Eine Ethnografie diplomaticher Lebenswelten (Bielefeld: transcript Verlag 2015).
[211] See, eg, William E Butler, 'Thomas Baty, Legal Adviser to the Government of Japan' (2020) 5 Jus Gentium: Journal of International Legal History 185.
[212] Murase (n 58).
[213] Margaret Kuo, 'Zheng Yuzxiu and the Diplomacy of Nationalism and Feminism', Ch. 35, in this volume.
[214] Shinohara (n 190).
[215] Sergey Vasiliev, Alexandra Kollontai, "New Woman", Ch. 37, in this volume.

policy by international law, and the League of Nations who had to face many disappointments.[216] Luiza Leão Soares Pereira aims at presenting, in the context of the gendered norms and prejudices of the British Foreign Office, 'a realistic photo of women in action'.[217] She analyses the ascension of Joyce Gutteridge (1906–1992) to the post of a Legal Adviser in light of her class, whiteness, and networks, most notably her father Harold Cooke Gutteridge, first Professor of Comparative law in Cambridge.

Portraits of Artists and Visionaries of International Law conclude the exhibition. Whereas in this volume, scholars and experts of law, history, and international relations experiment with portraiture, in the last hall the mirror is turned around: how did artists, visionary poets, avant-garde philosophers, authors of fiction and essays see international law, its institutions, and social practice? Outi Korhonen portrays Simone Weil (1909–1943) as a philosopher and a transgender avant-gardist, and also as an epistemological and ideological nonconformist. Dismissed from the preparation of the Universal Declaration of Human Rights, Weil saw rights as a paradoxical concept that separates rather than unites human beings with each other. The alternative consisted, for Weil, of a combination of human roots and 'duties', underlining 'the interplay of human responsibilities, rights, needs and trust'.[218]

Helene Halperin-Ginsburg (1883–1922) was a lawyer excluded from practice of law in Russia for being a woman and a Jew. Ksenia Shestakova narrates her as an activist for social justice, protection of children, and later also feminism, a journalist for progressive causes and an early supporter of liberal international law in opposition to the Soviet understandings of international law and politics.[219] Mai Taha's sitter was an Egyptian artist, communist, and feminist Inji Aflatoun (1924–1989) who invoked international human rights to advance her objectives. Not in an abstract, liberal internationalist frame, Taha underlines, but as a strategic instrument alongside others, such as armed resistance or surrealist political art activism.[220] Dianne Otto's portrait of Shirley Hazzard (1931–2016) features a young Australian typist at the UN who turns into a pungent commentator of the paradoxes of international law's ideals and the Cold War challenges. Hazzard became a best-selling author of fiction and essays. Her insider views of the UN, disillusioned but not hopeless, 'should today be compulsory reading for all'.[221]

Hilary Charlesworth's astute epilogue terminates the visit to the Portrait Gallery of International Law in the gift shop. She suggests precious thoughts to take home as gifts, such as 'the courage to question the content and quality of the ubiquitous galleries of great male international lawyers'.[222]

216 Andrei Mamolea, 'The Role of International Law in Paulina Luisi's Activism', Ch. 38, in this volume.

217 Luiza Leão Soares Pereira, 'Working from "Rooms of their Own": For a Realistic Portrait of Joyce Gutteridge CBE and Other Trailblazing Women', Ch. 39, in this volume.

218 Korhonen (n 58).

219 Ksenia Shestakova, 'Helene Halperin-Ginsburg: The Social Function of International Law', Ch. 41, in this volume.

220 Mai Taha, 'Human rights and Communist Internationalism: On Inji Aflatoun and the Surrealists', Ch. 42, in this volume.

221 Dianne Otto, 'Fearless Speech: A Portrait of UN Typist Shirley Hazzard', Ch. 43, in this volume.

222 Hilary Charlesworth, 'Epilogue: Exit through the Gift Shop', in this volume.

Back to the Future: Alternative Visions

This exhibition is a product of its moment. Its portraits are cramped in a tiny wing for temporary exhibitions, awaiting to be integrated in the prestigious Portrait Gallery of International Law—or not. It is now time for the visitors to look at the portraits, and their privilege to make conclusions of that experience. I shall simply share the curator's impressions at the eve of the vernissage.

The art of hanging portraits traditionally reflected status and wealth, taste in arts being considered an expression of class identity which contributes to the transmission of values, talents, and virtues. For it is the act of exposing a piece of work signed by the artist for view in the 'most sacred place', gallery or museum, that makes it become art, symbolically and financially. In that process, the name of the artist acts as a powerful sign: even if the sign/name does not change the physical character of the artwork, it affects its social nature.[223] A piece of research of international law, be it doctrine, theory, or history is also recreated at its reception, at the repetitive moments it is read and analysed. How, where, recommended by whom it becomes public counts, in today's academia where rankings, elite journals, expensive Global North conferences, and research funding competitions measure and express value, status, and resources.[224] Anodyne or petty as they seem, also the choices on whose portraits are to be cherished by professional communities serve as signposts for 'recognising the dynamics of our own contemporary cultural traditions'.[225]

International law, its diverse intellectual and professional contexts, are facing a transition whereby the semantic codes of traditions start to lose their bearings—as argued above. The most crucial changes do not concern visual memorabilia, but the management of the immaterial and material capital of the imagined collectivities they symbolize. Whereas art is believed to carry potential to engender changes in societies, by breaking the classed structures,[226] the same is seldom thought of history-writing. Histories of history-making show, nevertheless, how ever-present and at times drastic change is. Amongst the contingencies of history, fashionable topic also in international law,[227] the inclusions and exclusions in the spheres of knowledge and power of its professional and intellectual communities have not been addressed. By failing to identify and interrogate them, histories continue to take part in obscuring 'the way power works and make[s] particular intellectual or social hierarchies appear as natural aspects of our lives'.[228]

This exhibition tries to turn the tables. It disengages from the current practice of both deploring all 'women' for their predicament of cumulating intersecting

[223] Pierre Bourdieu, *Distinction. A Social Critique of the Judgement of Taste* (Routledge, 1986 [1979])).

[224] See, eg, Jan Klabbers, 'On Epistemic Universalism and the Melancholy of International Law' 29 EJIL (2018), 1057–069.

[225] Pointon, *Hanging the Head* (n 45) 5.

[226] See, eg, Norma Broude and Mary Garrard, *Feminism and Art History* (Routledge 1982).

[227] Ingo Venzke and Kevin Jon Heller (eds), *Contingency in International Law: On the Possibility of Different Legal Histories* (OUP 2021). See also Richard J Evans, *Altered Pasts: Counterfactuals in History* (Little, Brown 2014).

[228] Martti Koskenniemi, 'International Law: Constitutionalism, Managerialism and the Ethos of Legal Education' (2007) 1 European Journal of Legal Studies 1.

disadvantages with the other 'invisibles and silenced of histories'[229] and ignoring them. It abandons the expectation that everyone involved in international law today should acknowledge such reductive images of history, entering their biased frames and tacit assumptions. What are the alternatives? Searches for survivors after centuries of exclusion and marginalization continue to have their value and interest, but only with conditions. They should be combined with a critical identification of the formal and informal institutional practices, norms, and rituals of white masculinities in international law's past, in its research, and their eventual continuities. New names and forgotten faces do matter. Lost seeds of other family trees can be found. The goal of re-curation is not, however, to 'broaden agency' until everybody becomes, in one way or another, an international lawyer. The process has its limits. 'The Dazzling Aten', a city with treasures hidden in the sediments of sand in Egypt was discovered as this re-curation closes. In contrast, the quasi-exclusivity in the leading roles in international law that persisted until the 1990s is not likely to be reversed by excavations. Does this mean the re-curation lacks interest and consequences for today's international law and its research?

The opposite is argued here. Maintaining a gendered monopoly of the history of international law has been part of a broader political, economic, and social oppression that present international law carries traces of. Instead of assimilating and co-opting its hierarchies, in search for (a meagre) recognition, everyone has the choice to question, reject, or attempt to revise, not only the histories, but eventually the law. *What if* the excluded geared their energies from the strenuous struggles for inclusion—and the mourning and melancholia—to a collective celebration of their 'late birth'? Why seek to 'simply "occupy" a domain so enduringly grounded in their non-residence'[230]? A precious non-entanglement in an often-disastrous project and its consequences might be turned into a blessing, a cleaner basis to build future utopias on. The exhibition, of modest demeanour compared to libraries full of dominant intellectual history, foregrounds this question: Must one still climb up *that* family tree, many branches of which host ancestors condoning the destructive exploitation of the Earth, dominating its resources, and justifying the violence that protects *that* order?

Precursors of such a 'turn away from *that* history' of international law can be perceived in the portraits that follow. The limited space does not allow for rich details. The visitors are greeted by forty-two signs of existence, a scattered and sporadic presence in the imagined spaces and times of international law. In this, the work was inspired by the conviction of Virginia Woolf that with specific attention, it is possible to see women (and other marginalized subjects) in history: 'For one often catches a glimpse of them in the lives of the great, whisking away into the background, concealing, I sometimes think, a wink, a laugh, perhaps a tear.'[231] These forty-two tiny glimpses may disappoint or distort, but also leave the visitors hungry for more. They are but a beginning, an expression of the desire to disrupt the dominant gendered, racialized, and classed images of history in international law. The gallery is open for your visit, welcome!

[229] Rosalind Morris (ed), *Can Subaltern Speak? Reflections on the History of an Idea* (Columbia University Press 2010).

[230] Joan B Lands, *Women and the Public Sphere in the Age of the French Revolution* (Cornell University Press 1998) 206.

[231] Virginia Woolf, *A Room of One's Own* (Hogarth Press 1929) 45.

PART II
THE VESTIBULE OF THE LEGENDARY ANCIENTS

2
Christine de Pizan
The Law of Warfare as Seen by a Medieval Woman

Franck Latty

Christine de Pizan (*c*1365–*c*1430) remains largely unknown to legal scholarship. The daughter of a Bologna astrologist and physicist, Christine de Pizan was born in Venice, Italy. Her father having been invited to the court by Charles V, she joined the Kingdom of France at the age of five. Married at fifteen, she was widowed ten years later. She began writing to support herself and her family, including her three children. Her manuscripts (the printing press was invented some twenty years after her death) were distributed with great success to the princes and patrons of the time, many of whom were her protectors. A person of great erudition, Pizan is likely the first woman to have lived by her pen.

Her work in (old) French, abundant and varied, 'contains charming poems as well as austere philosophical and historical treatises'.[1] A contemporary of Joan of Arc, she dedicated a poem to her in 1429. She is also a renowned letter writer. Among her best-known works, *Le Livre de la Cité des dames* (*The Book of the City of Ladies*, 1405) is an allegorical treatise of a city inhabited exclusively by great women, which itself is sometimes presented as one of the first feminist works of literature.[2] In her writings, more generally, Pizan celebrates the moral qualities of women, refutes misogynistic clichés, and fights against those who make women inferior to men.[3] The question of women's rights was not discussed at that time, but Pizan's defence of women[4] is particularly inspiring from this perspective.

Even though Pizan never produced a full legal survey, the law is not absent from her work. One particularly noteworthy work is *The Book of Deeds of Arms and of Chivalry*[5] (which earns Pizan her place in the portrait gallery of women who have left a mark on the history of international law).

[1] (tr) Suzanne Solente, 'Christine de Pisan' [1969] Histoire littéraire de la France 40, 14.

[2] On the feminist interpretation of Pizan's work, see eg Rosalind Brown-Grant, *Christine de Pizan and the Moral Defence of Women: Reading beyond Gender* (Cambridge University Press 1999).

[3] Andrea Valentini, Edition of Christine de Pizan, *Le livre des epistres du debat sus le* Rommant de la Rose (Classiques Garnier 2014) 136.

[4] Isle Paakkinen, *Gender and Defence of Women in Christine de Pizan's Thought*, PhD dissertation (University of Helsinki 2016) 243 ff.

[5] I relied on the translation into modern English of the Book by Sumner Willard (tr) and Charity Cannon Willard (ed), *The Book of Deeds of Arms and of Chivalry* (The Pennsylvania State University Press 1999), and on the *édition critique* by L Dugaz, *Le Livre des fais d'armes et de chevalerie de Christine de Pizan. Edition critique* (Classiques Garnier, 2011).

Franck Latty, *Christine de Pizan* In: *Portraits of Women in International Law*. Edited by: Immi Tallgren, Oxford University Press.
 DOI: 10.1093/oso/9780198868453.003.0002

Figure 2.1 Christine de Pizan, *Livre des faits d'armes et de chevalerie, Mutation de Fortune*, c. 1410–1411, Paris, Bnf, fr 603, fol. 127v. Christine de Pizan-narrator in front of a mural painting. The picture is taken from one of her manuscripts offered to a patron.
Source: Bibliothèque nationale de France. Département des Manuscrits, France.

The Significance of *The Book of Deeds of Arms and of Chivalry* in the History of International Law

In 1410, Pizan finished *Le Livre des faits d'armes et de chevalerie* (*The Book of Deeds of Arms and of Chivalry*) which is a manual of warfare, intended primarily for those who are called upon to make war. It combines the art of warfare (strategic advice, qualities required of combatants, techniques of warfare, etc) with (a) the law of war at the time. Nevertheless, care must be taken not to fall into anachronism: in 1410, international law does not exist yet; *The Book of Deeds of Arms* refers to (b) rules permeated by religion.

(a) The Law of War in *The Book of Deeds of Arms*

The first part of *The Book* opens with comments on 'just war', a concept already well-known at the time, since Plato and Aristotle, then Cicero, and Saint Augustine and its 'successor'[6] Thomas Aquinas who laid the foundations for the concept. In this vein, Pizan writes that just wars are allowed: 'it seems manifest that wars undertaken for a just cause are permitted by God'.[7]

She then identifies five 'grounds' at the origin of wars, three of which 'rest on law': supporting law and justice (for example to defend the Church, or to help an ally or vassal); responding to attacks 'on the land and the people'; and launching military action to recover land usurped by others. In addition to these, there are two grounds 'of will': revenge for losses suffered; and conquering foreign lands or lordships.[8]

This is followed by guidelines of all kinds concerning the practice of warfare inspired by the writings of the Romans Vegetius,[9] and also Valerius Maximus and Sextus Julius Frontinus whose military narratives are presented in Part II of *The Book*, supplemented by oral sources collected by Pizan.[10]

More interestingly from an international law point of view, Parts III and IV of *The Book* address the 'laws governing deeds of arms',[11] the legal elements of which are largely taken directly from Honoré Bovet's *Battle Tree* (*L'arbre des batailles*).[12] In these parts of *The Book*, Pizan presents herself in an allegorical dream dialogue between a master (Bovet) and his pupil (Pizan). Some issues concerning the right or obligation to wage war are again addressed ('whether the Emperor has the right to make war on the Pope';[13] 'whether the vassal is by right obliged to go to war for his overlord at his own expense').[14] Apart from the important question of who should bear the costs of the war, these two parts are mainly devoted to the regulation of the conduct of hostilities.

Concerning tricks for example, Pizan states that 'one should conquer one's enemy by ruse, wiles, or tricks without doing wrong in arms' but that 'there are certain kinds of tricks that are unacceptable and forbidden' such as making an appointment for talks and taking the opportunity to capture the person and attack him, or feigning a truce or peace to kill another when his guard is released and he feels safe.[15] On the protection of prisoners of war, Pizan writes that 'it is against right and gentility to slay the one

[6] Martin Kintzinger, 'From the Late Middle Ages to the Peace of Westphalia' in Bardo Fassbender and Anne Peters (eds), *The Oxford Handbook of the History of International Law* (OUP 2012) 619 .

[7] Part I, Chapter II, Willard (n 5) 14.

[8] Part I, Chapter IV, ibid 16.

[9] eg Part I, Chapter XVIII ibid 53: 'the action a commander must take when it appears that battle is imminent'; Part II, Chapter XIV ibid 104: 'the way to fight in castles and towns'.

[10] eg Part II, Chapter XVI ibid 110: 'Particular needs for stocking a fortress with food supplies as well as weapons'; Dugaz (n 5) 31.

[11] Part III, Chapter I Willard (n 5) 143.

[12] Dugaz (n 5) 31. Note that the name of this author knows several spellings (Honoré/Honorat Bovet/Bouvet/Bonet).

[13] Part III, Chapter II, Willard (n 5) 145.

[14] Part III, Chapter V, ibid 148.

[15] Part III, Chapter XIII, ibid 163. cf First Protocol Additional to the Geneva Conventions relating to the Protection of Victims of International Armed Conflicts (1977), which permits 'ruses of war', but prohibits 'perfidy' (art 37).

who gives himself up'.[16] In the same vein, on the protection of civilian populations, she makes Bovet say in a very clear manner: 'those who engage in warfare may be hurt, but the humble and peaceful should be shielded from their force'.[17]

Several chapters in Part III and Part IV of *The Book* are also devoted to salient legal issues at that time, such as capture of individuals, ransom, inviolability of ambassadors, safe-conducts, truces, letters of marques (reprisals against individual), judicial combat, and coats of arms.

Although the law of war (*jus ad bellum, jus in bello*) is now materially part of international law, this was not the case in the late Middle Ages, when international law was at best 'a phenomenon *avant la lettre*'.[18] As shown in the *Book of Deeds of Arms and of Chivalry*, the law of warfare derives from a legal background inextricably linked to religion.

(b) Legal Background of the Law of Warfare in *The Book of Deeds of Arms and of Chivalry*

In 1410, the idea of a legal system governing international relations (including bellicose ones) between states had not yet taken shape. In France (the country that adopted Pizan), the state, as a form of territorial organization of political power, had not yet completely succeeded the feudal system when Christine de Pizan wrote her work, although the establishment of the monarchical state is particularly indebted to the reigns of Charles V and Charles VII, which respectively saw the birth and death of Pizan. However, at the risk of oversimplifying a complex process, it can be considered that the state, in the contemporary sense of the term, took shape during the reign of Louis XI (1461–1483), which marked the consolidation of royal authority over a unified population and territory. Many other European countries experienced, more or less belatedly, a similar process of assertion of the nation-state vis-à-vis the Pope and the Emperor, at the end of which sovereignty was assimilated to the king and the state.

The Book gives an edifying testimony to the lack of identity at that time between sovereignty and the authority, still contested, attached to the person of the king. Dealing with the right to wage wars, Pizan reserves this privilege for 'sovereign princes', to the exclusion of barons 'or any other person, however great he may be' if he has not 'the express permission and will of his sovereign lord'.[19] However, the 'sovereign prince' is understood in a broad way in so far as it includes 'emperors, kings, dukes, and other landed lords who are duly and rightfully heads of temporal jurisdictions'.[20] The sovereign presented here is indeed one who has no superior but, as feudalism only begins to come to an end, the quality of the head of temporal jurisdiction is not yet the prerogative of the sole king. The inclusion of dukes in this category served the interests of John

[16] Part III, Chapter XVII, ibid 169. cf Geneva Convention (III) relative to the Treatment of Prisoners of War (art 13).

[17] Part III, Chapter XVIII, ibid 172. cf Geneva Convention (IV) on Civilians (1949).

[18] Kintzinger (n 6) 608: 'international law in medieval Western Europe is to be described as a historical reality before its formal existence, that is, in the classical sense of a phenomenon *avant la lettre*'.

[19] Part I, Chapter III, Willard (n 5) 15.

[20] ibid.

the Fearless, who may have commissioned *The Book* with a view to the military education of the Dauphin Louis of Guyenne.[21] It nonetheless reflects the vague contours of sovereignty in these proto-state times.

Pizan's conception of law has been analysed as 'similar to the Thomistic and the Dantean conceptions of law', and it has been shown that in her works Pizan 'utilizes the standard division of law into natural, human and divine law, with the emphasis on law as right reason and law as justice'.[22]

In *The Book of Deeds of Arms and of Chivalry*, the right to have recourse to war seems to emerge first and foremost from 'divine law',[23] while the conduct of hostilities seems to be more governed by 'written law'.[24] However, the sources are not so clearly distributed. In any case, religion occupies a prominent place in the regulation of war, whether it is 'divine law',[25] the 'Holy Writ',[26] even morality,[27] and their less metaphysical declination through 'canon law',[28] body of written law produced by a very human institution: the Church. This is not surprising as at that time the Church controlled the whole of society and provided a framework for war, especially in order to limit conflicts between Christians. Among various sources, Gratian's decree (mid-twelfth century) is a masterful compilation of canon law, which includes a *Cause* 23 which deals with the legitimacy and justice of war.

'Laws drawn up by people' are occasionally referred to alongside canon law, as limits 'in the exercise of arms';[29] to clarify the vassal's obligations to his lord;[30] or from a penal perspective (cases in which people-at-arms deserve the death penalty),[31] or a civil one (eg to establish that the war booty should go to the sovereign who paid the men-at-arms).[32] Finally, precedents,[33] the 'law of nature',[34] battlefield customs,[35] even scholarship,[36] have an important place in *The Book of Deeds of Arms and of Chivalry*. '[D]ivine law' prevails in any event over what is 'customary in arms'.[37] The text navigates between one source and the other, without being bothered by 'precise references to legal texts, retaining only the references to the Scripture and sometimes to the

[21] Dugaz (n 5) 19.
[22] Paakkinen (n 4) 244.
[23] Part I, Chapter II Willard (n 5) 13. cf the quotation above concerning 'wars undertaken for a just cause' that 'are permitted by God'.
[24] Part III, Chapter I ibid 143: 'les loys et le droit escript' in the original version.
[25] Part I, Chapter IV, ibid 17.
[26] Part I, Chapter II, ibid 14 concerning just war.
[27] eg Part III, Chapter XVII, ibid 170 about the ransom amount.
[28] Part I, Chapter II, ibid 14.
[29] ibid.
[30] Part III, Chapter V, ibid 148: 'six principal covenants according to civil law' concerning the obligation of the vassal to go to war for his overlord at his own expense.
[31] Part III, Chapter IV, ibid 147, 'for what offenses men-at-arms may incur capital punishment'.
[32] Part III, Chapter XV, ibid 166–67.
[33] Part III, Chapter III, ibid 146 about Pope Alexander III who, persecuted by the Emperor, found refuge with the King of France 'who restored him to his place'.
[34] Part III, Chapter XXIII, ibid 180: right to liberty of every person, concerning the right of prisoners of war to escape.
[35] Part IV, Chapter III, ibid 189, concerning safe-conducts. See also about 'military custom': Part III, Chapter XX, ibid 175.
[36] Regarding the various opinions of the 'doctors' (no name appears) on the right of clerics to 'go into battle', see Part IV, Chapter XIV, ibid 214.
[37] Part IV, Chapter VII, ibid 198 about judicial duel.

Decree (*Decretum Gratiani*)'.[38] In most cases, solutions seem to be guided by an exegesis of the surrounding legal context rather than by a reference to a precise text. Thus, *The Book of Deeds of Arms and of Chivalry* not only offers a comprehensive account of the law of war in the early fifteenth century, it also reflects its religious sources, the importance of the law of nature, but also the role of other sources. Even if international law did not exist at that time, this certainly places Christine de Pizan in the genealogy of its thinkers.

Christine de Pizan's Place in the History of International Law

Pizan has disappeared from the 'radars' of international law scholars. At the end of the nineteenth century, the Belgian jurist Ernest Nys, 'the first professional historian of international law',[39] had nevertheless devoted several studies to her.[40] Alphonse Rivier echoed them,[41] as well as Dioniso Anzilotti who, in his famous *Corso di diritto internazionale*, briefly mentioned Pizan among the authors of 'special books [on war] in which the juridical aspect of the question is almost always mixed and confused with theological and moral considerations'.[42] Since then, Pizan—apart from very occasional mentions in certain surveys on the history of international law[43]—has fallen into oblivion, even though the rediscovery of her work is the subject of extensive studies in other areas of humanities (literature, linguistics, gender studies, etc).

The disappearance of Pizan from the family tree of international law authors, when the contributions of *The Book of Deeds of Arms and of Chivalry* to the history of international law of war are evident, may come as a surprise. It is a question of (a) identifying the causes, before considering (b) the rehabilitation of Pizan among the thinkers who have their place in the pantheon, haunted by men, of international law.

(a) Causes of Disappearance

From the outset, the issue of gender is inevitable. Pizan's '*Book*' is the work of a woman who tackles a subject traditionally considered 'masculine': war.[44] Pizan does not evade

38 Trs of Dugaz (n 5) 32.

39 Martti Koskenniemi, 'A History of International Law Histories' in Bardo Fassbender and Anne Peters (eds), *The Oxford Handbook of the History of International Law* (OUP 2012) 943.

40 Ernest Nys, 'Honoré Bonet et Christine de Pisan' [1882] Revue de droit international et de législation comparée XIV 451; *Les origines du droit international*, (A Castaigne/Thorin & Fils 1894); *Christine de Pizan et ses principales œuvres* (Martinus Nijhoff 1914).

41 Alphonse Rivier, *Note sur la littérature du droit des gens avant la publication du* Jus belli ac pacis *de Grotius (1625)* (Académie royale de Belgique 1883). He begins the chapter on the fifteenth century by writing (tr): 'Among the authors, we note an illustrious woman, the graceful [sic], learned and valiant Christine de Pisan', ibid 27.

42 Dionisio Anzilotti (tr Gilbert Gidel), *Cours de droit international* (Sirey 1929) 5.

43 eg in French legal literature Dominique Gaurier, *Histoire du droit international* (Presses universitaires de Rennes 2014) 120.

44 Françoise Le Saux, 'War and Knighthood in Christine de Pizan's *Livre des faits d'armes et de chevallerie*' in Corinne Saunders, Françoise Le Saux, and Neil Thomas (eds), *Writing War: Medieval Literary Responses to Warfare* (Brewer 2004) 194.

the issue since, not without irony, she pretends to leave aside 'cattails, spinning, and household duties', before invoking Minerva 'goddess of arms and of chivalry' to better justify a 'simple little woman' ('*simple femmelette*') coming to 'speak of such an elevated office as that of arms'.[45]

The supposed lack of legitimacy of a woman to 'treat such exalted matter'[46] no doubt explains that, subsequently, *The Book of Deeds of Arms and of Chivalry* was presented as the work of a man.[47] Similarly, it cannot be excluded that a gender bias has led international law scholars to judge of little interest a woman's thoughts on war and its law, all the more so as this scholarship remained almost exclusively male until the last quarter of the twentieth century. Among the great names who have been called the 'founders of international law',[48] there is no woman.

While Pizan's status as a woman may not be completely unrelated to the oblivion into which she has sunk, other explanations can be put forth, such as the fact that she has never been identified as a lawyer but rather as an intellectual all-rounder[49] or that the legal developments *The Book* contains lack fundamental originality in relation to earlier and later writings on the subject.[50] But in truth, the blacklisting of Pizan concerns more generally medieval legal thought.

The famous book *Les fondateurs du droit international*, for example, does not include any men of the Middle Ages among the founders of the discipline. Yet, medieval thought 'is far from being as sterile as is commonly thought'.[51] Indeed, many canonists and other 'learned men'[52] have dealt with various subjects concerning international law: war, peace, relations between sovereigns, embassies, etc.[53] Medieval writings on the law of war, in particular, have nourished the knowledge and reflection of later scholars (that of the famous 'founders' that followed the appearance of states and the birth of the law governing relations between these entities), whose approach based on natural law hardly marks a break from that followed by Pizan. 'Just war' in the works of Francisco de Vitoria (*c*1483–1546), Francisco Suárez (1548–1617), Alberico Gentili (1552–1608), and above all Hugo Grotius (1583–1645), great figures of the school of the law of nature supposed to have laid down the foundations of international law, is a continuation of the writings of the Middle Ages, including *The Book of Deeds of Arms and of Chivalry*, on the subject. Should Pizan therefore be rehabilitated?

[45] Part I, Chapter I Willard (n 5) 13.

[46] Part I, Chapter I ibid 11.

[47] See Everett L Wheeler, 'Christine de Pizan's *Livre des fais d'armes et de chevalerie*: Gender and the Prefaces' [2002] Nottingham Medieval Studies XLVI 119–61.

[48] See the book *Les fondateurs du droit international* (Giard & Brière 1904, rev edn Panthéon-Assas 2014), hereafter *Les fondateurs*. See also Part IV (People in Portrait) in Bardo Fassbender and Anne Peters (eds), *The Oxford Handbook of the History of International Law* (OUP 2012), where only one woman (with a minor role in international law) is portraited: the Austrian writer and peace activist Bertha von Suttner (1843–1914).

[49] See (n 1).

[50] See (n 55).

[51] Ernest Nys (tr), Introduction in L'arbre des batailles *d'Honoré Bonet* (Muquardt 1883) vi, hereafter Nys, Introduction.

[52] Kintzinger (n 6) 608.

[53] Rivier (n 41) 5.

(b) Grounds for Rehabilitation

What is the real contribution of Pizan and her *Book of Deeds of Arms and of Chivalry* to the history of international law? First of all, it is established that Pizan does not innovate much when it comes to the law of war. Like many of her predecessors, contemporaries, or successors (Grotius himself for instance),[54] she has taken up a lot of what others had already written. As previously noted, most of the developments relevant to the law of war are taken directly from Honoré Bovet's *Battle Tree*, who himself had largely 'plagiarised' the *Tractatus de insignis et armis* of Bartole of Sassoferrato, the *Tractatus de bello* of the Bolognese jurist Legnano, as well as, for canon law, the Decree of Gratian.[55] At least Pizan has the elegance to acknowledge that she has 'gathered together facts and subject matter from various books'[56] and even to stage, at her own side, her main source (Bovet) in the last two parts of *The Book*.[57]

But apart from the fact that Pizan proves to be a much better pedagogue than her teacher,[58] even if it means reducing the legal dimension of her prose (by selecting passages from *The Battle Tree* or by omitting references to textual sources),[59] the contribution of *The Book* lies in the ambition to cover the theme of war in its double technical and legal dimension. Pizan thus 'fills an intellectual and practical void and signs the first French full survey on military matters'.[60]

From the point of view of the history of international law, Pizan belongs to a lineage: that of the thinkers not only of just war,[61] but more generally of warfare and its framework by law. She is thus the first known woman to have written on these issues, long before the famous 'founding fathers' of international law.

In the footsteps of the historian of law Maria Teresa Guerra Medici, should Pizan thus be called the 'mother of international law'?[62] The formula, which sounds almost like a slogan, is seductive. It is unfortunately misleading, if not completely wrong. First of all, one can criticize the movement that leads to the birth of a branch of law being based on a single person: international law was born first and foremost from the legal practice of states, which some authors have been able to systematize successfully, not without relying on the writings of their predecessors. The absurdity of making Grotius the 'father of international law' is no longer to be established;[63] it would be

54 Jules Basdevant, 'Hugo Grotius', in *Les fondateurs du droit international* (n 43) 205 notes that Grotius owes much to his forerunners, especially Victoria, Vasquez, and Gentili.

55 Nys, Introduction (n 51) XVI.

56 Part I, Chapter I Willard (n 5) 12.

57 See (n 12).

58 Bernard Ribémont, 'Le *"Livre des faits d'armes et de chevalerie"*: droit et didactique' in Dominique Demartini et al (ed), *Une femme et la guerre à la fin du Moyen Age: Le 'Livre des faits d'armes et de chevalerie' de Christine de Pizan* (Champion 2016) 139 ff.

59 H Biu, '*Et la gist la maistrie*: de l'*Arbre des batailles* au *Livre des faits d'armes et de chevalerie*', in Demartini (ed), *Une femme et la guerre* (n 58) 152 ff.

60 ibid 150.

61 Cian O'Driscoll, 'Christine de Pizan (c.1364-c.1430)' in Daniel R Brunstetter and Cian O'Driscoll (eds), *Just War Thinkers. From Cicero to the 21st Century* (Routledge 2018) 64 ff.

62 Maria Teresa Guerra Medici, 'The Mother of International Law: Christine de Pisan' [1999] Parliaments, Estates and Representation 19 1 15–22.

63 Recently, see Charles Leben, 'Grotius: serait le père du droit international' in Hervé Ascensio and others (eds), *Dictionnaire des idées reçues en droit international* (Pedone 2017) 279 ff.

inappropriate to reproduce the same shortcomings by making Pizan the progenitor of the discipline. Her writings have, furthermore, left less of a mark on the history of international law than those of the Dutch jurisconsult.

If Pizan fits in well with a line of thought on war and its law, *The Book of Deeds of Arms and of Chivalry* is not such as to bring to the baptismal font a new legal system which, moreover, will not appear until several decades after her death. In other words, her '*Book*', which merely presents in a very pragmatic manner the material rules applicable to various war-related cases, does not propose any 'paradigmatic model of international law'[64] that could attribute to Pizan the origin of the discipline or even its theorization.

In short, Pizan deserves her place in the history of international law because she contributed substantially, with others, to the knowledge and reflection on the law of war, which is at the heart of the law of nations. She is one of the scouts who paved the way for the constitution of a discipline that will wait a few more centuries before being systematized by others and emancipated from natural law.

It is modest, but sufficient: in the male genealogical tree of international law thinkers, it is high time to recognize Christine de Pizan's rightful place, no matter if her legal thought on war was very classical and if she is not the ultimate author to refer to when addressing international law '*avant la lettre*' in the Middle Ages. Maybe Pizan's gender contributes to bring her now to the front of attention but this is a fair return after decades of collective amnesia.

[64] Trs of Emmanuelle Jouannet, *Le droit international libéral-providence: Une histoire du droit international* (Bruylant 2011) 21.

3
Olympe de Gouges
Beyond the Symbol

*Anne Lagerwall and Agatha Verdebout**

Introduction

At first glance, Olympe de Gouges hardly fits within the category of 'forgotten faces or names'. Born Marie Gouze in Montauban in 1748 and guillotined in Paris in 1793, the French playwright and political essayist is one of the famous figures associated with the French Revolution of 1789. She is mostly remembered for her pledges in favour of gender equality and against slavery. She is regularly labelled as the 'first modern feminist' in France[1]—an element which prompted the Francophone network of feminist studies in international law to choose the name of *Réseau Olympe*.[2] However, this label contrasts with how little her work is actually known, studied, and referenced in international legal scholarship.[3]

In this chapter, we try to underline what international lawyers can learn from the life and work of Olympe de Gouges, beyond the symbol that she has become.[4] Why do we not engage with her writings more? First, we briefly outline how de Gouges is remembered in international legal scholarship. Second, we argue that the original character of de Gouges's rewriting exercise of the *Declaration of the Right of Man and of the*

* The authors would like to thank all the participants to the webinar organized on 14 January 2021 by the University of Helsinki during which a draft version of this paper was presented and, more particularly, Immi Tallgren and Bérénice Schramm for their insightful comments.

[1] Dominique Godineau, 'Olympe de Gouges' in Sylvie Chapon and Christine Bard (eds), *Dictionnaire des féministes. France XVIIIe—XXIe siècles* (PUF 2017); Yannick Ripa, *Femmes d'exceptions: les raisons de l'oubli* (Le Cavalier Bleu 2018); Benoîte Groult, *Ainsi soit Olympe de Gouges: La déclaration des droits de la femme et autres textes politiques* (Grasset 2013); Olivier Blanc, *Marie-Olympe de Gouges: une humaniste à la fin du XVIIIe siècle* (René Viénet 2003); Jeanne A Ojala, 'Marie-Olympe de Gouges, 1745–1793' in Katharina M Wilson, Paul Schuelter, and June Schlueter (eds), *Women Writers of Great Britain and Europe. An Encyclopaedia* (Routledge 1997) 176–77; Natania Meeker, 'Olympe de Gouges (1745–1793). Women's Rights and Revolution' in Eugenia C DeLamotte, Natania Meeker, and Jean F O'Barr (eds), *Women Imagine Change: A Global Anthology of Women's Resistance* (Routledge 1997) 263–68.

[2] See website of the *Réseau Olympe*: <https://olympereseauinternational.wordpress.com/> accessed 20 May 2021. A brief biography of Olympe de Gouges by Dominique Gaurier can be found on the website, in French and English.

[3] Olympe de Gouges, however, has recently been the subject of a chapter in *The Faces of Human Rights* (2019): see Teresa Pizarro Beleza and Helena Peraira de Melo, 'Olympe de Gouges (1748–1793): Impressively Ahead of Her Time: A Visionary, Daring Activist and Martyr' in Kasey McCall-Smith, Jan Wouters, and Felipe Gómez Isa (eds), *The Faces of Human Rights* (Hart 2019) 33–40.

[4] The term 'symbol' is commonly defined as referring to 'a person, an object, an event, etc. that represents a more general quality or situation' (Oxford Learners Dictionary). When applied to a person, it can more specifically be understood as meaning that this person has become an embodiment of a broader idea or movement; in Olympe de Gouges's case, feminism.

Anne Lagerwall and Agatha Verdebout, *Olympe de Gouges* In: *Portraits of Women in International Law*. Edited by: Immi Tallgren, Oxford University Press. © Anne Lagerwall and Agatha Verdebout 2023. DOI: 10.1093/oso/9780198868453.003.0003

Figure 3.1 Olympe de Gouges in her hometown, Montauban, by Marika Gysbers.
Source: Courtesy of artist Marika Gysbers.

Citizen has so far been overlooked. Third, we seek to understand why her work has been neglected and suggest that the liberal philosophy of human and women's rights grounded in natural law that underlies de Gouges's work might not appeal to contemporary feminism. The conclusion offers some thoughts on what it takes for women to be remembered in international legal scholarship.

How International Lawyers 'Remember' Olympe de Gouges: On the 'feminist paradox' and de Gouges's Death

In international law, references to Olympe de Gouges are scarce and mostly located within feminist scholarship. If de Gouges's name is mentioned, it is usually in connection with two issues: the 'feminist paradox' and her death.

The 'feminist paradox' refers to the issue of strategy as to how to better further the cause of women. It has been defined as a contradictory attitude that seeks 'both to have "sexualised difference" acknowledged and to have it rendered irrelevant'.[5] This paradox is often traced back to Olympe de Gouges, and more particularly to her 1791 *Declaration of the Rights of Woman and of the Female Citizen*.[6] This genealogy seems to be the result of Joan W Scott's work on French feminism spanning the period from the French Revolution to the granting of the right to vote in 1944. In her book *Only Paradoxes to Offer* (1996), Scott argues that from the beginning the French feminist movement was torn on questions of strategy and gender mainstreaming. She identifies de Gouges as the origin of this dilemma.[7] Scott depicts the world of de Gouges as dominated by men (Voltaire, Rousseau, and Diderot). Some of them vividly negated women's capacity for imagination. In this context, she argues, de Gouges developed an ambivalent attitude towards her own femininity: negating her gender to be heard and emphasizing the same traits to represent her sex and its strengths.[8] Although other biographers agree that her attitude may resemble the 'feminist paradox', they doubt that Olympe de Gouges was aware of her own ambivalence. For instance, John R Cole shares Scott's analysis but draws the line at 'attributing to the author something like her own self-consciousness as a feminist caught on the horns of contrary theories'.[9] In this respect, Scott's study has been qualified as 'anachronistic' or as 'inappropriately theoretical and insufficiently historical'.[10] Likewise, Olivier Blanc regrets that Scott's work has had such an impact on the English-speaking literature, consolidating an image of Olympe de Gouges which he considers 'deceitful'.[11]

Another element that appears to enjoy relative consensus in international law is the story of de Gouges's execution. Olympe de Gouges was sentenced to death in November 1793 as a result of her opposition to Robespierre's *Terror*. She was the second woman to be guillotined after Marie-Antoinette. Her death was a consequence of the publication of the poster *Les trois urnes ou le Salut de la patrie* in July 1793. It proposed the organization of a three-choice ballot vote with the options of a sole indivisible republic, a federal republic, or the return to a constitutional monarchy. A few weeks before, however, a law had been passed imposing the death penalty

[5] Joan W Scott, *Only Paradoxes to Offer: French Feminists and the Rights of Man* (Harvard University Press 1996) 168.

[6] See, eg, Dianne Otto, 'Feminist Approaches to International Law' in Anne Orford and Florian Hoffmann (eds), *The Oxford Handbook on the Theory of International Law* (OUP 2016) 497; Shelley Kotze, 'Gender and Integration: The Ebb and Flow of Mainstreaming in Projects' in Mirek Dymitrow and Karin Ingelhad (eds), *Anatomy of a 21st Century Sustainability Project. The Untold Stories* (Mistra Urban Futures 2019) 54–62; Hilary Charlesworth, 'Inside/Outside: Women and the International Human Rights System' in Aristotle Constantinides and Nikos Zaikos (eds), *The Diversity of International Law: Essays in Honour of Professor Kalliopi K. Joufa* (Martinus Nijhoff 2009) 388; Sari Kouvo, *Making Just Rights?: Mainstreaming Women's Human Rights and Gender Perspective* (Lustu Forlag 2004) 84–85 and 104. See also Sundhya Pahuja, 'Decolonization and Eventness of International Law' in Fleur Johns, Richard Joyce, and Sudhya Pahuja (eds), *Events: The Force of International Law* (Routledge) 95–96; Stephanie Hennette-Vauchez's presentation of Charlesworth's work *in* Hilary Charlesworth, *Sexe, genre et droit international* (Pedone, *coll Doctrine(s)* 2013) 3 ff and 305.

[7] Scott (n 5) 19–56. See also Gregory S Brown, 'The Self-Fashionings of Olympe de Gouges, 1784–1789' (2001) 34 Eighteenth Century Studies 383–401.

[8] Scott (n 5) 19–56 in particular 23.

[9] John R Cole, *Between the Queen and the Cabby: Olympe de Gouges's Rights of Women* (McGill-Queen's University Press 2011) 17.

[10] ibid. See also Blanc, *Marie-Olympe de Gouges* (n 1) 251.

[11] ibid.

on any person questioning the idea of a republican government. The revolutionary tribunal's charges directly referred to this poster, as well as to an unfinished play, *La France sauvée ou la tyran détrôné* (1793), in which de Gouges openly attacked Marat and Robespierre.[12] Her political commitment, thus, went beyond the question of the place of women in society. She criticized not only the exclusion of women from the revolutionary process but also the violent and anti-democratic turn it had taken. Yet, her death has become a symbol of feminist resistance. It is interesting to note how it is sometimes said that right before being guillotined Olympe de Gouges claimed that if a woman is entitled to go to the scaffold, she should also be entitled to sit in the assembly.[13] She made such a claim, but in Article 10 of her *Declaration on the Rights of Woman and of the Female Citizen*. Her death, however, proved her point: if the words of women could be taken seriously enough to justify that they suffer the same consequences as men for their political ideas, they should enjoy the same political rights. Moreover, although her feminist writings were not part of the charges, her gender was certainly held against her. Shortly after her execution, Pierre-Gaspard Chaumette, prosecutor of the Paris Commune, warned:

> Remember this virago, woman-man, the impudent Olympe de Gouges who abandoned the care of her household to talk politics and committed crimes [...] This oversight of the virtues of her sex brought her to the scaffold.[14]

Through her death, de Gouges became a 'martyr' of the women's cause.[15] This symbol has possibly eclipsed her work, explaining why her name is mentioned but her writings rarely acknowledged by international legal scholarship. In the next section, we try to underline what international lawyers can learn from Olympe de Gouges, focusing on her rewriting exercise of the 1789 *Declaration of the Right of Man and of the Citizen*.

The *Declaration on the Rights of Woman and of the Female Citizen:* An Original Act of Feminist Rewriting

To claim that women should be entitled to equal rights was not common in 1791.[16] Such equality was not included in the 1789 *Declaration of the Rights of Man and of*

[12] The full text of the Criminal Revolutionary Tribunal's act of accusation against Olympe de Gouges is available at: <https://ledroitcriminel.fr/le_phenomene_criminel/crimes_et_proces_celebres/fichiers/gouges_acte_accusation.pdf> accessed 20 May 2020.

[13] See, eg, Sundhya Pahuja, 'Decolonization and Eventness of International Law' in Fleur Johns, Richard Joyce, and Sudhya Pahuja (eds), *Events: The Force of International Law* (Routledge) 95–96; Allison Kesby, *The Right to Have Rights: Citizenship, Humanity and International Law* (OUP 2012) 125.

[14] Quoted in Caroline Fayolle, 'La "femme-monstre": la République face à la peur de la confusion des sexes' in Lisa Bogani and others (eds), *La République à l'épreuve des peurs: de la Révolution à nos jours* (Presses universitaires de Rennes 2016) 112. Translation by the authors.

[15] As can be illustrated, for example, by the title of the chapter of Pizarro Beleza and Peraira de Melo (n 3) 33–40.

[16] See, inter alia, D'Alembert, *Des Femmes*, 1774, referred to in John Pappas, 'Condorcet, "le seul" et "le premier" féministe du 18ème siècle?' (1991) 23 Dix-Huitième Siècle 441–43; Condorcet, *Sur l'Admission des Femmes au Droit de Cité*, 1790: <gallica.bnf.fr> accessed 20 May 2021; Pierre Guyomar, *Le Partisan de l'Egalité Politique des Individus, ou Problème Très Important de l'Egalité en Droits et de l'Inégalité en Faits*, 29 April 1793: <gallica.bnf.fr> accessed 20 May 2021.

the Citizen, which prompted de Gouges to rewrite the text in a performative fashion. Keeping its structure and most of its substance, she systematically substituted *la femme* (the woman) for *l'homme* (the man) and *la citoyenne* (the female citizen) for *le citoyen* (the male citizen) and, less frequently, altered the meaning of the proclaimed rights. This creative text can be thought of as a path-breaking act of feminist rewriting. It made women the beneficiaries of rights and underlined that the original Declaration was drafted by men convinced that their particular position is universal: 'Man alone has raised his exceptional circumstances to a principle.'[17]

Her work comes close to the rewriting experiences, which feminists have regularly performed in the second half of the twentieth century: that is, reinvent works of literature[18] or judicial decisions by national[19] or international[20] institutions. Imagining these texts as freed from stereotypes about women and what they are (in)capable of, had women's concerns and interests been taken (more) into account. Such rewriting not only generates spaces in which human rights are shaped in innovative forms, it also empowers women as drafters, a position mainly held by men, whether as novelists, legislators, or judges.

Few contemporary rewriting projects refer to de Gouges. When they do, it is not to acknowledge her pioneering role in imagining such a performance.[21] Seldom do they capture the ingeniousness and boldness of de Gouges's rewriting. The latter arises not only of her choice to twist such a symbolic production of the French Revolution, but also of the style she uses in the dedication, postface, and postscript of her Declaration. She addresses the reader directly, not without generating a certain discomfort. In her dedication to the Queen—which amounts to less of an homage to Marie-Antoinette than to a call 'to give impetus to the launch of the Rights of Woman and to speed its success',[22] de Gouges wrote to her as an equal, a gesture of rare irreverence for the

[17] Preamble of the Declaration.

[18] See, eg, Angela Carter, *The Bloody Chamber and Other Stories* (Penguin 1979); Margaret Atwood, *The Penelopiad* (Canongate 2006); Madelein Miller, *Circe* (Little, Brown and Company 2018); Adrianna Cavarero, *In Spite of Plato* (Taylor and Francis 1995).

[19] Women's Court of Canada (2006) 18 Canadian Journal of Women and the Law 1-376; Rosemary Hunter, Clare McGlynn, and Erika Rackley (eds), *Feminist Judgments—From Theory to Practice* (Hart 2010); Heather Douglas and others (eds), *Australian Feminist Judgments: Righting and Rewriting Law* (Hart 2014); Kathryn M Stanchi, Linda L Berger, and Bridget J Crawford (eds), *Feminist Judgments: Rewritten Opinions of the United States Supreme Court* (Cambridge University Press 2016); Elisabeth McDonald and others (eds), *Feminist Judgments of Aotearoa New Zealand: Te Rino—A Two-Stranded Rope* (Bloomsbury 2017); Mairead Enright, Julie McCandless, and Aoife O'Donoghue (eds), *Northern/Irish Feminist Judgments: Judges' Troubles and the Gendered Politics of Identity* (Bloomsbury 2017); Bridget J Crawford and Anthony Infanti (eds), *Feminist Judgment—Rewritten Tax Opinion* (Cambridge University Press 2017); India, The Feminist Judgement Project: <https://fjpindia.wixsite.com/fjpi> accessed 20 May 2021.

[20] Eva Brems (ed), *Diversity and European Human Rights: Rewriting Judgments of the ECHR* (Cambridge University Press 2012); Loveday Hodson and Troy Lavers (eds), *Feminist Judgments in International Law* (Bloomsbury 2019).

[21] Loveday Hodson and Troy Lavers, *Feminist Judgments in International Law* (Hart 2019) 43, where the authors recall, for example, that she 'challenged male authority and demanded rights for women as long ago as her tract, the *Declaration of the Rights of Women and the Female Citizen* (1791)'. See also Marie-Bénédicte Dembour, *Who Believes in Human Rights? Reflections on the European Convention* (Cambridge University Press 2010) 5, where the author writes that 'despite Olympe de Gouges's "Declaration on the Rights of Woman" of 1790 and the writings of those such as Mary Wollstonecraft, a scholarly feminist critique of human rights has only started to provoke wide academic engagement over the last two or three decades'.

[22] Cole (n 9) 29.

time.[23] When she points at the male reader, she uses the personal pronoun '*tu*', which addresses him individually and informally, in a reprimanding fashion not devoid of anger, cynicism, and a mischievous sense of humour:

> Man, are you capable of being just? It is a woman who poses the question; you won't deprive her of at least that right. Tell me: Who gave you the sovereign empire to oppress my sex? Your strength? Your talents? Observe the creator in his wisdom; survey nature in all its grandeur, which you seem to want to emulate, and offer me, if you dare, an example of this tyrannical empire (Gouges' note added: From Paris to Peru, from Japan to Rome, the stupidest animal, in my opinion, is man).[24]

Her words to female readers are equally strong:

> Woman, wake up! The tocsin of reason is heard throughout the universe; Know your rights. The powerful empire of nature is no longer surrounded by prejudice, fanaticism, superstition, and lies. The torch of truth has scattered all the clouds of folly and usurpation. Enslaved man has multiplied his strength but needed recourse to yours to break his fetters. Having become free, he has become unjust to his companion. Oh, women! Women, when will you open your eyes? What have you gained from the revolution? A more marked contempt, a more public disdain.[25]

Her claims were norm-breaking, both in substance and style. She challenged indifference generally displayed towards women's rights. She voiced a feminist critique of human rights early in the process of their codification. From this perspective, her Declaration appears to be an essential text for feminist or human rights scholarship. Why then have international lawyers remained relatively inattentive or indifferent to her work? This might be partly explained by the way in which her texts—in particular, her *Declaration on the Rights of Woman and of the Female Citizen*—are rooted in theory and culture, as discussed next.

De Gouges's Liberal Approach to Equality Grounded in Natural Law of Divine Origin

Olympe de Gouges's liberal approach to human rights and gender equality can be illustrated by the first article of her Declaration: 'Woman is born free and remains equal to man in rights'.[26] Women are granted the same rights as men, whether it is access to public employment or to property, but also as stakeholders in the conception of these rights.[27] Faithful to the meritocratic ideas of the original text, de Gouges's Declaration also insists on subjecting women to the same responsibilities as men, such as

[23] Jürgen Siess, 'Un discours politique au féminin. Le projet d'Olympe de Gouges' (2005) 78 Usages politiques du genre 13–16.
[24] Cole (n 9) 30.
[25] ibid 34.
[26] Art 1, Cole (tr), ibid 31.
[27] See Article 16, ibid 34.

compliance with criminal law or the payment of taxes.[28] She sometimes appears even tougher on women. For instance, she erases the presumption of innocence guaranteed to all individuals in the 1789 Declaration and replaces it with the principle according to which 'if found guilty, every woman (must be punished with) all severity prescribed by the Law'.[29] Her intention was to take the revolutionary principle of equality seriously and extend it to all to confront men with the contradictions that arise when they exclude women from the rights and freedoms they recognized for themselves.[30] De Gouges only marginally adapts the rights of the 1789 Declaration to women's specific experiences, such as motherhood. Her declaration understands women's freedom of expression as a right to publicly reveal the identity of her children's father.[31] This freedom is thus given an unprecedented meaning, which many of de Gouges's biographers attribute to her personal life. She was born out of her mother's adulterous relation with Marquis Jean-Jacques Lefranc de Pompignan.[32]

De Gouges's Declaration, a product of the Enlightenment, is rooted in natural law and reason.[33] She draws on the observation of nature, highlighting the general absence of a sex hierarchy in the animal kingdom:

> Go back to the animals, consult the elements, study the plants, and finally cast a glance on all the modifications of organic matter. Then yield to the plain truth when I show you the way. Search, investigate, and distinguish, if you can, between the sexes in the workings of nature. Everywhere you will find them intermixed; everywhere they cooperate in this immortal masterpiece with a harmonious togetherness.[34]

She further suggests that women's role within their family links them to men in ways that justify including them as rights holders. It is 'the mothers, the daughters, the sisters' who demand to be represented in the national assembly, in her Declaration.[35] It is also 'the sex that is superior in beauty as in courage in the pains of childbirth' that 'declares, in the presence and under the auspices of the Supreme Being, the following Rights of Woman and of the Female Citizen'.[36] At the same time, she criticizes women's nature and calls on them to show more virtue. In so doing, she echoes the view of the government being corrupt as a result of the 'courtesans' alleged sway over state officials. For de Gouges, having recourse to their charms, 'women have done more harm than good' and were, to some extent, responsible for their own discredit.[37]

De Gouges's severe judgement of women and the liberal philosophy grounded in natural law that underlay her thought might be an element explaining why her writings have rarely been acknowledged by contemporary scholarship. Feminist

[28] Arts 7, 8, and 13, ibid 32–33.
[29] Art 9, ibid 32.
[30] Preamble, ibid.
[31] Art 11, ibid 33.
[32] See, eg, Guilia Pacini, 'Celle dont la voix publique vous a nommé le père: Olympe de Gouges's *Mémoire de Madame de Valmont* (1788)' (2001) 9 Women in French Studies 207–19.
[33] Art 4, Cole (tr), *Between the Queen and the Cabby* (n 9) 30.
[34] ibid.
[35] Preamble, ibid.
[36] Preamble, ibid 31.
[37] Postambule, ibid. 35.

international lawyers are diverse but they generally do not believe that women's rights should be grounded in 'nature'.[38] Unsurprisingly authors who pledge the reconciliation of feminist ethics with natural law identify Olympe de Gouges as an inspiring figure. Beattie, for example, writes that: 'the historical figure of de Gouges might provide a more fruitful legacy of revolutionary possibilities based on appeals to natural law as far as feminists are concerned'.[39]

More generally, the relative inattention of international lawyers to de Gouges's work may relate to the way in which her work has been perceived as relevant to literature, history, philosophy, or politics, but not so much to law. She is essentially identified as a playwright and political activist, as if these labels somehow deprived her writings of legal significance. However, such divisions of disciplines and writing styles did not exist in the eighteenth century. Authors freely wrote on society, power allocation, slavery, religion, ethics, and natural law in essays, books, or even theatre plays. This can possibly explain why de Gouges's contribution to our understanding of human rights is rarely acknowledged by international lawyers. Still, it did not prevent Montesquieu, Voltaire, Rousseau, or Diderot's work—which was indeed more extensive on the subject—to be mentioned in relation to modern international law of human rights.

Finally, even if de Gouges has become an important feminist figure in the Francophone and Anglophone world, her heritage varies. In France, although forgotten for the most part of the nineteenth and twentieth centuries, she is now remembered as a leading feminist. Following the celebrations of the bicentenary of the French Revolution and the emergence of new historiographies, the trajectories and lives of the women who took part came under increasing scrutiny.[40] In 1981, Olivier Blanc published a first biography of Olympe de Gouges,[41] paving the way for many other biographical studies[42] and her inclusion into women's dictionaries.[43] The Francophone network of feminist international lawyers chose the name of *Réseau Olympe* 'in homage to Olympe de Gouges as one of the first French feminists'.[44] The celebration surrounding the figure and name of Olympe de Gouges in France can be seen as a more general echo of the way French society sees the late eighteenth century as a founding moment of its history. The French republic, in fact, is grounded in a liberal understanding of human rights and equality which supposedly transcends origins

[38] For a project reconciling feminism and natural law, see Lisa Sowle Cahill, 'Natural Law: A Feminist Reassessment' in Leroi S Rouner (ed), *Is There a Human Nature?* (University of Notre Dame Press 1997) 80; Cristina LH Traina, *Feminist Ethics and Natural Law: The End of the Anathemas* (Georgetown University Press 1999).

[39] Tina Beattie, 'Justice Enacted Not These Human Laws (Antigone): Religion, Natural Law and Women's Rights' (2008) 3 Religion and Human Rights 263.

[40] For earlier works, see Marie-Paule Duhet, *Les femmes et la Révolution 1789–1794* (Gallimard 1971); Benoîte Groult, *Ainsi soit-elle* (Poche 1977).

[41] Olivier Blanc, *Olympe de Gouges* (Syros 1981).

[42] Benoîte Groult, *Ainsi soit Olympe de Gouges* (Grasset 2013); Sophie Mousset, *Women's Rights and the French Revolution: A Biography of Olympe de Gouges* (Transaction Publishers 2007); E Morin-Rotureau, *Olympe de Gouges*, (Histoire d'elles 2002); Paul Noak, *Olympe de Gouges: courtisane et militante des droits de la femme (1748–1793)* (Editions de Fallois 1993).

[43] Michelle Perrot et Georges Duby, *Histoire des femmes en Occident*, 5 vols (Plon 1991); Christine Fauré, *Encyclopédie politique et historique des femmes* (PUF 1997).

[44] Emmanuelle Tourme-Jouannet and others (eds), *Féminisme et droit international: Etudes du Réseau Olympe* (Société de législation comparée 2016) 13.

or gender. Article 1 of the French constitution still states that 'France [is] an indivisible [Republic]'.[45] In the French mindset, this not only means that no differences exist between 'French people', but also that any suggestion or attempt to have these differences recognized is groundless, if not illegitimate. Such an understanding can be illustrated through the recent debates on laicity, in the French Academy's refusal to support the feminization of professional titles until 2019, or in the *Ligue française pour la défense des droits de l'Homme et du Citoyen's* refusal to change its name in order to be more inclusive.[46]

Olympe de Gouges has also attracted attention from English-speaking authors investigating the role of women during the 1789 Revolution[47] and the Enlightenment era.[48] Nevertheless, she is not celebrated in the same way in the Anglophone literature, where feminist approaches to international law have predominantly developed.

Conclusion: What Is Required for Women to Be Remembered for their Contribution to International Legal Thinking?

Reading de Gouges whilst living in lockdown and becoming aware of how the Covid-19 pandemic has affected women more than men, including female researchers unable to invest as much time into their academic work and their writing as their male counterparts, has proven to be a troubling experience.[49] Her quest for equality remains as relevant today as it was 230 years ago, even if it might not be formulated in the same way. Her legacy, and her impressive literary output during the decade she spent as an author (dozens of plays, political essays, and manifestos), raises questions as to what is required for women to make a contribution to legal thinking.

Her life might suggest that such a contribution comes at the price of renouncing marriage, giving birth to only one child, securing financial resources through wealthy partners, and being beheaded. De Gouges began publishing at the age of thirty-five. She had by then been free of marital obligations for nearly twenty years since Louis-Yves Aubry, to whom she was married at the age of seventeen, died as a result of the

45 Art 1, Constitution de la République Française, 4 Octobre 1958.

46 In France, 'Notre nom', communiqué de la Ligue des droits de l'homme de Loudéac:<https://site.ldh-france.org/loudeac/accueil/nos-liens/notre-nom/> accessed 20 May 2021; by contrast, in Belgium, 'La ligue des droits de l'homme devient la Ligue des droits humains', Communiqué:< http://www.liguedh.be/la-ligue-des-droits-de-lhomme-devient-la-ligue-des-droits-humains-lasbl-aquarelle-remporte-le-prix-regine-orfinger-karlin/ > accessed 29 April 2020.

47 Sara E Melzer and Leslie Rabine, *Rebel Daughters: Woman and the French Revolution* (OUP 1992); Dorinda Outram, *The Body and the French Revolution: Sex, Class and Political Culture* (Yale University Press 1989).

48 Roland Bonnel and Cartherine Rubinger (eds), *Femmes savantes et femmes d'esprit: Women Intellectuals of the French Eighteenth Century* (Pieter Lang 1994); Dena Goodman, *The Republic of Letters: A Cultural History of the French Enlightenment* (Cornell University Press 1994); Samia Spencer (ed), *French Women and the Age of Enlightenment* (Indiana University Press 1985).

49 Alessandra Milnello, 'The Pandemic and the Female Academic', Nature 17 April 2020; Colleen Flaherty, 'No Room of One's Own', Inside Higher Ed 21 April 2020; Caroline Kitchener, 'Women Academics Seem to Be Submitting Fewer Papers during Coronavirus', The Lily 24 April 2020.

flood of the Tarn just one year into their union.[50] *Her only son, Pierre, was living away from home by the time she published her first text.*[51] Choosing not to be bound again by marriage, which struck her as 'the tomb of trust and of love',[52] she decided to publish whatever she wished. As a married woman she would have required her husband's consent. Whilst the distance from her son caused her grief and he continued to be a source of concern, her career as a published author was largely free of childcare. Her decision to change her name to Olympe de Gouges, a more personal and more aristocratic identity, which facilitated her access to influential literary and political circles illustrates her reinvention as an author. Her relationship with Jacques Biétrix de Rozières, a senior naval officer who supported her financially until the French Revolution, allowed her to write as much as she wanted. Equipped with economic independence and the assistance of a secretary to whom she dictated her writings, de Gouges was able to concentrate on her work in ways that would be difficult to imagine nowadays for most female researchers.[53]

Reading about her and her work has also served as a useful reminder of the risks faced by women who dare to step out of the position men have assigned to them and venture into spaces traditionally reserved for men. These risks involve being described as 'an original who was sometimes a mad woman and sometimes a psychic',[54] an image fed in part by medical diagnoses associating her with 'revolutionary hysteria'.[55] At her time, the risks included also execution. Though her feminist writings were not part of the charges against her, the words of warning spoken by Pierre-Gaspard Chaumette to any woman tempted to follow in de Gouges's footsteps surely illustrate how much she was also targeted for being a woman choosing not to conform to societal rules, and 'forgett[ing] the virtues appropriate to her sex'.[56]

[50] Kathleen Kuiper, 'Olympe de Gouges', *Encyclopaedia Britannica Online*:<https://www.britannica.com/biography/Olympe-de-Gouges> accessed 5 October 2020.

[51] Blanc, *Olympe de Gouges* (n 41).

[52] Postamble, Cole, *Between the Queen and the Cabby* (n 9) 37.

[53] Michael Head, 'Men Get Most of the Research Funding—It's a Serious Problem for Women and Science', The Conversation, 10 October 2017; 'Chercheurs vs Managers de la recherche: la guerre des mots', The Conversation, 24 May 2020.

[54] Leopold Lacour, *Les origines du féminisme contemporain. Trois femmes de la Révolution: Olympe de Gouges, Théroigne de Méricourt, Rose Lacombe* (Plon 1900), Préface, IV. See also Alphonse Aulard, 'Le féminisme pendant la Révolution' [1898] Revue bleue 311–16.

[55] Alfred Guillois, *Etudes psycho-médicale d'Olympe de Gouges* (thèse présentée à la Faculté de Médecine et Pharmacie de Lyon 1904) 88.

[56] Quoted in Fayolle (n 14) 113.

4
The Reign of Order and the Rights of Siege According to Rosa Luxemburg

Deborah Whitehall

Revolution and International Law

Although Rosa Luxemburg (1871–1919) did not identify herself as an international lawyer and made few remarks about international law, her struggles against the organizing logics of the capitalist state before the First World War assure her significance for international legal thought. She was a controversial tactician and theorist of socialist internationalism and by its plans for social and political change, a provocative antagonist of the global order created by states. She lasts for radical memory as a lost heroine of revolution and for aspirations for a revolutionary world order which did not eventuate in her life. For radical endeavour, she remains a vivid intellectual and tactical resource. The surprise of her inclusion in a compendium about the personalities of international legal history is also twofold and, in each detail, confirms the lasting pertinence of her different understanding of international order and of international siege for the development of international law. The specifics of Luxemburg's pre-war internationalism preceded the liberal international order as its nemesis and further, survive by the unexpected revival of her vision in the progressive projects of interwar—and then, more directly—post-1945 international law. Both attributions are necessary to correct the design monopoly assumed by liberal states after 1919 and by the clarification, reveal a richer, layered, and more contested international history and, for the contemporary world order, its radical inheritance. In each aspect, Luxemburg appears *for* the projects of two internationalisms.

A scene from a 1968 anti-war demonstration in West Berlin illustrates how Luxemburg figures as both an antagonist and a protagonist of the world order of states without confinement to her history moment or her ideological predilection. Her face on a placard held by a student protester against foreign aggression in Vietnam was apposite to the struggle for peace, and not only for socialism, then afoot worldwide. It also counted as a visual annotation for the emergent expectation among states that a free world entailed individual rights (everywhere), national independence and further, that civic and international toleration of military intervention abroad required special justification. Luxemburg's image in protest belonged to the impetus for a broader kind of social freedom agreed by states and checked its evident contradictions in a world order still prised for ideological wars. It signals to the life and to the afterlife of her radical question for the world designed and governed by states and its shifting imaginative hold.

Deborah Whitehall, *The Reign of Order and the Rights of Siege According to Rosa Luxemburg* In: *Portraits of Women in International Law*. Edited by: Immi Tallgren, Oxford University Press. © Deborah Whitehall 2023.
DOI: 10.1093/oso/9780198868453.003.0004

Figure 4.1 Vietnam Demonstration, Berlin: Protesters carry portraits of Lenin and Rosa Luxemburg (Berlin, 18 February 1968).
Source: Ullstein Bild/Getty Images [2255427]

Socialist Internationalism Before 1919

Luxemburg most clearly exists for international legal history as a singular and sometimes controversial agent of socialist internationalism before the language of internationalism was the principal domain of states. A reference to 'internationalism' after Marx and until 1919 prompted immediate association with the ambitions of revolutionaries for the global realization of social democracy via world siege. European Marxists in the First International (1864–*c*1876) and Second International (1889–1916 and later regroupings) described themselves as internationalists and used socialist internationalism as a rubric for their collectivist ideology. Those internationalists were also the European leaders of national movements for social democracy who debated and agreed upon a common intellectual strategy for a world without the capitalist state. Their radical internationalism anticipated the final breakdown of the capitalist order including its international expression in law, in imperial geographies, and of course, in imperialist wars. The appropriation of the socialist vocabularies ('internationalist' and 'internationalism') by the capitalist state and by international historians after 1919 confirms the ideological victory that was simultaneous with the receding of the revolutionary vision to certain states after October 1918. Luxemburg figures for the legal internationalism of states as an earlier agonist from whom it borrows its lexis and who clarifies its historically contingent root.

Luxemburg entered the scene of radical European politics from the mixed vantage of being a bourgeois woman who was also a Jewish Pole born in Poland under

Tsarist rule. She became a prominent member of the Second International for more than twenty years in parallel to her efforts at the frontiers of the working class movement in Poland and when Social Democracy became legal in Germany in the 1890s, in the extra-parliamentary campaigns of the German Socialist Party (SDP), as co-leader of its more radical splinter, the *Spartakusbund* (Spartacus League) from August 1914 (first as the International Group), and in 1917, after changing its name to the Spartacus Group in 1916, at the helm of its fracture and refiguration further Left with the radical offshoot of the SDP (USPD), and then again from late 1918, as a leader of the independent Spartacus League that led the failed rebellions in Berlin (of which she was a prominent fatality in 1919) and which was the precursor of the German Communist Party (KPD) in the Weimer Republic. She achieved such status despite the social barriers of chauvinism, racism, and anti-Semitism which raided radical politics in the first decades of the twentieth century and exaggerated the hostility produced by her unorthodox readings of Marx. Her most famous intellectual adversary, Vladimir Lenin, bracketed her as an 'eagle' among socialists despite her faults.[1] Another, August Bebel, thought that her 'wretched female's squirts of poison' were the very reason he 'wouldn't have the party without her'.[2] Luxemburg's acerbic and provocative polemic confirms her reputation as an agonist who fearlessly targeted the existing centres of ruling power and any socialist who she judged as reactionary or too conservative in its revolutionary ambitions. Her unwillingness to concede to radical as well as governmental opposition is consistent with her murder by counterrevolutionaries in January 1919.

The indiscretions of Luxemburg's double margin (against the state and against radical standards) were impossible to ignore due to her resolute tethering of ideas and practice. She routinely emphasized the practical imperative of philosophy by insisting the 'program would be a miserable scrap of paper if it could not serve us in *all* eventualities, at *all* moments of the struggle, and if it did not serve us by its *application* . . . ' and further, in reverse, the 'entire strength of the modern labor movement rests on theoretical knowledge'.[3] Ideas mattered for Luxemburg not only hypothetically but also as the guide *for* realizing revolution by inspiring and organizing revolutionary action. She thought the translation from theory into practice was also the distinctive way the revolutionary thinker makes *use* of his or her talents by entering the process of history as an activist who educates, campaigns, rallies, and mobilizes the disenfranchised classes to spontaneous rebellion. Luxemburg's pamphlets and other works comprise the written archive of her activism which, despite early posthumous hostilities to her propagated by prominent socialists, never went out of print.

She campaigned on the street and by her pen for 'the two rules of life' which were relative to the existing centres of state control. Together, these defined the tasks of international socialism (or international social democracy) as internationalist on account

[1] VI Lenin, 'Notes of a Publicist' (Marxists' Internet Archive, written February 1922) <https://www.marxists.org/archive/lenin/works/1922/feb/x01.htm> accessed 6 February 2023.

[2] Letter, August Bebel to Viktor Adler (16 August 1910) cited in Raya Dunayevskaya (ed), *Rosa Luxemburg, Women's Liberation and Marx's Philosophy of Revolution* (Illinois University Press 1991) 26–29.

[3] Rosa Luxemburg, 'Reform or Revolution' in Helen Scott (ed), *The Essential Rosa Luxemburg: Reform or Revolution and The Mass Strike* (Haymarket 2008) 41, 43–47, 94, hereafter Luxemburg, 'Reform or Revolution'.

of its national mission 'against the ruling classes within the boundaries of the bourgeois states' and beyond any one state, for the 'international solidarity of the workers of all countries'.[4] Luxemburg conceived the world of revolution to be continuous with the world of capitalist rule and necessarily, whatever advance by radical struggle within the bourgeois state, must follow the strategic precepts set by the International organization for world revolution. The project was necessarily international because, as she clarified in a 1915 policy document for the Second International, 'there is no socialism without international proletarian solidarity, and there is no socialism without class struggle' against the national bourgeoisie.[5] A piecemeal approach to insurrection that did not align the two rules within and beyond the state was fatal to revolution because it separated the proletariat from its cause. The objective of radical struggle, according to Luxemburg, was never principally about spatial or legal control within a state but rather against the invidious rules of modern capitalist production and its rippling imprint on every corner of modern life.

Luxemburg's prominence (and notoriety) within radical circles also placed her at the historical frontier between contested internationalisms. Her alternative vision of global order resists the unitary tale of one internationalism orchestrated by post-war internationalists. Her history elucidates the prominence of the ideological contests between international socialism and capitalist states before war. Those states directed the post-war international legal order and the redesignation of 'internationalism' as their internationalism and as the privilege of military victory *and* the setbacks of the revolutionary's worldwide programme. To remember Luxemburg's internationalism for legal history means recognizing international law as the ledger of a prior ideological struggle in addition to being a referent for the organizational achievements of states. The struggle for organizational design began with the internationalist projects of international social democracy against the imperialist and capitalist state that required international working-class solidarity and adherence, by the working class in every state, to the principles articulated by the umbrella organization for its achievement. Noting the struggle clarifies the contests from which twentieth-century international law emerged as the achievement of states rather than from revolution or from a radical mindset that envisaged a world without state boundaries or state-made international laws.

Luxemburg gestures to the historical opposition between internationalisms by criticizing, for instance, the regulatory initiatives of states to avert war or for the achievement of global justice. She said at the outset of the First World War that: '[w]orld peace cannot be assured by projects utopian or, at bottom, reactionary, such as tribunals of arbitration by capitalist diplomatists, diplomatic "disarmament" conventions, "the freedom of the seas," abolition of the right of maritime arrest, "the United States of Europe," a "customs union for central Europe," buffer states, and other illusions'.[6] The same conclusion inspired her probing of international relations in the preceding

[4] Rosa Luxemburg, 'Theses on the Tasks of International Social-Democracy' (Marxists' Internet Archive, written late 1915) <https://www.marxists.org/archive/luxemburg/1915/xx/theses.htm> accessed 6 February 2023, hereafter Luxemburg, 'Tasks of International Social-Democracy'.

[5] ibid.

[6] Luxemburg, 'Tasks of International Social-Democracy' (n 4) pt 8.

decades to find 'any tendency toward peace, toward disarmament, toward settlement of conflicts by arbitration'.[7] She discovered that the promises of bilateral agreements and interstate law dissolved in recurring global patterns of conflict, the up-scaling of imperialism and diplomatic disappointments. The circumstances and patterns of geopolitical crisis indicated that 'a little order and peace' in a disordered system of production motored by class antagonisms was 'just as impossible, just as much a petty-bourgeois Utopia, with regard to the capitalist world market as to world politics, and with regard to the limitation of crises as to the limitation of armaments'.[8] Luxemburg defined a 'little order and peace' as a world without boundaries, international relations, or international law. Her idea of order meant social freedom in its broad radical compass and hinged, consistent with her reframing of Marxist agendas, on the world-wide success of proletariat revolution and the end of the capitalist-imperial state.

Post-War Internationalism

Socialism survived Luxemburg in the intermittent, sometimes networked, insurrections she predicted. It also organized in the immediate aftermath of the First World War as an international phenomenon via the existence of socialist states within the liberal international matrix of a world dramatized by borders, capitalism, industrialization, environmental degradation and catastrophe, pandemics, markets, exploitation, spheres of influence, wars, diplomacy, and necessarily, the legal idea of a state. To be radical and international after Luxemburg arguably means conceding elements of her utopian world vision by agreeing to utilize the rubrics of international law, including its logic of international organization and its regulatory tools (treaties, rights, arbitration, humanitarianism, or expert agencies) or norms (democracy, responsibility, sovereignty, cooperation, independence, nation, equality, humanism, or peace) to enter international relations. The radical root of the contemporary order is counterintuitive, by those details, given the prevalence of the capitalist state. States still control the normative and political bases of international legal design. States marginalize the revolutionary's claim. States are also the protagonists and self-announced protectors of humanity and problem solvers of a world in conflict and crisis.

Against the prevailing intuition that law and revolution are oppositional and that states condition both the existence and character of order, Luxemburg's radical sensibility imprints on the spaces, projects, and thematic preoccupations of legal internationalism after her. There is no perfect match between her vision and the international legal system. Neither, evidently, is the revolutionary project complete nor is the revolutionary's disquiet, quietened by noting the coincidence of purposes between the different ideological projects at different times. The coalescences between pre-war radicalism and post-war international law arise, however, in numerous contexts despite continuing ideological disagreements and the earlier failures of revolutionary

[7] Rosa Luxemburg, 'Peace Utopias' (Marxists' Internet Archive, written 6 and 8 May 1911) <https://www.marxists.org/archive/luxemburg/1911/05/11.htm> accessed 6 February 2023, hereafter Luxemburg, 'Peace Utopias'.

[8] ibid.

internationalism. The legal vocabularies of internationalism relevant today resonate, though often with different motivating criteria, with the broad particulars of Luxemburg's singular strategic vision.

Spaces

Luxemburg's response to the imperial impulse of accumulating capital was to ask for a new regulating logic for the whole world. Superficially, her vision for a networked, cooperative, and more humane world order extends to the same geographical space of post-war international law and envisaged more than the overthrow of a specific government or for insurrection in any one European state. Though she did not invent the radical possibility of a world order premised on universal justice and peace, and was merely one agonist in the contest to settle its terms, her vision of an international proletariat order contemplated a world geography. That is, it targeted the same geographical space as post-1919 international law. How Luxemburg arrived there was very different. She expected the achievement of international proletariat revolution in every capitalist and non-capitalist country and on every continent. Those concerns prompted her study of a myriad of global situations. A scan of her collected works notes her location (in Europe) and concern with European politics and the politics of various European states (Poland, Germany, Russia, but also, England, France, Spain, etc) but also, the extension of her theoretical vision and comment to non-western states targeted or vulnerable to the reproductive logics of capital.

Her controversial reinterpretation of Marx directed her geographical vision, ensuring its distinctiveness for radical thought and emphasized the spatial patterns of capitalist accumulation were without spatial limit. She looked further than the European state, which framed Marx's conception of economic reproduction, to suggest '[f]rom the very beginning, the forms and laws of capitalist production aim to comprise the entire globe as a store of reproductive forces'.[9] This meant capital 'ransacks the whole world, it procures its means of production from all corners of the earth, seizing them, if necessary by force, from all levels of civilization and from all forms of society'.[10] Luxemburg saw the whole globe as the site of potential contest, from Europe to Africa, Asia, America, the Middle East, or even Australia, because the processes of capital constantly needed to refresh its means of production (quantity and quality) to expand, and then to find use for the surplus it establishes. Accordingly, the accumulative pattern of capital was both 'elastic and spasmodic' (both spatially and in its organic mechanisms of production and control) *and* rigid in its objectives, regulating apparatus, and social system.[11] Luxemburg identified the sphere of capitalist influence to be continuous with its exploitative productive logic and consequently, constantly enlarged by its pursuit of new resources and markets.

[9] Peter Hudis and Kevin Anderson (eds), *The Rosa Luxemburg Reader* (Monthly Review Press 2004) 55–56.
[10] ibid.
[11] ibid 47–61.

Themes

Luxemburg did not predict that her answers for the spatial patterns of capitalist accumulation would resurface in post-war international law. The prescience of her thought for the global order designed by states is the unexpected sequel to the Marxist suggestion that the existing order is subject to historical processes which predict its end and which the working-class struggle can quicken. The refiguration of key elements of her programme for post-1919 international law is a spontaneous appropriation that resonates with the broad thematic spectrum of Luxemburg's internationalism but more especially, in the details which distinguish her for socialist thought. These overlap with the humanist, collectivist, spatial, pacifist, and democratic ambitions of international law. The surprise for the earlier ideological contests is how the revolutionary claim renews by becoming a living element of post-revolutionary international legal history. That is, the rights of siege persist (according to Luxemburg's expectation) though not as insurrection but rather in new regulatory causes which progressively reform the experience of international society.

The thematic intersections between post-1919 international law and revolution share the logic of Luxemburg's spatial pattern and, consequently, extend to any issue affected by class. Luxemburg studied how exploitative economic practices reproduce in the broadest spectrum of political, social, environmental, cultural, and legal injustice. Such injustices exist in networked patterns within states and more broadly, beyond the state by the networked patterns of globalizing capital. The inside-outside paradigm explains why she thought that the revolutionary programme must assume 'an international footing' and seek out 'fraternal parties in other countries' to exploit 'the means of international brotherhood' to achieve peace and 'win' a new world.[12] The model set the details of the revolutionary programme and distinguished Luxemburg's agenda from the tendency of European socialists to prioritize 'detail work, the petty daily struggle in the political and economic realms' within the European state.[13] The socialist who is content to progress by such 'degrees' forgets, she says, the 'distant guiding star, the ultimate goal' of revolution which requires immediate transformation of the whole world.[14]

For Luxemburg, the immediate tasks of revolution particularized in fields familiar to post-war international law including world peace (where belligerence = the contest for territory and resources); environmental protection (where natural resources = the opportunity for industrial growth and new markets); universal franchise (where working class women = a potential vote or voice in parliament); racism (where non-industrial communities = a new worker, a new consumer, a custodian of unexploited resources); world economy (where networked capital = networked exploitation); labour rights (to liberate workers); decolonization (where imperialism in/beyond Europe = hegemony of capitalist states and capitalist exploitation of resources); redistribution of basic needs (where adequate housing, food, healthcare,

[12] ibid 355–57.
[13] ibid 359.
[14] ibid.

education = equality); freedom of expression, association, and movement (where censorship = limitation of revolutionary opposition); abolition (where slavery = colonialism, servitude, displacement, exploitation of primitive labour economies), and in numerous incidental ways, cultural and national rights (where culture, education, language, national minorities, religion = triggers to enhance or inhibit working class solidarity among minorities or indigenous communities).[15] The surprising postscript to the revolutionary world programme imagined by Luxemburg was that its broad-ranging thematic coordinates could map into the utopian projects of post-war international law. These reappear as the ironic, belated initiative of the most powerful states which still control the world economy and the legal meaning of peace, freedom, and distributive justice.

Projects

Though Luxemburg's list of specific tasks, like the spatial reach of capitalist accumulation, extends wherever capital goes, it begins with the overthrow of the institutional apparatus which secures or gives expression to the status quo, especially capitalist law. She was adamantly anti-law because bourgeois rules outlaw or exclude radical opposition and structurally, because law shields the self-regulating habits of class. Luxemburg reiterates the Marxian point that bourgeois law *allows* injustice even when it secures civil rights of property, religion, education etc. because such entitlement does not cancel the automated processes of capitalist production and exploitation. A right to own property or resources, for example, does not promise prosperity but permits capitalism to expand and flourish. A right to education does not assume the proletariat class will enjoy the privileges of knowledge or access to the system of professional opportunity which regulates who governs the decisions of politics, culture, law, administration etc.[16]

Luxemburg's concern for the unregulated zones of capital included specific projects that reappear in post-war international legal reforms. Three examples helpfully scope the overlap and the difference that Luxemburg's argument makes for pre-war and post-war internationalism. She theorized peace, the rights of peoples to self-determination, and environmental protection (unlike parliamentary socialists and unlike international law in any historical phase) as class questions which always exceed the spatial limits of the state.

World peace

The progressive inhibition of the legal right to war during the twentieth century reflects the normative and political commitment of states to peace after two world wars determined (and adjusted) the balance of world political power. Luxemburg's objection to war arose as a working-class question before the score was clear. As early as

[15] For an overview of the plurality of the thematic and spatial spectrum of Luxemburg's thought see a cross-section of her writings, eg, the list of pamphlets published at *Marxists' Internet Archive* <https://www.marxists.org/archive/luxemburg> accessed 6 February 2023.

[16] eg, Luxemburg, 'Reform or Revolution' (n 3) 90.

1899, she said: '[a] standing army and militarism are indeed indispensable—but for whom?'.[17] The rhetorical question exaggerated in her opposition to the First World War which she saw as exemplifying the 'reversion to barbarism' that Friedrich Engels identified with capitalist society.[18]

Luxemburg was adamantly anti-war because militarism sacrifices the proletariat classes on the battlefield, as workers in the munitions' factories, calms insurrection, and further, exploits patriotism or nationalism to advance the imperial objectives of the bourgeois state for territory, natural resources, labour power and, evidently and in every case, to realize surplus value. That is why, for instance, Luxemburg objected to militarism and conscription; why she disagreed with parliamentary socialists who supported the German government's bid to increase war credits in 1915; why her response to war was to escalate the working class struggle by inciting riot, desertion, and seizure of ports etc. by the proletariat ranks of the armed forces; or why she cites every international situation (eg, Boer War, Morocco, Japan, China, Franco-Prussian etc.) as an imperial war in the competitive struggles of capitalist states for economic influence in Europe and non-European regions.[19] The reason she distrusted international legal initiatives designed to encourage peace was because militarism always persists, being a 'province of accumulation' which serves the interests of capitalist world domination and the capitalist state.[20]

Self-determination of peoples

Self-determination and decolonization figure in pre-1919 socialist thought as working-class questions. Socialists did not share the ideological footing of the legal articulation of inter-war minorities protections (in Europe), or the mandates system (in the colonial world), or its later refinement as a right to national independence. International legal history links national independence to statehood and more particularly, to the proposals at the end of the First World War to use national rights to suppress nationalist division and secure peace in Europe. The hesitation of post-war international law to afford full independence to all peoples, everywhere, affirms Luxemburg's prior circumspection about the usefulness of self-determination as a class strategy.

Her idiosyncratic approach to national rights shifted depending on the impact of national independence on the relevant people—the mass comprised of ordinary workers or indigenous communities—in specific instances. She disagreed with socialist policy that independence from imperial rulers in any state always serves the immediate goals of revolution by harnessing nationalism against imperial rulers. Neither did Luxemburg believe the concept of the nation-state was immune from class

[17] Rosa Luxemburg, 'The Militia and Militarism' (Marxists' Internet Archive, 20–26 February 1899) <https://www.marxists.org/archive/luxemburg/1899/02/26.htm> accessed 6 February 2023, hereafter Luxemburg, 'Militia and Militarism'.

[18] eg, Rosa Luxemburg, *The Crisis in German Social Democracy: The 'Junius' Pamphlet* (NY Socialist Publication Society 1919) 18, written 1915 while in prison, hereafter Luxemburg, *Juniusbroshüre*; Luxemburg, 'Militia and Militarism' (n 17); and Luxemburg, 'Tasks of International Social-Democracy' (n 4).

[19] Rosa Luxemburg, *The Accumulation of Capital* (Routledge 2003, 1st edn 1913), hereafter Luxemburg, *Accumulation of Capital* 394–98.

[20] ibid 434.

interests. The flag of peoples could, in her estimation, function furtively as a new tool of class domination or colonial control. She thought that the 'rights of nations' should not be a 'yardstick' or figure as a blanket-good for socialism in every case even though the 'nation' should have, in principle, the 'right' to self-determination.[21] That right meant, for a working-class perspective, equality before the law for all nationalities and the free development of culture and democracy via cooperation and solidarity, not domination or control.[22]

Luxemburg's question was always '[w]here is there a nation in which the people have the right to determine the form and condition of national, political and social existence?'.[23] The identification of the people as the proletariat majority supplied her answer.[24] Luxemburg objected to Polish independence from Russia and criticized decolonization in South America, (eg, Brazil, Argentina, Uruguay, or Paraguay) because 'freedom' entailed merely the substitution of an imperial ruler with another capitalist regime (in Poland) or another regime closely aligned with the interests of colonial landholders (in South America).[25] In her radical perspective, independence substantiates as a working class good—which is a different inquiry from the juridical concern with territorial integrity and indigenous self-government—only where freedom from imperial rule facilitates and couples with the internal freedom of the people from commodity interests.[26]

Environmental protection

Luxemburg envisaged the world environment as another context for tracking the dangers of capitalist accumulation. Her interest in the natural world relates to the social record of the Anthropocene, especially in the imperial regions previously untouched by class, that parallel changes to ecosystems and foreshadows, without detailing, regulatory concern for environmental degradation. For Luxemburg, the imprint of capital on nature was acute in the imperial advance of European capitalists beyond Europe due to the visibility of the shift from natural to commodity economies in the pre-industrial and industrializing regions of the world. Nature recorded the recent arrival of colonial interests and government as the uninvited scars of industrialization, urbanization, railways and roads, cultivation, and slavery.

The environmental consequences of imperialism mirrored the social dangers for the proletariat class in Europe and extended those dangers to the new underclass in the undeveloped world. There, indigenous communities lost economic, cultural, and political independence in parallel to the desecration of local ecosystems and exportation of natural resources to European factories. A peasant who was once isolated, self-sufficient, and dependent on nature became a new source of labour, his or her lands appropriated for resources and cultivated with machines, and a new market or consumer for the new surplus. The environmental register of imperial exploitation

[21] Rosa Luxemburg, 'The National Question' in Rosa Luxemburg, *Writings of Rosa Luxemburg* (Red-Black 2010), hereafter Luxemburg, 'National Question' 109, 132, 136.

[22] ibid 160–61.

[23] Luxemburg, *Juniusbroshüre* (n 18) 94–95.

[24] ibid 19.

[25] Luxemburg, 'National Question' (n 21) 159–60.

[26] Luxemburg, *Juniusbroshüre* (n 18) 94–95.

included the new roads or railways 'which cross forests and tunnel through the mountains, telegraph wires which bridge the deserts', the fortifications, villages, factories and towns, or the 'opening' of oceans or lands to trade-routes and war.[27] These interventions counted for Luxemburg as the outward signs of the social wrongs of class and its networked pattern of exploitation that extends across the whole world. Environmental integrity mattered for Luxemburg not scientifically as a question of human survival or sustainability (of food, of resources, of climate control), but because natural degradation is symptomatic of the extension of capital and its widening field of social harm.

The Meaning of International Praxis

The fact of Luxemburg's prior claim does not contest that the design and advances of twentieth-century international law belong to states. Her citation is one of earlier opposition for a different international order and for a different mechanism for organizing the world without the institutional tools of states or the bureaucratic apparatus of world government or global law. Consequently, her thought complicates without changing the historical seam from which international law emerged as the post-war project of states. Luxemburg's struggles against the capitalist state makes visible the prior ideological contests between two internationalisms to organize the world and in certain unexpected respects, details the spaces, themes, and projects the contemporary world order now shares with earlier, radical utopias. Arguably more interesting, however, is how the deficits of present-day international legal praxis become visible by introducing Luxemburg's social measure. Her ideological question against the state becomes what international law does not yet achieve, and further asks, which groups remain disenfranchised despite the progress states make toward a better, more collaborative, more peaceful, less exploitative, less imperial, more sustainable, and more humanistic world. International legal reform towards those goals is not—consistent with Luxemburg's account—the equivalent to international order. Nor does it eliminate the social objectives of revolution or the recurrence of siege.

[27] eg, Luxemburg, *Accumulation of Capital* (n 19) 366–98.

5
Maria van Reigersberch
Wife of Hugo Grotius

Henk Nellen

Maria van Reigersberch owes her fame to the role she played in the eventful life of her husband Hugo Grotius (Hugo de Groot, 1583–1645), statesman, theologian, lawyer, theorist of international law, and one of the most accomplished humanists of his age.[1] Maria herself did not have any education in the work of classical or legal writers, as can be inferred from the spelling of words like 'Seneka' (Seneca), 'contenweren' (to continue), and 'konscentie' (conscience) in her letters. In 1608, Hugo did his wife a favour by translating the Latin poetry he had written on the occasion of their marriage into Dutch.[2] The only sources Maria has left behind are a testament, official requests to public institutions, and a collection of letters, about ninety in total. She always wrote these letters spontaneously to settle her daily affairs. In 1639, her husband Hugo reported that Maria was working on an autobiography, but this document disappeared without any trace.[3]

Maria was born in Veere, Zeeland or in Boulogne-sur-Mer, France on 7 October 1589. She was the daughter of Pieter van Reigersberch (1547–1602), alderman and mayor of Veere, and Maria Nicolai, also known as Mayken Claesdochter (died 1638). Maria was presumably the second youngest child in a family of four boys and four girls. Pieter van Reigersberch played a significant role in urban and regional politics. He was known as a supporter of William of Orange. In the period when governor-general Leicester was in power in the Northern Netherlands, he fled to France together with his family. Therefore, it is believed that, if Maria was not born in Boulogne-sur-Mer, she spent at least part of her early childhood there (or in the neighbouring Calais). As her year of birth is not entirely certain either and any sources on her early years are

[1] See, for short biographical introductions, AJ van der Aa, *Biographisch Woordenboek der Nederlanden* 16 (Haarlem 1874) 189–96; *Nieuw Nederlandsch Biografisch Woordenboek* 2 (Leiden 1912), cols 1181–85; *Encyclopedie van Zeeland* 2 (Middelburg 1982) 556–57, and Henk Nellen, 'Maria van Reigersberch, heldhaftige vrouw van Hugo de Groot', in Els Kloek (ed), *1001 Vrouwen uit de Nederlandse Geschiedenis* (Nijmegen 2013) 293–97, also accessible through: <http://resources.huygens.knaw.nl/vrouwenlexicon/lemmata/data/Reigersberch> accessed 4 October 2022. I feel indebted to Anna van der Velde for revising my English.

[2] *De dichtwerken van Hugo Grotius/The Poetry of Hugo Grotius*, I 2 ab 4, *Original Poetry 1604–1608*, E Rabbie (ed) (Assen 1992) 437.

[3] MJ van Ittersum, 'Knowledge Production in the Dutch Republic: The Household Academy of Hugo Grotius', (2011) 72/4 Journal of the History of Ideas 523–48, at 538; PC Molhuysen and others (eds), *Briefwisseling van Hugo Grotius*, 17 vols (Rijks Geschiedkundige Publicatiën, Grote serie, The Hague 1928–2001) also accessible through <http://grotius.huygens.knaw.nl/years>, vol 10, no 3943: 'Mijn huisvrouw neemt bij tijdt en wijlen wat tijdts om haar Historie te dicteren'. Hereafter Grotius' *Briefwisseling* is referred to as *BW*.

Henk Nellen, *Maria van Reigersberch* In: *Portraits of Women in International Law*. Edited by: Immi Tallgren, Oxford University Press. © Henk Nellen 2023. DOI: 10.1093/oso/9780198868453.003.0005

Figure 5.1 Maria van Reigersberch, Elsje van Houweningen and Hugo Grotius, preparing the escape from Loevestein, 1621, by Gerard Sibelius. Engraving, 15.5 × 10.4 cm, dated 1768–1771. Rijksmuseum, Amsterdam.

Source: Gift of Mrs Brandt. Rijksmuseum, Amsterdam.

missing, her life remains shrouded in mystery until July 1608.[4] After a short courtship, she married Hugo Grotius who had just been appointed as general prosecutor ('advocaat-fiscaal') at the Supreme Courts of Justice in Holland and Zeeland. Thanks

[4] cf PJ Meertens, 'De Groot en Heinsius en hun Zeeuwse vrienden', *Archief. Vroegere en Latere Mededelingen voornamelijk in betrekking tot Zeeland* (Middelburg 1950) 53–99, at 54–61.

to a fixed and generous salary, Grotius was able to enter into an advantageous marriage. Most likely the marriage took place on, or shortly after, 20 July 1608. Four of their nine children died in infancy.

A Stratagem Inspired by Love

The young couple settled in The Hague. Here Maria van Reigersberch gave birth to her first three children: Pieter (who lived only briefly), Cornelia, and Cornelis. Under the guidance of the Secretary of the States of Holland, Johan van Oldenbarnevelt, Grotius' career advanced quickly in the administration of Holland, the leading province of the Dutch Republic. In June 1613, he was appointed as the leading legal advisor ('pensionaris') in Rotterdam, a job that placed him in the midst of turbulent politics. The family moved to the new location, where in the following years the children Pieter, Maria, and Dirck were born. Maria gave birth to the latter on 10 October 1618, at the height of the Truce struggles, only a few weeks after Hugo had been arrested and imprisoned on suspicion of high treason. During the subsequent trial, Maria supported her husband, but oral contact was not allowed.[5] Despite the pressures exerted on her by friend and foe, she refused to submit a request for pardon as she believed that her husband was innocent. She was reaffirmed in this conviction when rumours reached her that a majority of the special court, created to condemn Oldenbarnevelt and his main followers, intended to vote against a death penalty for Grotius.[6] On 12 May 1619, Oldenbarnevelt was sentenced to death. Meanwhile, his right-hand man Grotius had to fear for his life. After the decapitation of Oldenbarnevelt on 13 May, his sentence, pronounced on 18 May, came as a relief: lifelong imprisonment and confiscation of all his goods.

On 12 June, Maria joined her husband in the state prison Loevestein with some of her children. Life in jail was a daily struggle for the family because the rooms in the castle were chilly and uncomfortable. The commander in chief, Jacob Prouninck van Deventer, restricted Maria's and the children's freedom of movement. Further, the state allowance for Grotius' livelihood was only 24 stivers a day, a meagre sum that the prisoners proudly refused to cash in. In a fierce confrontation, Maria blamed Prouninck for his cruelty: now that she saw how her husband suffered, she would have preferred to see him die on the scaffold just like Oldenbarnevelt.[7] In April 1620, the Rotterdam city administration summoned Maria to evacuate the official residence in

[5] Hugo Grotius, *Verantwoordingh van de wettelijcke regieringh van Hollandt ende West-Vrieslandt* ([Hoorn] 1622) 14.6 (141) and 16.2 (154).

[6] Grotius, *Verantwoordingh* (n 5) 16.6 (157–58); Robert Fruin (ed), *Verhooren en andere bescheiden betreffende het rechtsgeding van Hugo de Groot*, Werken uitgegeven door het Historisch Genootschap, gevestigd te Utrecht, Nieuwe reeks 14 (Utrecht 1871) 71 and 73. See also P Scheltema, 'Dagboekje van Willem de Groot, door hem gehouden tijdens de regtspleging van zijnen broeder Hugo de Groot, Johan van Oldenbarneveld en Rombout Hoogerbeets, uit het onuitgegeven hs. medegedeeld', in NC Kist and HJ Royaards (eds), *Nieuw Archief voor Kerkelijke Geschiedenis, inzonderheid van Nederland* 1 (1852) 331–54 at 341 and 344.

[7] A Th van Deursen, JG Smit, and J Roelevink (eds), *Resolutiën der Staten-Generaal*. Nieuwe reeks 1610–1670, Rijks Geschiedkundige Publicatiën, Grote serie (The Hague 1971), vol 4, no 943 (150–51) and no 1504 (228); Grotius, *Verantwoordingh* (n 5) 18.3 (161); *Verhooren en andere bescheiden* 77; Caspar Brandt and Adriaan van Cattenburgh, *Historie van het leven des heeren Huig de Groot*, 2 vols (Dordrecht/Amsterdam 1727) 1 211–13.

Rotterdam. She obeyed, but asked a local notary to draw up an official protest.[8] This was the first step in a long drawn-out campaign to obtain financial compensation after Grotius' dismissal from the city's service.[9]

On Monday morning 22 March 1621, Maria helped her husband to escape from Loevestein by hiding him in a book chest. To deceive the porters, she had placed her husband's clothes and slippers in front of the curtained bed. In addition to Maria, other women were also involved in this spectacular scheme. Her maidservant Elsje van Houweningen accompanied the chest on a carefully prepared escape route, which led over the water to Gorinchem. There, a merchant's wife, Johanna Daetselaer-Van Erp, sister of the Leiden orientalist Thomas Erpenius, helped Hugo Grotius on his way to the southern border. After a short stay in Antwerp he settled in Paris, where Maria soon followed him. In a Neo-Latin poem, the *Silva ad Thuanum* (Paris 1621), Grotius gratefully made public that Maria had devised the ruse with the book chest.[10]

In exile, Maria was primarily concerned with her children's future, while her husband went to great lengths to defend the politics of the defeated party. Just like other supporters, he pointed out the illegality of Oldenbarnevelt's elimination in numerous letters, pamphlets, and historical works. Maria played a supporting role in his political campaign. In the often reprinted apology *Verantwoordingh* (1622), Grotius provided detailed information that enabled the Dutch readership to construct an 'exemplum' of Maria as the epitome of an ideal woman. Diligence, courage, and marital fidelity were named as the most important traits: immediately after his arrest Maria had decided to share the prison with him, in Loevestein she bravely resisted Prouninck's harassments, and thanks to her repeated complaints the harsh prison regime was softened considerably.[11]

Exile

As a jobless citizen, Hugo Grotius waited in vain for an honourable return. After ten years, he tried to force a way out of the impasse by returning to Holland in person, but the attempt failed. Before long, he had to flee again, this time to Hamburg. In the end, after many negotiations, Grotius succeeded in acquiring an office that befitted his international reputation as a scholar and statesman: he entered the diplomatic service of Sweden. In the spring of 1635, he travelled to Paris, accompanied by Maria and some of their children, as the ambassador of the young Queen Christina. For a period of ten years, he fulfilled an important diplomatic task that also reflected on the status of Maria. The family rented a comfortable house in the French capital and

[8] Brandt and Cattenburgh, *Leven* 1 (n 7) 221–22.

[9] Van Ittersum, 'Knowledge Production' (n 3) 532–33 and 542. See also Brandt and Cattenburgh, *Leven* 2 (n 7) 1–74 (second pagination): 'Aenhangsel', and *Vertoogh bij de weduwe van wijlen de heer Hugo de Groot, over-gegeven aen de ed. achtbare heeren burgemeesters ende vroetschappen der stede Rotterdam. Daer bij gevoegt zijn de authentycke stucken, dienende tot justificatie van 't selve vertoogh* (The Hague? 1649, Knuttel, Pamphlet no 6486, re-edited in 1652).

[10] Moniek van Oosterhout, *Hugo Grotius' Occasional Poetry (1609–1645)*, diss Nijmegen (Nijmegen 2009) 406–07, lines 80–118. On the escape, see Brandt and Cattenburgh, *Leven* 1 (n 7) 242–55.

[11] Grotius, *Verantwoordingh* (n 5) 18.4 and 18.5 (161–62); 18.7 and 18.8 (163–67).

Maria took command of a crowded and busy household filled with embassy and service personnel.

Meanwhile, she assisted her husband in receiving numerous diplomats, scholars, and travelling compatriots. Reports in letters on the discussions with visitors from Holland attest to Maria's commitment to the career of Hugo, especially when it came to defending his contentious role during the Truce controversies. Many times, she visited the court on her own to attend audiences with the French Queen Anna of Austria.[12] When one of her journeys to Holland brought her to The Hague in 1639–1640, she moved around in a carriage with no less than six horses, as befitted an ambassador's wife. She realized that her opulent retinue was being watched with crooked eyes: 'The sight of my driving around in a decent carriage has infuriated those Hollanders, and I know well there were those who said: they should have chopped off his head as well, then his wife would not defy and annoy us with a carriage with six horses.'[13]

This quotation characterizes Maria van Reigersberch perfectly. Her letters contained strong statements, showing that she was an energetic, self-assured, and strident woman who enjoyed telling her critics the truth straightforwardly. She wholeheartedly approved of the politics her husband had advocated for in Holland and always endorsed his stubborn refusal to confess his guilt, thus blocking the way for a smooth return. At the same time, she was also a dedicated mother, who was deeply saddened by the impact the exile had on the life of her children: 'It is in our children that we feel most of the misery that the Dutch have brought over us', she once wrote in a mood of bitterness.[14]

She made every effort to put her children's affairs in order so as not to let their father's fate affect them. Pieter was destined for a career in maritime commerce, but he found employment in the legal profession against the wishes of his parents. As he initially had trouble earning a decent living, he was a constant source of sorrow for his parents. Maria had to act as an intermediary because she thought of Hugo as too complaisant,[15] which affected the relationship with his son in a negative way. Pieter, limp and pockmarked as a result of a life-threatening childhood illness, even thought that his mother kept him at bay because of his appearance.[16] The other two sons, Cornelis and Dirck, entered a career in the army. Dirck soon turned out to be an unlucky soldier, who repeatedly became a prisoner of war, while Cornelis led a rudderless, spendthrift life that did not bring him any material certainty. 'Oh', Maria complained about him, 'that I could have him the way I wish he would be: how happy would he be!'.[17] Maria was repeatedly forced to solve their problems by opening her purse. Despite her well-meaning efforts, she received ingratitude and for that reason concluded in a letter to her husband that as a governess in another family she would have gained more appreciation.[18] Contrary to her unruly sons, the daughters Cornelia and Maria led a quiet and uneventful life leaving only sporadic traces in the sources. The youngest daughter Maria died in 1635 at the age of eighteen. Cornelia lived long enough to

[12] See for example *BW* (n 3) 9 nos 3464, 3550, 3594, and 3747, discussing Maria's visits to Queen Anne of Austria, who would soon give birth to Louis XIV.

[13] HC Rogge (ed), *Brieven van en aan Maria van Reigersberch* (Leiden 1902) 245.

[14] ibid 242.

[15] ibid 183: '... mijn man is al te saght'.

[16] *BW* (n 3) 11 no 4747.

[17] *Brieven* (n 13) 227.

[18] *BW* (n 3) 11 no 4605.

marry a French military officer, Jean Barthon de Montbas. In her last will, Maria referred to the 'friendship and comfort' she had always enjoyed in Cornelia's company.[19]

De iure belli ac pacis

Maria was always ready to attend to Hugo's needs, even though the uncertainty of a life in exile weighed heavily on her. She was afraid that they were wasting their time by waiting for a regime change in the fatherland.[20] During her travels in Holland, she urged the payment of the arrears of salary owed to Grotius by the municipality of Rotterdam, tried to reverse the confiscation of his property stipulated in the verdict of 1619, and showed genuine practical commitment to Hugo's scholarly enterprises. She consulted Gerardus Joannes Vossius, Thomas Erpenius, and two Leiden printers, Franciscus Raphelengius and Jean Le Maire, on the publication of *De iure belli ac pacis* (Paris 1625). She even toyed with the idea of publishing the book in-house, when she was told by a Rotterdam printer that such an enterprise might render a considerable profit, no less than 2,000 guilders. However, the plan proved to be unfeasible because the distribution of the print run would cause insurmountable problems.

In the end, due to Maria's resourcefulness, another solution was opted for and an agreement was made with the printer Nicolas Buon in Paris. He was allowed to publish the work provided that he handed over a large number of copies to the author who could supply some bookshops in Holland for his own gain.[21] Much later, Grotius again suggested the idea of his own printing company to publish his annotations on the Bible in order to avoid French censorship.[22] Again, the plan failed, but Maria continued to keep an eye on her husband's finances. She angrily reproached Hugo for promising the Amsterdam printer Johan Bleau the production and sale of the *Historiae et Annales* (Amsterdam 1657) without negotiating any financial compensation.[23]

A Happy Marriage

Hugo Grotius described his wife as eloquent and blessed with a good memory.[24] He loved her and at times referred to the harmony ('concordia') that existed between them.[25] As a rule, however, he only indicated between the lines that he was happily married, while Maria van Reigersberch, especially in her early letters, did not shy away from expressing her affection for Hugo: 'Oh, if only I could fly over to you, don't think I would fail to do so!'[26]

[19] JW Des Tombe, 'Een autograaf en het testament van Maria van Reigersbergh' (1904) 54 De Navorscher 583–92, at 589: 'Ende naedemael ick altijd vriendschap en troost gehad hebbe van mijn dochter ...'.

[20] *Brieven* (n 13) 140–41, 183.

[21] ibid 93–95; 102–03.

[22] *BW* (n 3) 10 no 4196 and 11 no 4918.

[23] *BW* (n 3) 11 no 4605.

[24] *BW* (n 3) 10 no 4132: '... et neque memoria neque facundia ei (meae uxori) desit ...'.

[25] *BW* (n 3) 9 no 3758.

[26] *Brieven* (n 13) 117.

She often had to go north to arrange all kinds of family matters because her husband saw a return with honour to the fatherland thwarted. She travelled at least seven times, mostly by land, because according to her husband she was 'an insular animal that shunned water'.[27] In addition to negotiating with printers and booksellers, she followed up on her three sons, who all went to school in Holland, and strengthened ties with numerous relatives and friends. Her letter of 12 August 1624, for example, offers detailed accounts of dinners, visits, and conversations with city magistrates, scholars, and powerful patricians.[28] While Maria was abroad, Hugo eagerly awaited her homecoming, acknowledging how much his busy household was in need of the diligent hands of his wife.[29]

It is clear from Maria's letters that she was in charge of her own finances. The confiscation of Grotius's property and assets ordered in 1619 also affected her financial position. The seizure was lifted, first for her part in 1625, and for Grotius' properties in 1630–1631.[30] Contrary to Hugo, Maria came from a well-off family and probably possessed considerable financial resources. Although her correspondence does not provide detailed information, she must have enjoyed income from land and shares in trade and fishing companies. Without her husband's knowledge, she invested large sums in the business of a sugar merchant in Rouen, Daniel Tresel, one of Grotius' co-convicts, who went bankrupt in 1641.[31]

In the autumn of 1645, Maria van Reigersberch stayed in Spa for a medical cure in the company of her daughter Cornelia. There she was informed that her husband, after resigning from the Swedish service, had died in Rostock on 28 August 1645. Maria was absent from Grotius' well-attended funeral on 3 October in Delft.[32] For some time she kept Paris as her residence. Around 1648, she moved to The Hague where she passed away on 19 April 1653. As her last will shows, she was a wealthy widow who, at the end of her life, married her daughter Cornelia off with a large dowry and granted her three sons equivalent bequests.

The provisions of this will show that she cherished her distinguished ancestry. In an attempt to rule beyond the grave, she included detailed financial restrictions meant to prevent her sons from entering into marital unions that would disparage the status of the patrician family De Groot-Van Reigersberch. She also encouraged her next of kin to follow up on her efforts in obliging the city of Rotterdam to pay the arrears of Grotius' salary. In her last years, she did her best to ensure that the manuscripts that Grotius had left were sent to the press. After her death, her sons took over this task.

[27] *BW* (n 3) 10 no 4059: '... animal insulare sed minime aquaticum'. See also ibid 9 nos 3503, 3514 ('Uxor maris est impatiens'), and Des Tombe, 'Een autograaf' 586.

[28] *Brieven* (n 13) 93–102.

[29] *BW* (n 3) 10 nos 4198, 4328, and 4433.

[30] G Moll, 'De confiscatie der goederen van Hugo de Groot', (1902) 20 Oud-Holland 83–112.

[31] *BW* (n 3) 12 no 5168.

[32] Henk Nellen, *Hugo Grotius: A Lifelong Struggle for Peace in Church and State, 1583–1645* (Leiden 2014) 734.

National Fame

In later centuries, the public image of Maria van Reigersberch was based on elements like loyalty, decisiveness, and self-sacrifice. In their literary works supporters of the republican States party, successor to the Oldenbarnevelt faction, heralded her as a heroine: this independent and proud woman had shown great courage by standing up against oppression and advocating for national reconciliation. In the nineteenth and twentieth centuries, public interest in Maria as an archetypical example of a brave and even emancipated woman who never left the side of her demanding husband was greatly stimulated by the publication of her letters,[33] which influenced the interpretation of her eventful life.[34] Robert Fruin,[35] and after him Annie Romein-Verschoor,[36] portrayed Maria as a tragic figure embittered by the setbacks of a long-lasting exile. Although truthful, this image is also one-sided as in a correspondence the daily annoyances and disappointments of a family in exile receive the most prominent attention, whereas periods of happiness ordinarily do not provoke much discussion.

Being a thrifty, energetic, and confident woman, Maria always used letters to settle her affairs. Faced with a family that was torn apart by exile, without much practical support from a man who preferred to remain in the background or stubbornly held on to his position, she sometimes found it necessary to intervene firmly and cut the knot. That was, at least according to Maria, the only way to solve life's problems. Indulging in her preference for outspoken statements, she noted in plain Dutch: 'that's where the mussels are'.[37] Undoubtedly, this expression, equivalent to the English 'there's the rub', was rather common in seaside areas like Zeeland.

[33] The standard edition of Maria's letters is *Brieven* (n 13). For other editions see H Vollenhoven, *Broeders gevangenisse. Dagboek van Willem de Groot, betreffende het verblijf van zijnen broeder Hugo op Loevestein, uit echte bescheiden aangevuld en opgehelderd* (The Hague 1842), with a letter and many requests in the name of Maria van Reigersberch; H Vollenhoven and GDJ Schotel (eds), *Brieven van Maria van Reigersbergh* (Middelburg 1857); GW Hellinga and WGs Hellinga (eds), *Allerliefste van Hugo de Groot* (The Hague 1957) 111–72; FF Blok, 'Deux lettres en français de Marie de Reigersberg, veuve de Hugo Grotius' (1990) 20 Quaerendo 4–23, 87–95; MB Smits-Veldt and MS Bakker (eds), *In een web van vriendschap. Brieven van Nederlandse vrouwen uit de zeventiende eeuw* (Amsterdam 1999) 35–52, 103–114, also accessible through Digital Library for Dutch Literature, <https://www.dbnl.org/tekst/smit040webv01_01/colofon.php>, accessed 24 January 2023.

[34] MB Smits-Veldt, 'Maria van Reigersberch. De canonisering van een vaderlandse echtgenote' (1997) 2 Nederlandse Letterkunde 271–91; Lia van Gemert, 'Echte helden zie je zelden. Idolen in het Nederlandse epos' (2006) 38/1 De Achttiende Eeuw 22–38, 104–05.

[35] Robert Fruin, 'Hugo de Groot en Maria van Reigersbergh', in: Robert Fruin, *Verspreide geschriften* 4 (The Hague 1901) 1–94, also published in: *Allerliefste van Hugo de Groot* 7–103.

[36] Annie Romein-Verschoor, *Vaderland in de verte. Historische roman* (Amsterdam 1948).

[37] *Brieven* (n 13) 162: '... daar leggen de mosselen'.

PART III
FIGUREHEADS OF FIGHTING FOR PEACE

6

Bertha von Suttner

Locating International Law in Novel and *Salon*

Janne E Nijman

Introduction

Austrian feminist and pacifist Baroness Bertha von Suttner, née Countess Kinsky von Chinič und Tettnau (1843–1914), is not completely absent from the historiography of international law. She is portrayed—as the only woman—in the *Oxford Handbook of the History of International Law* (2012) as 'one of the leading figures of the late 19th-century [international] peace movement', a friend and love-interest of Alfred Nobel, an 'important initiator' of the Nobel Peace Prize, and its first female recipient (1905).[1] But this is about it. In spite of the flurry of intellectual histories of international law in recent years, Bertha von Suttner has remained largely unstudied in international legal historiography.

In *The Gentle Civilizer of Nations*, Martti Koskenniemi examines the intellectual scene to which she was both insider and outsider.[2] When exploring late nineteenth-century liberal internationalism, his focus is on the 'Men of 1873' and Suttner does not feature in any way. Similarly, I failed to mention Suttner when I explored the early twentieth-century intellectual and legal context of Viennese and neo-Kantian constitutional and international law scholar, Hans Kelsen (1881–1973).[3] This short portrait shows that her ideas on international law deserve serious discussion. Together with the 'Men of 1873', she stood—literally and figuratively—at the foundations of the international legal institutions in The Hague. Like these liberal internationalists, she adhered to international law's 'civilizing mission' and had a certain ambivalence about colonialism. She strongly opposed the warfare, 'imperialist violence', and exploitation of European expansion, and rejected a plan to divide China among European powers.[4] Yet she also seemed to have accepted colonialism as part of humanity's civilizing

[1] Simone Peter, 'Bertha von Suttner (1843–1914)' in Bardo Fassbender and Anne Peters (eds), *The Oxford Handbook of the History of International Law* (OUP 2012) 1142–46.

[2] Martti Koskenniemi, *The Gentle Civilizer of Nations. The Rise and Fall of International Law 1870–1960* (Cambridge University Press 2001).

[3] Janne E Nijman, *The Concept of International Legal Personality: An Inquiry into the History and Theory of International Law* (T.M.C. Asser Press 2004), ch 3.

[4] Brigitte Hamann, *Bertha von Suttner: Ein Leben für den Frieden* (Piper München 1986) 254–56, 255: 'Unsere sogenannte europäische Zivilisation kommt aus dem Orient. Sie sind uns einige Jahrhunderte voraus.' One recognizes similar wording by Kant, Leibniz, and Wolff. In Bertha von Suttner, *Memoirs of Bertha von Suttner: The Records of an Eventful Life* (Ginn & Co Boston and London 1910) vol II 402, hereafter *Memoirs*, she cites a Chinese attaché, who tells her success of the 1899 conference is 'highly desirable' for China 'is particularly threatened by the most serious dangers of the European policy of force.' ibid 263.

Janne E Nijman, *Bertha von Suttner* In: *Portraits of Women in International Law*. Edited by: Immi Tallgren, Oxford University Press.
 DOI: 10.1093/oso/9780198868453.003.0006

Figure 6.1 'Finally, in 1907, just as eight years earlier, I was present at The Hague during the time of the Peace Conference': in footnote Bertha von Suttner, Memoirs of Bertha von Suttner: The Records of an Eventful Life (Ginn & Co Boston and London 1910) vol II, 402.
Source: Library of Congress, Prints & Photographs Division, [LC-DIG-ggbain-07508], George Grantham Bain Collection.

process of international organization and integration.[5] The distinction between civilization and savagery, she appears to have drawn between '*Rechtsmenschen*' and '*Gewaltmenschen* überall'.[6] At the same time, she considered many of the Austrian and German law professors '*Friedensbremser*'.[7]

[5] ibid, Hamann at 256: Wenn er aber Europa vereinen will, um *Raubpolitik* in Asien und Afrika zu vertreten, so bin ich dagegen. Aug die Kolonisierung muß auf das ethische Gebiet hinübergebracht werden, sonst sind wir mit uns selber in Widerspruch. […] Auch für Kolonial-Streitigkeiten müßten unsere Prinzipien gelten.' See for a brief conversation in The Hague with a physician of the Dutch Colonial Army, who had been stationed in Borneo, Indonesia, about the violence and suffering he had seen there, ibid, *Memoirs* at 297.

[6] Suttner as cited in Hamann (n 4) 257.

[7] ibid 260.

Similar to many women in the history of international (legal) thought, Suttner and her work have been largely ignored, as not fitting traditional understandings 'of what counts as international thought and [. . .] of who counts as an international thinker'.[8] To include Suttner in this historiography, requires us to move outside the gendered frame of international law and international legal history and to study sources traditionally not considered relevant within the scope of international legal history. That is, female diaries, journal, and magazine articles, and in this case a bestselling novel *Die Waffen Nieder!* (*Lay Down Your Arms*) (1889) with a female protagonist. From reading this one realizes Suttner held a rather well-developed—and at times fairly sceptical—outlook on international law (see 'International Law in *Die Waffen Nieder*' below). The novel contributed to her standing as a world-leading peace activist, 'the only woman permitted' at the opening ceremony of the 1899 conference at Queen Wilhelmine's *Huis ten Bosch*.[9] In The Hague, not allowed access to the formal sessions, she resorted to a typical female practice to influence intellectual and political debates. As salonnière, she created an informal social space[10] for frank conversations among the small cosmopolitan elite of diplomats, journalists, and international legal experts to contribute to the 'peace through law' project (see 'Salonnière Agency during the 1899 and 1907 Peace Conferences' below). With this focus on international law in her novel and *Salon*, this portrait connects loosely with a more socio-legal and materialist approach to international legal history.[11] The following section first briefly situates Suttner's life and work.

Situating '*Friedensbertha*'

Born in Prague, one of the capital cities of the Austro-Hungarian Empire, Bertha grew up in Brno (Moravia), in Vienna, and in the spas and casinos of Europe with her gambling bourgeois mother. Her father died at the age of seventy-five, shortly before Bertha was born. He came from a Bohemian, high nobility family with a long military tradition. Her whole life, Bertha would be much aware of the implications of class-society being an outsider to both imperial aristocracy and bourgeois middle class. She received, however, an excellent education thanks to private tutoring and together with her cousin Elvira she read Kant, Hegel, and Shakespeare. When Bertha's first professional love, opera singing, did not lead to a career, her excellent education helped her to find work as a governess to the Von Suttner family in 1873.

She avoided marriages without love, a deviation from the social convention she criticized in *Die Waffen Nieder!* (1889),[12] to then fall in love with the eldest Von Suttner

[8] Valesca Huber, Tamson Pietsch, and Katharina Rietzler,'Women's International Thought and the New Professions, 1900–1940' (2019) Modern Intellectual History 1–25 at 1; <https://doi.org/10.1017/S1479244319000131> accessed 5 October 2022.

[9] *Memoirs* (n 4) 250.

[10] See, eg, *Memoirs* (n 4) 283–84, for how she creates her salon in the Kurhaus.

[11] See, eg, DR Quiroga-Villamarín, 'Beyond Texts? Towards a Material Turn in the Theory and History of International Law' (2020) Journal of the History of International Law 1–35 available at <https://doi.org/10.1163/15718050-12340172> accessed 5 October 2022.

[12] Bertha von Suttner, *Lay Down Your Arms. The Autobiography of Martha von Tilling*, T Holmes (authorized tr, 2nd rev edn Longmans, Green and Co 1908) 30, 423. Hereinafter LDYA, and references in main text are page numbers of this edition. A first English translation appeared in 1892.

son, Arthur (1850–1902), seven years her junior. When she was ordered to leave the house, her command of English, French, German, and Italian *inter alia* enabled her to start as private secretary with Alfred Nobel in Paris in 1875. Alfred and Bertha would stay in touch throughout their lives. Within a few weeks, however, Bertha and Arthur reunited, married, and moved to the Caucasus. Here Bertha's aristocratic network was helpful but did not provide sufficient financial stability, so the couple worked as journalists and teachers. They lived an austere life from 1876 till 1885. During the Russo-Turkish War of 1877–1878, Arthur reported on the war for the leading newspaper of the establishment, the *Neue Freie Presse*. Next to her journalistic and *feuilleton* writing, Bertha transformed their home into a hospital for wounded Russian soldiers. From 1885 onwards, after reconciliation with Arthur's conservative family, the couple lived at Schloss Harmannsdorf a little over eighty kilometres northwest of Vienna in a rural, conservative, and intensely Roman Catholic area. With the success of *Die Waffen Nieder!*, Bertha also travelled Europe as an activist for peace and social justice and founded, for example, the Austrian and German peace societies. Bertha left Harmannsdorf for Vienna after Arthur's death in 1902 and lived there until she died in 1914 just a few days before the First World War broke out.

Late Habsburg Vienna—or *Kakania* as Robert Musil called it—was marked by cultural, intellectual, social, and political paradoxes and fault lines. It was the imperial-royal capital of a multinational empire in decline. The old social and political order was held together by a class-based social scaffolding, a clerical system of government, dynastic bonds among the ancient Catholic aristocracy, '*schwarz-gelb*' loyalty to Emperor and imperial army, and by salons and perpetual waltzing.[13] This deeply conservative imperial society was challenged by progressive liberals, who were of an anti-clerical, internationalist, capitalist, and rationalist mindset and who wanted to reform the Habsburg Empire into a constitutional parliamentary monarchy.[14] In *Die Waffen Nieder!*, Frederick, Arthur von Suttner's alter ego, represents this 'democratic and liberal point of view' (351). Both progressive liberals and 'modernist' artists and intellectuals suffocated in what Kelsen would later call the 'the polluted political atmosphere'.[15] Anti-Semitism was fanned by the toxic politics of the Christian Socialists and their German-Nationalist friends. Bertha and Arthur responded with the foundation of the *Verein zur Abwehr des Antisemitismus* in 1891. Like Freud, they too were friends with Theodor Herzl, an editor at the *Neue Freie Presse*, to which both Bertha and Arthur contributed. Herzl would finance their stay in The Hague in 1899.

Bertha von Suttner was a harsh critic of the old social and political order. Her work testifies to the 'misery' underlying all the 'pomp and circumstance', all the 'sensuous worldly splendor and glory' of the Dual Monarchy.[16] One only has to read in *Die Waffen Nieder!* Martha's repudiation of the imperial couple's theatrically washing of the feet of the poor—a 'sham' through which they compared themselves with God: not

[13] Allan Janik and Stephen Toulmin, *Wittgenstein's Vienna* (Touchstone 1973) 33, ff.

[14] ibid.

[15] Hans Kelsen, 'The Pure Theory of Law, "Labandism", and Neo-Kantianism. A Letter to Renato Treves' (1933) in Paulson and Litschewski Paulson (eds), *Normativity and Norms: Critical Perspectives on Kelsenian Themes* 172 (OUP 1998).

[16] *Wittgenstein's Vienna* (n 13) 37.

'peculiarly humble' (86–9) —to realize how critical she was of 'the unshakable commitment of the ruling dynasty to the Habsburg concept of *Hausmacht*, that is, the idea that the Habsburgs were the instrument of God on Earth'.[17] That said, Bertha was not part of the 'modernist' cultural and social scene either. She rejected the attitude of 'therapeutic nihilism', so popular an antidote among Viennese artists and thinkers, such as Sigmund Freud, for failing to provide answers to the problems of the day.[18] Bertha and Arthur were well-read, they studied the latest scientific articles and books together on a daily basis. With an optimism about human reason and humanity's progress, inspired by the political philosophy of Immanuel Kant, Charles Darwin's theory of evolution,[19] and by the evolutionary sociology of Herbert Spencer and Thomas Buckle. She mocks the 'barbarism' of self-acclaimed 'civilised nations' and calls for 'the triumph of the intellect' over the irrationality of war.[20] While this rationalism was shared by many Viennese intellectuals, prominent authors such as Karl Kraus and Rainer Maria Rilke ridiculed '*Friedensbertha*' for her utopian and 'low-culture' writings.[21] Similarly, modernist Arthur Schnitzler depreciated her belief in reason. After Bertha's visit in March 1914, he penned down '[s]he is a good though doubtless fundamentally banal person', which he related to her lack of nihilism: 'like people who "have to believe something", even in the triumph of reason'.[22] While celebrated by many in the national and international 'peace through law' movement, German international lawyer, Felix Dahn (1834–1912), famously snarled at her '*Wo Männer fechten, hat das Weib zu Schweigen!*'.[23]

It is against this background of fin-de-siècle Vienna and the disintegrating Austro-Hungarian Empire that Bertha von Suttner became a leading international peace activist, who advocated social justice and a Kantian transformation of the old international order: '*Gestern: Gewalt als Recht. Morgen: Recht als Gewalt*'.[24]

International Law in *Die Waffen Nieder!*

Die Waffen Nieder![25] is a first-person novel that tells the life-story of Martha von Tilling amid four European wars—1859, 1864, 1866, and 1870–71. It describes in very realistic terms the suffering war brings to both men and women. While this largely

[17] ibid.

[18] William M Johnston, *The Austrian Mind: An Intellectual and Social History 1848–1938* (University of California Press 1983) 223, ff. One cannot help but think Bertha was familiar with Sigmund Freud's incipient ideas. Frederick explains how war 'electrifie[s]' in Freudian terms: united in 'love' and peace as an alternative for Id, LDYA (n 12) 388.

[19] eg LDYA (n 12) 44, 65–69.

[20] eg LDYA (n 12) 47–48, 74, 201, 261; also the Preface to *Memoirs* vol 1 (n 4).

[21] See eg Stefan Zweig, *The World of Yesterday* (4th edn, Cassell 1943, 1947) 163: 'the old lady, *who was not taken seriously in Vienna*' (emphasis added).

[22] Peter Gay, *Schnitzler's Century: The Making of the Middle-Class Culture 1815–1914* (WW Norton 2002) 288.

[23] Hamann (n 4) 141, 264.

[24] Jemand [B von Suttner], *Das Maschinenalter: Zukunftvorlesungen über unsere Zeit* (1889), 292, as cited in Peter (n 2) 1145. cf Hamann (n 4) 234 for Suttner's commitment to the development of the international legal order to constrain states.

[25] Like many female authors at the time, Von Suttner was initially turned down by publishers. She had published *Das Machinenalter* anonymously. *Memoirs* (n 4) 275–76. She resisted, however, the prejudice of women as 'the weak-minded sex' and published the 'women's novel' under her own name. See *Memoirs* vol

explains its world fame, it is also a novel of international (law) ideas. Martha examines contemporary international law issues such as the problem of secret treaties (359–60), the right to self-determination of the people of Schleswig-Holstein (195), 'historic rights' claimed by Denmark as a 'right cause' (135–36, 157), or other *causa belli* (eg 386) claimed by European states to justify war. She passionately attacks the conservative perspectives on state, war, and international order, so all-pervasive in the German-language world—Austria, Germany, 'it is all the same school' as Martha's husband Frederick observed (300). In the novel, Martha's father, *K.u.K.* (*Kaiserlich und Königlich*) General Count Althaus represents the old outlook on society and international order steeped in Hegelian and Clausewitzian thought.[26] Martha and Frederick draw on Kant's teleological conception of universal history and nature and his claim that 'reason' obliges humanity to 'progress' morally towards 'enlightenment' and 'perpetual peace'.[27] A rationalism that morally commands a law-governed national and international society and institutions that administer justice. They study the Swiss liberal international lawyer Johann Caspar Bluntschli (1808–1881), who they read in the Kantian tradition of legal pacifism and argued for an international legal order (*Rechtszustand*) that outlaws war (433).[28]

For Martha, war is the negation of 'civilisation' and she mocks the sense of superiority of European 'civilised nations' (261). Through her eyes the reader learns how society maintains this 'savagery' (315): by social conventions that define a woman's role by her (breeding) function to the military, by a culture of patriotism and militarism, and by a Roman Catholic clergy who treats warfare as a product of the will of God.

In a state organized for warfare, women are belittled and silenced: 'What a cowardly lot you women folk are!' or 'politics is [...] far "too high a thing" for ladies'.[29] Martha resists fervently to 'educate' her children in patriotism and militarism, as is clear for example when her father brings her son Rudi a box of tin soldiers 'to awaken the love for the trade [of war]'.[30] While she refuses to raise her son for military service, she refuses to indoctrinate her daughter to adore military uniforms and to cry to her future husband ' "Go on, die for your country that is the most glorious of deaths" '.[31] Martha is

1 (n 4) 289. The cry of the title '*Die Waffen Nieder!*' is penned down by Martha in her diary for the first time in 1864. LDYA (n 12) at 143; subsequently, it is on her lips a few times throughout the book, eg at LDYA (n 12) 150, 209, and 277.

[26] In LDYA (n 12) Carl von Clausewitz is represented by his follower, the *Schlachtendenker*, Helmuth von Moltke, whose view on war is captured here by his famous adage 'Everlasting peace is a dream, and not a pretty dream either', LDYA (n 12) 423. See eg on nineteenth-century perspectives on international law, including the Hegelian and Clausewitzian perspectives, Hendrik Simon, The Myth of Liberum *Ius ad Bellum*: Justifying War in 19th-Century Legal Theory and Political Practice (2018) 29(1) EJIL 113–36.

[27] Immanuel Kant, 'Idea for a Universal History with a Cosmopolitan Purpose' and 'Perpetual Peace' in HS Reiss (ed), *Kant Political Writing* (Cambridge University Press 1997) 41–53 and 93–130.

[28] See for international legal thought of Bluntschli and Kant, Hendrik Simon, 'Theorising Order in the Shadow of War. The Politics of International Legal Knowledge and the Justification of Force in Modernity' (2020) 20 *Journal of the History of International Law* 218–45. See also for Bluntschli as also one of the founders of the *IDI*, the 'Men of 1873', Koskenniemi (n 3), at 42–47; colonization 'to promote civilization and the extension of culture', in Bluntschli, *Droit international codifié* (4th edn 1886) 176–77.

[29] LDYA (n 12) 30 and 350; cf Bertha von Suttner, 'Universal Peace: From a Woman's Standpoint' (1899) 169 (512) *The North American Review* 51.

[30] LDYA (n 12) 62; on the same theme of raising sons into soldiers and nationalists, 171, 190, 196, 229.

[31] LDYA (n 12) 228, cf Suttner, Universal Peace (n 29) 51.

often furious when 'for [her] female weakness of intellect' she is told not to think about politics and war: '"don't think about it" that is the support of all kinds of barbarity'.[32]

The novel character of aunt Mary gives us an insight in the toxic entanglement of militarism, patriotism, the 'loyal love' of the imperial Habsburg family, and the doctrine of Divine Providence: '"What is the will of God[, m]ust be borne with composure and resignation"'.[33] This is an attitude Martha qualifies as '"[. . .] folly. All savagery, all the arbitrary action of men, hiding itself under the shield of God's will"'(321). Martha unravels the influential doctrine/ideology in a conversation with a clergyman in which 'the lawfulness of war' (339) is discussed within the Roman Catholic just war tradition. One recognizes Thomas Aquinas' *Summa Theologiae* II.II. Qu 40 to structure the clergyman's discussion of nineteenth-century wars.[34] Martha rejects the 'suppression' of 'the gift of reason' by religion (227–28).

Throughout the book, Martha fights the old order by quarrelling with her father. This aristocratic, *K.u.K.* General features as the embodiment of the 'war spirit' that infects society with '*la haine sacrée de l'ennemi*' and 'patriotic egotism' (402–03). He sets out the 'old idolatry of war' (48) in Hegelian terms: 'Continual peace relaxes, effeminates, produces like stagnant water corruption; especially the degeneration of morals. [. . .] Wars are the best means for putting in practice self-sacrifice, heroism in short, the firmer elements of the character.'[35] Count Althaus defends the so-called *liberum ius ad bellum*: the international '*right* to go to war'.[36] He stands for mainstream nationalism and glorification of the state. He reasons about European politics as a zero-sum game (211), a 'contest for hegemony' and 'honour',[37] and with the 'European equilibrium' or 'balance of power' logic as his guiding principle.[38] In this outlook, war is a regular instrument of international and dynastic politics.[39] Sovereignty and territorial integrity of the state are sacred[40] and the normative force of treaties is extremely limited.[41]

As an alternative, Martha and Frederick argue for a peaceful order based on international law. Once retired from the *k.u.K* army, Frederick starts to study international law and to correspond with Bluntschli, who published *Das moderne Völkerrecht der civilisierten Staaten als Rechtsbuch dargestellt* in 1868 and argued that peace through international law was possible (368). In Martha's red diaries, she copies excerpts of international legal documents of her time. In a blue cahier, Frederick and Martha develop their 'peace through law' argument by engagement with peace studies authors from Aristophanes to Kant (365–7). In the international legal order, they advocate, war is not a natural disaster but inflicted by human choice, it is 'a crime' or '*Völkermord*' as Martha phrased it at the graveyards of Königgrätz (1866).[42] War does

[32] LDYA (n 12) 218, also 225, 287, 297.
[33] ibid 133 and 20; also 112, 337.
[34] ibid 338–46.
[35] ibid 197; see also 41–43, 124–25, 228, 385–86; cf *Hegel's Philosophy of Right*, TM Knox (tr) §§ 324–25.
[36] LDYA (n 12) 434 emphasis added; see also Simon (n 26).
[37] LDYA (n 12) 126, 135.
[38] ibid 126, 135, 208, 368, 372, 383.
[39] ibid 135, 146, 204.
[40] ibid 41, 386.
[41] cf Hegel (n 35) §§ 330–40.
[42] LDYA (n 12) 279; cf Kant (n 28).

not morally improve humanity, it 'dehumanises'.[43] Bertha von Suttner was more radical than those contemporaries who argued for the development of international humanitarian law: progress lies in a positive *ius contra bellum* not in *ius in bello*. Martha fulminates against the assumption that the 'humanisation' of war as envisioned by Henry Dunant and in the Geneva Convention (1864) is at all possible.[44] She attacks the international *right* to go to war.

With their '*Protocol of Peace*', Martha and Frederick aimed to change the minds of humanity. Martha invoked Kant's *Project for a Perpetual Peace* (1795) to argue against the natural 'right' of sovereign states to go to war and for 'general disarmament' in Europe (362, 390), and to suggest that 'the civil constitution in every state should be republican' to avoid war provoked by dynastic conflicts (387).[45] She quotes moreover from paragraph 3 of its Preliminary Article, which argues for the abolition of standing armies.[46] Nations with armies would become 'armed nations' (351–53). Martha protests against the arms race and the industrialization of weaponry (351). She draws on Kant's cosmopolitan outlook when she calls for a confederation or 'union' of states, a 'league of peace', in Europe (177, 298).[47]

Here, I want to end with Martha's plea for the peaceful settlement of international disputes by an international 'court of law' (198–99). She refers a few times to the Alabama Claims (1872) and the Caroline Islands (1885) cases to oppose the traditional view that 'Sovereign states and nations will never accept such a court's decision'[48] and that arbitration is 'a utopian […] dream' (296, 386, 424). At the end of the novel, Martha explicates the agenda of the peace movement and pleads one last time: 'to move the Governments to submit their differences in future to an Arbitration Court, appointed by themselves, and so once for all to enthrone justice in place of brute force'.[49] With this agenda of arbitration, disarmament, and the abolishment of the *ius ad bellum*,[50] Bertha went to The Hague to work them through her salon in 1899 and 1907.

Salonnière Agency during the 1899 and 1907 Peace Conferences

The salon was an important social institution in the circles of Bertha and her alter ego Martha, and as such very present in *Die Waffen Nieder!*.[51] Throughout her life, Martha visited and hosted salons in Berlin, Paris, and Vienna. In the seventeenth and eighteenth century, aristocratic ladies ran salons in European patriarchal, monarchical societies. Gradually, first in France and later also elsewhere in Europe, other than aristocratic women came to lead cultural and intellectual salons with their art of

[43] LDYA (n 12) 197–98, 227.
[44] ibid 220–27, 295.
[45] cf Kant (n 28).
[46] LDYA (n 12) 362; cf Kant (n 28); Hegel (n 37) § 326.
[47] cf *Memoirs* (n 4) 221.
[48] LDYA (n 12) 126–27; also, *Memoirs* (n 4) 247.
[49] LDYA (n 12) 424, and throughout the book. See also Kant (n 28).
[50] cf Suttner, Universal Peace (n 29) 50–61. Bertha wrote this article while being in The Hague for the Peace Conference.
[51] LDYA (n 12) 357, 382.

conversation and sociability skills. As such, the salon was instrumental to female—often Jewish—emancipation and the development of a bourgeois 'public sphere'.[52] By the second half of the nineteenth century, Martha 'would gladly have drawn into [her salon] a few persons from the world of literature and scholarship, —[... but ...] that could hardly be done in the society in which [she] moved. Bourgeois elements could not be mixed with what was called "the circles" of Vienna'. (51–52) What Martha as an aristocratic lady could not do in her Viennese salon in the 1860s (later it changed also in Vienna), which led to what she considered 'intolerably dull' conversations,[53] Bertha could do later in The Hague. In the tradition of 'salon diplomacy', there she used her salon as a 'diplomatic tool' during the Peace Conferences.[54]

Prior to the 1899 Conference, she wrote letters to all corners of the world to invite prominent peace activists to join her in The Hague.[55] She held salon at the *Grand Central Hotel* and later at the *Kurhaus* hotel at Scheveningen beach.[56] Her salon was 'always full of callers, and from early in the morning with interviewers' for international newspapers.[57] With her '*Geselligkeit im aristokratischen Stil*', Suttner offered an informal space for the worlds of diplomacy, journalism, international law, political economy, industry, military, civil society, and the arts to meet and discuss the latest developments that were at issue in the formal sessions of the Peace Conference.[58] As the most prominent woman of the international peace movement, she could as a salonnière lead authoritatively the exchange of progressive (legal) pacifist ideas in a private setting, thus contributing to the creation of an *international* public sphere *avant-la-lettre*. 'Journalists [were] not admitted to the [Conference] deliberations',[59] but at her salon they informed themselves, spoke with delegates and consulted international lawyers and peace activists. The latter in turn hoped to mobilize 'public opinion' through the press and to influence the representatives.[60]

With her salon, Suttner gave a great platform to people like Johann Bloch, author of *Die Zukunft des Krieges*, who rejected war from an economic perspective: 'My guests also listen with lively interest to Bloch's remarks and elucidations.'[61] Among her most regular callers were her journalist friends William Stead and Alfred Fried and pacifists Nowikow, Frederic Passy, Hodgson Pratt. Among the many diplomats, activists, and international lawyers credited in her *Memoirs* is the French delegate and former minister, Léon Bourgeois, who became influential in international law scholarship with

[52] Jürgen Habermas, *The Structural Transformation of the Public Sphere: An Inquiry into a Category of Bourgeois Society* (The MIT Press 1991) 31–51.

[53] eg LDYA (n 12) 52, 63–64, 70, 84.

[54] Glenda Sluga, *On the Historical Significance of the Presence, and Absence, of Women at the Congress of Vienna, 1814–1815*, in: L' homme: Zeitschrift für feministische Geschichtswissenschaft, Jg 25 (2014) Nr 2, 49–62, at 54 and 50, available at <https://doi.org/10.25595/1868> accessed 5 October 2022. cf also, Antoine Lilti, *The World of the Salons. Sociability and Worldliness in Eighteenth-Century Paris* (OUP 2015) which includes a chapter on politics in the salon and a space for diplomats.

[55] *Memoirs* (n 4) 235–36.

[56] Annemarie van Heerikhuizen, 'World Peace in the Eyes of Bertha von Suttner and Bertha Waszklewicz' (2017) 2(7) Women's History 25–31.

[57] *Memoirs* (n 4) 255.

[58] Hamann (n 4) 260.

[59] *Memoirs* (n 4) 251.

[60] ibid 236–40.

[61] ibid 257.

his solidarist theory. Suttner writes, 'I hardly ever had a more interesting table companion than Bourgeois.'[62]

For Suttner and the '*groupe du high-life pacifique*', the mission was clear: 'to talk the delegates over, to win them one by one'—in the words of Henry Dunant whose letter she copied in her memoirs—to establish an international court of arbitration. As letters by Ducommen, Pratt, and Dunant show, all counted on Suttner's 'special gifts' to shape global public opinion on the issue. Dunant writes: 'You alone, madam, are capable of doing this.'[63]

The Conference delegates established three Commissions. One on disarmament, one on the laws of war, and the Third Commission, presided over by Bourgeois, on the pacific settlement of international disputes.[64] Their work—the foundation of an international court—was Suttner's main target as Salonnière of the 1899 conference. She organized numerous social events, including a small dinner for the Austrian representative and the French delegation, hoping the latter would inspire the former to support the court.[65] Austria had appointed international law professor Lammasch (1853–1920) as delegate, and Germany his colleague Stengel (1840–1930), both of a more conservative leaning. The latter's pamphlet, 'Perpetual Peace', summed up 'all glorification of war and of disarmament'.[66] Both delegations argued that arbitration 'is directly contrary to the principle of state sovereignty',[67] while Great Britain, Russia, and the United States were among those delegations coming with plans to establish a permanent court of arbitration.

When the formal negotiations were at their most critical point, on 15 June 1899, United States Ambassador Dr Andrew White called on Suttner to use her clout and move Austria and Germany to support the court and in particular its obligatory nature:

> If you can bring pressure to bear on influential persons, Baroness, do it now. Every possible measure must be employed to clear away the difficulties that are springing up.... The most important question before our Congress—that of a court of arbitration—has reached a turning point; [...].[68]

Two weeks later, White urged Suttner not just to apply pressure on the German and Austrian emperor but also to attend to the formation of public opinion:

> [he] urges me, in case I have the opportunity, to oppose those pessimistic prejudices which have gone abroad regarding the Conference, and which render more difficult the possibility of further work and the assembling of new conferences.[69]

[62] ibid 290.

[63] ibid 240 and 243; see also Passy's letter to Queen Wilhelmine of the Netherlands in which he calls on her to conclude a treaty with Belgium or Switzerland to establish such a court to set an example, in Hamann (n 4) 254.

[64] Shabtai Rosenne (ed), *The Hague Peace Conferences of 1899 and 1907 and International Arbitration. Reports and Documents* (TMC Asser Press 2001) at xvii–xviii.

[65] *Memoirs* (n 4) 256.

[66] ibid 239.

[67] ibid 293.

[68] ibid 294.

[69] ibid 315.

Only to repeat this in a letter written a few days later from *Huis ten Bosch*, where the negotiations were taking place. Soon after, upon another 'persuasive speech' by *inter alia* Bourgeois,[70] the much fought over article 27 was adopted: 'The Signatory Powers consider it their *duty*, if a serious dispute threatens to break out between two or more of them, to remind these latter that the Permanent Court is open to them.'[71]

Conclusion: A *'Cassandra of our time'*

By locating international law in Bertha's novel and in her salon, this chapter provides a portrait of a woman who imagined, argued, and contributed to the development of international law and institutions. *Die Waffen Nieder!* makes for a valuable source in the history of international law as it presents nineteenth-century wars and international law (theory) as lived experience presented by Martha. It also gives another insight in the agenda of the 'peace through law' movement Suttner advocated parallel to the formal sessions of the Peace Conferences in and through her Hague salons.

Von Suttner built on a long European Enlightenment tradition in which salons had become strategic spaces—also for the diplomatic world—where (international) politics was critically discussed, the representatives of the world's powers informed and lobbied, and public opinion formed. With her Hague salon, she deliberately created such a space to influence the 1899 negotiations and shape global public opinion. The importance of that role has been recognized widely. For one, she received the Nobel Peace Prize in 1905.

Bertha von Suttner was not an international lawyer in the classical sense. Yet with her novel and other writings she did contribute to what Lassa Oppenheim in 1908 claimed to be one of the main tasks of the science of international law: 'popularization of international law'.[72] In the course of her life, the ambivalence about international law did not diminish. In 1912, she wrote to Fried about international lawyers in what seems an echo of Kant's complaint about natural lawyers: '*Das sogenannte> Völkerrecht<—trockene Juristerei—past nicht in die Friedensbewegung, ungefähr wie das Rote Kreuz*.' And, four weeks before her death: '*Die Völkerrechtslehrer werden den Pazifismus erdrosseln* [suffocate].'[73] In Suttner's view, the development of the laws of war to 'humanis[e] war' had gummed up the works of the peace movement and driven 'a wedge (surely not without purpose)' into 'the deliberations of the Peace Conference'.[74] In her view, only a ban on war, disarmament, and the pacific settlement of international disputes by an international court of arbitration would do. She would fight for it until the end of her life.

[70] ibid 319–20.

[71] Convention for the Pacific Settlement of International Disputes, The Hague, 29 July 1899, in Rosenne (n 64) 415, 417 (emphasis added).

[72] Lassa Oppenheim, 'The Science of International Law: Its Task and Method' (1908) 2 AJIL 323.

[73] Hamann (n 4) 265.

[74] *Memoirs* (n 4) 228–29.

In 1913, Stefan Zweig run into Suttner in the streets of Vienna. She called him to action: 'The war is already upon us, and once again they have hidden and kept it from us. Why don't you do something, you young people? It is your concern most of all. Defend yourselves! Unite! Don't always let us few old women to whom no one listens do everything. [. . .] Things are worse than ever, the machine is already in motion.'[75]

[75] Zweig (n 21) 163.

7

Jane Addams

Positive Peace from the Everyday to the International

Kate Grady and Gina Heathcote

Introduction

In this image Jane Addams holds her pen, looking at you from another century, from a life built around engagement in the politics of care and careful politics. In this chapter, following Ruby, we approach international law by asking, 'how might Jane approach this situation?'.[1] In Yemen, food insecurity, arms sales, and political apathy perpetuate a conflict that produces and compounds gender insecurity, violent everydays, and new sites of Othering. In the UK, the politics of austerity, the fanning of populism through exclusionary nationalism, and the withdrawal of public funding for essential services are compounded by the uncertainty of a global pandemic. Whether in the midst of conflict or supposed peace, nations have yet to solve the everyday crises that exclude, that harm, that discriminate, and that so often underpin the turn to military solutions.

Addams was an important early feminist theorist of international law, linking domestic and international activism, identifying labour rights, citizenship, arms control, and gender equality as components of peace. Addams was also the recipient of the Nobel Peace Prize in 1931. As a founding member of the Women's International League for Peace and Freedom (WILPF), she is recognized as holding a crucial role in the development of transnational feminist movements and anti-militarism that continue to this day, ultimately influencing contemporary international norms including UN Security Council Resolution 1325 (2000) and the Treaty on the Prohibition of Nuclear Weapons 2017.

Addams was a social worker and activist who led the settlement movement in the United States and was instrumental in the organization of labour movements in the early decades of the twentieth century. She took up work on women's suffrage and, as a pacifist, joined activists touring warring nations during the First World War. She took a central role in the organizing and hosting of the International Congress of Women Peace Conference in The Hague in 1915, leading the United States delegates, becoming President of the Congress, and campaigning for arms control, women's equality, and the prohibition of the use of force.[2] Many of the ideas from

[1] Felicity Ruby, 'Security Council Resolution 1325: A Tool for Conflict Prevention?' in Gina Heathcote and Dianne Otto, *Rethinking Peacekeeping, Gender Equality and Collective Security* (Palgrave 2014) 175.

[2] See: Lela B Costin, 'Feminism, Pacificism, Internationalism and the 1915 International Congress of Women' (1982) 5(3–4) Women's Studies International Forum 301; Anne Wiltsher, *Most Dangerous Women: Feminist Peace Campaigners of The Great War* (Thorsons 1985) 103.

Kate Grady and Gina Heathcote, *Jane Addams* In: *Portraits of Women in International Law.* Edited by: Immi Tallgren, Oxford University Press. © Kate Grady and Gina Heathcote 2023. DOI: 10.1093/oso/9780198868453.003.0007

Figure 7.1 Jane Addams ca. 19.
Source: Library of Congress, [LC-USZ62-13484], Gerhard Sisters.

the Peace Resolutions of this conference are now enshrined in international legal documents.[3]

Addams' commitment to peace, women's rights, and transformative international law is captured in those Peace Resolutions, and the work of WILPF, which she founded and of which she was President (1919 to 1929) and then Honorary President (1929 to 1935) until her death. A prolific scholar, Addams' texts *Newer Ideals of Peace* (1907), *The Revolt against War* (1915), and *Peace and Bread in the Time of War* (1922) are of specific relevance to international lawyers. In this short intervention, we reflect on the larger contribution of Addams through her social justice initiatives, her conception of positive peace, her distinctly feminist approach to international law in the early twentieth century, and the relevance of these ideas for contemporary international law. The chapter proceeds through three themes: peace, the everyday, and plural subjectivities.

[3] Freya Baetens, 'International Congress of Women (1915)' in Rüdiger Wolfrum (ed), *Max Planck Encyclopedia of Public International Law* (OUP 2011).

Peace

In this section, we situate Addams' conception of peace within the longer timeline of feminist methodologies, recognizing the history of feminist engagement with the structures of international law and the centrality of peace as an organizing principle across transnational feminist spaces. In so doing, we identify both the silence of mainstream international legal knowledge and histories on the contributions of feminist thinkers and actors, and the transnational nature of feminist knowledge. That silence seems all the more curious given that to read the Peace Resolutions from The Hague in 1915 at a distance of a century later is to identify numerous ideas now embedded within the international legal order.[4] The Resolutions asserted that, since each warring state believed itself to be acting in self-defence rather than as aggressor, there was no irreconcilable difference between them and therefore an honourable, permanent peace should be established. This peace settlement would preclude rights of conquest and the transfer of territory without the consent of those within it and would ensure the right of peoples to autonomy and democracy. This framing foregrounds future understandings of decolonization and the need for self-determination with both internal and external legitimacy.[5] Addams' influence on the Peace Resolutions reminds us that awareness of and engagement with the profound influence of colonialism on international law is not a twenty-first century turn to decolonizing, or even an institutional turn of the 1960s and 1970s, but embedded in counter-narratives from the earliest decades of the twentieth century.

Simultaneously, we shift from identifying Addams as a necessary addition to the intellectual history of international law towards articulating a prehistory of feminist approaches to the discipline, both disrupting and underpinning Charlesworth, Chinkin, and Wright's seminal article on feminist approaches to international law.[6] The call, in 1991, for recognition of 'the immunity of international law to feminist analysis' and a need for an account of the 'organizational and normative structure of the international legal system', has engendered a vast body of scholarship in the subsequent decades.[7] We define these feminist approaches as 'a process and a series of ongoing, mutating, critical interventions',[8] and link this with transnational feminist knowledge production; a horizontal, activist, legal, global, and local project.[9]

Importantly, Otto's work embeds feminist activist histories within international law as an important element of the feminist analysis of both the organizational and normative structures of international law.[10] Otto's account of the feminist vision of

[4] WILPF Resolutions, 1st Congress, The Hague, Netherlands, 1915 available online at <https://wilpf.org/wp-content/uploads/2012/08/WILPF_triennial_congress_1915.pdf>, accessed 5 October 2022.

[5] Catriona Drew, 'The East Timor Story: International Law on Trial' (2001) 12(4) EJIL 651.

[6] Hilary Charlesworth, Christine Chinkin, and Shelley Wright, 'Feminist Approaches to International Law' (1991) 85(4) AJIL 613.

[7] ibid 614.

[8] Gina Heathcote, *Feminist Dialogues on International Law: Success, Tensions, Futures* (OUP 2019) 24.

[9] Sydney Calkin, Fiona de Londras, and Gina Heathcote, 'Abortion in Ireland: Introduction to the Themed Issue' (2020) 124(1) Feminist Review 1, 8–10.

[10] Dianne Otto, 'A Sign of "Weakness"? Disrupting Gender Certainties in the Implementation of Security Council Resolution 1325' (2006) 13 Michigan Journal of Gender and the Law 113.

peace at The Hague in 1915 is informative, placing gender-equal participation as a necessary first component to 'address the global patterns of inequality and injustice that create the insecurities that lead to armed conflict and, second, to bring the interlinked projects of militarism and women's inequality to an end'.[11] It is this placement of gender equality as a project interconnected with addressing global inequalities and challenging militarism that epitomizes Addams' contribution and which can be recognized as a distinctly feminist peace agenda.

Addams' views on peace diverged in important ways from the contemporary mainstream peace movement in the United States.[12] As Fischer explains, the mainstream viewed states as evolving in a process of social Darwinism from militarism—with a militarized state concerned with external threats—to industrialism—with a state concerned to sustain its members through its economic relations.[13] As a consequence, dispute settlement and international commerce were seen as vehicles for improving international relations. In contrast, in *Newer Ideals of Peace*, 'Addams's operative question was: as a matter of daily, lived experience, do those at the bottom experience industrialism as a time of peace?'.[14] Addams argued that United States industrialism was not peaceful, charting all manner of ways in which the lives of women, workers, and children continued to be militarized. Moreover, international commerce was inseparable from imperialism being, in Addams' words, 'the modern representative of conquest'.[15]

Addams' contribution to the formation of a feminist organization of peace, thus, centres a co-ordinated international agenda that foregrounds the pacific settlement of disputes and that undoes the history of colonialism while prioritizing the de-escalation of disputes through the shift away from the investment in arms, driven by an international ethos of community rather than by individual state interests.

Everyday Security

Importantly, Addams' contribution straddles an understanding of the nexus between these global strategies for peace and everyday insecurity—including the nexus to poverty and race discrimination. In this section, we incorporate a conscious bridging of wider feminist and gender scholarship, linking contemporary international legal histories with feminist approaches to international law.[16] This wider feminist and historical scholarship draws us toward Addams' domestic politics as a mechanism for

[11] ibid 119; Dianne Otto, 'Rethinking "Peace" in International Law and Politics from a Queer Feminist Perspective' (2020) 126(1) Feminist Review 19, 20.

[12] For accounts of this mainstream movement, see David Kennedy, 'The Move to Institutions' (1987) 8 Cardozo Law Review 841.

[13] Marilyn Fischer, 'The Conceptual Scaffolding of Newer Ideals of Peace' in Marilyn Fischer and others (eds), *Jane Addams and the Practice of Democracy* (University of Illinois Press 2008) 165.

[14] ibid 169.

[15] Jane Addams, *Newer Ideals of Peace* (1st edn, University of Illinois Press 2007) 64. See also: Jane Addams, 'The Revolt against War' (1915) 34 The Survey 355.

[16] On international legal histories, see: Matthew Craven, 'Theorizing the Turn to History in International Law' in Anne Orford and Florian Hoffman (eds), *The Oxford Handbook of the Theory of International Law* (OUP 2016).

understanding her approach to international security, anti-militarism, and positive peace. Given the role of 'highly qualified publicists' in the formation of international jurisprudence,[17] there is significant value in tracing the ideas of feminists, such as Addams, who were active in shaping the League of Nations,[18] instrumentalizing it as a space of civic engagement, and who articulated an understanding of peace that resonates with contemporary concerns of international lawyers.

Today, WILPF is an international movement which seeks to redefine security, promote socio-economic justice, and establish lasting, feminist, peace.[19] Just as the history of WILPF is told, and personified, through the life of Jane Addams, the history of social work is often articulated through the history of Hull House and also personified in the life of Jane Addams. Hull House, whilst now operating as a museum, was a settlement house so varied it almost defies explanation—private home, gathering place for immigrants, public kitchen, nursery, library, research institute, debate salon, public bath, playground, cultural centre, and place for learning everything from languages to politics to sewing.[20]

There remains, however, a silence in mainstream international legal knowledge (and histories) on the contributions of feminist thinkers and actors as authors, as thinkers, as writers, as contributors to legal knowledge, rather than simply as doers. This strange gendering of knowledge, where men are understood for their intellectual contribution and for the shaping of knowledge, is worthy of further attention.[21] How is it that Hull House receives equal attention to that given to Addams and that her writing receives so little attention? How is it that her contribution to social work, as a field of knowledge, is understood through the act of founding Hull House (after travelling to England and drawing from the model established at Toynbee Hall) and her contribution to peace through the act of founding WILPF, and not the ideas beneath either founding act or the philosophical nexus between the two? Examining Addams' influence on feminist peace trajectories and the relationship between gender and security highlights the failure of international law as a discipline to see and incorporate the histories of feminist activism into its development. Further, this renders women's lives as exceptional should they enter public consciousness while entailing a continued forgetting of feminist thinking and praxis.

To elevate and consider transnational translations of knowledge, thus drawing in Knop's account of the transnational,[22] we use Addams' transplanting of the Toynbee Hall model into the United States context as a motif for how transnational feminist accounts, from suffrage, to security issues, to violence against women, and the trajectories of intersectionality, move sideways, are ever re-imagined and yet are traceable in a horizontal fashion. This is a feature of transnational feminist organizing that is

[17] Statute of the International Court of Justice 1945, art 38(1)(d).

[18] See Kennedy (n 12).

[19] For information, see WILPF, 'Work Areas', available at <https://www.wilpf.org/work-areas/>, accessed 5 October 2022.

[20] Hull House Museum, 'About Jane Addams', available at <https://www.hullhousemuseum.org/about-jane-addams>, accessed 5 October 2022.

[21] See also Christopher Gevers, 'Anna Julia Cooper: A Voice from the (Global) South', in this volume.

[22] Karen Knop, 'Here and There: International Law in Domestic Courts' (2000) 32 New York University Journal of International Law and Politics 501.

central to the flows of knowledge and its reproduction in new contexts, and that responds and adapts to different legal, cultural, and political realities (amongst others). This is, in effect, a gendering of what is valued and how knowledge is understood to persist and travel. As such, the story of security produced within international law across the twentieth century remains focused on states, while Addams' conception of positive peace, drawn from local engagements with the 'Other' (migrant, poor), remains domestic in orientation. Addams, however, built her conception of the political in the international legal frame through her understanding of poverty, race, and inequalities in the everyday, while using Hull House as a means to build strategies for change.

Addams rejected the notion of peace as simply negative peace—the absence of violence—and instead formulated a concept of positive peace built on foundations of social justice, equality, freedom, cooperation, care, and the absence of militarism.[23] For Shields and Soeters, the term 'peaceweaving' usefully describes Addams' conception of peace and incorporates five of the ideas practised at Hull House. First, peace is concerned with relationships, and maintaining peace requires sustaining human relationships with care and attention, including through conflict resolution. Second, peace requires social transformation and dogmatism prevents this. Third, peace requires the empathetic capacity to see the world from another's point of view, in order to build relationships and resolve conflict. Fourth, participatory democracy and cooperative, experimental, problem-solving, rather than ideology, are necessary for peaceful communities. And fifth, peace may only be secured through 'lateral progress' which involves improvements for those at the bottom rather than merely those at the top.[24]

This conception of peace, however, has limited purchase within international legal structures. When feminist voices gained access and audience in the Security Council in 2000, the actions and histories of WILPF were instrumental to that happening. Nevertheless, the pinpointing of Security Council Resolution 1325 as springing forth in 2000 often re-purposes the history of feminist peace projects as secondary to the 'moment' the international community understood the importance of women's lives and contributions to peace and security. The Security Council then deployed a range of interventions and policies into/onto post-conflict and conflict states that often silence the existing frames and applications of understandings of gender, of conflict, of peace within feminist networks within those states. Addams' desire to build a peace involving 'the displacement of the military ideals of patriotism by those of a rising concern for human welfare'[25] seems unlikely to be realized in a context where it is the militarized Security Council that is the guardian of the women, peace, and security agenda.[26]

Furthermore, everyday insecurity within communities is distanced from the lens on women, peace, and security that is filtered through the international legal form to imagine security as pertaining to states. Yet, the convergence of the women, peace, and

[23] Addams, *Newer Ideals of Peace* (n 15).

[24] Patricia M Shields and Joseph Soeters, 'Peaceweaving: Jane Addams, Positive Peace, and Public Administration' (2017) 47(3) American Review of Public Administration 323.

[25] Addams, *Newer Ideals of Peace* (n 15) 8.

[26] Dianne Otto, 'Power and Danger: Feminist Engagement with International Law through the UN Security Council' (2010) 32(1) Australian Feminist Law Journal 97.

security framework with the Security Council's counter-terrorism agenda[27] has served to reinforce what Nesiah describes as the 'double life' of state sovereignty. In particular, those states found to be in conflict are deemed to have abdicated sovereignty whilst the members of 'the Security Council are authorized … to exercise imperial sovereignty' over them.[28] This reifies state security for some states whilst simultaneously reinforcing the unequal distribution of power within the international legal order—the very opposite of Addams' 'lateral progress'.

Nesiah's attention to the differing effects of women, peace, and security for different states reminds us of the necessity of understanding gender as a form of structural power intimately connected to other forms of power—a view also encapsulated in the 1915 Peace Resolutions with their focus on the interconnections between gender inequality, militarism, commerce, and conquest, and in Addams' argument about the relevance of social context for understanding conflict.[29] This invocation of the relationship between hegemonic power structures, and between the local and the global, reminds us today of the rich Black feminist scholarship in the United States which has drawn out the symbiosis between state violence at home and abroad, underpinned by gendered, racialized, and capitalist power structures.[30] Addams' investment in the Hull House project reminds feminist actors and authors working on international law, peace, and conflict, that the everyday violence within our communities functions in a continuum of violence underpinned by the multiple subjectivities constructed, alienated, and carrying harm in our communities.

Plural Subjectivities

Drawing on Addams' work on peace within the League of Nations addresses not gendered subjects but feminist peace. We understand this to be a feminist project for peace that does not fixate on women's lives but understands a feminist appraisal of peace as the universal/international trajectory of feminist thinking. The tendency of mainstream feminist accounts to dislodge feminist diversity is often a consequence of the restraints that gender law reform imposes on the language and possibilities for change. In particular, the framing of gender reforms through the subject of woman reproduces a narrow approach to equality that is often unable to encompass the range of issues and experiences to which transnational feminist approaches respond. This is well documented in contemporary feminist legal thinking but is also found in pro-feminist spaces such as the early work of WILPF. That is, the transformation of transnational feminist activism and thinking into legal tools often results in a filtering out of the methods and structures that inform the localized modes.

[27] United Nations Security Council Resolution 2242 (13 October 2015) UN Doc S/RES/2242.

[28] Vasuki Nesiah, 'Gender and Forms of Conflict: The Moral Hazards of Dating the Security Council' in Fionnuala Ní Aoláin and others (eds), *The Oxford Handbook of Gender and Conflict* (OUP 2018) 298.

[29] Addams, 'The Revolt against War' (n 15).

[30] Angela Y Davis, *Are Prisons Obsolete?* (Seven Stories Press 2003); Ruth Wilson Gilmore, *Golden Gulag: Prisons, Surplus, Crisis, and Opposition in Globalizing California* (University of California Press 2007); Julia Sudbury, 'A World Without Prisons: Resisting Militarism, Globalized Punishment, and Empire' (2004) 31(1–2) Social Justice 9.

Addams' work centred on the living of an alternative type of peace that welcomed immigrants, transformed communities through attention to—and working in conjunction with—the least well off in her community, while ignoring the conventions of heteronormative respectability. This is a fascinating record of feminist praxis that has otherwise been subsumed into a trajectory of women at the League, and then the United Nations, without a sufficient account of the methods and thinking behind Addams' work. That Addams produced an oeuvre that records and centres this politics is not generally regarded as a matter of relevance to international lawyers, although her influence and work are well understood within the work of WILPF.[31] Addams is regarded as a gendered subject but not a thinker on feminist peace that might inform international law today. Yet, as such a thinker, Addams offers a blueprint for organizing the global order differently, with attention to those not recognized by the practices of statehood, with attention to the relationship between poverty and insecurity, with an emphasis on cooperative solidarity and with a rejection of the role of heteronormativity as a means to order dominant world frames.

Indeed, Addams' understanding of the concept of the 'international' challenges international law and lawyers in potentially fruitful ways. For Addams, the word referred not just to sovereign states but also to cross-community cosmopolitan solidarity and, in consequence, international peace was not merely about regulating interactions between states, but connected to social justice, anti-nationalism, and anti-militarism.[32] Addams' scholarship emphasized mutual-aid, cooperation, and nurture between social citizens beyond borders, arguing that, in Sarvasy's words, 'the politicization and socialization of nurture, practiced in diverse neighborhoods and through bread provision, would enhance its ability to counter and ultimately to replace the aggressive urges as they played out in international affairs'.[33] To achieve peace therefore required transcending the nation-state, 'strengthening of ties between transnational institutions and local world social citizenship to pressure nations to join the globalizing of the second stage of democracy'.[34]

Within Addams' scholarship and activism this attention to subjectivity beyond states not only centres everyday violence but also, ultimately, prefigures feminist accounts of legal subjectivity that disrupt the male subject, the whiteness of legal subjectivity, and the inherent exclusions that extend from dominant Western legal paradigms. At the same time, a contemporary reading of Addams' work also requires an explicit rejection of the racist terminology that was used by Addams at times. Whilst Addams often allied herself with black and immigrant communities, and worked closely with WEB Du Bois, some of her writings also reveal pejorative language, racialized stereotypes and myths,[35] and instances where, in contrast to her staunch support of women's equality, she was accused of being an 'accommodationist'

[31] See further: WILPF, 'Early WILPF Women' available at <https://wilpf.org.uk/wp-content/uploads/2015/03/Addams-Jane.pdf>, accessed 5 October 2022.

[32] Fischer (n 13) 176–78.

[33] Wendy Sarvasy, 'A Global "Common Table": Jane Addams's Theory of Democratic Cosmopolitanism and World Social Citizenship' in Marilyn Fischer and others (eds), *Jane Addams and the Practice of Democracy* (University of Illinois Press 2008) 197.

[34] ibid.

[35] Ralph E Luker, 'Missions, Institutional Churches, and Settlement Houses: The Black Experience, 1885–1910' (1984) 69(3/4) Journal of Negro History 101; Wilson Record, 'Negro Intellectual Leadership in the National Association for the Advancement of Colored People: 1910–1940' (1956) 17(4) Phylon 375; Dorcas

on matters of race.[36] As a mechanism for rethinking international law, Addams' scholarship simultaneously reminds us of the whiteness of international legal histories, and the complicity of whiteness in many of international law's more dangerous legacies, while opening an aperture to the way in which feminist knowledge is filtered out of dominant international legal histories.

Simultaneously, we are aware that in framing Addams' contribution to peace studies, to social work, and to international law there is a further silencing of those transnational feminist acts, writings, and activisms that were not in the United States, not awarded a Nobel Peace Prize, and not articulated in English. Plural feminist methodologies require both a re-examination of the knowledge projects of those sitting within international spaces but gendered female, and thus excluded from the canon, and the voices not held and not centred in Addams' engagements with the League, and beyond. Recognizing plural subjectivities calls for attention to the risk that feminist engagement with international legal structures will be limited to those least likely to threaten the status quo and most willing to uphold the present international order. For Otto, this requires feminist praxis to make space for marginalized voices and to take on the political responsibility of listening[37]—a notion that resonates with Addams' ideas of empathy, cooperation, and participation as components of peace; not speaking to, or for, or on behalf of, but problem-solving in relationship with.

Conclusion

Addams' scholarship and activism, spanning feminist spaces internationally and migrant and poor communities in Chicago, seem more relevant as a practice for peace than ever; fostering communities of inclusion that build platforms for understanding difference and for undoing the legacy of European colonial histories that have for too long foregrounded exclusion based on race, gender, ableism, sexuality, and religion while speaking the language of the universal. As an entry into the Portrait Gallery of International Law, Addams stares at us from another century with a serious question about the praxis and role of our personal biographies as the space where methodologies are felt and remembered in the everyday.

Davis Boles and others, 'The Dance Between Addams and Du Bois: Collaboration and Controversy in a Consequential 20th Century Relationship' (2016) 53(2) Phylon 34.

[36] Boles (n 35) 48.

[37] Dianne Otto, 'Beyond Legal Justice: Some Personal Reflections on People's Tribunals, Listening and Responsibility' (2017) 5(2) London Review of International Law 225; Heathcote (n 8) ch 6.

PART IV
THE WINTER GARDEN OF ABOLITION AND RESISTANCE: WOMEN AGAINST SLAVERY, RACISM, AND IMPERIALISM

8
Anna Julia Cooper
A Voice from the (Global) South

Christopher Gevers

Anna Julia Cooper began her address to the 'Congress of Representative Women' assembled at the 1893 World's Columbian Exposition in Chicago by recalling the 'yet unwritten history' of Black women—'full of heroic struggle, a struggle against fearful and overwhelming odds', of 'painful, patient and silent toil'—that 'would furnish material for epics'.[1] The thirty-four year old Cooper—who had already published her pathbreaking collection of essays *A Voice from the South by a Black Women of the South* (1892) and founded the *Colored Women's League*—would herself go on to live a life fit 'for epics'.[2] Born into slavery in 1858, Cooper would receive her doctorate from the Sorbonne in 1925 at the age of sixty-six (later translated as *Slavery and the French and Haitian Revolutionists*),[3] and would live another forty years, dying a few months before the United States' Civil Rights Act was passed. She was twenty-six at the time the Berlin Conference formalized the colonization of Africa, participated in the first Pan-African Conference in London fifteen years after that, and lived through two World Wars to see the formal 'decolonization' of most of Africa over sixty years later.

While Anna Julia Cooper is rightly celebrated as a Black feminist icon, an educator, a literary theorist, and a pioneer of Africana philosophy,[4] less attention has been paid to her influence on (Black) Internationalism and, by extension, her (still) pioneering critiques of international law.[5] In 1900 Cooper was one of two Black women to address the inaugural Pan-African Conference,[6] where she presented a paper on 'The Negro

[1] Anna J Cooper in May Wright Sewall (ed), *The World's Congress of Representative Women* (Rand, McNally & Company 1894) 711, hereafter Sewall, *World's Congress*. The Congress was convened as part of the 1893 'World's Columbian Exposition', and claimed to be 'without doubt, the largest and most representative gathering of women ever convened in this or any other country'. ibid v.

[2] As Lewis R Gordon succinctly puts it: 'The life of Anna Julia Cooper ... defies belief'. Lewis Gordon, *An Introduction to Africana Philosophy* (Cambridge University Press 2008) 69, hereafter Gordon, *Africana Philosophy*. See further Vivian M May, *Anna Julia Cooper: Visionary Black Feminist* (Routledge 2012) 13–36, hereafter May, *Anna Julia Cooper*. See also (n 10).

[3] Anna Julia Cooper, *Slavery and the French and Haitian Revolutionists (1788-1905)* (Frances Richardson Keller tr, Edwin Mellen Press 1988), hereafter Cooper, *Slavery and the French and Haitian Revolutionists*. The French title was 'L'Attitude de la France a l'egard de l'esclavage pendant la revolution'. In an earlier 1988 translation Keller used *Slavery and the French Revolutionists (1788–1805)*, references herein are to the 1988 version.

[4] See Gordon, *Africana Philosophy* (n 2) 69–73.

[5] For example, Shirley Moody-Turner recently suggested that future scholarship on Cooper should consider 'how she developed her theories about the interlocking nature of racism and sexism in an international context'. Shirley Moody-Turner, 'Prospects for the Study of Anna Julia Cooper' (2018) 40 Resources for American Literary Study 1–29, 17–18.

[6] Along with Anna H Jones. May, *Anna Julia Cooper* (n 2) 23.

Christopher Gevers, *Anna Julia Cooper* In: *Portraits of Women in International Law*. Edited by: Immi Tallgren, Oxford University Press. © Christopher Gevers 2023. DOI: 10.1093/oso/9780198868453.003.0008

Figure 8.1 Anna Julia Cooper in Paris.
Source: Scurlock Studio Records, Archives Center, National Museum of American History, Smithsonian Institution.

Problem in America' and was elected to the Executive Committee of the resultant, short-lived Pan-African Association (notably WEB Du Bois—who would become the 'Father of Pan-Africanism'—was not).[7]

These remarkable achievements of Anna Julia Cooper demand further attention, and study, however this short essay will focus primary on two aspects of Cooper's intellectual *ouvre* as they relate to international law. It does so in order to counter the practice that Brittney Cooper describes as 'triaging Black women's histories', whereby 'when we have *recovered* a black woman figure, that is, when we have saved her from being buried and lost to the annals of history, when we know her name and as many

[7] WEB Du Bois was elected as the 'Vice President' of the United States branch of the Pan-African Association. See *Report of the Pan-African Conference* (London 1900). Little has been written about Cooper's role in the Pan-African Association, and she appears to be confused with Alice Kinloch at times. In contrast, quite a bit of attention has been paid by historians in recent times to figuring out precisely which white man was elected as the Association's Treasurer (between Robert Colenso and his brother Frank). See Gwilym Colenso and Christopher Saunders, 'New Light on the Pan-African Association: Part 1' (2008) 107 African Research & Documentation (2008) 27; and Gwilym Colenso and Christopher Saunders, 'New Light on the Pan-African Association of 1900: A Further Note' (2011) 115 African Research & Documentation 77.

details as we can about her life and work, we... move on to the next patient'.[8] Rather, paraphrasing Brittney Cooper, this essay aims to engage with the content of what Anna Julia Cooper *said*, and its 'critical scholarly utility', even as it celebrates all that she *did*.[9] In particular it will focus on two concepts introduced (or perhaps anticipated) by Cooper's work that are central to contemporary understandings of human rights and international law (or should be), namely: 'intersectionality' and 'racial capitalism'.

The 'doubly enslaved': Race, Gender, and Human Rights

> The colored woman of to-day occupies ... a unique position... She is confronted by both a woman question and a race problem, and is as yet an unknown or an unacknowledged factor in both.
>
> Anna Julia Cooper, *A Voice from the South* (1892)[10]

The history of human rights is contested, to say the least. However, few would omit Hersch Lauterpacht's *An International Bill of the Rights of Man* (1945) from an account of their emergence and consolidation as enforceable international legal entitlements. Those looking to complicate matters will likely point out that it was the White Supremacist Jan Smuts who introduced the reference to 'human rights' into the UN Charter's Preamble. What these apparently contrasting figures had in common, however, was that in 1945 neither intended human rights to apply fully (or at all) to women and Black people. Not only did Lauterpacht deliberately avoid prohibiting 'discrimination on account of sex' and strategically sidestepped the 'problem' of the 'full equality of women',[11] he deliberately made the right to self-government subject to 'the law of the State' with the denial of this right to Black South Africans and Americans in mind.[12] Whether as a necessary compromise (in light of 'existing possibilities', with 'the necessity of not impeding the acceptance of the Bill'),[13] or more disturbingly in the case of '*sui generis*' South Africa, in an effort to ensure its survival as a 'White man's country',[14] Lauterpacht's was ultimately an *International Bills of Rights of [White] Men.* As such it continued the long exclusionary tradition of Western 'human rights', wherever it is said to start.

[8] Brittney C Cooper, *Beyond Respectability: The Intellectual Thought of Race Women* (University of Illinois Press 2017), hereafter Cooper, *Beyond Respectability*. Similarly, Lewis Gordon has criticized the 'ongoing practice of locking black intellectuals and their productions in the biographical moment'. Lewis R Gordon, *Existentia Africana: Understanding Africana Existential Thought* (Taylor & Francis 2000) 26.

[9] Cooper, *Beyond Respectability* (n 8).

[10] Anna Julia Cooper, *A Voice from the South By a Black Woman of the South* (Aldine Printing House 1892) 134, hereafter Cooper, *Voice from the South*.

[11] Hersch Lauterpacht, *An International Bill of the Rights of Man, With an Introduction by Philippe Sands* (OUP 1945, rev edn 2013) 119, hereafter Lauterpacht, *International Bills of Rights*.

[12] ibid 137–38.

[13] ibid 121–22.

[14] According to Lauterpacht, '[t]he position in South Africa [was] *sui generis*, and it would be fatal to adapt fully the fundamental purpose of the Bill of Rights to exceptional situations of this nature'. ibid 140.

According to contemporary defenders of Lauterpacht (and Smuts) we are to avoid passing judgement on these exclusions based on 'more contemporary standards',[15] like the slave-owning Founding Fathers of 1776 they are to be properly 'contextualised'.[16] However, fifty-years before Lauterpacht and Smuts, Anna Julia Cooper was able to imagine the 'universal triumph of justice and human rights' *without compromise or exclusion*,[17] and call for 'the final triumph of all right over might, the supremacy of the moral forces of reason, and justice, and love in the government of the nations of the earth'.[18] What is more, Cooper did so while recognizing both the limits of formal rights and the 'intersectional' nature of regimes of domination, and those based on race and gender in particular.

In her seminal *A Voice from the South: By a Black Women of the South*, published in 1892, Cooper insisted that '[o]nly the Black Woman can say "when and where I enter, in the quiet, undisputed dignity of my womanhood, without violence and without suing or special patronage, then and there the whole *Negro race enters with me*" '.[19] The following year, in her address to the 'World Congress of Representative Women' she boldly pointed out to her audience (referencing *Dred v Scott*) that 'in the eyes of the highest tribunal in America [the 'Afro-American woman] was deemed no more than a chattel, an irresponsible thing, a dull block, to be drawn hither or tither at the volition of an owner', and as such, while 'white woman could at least plead for her own emancipation; the black women, *doubly enslaved*, could not but suffer and struggle and be silent'.[20]

In doing so, Cooper anticipated Kimberle Crenshaw's critique of the shortcomings of both anti-racist and feminist discourses and mapping of the 'intersections' of race and patriarchy a century later (and Cooper did so using the language of 'human rights', for what it's worth).[21] As Crenshaw put it:[22]

> Feminist efforts to politicize experiences of women and antiracist efforts to politicize experience of people of color have frequently proceeded as though the issues and experiences they each detail occur on mutually exclusive terrains. Although racism and sexism readily intersect in the lives of real people, they seldom do in feminist and antiracist practices. And so, when the practices expound identity as woman or person

[15] Phillipe Sands, 'Introduction', in Lauterpacht, *International Bills of Rights* (n 11) xvi. On Jan Smuts, see Christof Heyns and Willem Gravett, ' "To Save Succeeding Generations from the Scourge of War": Jan Smuts and the Ideological Foundations of the United Nations' (2017) 39 Human Rights Quarterly 574, 577 (noting: 'Taking the view purely from the present ignores the real constraints that historical figures face and few, if any, would pass the test').

[16] For a response to this form of *historicism*, see Lewis R Gordon, 'African-American Philosophy, Race, and the Geography of Reason' in LR Gordon and JA Gordon (eds), *Not Only the Master's Tools: African American Studies in Theory and Practice* (Routledge 2006).

[17] As Cooper put it, the demand was for 'an entrance not through a gateway for ourselves, our race, our sex, or our sect, but a grand highway for humanity'. Sewall, *World's Congress* (n 1), 714–15.

[18] ibid.

[19] Cooper, *Voice from the South* (n 10) 31.

[20] Sewall, *World's Congress* (n 1) 712.

[21] See Kimberle Crenshaw, 'Demarginalizing the Intersection of Race and Sex: A Black Feminist Critique of Antidiscrimination Doctrine, Feminist Theory and Antiracist Politics' (1989) 1 University of Chicago Legal Forum 139; and Kimberle Crenshaw, 'Mapping the Margins: Intersectionality, Identity Politics, and Violence against Women of Color' (1991) 43(6) Stanford Law Review1241–99.

[22] ibid 1242.

of color as an either/or proposition, they relegate the identity of women of color to a location that resists telling.

The notion of 'intersectionality' has, for better or worse gone mainstream in recent years—even permeating the inner workings of the UN human rights mechanisms[23]—yet it remains under-utilized, too often amounting to adding gender and (less often) race 'to the mix' of pre-existing categories and conceptions of domination, or 'adding up' gendered and racialized violence rather than considering how 'race and gender intersect'—as regimes of both domination and empowerment— 'in shaping structural, political, and representational aspects of violence[s] against women of color'.[24] Moreover, as Crenshaw and Cooper plainly stated, their concern was with the silencing and marginalization of 'women of color'—representationally and analytically—in conversations about 'justice and human rights', and on this score international law (and human rights) have some distance to go.

As a 'voice from the South'—and, along with her fellow 'Race Women Internationalists'[25] Alice Kinloch and Jane Nardal, a collective 'voice from the *Global* South'—Anna Julia Cooper was at the forefront of 'advanc[ing] the telling of that [marginalized] location',[26] and mapping the intersections of regimes of racial and gendered domination both domestically and internationally.[27] Yet, international lawyers continue to excuse Lauterpacht and Smuts, and exclude Cooper.

The Haitian Revolution and 'racial capitalism'

> It was necessary to deal justly by their brothers and fellow citizens beyond the sea. One could not despoil the planters of their properties not to speak of the interests of the commercial cities and of proprietors in France.... *The slaves—they too were men—men to be reckoned with.*
>
> Anna Julia Cooper, *The Third Step*[28]

[23] Both *Committee on the Elimination of Racial Discrimination* (CERD) and the *Committee on the Elimination of Discrimination Against Women* (CEDAW) have acknowledged 'intersectionality' in the substance of their General Recommendations 25. See Aisha Nicole Davis, 'Intersectionality and International Law: Recognizing Complex Identities on the Global Stage' (2015) 28 Harvard Human Rights Journal 205, 220–22.

[24] Crenshaw 'Mapping the Margins' (n 21) 1244. I use the term 'violences' to mark a broader understanding that includes structural violence, cognizant of the risks and limitations of reproducing the 'victim subject', particularly in respect of the 'native', Third World subject. See Ratna Kapur, 'The Tragedy of Victimization Rhetoric: Resurrecting the 'Native; Subject in International/Post-Colonial Feminist Legal Politics' (2002) 15 Harvard Human Rights Journal 1–38. See further Vasuki Nesiah, 'Toward a Feminist Internationality: A Critique of the U.S. Feminist Legal Scholarship' (1993) 16 Harvard Women's Law Journal 189.

[25] See Imaobong D Umoren, *Race Women Internationalists: Activist-Intellectuals and Global Freedom Struggles* (University of California Press 2018), hereafter Umoren, *Race Women Internationalists*.

[26] Crenshaw 'Mapping the Margins' (n 21) 1242.

[27] See further Adrien Katherine Wing (ed), *Global Critical Race Feminism: An International Reader* (New York University Press 2000).

[28] Anna J Cooper, *The Third Step (Autobiographical)* (Manuscripts and Addresses 24, 2017) 13, available at <https://dh.howard.edu/ajc_addresses/24>.

In September 1924 Anna Julia Cooper wrote excitedly to WEB Du Bois informing him that she had 'come across a very interesting history of Haiti' in the French National Archives (Garran-Conlon's *Rapport sur les troubles de Saint Dominique*), and surmised: 'It seems to me splendid propaganda material for our cause.'[29] As such, Cooper was planning to translate it into English and asked for Du Bois' assistance (and that of the NAACP perhaps) in doing so.[30] Cooper was cognizant of the racial and gendered obstacles that were up against her being the one to tell this history, so perhaps the translation of a long-dead white man's account seemed the best way to circumvent these; but even this proved to be too much. Cooper's failed attempt to translate Garran-Conlon's account of the Haitian Revolution—and the failure of Du Bois to see its full potential[31]—is all the more compelling in light of her failure to translate and publish her own work on the subject. In fact, as Cooper told Du Bois in the opening lines of her 1924 letter, she had come across Garron-Conlon's account as 'a by-product of [her] thesis for the Sorbonne', complete the following year, on *Slavery and the French and Haitian Revolutionists* (as translated).[32]

To this day, Cooper's *Slavery and the French and Haitian Revolutionists* (1925) sits at the center of a 'bundle of silences':[33] of Black Internationalism in international (legal) thought;[34] of 'Race Women Internationalists' in Black Internationalism;[35] and of the Haitian Revolution in 'Global History'.[36] While the 'Haitian turn' of the last few years has begun to address the latter—with works like CLR James' *The Black Jacobins* and Eric Williams *Capitalism and Slavery* (1944) finally receiving due attention—Cooper's 1925 thesis remains largely ignored.[37] This is not simply an oversight in the historical record, as Cooper's study offers insights that are not readily gleaned from those of CLR James, Eric Williams, and others. International lawyers await their own 'Haitian turn', but when they do so Anna Julia Cooper's 1925 study stands to enrich their understanding *both* historically and *historiographically*.[38] For present purposes, however,

[29] 'Letter from Anna J. Cooper to WEB Du Bois' (10 September 1924), *WEB Du Bois Papers*. They were, perhaps, on poor terms at the time; following Cooper's inability to attend the 1921 and 1923 Pan-African Congresses (see below).

[30] Cooper asked: 'Do you think if it has been translated? Do you think the present interest in Haiti would make such a work worthwhile? Would the NAACP care to promote such an undertaking?'. Ibid.

[31] Du Bois' response was supportive yet hardly enthusiastic, and in any event he indicated that the NAACP did not support publishing. See 'Letter from W. E. B. Du Bois to Anna J. Cooper' (12 September 1924), *WEB Du Bois Papers*.

[32] Cooper's 1925 thesis, which resulted in her becoming the first Black American women to receive a doctorate from the Sorbonne.

[33] Michel-Rolph Trouillot, *Silencing the Past: Power and the Production of History* (Beacon Press 1995).

[34] See further Adom Getachew, *Worldmaking after Empire: The Rise and Fall of Self-Determination* (Princeton University Press 2019).

[35] See further Vivian M May, '"It Is Never a Question of the Slaves": Anna Julia Cooper's Challenge to History's Silences in Her 1925 Sorbonne Thesis' (2008) 31(1) Callaloo 903–18, 903–04; Umoren, *Race Women Internationalists* (n 25); and Brent Hayes Edwards, *The Practice of Diaspora: Literature, Translation, and the Rise of Black Internationalism* (Cambridge University Press 2003) 127–28, hereafter Edwards, *Practice of Diaspora*.

[36] See generally Trouillot, *Silencing the Past* (n 33).

[37] Ironically, in fact, the scholar who has perhaps done the most to un-silence the Haitian Revolution in recent times, and written persuasively on the conditions of its silencing more generally—Michel-Rolph Trouillot—does not include Cooper's study in his landmark *Silencing the Past*. Ibid.

[38] See further May, "It Is Never a Question of the Slaves" (n 35); and Nathifa Greene, 'Anna Julia Cooper's Analysis of the Haitian Revolution' (2017) 23 (1–2) The CLR James Journal 83–104.

I want to focus on one aspect of *Slavery and the French and Haitian Revolutionists* that speaks to a silenced, or at least muted, aspect of both international law and accounts of the Haitian Revolution, namely how Cooper anticipates the concept of 'racial capitalism'.

As Hudson describes it, 'racial capitalism' refers to 'the simultaneous historical emergence of racism and capitalism in the modern world and their mutual dependence'.[39] Or, as Fanon put it: 'The cause is the consequence; you are rich because you are white, you are white because you are rich'.[40] Like 'intersectionality', the concept of 'racial capitalism' risks becoming a victim of its own success, more often cited that engaged. The term itself emerged in debates amongst anti-apartheid activists in the 1970s, but was popularized by Cedric Robinson in *Black Marxism: The Making of the Black Radical Tradition* (1983).[41] To paraphrase Robin Kelley, the emergence of the term racial capitalism was 'more of an act of recognition than invention',[42] recording the intimacies of regimes of racial and economic domination that scholars within the Black Radical Tradition had begun to map long before the term itself emerged.

Following Robinson, many scholars point to WEB Du Bois' *Black Reconstruction* (1935)—where he set out the 'color caste founded and retained by capitalism . . . [which] resulted in subordination of colored labor to white profits the world over'[43]—as the origins of conceptualizations of the 'subtle and dynamic relationship between capitalist exploitation and white supremacy'[44] that became known as racial capitalism (although it is possible to find both earlier and more comprehensive accounts in Du Bois' extensive oeuvre).[45] However, Cooper's 1925 thesis on *Slavery and the French and Haitian Revolutionists*[46] anticipated the insights of *Black Reconstruction* and subsequent writings on 'racial capitalism' (and continues to exceed accounts of the Haitian Revolution in many respects).[47]

Like Du Bois did generally (and CLR James and Eric Williams later did in respect of the Haitian revolution in particular), in *Slavery and the French and Haitian Revolutionists* Cooper located slavery and colonialism in the broader global political

[39] Peter James Hudson, *Bankers and Empire: How Wall Street Colonized the Caribbean* (University of Chicago Press 2017) 13–14.

[40] Frantz Fanon, *The Wretched of the Earth* (Grove Press 1963) 40.

[41] See Peter James Hudson, 'Racial Capitalism and the Dark Proletariat' in Race Capitalism Justice (2017) 59–65.

[42] Robin DG Kelley, 'Foreword' in Cedric J Robinson, *Black Marxism: The Making of the Black Radical Tradition* (Chapel Hill 2000) xv.

[43] WEB Du Bois, *Black Reconstruction: An Essay toward a History of the Part which Black Folk Played in the Attempt to Reconstruct Democracy in America, 1860–1880* (Harcourt, Brace and Company 1935) 30, hereafter Du Bois, *Black Reconstruction*.

[44] Walter Johnson, 'To Remake the World: Slavery, Racial Capitalism, and Justice' in *Race Capitalism Justice* (Boston Review 2017) 22.

[45] See, for example, WEB Du Bois, 'Of the Culture of White Folk' (1917) 7(4) Journal of Race Development 434–47; WEB Du Bois, *Black Folk: Then and Now* (OUP 1939); and WEB Du Bois, *The World and Africa* (OUP 1947), hereafter Du Bois, *World and Africa*.

[46] Cooper's original proposed topic was the French attitude towards Equality of the Races *generally*. However, her supervisors said the topic was 'too vast and too vague', so Cooper pinned it down to 'Slavery' (as the 'Definite Title'), and 'The Revolution' (as the 'Time Limit'). See Anna J Cooper, *The Third Step* (n 28) 8–9.

[47] According to Trouillot: 'French historians continue to neglect the colonial question, slavery, resistance, and racism more than the revolutionary assemblies ever did.' Trouillot, *Silencing the Past* (n 33) 101.

economy it undergirded. At the outset Cooper noted that '[i]mmense interests were at stake' given that 'Santo Domingo was certainly the richest of the French possessions', where 'work and profits had been organised in such a way that at first glance it could have appeared impossible to get along without [slavery and] the black man'.[48] Notably, given her audience and examiners at the Sorbonne,[49] some of Cooper's most powerful connections in this regard were made indirectly: in the letters from white planters and mercantilist that she annexed to her PhD. These included their complaints that ending the slave trade and extending 'human rights' to the enslaved and free Black people would 'bring total ruin to our commerce and to our port cities, the loss of our colonies, bankruptcy, uprisings . . . , anarchy and all the horrors which follow it', warning that 'France was to have been regenerated [by the Revolution], and she will be *forever lost*'.[50]

Cooper did not *reduce* the question of slavery to these economic structures, however, pointing out how white supremacy trumped capitalist interests and class alliances on various occasions. For example, Cooper pointed out how the 'white colonist-proprietors' and the '"petits-blancs", or lower middle-class whites' forged a common 'white' identity, despite their class differences, as both 'took pride and pleasure in humiliating the mulattoes with the most contemptuous terms, referring to them as dogs, ugly ones, big-bellies, quarter-breeds, half-castes, and so on, further lumping all these odious implications together in the general term "colored men"'.[51] Similarly, Cooper notes:[52]

> The 'petit-blancs' were not owners; rather they were artisans, shop-keepers, policemen, and former soldiers. Their ranks were swollen with fortune-hunters, come from all over. All these people were confirmed enemies of the [freed] blacks, whom they understood very little, and whom they never sought to understand. Nor did they wish to understand the mullatoes, whom they reproached with owning property and being rich. For the blacks they felt an extreme contempt, for the mulattoes an intense jealousy. The mullato class was restless and active; it was composed principally of landholders who were sometimes well educated and extremely desirous of affirming their equality with the whites; but the whites refused to have anything to do with them, obstinately opposing any reasonable sharing of their civil or civic rights.

In doing so Cooper anticipated Du Bois' observation in *Black Reconstruction* of how white workers 'received a low wage, [but] were compensated in part by a sort of public and psychological wage'.[53] These 'wages of whiteness' that, in Cooper's analysis,

[48] Cooper, *Slavery and the French and Haitian Revolutionists* (n 3) at 46, 38.

[49] As May puts it: 'Cooper's approach is, at times, quite understated: she had to find a way to assert her own approach to French history and to present her critiques of Bougle (her major professor), yet still pass her defence and receive her diploma.' May, '"It is Never a Question of the Slaves" (n 34) 8.

[50] 'Letter from an Inhabitant of Nantes, November 21, 1789' (reprinted in Cooper *Slavery and the French and Haitian Revolutionists* (n 3) 169–70.

[51] ibid 46–47.

[52] ibid 46.

[53] Du Bois, *Black Reconstruction* (n 42) 700. See further Cheryl I Harris, 'Whiteness as Property' (1992–1993) 106 Harvard Law Review 1707, 1741–42 (noting: 'Whiteness produced—and was reproduced by—the social advantage that accompanied it').

made the Haitian Revolution *inevitable* at the end of the eighteenth century,[54] made Reconstruction at the end of the nineteenth century *impossible* according to Du Bois, as 'the theory of race supplemented by a carefully planned and slowly evolved method, ...drove... a wedge between the white and black workers'.[55] Moreover, according to Du Bois, this evolving system of racial capitalism would go global, in part due to the 'astonishing triumph of revolution in Haiti'.[56] As Du Bois later argued in *The World and Africa* (1947), over the course of the nineteenth century 'slavery and the slave trade were abandoned in favor of colonial imperialism', with 'the transfer of capital from sugar plantations to colonial imperialism in Africa and Asia' and the development of 'a method of control of human labor and material which proved more profitable than slavery'.[57] As Du Bois put it, by 'thinking in world terms':[58]

> ... the captains of industry saw new opportunity for capital... [With] vaster profits from spices, gold, diamonds, and copper; they could replace wasteful slavery with local black labor paid at wages from one-half to nine-tenths cheaper that white labor in Europe and America and make white labor like it because all this could be done to the glory of God and the superiority of the white race.

In his 1947 account Du Bois recognized that it was the Haitian Revolution against French rule that catalyzed the 'new imperialism' of the British that would become global racial capitalism.[59] Two decades earlier—addressing the heart of the French intellectual establishment and amidst her own country's ongoing military occupation of Haiti (and doing so in French, no less)—Cooper did not only upend the orthodox view of the French Revolution and challenge the prevailing white supremacist views (including those of one of her examiners), she set out the historical and theoretical coordinates that her Black Internationalist counterparts would later use to map the system of global racial capitalism (one that international lawyers are, slowly, catching up with). In its *articulation*[60] of the subtle and intimate relations between emerging global regimes of racial and economic domination—or of 'racial capitalism'—Cooper's account of the Haitian Revolution is not simply overlooked, it is unsurpassed.

[54] As Cooper later put it, in summarizing her thesis: '[A]ll might have gone well but for the irreducible obsession of the colony of St. Domingo with regard to their prejudice toward the men of color. The mother country was disposed to grant all the rights for local self government... But this was a problem too grave to be resolved by the force at hand; too dangerous to await force from the Metropolis. In fact force was fire to powder.' Anna J Cooper, *The Third Step* (n 28) 13.

[55] Du Bois, *Black Reconstruction* (n 43) 700.

[56] Du Bois *World and Africa* (n 45) 41.

[57] ibid 44, 40.

[58] ibid 42, 47.

[59] ibid 41–44. Noting that '[i]t was this revolt more than any other single thing that spelled doom not only of the African slave trade but of slavery in America as a basis of an industrial system', which led to 'the transition from the century of human slavery in America to the century of the transfer of capital from sugar plantations to colonial imperialism in Africa and Asia', with the 'main end of both enterprises [being] profit to the owner and exploiter, mainly at the expense of poverty, ignorance, and pain for the slave and native subject' (ie the Dark Proletariat').

[60] See Stuart Hall, 'Race, Articulation, and Societies Structured in Dominance' in United Nations Education, Scientific and Cultural Organization (ed), *Sociological Theories: Race and Colonialism* (UNESCO 1980) 305–45.

Conclusion

Anna Julia Cooper's life was at once singular and symptomatic of the silencing of the lives and thoughts of 'Race Women Internationalists' more generally, in international law and beyond. For example, the 1900 Pan-African Conference—in which Cooper played an active, and unacknowledged role—is almost universally credited to the singular efforts of Henry Sylvester Williams of Trinidad, following his formation of the African Association in London three years prior.[61] However, the 'principal actor' in both the formation of the African Association in 1897 and the subsequent organization of the Pan-African Conference was Alice Kinloch, a Black woman from South Africa: a 'unnamed name' of whom there are very few portraits at all, who has been all but erased from the historical account of the event that set in motion twentieth-century Black Internationalism.[62] Later on, when Anna Julia Cooper defended her PhD at the Sorbonne in 1925, she inspired the young Jane Nardal (who was sitting in the public gallery) who credited Cooper with her 'awaken[ing]'.[63] Nardal, along with her sister Paulette, was one of the founders of the *Negritude* movement whose contributions continue to be overlooked; in fact, according to her sister, the movement was Jane Nardal's idea.[64] Yet, even as these alternative internationalisms are (slowly) making their way into the canons and consciousness of international lawyers—often as appendages to what remain white, western accounts—the role of Alice Kinloch, Pauline Hopkins, Anna Julia Cooper, Ida Gibbs Hunt, Jane and Paulette Nardal, Eslanda Robeson, Amy Ashwood Garvey, and others remain 'unknown or unacknowledged'.[65]

[61] See, eg, Marika Sherwood, 'Pan-African Conferences, 1900–1953: What Did "Pan-Africanism" Mean?' (2012) 4(10) Journal of Pan African Studies 107–08.

[62] Kinloch was unable to attend the 1900 Conference having returned to South Africa. Alice Kinloch's husband was listed as the Vice President of 'South Africa, Natal'.

[63] See letter from Jane Nardal to Alain Locke, re-printed and translated in Edwards, *Practice of Diaspora* (n 35) 127–28.

[64] ibid 122.

[65] Cooper, *Voice from the South* (n 10) 134.

9
Homelands of Mary Ann Shadd

*Sarah Riley Case**

Introduction

I had been planning to walk the lands where Mary Ann Shadd (1823–1893) lived when the possibility of writing this chapter arose. Mary Ann Shadd was a Black abolitionist who moved between the United States and British colonies to the north during the nineteenth century before Canada became a nation. The transatlantic slave trade would be abolished in her lifetime. For most of her life, slavery was permitted or limited within the bordered authority carved out by states and colonies. Shadd crossed these boundaries in search of a homeland that would provide freedom for her people. I am of Caribbean descent and I wished to trace the paths that she took because of our shared history of slavery and migration.

The transatlantic slave trade persisted for four centuries fuelling capitalism and the modern world.[1] Today this is unfathomable. But there is 'a memory of slavery not too far removed from the present-day reality for many of us'.[2] Only two generations back my grandfather was raised by family members who were enslaved in British Guiana. I was born in Canada after my family sought refuge from British Guiana elsewhere under the empire and later the Commonwealth. I live a drive away from the borderlands where Black fugitives from slavery, and some born free, crisscrossed the British colony of Canada West and the United States to leave oppression behind.

Mary Ann Shadd was one such fugitive. She was an emigrationist who counselled Black people to leave the United States while slavery was legal there in her book, *A Plea for Emigration: Notes on Canada West*.[3] She organized in abolitionist circles with figures such as Frederick Douglass, she furnished education to those in need, she recruited Black soldiers during the American Civil War, and she was a rare woman to publish an abolitionist newspaper, the *Provincial Freeman*, in the tradition of the Black

* Assistant Professor, McGill University Faculty of Law. Throughout this chapter, I refer to British colonies where Mary Ann Shadd sought refuge, which it is crucial to emphasize from the outset were established on territories of the Three Fires Confederacy: the Ojibwe, Odawa, and Potawatomi nations. I am grateful to several people who helped this chapter come to fruition. Foremost among them is Anne-Charlotte Martineau who is dedicated to uncovering histories of slavery in international law and whose vision led to featuring Mary Ann Shadd in this book. I also benefited immensely from the support of Immi Tallgren, Karen Knop, Martti Koskenniemi, Christopher Gevers, Parvathi Menon, Brenda Cossman, Daniel del Gobbo, Maurice Riley Case, and the Buxton Museum and the Chatham-Kent Black Historical Society, which hosted me.

[1] Cedric Robinson, *Black Marxism: The Making of the Black Radical Tradition* (University of North Carolina Press 2000); Eric Williams, *Capitalism and Slavery* (University of North Carolina Press 1944); Adelle Blackett, 'Slavery Is Not a Metaphor' (2018) 66(4) The American Journal of Comparative Law 927.

[2] Rinaldo Walcott, *On Property* (Biblioasis 2021) 17.

[3] Mary Ann Shadd, *A Plea for Emigration: Notes on Canada West* (1852).

Sarah Riley Case, *Homelands of Mary Ann Shadd* In: *Portraits of Women in International Law*. Edited by: Immi Tallgren, Oxford University Press. © Sarah Riley Case 2023. DOI: 10.1093/oso/9780198868453.003.0009

press. After emancipation in the United States, Mary Ann Shadd graduated among few women from Howard University law school to fight for suffrage and racial equality.

As I said, I was planning to visit the places where Shadd lived before this chapter came into view because of our bond through slavery. She was a destination in my imaginary about the past, *my past*. Black diaspora shares a history of dispossession, a long dispersal, and the search for a homeland where the dispossessed might flourish—however ephemeral such a homeland may be.[4] Fugitives from slavery had dreams of a place that would exceed the plantation logics behind all manner of borders patrolled by governments and white citizens.[5] It is through my family that I know their descendants sustain this tradition by crossing borders that continue to subjugate Black people.

I was therefore inspired to translate my personal search into the theme of this book. But I unexpectedly suffered from discomfort throughout the process of writing. I have come to think there are two reasons why. For one thing, Mary Ann Shadd eludes me because few archival materials tell her story. Contemporary policies of multiculturalism in the West have done little to redress the systematic erasure of Black people in the discipline of history. It took Shadd's family to begin recovering her story and important gaps remain.[6]

Erasure also marks the visual record of her life. There is a single photo of Mary Ann Shadd without attribution or a date.[7] On my pilgrimage to visit the places where she lived, I found sparse relics in museums and outdoors. Her home is gone. There is a plaza where she ran her newspaper. I took photographs of these places, my camera framing modern absences instead of the past. Nonetheless, my image of a bust erected in 2015 attests to the dedication of some to fill out the archive, to refashion, to take up space. I had hoped that my visual and textual portraits would serve a similar purpose.

In writing this chapter, I had expected to suffer from historical erasure. But I did not fully appreciate how much I would suffer from discomfort about my project to locate Shadd in *international law*. What troubled me on this other register was the drive to fuse two parts of my life—Black diaspora and international law—that may not be easily reconciled.

There is a normative connection between abolition and international rules prohibiting slavery. However, states adopted global rules against slavery after the transatlantic slave trade was abolished.[8] States had made piecemeal agreements to limit the trade (a euphemism and an international legal practice) in persons during the nineteenth century.[9] The British sought to abolish the trade then through enforcement on

[4] Rinaldo Walcott, 'Who Is She and What Is She to You?' Mary Ann Shadd Cary and the (Im)possibility of Black/Canadian Studies' (2000) 24(2) Atlantis 137, 144.

[5] Katherine McKittrick, 'Plantation Futures' (2013) 17(3) Small Axe 1, 3.

[6] Jane Rhodes, *Mary Ann Shadd Cary: The Black Press and Protest in the Nineteenth Century* (Indiana University Press 1998) 1.

[7] Library and Archives Canada <https://recherche-collection-search.bac-lac.gc.ca/eng/home/record?app=fonandcol&IdNumber=3191895>, accessed 8 October 2022.

[8] Notably, the Slavery Convention of 1926 (entry into force 9 March 1927).

[9] Such as the 1815 Declaration Relative to the Universal Abolition of the Slave Trade. European powers also used bilateral and multilateral treaties to prohibit the trade. Oji Umozurike, 'The African Slave Trade and the Attitudes of International Law Towards It' (1971) 16:2 Howard Law Journal 334; Jean Allain, *Slavery in International Law: Of Human Exploitation and Human Trafficking* (Brill 2013) 64–74; Saidiya Hartman, *Lose Your Mother: A Journey Along the Atlantic Slaver Route* (Farrar, Straus and Giroux 2007) 113.

Figure 9.1 Bust of Mary Ann Shadd Cary by Artis Lane in B.M.E. Freedom Park, Chatham, Ontario.
Source: Courtesy of the photographer Sarah Riley Case.

the seas. Europeans also, monstrously, justified the colonization of Africa with abolition into the twentieth century.[10] But for centuries international law was complicit—by condoning slavery or by remaining silent about this vast international structure that could not be ignored.[11]

Meanwhile the labours of Black abolitionists and allies were crucial to dismantling slavery. Shadd worked across the small places of her life: homes, schools, abolition conventions, army bureaus, newspaper offices. I was anxious about the possibility that tying her to international rules against slavery would instrumentalize her efforts, which came from *elsewhere*. My solace was in this elsewhere, which is to say the self-determined practices of Black abolitionists, among other radical thinkers who still struggle against slavery's afterlives.[12]

This chapter therefore presents the life of Mary Ann Shadd through the frame of a Black radical tradition, to use Cedric Robinson's term, which I will explain. Black abolitionists and fugitives were radicals who implicitly engaged with international law

[10] Hartman (n 9) 210; Adom Getachew, *Worldmaking After Empire: The Rise and Fall of Self-Determination* (Princeton University Press 2019).

[11] The trade in enslaved persons was sustained through international instruments, such as the *asiento*. European jurists also articulated justifications for slavery. For example, Vitoria condoned slavery on the basis of race. Others, such as Grotius, condoned the enslavement of prisoners of war and persons in enemy territory, while remaining silent about the international trade their governments engaged in. This is notable because many people were enslaved as prisoners of war and through raids. See Hartman (n 9) 210; Afua Cooper, *The Hanging of Angelique: the Untold Story of Canadian Slavery and the Burning of Old Montreal* (University of Georgia Press 2006) 30; Allain (n 9) 9–56.

[12] Hartman (n 9) 5.

by refusing conditions that international law historically condoned, including slavery and the borders carved out by states and empires that slavery facilitated. More than refusing international rules, however, Shadd and her peers acted in a 'self-assured' way,[13] inspired by thoughts of liberation.

In addition to abolitionists such as Frederick Douglass, her fellow travellers in a radical tradition might include dreamers who sought to dismantle the legacies of colonialism worldwide by carving out self-determined spaces for Black people—Pan Africanists, the Back to Africa movement, the Black Power movement that fought for a nation within a nation.[14] I have sought to capture Mary Ann Shadd's life through this lens, focusing on her abolitionism and her fugitive dreams of a homeland for Black community.[15]

Growing Up in the Black Abolitionist Movement

Mary Ann Shadd was born to free parents in 1823 Delaware, where slavery was legal as it then was across most places.[16] Colonial authorities outlawed forms of slavery during the preceding century in parts of British North America.[17] But Mary Ann grew up with slavery as a deeply entrenched state of affairs. She would have lived nearby people who were enslaved because in her day 'there were people of African descent with conflicting statuses living in close proximity to one another—at times within the same family'.[18]

Mary Ann's childhood was relatively stable since her family had experienced generations of freedom. The family name came from her great-grandfather, Hans Schad, a German soldier hired by the British before the American Revolution. When Hans was injured in battle, two free Black women aided his recovery, one of whom would become Mary Ann's great-grandmother, Elizabeth Jackson. The couple practiced trades, such as shoemaking and butchery, and by the time Hans passed away, he left meagre property to his children. Her father Abraham Shadd took over the shoemaking business from his forebears. Little is known about her mother Harriet Parnell, although she also had mixed racial parentage, which may have eased the family's social status.

But the conditions of free Black people, such as the Shadds, were not entirely free. Mary Ann was a young Black woman who inevitably suffered horrors of white supremacy. Heinous abuses stripped enslaved Black women of mothering, sistering, marrying, learning, and bodily integrity. Governments and white citizens policed the movement of *free* Black people as well through the violence of 'patrols', criminalization, and forcible bondage. This violence was increasingly legalized as communities of free Black people steadily grew.

[13] Walcott (n 4) 142.

[14] Robin Kelley locates Mary Ann Shadd within a radical emigrationist tradition: Robin Kelley, *Freedom Dreams: The Black Radical Imagination* (Penguin Random House 2002).

[15] Hartman (n 9) 211.

[16] The biography in this chapter draws on Rhodes (n 6) and primary research, unless another attribution is made.

[17] For example, An Act to Limit Slavery in Upper Canada of 1793 and prohibitions in Vermont, Pennsylvania, New Hampshire, Massachusetts, Connecticut, and Rhode Island.

[18] Natasha Henry, 'Chloe Cooley and the Act to Limit Slavery in Upper Canada' *The Canadian Encyclopedia* (30 October 2013) (writing on Upper Canada).

Free Black people in Delaware were severely repressed under the Black Codes enacted while Mary Ann was a child. These laws stripped the Shadd family of allowances that they experienced before. Under the codes, free Black people would be enslaved or imprisoned if they did not carry proof of their status. They would be punished for gathering. They were excluded from white spaces. What is more, Delaware officials barred free Black people from entering the state. The purpose of the laws, according to one minister, was 'to degrade, to crush, and to render them ignorant and powerless'.[19]

Deepening this repression were programmes to remove free Black people from the country altogether. A few years before Mary Ann was born, a coalition of slaveholders, abolitionists, and proslavery politicians inaugurated the American Colonization Society to relocate free Black people to Africa. They founded the colony of Liberia in 1822 for this purpose and to 'civilize' African peoples. Within a decade, the Society relocated 1,400 people to Liberia.[20] In Delaware, the legislature endorsed the colonization programme: 'the state where the Shadd family had grown and thrived was rapidly becoming hostile to their presence'.[21]

This calculated dislocation was denounced by Black and white abolitionists who began to hold conventions to improve conditions at home. Mary Ann's father became involved with the Black convention movement and he helped found the American Anti-Slavery Society. Her father believed that Black people should be recognized as equal rights holders on American soil. Abraham and other abolitionists condemned colonization for this reason and because the welfare of Black people was tangential to the plans of proslavery forces.

Mary Ann was profoundly shaped by her upbringing within the abolition movement. If her father opposed deportation, her family was always already moving across jurisdictions because of repression and Abraham's activism.[22] When Mary Ann was ten years of age, her family moved from Delaware to evade the Black Codes and to find a school for her, since the school for Black children in Delaware did not admit girls. So, her family went north to a town near Philadelphia where the convention movement was centred.

It is believed that Mary Ann received her education from Quakers, who were antislavery Christians devoted to education and self-reliance. The Shadd family is known to have shared these ethical commitments. Mary Ann would come to ground her own abolitionist politics in Christian morality, Victorian temperance and, above all, the belief that 'racial uplift' was the path to emancipation.[23] She believed that her people would be free if they accessed education, did hard work, and acted respectably. This, she thought, would convince white citizens to make equal rights possible.

By the age of seventeen, Mary Ann put her beliefs into practice as a schoolteacher. She taught Black children and adults who might not have learned otherwise—they were often living in destitute conditions. Although hers was an accepted profession for women, she travelled across state borders to reach them at great risk to herself. Around

[19] Rhodes (n 6) 6–7.
[20] ibid 9.
[21] ibid 10.
[22] ibid 105.
[23] Maria del Rosario Fraile, 'Self-Reliance Is the True Road to Independence: Freedom and Independence in Mary Ann Shadd's Writings' (2013) 34 *Spanish Journal of English Studies* 227.

this time Mary Ann also began to intervene in public discourse. She joined her father at conventions where she developed oratory skills.[24] She also published a treatise in Frederick Douglass' newspaper, the *North Star*, proposing that free Black people could overcome subjugation through self-reliance. Mary Ann lamented the little progress that conventions had made in the decades since her childhood, remarking 'We should do more, talk less.' Her message was similar in a pamphlet published shortly after, *Hints to the Colored People of the North*, where she developed ideals of racial uplift by critiquing leadership within Black community. Using the same pen to encourage upward social mobility, she admonished her peers for pursing material goods instead of devoting themselves to the cause. She denounced churches, especially, for 'minister[ing] to our vanity' through public events, rather than labouring for conditions necessary to racial uplift.

Mary Ann's critique of community leaders was unconventional because she was a woman and they were men.[25] But if she was deviant, she was also a conformist who elevated white liberal values in her appeals to respectability. Mary Ann's ideals of racial uplift would carry through future generations from the Reconstruction era to the civil rights movement until now. And while, from my perspective, there are good reasons to question her priorities—including her faith that liberalism would bring justice to Black people—Mary Ann clearly believed that she was unifying her people by debating 'how best to build community'.[26]

Given my sense of belonging to Black diaspora, it is important for me to remark that Black community was Mary Ann's audience, not white citizens and governments, nor international law. Mary Ann's declaration in her pamphlet is telling. What she wrote there was, 'My destiny is that of my people, it is a duty to myself.'[27] Mary Ann sought to unite diaspora shortly after she published her two opinions by making a homeland of Canada West, near to where I live now. Her abolitionism must therefore be understood through the lens of racial uplift and liberalism as well as the radical imaginary of fugitives.

Mary Ann Shadd's Plea for Emigration

Black people have for centuries followed fugitive dreams of a homeland beyond authorities that oppress us. But you will recall that emigration was *unpopular* in the convention movement because of the American Colonization Society. Mary Ann's plea for emigration was therefore 'as much about her effort to secure a place in the movement as it was about finding new geographic location for transplanted [people]'

[24] Carol Conaway, 'Rhetorically Constructed Africana Mothering in the Antebellum: The Racial Uplift Tradition of Mary Ann Shadd Cary' (2007) 2 Journal of Pan African Studies 4, 8.

[25] Elizabeth Cali, '"Why Does Not Somebody Speak OUT?": Mary Ann Shadd Cary's Heteroglossic Black Protofeminist Nationalism' (2015) 32(2) Vitae Scholasticae 32.

[26] Shirley Yee, 'Finding a Place: Mary Ann Shadd Cary and the Dilemmas of Black Migration to Canada, 1850–1870' (1997) 18(1) Frontiers 1.

[27] Jane Rhodes, 'At the Boundaries of Abolitionism, Feminism, and Black Nationalism: The Activism of Mary Ann Shadd Cary', in Kathryn Kish Sklar and James Stewart, *Women's Rights and Transatlantic Antislavery in the Era of Emancipation* (Yale University Press (2007) 350.

threatened by anti-Black violence.[28] Some Black abolitionists were recruiting people to move onto places such as Haiti, South America, Africa, and the British Empire. Mary Ann hoped that Canada West would be a 'fugitive *elsewhere*' for her people,[29] a place of safety where they could fight for abolition and thrive.

Mary Ann favoured British colonies to the north because of proximity, laws of formal equality, the climate, the English language, and the presence of Black people. Black 'loyalists' had arrived in Nova Scotia during the eighteenth century after fighting for British North America. British authorities had deported Jamaican freedom fighters there too for sedition. In each case, the colonial government brutalized Black people, and many moved on elsewhere.[30] But Mary Ann would have known Canada West as a hopeful destination on the Underground Railroad because her family provided refuge to brave individuals escaping bondage for the north. Emigration to Canada West was also discussed at the conventions in response to mass incidences of anti-Black violence. Discussions about a larger exodus then became real when the British prohibited slavery across most colonies in 1834, including in the Canadas,[31] while conditions that Black people endured were worsening in the United States.

The introduction of legislation in 1850 to obstruct the movement of Black individuals across the United States forced tens of thousands to make the voyage. The *Fugitive Slave Act* empowered white citizens to detain people accused of stealing themselves from slaveholders for prosecution—given the status of enslaved persons as property. 'Slavecatchers' could recover a fee for this work, a cruel incentive, and they might sell captives into slavery. This imperilled fugitives *and* free Black people in places where slavery was legal *and* illegal. Any Black person in any state might be sold into bondage. Because of the Act, the possibility of a home in the Republic had become, in Mary Ann's words, 'dangerous in the extreme'.[32] She agonized that the 'pro-slavery administration' was 'bearing upon them with fatal effect'. She travelled to Toronto a year later with her father to attend a convention where they would discuss the state of abolition and migrating to Canada West.

The North American Convention of Colored Freemen was held in Toronto in 1851, months after Black abolitionists and allies formed the Anti-Slavery Society of Canada to support refugees entering the colony. Sources claim that as many as 20,000 fugitives moved to Canada West around this time.[33] Six million Black people would move from the southern to the northern United States in the twentieth century because of Jim Crow laws and poverty, as the painter Jacob Lawrence documented in The Migration Series.[34] In the 1850s, many claimed freedom by migrating to Canada West.

When she arrived, Canada West already hosted Black communities living in cities and farming the surrounding lands. Abolitionists had set up residences dedicated to

[28] Yee (n 26) 1.

[29] Hartman (n 9) 97.

[30] Barrington Walker, *The African Canadian Legal Odyssey: Historical Essays* (University of Toronto Press 2012) 16–20.

[31] An Act for the Abolition of Slavery throughout the Colonies of 1833. Albeit forms of slavery were prohibited in the eighteenth century.

[32] Shadd (n 4).

[33] Natasha Henry, 'Fugitive Slave Act of 1850' *The Canadian Encyclopedia* (10 February 2015).

[34] Museum of Modern Art, 'One-Way Ticket: Jacob Lawrence's Migration Series' available at <https://www.moma.org/interactives/exhibitions/2015/onewayticket/>, accessed 8 October 2022.

supporting fugitives. The region of Chatham especially flourished with farms, houses, stores, medical practices, churches, free masons, taverns, hotels, women's associations, newspapers, and music.[35] I saw fragmented relics of this community on my visit to Chatham, where some descendants of the people who made the community now live in very different circumstances.

Soon after arriving, Mary Ann published her book describing her adopted community, *A Plea for Emigration*. In some ways, her book is an homage to formal equality for enabling Black men (who enjoyed legal rights) and their families to prosper. She praised the British Empire for guaranteeing rights to all men. In Canada West, slavery would not be tolerated as it was in the United States. Men could own property and property owners could vote. Citizenship was a birth-right. The conditions for racial uplift through business and labour were fair; Black men, Mary Ann claimed, were not 'obliged to work a little better, for a lower rate'.

Mary Ann was trying to persuade her people to immigrate to Canada West because it would provide a better home. However, her words glossed over dreadful conditions that Black, Indigenous, and other people of colour experienced there. The mid-nineteenth century was a period of intense nation-building before the confederation of Canada in 1867. The British were dispensing programmes throughout this time to subordinate non-whites. This was the period when the British began appropriating territories from Indigenous peoples under false pretences.[36] This was the start of residential schools that effected genocidal policies by removing Indigenous children from Indigenous nations. This was the period when thousands of Chinese workers with limited rights laboured to build a national railway that would define the state's borders. This was when the Supreme Court of Canada affirmed the doctrine of discovery.[37]

There was a pervasive culture of eugenics that operated alongside, and through, the legal liberalism that Mary Ann praised. Black refugees often lived in dismal conditions without food, clothing, schools, and shelter. Racism did not improve as more fugitives arrived in the region. In fact, white citizens petitioned the government to stop people from seeking refuge. If Mary Ann avoided writing about this in her book, she did increasingly 'question the degree to which the Canadian and British governments supported the antislavery movement and the presence of black settlers'.[38]

Telling this past is important for me because it reveals the historical trajectory of racism that persists in contemporary 'multicultural' states despite, and through, facially neutral laws of formal equality. It also begins to explain the imaginary that Black radicals foster beyond liberalism, while necessarily living within nation-states and empires.

[35] See Peggy Bristow and others (eds), *We're Rooted Here and They Can't Pull Us Up* (University of Toronto Press 1994).

[36] See Glen Coulthard, *Red Skin, White Masks: Rejecting the Colonial Politics of Recognition* (University of Minnesota Press 2014).

[37] *St Catherines Milling and Lumber Co v R* (1887) 13 SCR 577.

[38] Yee (n 26) 10.

Her Acts of Refusal against States and Empires

Mary Ann refused to live in places that threatened her safety, which is why she went to Canada West. Then, when confronted with anti-Black racism there, she asserted her community's authority through other radical acts. I am inspired to think of these acts as part of a Black radical tradition because they were refusals to be subordinated by colonial authorities that oppressed Black people and continue to do so through different techniques in the afterlives of slavery— 'skewed life chances, limited access to health and education, premature death, incarceration, and impoverishment'.[39]

Mary Ann's resistance to laws that condoned segregated schools must be understood in this context. Mary Ann faced difficulties accessing education as a child and, in Canada West, laws legitimized the practice of refusing Black children access to public schools. Black people were permitted to have their own schools, but their taxes went to the public schools, which did not admit their children. Teaching had always been part of Mary Ann's abolitionism because her people had for centuries been denied possibilities to learn. In Canada West, she drew upon her experience as a schoolteacher to repudiate colonial laws by opening an integrated school.[40] But the realities of funding her school were harsh. She spent years struggling to raise funds. She allied with a Christian society to gain a stream of funds that dried up soon enough. She closed her first school in Canada West because the money was insufficient only to later open another school that closed for similar reasons.

Mary Ann also supported radical acts of outright insurrection. For instance, she was the Secretary of the Chatham Vigilance Committee, which rescued people from slavery. In the United States, vigilance committees assisted fugitives along their escape route. In the British colonies to the north, 'slavecatchers' would kidnap Black people to take them south. Shadd's committee intercepted their attempts. After one rescue aboard a train, colonial authorities prosecuted committee members, including Mary Ann's brother, and she rallied to fund the defence.[41] The committee was enforcing laws against slavery, but members were charged anyway under laws of property and public respectability, which charges Indigenous and Black activists routinely face, still, for taking direct action.

In another example, Mary Ann published a first-hand account of a failed attempt planned in Chatham to inspire a plantation revolt across the United States, known as the Harper's Ferry raid.[42] The idea was that by raiding the Harper's Ferry military base, abolitionists would begin an uprising that would end slavery.

The fact that Mary Ann published and ran a newspaper was no small part of her activism. The press was crucial to sharing ideas and organizing across nineteenth century Black communities. Mary Ann rarely published under her name because community

[39] Hartman (n 9) 5.

[40] Carol Conway, 'Racially Integrated Education: The Antebellum Thought of Mary Ann Shadd Cary and Frederick Douglass' (2010) 27(2) Vitae Scholasticae 86.

[41] John Farrell, 'The History of the Negro Community in Chatham Ontario: 1787–1865' (PhD thesis, University of Ottawa 1955).

[42] Heike Paul, 'Out of Chatham: Abolitionism on the Canadian Frontier' (2011) 8 Atlantic Studies 165, 179–80.

leaders admonished her 'unladylike' behaviour. However, she allied with Black and white abolitionists to publish her newspaper, where she voraciously debated community leaders as she did in her youth. She took particular aim at charitable groups that asked for donations instead of fostering independence. At the same time, she passed years travelling across borders to gain subscriptions for her newspaper. Like with her schools, dire material conditions eventually stifled her efforts to nurture community through the Black press.

Mary Ann also supported abolition by force in the Republic. Not long after the American Civil War broke out in 1861, she returned to recruit Black soldiers for the Union army. Her labours again involved travelling to reach Black communities, where she would use the oratory skills she developed earlier in the convention movement to persuade Black men to enlist.[43] It was only after the war that Mary Ann became a lawyer, motivated to further racial equality and women's suffrage during the Reconstruction era.

International Law and Belonging (to a Black Radical Tradition)

I believe it is important to acknowledge that Mary Ann Shadd is unlike other women described in this book. Her efforts implicitly responded to and unfolded alongside international law but Black community was her 'inspiration'.[44] I would therefore ask readers to reflect upon her life in this way. It is also important to note that other Black radicals *have* offered imaginaries of international law, such as Kwame Nkrumah, Paulette Nardal, and WEB Du Bois.[45] The latter acknowledged Mary Ann Shadd's 'pilgrimages' across borders in an essay dedicated to Black women.[46]

In reflecting upon Mary Ann's labours within Black community, I have grappled with difficult questions about how I might do justice to her *politics of law*. I have not said much about her legal career because her graduation was delayed for years and she practiced little due to sexism and anti-Black racism. When thinking about her engagements with law, I wish to sit instead with Mary Ann's acts of refusal: emigrating, publishing, fighting, and teaching for abolition. These acts I believe prefigured laws of Black community within and beyond imperial jurisdictions that assume the authority to define law. Mary Ann had visions of emancipation that exceeded these jurisdictions. She refused the plantation logics that imperiled her movement and her life.

She also defied binaries *within* the diaspora. Often Black resistance movements are described along factional binaries, for example between integration and separation, respectability and force. Readers might think here of differences between the Black Power movement and the civil rights movement. Mary Ann Shadd reveals the

[43] Rhodes (n 6) 154–60.

[44] Robinson (n 1) 72.

[45] For but a few references: Getachew (n 10); Henry J. Richardson III, 'Two Treaties, and Global Influences of the American Civil Rights Movement, Through the Black International Tradition' (2010) 18(1) Virginia Journal of Social Policy and the Law 59; Imaobong Umoren, *Race Women Internationalists: Activist-Intellectuals and Global Freedom Struggles* (University of California Press 2018).

[46] WEB Du Bois, *Darkwater: Voices from Within the Veil* (Harcourt, Brace and Howe 1920).

fluidity of these concepts. She was for allyship *and* she pledged her life to her people. She was committed to abolition *and* to living elsewhere. She praised temperance *and* transgressed colonially defined genders. She supported formal equality *and* she was a freedom fighter. She was not unlike other radicals who seek freedom through any means that might advance the cause.

In the process of writing, this sense of betweenness became important to my own identity, because I am a lawyer and I know well that there are real constraints around how Black people can live in places while pursuing justice. Still today, people advancing the movement for Black life seek justice through law *and* they have transformational ways of doing abolition in the ongoing struggle for emancipation. I want to capture how Mary Ann Shadd used means that are full and radical.

With the term Black radical tradition, Cedric Robinson identified revolutionary acts that may seem discrete but are connected through the 'presence of a historical or political consciousness' across African peoples.[47] Slavery and colonialism are relevant to Black radicalism because they are its objects. However, resistance to the West is 'not the foundation for Black radicalism's nature or character'. Rather, Black radicalism is a *specific* response: it is a 'social tradition' across communities that are dispersed, plural, *and* share experiences.

Robinson's examples of this social tradition include plantation revolts, rebel organizing, and fugitive acts of emigration. In the intellectual strand of Black radicalism, he counts Du Bois and CLR James. The scholar Robin Kelley expands upon Black radical imaginings to capture Third World dreamers, reparations seekers, and Black feminists.[48] The Black radical tradition includes revolutions, uprisings, arson, and everyday refusals. It spans plantations, bridges, streets, buses, sports arenas, theatres, and universities. Black radicals move between institutions and insurrection; they cross over them because of the dispossession and displacement of Black people, and our desire for something approaching home.

The scholar Saidiya Hartman says that the search for a homeland explains why 100 square blocks of Los Angeles can be destroyed in a night.[49] Freedom has required people 'to burn the cane fields, or to live in a garret for seven years, or to stage a general strike, or to create a new republic'. This is because 'We may have forgotten our country, but we haven't forgotten our dispossession. It's why we never tire of dreaming of a place that we can call home, a place better than here.' The longing for home explains why people in the twenty-first century protest in the streets despite threats posed by COVID-19 and laws of property and public respectability.

In this chapter, I wanted to share how Mary Ann Shadd has helped me to refocus on the collective betweenness of Black diaspora. Her life reveals conditions of Black life that exist alongside an international order that has not alleviated global anti-Black violence through borders, policing, labour, health, education, and climate change—although courageous people work towards repair.[50]

[47] Robinson (n 1) 73.
[48] Kelley (n 14).
[49] Hartman (n 9) 87–88.
[50] For example, UN Special Rapporteur on Contemporary Forms of Racism, Racial Discrimination, Xenophobia and Related Intolerance, 'Reparation, Racial Justice and Equality' UN Doc A/74/321; Adelle

Fundamentally, her story is about constructing different futures. And that is where I wish to end this chapter. The theorist Fred Moten frames the discipline and project of Black Studies as a mission to save the earth and to save human existence on the earth.[51] It is a big claim. But his claim is apparent in movements for Black life and movements to repatriate Indigenous lands. These projects continue the legacies that pathbreakers, such as Mary Ann Shadd, began. They might foster just relations among peoples that risk being captured by a 'politics of recognition' that keeps people down under capitalism and liberal governance.[52] Readers can look to social movements for this kind politics of law. They might also take a pilgrimage to places such as Chatham to inform themselves about the past and about ongoing harms to imagine some fugitive elsewhere from the present condition.

Blackett, *Everyday Transgressions: Domestic Workers' Transnational Challenge to International Labor Law* (Cornell University Press 2019).

[51] Robin Kelley and Fred Moten in Conversation, University of Toronto <https://youtu.be/fP-2F9MX jRE>.

[52] Coulthard (n 36).

10
Avabai Wadia
A Gentle Rebel of (Other) Nations?

Vasuki Nesiah

> We were totally unaware then that we were history makers.
>
> Avabai Wadia
> 147 of *The Light is Ours*

> You don't change the course of history by turning the faces of portraits to the wall.
>
> Jawaharlal Nehru

In her 2020 book, *Feminist Internationalism: How to Change Everything,* Verónica Gago writes that this is a moment where women's struggles across the world have developed an intensity and interconnectedness that brings a radical potential for change. Gago writes the book from Buenos Aires just as the Argentinian feminist movements fight for abortion rights moves to success, alongside a range of women's movements across the world on a diverse range of issues that speak to a radical potential for social transformation. The struggles Gago's book describes and engages with, are animated by feminist movements' insights that the politics of the body are central to the body politic at every scale of political society from the local to the global. Indeed, in all of these contexts intimate decision about sexuality and reproduction have become central to fraught political debates. They determine supreme court appointments and presidential politics, foreign aid, and international labor mobility.

One important backstory to these contemporary struggles to 'change everything' in Buenos Aires and beyond has been the transnational struggle for reproductive rights and sexual self-determination. One of the most significant events in the history of these struggles was the founding of the International Planned Parenthood Federation (IPPF) approximately seventy years ago on 29 November 1952, in a meeting of women's rights activists from across the globe in Mumbai, India for the Third International Conference on Planned Parenthood.[1] Avabai Wadia, an organizer of the Conference worked with Margaret Sanger and others to pass the conference resolution that formally founded IPPF. Wadia's belief in the centrality of the IPPF agenda

[1] For a history of IPPF see Beryl Suitters, *Be Brave and Angry: Chronicles of the International Planned Parenthood Federation* (International Planned Parenthood Federation 1973).

Vasuki Nesiah, *Avabai Wadia* In: *Portraits of Women in International Law.* Edited by: Immi Tallgren, Oxford University Press.
 DOI: 10.1093/oso/9780198868453.003.0010

Figure 10.1 Miss Avabai Menta, a nineteen-year-old girl from Colombo, Ceylon passed the examination for a call to the English Bar. Photo shows Miss Avabai Mehta photographed at her London home after her success had been announced.
Source: Smith Archive / Alamy Stock Photo.

to international law and policy reflected her insistent feminist challenge to the zoning of social life into the categories of public and private.

Wadia was a lawyer and activist whose engagement in the arena of international law and policy reflects how her political priorities made connections between law and public health, feminist, and anti-colonial struggles. Her style of engagement forged solidarities in the cities she lived in—Colombo, Bombay, and London—alongside transnational solidarities with activists across the world. Her own home, politically and otherwise, was located in women's movements across the world and the paths they forged towards each other, and away from the world they had inherited. They sought to develop nothing less than a new international order, from the most intimate arenas of women's lives to the most public and global arenas of international law and policy that determined possibilities for their future.

Background

Avabai Wadia was born in Colombo, Sri Lanka (then colonial Ceylon) in 1913, on the eve of the First World War, into a peripatetic Zoroastrian family. That same year

Gandhi was in South Africa helping lead a minor's strike; Pancho Villa helped ignite the Mexican revolution; the Vietnamese attacked Saigon in the battle against French colonialism; labour activists formed the Irish Citizens Army to advance and defend labor activism; and the Woman Suffrage Association in America marched in Washington DC for the right to vote. There was increased unrest in Sri Lanka against the oppressions of colonial rule, as well as the struggle for women's franchise.[2] All of these struggles transformed the landscape of international law and the histories of the world's peoples in ways that inspired Wadia and her engagement in these world-transforming struggles.

In a 1985 article on debates in the UN with the Reagan administration, *The New York Times* describes Wadia as 'something of a grande dame on the international women's scene'; in her seventies then, she was still travelling the international circuit of women's conferences mobilizing support for reproductive rights.[3] Wadia is probably most famous for co-founding and then leading the IPPF, arguably the foremost international public health institution for women across the globe. However, long before IPPF came into being, she was already an active contributor to internationalist women's organizations such as the Women's International League for Peace and Freedom (WILPF), representing WILPF at League of Nations meetings in Geneva, and elsewhere as a pioneering young lawyer in London. After gaining her schooling at Ladies College in Colombo, Wadia moved to London to complete her studies and subsequently, to take the bar. She is not just the first women lawyer from Sri Lanka to pass the bar exam, but in fact one of the first women to pass her barristers in London, and that too with a first class.[4]

Wadia joined the Inns of Court and practised at the High Court of Justice as one of the first female lawyers in England.[5] She soon plunged into London's radical inter-war political milieu as an activist in the women's movement, the labour party, and anti-colonial solidarity struggles. The inter-war years were an exciting time to be in England as 'London became the epicentre of an anti-imperial internationalism' as colonial subjects infused metropolitan politics with anticolonial solidarities.[6] Claude McKay described these insurgent dynamics as 'the great destructive forces within while the subject races are fighting without... We have a great wall to batter down, and while we are working on one side, we should hail those working on the other'.[7] Wadia plunged into these transnational anti-colonial networks in ways that pivotally shaped her own political identity and her approach to the promise and possibilities of internationalism.

[2] One early institutional expression of women's struggle for franchise was the 1919 Ceylon National Congress resolution supporting female suffrage. Malathi de Alwis and Kumari Jayawardena, *Casting Pearls: The Women's Franchise Movement in Sri Lanka* (Social Scientist Association 2001, new edn 2021).

[3] <www.nytimes.com/1985/09/23/style/a-voice-for-control-of-the-population-explosion.html> accessed 1 October 2022.

[4] Her success impacted opened doors for women back at home. 'As a direct consequence of her success, the Law College in Colombo opened its doors to women.' < www.open.ac.uk/researchprojects/makingbritain/taxonomy/term/50> accessed 1 October 2022.

[5] <www.theguardian.com/news/2005/aug/11/guardianobituaries.india> accessed 1 October 2022.

[6] Miles Taylor, Insurgent Empire by Priyamvada Gopal review—a superb study of anticolonial resistance, *The Guardian*, 11 July 2019

[7] Quoted in Priyamvada Gopal, *Insurgent Empire* (Verso 2019) 295. Gopal draws attention to figures like McKay and George Padmore, as well as Shapurji Saklatvala, who, like Wadia, was a Parsee. Originally hailing from the Parsee community in Bombay, Saklatvala was a radical voice in the House of Commons as the Communist party MP for Battersea. For an excerpt from the book that focusses on Saklatava's contribution see Gopal's 'Shapurji Saklatvala, the First British MP to Uncompromisingly Refute Imperialism', *The Wire* 30 October 2019.

Eventually, Wadia's anti-colonial activism got her blacklisted with London law firms.[8] She moved back to Colombo and practised in the Supreme Court there for two years while becoming increasingly active with the All Ceylon Women's Association (ACWC). As the war intensified the family relocated to Mumbai which was already home to a large Parsee community. In India Wadia joined the All-India Women's Conference and co-founded the International Planned Parenthood Federation (IPPF). She helped organize the Asian-African Conference of Women in Colombo in 1958 and remained an active member in transnational women's movements for the rest of the century; she died in 2005 aged ninety-one.

In this chapter, I read Avabai Wadia's life and work in the anti-imperialist international women's movement as a window into the 'negative space' around the dominant voice of twentieth-century international law, casting it into relief and illuminating what it marginalizes and excludes. In this way it re-reads international law as centrally constituted through these 'negative space' movements and demands. I highlight how Wadia's professional and political engagements illuminate the significance of feminist internationalisms, shaped both by the struggle for decolonization and the struggle for women's rights, in this portrait of twentieth-century international law.

The Internationalism of Anti-Imperial Feminism

The 1955 Bandung conference and the Non-Aligned Movement (NAM) meetings that followed offered a central platform for postcolonial states to present a collective anti-imperial voice on the world stage.[9] Their most prominent descendants were states and social movements such as the ongoing national liberation movements that constituted the Afro-Asian People's Solidarity Organization (AAPSO) and the Tricontinental that drew from NAM, AAPSO, and a range of other radical anti-imperialist currents around the world. A number of important non-state actor meetings and networks—the shadow Bandungs—emerged around these conferences.[10] The meetings of the anti-imperial women's rights internationalists were amongst the most noteworthy of these formations and Wadia was amongst the most significant convener of these networks.

Garima Karia describes women's diplomacy in the Afro-Asian World as the 'Forgotten Femissaries'.[11] The three most central meetings of Afro-Asian women's meetings took place in Beijing (1949), Colombo (1958), and Cairo (1961) at a moment where anti-colonial movements were bringing sweeping changes to the international order. Wadia was the chief organizer of the 1958 conference, which had representation from fourteen countries. These meetings emerged from national women's rights organizations such as the All Ceylon Women's Conference (ACWC) and the All China

[8] <en.wikipedia.org/wiki/Avabai_Bomanji_Wadia> accessed 1 October 2022.

[9] Bandung and NAM are often relegated to the footnotes of dominant histories of international law. For a counter to this dominant narrative, see Luis Eslava, Michael Fakhri, and Vasuki Nesiah (eds), *Bandung, Global History and International Law: Critical Pasts and Pending Futures* with Luis Eslava and Michael Fakhri (co-eds, Cambridge University Press (2017)).

[10] www.thetricontinental.org/about> accessed 1 October 2022.

[11] See Garima Karia in < www.mcgill.ca/arts-internships/files/arts-internships/aria_final_poster_garim a_karia.pdf> accessed 1 October 2022.

Women's Democratic Federation, and transnational women's rights networks such as the Women's International Democratic Federation (WIDF). These groups worked in close collaboration with NAM and APPSO, and leaned on NAM countries such as Egypt and India for funding and support.[12]

There were important ideological differences amongst the women involved and the women's groups that participated in these conferences; these were amplified because of two dynamics, national and international. On the international stage, the Cold War dominated political alliances and those who allied in nationalist movements across Asia and Africa chose one or the others side of the Cold War. Some sought to retain the 'Spirit of Bandung' in charting a third way that challenged Cold War alliances. Moreover, on the national stage, many countries won their independence in this same period and civil society actors, including women's groups, were absorbed into the state or state-allied welfare activities. Others got absorbed into social and political movements that challenged the state from a range of ideological directions, from temperance movements to labour movements.[13] Wadia's own political coming of age had been incubated in the London anti-colonial movements during her student days and this political formation shaped her own positionality viz-a-viz the dominant world order. At the same time, the movements that were most critical to her formation were those that were institutionalized—be it political parties such as the Indian National Congress or transnational civil society groups such as the WILPF. Thus, Wadia was both an activist seeking to change the post-war world order through women's organizations and others, but also an institutional player who channeled her activism through these established organizations and networks.

Wadia's presence in these networks was shaped by her combination of pioneering professional and academic achievement, a deeply solidaristic ethos, and sheer charisma. Although she hailed from a minority community, she was often chosen as the representative of the local and national groups she was a part of at international

[12] Elizabeth Armstrong, 'Before Bandung: The Anti-Imperialist Women's Movement in Asia and the Women's International Democratic Federation' (2016) 41(2) Signs . The Beijing conference was preceded by the Nehru sponsored Asian Relations Conference in New Delhi in March–April 1947 that was not focused on women but included women and therefore gave the women present an opportunity to meet and plan next steps on the eve of Indian independence in August of that same year. See Garima Karia in<www.mcgill.ca/arts-internships/files/arts-internships/aria_final_poster_garima_karia.pdf> accessed 1 October 2022. This, of course, was in addition to the many women's conferences in Asia and Africa that brought women's groups together such as the pan-Asian Women's Conference in Lahore in 1931 and the pan-Arab Women's conference in Cairo in 1944, Armstrong ibid 313. These conferences were not only about so called 'women's issues' such as equal suffrage and non-discriminatory property rights, but also anti-imperialism.

[13] In both colonial Ceylon and colonial India temperance movements were an important dimension of anti-colonial agitation with liquor and sexual licentiousness often associated with the colonizer or the West in influential strands of the nationalist movement. Women had a leading role in these movements and were often positioned as the moral guardians of the nation in ways that echoed Victorian models of bourgeois womanhood that were transmitted through missionary schools and other outlets, while also invoking local religious traditions. It was not surprising that many women took on welfare activities in the postcolonial period, in roles that were traditionally gendered while also leveraging these for a voice in the public sphere. For further discussion of the Sri Lankan context see Kumari Jayawardena and Malathi de Alwis, 'Embodied Violence: Communalising Women's Sexuality in South Asia' (1996) 4(8) Reproductive Health Matters: An International Journal on Sexual and Reproductive Health and Rights. For an interesting subaltern challenge to the gendered legacies of constitutional morality in the Indian context see the discussion of sex worker rights Rohit De, *A People's Constitution* (Princeton 2018) ch 4. My thanks to Parvathi Menon for making the valuable connections with De's work.

meetings. In her London days, she represented WILPF at the League of Nations and other meetings; when she returned to Colombo, she represented the All Ceylon Women's Association (ACWC) at meetings of the All India Women's Conference (AIWC). When Wadia moved to Bombay she was nominated as a delegate of AIWC at the meetings of the Women's International Democratic Federation (WIDF). Despite her origins in Sri Lanka (then Ceylon), she soon became a full voting member of the AIWC Standing Committee and an influential figure in the Indian women's movement. Most significantly, she became the head of the first AIWC office in 1944. As she acknowledges in her memoir, she was thrust into this leadership position on the basis of her long history of linkages with the upper echelons of the Indian nationalist movement who she met while studying in London, and in her early years of practice in the Inns of Court.[14] In this period, she met Mahatma Gandhi, Jawaharlal Nehru, and Mohammed Ali Jinnah, as well as many women in influential positions in independent India such as Lady Rama Rau and Mrs Rameshwari Nehru.[15]

The milieu that shaped Wadia's anti-colonial feminism as a young adult in London included a vibrant mix of socialist and liberal intellectual and political traditions and institutions in South Asia and England. These included the Labour Party, the Fabian Society, and the London liaisons of the Indian Congress Party. These groups were marked by the tensions navigating the complexities of their historical moment. Nothing embodied the intersection of progressive and reactionary ideas and movements as powerfully as the traction that Malthusian ideas gained amongst social reformers who were colonial in outlook and anti-colonial in their professed politics.[16]

Wadia was inspired and influenced by these figures' anti-colonial sentiments. Yet, as she became more deeply involved with the international reproductive rights movement, she also learned of the Malthusian League and the formative influence of Malthusian ideas in propelling public health policy regarding reproduction across the world,[17] including in India where there was a Neo-Malthusian League established in 1928.[18] In tracing the history of reproductive rights work, Wadia notes the racist history of industrial scale forced sterilizations in many parts of Europe, such as Nazi Germany and Sweden where these were undertaken as national public health policy with varying degrees of Eugenicist discourses of legitimation. While critical of such practices, Wadia is strikingly silent on the racist dimensions of many Malthusian ideas

[14] Avabai Bomanji Wadia, *This Light is Ours* (International Planned Parenthood Federation 2001) 102.

[15] Through her mothers' involvement in theosophical networks, Wadia met the feminist and socialist Annie Besant when she was just a schoolgirl in Colombo and it was Besant who influenced Wadia's family to send Wadia to England for higher studies.

[16] For instance, under the leadership of Harold Laski, the Fabian Society collaborated with many members of the radical anti-colonial leadership in Ceylon such as NM Perera and Colvin R de Silva, students of Laski at the London School of Economics. In India too leading figures such as Nehru had been members of the Fabian Society and found that many British Fabians were comrades in the fight against colonialism. At the same time, historically, the Fabian Society supported Malthusian ideas of social reform and the pre-Laski Fabian Society subscribed to various eugenicist theories that remained a significant dimension of reproductive politics.

[17] Wadia (n 14) 130–31. As she notes in her memoir, the *Malthusian League* convened the first international conference on reproduction in 1900; subsequent conferences drew people like the American Margaret Sanger who until then had been operating primarily in their national contexts. Sanger herself became a noted supporter of eugenicist ideas.

[18] ibid 496.

in her everyday political engagement. She seems to have focused her alliances on the fact that many of these individuals and groups (such as the Madras branch of the Neo-Malthusian League) were strong advocates of women's education.[19] In areas such as public health and public education, racist and classist notions of civilization got baked into technocratic notions of social reform and progress. In the post-colonial context, these shaped the developmental state and the postcolonial vision of modernity central to figures like Jawaharlal Nehru. It is significant perhaps that Wadia's direct exposure to reproductive rights circles took place not in London where she was fighting racism and colonialism but decades later in India. Moreover, her own reproductive politics were shaped by women's groups who situated it as a political issue in relation to a range of women's rights issues (such as sexual freedom), rather than by public health technocrats developing programs for population control.

Wadia met some of the key Indian women's rights activists who drew her into more concerted engagement on reproductive rights in London as they travelled there as part of the Indian anti-colonial movement. Wadia was effectively adopted as their protegee and got an extraordinary front seat view of a transnational anti-colonial and proto-feminist community that she helped shape further. The ties she established with women leaders proved especially significant in defining her trajectory and the opportunities available to her when she returned to South Asia. Wadia emerged thus from an 'old girls network' that drew on an elite, cosmopolitan community that moved through the world with ease even when opposing the empire. For her these Indian networks soon grew to be global in reach—Wadia describes hosting Madam Soong Ching-Ling who later became Vice President of China, and then Wadia herself being hosted by Princess Ashraff and the High Council of Women's Associations in Iran. AIWC is also in correspondence with women's rights groups all over the world as they collaborate on feminist and anti-colonial agendas—for instance, Madam Pasha of Egypt writes to the AIWC expressing hope of a transnational alliance—or 'a strong block to work for the good and betterment of the oriental world, and realize peace, plenty and justice for all of us'.[20]

As noted above, one of the most significant dimensions of this community emerged precisely from the anti-imperial struggles that fueled their place in the public sphere. For these groups, women's activism, the national freedom struggle, and transnational solidarities were deeply intertwined. Thus Wadia describes the 18th national AIWC meeting in Hyderabad, in December 1945 as involving leaders of the South Asian women's movements as well as representatives of the women's movement from across Asia. They drew on this transnational community in seeking to pressure international institutions such as the International Labor Organization on labor conditions in sectors central to colonial economies such as tea plantations and mines, and basic welfare policy in relation to questions of poverty relief and food distribution. Similarly, Wadia was an AIWC delegate at the Asian Relations Conference that Nehru convened in Delhi; this was yet another meeting that in hindsight we can plot as being on the road to Bandung. Wadia's own reports of these meetings at the dawn of Indian

[19] This is equally true of her international alliances; thus when she speaks of Helvi Sipilä (also profiled in this book) she speaks not of any alliance between Sipilä and Scandinavian neo-Malthusian projects but of Sipilä's gracious hosting as the Secretary General of the 1975 Mexico conference on women's rights.

[20] Pasha's letter to the AIWC quoted in Wadia (n 14) 107.

independence capture the electrifying sense of possibility that marked the hopes for a Pan-Asian renaissance in that moment.[21]

Against the backdrop of Asian and African countries attaining independence and shaping national policy for their postcolonial futures, internationalist feminist activists such as Wadia saw international organizations as an important arena for legal and policy development. These activists impacted the lawmaking function of international organizations on a range of topics, from global public health to the new regulations relating to nightwork in mines. When looking at the shaping of the human rights covenants that finally passed in 1966, the lines of influence between civil society initiatives and hard law is not always direct and immediate but they are significant in shaping the enabling milieu for such international legal developments. AIWC was the first national organization in the world to be granted consultative status with the United Nations Economic and Social Council (ECOSOC) and as head of its Mumbai office Wadia was responsible for drafting and submitting reports to ECOSOC for the first several years.

AIWC developed a women's charter that set out principles and priorities for independent India—its significance was amplified because AIWCs ECOSOC role was also seen as a form of representation for women in Asia more generally. The women's charter and other AIWC initiatives developed in the Indian context brought to the fore issues such as gendered poverty in rural areas, public health policy addressing maternal mortality, and priorities and programs for girls' education. As similar questions were being grappled with in countries emerging from colonialism, the Indian discussions also shaped the global conversation about the postcolonial development agenda at the newly formed United Nations (UN). As Wadia notes, in 1952 when IPPF was founded India was the only country 'promoting a family planning program and there was no UN program' but just twenty years later there were forty such national programs.[22]

India played an outsize role in this inaugural moment of the UN.[23] While the UN had been established in the Allies' moment of military triumph over Germany, the Second World War took place against the backdrop of anti-colonial struggles across the world and figures like Nehru believed that the UN's postcolonial future was worth fighting for. Even as colonial forces were repeatedly defeated in colonial theatres across Asia and Africa, the UN itself became the new battleground: was it going to be a new institutional vehicle for neocolonial management of insurgent nations or the platform for a new international order premised on an anti-imperial ethos? These battles would unfold over the next few decades with the General Assembly's 1974 passage of the NIEO declaration as the initially triumphant, if eventually doomed, expression of the latter vision.

In the first years of the UN, there was real hope that the General Assembly could be the route to democratizing the global public sphere. Assessing India's successful defeat of South African agendas for the UN's approach to questions of apartheid,

[21] Nehrus speech at the Asian Relations Conference quoted in Mark Mazower, *No Enchanted Palace: The End of Empire and the Ideological Origins of the United Nations* (Princeton 2009) 187.

[22] Wadia (n 14) 256.

[23] Mazower (n 21); Manu Bhagavan, *The Peacemakers: India and the Quest for One World* (Harper Collins 2012).

Mark Mazower notes that the Nehruvian strategy of using the General Assembly to mobilize support amongst countries from the global south blazed a trail for institutional manoeuvering and influenced soft law developments for decades to come. South-South solidarities shaped General Assembly positions regarding the political situation in countries such as South Africa and Palestine; it was also pivotal in treaty development such as the shared first article on the right to self-determination in the 1966 human rights covenants or, in the next decade, negotiations over the law of the sea. In the heyday of non-alignment, looking back and looking forward, the General Assembly passed a dizzying array of global south generated resolutions such as the 1960 Declaration on Decolonization, the 1973 resolution in support of the New International Economic Order, and the 1986 Declaration on the Right to Development. Adom Getachaw argues that the 1960 Declaration on Decolonization was indication that 'Within fifteen years anticolonial nationalists had successfully captured the UN and transformed the General Assembly into a platform for the international politics of decolonization.'[24]

Wadia was shaped by Nehruvian modernism in her view of the design of international institutions and their potential for shaping lives and nations—she treated it as a sacred responsibility. If Wadia's law school years and early adulthood was shaped by the anticolonial solidarities and resistance networks in London in the inter-war period, it was the prospect of postcolonial institutionalism that emerges as the signature dimension of her career in the post-war era. For Wadia this was not about being a functionary within international institutions. The UN assiduously tried to recruit her to become Director of UNESCO's Education department, begging her to reconsider when she turned them down. Instead, Wadia was interested in shaping international institutions such as the WHO and the ILO from the South. Nehru famously aligned his nationalism and internationalism: 'We march to the one world of tomorrow where national cultures will be intermingled with the international culture of the human race.... we shall remain true Indians and Asiatics, and become at the same time good internationalists and world citizens.'[25] Wadia was recruited to this fundamentally optimistic and humanistic Nehruvian notion of being citizens of their counties but also of the world.

Reproductive Rights Activism on the International Plane

The control of intimacy has always been a central dimension of global governance in a wide range of contexts and historical circumstances, be it in the Code Noir's rules regarding parentage in the context of slavery, or refugee law rules about family reunification. Yet, as feminist international lawyers have argued, the most powerful rule in this governance regime is the public/private dichotomy. Three decades ago, Hilary Charlesworth, Christine Chinkin, and Shelley Wright argued, in a now canonical article, that contesting the work of the public/private distinction 'to redefine the

[24] Adom Getachaw, *Worldmaking after Empire: The Rise and Fall of Self-Determination* (Princeton University Press 2020) 73.

[25] Nehru, *The Discovery of India* (John Day Co 1946) 540.

traditional scope of international law' was central to re-imaging the possibilities for international law, and realizing its promise.[26] Wadia's feminist internationalism found its most powerful expression in engaging precisely in this contestation through her work on reproductive rights. Characteristically, Wadia didn't frame her work and vision in antagonistic terms but she advocated for a certain ideological revolution prioritizing matters of contraception and reproductive rights in international bodies such as the World Health Organization.[27] Today these issues have become so normalized in development and international public health agendas that it might be difficult to appreciate the extraordinary activism and advocacy that took place over many decades to ensure these intimate matters of family planning became such an important part of the work of international institutions.[28]

Wadia channeled all her previous work on a range of women's rights issues into a focus on reproductive rights with the founding of IPPF in 1952. IPPF was founded in collaboration with reproductive rights activists from around the world, including Margaret Sanger who founded the first American birth control clinic and the Planned Parenthood Federation of America. The IPPF built on eight such national initiatives and its 1952 founding was at a Conference on Planned Parenthood that brought together reproductive rights activists from sixteen countries. The work IPPF undertook was at the intersection of legal, medical, and development work. Since then, reproductive rights have remained central to international law, global public health, and international development. Within international law, its most prominent articulation emerged at the Fourth World Conference on Women convened in Beijing, 1995. After extensive debate and much controversy, The Beijing Platform for Action recognized the right 'to be informed and to have access to safe, effective, affordable and acceptable methods of family planning of their choice, as well as other methods of their choice for regulation of fertility which are not against the law'.[29]

In the fifty years following the founding of IPPF Wadia devoted her life to its work. In the early years much of her work focused on developing the institutional infrastructure, consolidating the IPPF charter, establishing its regional chapters, and various policies and protocols enabling IPPF to expand globally and implement its mandate. Her memoir describes a busy agenda advancing this mission through visits to reproductive health clinics worldwide, local and regional conferences on topics such as healthcare, contraception, and sex education, conversations in conference corridors and post-conference receptions, forming alliances with local groups in Korea, Kenya, Ceylon, Singapore, Nepal, China, and elsewhere over the course of several years.

[26] Hilary Charlesworth, Christine Chinkin, and Shelley Wright, 'Feminist Approaches to International Law' (1991) 85(4) AJIL 613–45.

[27] In 1965, after many uphill battles reproductive rights became a part of WHO work (241, 245). See Wadia's notes for the May 1965 Geneva meeting of the World Health Assembly (246).

[28] It was a political vision that foregrounded public health and development expertise as core to its interventions, be it in relation to national policy agendas for technocratic social reform that we noted earlier, or in relation to the complementary work of international institutions in supporting the modernist developmental state model, Wadia's work offers a case study of the reach of expertise in reproductive rights in impacting international law and policy. David W Kennedy, *A World of Struggle: How Power, Law and Expertise Shape Global Political Economy* (Princeton 2016).

[29] Beijing Declaration and Platform for Action, art 94 at 57 <https://www.unwomen.org/sites/default/files/Headquarters/Attachments/Sections/CSW/PFA_E_Final_WEB.pdf> accessed 1 October 2022.

Wadia's work offers a powerful instance of Sally Merry's anthropological portrait of women's rights law making at the UN through the circulation of transnational networks of women's rights activists who convene in conferences and boardrooms to frame agendas, debate language, and develop model legal frameworks before dispersing to their national contexts where they broker knowledge and negotiate priorities in ways that traverse and shape the boundaries between local and global.[30]

IPPF encountered a minefield of political debates across the globe. Reproductive rights remained a fraught arena characterized by diverse challenges such as Euro-American eugenics theories, Malthusian economic development models, China's one child policy, the Vatican's opposition to birth control, and the Reagan administration's 'family values' campaign. Wadia delicately negotiated around these challenges through a focus on solidarity with local women's groups, material support to regional offices and their local health clinics, alongside active use of her international platform to make the case for reproductive rights. After consolidating the organizational structure of IPPF, Wadia's focus turned to institutionalizing the IPPF agenda within the UN, development agencies, public health organizations, and perhaps most critically, ensuring it remained a priority for the international women's movement. Wadia travelled across the world and took the IPPF platform to all the key conferences on population, development, and women, from Nairobi to Mexico.

Ten years prior to Beijing, in one of many efforts to lay the groundwork for the Beijing conference at the UN, Wadia visited New York in the middle of the Reagan years for meetings and negotiations with different stakeholders battling concerted pushback from the American administration. *The New York Times* reported on one of these meetings noting that 'At first glance, Wadia does not strike those around her as a person in the vortex of one of the world's most divisive issues—population control. Refined, small in stature and ever so slightly stooped as she begins her seventy-third year, she does not look like an advocate of any sort. Indeed, when she attended an awards ceremony at the United Nations, she sat on the dais, a lone woman dwarfed by the gray-suited men on either side.'[31] The report then adds that those first impressions are dramatically revised once Wadia takes the podium to powerfully and persuasively make her case. She comes armed with statistics about maternal mortality and rising populations, and the political and ethical case for women and families to have control over their bodies and reproductive futures. Noting the rapt audience, *The New York Times* says that 'when it comes to promoting family planning worldwide, Mrs. Wadia, president of the [IPPF], has few equals'.[32]

Wadia was a 'grand dame' of this world—anchored in the global south but also a global player, who helped found the networks and pathways through which those agendas and knowledges were circulated. One of the distinct aspects of Wadia's approach to IPPF was what we might call a philosophy of 'vernacularization', to borrow Merry's term for this bridging discourse. From its inauguration in 1952, she pushed

[30] Sally Engle Merry, 'Transnational Human Rights and Local Activism: Mapping the Middle' (2006) 108(1) American Anthropologist 38–51.

[31] <www.nytimes.com/1985/09/23/style/a-voice-for-control-of-the-population-explosion.html> accessed 1 October 2022.

[32] ibid.

back against the efforts of Sanger and others to develop a more centralized model and instead advocated successfully to ensure the regional IPPF chapters had the autonomy to develop agendas in ways that were embedded in local approaches. Wadia says that 'think globally act locally' was the motto guiding IPPF staff and described the organization as a 'decentralized federation' that took 'into account the realities of geographical, cultural, ethical, religious and linguistic differences in a world setting'.[33] She describes an ongoing and delicate negotiation with western dominance—by staff in the London office or by donors and donor agendas—and the need to steer the organization in ways that retained organizational unity and the flow of funding while being anchored in 'third world aspirations'.[34]

Wadia's work as a representative of an NGO and an advocate of a social movement offer a testament to the central, yet underappreciated, role of non-state diplomatic initiatives in the making of international law and policy. In all these small and big engagements and negotiations, Wadia and the institutional offices of the IPPF constituted a very real continuation of the substantive transnational engagements that Karia described in speaking of women's diplomacy in terms of the " 'Forgotten Femissaries' of the Afro-Asian World".[35]

Conclusion

The title of this chapter is a nod to Martti Koskenniemi's pioneering project of telling the story of international law through the work of individual protagonists in the international law story.[36] This chapter is influenced by that methodology but is also in conversation with the questions it raises about which protagonists we foreground in such an effort. In *The Gentle Civilizer of Nations*, Koskenniemi uses the story of four influential European lawyers/academics to argue that international law developed through an evolving conception of its mission as a gentle civilizer, providing liberal scaffolding for a world in motion, from the era of empire to a community of sovereign nations.[37] Wadia was a co-traveller of international law in the twentieth century and could be seen as a gentle rebel against that vision of liberal cosmopolitanism. From a minority Parsee community, from the small country of Ceylon, she made the world her own by creating or finding networks of allies and comrades wherever she went. Perhaps most radically, for over five decades, her work determinedly underscored that the personal was political, challenging an international law and policy landscape framed through the public/private dichotomy. Her feminism and anti-imperialism offer a different way

[33] Wadia (n 14) 259, 291.

[34] ibid 292. Moreover, Wadia's feminist internationalism continued to be her load star in this work—she recalls being in Belgrade for the 1965 Population Conference when war broke out between India and Pakistan and her very conscious overtures to Begum Salim Khan of Pakistan in Belgrade, and then in London because her IPPF solidarities trumped her nationalism.

[35] <www.mcgill.ca/arts-internships/files/arts-internships/aria_final_poster_garima_karia.pdf>accessed 1 October 2022.

[36] Martti Koskenniemi, *The Gentle Civilizer of Nations: The Rise and Fall of International Law 1870-1960* (Cambridge University Press 2001).

[37] The protagonists of Koskenniemi's story are Hans Kelsen, Hersch Lauterpacht, Carl Schmitt, and Hans Morgenthau.

of engaging international law that both extended its promise for forging internationalist solidarities, but also illuminated the limits of its historic inheritances, including the vision of civilizational hierarchies that animated international law's dark side.

However, the story of Wadia's legacy of rebellion is much more complicated given the white supremist, Brahminical,[38] and classist narrative on family planning that were also co-travellers to her life's work with IPPF. There were civilizational narratives embedded in conceptions of the modern family and the modern nation, and many of Wadia's most prominent collaborators were advocates of Malthusian and eugenicist arguments regarding the need to curb populations in the global south.[39]

In Wadia's work reproductive self-determination was tied to questions of national self-determination. Her feminist internationalism emerged from solidarities forged in resistance movements and her strong commitment to local self-determination shaped her approach to IPPF's organizational structure. Thus, she did not challenge Margaret Sanger's eugenicist views directly and considered Sanger a valued ally; however, her pushback against Sanger's centralizing vision for IPPF could be seen as a gentle back-door negotiation against white supremist or global North dominance.[40] These themes recur in her resistance to the Reagan administration seeking to projects its own 'family values' policies onto international public health programs. Wadia herself did not subscribe to racist and castist arguments and her approach to reproductive rights foregrounded feminist solidarities with women seeking self-determination over their reproductive capacities, often against patriarchal efforts to undermine that self-determination. The reproductive freedoms Wadia fought for remain especially significant for women of colour, minority women, Dalit women, tribal women, and indigent women all over India.

Nevertheless, Wadia was also willing to build strategic alliances with activists and policy makers (such as Sanger) whose family planning politics were infused with racial, caste, and class prejudice. Not unlike the white men from the global North who have a starring role in the plot of *The Gentle Civilizer of Nations*, Wadia too was willing to move in elite circles of international and national law and policy and collaborate with actors and institutions constituted by the structures and ideologies of white supremist and Brahminical projects. Her rebellious legacy therefore warrants

[38] Brahminical refers here to the beliefs and structures that undergird the structures of caste oppression. Uma Chakravarti's conceptualization of Brahminical patriarchy captures how 'Caste hierarchy and gender hierarchy' are interlinked in controlling women's sexuality to ensure caste purity and patrilineal succession. Thus the realm of family planning carried important stakes for a Brahminical social order. A 'combination of consent and coercion' secured the participation of upper cast women in policies directed at controlling the sexuality and reproductive capacity of dalit women or women deemed lower caste: Chakravarti, 'Conceptualising Brahmanical Patriarchy in Early India: Gender, Caste, Class and State' (3 April 1993) 28(14) Economic and Political Weekly. As a Parsee, Wadia herself was not part of the Hindu caste system. However, much of the early AIWC leadership were upper caste Hindu women, some of whom contested the caste system, while others were complicit.

[39] Relatedly, in India neo-Malthusian logics gained traction with those seeking to curb dalit and tribal populations; it is not difficult to see contemporary Hindutva efforts to curb Muslim populations as carrying a related provenance.

[40] In her own tribute to Sanger, Wadia speaks of Sanger in ways that reflect on their shared history of activism as no linear progress narrative 'towards a distant light'— rather it is a more complicated story of 'hard and self-sacrificing decisions, over and over again, having to contend with self-doubts and fears which crop up in any creative undertaking'. <alexandersanger.com/2005/09/08/tribute-to-avabai-wadia> accessed 3 October 2022.

a question mark; it is a question mark that haunts Wadia's story and the biases baked into the perspective of international law and policy that IPPF has represented at different stages in its history. Wadia's story is complicated and her rebellion against the imperial ambitions of the discourse and projects of imperial 'civilization' is not a story of determined resistance at every turn. The gentleness of her rebellion might be both compliment and indictment.[41]

[41] My thanks to Immi Tallgren and Parvathi Menon for comments on this piece as a whole but especially for their encouragement that I mark the complications in the Wadia story in relation to questions of race and caste.

PART V

THE HALL OF DIVERSITY OF FEMINIST ACTIVISM IN INTERNATIONAL LAW

11

Ghénia Avril de Sainte-Croix

Abolitionism and the League of Nations

*Frédéric Mégret**

Ghénia Avril de Sainte-Croix (full name: Adrienne-Pierette-Eugénie Glaisette Avril de Sainte-Croix; nom de plume: Savioz) was a Swiss-born, leading French feminist of the late nineteenth and early twentieth centuries. An author and journalist of Protestant background, she was heavily involved in social reform and philanthropic work. She headed the Conseil National des Femmes Françaises (CNFF) between 1922 and 1932 and was very active in the International Council of Women (ICW). Whilst her status as a formidable feminist activist and thinker has been bolstered in the last decades,[1] she is not typically associated with the world of international law.

Nonetheless, as a founding member of the International Abolitionist Federation which argued against state regulated prostitution (notably licensed *maisons closes*), de Sainte-Croix translated her considerable domestic and transnational expertise in Versailles and, subsequently, at the League of Nations. She was recognized in 1922 after becoming a member of the League's Permanent Advisory Committee on Traffic in Women and Children. Her contributions there, especially her highly influential reports, included nudging the League away from referring to *la traite des blanches* towards a defence of all women, connecting the issues of sexual exploitation and migration, and shifting arguments about prostitution from one concerned with public health to one focused on women's dignity.

This chapter examines de Sainte-Croix's role as an early feminist in international law at a time of great optimism in international circles about the prospects of international regulation when the League was tempted to defer to strong early feminist voices on social issues. To examine the story of de Sainte-Croix from the perspective of international law is, nonetheless, to ask for intellectual trouble. De Sainte-Croix was not a lawyer, let alone an international lawyer, and likely had only a lateral familiarity with the discipline. Although often noted as influential, it remains hard to gauge her exact impact in what remained above all a collective endeavour by civil society representatives to change the international status quo.

What, indeed, does it mean to tell the story of international law beyond its canon by including figures who have traditionally not been associated with it? Is it, to use the

* I am grateful to Karen Engle for very useful feedback on an earlier draft of this chapter.

[1] Karen Offen, 'Madame Ghénia Avril de Sainte-Croix, the Josephine Butler of France' (2008) 17 Women's History Review 239.

Frédéric Mégret, *Ghénia Avril de Sainte-Croix* In: *Portraits of Women in International Law.* Edited by: Immi Tallgren, Oxford University Press. DOI: 10.1093/oso/9780198868453.003.0011

Figure 11.1 Portrait of Eugénie Avril de Sainte-Croix.
Source: Bibliothèque nationale de France, département Estampes et photographie, N-2.

words of Immi Tallgren, to highlight either an 'absence' or an 'invisibility', or both, or something in between?[2] What would it mean to write the history of international law if we were to take seriously the role that a priori relatively marginal figures such as de Sainte-Croix played (or did not play) in it?[3] What might writing more 'comprehensive

[2] Immi Tallgren, 'Absent or Invisible? Women Intellectuals and the "Dawn of the Discipline"' in Immi Tallgren and Frédéric Mégret (eds), *The Dawn of the Discipline: International Criminal Justice and its Early Exponents* (Cambridge University Press 2020).

[3] ibid.

histories' tell us about how international law could be conceived differently and about its implicit gendering?

What de Sainte-Croix was for certain, was a feminist social crusader who frequented the high temples of international governance. She rightly believed that a particular kind of inter-war internationalism would help her lifelong fight against sexual slavery. She was more than a footnote in the history of the League of Nations, its emerging humanitarian sensitivity, and its attempt to foster peace through law. Much of her earlier work concerned the unequal gendered application of sexual laws, including policing prostitution. Her relevance to international law, then, goes beyond simply 'having been there'.[4] Though she did not articulate a specific legal doctrine in the way conventional international lawyers might, she interacted dynamically with the law throughout her life.

To study her life, then, is to study how an influential early feminist could both seize the opportunities afforded to her by the League of Nations to shape its international legal regime and experience the limitations imposed on women in the higher reaches of international governance. This chapter draws on the work of researchers who have studied de Sainte-Croix's life as part of the history of early European and French feminism[5] as well as research on the work of the League in the area of prostitution and human trafficking.[6] It complements prior archival research on the League by paying attention to the historiography of international law and what de Sainte-Croix's trajectory may mean for international law in general. To understand said trajectory, it is important to (a) contextualize the social and political struggles in France , and then (b) examine how her work gradually matured into a more explicit, even if limited, public international element.

Early Feminist and Abolitionist

De Sainte-Croix was one of the founders of the CNFF in 1900, in the crucible of the French Third Republic. Over the span of her career, she would become associated with the entire arc of the effort to abolish prostitution. The 'abolitionist' movement, as it was then known, had emerged in the UK under the influence of Josephine Butler against the so-called 'regulatory approach' and in particular the tolerance of *maisons closes*. It was a complex movement traversed by contradictory currents, but its inspiration included early liberal ideas hostile to state intervention in private

[4] ibid 382.

[5] 'Offen (K.), "La plus Grande Féministe de France" (...) Mme Avril de Sainte-Croix | Archives Du Féminisme' <https://www.archivesdufeminisme.fr/sommaires-des-bulletins/bulletin-09/offen-k-grande-feministe-france-mme-avril-sainte-croix/> accessed 9 September 2020; Karen Offen, 'Intrepid Crusader: Ghénia Avril de Sainte-Croix Takes on the Prostitution Issue' (2005) 33 Proceedings of the Western Society for French History <http://hdl.handle.net/2027/spo.0642292.0033.022>> accessed 9 September 2020.

[6] Monique Constant, 'Combats contre la traite des femmes à la Société des Nations (1920-1940)' (2007) 131 Relations internationales 39; Magaly Rodríguez García, 'The League of Nations and the Moral Recruitment of Women' (2012) 57 International Review of Social History 97; Magaly Rodríguez García, 'La Société des Nations face à la traite des femmes et au travail sexuel à l'échelle mondiale' (2012) 241 Le Mouvement Social 109.

affairs; conservative-moral ideas about redemption of prostitutes; Western paranoia about imagined exploitation of European women by the 'Orient;' concerns about uncontrolled migration and competition by 'foreign prostitutes'; and prophylactic ideas about 'social hygiene' particularly associated with fears over venereal diseases. Parts of the movement targeted the very idea of prostitution, whilst other strands were primarily concerned with trafficking.

De Sainte-Croix was undeniably one of the intellectual leaders of the abolitionist camp, especially in the French speaking world. In France, she had founded the Oeuvre Libératrice which sought to provide prostitutes with a refuge, income, and training to escape prostitution. She was chosen as a member of a governmental mission which, from 1904 to 1909, investigated the role of the *police des moeurs* (the vice squad). She was also very active in early transnational feminist networks which had blossomed following the emergence of like-minded initiatives in European countries and the United States. She was associated with the Fédération Abolitionniste Internationale and had participated in an international congress on the White Slave Trade in London as early as 1899. She was a leading figure in the International Council of Women and chaired its committee on the 'White Slave Traffic' and 'Equal Moral Standard' and subsequently became its vice-president for decades.

In 'La Serve', an especially vigorous early article published in 1898 in the feminist Dreyfusard newspaper *La Fronde*, Sainte-Croix drew an explicit analogy between feudal serfdom and the condition of women in prostitution. She appealed to her fellow women to 'shed these shameful chains, the last official ones, of the most pitiable of slaves.[7] Her prose was steeped in references to history and the classics, leaving no doubt about the longevity of the issue. She deplored the existence of a 'double morality': 'the prostitute is always the target, forgetting the *prostituting*' leading to a 'duality of state morality which punishes severely in women that which it tolerates, protects, with men'.[8] This displayed society's hypocrisy. Sainte-Croix, who was the 'particularly competent'[9] head of the commission for the 'unity of morality' at the Conseil International des Femmes, was incensed by claims that legalized prostitution would protect the sanctity of the sacred family 'foyer', when exactly the opposite was true (notably as a result of the spread of syphilis to wives via their bordel-patronizing husbands).

Sainte-Croix's rhetoric was strongly influenced by a certain spiritual register. She often described prostitutes as 'fallen' (*soeurs déchues*). Although one would hesitate to describe her feminism as paternalistic, it could be described as maternalistic. She regretted some women's false consciousness and tendency to 'simply repeat, without fully understanding them, the aphorisms produced by the male ego'.[10] At the same

[7] Savioz, 'La Serve' *La Fronde* (21 January 1898). (author's translation: '"faire tomber les chaînes honteuses, les dernières officielles, des plus pitoyables de toutes les esclaves"').

[8] ibid. ('"toujours on frappe la prostituée, oubliant le *prostituant*" leading to a "dualité de (la) morale d'Etat qui réprime sévèrement chez la femme ce qu'elle tolère, protège, chez l'homme"').

[9] Magdeleine Auteur du texte Boy, *Les associations internationales féminines: thèse soutenue... pour le doctorat en droit / par Magdeleine Boy; Université de Lyon, Faculté de droit* (1936) 60 <https://gallica.bnf.fr/ark:/12148/bpt6k9806545x> accessed 9 September 2020.

[10] Savioz (n 7) ('"répéter simplement, sans parfois les comprendre, les aphorismes émis par l'égoïsme masculin"').

time, she called for a genuine feminist political awakening to address prostitution. This would, in language evocative of much later debates on intersectionality, involve solidarity between women, particularly privileged women with their 'more desperate sisters'.[11] She urged women to speak publicly and loudly about matters of sexuality 'so that men will hear—men who have usurped the title of moralists'.[12] She denounced the patriarchal, neo-regulationist defence of *maisons de tolérance* based on the need to protect 'honourable women' from disrespectable *filles publiques*. Women should shun male protection of this sort, which came at the high cost of ratifying male behaviour that was at the heart of the problem. Male continence—rather than female sexual liberation—would be required. The 'woman question', as Karen Offen put it, ought to be reframed as much as possible as the 'man problem'.[13]

De Sainte-Croix emphasized the importance of sexual education and insisted on equal pay to better protect women from prostitution. She raged against the unintended and pernicious effects of regulated prostitution and the policing of women. First and foremost, she was an ardent defender of feminism, which was sometimes ridiculed in French political debate ('Feminism abroad, with its noisy manifestations, seemed perfectly ridiculous in our measured country').[14] Although her feminism was largely 'conservatism tainted social feminism' described by Monique Constant,[15] its intonation when it comes to the issue of prostitution was strikingly modern.

But perhaps de Sainte-Croix's most notable intellectual contribution to the history of the fight against prostitution, particularly its legal dimensions, was the explicit connection she forged with human rights. Her main target at times was not so much prostitution as officially sanctioned, state-organized prostitution—*lès prostituées officielles*. She revealed a stark liberal sensitivity, one that considered that 'the role of the police must be confined to suppressing scandal in the street; if it goes further, it exceeds its rights'.[16] In 'La Serve', she had noted that even if the prophylactic regulation of prostitution was successful in limiting the spread of venereal diseases, it should still be fought on dignity grounds: women could under no circumstance be made into the government's slaves.[17]

Pushing the French revolutionary analogy, she gladly compared *maisons closes* with *Bastilles*. In 1900, at the Paris Congress on the condition and rights of women, she was one of the first to analyse the fate of prostitutes from a rights perspective.[18] In 1907, she

[11] Karen Offen, 'Is the "Woman Question" Really the "Man Problem"?' in Christopher E Forth and Elinor Accampo (eds), *Confronting Modernity in Fin-de-Siècle France: Bodies, Minds and Gender* (Palgrave Macmillan UK 2010) 55 <https://doi.org/10.1057/9780230246843_3> accessed 9 September 2020.

[12] Andrea Mansker, 'Shaming Men: Feminist Honor and the Sexual Double Standard in Belle Epoque France' in Christopher E Forth and E Elinor Accampo (eds), *Confronting Modernity in Fin-de-Siècle France: Bodies, Minds and Gender* (Palgrave Macmillan UK 2010) 176.

[13] Offen (n 11).

[14] Marie-Louise Puech, 'La Femme Française et La Société Des Nations' [1922] France & Monde. ('Le féminisme à l'étranger, avec ses manifestations bruyantes paraissait parfaitement ridicule et déplacé dans notre pays de mesure').

[15] Monique Constant, 'Combats contre la traite des femmes à la Société des Nations (1920–1940)' (2007) 131 Relations internationales 39. ('féminisme social fortement teinté de moralisme').

[16] ('Le rôle de la police doit se borner à supprimer le scandale dans la rue; plus loin, elle outrepasse ses droits.').

[17] Savioz (n 7).

[18] Une morale pour les deux sexes.

published a book, 'Le Féminisme', in which she compared the abolitionist movement to the struggle for *les droits de l'homme* and in particular the Etats Généraux of 1789. One of de Sainte-Croix's leading beliefs was that the state's function should be limited to maintaining public order and that going beyond this task denoted a violation of several articles of the Declaration of the Rights of Man. This meant above all that the prostitute herself should not be rendered responsible for an ill of which she was the principal victim.

In this context, she was particularly indignant that France was, since the Napoleonic campaigns that had first given rise to state regulated prostitution, an outlier. She pointed out that no member of Parliament had risen against prostitution since the adoption of the Déclaration des Droits du Citoyen.[19] At the same time and precisely because of this French precedent, she was not easily duped by modernity's false promises. Although appealing to the Rights of Man, she noted that the French Revolution had systematically ignored prostitution and in fact prolonged its punishment, regularly condemning prostitutes to infamy and ridicule.[20] Indeed, the French Revolution had invented its own, 'modern' reasons to keep control over prostitutes no longer 'in the name of the King, of religion, or of morality' but in that of 'public health'.[21]

At the League of Nations

After the First World War, de Sainte-Croix, who had been on all fronts of the feminist struggle in France, was well poised to take advantage of new international opportunities afforded by the 1920s. She briefly met Woodrow Wilson in Paris on the margins of the Versailles Conference as part of a delegation of 'grateful' French women, although Wilson told them he could not do much to favour women's suffrage within sovereign countries.[22] At any rate, the inter-war period bristled with early feminist projects. Though not necessarily in the jargon of international law, these projects certainly impacted it. The feeling among the CNFF, which encountered much resistance from the French government towards abolitionist ideas, was that 'the League of Nations is the best forum for women's activism to manifest itself'.[23] The state could in fact be circumvented to directly reach the international milieu.[24]

De Sainte-Croix on the international stage may have picked her fights carefully and her strategy was shaped by the limited opportunities available to her. There was no opening at the League for example to push a woman's suffrage agenda, and she largely left questions of international peace to others. In that respect, her international action

19 Savioz (n 7).
20 ibid.
21 ibid.
22 Mona L Siegel, *Peace on Our Terms: The Global Battle for Women's Rights After the First World War* (Columbia University Press 2020).
23 Pichon-Landry, 'Rapport Du Secrétaire Général' *Conseil national des femmes françaises—revue trimestrielle* (1 January 1922) 7: ('la Société des Nations est le meilleur terrain où puisse s'exercer l'action des femmes').
24 Christine Machiels, '"Protégeons la jeunesse!". Maria Vérone, une avocate féministe face à la prostitution des mineur(e)s (1907–1938)' [2008] Revue d'histoire de l'enfance 'irrégulière'. Le Temps de l'histoire 119.

was very much a prolongation of her domestic and transnational work on abolition[25] and a good fit for the League's new responsibilities. As with the abolition of slavery, the international character of trafficking made it particularly susceptible to international regulation and was as such an obvious tactical starting point for abolitionists. De Sainte-Croix and other abolitionists may have thought that eradicating *la traite des femmes* would be conducive to eliminating prostitution altogether. They spared no energy in trying to convince the powers-that-be that the two were intimately linked.

Article 23c of the Covenant entrusted the League with the task of 'the general supervision over the execution of agreements with regard to the traffic in women and children'. A 1921 conference had led to the International Convention for the Suppression of the Traffic in Women and Children which reprised, modernized, and broadened an earlier 1910 treaty. Sainte-Croix had been considered as a member of the French delegation but was ultimately deemed too radical and replaced by Marguerite de Witt-Schlumberger.[26] The conference witnessed an internationalization and rekindling of the controversy between abolitionists (mostly Northern European countries) and those supportive of a regulatory approach (first among which were France's *réglementaristes*) which created tensions between former allies. Women's NGOs tended to fall on the side of abolitionism, drawing a necessary link between brothels and trafficking.[27] A Consultative Commission on the Traffic of Women emerged which would serve as the background against which some of these controversies continued to crystallize.

Within the sites of international governance, de Sainte-Croix occupied three roles. First, she acted as a leading member and agitator for French and international feminist organizations and never abandoned that position despite her relatively constant institutional presence in Geneva. Second, she was part of early efforts to institutionalize civil society representation within the League. Specifically, she ended up being the representative of the Committee of Women's International Organizations before the League of Nations 1925–1931. Third, de Sainte-Croix was an emerging 'international expert', co-opted by the League to participate in some of its standard-setting activities. For example, she was made a delegate in the League's sub-commission on social questions. She was also a member of the Commission on the Protection of Childhood. Most importantly, she was a member (*assesseur*) of the Advisory Committee on the Traffic in Women and Children of the League which was composed of (mostly male) governmental delegates but also five civil society assessors supposed to represent major organizations invested in the issue. This was in itself a remarkable achievement.[28]

As the *assesseur* for International Women's Organizations, sitting alongside more confessionally specific organizations (such as the International Catholic Association for the Protection of Girls or the Jewish Association for the Protection of Girls and Women) and some more compromised by their commitment to the regulation of prostitution (the International Bureau), de Sainte-Croix's position was particularly

[25] Yolande Cohen, 'De parias à victimes. Mobilisations féministes sur la prostitution en France et au Canada (1880–1920)' [2014] Genre, sexualité & société <http://journals.openedition.org/gss/3157> accessed 10 September 2020.

[26] Constant (n 15).

[27] Henry Ruffin, *Croyez-vous à la Société des Nations?* (Plon-Nourrit et Cie 1924) 66.

[28] Offen, 'Intrepid Crusader' (n 5).

strategic. She behaved as a true representative of the civil society organizations (including the 200,000 strong association of French women), faithfully relaying their views. She did not hesitate, as she was frequently called upon to do, to adopt a stance at odds with that of the French government.[29] Indeed, her presence as a woman at the League in these various positions owed very little to France, which had only nominated men at the League Council or annual Assembly as representatives, and few women even in League commissions.

De Sainte-Croix's involvement with the League must be understood as part of the inter-war era's newfound enthusiasm for international solutions to complex domestic and transnational issues. At that time, although not all French women's organizations embraced the League,[30] those who did tended to conceive the League as a hospitable site for their project to 'create a binding supranational law when it came to social issues'.[31] The context was also one of domestic exclusion of women's political voices for most purposes, but where their expertise on 'women's issues' was beginning to be recognized.[32] A form of co-optation—what Magaly Rodríguez García described as the League's 'moral recruitment of women[33]—occurred which simultaneously gave some women a strategic opportunity to make their voices heard. At the same time, women's organizations were quite clear that the League needed them and that the CIF, with its 40 million members, could become the 'surest support' in international efforts.[34]

De Sainte-Croix soon emerged as a force to be reckoned with in the Committee on Trafficking where her particular mix of moral conservatism and feminist progressivism was evident. She wasted no time to point out that the International Council of Women had long been involved on a transnational basis in exactly the sort of efforts to fight trafficking that the League was now beginning to engage in. She relentlessly sought to tie the question of trafficking with that of licensed houses and regulated prostitution. In co-operation with fellow abolitionist Paulina Luisi from Uruguay, for example, she opposed a prohibition of the recruitment of foreign prostitutes in *maisons closes* because it seemed to imply that such places of prostitution were otherwise acceptable.[35] All in all, abolitionist slogans may have gotten more exposure internationally in the relatively rarefied air of Geneva than they might have elsewhere. The medical/hygienist justification for the *maisons closes* was gradually and effectively debunked.

More importantly, de Sainte-Croix seems to have taken to heart the need to gather and compile large amounts of information concerning governmental practices on prostitution. She dutifully assembled reports for the international women's organizations that she represented. The League of Nations Official Journal gives regular accounts throughout the 1920s and early 1930s of de Sainte-Croix presenting such

[29] Ruffin (n 27) 66–67.

[30] Puech (n 14) 483–84.

[31] Constant (n 15).

[32] Anne R Epstein, 'Gender and the rise of the female expert during the Belle Époque' (2011) 14 Histoire@Politique 84.

[33] García, 'The League of Nations and the Moral Recruitment of Women' (n 6).

[34] Pichon-Landry, 'Rapport' *Conseil national des femmes françaises—revue trimestrielle* (1 January 1926) 10.

[35] Report on the Work of the Committee on Traffic in Women and Children, Report on the Work of the Advisory Committee During Its Second Session (Geneva, 22–27 March 1923) (A.36.1923.IV).

reports, alongside other assessors, to the Committee. For example, in July 1932 she was credited with conveying international women's organizations' viewpoints on the forced or free repatriation of foreign prostitutes (opposed), the ratification of the 1923 Convention on obscene publications (in favour), the closure of brothels (in favour), or the creation of women-only police forces (in favour).[36] Much of the correspondence that the League archives have conserved involve her writing to various organizations and countries to elicit responses over questionnaires. The goal of such investigations was not to elucidate customary international law in the narrow sense but to highlight an emerging consensus on best practices.

The Committee, no doubt in part as a result of her work, departed from the public health approach favoured by many governments at the time to emphasize instead the need to protect women and children—a position that was still marginal among some League members but became dominant at the League itself.[37] De Sainte-Croix was obviously not alone and it helped that many other assessors, some governmental delegates (Paulina Luisi for example), and the staff of the social section of the League (headed through most of the 1920s by Dame Rachel Crowdy) were also women. The abolitionist position also had powerful representatives among states, notably Nordic ones. But it is not vain speculation to think that her work bore fruit in at least rallying more participants to the abolitionist cause. In the process, she had to contend not only with regulationist voices, but also 'paternalist abolitionists' who would have dealt with the problem of trafficking by doubling down on controls over women's mobility.[38]

It remains unclear nonetheless whether her painstaking work of information collection and representation ultimately shifted the lines of the debate. Certainly, de Sainte-Croix's international work had to deal not just with masculine hegemony but also nationalism and sovereignty (understood here as masculine claims to knowing what was best 'at home'), and the wariness of states to have the League dictate matters of social organization, especially those involving gender relations. By the 1930s her and other feminists' work would succumb to the rise of nationalism and the gradual evisceration of the League.

The Committee, whose reorganization had long been mooted much to de Sainte-Croix's dismay, disbanded and was replaced by a Social Questions Committee without the presence of civil society assessors. This was unmistakably part of a regulationist governmental ploy to reclaim the reins of policy-making at the League.[39] De Sainte-Croix's life ended in 1939 on the eve of the Second World War but also of some of the major changes in the condition of women that would take hold in the second half of the twentieth century. She would not witness the abolition of the *maisons closes* in France by Loi Marthe Richard in 1946, although she can certainly be credited with paving the way for such a change, both domestically and internationally.[40]

[36] League of Nations, Official Journal, 1932/07 (A13, N7) 1289.

[37] Jessica R Pliley, 'Claims to Protection: The Rise and Fall of Feminist Abolitionism in the League of Nations' Committee on the Traffic in Women and Children, 1919–1936' (2010) 22(4) Journal of Women's History 25.

[38] ibid 97.

[39] ibid 37.

[40] Interestingly though the abolition of *maisons closes* in France was in part related to the perception that the prostitution 'mafia' had been compromised with the Nazi occupier during the Second World War, an event not strictly related to the concern for women's dignity that de Ste Croix had historically championed.

Conclusion

A tireless advocate, de Sainte-Croix continued to be a vice-president of the Conseil International des Femmes and delegate at the League into her eighties, and was an object of occasional devotion by fellow French feminists.[41] Her legacy is obscured today by many new generations of feminists that have brought more radical ideas to bear, particularly on the questions of prostitution and trafficking. However, it is also remarkable how little has changed since the inter-war period and how the debate continues to be structured by an opposition between anti-trafficking and anti-prostitution camps.

The particular brand of feminist governance that was successfully inaugurated in the 1920s gradually fell apart in the 1930s, although one must be mindful that this was true of League structures in general. De Sainte-Croix was not invested in international legal structures for their own sake but because she saw that international governance and law had the potential to nudge countries towards a common position, which was much required to deal with the problem of prostitution. Foreshadowing later feminist theorizing, her career in a sense transcended the private (the morality of men and the lives of women) and the public (the regulation of women's bodies) as well as the domestic and the international, across which she moved seamlessly. She was spurred by feelings of moral indignation at the unequal treatment of women rather than abstract theorizing about the international system.

However, de Sainte-Croix may have been too busy, too genuinely committed to her single-minded desire to abolish prostitution and sex trafficking to emerge as a voice in the broader debates that structured the League. She was a meaningful participant, but a highly specialized one. It is not clear what her views were on an early form of international criminal law that emerged around the 1921 Convention. She was seemingly more concerned with not punishing women for prostitution than punishing male clients, and with broad social reforms than with wielding the power of criminal repression. Ultimately it might be argued that she was to be found where she was expected, 'in her place' as a woman specializing in 'traditionally feminine' issues, allowed a relative relevance and prominence only to the extent she did not overstep the bounds of her expertise.

Indeed, she did not stray much beyond a relatively siloed vision of the League's functionalism, which might have led her to critique the very international governance institutions within which she hoped to achieve progress for her cause. The organization of international society and attendance to the ever-crucial questions of war and peace, she was content to leave to men as part of a well understood division of labour. And although she rejected the term *traite des blanches* as too racially connoted, for all intents and purposes this was her primary concern and we have no reason to think that the question of the colonies (except as further outlets for male debauchery) was foremost in her mind.

[41] Comtesse Jean de Pange, 'Hommage à Mme Avril de Ste Croix' *La Presse* (13 February 1935).

Even when it came to the crucial issue of prostitution, her decade-long investment in the international struggle against trafficking did not fundamentally challenge its tolerance. Her feminism had to be toned down somewhat internationally, and the earlier fiery articles of 'Savioz' seem to have been tempered by age, socialization, and the weight of institutional logics. She may have been hamstrung by the sort of compromises that, paradoxically, made way for her expertise and suffered from a sort of self-perpetuating exclusion as a price of inclusion,[42] a price often paid by women experts in her time.[43] At worst, de Sainte-Croix may have served to merely prolong fruitless debates which states such as France never intended to take seriously, even as they enjoyed the benefits of appearing part of ongoing, progressist, and humanitarian, even feminist, conversations.

Nonetheless, within the limits of her role, she was certainly active, mobilized others, and made the most of the available opportunities. She helped develop tools such as state reporting that would become hallmarks of the monitoring of human rights or corruption much later in the twentieth century. She tirelessly invoked vague but meaningful trends in state practice and sought to bridge the gap between her strong moral and political views, human rights, and international law.

[42] Tallgren (n 2) 411.
[43] Epstein (n 32).

12

Yayori Matsui

Challenging the Silences of International Law through Pan Asian Feminist Solidarity

Keina Yoshida[*]

Introduction

This portrait sketches out the work carried out by Yayori Matsui (1934–2002), a Japanese journalist, women's rights activist and organizer of women's tribunals in Asia. Matsui is an important feminist figure who founded many women's rights organizations in Japan.[1] Significantly, the organization Violence against Women in War-Network, which Matsui founded, was the principal sponsor of the Women's International War Crimes Tribunal on Japan's Military Sexual Slavery held in Tokyo in 2000.[2] The Women's Tribunal, a peoples' tribunal, was held in December 2000 with the objective of putting Emperor Hirohito on trial for crimes against humanity and war crimes committed against the so-called 'comfort women'.[3] It looked to determine the state responsibility of Japan, putting pressure on the Japanese government to take legal responsibility for military sexual slavery. This portrait introduces Matsui's work and legacy through an exploration of her own words, her activism towards creating an anti-racist pan-Asian feminist solidarity movement, and her work to establish the Women's Tribunal.

Although Matsui was not an international lawyer by education or professional status, her impetus in establishing the Women's Tribunal in conjunction with others, was a significant moment in 'breaking the silence' around gender crimes, thus contributing to the development of a gender jurisprudence in international law.[4] Through her

* * Research for this piece was conducted in Tokyo and Kyoto in September 2019. A return trip to Yayori's archives was made impossible by the global pandemic. The author would like to thank Christine Chinkin, Mina Watanabe, Yoko Hayashi, and Miwa Atsuko. I visited the Kyoto Museum for World Peace, Ritsumeikan University and I am grateful to Professor Shinichi Ago for his guidance to the exhibition. I also visited the Women's Active Museum on War and Peace where Matsui's works are available.

[1] https://wam-peace.org/en/aboutaccessed 4 October 2021.

[2] Judgment on the Common Indictment and the Application for Restitution and Reparation, (4 December 2001) (Women's Int'l War Crimes Tribunal for the Trial of Japan's Military Sexual Slavery). Ustinia Dolgopol 'The Judgment of the Tokyo Women's Tribunal' (2003) 28(5) Alternative Law Journal 242; Karen Knop 'The Tokyo Women's Tribunal and the Turn to Fiction' in Fleur Johns, Sundhya Pahuja, and Richard Joyce (eds), *Events: The Force of International Law* (Taylor and France 2011) 45–164; Rumi Sakamoto 'The Women's International War Crimes Tribunal on Japan's Sexual Slavery: A Legal and Feminist Approach to the "Comfort Women" Issue' (2001) 3(1) New Zealand Journal of Asian Studies 49.

[3] Ianfu is the term used in Japan 慰安婦.

[4] Matsui is credited with having the idea of the Women's Tribunal in Tokyo. See the recent documentary Gendered Peace, the legacy of the Tokyo Women's Tribunal, available here: <https://www.lse.ac.uk/women-peace-security/research/Gendered-Peace-the-legacy-of-the-Tokyo-Womens-Tribunal>.

Keina Yoshida, *Yayori Matsui* In: *Portraits of Women in International Law.* Edited by: Immi Tallgren, Oxford University Press.
 DOI: 10.1093/oso/9780198868453.003.0012

Figure 12.1 Matsui (middle) at a dinner with judges and participants after the Women's War Crimes Tribunal, Tokyo, in December 2000.
Source: Courtesy of Christine Chinkin, personal archives.

activism Matsui expressed her deep belief in the power of international law to bring justice including in alternative forums such as women's tribunals. According to one Japanese international lawyer I spoke to, she also played a significant role in bringing international legal developments on gender crimes and its discourses into Japan.[5] This chapter introduces Matsui's life and journey towards working for gender equality within Japan in conjunction with feminist activists in Asia. Following an introduction to her background, the chapter explores how and why Matsui turned to alternative forums to develop international law in the quest for justice for gender crimes perpetrated by the Japanese imperial army.

[5] More generally on comparative law and Western legal influences in Japan see Annelise Riles 'From Comparison to Collaboration: Experiments with a New Scholarly and Political Form' (2015) Law and Contemporary Problems 78, 147–83. There is of course a long and independent history of international law in Japan. See Soji Yamamoto, International Law (2nd edn 1994), in English Soji Yamamoto, 'Japanese Approaches and Attitudes Towards International Law' (1991) 34 Japanese Annual Yearbook of International Law 115. Urs Mattias Zachermann 'The Reception and Use of International Law in Modern Japan, 1853–1945 ZJapanR Bd 19 Nr 37 (2014).

A Short Biography

The biographical information on Matsui's life is readily available in Japanese following the publication of her autobiography published one year after her death.[6] Visitors to Tokyo who are interested in Matsui's life can visit the Women's Active Museum on War and Peace (WAM) located near Waseda University which holds her books and archives, as well as Matsui's desk.[7] As part of the preparation for this chapter, I visited WAM in September 2019 and spoke to a number of Japanese women who knew Matsui. My interest in Matsui's work came from my own curiosity to know why she had advocated for the Tribunal. Through my conversations with feminist activists and Japanese international lawyers, I discovered that Matsui had been both an inspirational and controversial figure in Japan. I was told how her work on the Tribunal led to protests at her funeral from Japanese far right groups. I was also sent a number of biographies that Matsui had written of Japanese international female lawyers, including one who would later become a member of the Committee on the Elimination of Discrimination against Women.[8]

Yayori Matsui was born in Kyoto, in the Iwakura district (岩倉) on 12 April 1934. Iwakura is a quiet district in the North East of Kyoto, outside of the tourist map. Matsui's father was originally from a farming village and studied ceramics before disappointing his father and turning to Christianity. Matsui's mother was the youngest of six children. Her mother's father died when she was three years old and she had to give up her studies when she was young. Matsui's mother and father would meet at the prestigious Doshisha University in Kyoto, the old capital.

Following Matsui's parents' graduation from university the family moved to Tokyo where her father got a job in a church in Akasaka, Tokyo. That Matsui comes from a Christian household is immediately discernible to readers of Japanese from the kanji in her first name.[9] Matsui would instead use and publish under a *hiragana* version of her first name Yayori (やより) to avoid the immediate and 'heavy' Christian connotation.[10]

Matsui studied both in Japan and at universities in the United States and Paris which had a profound effect on the trajectory of her career. In Japan, she studied in the Department of English and American Studies in Tokyo University of Foreign Studies. Matsui went to the United States on a study abroad programme in 1957, to Harvard

6 『愛と怒り闘う勇気』岩波書店、2003年—YayoriMatsui,*CouragetoFight:LoveandAnger*(Iwamani Shoten Publishers 2003), hereafter *Courage to Fight*. There are also a number of obituaries which include biographical and personal information. For example in English see Yumiko Mikanagi 'In Memory of Matsui Yayori who 'Loved, Angered and Fought Courageously' International Feminist Journal of Politics (2010) 6(1) 141–49.

7 For more information see: Mina Watanabe 'Passing on the History of "Comfort Women": The Experiences of a Women's Museum in Japan' Journal of Peace Education (2015) 12 236–46.

8 Matsui wrote a biography of Yoko Hayashi who would become the Chair of the CEDAW Committee.

9 Kanji is one of the Japanese scripts which uses Chinese characters. [漢字]. 松井耶依 is the kanji script of Matsui's name.

10 Christianity is called Yaso-kyo (耶蘇教) in Japanese, and 耶is a rare kanji used in Japanese names. A link with Christianity is immediately presumed for Japanese readers of this symbol. My thanks to my Japanese colleagues for discussions over the kanji.

and in Minnesota where she attended classes in politics, economics, history, and on the United Nations. This trip was the beginning of a number of important revelations for Matsui.

First, she was shocked at how affluent the United States was compared to Japan before the latter's period of economic growth. Secondly, she was surprised at how women in the United States were outspoken and opinionated. She details in her autobiography particular surprise at seeing a man, a Czech professor, doing housework and the dishes. This second aspect forms an important part of Matsui's own trajectory as she would later discover the women's liberation movement in the United States. Thirdly, her time in the United States led to consciousness of being an Asian woman. Matsui recounts that she went on a trip to the southern states and during that trip

> there were two different waiting rooms in the bus terminal in Memphis, White and Colored, and I thought I should go into the Colored one, but I saw only Black people there and I was told to go to the other room. So I went to the other one, with White people. In that room, the White people stared at me and said nothing. I felt really uncomfortable.[11]

Through that experience Matsui explains that she began to identify herself as Asian, and that this experience and realization would influence her life in her aims to build a pan-Asian feminist solidarity movement.

This formative period of Matsui's life also led her to Europe as she sailed from New York to Southampton and then to Rotterdam. She arrived in Paris on 14 July 1958, on Bastille day.[12] She had arrived more or less by accident after learning that it would be months before a ship would set sail back to Japan. She decided to stay to learn French after deciding that she would like to work for an international organization in the future (something that never happened). After three months, she enrolled in the Sorbonne to study history. She found a part-time job working for a professor in Nagoya University, typing letters and translating the works of the French dramatist Romain Rolland.

Her time in France was extremely mixed. On the one hand, it allowed her to explore Europe and travel to Italy and Germany, and to meet students from around the world, including from Latin American student movements. In this way she became alert to the Cuban revolution and discourses on United States imperialism. On the other hand, and on a personal level, Yayori would encounter chauvinism, racism as an Asian woman, and also recount nearly being raped by a stranger.[13] After nearly two years abroad, and running out of money in Autumn 1959, she decided to return to Japan.

When Matsui returned to Japan from the Sorbonne she embarked on a journey by boat which would change the course of her life. The boat made many stops and she was profoundly affected by the contrast in the wealth of Western Europe to the poverty and conditions that she saw in Bombay, Colombo, and Vietnam. She recounts:

[11] 『愛と怒り闘う勇気』岩波書店、2003年 30 (Matsui uses the words 'White' and 'Coloured' in English in the Japanese text. The translation is my own and it is a rough translation.

[12] ibid 33.

[13] ibid 38–39.

> A month long journey by ship from Marseilles took me to various Asian ports on the way. This was in the late 1950s and my encounter with the reality of Asia during this journey was one of the most shocking events of my young life. I saw unimaginable poverty. In Bombay, I saw people curled up in foetal positions dying on the streets. Noisy crowds of begging children followed me in Colombo, Sri Lanka and squatting Vietnamese women selling food in the streets of Saigon looked exhausted. These scenes were in striking contrast to the ostentatious wealth I had observed in countries in Europe and the United States during my two-year stay there.[14]

In 1961, Matsui became a journalist at a leading newspaper, *The Asahi Shimbun* by taking their open entrance exam. She was the only woman hired as a journalist by the paper that year. She extensively covered the Minamata disaster, mercury spills by a petrochemical company in the 1950s which resulted in the poisoning of a Japanese village.[15] Minamata would mark one of the important currents of Matsui's work which brought together the impact of colonialism on women's rights and environmentalism. She wrote about industrial pollution and the importance of women's interventions in the realm of environmental protection in the United States, Europe, the Soviet Union, and Japan. In fact, Matsui often writes that the feminist movement in Japan was born from the environmental movement which was more advanced in the 1960s and 1970s than activism around gender equality.

It was during a subsequent trip to the United States as a journalist that she encountered the Women's Liberation movement. This discovery led Matsui to develop her thoughts that Japan's economic development was achieved by discrimination against women, exploitation and oppression of women in Asia, as well as the export of pollution. This feminist awakening led Matsui to cover the United Nations International Women's Year Conference in Mexico City 1975 on which she has written with respect to the debate between the Latin American and Third World Women and those from the United States. The former accused women from the United States of taking wealth from Third World countries where poor women struggle to survive:

> So acrimonious was the confrontation between Latin American and US women that at times they physically struggled for possession of the microphone. Listening to the debate forced me to realize that this condemnation by women in the South applies also to Japanese women, and I had to think of Japanese women belonging to the North in this conflict of values.[16]

Matsui was *The Asahi Shimbun*'s Asia correspondent working during the UN Women's Decade (1975–1985). She attended the Nairobi Conference and through these conferences met other feminists from around the world. Matsui was extremely productive and would write about the threefold types of oppression women faced in Asia which

[14] ibid, Introduction.

[15] International lawyers will be familiar with the Minamata disaster from the Minamata Convention on Mercury adopted 2013 and entered into force in 2017. In 2017, the UN Minamata Convention on Mercury was effectuated.

[16] Yayori Matsui, *Women in the New Asia: From Pain to Power* (Zed Books 1999) 4.

included class discrimination, sex discrimination, and economic, political, and military control by countries in the Global North both for the newspaper and in pamphlets that she produced for the organizations that she founded. She sought to draw attention to stories of women's activism, such as that of the Chipko movement, and other Asian women's movements in the 1970s. She exposed the exploitation of women in palm oil plantations in Malaysia, banana plantations in the Philippines, domestic workers for Japanese families in Singapore, tea plantations in Sri Lanka, the violations of indigenous peoples' rights and their fight in Sarawak (visiting again and again), and women's labour conditions in Japanese-owned factories abroad.

Matsui's books, newspaper articles, newsletters, and pamphlets aimed to bring awareness to the hunger, exploitation, and poverty of Asian women to a Japanese audience who enjoyed abundant affluence in the 1980s.[17] Matsui wanted to make them aware of 'Japan's direct involvement in their lives' and Japan's role as oppressor in Asia.[18] For example she wrote:

> ... we cannot ignore the blood and tears shed in Mindanao: the island into which huge amounts of Japanese ODA (Official Development Assistance) have been poured and to which many Japanese companies have flocked, in order to serve as the food-producing base for Japan and enrich Japanese dinner tables.[19]

A particular focus of Matsui's work as Asia correspondent was on 'sex tourism' as it was known then and trafficking in women and girls. Matsui wrote of desperate parents selling their children and met with young girls who were kept in brothels in Thailand and India. She wrote about the explosion of sexual exploitation in Cambodia following the United Nations Peacekeeping Operation in 1992 and recounted she witnessed white men working for NGOs having dinner with young Cambodian girls.[20] But it was her advocacy on the issue of Japanese guided tours to Korea to visit 'kisaeng' that formed the focus of her attention. She described these tours as a 'sexual invasion' and part of a colonial practice that signified that nothing had changed since the war. Justice for the comfort women was therefore necessary in order to prevent the sex tourism and trafficking that was taking place today.[21]

Matsui left Asahi Shimbun retiring in 1994, and turned to feminist organizing. She founded the Asian Women's Association which focused on Japan's wartime responsibility, militarized prostitution, sex tourism by Japanese men in Asia, and human trafficking.[22] In 1995 she founded the Asia-Japan Women's Resource Centre.[23] That same year she attended the Fourth UN World Conference on Women held in Beijing, which concluded with the adoption of the Beijing Declaration and Platform

[17] Ibid.

[18] ibid, Preface to English Edition.

[19] ibid 86. Official development assistance. There is now an Independent Expert on the effects of foreign debt and other related international financial obligations of states on the fully enjoyment of all human rights, particularly economic, social, and cultural rights.

[20] ibid 38.

[21] Yayori Matsui, 'Sexual Slavery in Korea' Frontiers: A Journal of Women's Studies (1997) 2 22–30. Translation by Lora Sharnoff. *Courage to Fight* (n 21) 190.

[22] ibid 49.

[23] *Women in the New Asia* (n 16) viii.

for Action. Matsui wrote extensively about feminist advocacy in the run up to and during Beijing.[24] She was involved in campaigning against ODAs and the structural adjustment programmes of the World Bank. Matsui argued that Japan's provision of ODAs to countries like Thailand resulted in large infrastructure projects which in turn caused environmental damage and a feminization of poverty, particularly affecting rural women and their vulnerability to being trafficked and exploited.[25]

Organizing of Women's Independent Tribunals

The Beijing Platform for Action included as one of its twelve thematic areas the issue of armed conflicts. As part of this theme at the Beijing NGO Forum in Huairou (held about 50 kilometres outside of the capital) former 'comfort women' organized a small War Crimes Tribunal, at which Korean and Filipino women testified to their experiences and demanded compensation from the Japanese government. This was a precursor to two other tribunals which would take place in Tokyo, most famously the Tokyo Women's Tribunal in 2000.

Andrew Byrnes and Gabrielle Simm have described the Women's Tribunal as 'probably the best-known international peoples' tribunal in Asia'.[26] Matsui's own journey demonstrates that this status within international law scholarship was the result of many years of organizing and attending women's tribunals in Asia in the 1990s. At the Asian Women's Tribunal held at Chulalongkorn University in Bangkok in December 1994, Matsui acted as one of the tribunal's judges and heard harrowing testimonies from women trafficked from Thailand to Japan, sold into sexual slavery, and infected with HIV, and subsequently deported with no justice or resources.[27]

Matsui was also involved in organizing the Asian Tribunal on Women's Human Rights (Traffic in Women and War Crimes against Asian Women) held in Tokyo, in March 1994 which lasted for six days. She was part of the Women's Human Rights Committee of Japan who organized the tribunal together with the Asian Women Human Rights Council.[28] The aim of this Tribunal was to 'reveal the connections between the different forms of violence against women—where women are subjected to patriarchal socio-economic arrangements'.[29] The Tribunal also sought to draw to

[24] In the Court of Women II: Asia Tribunal on Women's Human Rights in Tokyo: Proceedings of the International Public Hearing on Traffic in Women and War Crimes Against Woman, March 12, 1994.

[25] Matsui contrasted the situation of countries like Thailand and the Philippines with Burma, which she argued had a more egalitarian society rejecting Japan's economic model in the 1980s. This changed, however, in the 1990s with Burmese girls increasingly being targeted and trafficked into Thailand.

[26] Simm and Byrne, International Peoples' Tribunals in Asia: Political Theatre, Juridical Farce, or Meaningful Intervention?' Asian Journal of International Law (2014) 4 103–24, at 110. Dianne Otto, 'Impunity in a Different Register: People's Tribunals and Questions of Judgment, Law, and Responsibility' in Karen Engle, Zinaida Miller, and DM Davis (eds), *Anti-Impunity and the Human Rights Agenda* (Cambridge University Press 2016),

[27] *Women in the New Asia* (n 16) 13.

[28] See In the Court of Women II: Asia Tribunal on Women's Human Rights in Tokyo: Proceedings of the International Public Hearing on Traffic in Women and War Crimes Against Woman, March 12, 1994, written by Asian Women's Human Rights Council (Manila, Manila (National Capital Region): Asian Women's Human Rights Council, 1994), 122 pp, 8.

[29] ibid. The Tribunal was composed of a jury from Korea, India, Croatia, and Japan. This focused on the violence committed against women in the family and in the community.

attention the linkages between United States militarism and military prostitution.[30] The women argued that the ongoing presence of United States military bases in Okinawa, Korea, and the Philippines was based on national, racial, class, and gender oppression. The verdict was read out by a jury which included VR Kirshna Iyer (former justice of the Supreme Court of India), Yoko Hayashi (future member of the Committee on the Elimination of Discrimination against Women), and Vesna Kesic (Centre for Women War Victims, Zagreb).

It was Matsui's meeting with a number of Filipino and Korean activists at the World Conference on Human Rights in Vienna in 1993 which led to their joint advocacy around the comfort women issue. In her autobiography Matsui states that it was Indai Sajor from the Philippines who asked for a conference in Tokyo on wartime violence against women. This became the 1997 International Conference on Violence against Women in War and Situations of Armed Conflict, held in Tokyo. Sajor and others such as Heisoo Shin from South Korea, a third coordinator of the Tribunal and now member of the UN Committee on Economic, Social and Cultural Rights, have recalled that the idea for a women's tribunal in Tokyo came from Yayori in 1998. Sajor has recounted in a documentary made in 2020 recalling the importance of the Tribunal: 'Yayori Matsui came to me and said, "Indai, we have to organise a war crimes tribunal". I said to Yayori immediately, "yes why not".'[31]

Matsui conceived of the Women's Tribunal as 'an addendum, or a continuation' of *the International Military Tribunal for the Far East* (IMTFE), also known as the Tokyo Tribunal.[32] Matsui viewed peoples' tribunals and women's tribunals in particular as an important mechanism for filling in some of the gaps of formal international legal processes, and as an urgent contemporary space for the survivors of gender-based violence in Asia. This gap was particularly wide with respect to impunity for gender-based and sexual crimes, with Matsui writing that 'only in recent years have female scholars of international law and history begun to question why the systematic wartime violence such as sexual slavery committed by the Japanese Imperial Army on such a large scale was not prosecuted at the Tokyo Trial . . . '.[33]

Even though some Japanese defendants were prosecuted for rape in the IMTFE,[34] scholars have brought attention to the fact that the so-called Rape of Nanking was

[30] There are of course many legacies. See, eg, Margo Okazawa-Rey, 'Amerasian Children of GI Town: A Legacy of U.S. Militarism in South Korea' Asia Journal of Women's Studies (1997) 3(1) 71–102.

[31] Gendered Peace: the legacy of the Tokyo Women's Tribunal. Documentary available here: <https://www.youtube.com/watch?v=pfLfZ87e1O8> 10 December 2020.

[32] Yayori Matsui 'Women's International War Crimes Tribunal on Japan's Military Sexual Slavery: Memory, Identity, and Society' East Asia: An International Quarterly (Winter 2001) 19(4) 119. On the prosecution of gender crimes generally see: Patricia Viseur Sellers, 'Sexual Violence and Peremptory Norms: The Legal Value of Rape' (2002) 34 Case Western Reserve Journal of International Law 287. See 'A History of Silence: The Nuremberg and Tokyo Trials' in Nicola Henry, *War and Rape: Law, Memory, and Justice* (Routledge 2011) 28–60; Kelly Dawn Askin, *War Crimes against Women: Prosecution in International War Crimes Tribunals*, vol 1 (Martinus Nijhoff Publishers 1997).

[33] Matsui, 'Women's International War Crimes Tribunal' (n 32) 131.

[34] Rape was charged as 'inhumane treatment' and 'failure to respect family honour and rights'. General Iwane Matsui, Commander Shunroku Hata, and Foreign Minister Hirota were held criminally responsible for rape, as was Yamashita in separate and controversial trial proceedings. On Yamashita see: Ann Marie Prévost, 'Race and War Crimes: The 1945 War Crimes Trial of General Tomoyuki Yamashita' (1992) Human Rights Quarterly 303.

considered in only one short paragraph in the judgment.[35] Moreover, none of the twenty-eight Japanese war criminals were prosecuted for the human rights violations suffered by the 'comfort women'.[36] It would take five decades for the crimes perpetrated against comfort women to be recognized as war crimes and crimes against humanity by a Women's Tribunal created by civil society.[37] Intersecting factors including sexism, self-interest, nationalism, and colonialism colluded in order to silence Asian women's experiences of the crimes perpetrated by Japanese forces.[38] It had also failed to prosecute Emperor Hirohito.

Since Nuremberg and Tokyo, the developments of international criminal law led to advances in the prosecution of gender crimes.[39] The Women's Tribunal sits within this context, with Matsui purposely seeking out an international participation by Patricia Viseur Sellers who was the Gender Advisor to the International Criminal Tribunal for the Former Yugoslavia and Rwanda Tribunals at the time she took on the role of prosecutor for the Tokyo Women's Tribunal and Gabrielle Kirk Macdonald who was a judge in the ICTY and ICTR. Matsui was instrumental in ensuring that the judges were eminent international lawyers. This in turn, according to some of the Japanese lawyers I spoke to, had an important impact on the development of international human rights law and women's rights on Japan's legal community.

The Tribunal's existence has since been cited by formal legal processes and sexual slavery has now been enshrined in international criminal law.[40] In this way, the Tribunal's legacy and Matsui's vision on sexual slavery has infused international criminal justice, partly by way of individuals such as Patricia Sellers, prosecutor at the ICTY *Foca* case, establishing criminal responsibility for sexual slavery or enslavement as a crime against humanity. But as Matsui has explained the importance of the Tribunal to international law goes beyond gap filling:

> It is vitally important to realize that a people's tribunal does not merely play a supplementary role in filling the gaps in the order of states. Rather, it can participate in the

[35] On the marginalization of the 'rape of Nanking' see: Yuma Totani 'The Case against the Accused' in Yuki Tanaka, Tim McCormack, and Gerry Simpson (eds) *Beyond Victor's Justice? The Tokyo War Crimes Trial Revisited* (Brill/International Humanitarian Law Series 2011) vol 30 160.

[36] Yuma Totani, *The Tokyo War Crimes Trial: The Pursuit of Justice in the Wake of World War II* (Harvard University Press 2008) 176–88. See also Immi Tallgren 'Watching Tokyo Trial' (2017) 5(2) London Review of International Law 291–316, at 311.

[37] Christine Chinkin, 'Women's International Tribunal on Japanese Military Sexual Slavery' (2001) 95(2) AJIL 335. There seems to be one documented case of prosecution for comfort women: Washio Awochi, was prosecuted by a Dutch court for forcing a Dutch woman into prostitution. Case No 76. Netherlands Temporary Court Martial at Batavia (judgment Delivered on 25 October 1946.

[38] N Henry, 'Silence as Collective Memory: Sexual Violence and the Tokyo Trial' in *Beyond Victor's Justice?* (n 35) 263.

[39] Kelly D Askin, 'Prosecuting Wartime Rape and other Gender-related Crimes under International Law: Extraordinary Advances, Enduring Obstacles' (2003) 21 Berkeley Journal of International Law 288. Patricia Viseur Sellers, 'Gender Strategy Is Not Luxury for International Courts' (2009) 17 American University Journal of Gender, Social Policy and Law 301.

[40] Sellers, 'Gender Strategy' (n 39) 301. *Prosecutor v. Kunarac, Kovac and Vukovic*, IT-96-23 (October 22, 2001). See *Isabelita Vinuya et al v Executive Secretary of Philippines et al Supreme Court of Manila.* GR No 162230 28 April 2010. While mentioning the Tribunal and its outcomes Judge Castillo states 'It bears stressing, however, that although the tribunal included prosecutors, witnesses, and judges, its judgment was not legally binding since the tribunal itself was organized by private citizens.'

> formation of a new order of states. Thus, the Tribunal showed that international law is not an order created and implemented only by states; the people can and do play an increasingly important role in forcing states to abide by international law.[41]

Matsui argued that women had an important role to play in forming this new state order but that justice for the comfort women and others would need to be obtained in order for this to happen. The Tribunal's findings resulted in a political and media backlash within Japan. Matsui faced threats on her life and had to go into hiding. Matsui's funeral was picketed by members of right wing groups who were outraged by the conviction of Emperor Hirohito.[42]

Conclusion

Matsui, alongside women and men from countries including North and South Korea, China, Taiwan, and the Philippines who organized the Tribunal made a key contribution to feminist international law both methodologically and substantively, closing the gaps and breaking the silences on wartime sexual violence carried out by the Japanese Imperial Army.[43] The Tribunal acts as both a prequel and sequel within the story of international criminal law. Within international legal scholarship, Karen Knop has approached the Women's Tribunal as an instance of performing 'the act of going back in time and taking another path ...*as if* it were a reopening or a continuation of the official IMTFE and subsidiary trials'.[44] In doing so the Tribunal not only created legitimacy by adopting a consistent legal approach to the original IMTFE, but also created a factional which have broader effects.[45]

Despite the important contribution which Yayori Matsui made to peoples' tribunals, her personal work and activism remains relatively unacknowledged within the international legal canon.[46] Lastly, it would be remiss not to recall that Matsui was adamant that the Tribunal had to take place in Tokyo, as the capital of the perpetrator country and that the comfort women should attend. Her dream came through, as thousands of people from all over Asia and of different generations attended.

[41] Yayori Matsui 'Women's International War Crimes Tribunal on Japan's Military Sexual Slavery: Memory, Identity, and Society' East Asia: An International Quarterly (Winter 2001) 19(4) 133.

[42] Mina Watanabe speaking in the documentary *Gendered Peace, the Legacy of the Tokyo Women's Tribunal* (n 4).

[43] Hilary Charlesworth and Christine Chinkin, *The Boundaries of International Law: A Feminist Analysis* (Manchester University Press 2000). See also http://www.iccwomen.org/wigjdraft1/Archives/oldWCGJ/tokyo/chinkin.htmlaccessed 4 October 2021.

[44] Karen Knop, 'The Tokyo Women's Tribunal and the Turn to Fiction' in Fleur Johns and others (eds), *Events: The Force of International Law* (Routledge 2011) 145, 145 and 149. See also the documentary on the Women's Tribunal *Breaking the History of Silence* (2001).

[45] ibid 149.

[46] Andrew Byrnes and Gabrielle Simm (eds), *People's Tribunals and International Law* (Cambridge University Press 2018). See fn 38, at 92. Christine Lévy, 'Le Tribunal international des femmes de Tokyo en 2000. Une réponse féministe au révisionnisme?' Clio Women, Gender, History (2014) 39(1) 129–150.

13

Canonizing the Memory of Annie Ruth Jiagge in the Global Efforts towards Gender Equality

Michael Addaney

Introduction

On 12 June 1996, an influential lawyer, judge, and women's rights activist, Justice Annie Ruth Jiagge passed away in Accra, Ghana, after half a century of dedicated public service. She was the first Ghanaian woman lawyer and the first woman in Ghana,[1] and second in the Commonwealth of Nations, to become a high court judge.[2] On her passing, prominent personalities across the globe poured tributes to her unwavering devotion to promoting women's rights, including the former UN Secretary General Boutros Boutros-Ghali.[3] Being a black African woman from a minority background in Ghana, there are concerns that her memory may fade if her five decades of service and contribution to the codification of women's rights law at the international level would not be etched by scholars, activists, and policymakers.[4]

African women have a long history of active participation in politics—overcoming colonialism and patriarchal structures—and have had a profound impact on national and global political activism. However, they remain noticeably absent from canon in international law and politics. Women such as Funmilayo Ransome-Kuti, Bibi Titi Mohammed, Mabel Dove-Danquah, Vera Chirwa, and Graca Machel mobilized others in their struggle against colonialism and apartheid in Africa. In more contemporary times, Winnie Madikizela-Mandela, Ellen Johnson Sirleaf, and Nkosazana Dlamini-Zyma have led the fight to ensure gender equality and women's representation in parliament and general political leadership. Despite their trailblazing and vast contributions to African society, they have most times gone unnoticed.

This chapter joins the larger discourses on women, politics, and international law, their origins, and how they transformed international judicial, legal, and social

[1] 'Meet Annie Ruth Baeta; Ghana's First Female Lawyer and Judge' African Post, 7 January 2020 https://africanpostonline.com/meet-annie-ruth-baeta-ghanas-first-female-lawyer-and-judge/> accessed 10 October 2020.

[2] After Anna Chandy who became Judge on 9 February 1959 at the Kerala High Court, Saumya Anand 'Justice Anna Chandy: The First Female High Court Judge of India' Feminism in India 18 October 2018 <https://feminisminindia.com/2018/10/18/justice-anna-chandy/> accessed 10 October 2020.

[3] See Tribute by the UN Secretary-General, Dr Boutros Boutros-Ghali, on the occasion of the memorial for Mrs Justice Annie Ruth Jiagge, 3 August 1996 <https://www.un.org/womenwatch/daw/news/jiagge.htm> accessed 10 October 2020.

[4] See Kate Skinner 'Women's Rights as International Human Rights: Justice Annie Jiagge of Ghana' 23 July 2019 <https://blog.bham.ac.uk/archiveofactivism/2019/07/23/womens-rights-as-international-human-rights-justice-annie-jiagge-of-ghana/> accessed 10 October 2020.

Michael Addaney, *Canonizing the Memory of Annie Ruth Jiagge in the Global Efforts towards Gender Equality*
In: *Portraits of Women in International Law.* Edited by: Immi Tallgren, Oxford University Press. © Michael Addaney 2023.
DOI: 10.1093/oso/9780198868453.003.0013

institutions across the world. How did Jiagge's journey take her from Lomé, Togo, through to Keta, Ghana, and London, Britain, to the highest court of Ghana, and the president of the UN Commission on the Status of Women (UNCSW)? What challenges did Jiagge encounter and how did she overcome these barriers? How did Jiagge's appointment to several prestigious positions contribute to efforts towards international gender equality? In discussing these issues and considering what might have shaped Jiagge's career, this chapter is situated within the broader context of existing scholarship that *inter alia* explores the extent to which the perspectives and careers of judicial appointees are shaped by their experiences.

Considering the role of Jiagge as the representative of Ghana on the UNCSW from 1962 to 1972 and her involvement in drafting the working document which became the Declaration on the Elimination of Discrimination Against Women, this chapter underscores the significant contributions she made to the formulation of women's rights as human rights, enshrined in international law. The challenges faced by the late Jiagge and their implications for women's rights activism in Africa are also discussed. This chapter begins by placing Jiagge's background within the broader context of women judges and women in international law. This is followed by an in-depth presentation of her educational and professional experiences considering that the lived experiences of women judges are significant, not only in setting an example for female judges and legal practitioners to come, but in understanding the perspectives and legal philosophies of the judges.

African Women and the Making of Gender Responsive International Law

The turn of the twenty-first century ushered in a growing number of women appointed to serve on international judicial and quasi-judicial bodies.[5] Among the women judges that were nominated by their countries and served on these international bodies were prominent African women judges, drawn from across the continent, with diverse judicial and professional backgrounds. Much remains unknown about the roles and contributions of these pioneering women who served various international bodies and sat on influential committees. Some studies have provided rich empirical and theoretical knowledge on how women have entered judiciaries along with some discussion on what contributions they bring to the bench.[6] As international human rights law is still evolving, especially in relation to women's human rights in developing countries, discourses on the scantiness of women's participation in international treaty-making and standard settings have gained traction among scholars.[7] It

[5] Nienke Grossman, 'Shattering the Glass Ceiling in International Adjudication' (2016) 56 Virginia Journal of International Law 344, 354.

[6] See, for example, Mary L Clark, 'Changing the Face of the Law: How Women's Advocacy Groups Put Women on the Federal Judicial Appointments Agenda' (2002) 14 Yale Journal of Law and Feminism 243; International Commission of Jurists, Ser No 1, Women and the Judiciary (2014) <https://www.icj.org/wp-content/uploads/2014/10/Universal-Women-and-Judiciary-Gva-For-1-Publications-Conference-Report-2014-ENG.pdf> accessed 10 October 2020.

[7] Grossman (n 5) 650.

Figure 13.1 WCC president (1975–1983) Annie Ruth Jiagge with president José Miguez Bonino from Argentina at the central committee meeting of the World Council of Churches, Geneva, 14–22 August 1980.
Source: Marc Van-Appelghem/World Council of Churches archives 1770/8/80.

is suggested that the low number of women on international judicial bodies and committees is a global phenomenon that cuts across the wide spectrum of international law with only a few exceptions.[8]

Women judges are 'trickling in' on international courts and other institutions making it clear that they are not token women but rather that they are well qualified to be in those positions.[9] The profiles of these women indicate that they have stellar academic backgrounds and significant professional accomplishments, some being trailblazers who earned the status of 'first' in their various professional endeavors.[10] Notwithstanding these observations, women's entry onto international positions remains a long and bumpy road for various reasons.[11] For one, the process of electing and appointing members to international positions involves a great deal of domestic politics, and women must find strategies to combine their professional experiences with other political considerations in creative ways.[12] For instance, Fionnuala Ní Aolái[13]

[8] See Josephine J Dawuni, 'African Women Judges and Gender Parity on the African Court on Human and Peoples' Rights' INTLAWGRRLS, 1 February 2017 <https://ilg2.org/author/jdawuni/> accessed 10 October 2020.

[9] Josephine J Dawuni 'African Women Judges on International Courts: Symbolic or Substantive Gains?' (2018) 47(2) University of Baltimore Law Review 208.

[10] ibid.

[11] Sally J Kenney, 'Choosing Judges: A Bumpy Road to Women's Equality and a Long Way to Go' (2012) Michigan State University Law Review 1499.

[12] ibid.

[13] Fionnuala Ní Aoláin, 'More Women—But Which Women? A Reply to Stéphanie Hennette Vauchez' (2015) 26 EJIL 229, 231–32.

observed that 'by accessing elite judicial institutions, women exert agency by taking strategic, creative and intuitive action, to generate individual opportunity as well as to enable dynamic entry to gendered institutional environments that have been, as a practical matter, closed to the female sex since their inception'.[14]

Judges and members serving on international courts and judicial committees play a crucial role in norm setting, hearing, and disposing cases guided by principles of international law and rules of procedure for the respective courts and committees.[15] Considering the poor record of international judicial bodies in attaining an equitable distribution of the sexes, actors and framers of the treaties establishing these bodies usually put in place parameters to ensure adequate gender representation in the nomination and selection processes.[16] However, the definition of 'adequate' remains dubious, and thus leaves room for political manoeuvring by states.[17] Practically, on some courts and committees, all or some governments have a *de jure* or *de facto* right to appoint a judge but most international judges are appointed on a merit-based case-by-case basis considering educational background and professional experience in conjunction with regional and geographic balance; others for relatively short renewable terms, and some for longer non-renewable terms.[18]

At both international and local spheres, African[19] women judges are caught at the intersection of race, gender, and class relations.[20] Shedding light on the experiences and contributions of African women judges and probing the trajectories and contributions of African women who contributed to international legal developments enrich the discourse in scholarly efforts to understand what women judges generally, and African women in particular, do once they are nominated and accepted to serve on international judicial and quasi-judicial bodies.[21] Due to limited scholarship and documentation, it is difficult to quantify in a tangible form what African women contributed to international legal development. Attention to African women and their contributions to international law, women's rights, human rights, and the transformation of gender hierarchies within international law underscores the contribution of the Global South and minority voices in addressing marginalization and gender inequality through international law. The inspiring story of Annie Ruth Jiagge demonstrates, through various ways, what African women do once they are appointed to such bodies and how.

[14] ibid at 229.

[15] See Josephine J Dawuni 'African Women Judges on International Courts: Symbolic or Substantive Gains?' (2018) 47(2) University of Baltimore Law Review 199–246.

[16] ibid 204.

[17] See Josephine J Dawuni, Vive La Diversité! A Roadmap to Gender Parity on African Regional Courts?, Völkerrechtsblog (May 15, 2017) <https://voelkerrechtsblog.org/vive-la-diversite/> accessed 10 October 2020.

[18] Erik Voeten 'The Politics of International Judicial Appointments' (2009) 9(2) Chicago Journal of International Law 389.

[19] 'African woman' is conceptualized as one who self-identifies as an African and is placed in a category that qualifies her for judicial selection as an African. See Dawuni (n 10) 211.

[20] ibid 212.

[21] ibid.

Justice Annie Ruth Jiagge: Educational and Professional Experience and Contribution to International Law

Jiagge was born Annie Ruth Baeta in Lomé, Togo on 7 October 1918.[22] Her father, Reverend Robert Domingo Baeta, was a teacher and minister and her mother, Henrietta Baeta (née Sedode), was also a teacher. On 10 January 1953, Annie Ruth Baeta married Fred KA Jiagge. Jiagge began her early education in Lomé and later went to live with her maternal grandmother, Julia B Sedode, in Keta, Ghana (then Gold Coast) to be educated in English.[23] Obtaining a Teacher's Certificate from the Achimota College in 1937, Annie Jiagge's career began in 1938 when she took up a teaching post in the Presbyterian Girls' School in Keta where she was later promoted to the position of head teacher.[24] Although Annie Jiagge achieved excellence as a professional teacher, she decided to pursue legal education. She received financial support from her mother to study at the London School of Economics and Political Science (LSE) and Lincoln's Inn.[25] Annie was confronted by her male colleagues from the then Gold Coast to drop her academic pursuits.[26] They felt the law was too much for a woman like Jiagge. One of her colleagues even went as far as proffering unsolicited advice by asking her to study dressmaking at the Paris Academy.[27] Rather than pay heed to their callous remarks she assured her colleagues that she would return to the Gold Coast if she failed her first examination. Unfortunately for them, she passed, and they had no choice but to stop bothering her. Being a daughter of teachers, Jiagge was said to be ubiquitous and fierce, refusing to be intimidated by her male colleagues during her sojourn at LSE.[28]

While in London, Jiagge encountered the Pan-African movement and built alliances including leading people who would return to Ghana to join the anti-colonial struggle such as Kwame Nkrumah and JB Danquah. The Pan-African movement spanned the twentieth century ideological spectrum, ranging from more right-wing, pro-capitalist, race-based nationalism to more revolutionary socialist discourses advanced by men like George Padmore, Walter Rodney, Kwame Nkrumah, Julius Nyerere, Amilcar Cabral, Stephen Bantu Biko, and Frantz Fanon, all of whom

[22] Seth Bokpe 'She Called the Bluff of Chauvinists to Become Ghana's First Female Lawyer, Judge' The Ghana Report, 19 January 2020 <https://www.theghanareport.com/she-called-the-bluff-of-chauvinists-to-become-ghanas-first-female-lawyer-judge/> accessed 10 October 2020.

[23] Josephine Dawuni, 'Jiagge, Annie Ruth locked (1918–1996)' The Dictionary of African Biography <https://oxfordaasc.com/view/10.1093/acref/9780195301731.001.0001/acref-9780195301731-e-49036> accessed 10 October 2020.

[24] DEK Amenumey, *Outstanding Ewes of the 20th Century: Profiles of Fifteen Firsts* (Woeli Publishing Services 2002) 90–93.

[25] 'Justice Annie Jiagge: The First Ghanaian Woman to Become a Lawyer by Defying Patriarchy' *The Independence Ghana*, 18 July 2020 <https://theindependentghana.com/2020/07/justice-annie-jiagge-the-first-ghanaian-woman-to-become-a-lawyer-by-defying-patriarchy/> accessed 10 October 2020.

[26] Ibid.

[27] Christopher Sam 'Meet the First Woman to Become a Lawyer and a Judge in Ghana' *African Times*, 31 December 2019 <https://gh.opera.news/gh/en/justice/276d5e18a1c5b7f53f3df358f8e3c37f> accessed 10 October 2020.

[28] 'Meet Annie Ruth Baeta; Ghana's first female lawyer and judge' *African Post*, 7 January 2020 <https://africanpostonline.com/meet-annie-ruth-baeta-ghanas-first-female-lawyer-and-judge/> accessed 10 October 2020.

locate Africa's underdevelopment in capitalism, challenging the class system, racism, and in the case of Fanon, race-based nationalism.[29] Yet an accurate historic record must include women like Mable Dove Danquah, Adelaide Caseley-Hayford, Bibi Titi Mohamed, Funmilayo Ransome Kuti, Gambo Sawaba, Muthoni Likimani, Thenjiwe Mtintso, Djamila Bouhired, Charlotte Maxeke, Albertina Sisulu, and the other uncounted numbers of women who mobilized for Africa's liberation.[30]

Feminism and Pan-Africanism intersect in various ways but follow different paths as they jointly challenged entrenched systems of colonial and gender domination.[31] Women have been, however, steadily erased from the history of Pan-Africanism despite their active presence from the very start of Pan-Africanism.[32] Women had to practice the art of navigating a variety of complex positions around race, gender, class, national origin, and culture within the larger goal of the liberation of African peoples globally. Historically, all over the Third World, there has been a close connection between the anti-colonial and feminist movements.[33] As a Pan-African Christian advocate for gender equality, Justice Jiagge's work demonstrates that there has always been, and continues to be, room for activist women from all walks of life. Moreover, her work consistently created theoretical and lived links at the intersections of nationalism, feminism, and early communist thought. However, she is not known in Ghana as a Pan-Africanist but deserves, in my view, to be recognized as such. The life, achievements, and lack of recognition of Justice Jiagge reflect contemporary rhetoric of women's substantive but neglected contributions to Pan-African and feminist movements.

In 1950, she returned to the then Gold Coast to practice as a barrister and later became a magistrate soon after marriage in 1953. Upon Ghana's independence from the British on 6 March 1957 under the Kwame Nkrumah-led Convention People's Party, Annie Jiagge was elevated to the position of High Court Judge in 1961.[34] Being the first female judge in Ghana in the 1950's and second in the Commonwealth, was an achievement considering just how male-dominated the public domain and the legal sphere were at the time. Her story offers insights into how much women have contributed in history and how many are not known, let alone publicly celebrated.

Jiagge served from1962 to 1972 as Ghana's representative on the UNCSW and chaired its 21st Session in 1968. While a member, she was exposed to the nature of violence against women worldwide. She recounted how she could not sleep after reading a disturbing report of a man who had killed his sister because of her involvement in an extramarital affair.[35] On another occasion, she was furious to learn that in

[29] Hakima Abbas and Amina Mama 'Feminism and Pan-Africanism' (2014) 19 Feminist Africa 2–6.

[30] Ibid.

[31] Yolande Bouka 'Women, Colonial Resistance, and Decolonization: Challenging African Histories' in O Yacob-Haliso and T Falola (eds), The Palgrave Handbook of African Women's Studies (Springer Nature 2020).

[32] Carole Boyce Davies 'Pan-Africanism, Transnational Black Feminism and the Limits of Culturalist Analyses in African Gender Discourses' (2014) 19 Feminist Africa 78. Davies argues that many of these women explicitly indicated women's rights positions in their work and activism. She classifies them as Pan-Africanists who were feminists or feminists who were Pan-Africanists.

[33] ibid.

[34] Amenumey (n 23) 94.

[35] Margaret Snyder and Mary Tadesse, *African Women and Development.* (Zed Books 1995).

some countries women were not included in head counts.[36] Jiagge took advantage of the international concern for gender-related issues to challenge oppressive national practices. By acquiring enviable domestic acumen, she tried to reshape international agendas in her own terms and interests, and by so doing carved out great professional and political positions domestically and internationally.

History has, in particular, credited Jiagge with authoring the first draft of the UN Declaration on the Elimination of Discrimination against Women in 1967. According to Jiagge, it all began in 1966, when she was elected rapporteur of the UNCSW. Meeting in Iran, the Commission was charged with preparing a document on the elimination of discrimination against women. After two weeks of discussing country reports, the team had not yet produced a draft document. As rapporteur, Jiagge feared that the group might leave Iran without a document and decided to attempt a draft to serve as a discussion paper. After consulting with team members, including Princess Ashraf Pahlavi of Persia (Iran), Jiagge stayed up from 9 pm to 7 am, struggling with the draft. By midmorning, the document was typed and distributed. A decision was taken to send the document to all UN member-states for comment, and it was later adopted.

Interchanges between feminists in Africa and other Third World contexts, and feminists in the First World are both inevitable and necessary. The works of Jiagge point to the need to develop approaches that are rooted in local experiences and practical situations, as possibility for changing the landscape remains contingent on the popularization of women's struggles and engagement with key sites of power from a strategic base. As an African feminist, Jiagge worked to develop truly transformative critiques of and interventions into patriarchal and elitist structures and organizations nationally and globally. Her exposure and alliances with the Pan-African movement and World Council of Churches demonstrate her tolerance and acceptance of different ideas and understandings whilst popularizing African women's struggles globally. For instance, recounting her experiences of the daily struggles women in Ghana face, she noted that the real battles women face were local and personal.[37] The division between the private sphere, where women's labour is traditionally undervalued, and the public sphere, where they have limited legal and political access and little opportunity to challenge their unequal status, has kept women's experience of oppression at the level of the personal instead of the political.[38] Jiagge thus sought to dismantle such structures and shine a light on the personal struggles of women in the Third World at the global level.[39]

[36] ibid.

[37] ibid.

[38] Shireen Essof 'African Feminisms: Histories, Applications and Prospects', (2001) 16(50) Agenda 124–27; Emmanuelle Bouilly, Ophélie Rillon, and Hannah Cross 'African Women's Struggles in a Gender Perspective' (2016) 43(149) Review of African Political Economy 338–49.

[39] Ailli Mari Tripp and others, *African Women's Movements: Transforming Political Landscapes* (Cambridge University Press 2009); Elizabeth Schmidt, '"Emancipate Your Husbands!" Women and Nationalism in Guinea, 1953–1958' in J Allman, S Geiger, and N Musisi (eds), Women in African Colonial Histories (Indiana University Press 2002) 283–304; BM Cooper, 'Anatomy of a Riot: The Social Imaginary, Single Women, and Religious Violence in Niger' (2003) 37(2–3) Canadian Journal of African Studies 467–512; KA Snyder, 'Mothers on the March: Iraq Women Negotiating the Public Sphere in Tanzania' (2006) 53(1) Africa Today 59–79.

In 1968, Jiagge was asked to write an introduction to the International Convention on the Elimination of all Forms of Discrimination against Women (CEDAW). The UN General Assembly adopted the CEDAW in 1979 with some sixty-three states including Ghana and it was signed in July 1980 during the Copenhagen Conference that marked the mid-term of the *UN Decade for Women*. Conversely in Ghana, Justice Jiagge was influential in instituting the National Council on Women and Development as mandated by the UN resolution 3275 (XIX).[40] With inspiration from the upcoming *International Women's Year*, the resolution pressured member states that had not established domestic frameworks to set up 'national machinery to accelerate the integration of women into development and to eliminate discrimination on grounds of sex'.[41] The 'national machinery' adopted in most African countries, including Ghana, were strongly criticized.[42] Nonetheless, Jiagge manoeuvred her way working under the constrictions of the then military government led by General IK Acheampong through holding consultations with Ghanaian women in the build-up to the first *World Conference on Women* in 1975 in Mexico City where Jiagge led the Ghanaian delegation.[43] These consultations pressed Annie Jiagge and Esther Ocloo[44] to focus on working to improve women's access to microcredit through the Women's World Banking initiative.[45] In 1980, Jiagge was again the leader of Ghana's delegation in Copenhagen. In 1993, she was a member of the UN Secretary-General's advisory group to plan the Fourth World Conference on Women that took place in Beijing in 1995.[46]

Through her activism and career as Justice of the High Court of Ghana, Jiagge contributed to the socio-economic development of women as well as efforts in addressing gender inequality. Jiagge was awarded the Grand Medal of Ghana in 1969, the country's highest honour and the Gimbles International Award for Humanitarian Works. In 1975, she founded and served as the First Chair of the Ghana National Council on Women and Development, a state-supported organization that promoted the interests and well-being of Ghanaian women.[47] The government of Ghana called on her expertise several times; in 1966, she was asked to chair a Commission to Investigate the Assets of Senior Public Servants and Named Political Leaders. From 1961 to 1976,

[40] UN resolution 3275 (XIX).

[41] ibid.

[42] Dzodzi Tsikata, 'National machineries for the advancement of women in Africa: Are they transforming gender relations?', <https://www.socialwatch.org/sites/default/files/pdf/en/nationalmachineries2001_eng.pdf>. accessed 10 October 2020.

[43] Snyder and Tadesse (n 29).

[44] Dr Esther Ocloo (neé Nkulenu) was a business woman with an enviable entrepreneurial legacy, an industrialist and philanthropist. See Mary Anane-Amponsah 'Esther Ocloo remembered' Graphic, 7 April 2019 <https://www.graphic.com.gh/news/general-news/ghana-news-esther-ocloo-remembered.html> accessed 10 October 2020.

[45] Deborah Atobrah and Albert K Awedoba, 'A Trail-Blazer, An Outstanding International Jurist, A Humanitarian, An Ecumenical Christian and More: The Life of Justice Annie Jiagge (Née Baëta)' in Mercy Akrofi Ansah and Esi Sutherland-Addy (eds), *Building the New Nation: Seven Notable Ghanaians* (Digibooks Publishing 2018) 47–9.

[46] ibid.

[47] Unpublished Order for Memorial, Thanksgiving and Burial Service for the Late Mrs Justice Annie Jiagge, with Tributes. Prepared by the Baeta and Jiagge families. Designed by Orlando Baeta, printed by Buck Press, Accra, Ghana, 1996.

she was a member of the Council of the University of Ghana. The university honored her with a Doctor of Laws degree in 1974. In 1979, she served on the Constituent Assembly whose work ushered in Ghana's Third Republic. After her retirement from the Bench in 1983, she continued to serve. In 1985, she was a member of a UN Panel to conduct Public Hearings on the Activities of Transnational Corporations in South Africa and Namibia. In 1991, she served as a member of a Committee of Experts that drafted Ghana's 1992 Constitution. From 1993 until her death in 1996, Justice Annie Jiagge was a member of Ghana's Council of State.

Through her writings, aspects of Jiagge's life can be mapped out, including her seminal work on women's political rights. She also granted several interviews and was involved in many documentaries such as the UN-sponsored film *Fear Woman* featuring Annie Jiagge and two other prominent Ghanaian women, Nana Okosampa VI[48] and Esther Ocloo.[49] After her passing in 1996, tributes poured from across the globe to Annie Jiagge and biographical scholars have been attracted to her. Jiagge was identified by Amenumey as one of the 'Outstanding Ewes of the 20th Century'.[50] Similarly, Dawuni wrote an entry for Jiagge in the Dictionary of African Biography in 2012.[51]

A recent work articulates selected cases that Jiagge presided over in Ghanaian courts and the judgments that she delivered.[52] The fact-based narration of her works connects how the life and lived realities of Jiagge as a school teacher and Justice of the High Court reflect those of other Ghanaian women in the public space. For instance, in her generation, teaching was regarded as a reputable occupation for women and offered a level of preparation, technical skills development, an experience that enabled her to pursue law and involve herself in many other public activities. Furthermore, being a devout Christian, faith was central to Annie Jiagge's professional life. At the time, the Church, as a movement, provided opportunities at the global, national, and local level for women from the Global South to demonstrate leadership in diverse contexts through exposure and opportunities for professional development. Justice Annie Jiagge's devotion to and involvement in Church activities led to her forming an all-girls' choir in her hometown of Keta and establishing the Young Women's Christian Association Hostel to address the housing needs of migrant girls in Accra after her election as the president of the World Council of Churches in 1980.

There are contentions concerning the relationship between Christianity and feminism and whether a mutually beneficial connection between the two can be maintained at all, and if so, in what ways.[53] Justice Jiagge negotiated a careful balance in maintaining her alliances with the World Council of Churches and local and international feminist movements. Scholars, such as King, have explained how besides the

[48] She was a prominent Fante chief.

[49] See (n 44).

[50] Amenumey (n 24) 90–93.

[51] Josephine Dawumi, 'Annie Jiagge' in Emmanuel Akyeampong and Henry Louis Gates (eds), *Dictionary of African Biography* (OUP 2012).

[52] Atobrah and Awedoba (n 45) 19–28.

[53] Ursula King 'Christianity and Feminism: Do They Need Each Other?' (2004) 4(3) International Journal for the Study of the Christian Church 194–206.

historical, denominational, and geographical diversities, there are conceptual complexities affecting the understanding of Christianity and feminism. There are also the very real limitations of personal biases created through experiences, education, and environmental conditions which shape how each individual sees the world and understands particular issues.[54] Clearly, Justice Jiagge's upbringing, education, career, and alliance with the Pan-African and feminist movements in the Global South shaped her world view.

Some feminist scholars maintain that feminism responds to the patriarchal structures and androcentric forms of all religions, not only Christianity, although the critique has gone furthest in the Judeo-Christian tradition.[55] There exists a long historical connection between Christianity and the women's movement regarding the impact of particular Christian teachings and the contribution of women from different Churches, especially from nonconformist backgrounds, in advancing the equal legal and educational status of women in modern society.[56] The documentaries and writings about Justice Jiagge suggest that her belief in and advocacy for social reforms were not the primary goals of her life, but the consequence of her deep Christian faith and commitment, driven by a revolutionary theology, looking for a new concept of God and a new understanding of divine presence in human life and action.[57] Jiagge recounted an experience with impoverished and suffering people whom she not only helped, but who made her rethink her own faith, and by so doing becoming an innovative and progressive Christian. Her career as a judge, Christian faith leader, and gender activist challenged the religious and cultural assumptions about women in her time and beyond.

The contributions of Jiagge as a judge and in the formulation and adoption of the CEDAW concretely illustrate how national and international legal frameworks act together and how artificial segregation into 'public' and 'private' are challenged by women's activism. Discrimination against women was rife in her time and continues to be an issue of concern at the local and international level including gender-based violence, child marriage, family life, and employment. The primary preoccupation of Jiagge regarded the legal regulation of age of marriage, consent to marriage, registration of marriages, maintenance and custody of children, and inheritance and divorce, typical examples of discrimination against women and girls. Her activism on these issues in Ghana, reinforced by Article 16 of the CEDAW, facilitated new initiatives to be advanced in the 1980s and 1990s. It can be argued that the CEDAW which influenced the adoption of the Protocol to the African Charter on Human and Peoples' Right on the Rights of Women in Africa, remains fundamental in defining discrimination and outlining the obligations on states to enact suitable legislation and other policies addressing discrimination against women.

[54] ibid.

[55] ibid.

[56] King argues, for instance, that 'both Christianity and feminism as movements of liberation, defending the intrinsic worth and dignity of every human being—and half of all human beings are women.' Ibid 197.

[57] See Atobrah and Awedoba (n 45) 19–28.

Conclusion

The story of Annie Ruth Jiagge from her humble beginning as a teacher through to her education in London, her appointment as a Justice of the High Court of Ghana, and her rise to the UNCSW demonstrate that despite the odds against them, with determination and dedication to service, women can overcome the socio-cultural and structural barriers to achieve professional excellence at the local and global levels. It can therefore be argued that prospects exist for women in the legal profession in Ghana and other African countries to occupy positions in the development and reformation of international law. Kuukuwa Andam and Sena Dei-Tu argue that in the Ghanaian and African contexts, the challenge is not essentially that institutional and social structures do not allow for women to be nominated and appointed as judges or diplomats, but rather that female lawyers and judges often feel apprehensive about applying for international jobs.[58] It seems that the combination of Jiagge's education and her lived realities growing up in one of the most patriarchal and marginalized regions of Ghana positioned her to champion causes relating to gender equality in a developing country. For her contribution to eliminating discrimination against women, Jiagge should be in textbooks along with many other women. Through her contribution to the legal protection of the rights of women, there are national laws, policies, and institutions that are assiduously working to empower women to break barriers and stereotypes. As Jiagge once said 'we can do so much, we must do it as women. Not as imitation of men. Women are playing a big role in development because they bring an extra ingredient of femininity.'[59] Every person should hold this closely to heart and fight against all forms of discrimination against women.

[58] Kuukuwa Andam and Sena Dei-Tu 'Sophia Akuffo: Balancing the Equities' in Josephine Jarpa Dawuni and Akua Kuenyehia (eds), *International Courts and the African Woman Judge* (Routledge 2017) 105.

[59] Cited by Atobrah and Awedoba (n 45) 19–28.

PART VI

THE HALL OF WOMEN FOR SOCIAL AND ECONOMIC DEVELOPMENT BY INTERNATIONAL LAW: A NORDIC DREAM?

14
Alva Myrdal
The Rise and Fall of Social Democratic Internationalism

Anne Orford

Alva Myrdal was a feminist public intellectual, social policy researcher, ambassador, socialist internationalist, and eventual Nobel Peace Prize Laureate. She is remembered both as one of the major architects of the Swedish welfare state and as a significant figure in international disarmament. For much of her life she was engaged in debates about social policy, initially in the Swedish context and then, after the Second World War, on the international stage, first as principal director at the UN Department of Social Affairs in New York from 1949, then director of the Department of Social Sciences at the United Nations Educational, Scientific, and Cultural Organization (UNESCO) from 1951, and finally as Swedish Ambassador to India from 1955 to 1961. She was the head of Sweden's delegation to the UN Committee on Disarmament from 1962 to 1973, and in 1982 was awarded the Nobel Peace Prize for her work on disarmament. Alva Myrdal was a frequent contributor to Swedish newspapers and the author of numerous books and articles in Swedish and English.[1]

Alva Myrdal's life and work offer a window into Scandinavian social democratic internationalism at the period when it was at its most idealistic and influential. As this chapter will show, the struggle over how to interpret Alva's legacy is closely tied up with the rise and fall of social democracy in Sweden and beyond over the course of the twentieth century. An image of Sweden as social laboratory and modernist utopia continues to have a pervasive grasp on the imagination of many people in Western countries.[2] Indeed, Alva was well aware that the wide interest in Sweden's social and political experiments was rarely objective, noting that 'some people in some countries will accept only idealized truths about Scandinavia', while others are quick to criticize and watch for 'exaggerations and embellishments'.[3]

Within Sweden, Alva Myrdal is a household name. Outside Sweden and in international law circles, her work is less well known than that of her husband, Gunnar Myrdal, despite the interconnected nature of their thinking and research. I focus throughout the chapter on the interrelation of the personal life, politics, and ideals of Alva Myrdal, because it was in part her insistence on the need to take material

[1] Alva Myrdal's works from 1932 to 1961 are listed in Barbro Terling, *Alva Myrdal: Kommenterad Bibliografi, 1932–1961 med engelsk parallelltext: Alva Myrdal: An Annotated Bibliography, 1932–1961 with Parallel Text in English* (Alva och Gunnar Myrdals Stiftelse 1987).

[2] Carl Marklund, 'The Social Laboratory, the Middle Way and the Swedish Model: Three Frames for the Image of Sweden' (2009) 34 Scandinavian Journal of History 264.

[3] Alva Myrdal, *Nation and Family: The Swedish Experiment in Democratic Family and Population Policy* (MIT Press 1968 [1941]) 15.

Anne Orford, *Alva Myrdal* In: *Portraits of Women in International Law.* Edited by: Immi Tallgren, Oxford University Press.
 DOI: 10.1093/oso/9780198868453.003.0014

Figure 14.1 Swedish Delegate Mrs. Myrdal at the Geneva Conference on Disarmament in 1966.
Source: Unknown photographer, National Archives of the Netherlands, Photo collection Anefo.

questions of reproduction seriously in an institutional form that shaped Sweden as a state unlike almost any other.

The Education of a Social Democrat

Alva was born in Uppsala in 1902.[4] She was the first child of a couple from rural Sweden who struggled economically during a period of rapid urbanization and industrialization. Alva's father, Albert Reimer, came from a landless peasant family, and was deeply involved in the three people's movements (*folkrörelser*) that helped transform Sweden—the cooperative movement, the temperance movement, and the Social Democratic labour movement. He read Kropotkin and Rousseau, was a lifelong atheist, and saw himself as a 'barricade socialist'. Alva's mother, Lova Larsson Reimer, came from a landowning farming family and was politically liberal and socially conservative. The clash between her parents' perspectives deeply shaped Alva's view of the politics of the personal. Alva

[4] The details in this section are drawn from Sissela Bok, *Alva Myrdal: A Daughter's Memoir* (Perseus 1991), chs 2–4. As Alva's biographer Yvonne Hirdman notes, Alva's childhood 'comes to us mediated via her daughters, which makes it a fairy tale': Yvonne Hirdman, *Alva Myrdal: The Passionate Mind* (Indiana University Press 2008) 7.

called herself 'a child of the people's movements' and would later recall political meetings being held in her home while she sat under the dining table, listening to debates about social democracy, voting rights campaigns, or the running of the communal board for food and the cooperative store. Under that table, she learnt at least two lessons: to take popular movements seriously, and 'that Father plans the world, not Mother'.[5]

Alva emerged from a milieu that did not nurture young women or support their education. She was expected to leave school at fourteen after completing her allotted seven years of elementary school education. While the nearest town of Eskilstuna had a public gymnasium (or high school), it was only for boys. Neither of Alva's parents saw this as a problem. Her father wanted his five children to grow up to be farmers, and her mother, who had lost two siblings to tuberculosis, was opposed to her children using the town library (for fear of infection) or leaving home to go to school elsewhere. At fifteen, Alva began working as a bookkeeper in the Eskilstuna tax office, took orders for embroidery and sewing, spent any spare money on second-hand books, smuggled library books home under the wide skirts worn at the time, and in the end persuaded her father to join with other parents and urge the town board to establish a gymnasium for girls. As a result, Alva began her high school studies at seventeen, at a cost of 900 crowns a year (for a course that cost boys 80 crowns). The girls were not allowed to take classes in the high school building established for boys and were required to travel across town to various makeshift classrooms during the day. Alva continued working in the tax office to pay for the school fees, compressed the final two years of her course into one, and graduated from high school at twenty with highest honours.

In 1919, while still finishing her high school studies, Alva met Gunnar Myrdal, then a university student. Gunnar was the oldest son of a conservative, prosperous family. He considered himself and was considered by his parents to be exceptionally gifted. He was the first person in his family to attend high school, and for his parents that goal was thought to be worth every sacrifice. Gunnar had received an excellent education in the natural and social sciences at the Stockholm gymnasium, where his teachers took him seriously and carefully guided his studies. By the time he met Alva, Gunnar was studying law at Stockholm's Högskola (now the University of Stockholm). Yet during his first conversations with Alva, it was clear that Gunnar had 'met his match in her'.[6] He had read very few of the books about which she wanted to talk so excitedly (although he pretended he had), and throughout the rest of their lives he would rely on her as a 'fountain of ideas'.[7] He was also strongly influenced by her passion for equality and social justice—meeting her challenged, at least in theory, his elitist condescension towards both women and 'the masses'.[8]

After finishing high school, Alva enrolled at the University of Stockholm and earned her Bachelor of Arts in 1924, the year she and Gunnar were married. She planned to write a critical study of Freud's *Interpretation of Dreams* as a doctoral dissertation at Uppsala University supervised by Bertil Hammer, but Hammer died while she was in the United States as a Rockefeller Fellow undertaking preparatory research.[9] The

[5] Bok, *Alva Myrdal* (n 4) 26.
[6] ibid 52.
[7] ibid 108.
[8] ibid 52.
[9] ibid 80, 83, 95.

professor who replaced Hammer thought Freud unworthy of attention and rejected any thesis proposal that was not designed to test the professor's own theories. Alva instead earned a Master of Arts from Uppsala University in 1934 but felt herself once again 'shut out from continued studies'.[10] While she became a prolific author, she subsequently had only limited involvement with Swedish universities.

Alva and Gunnar Myrdal had three children: Jan (born in 1927), Sissela (born in 1934), and Kaj (born in 1936). Although 'Gunnar accepted her as an intellectual equal from the start', Alva's daughter Sissela would recall that 'neither he nor anyone else fully honoured that equality in practice', particularly when it came to caring for children or running the household.[11] That was not unusual in early twentieth-century Europe. To the extent that there were prominent women with leadership roles in politics, science, literature, religion, or education, they generally did not have children. The availability (if not yet legality) of improved contraceptives in the 1930s meant that women could begin to imagine taking on public roles while having children, yet without any models or guides as to how such roles might be combined. As a result, Alva Myrdal was one of the first women to experience, analyse, and write about the contradictions and dilemmas to which a social democratic approach to reproduction gave rise.

The Population Question

In the 1930s, Alva began to focus on developing concrete proposals aimed at social reform. She joined the Social Democratic Party in 1931, during the period when the party, led by Per Albin Hansson, developed its *folkhemmet* model. This was based on the idea that the emergent Swedish social democratic state was the People's Home, in which solidarity, equality, and mutual support were natural. It would prove to be the foundation for a long period of Social Democratic rule.[12]

In 1934, when Alva was thirty-two, she and Gunnar published a hugely influential book entitled *Kris i befolkningsfrågan* (Crisis in the Population Question).[13] It has been said that 'no other book is as much a manifesto of the Swedish Welfare State' and that it 'is invaluable as a document for understanding Swedish modern history'.[14] The book attracted a great deal of public attention and was at the centre of deliberations over the welfare state for the remainder of the 1930s.[15] *Kris i befolkningsfrågan* was reprinted several times during the 1930s and would become the best-selling social science book in Sweden of the twentieth century.[16]

[10] ibid 96.
[11] ibid 71.
[12] See generally Gøsta Esping-Andersen, 'The Making of a Social Democratic Welfare State' in Klaus Misgeld, Karl Molin, and Klas Åmark (eds), *Creating Social Democracy: A Century of the Social Democratic Labor Party in Sweden* (Pennsylvania State University Press 1992) 35.
[13] Alva Myrdal and Gunnar Myrdal, *Kris i befolkningsfrågan* (Albert Bonniers Förlag 1934).
[14] Hedvig Ekerwald, 'The Modernist Manifesto of Alva and Gunnar Myrdal: Modernization of Sweden in the Thirties and the Question of Sterilization' (2001) 14 International Journal of Politics, Culture and Society 539, 542.
[15] ibid 542.
[16] Hedvig Ekerwald, 'To Build a Nation: Alva Myrdal and the Role of Family Politics in the Transformation of Sweden in the 1930s' in Sven Eliaeson, Lyudmila Harutyunyan, and Larissa Titarenko (eds), *After the Soviet Empire* (Brill 2015) 108, 109.

The book began by contrasting two dominant positions in the debate over population. One position, asserted mainly by a coalition of conservatives and clergy, warned of the dangers of declining birth rates in Sweden and many European nations, particularly in the aftermath of the Great War and the Depression. In a move that is very familiar from the overt anti-feminism and social conservativism of twenty-first century right-wing movements, that coalition called for punitive laws to discourage contraception and abortion, and opposed reforms that would give women greater freedom or control over reproduction, in the name of defending the nation. A second group, including many Social Democrats, advocated for greater freedom for women with respect to birth control and for public funding for schools, housing, and better working conditions. Alva and Gunnar sought to transcend the terms of that debate, by accepting the conservative view that declining birth rates were a bad thing, but concluding that this presented 'the most forceful argument for a profound and radical socialist reshaping of society'.[17] *Kris i befolkningsfrågan* called for radical reforms including housing subsidies for families with children, free school lunches, the legalization of contraceptives, public health care, and sex education in schools, while presenting the rights of women and children as the foundation for those reforms.

However the Myrdals' manifesto abandoned their commitment to rights and liberty when it came to their proposal of forced sterilization on 'racially hygienic' grounds for those who, because of genetic disease or intellectual disability, would offer children an 'unsuitable milieu for child-rearing'.[18] The authors were aware of the potential similarities between their proposals and the social conservatism of the right. They took care to warn against Germany's 'political barbarism of race and class' and dismissed the notion that some races might be more advanced than others.[19] Nonetheless, their vision mirrored the conservative nostalgia for community and family and the biopolitics of modern statecraft, while seeking to transform those institutions and methods into state-based forms of social protection.[20]

Kris i befolkningsfrågan had an enormous influence in Sweden, was discussed in reading groups and collectives around the country, and led to significant policy reforms. Alva travelled the country giving speeches, conducting workshops, and writing newspaper articles about the book, often being heckled by audience members for not being at home with her children and attacked in the press as a threat to family values. It was Gunnar, however, who received new invitations based on the book's success. In 1935 Gunnar was asked to chair Sweden's new Housing Commission and was made a member of the newly formed Population Commission, which implemented many of the book's proposals. In 1938, Gunnar was invited to give the prestigious Godkin Lectures at Harvard University, which he titled *Population: A Problem for Democracy*. The subsequent publication of the lectures by Harvard University Press under Gunnar's name has been called 'the mature form of the couple's thinking on

[17] Bok, *Alva Myrdal* (n 4) 117, citing Myrdal and Myrdal, *Kris i befolkningsfrågan* (n 13).

[18] ibid 118.

[19] ibid 118.

[20] For an analysis of that tendency in social democratic thought more broadly, see the discussion in Melinda Cooper, *Family Values: Between Neoliberalism and the New Social Conservativism* (Zone Books 2019).

these matters',[21] although only one member of 'the couple' was named on the cover. When he was asked to chair the National Parents' Association of Sweden, Gunnar inquired whether the board had really meant the post for Alva. Its members sheepishly replied 'that of course they took for granted that she would be the one who would do the actual work'.[22]

In 1941, Alva published an English-language sequel, entitled *Nation and Family: The Swedish Experiment in Democratic Family and Population Policy*,[23] the research for which was funded by the Carnegie Corporation. *Nation and Family* was written for an American audience and offers Alva's reflections on the implementation of population policies in Sweden. *Nation and Family* is built upon a modernist conviction that social planning based upon factual knowledge and explicitly articulated values is not only desirable but also necessary if the modern state is to be made hospitable for women and children. A capacity and willingness to plan for social organization was central to addressing potential population crises—whether of depopulation, as was perceived to be the case in the Sweden of the 1930s, or overpopulation. Alva argued that governments of modern industrial societies cannot avoid having policies that impact upon families—the only question was 'whether these will be purposeful, intended policies'.[24]

According to *Nation and Family*, 'the population crisis is only the external aspect of what is really a crisis in the family as an institution'.[25] The family is a 'deep-rooted and fixed' 'system of human relations' which 'has necessarily lacked the plasticity to adapt itself to the fundamental and pervasive economic changes of the last century. The family even in its modern structure has its moorings in a preindustrial agrarian society.'[26] The differentiated status of women was one of the last remaining vestiges of that society. Thus Alva argued that in order to address the status of women, the state as the vehicle of social planning must address the crisis of the family as an institution.

> Since we cannot, and do not want to, revert to an agrarian or patriarchal order, some collectivist devices must be instituted in the larger national household to substitute for the relative security enjoyed in the family household of old.[27]

As a result, 'a population policy had to be nothing less than a social policy at large'.[28] Alva's vision of the issues that such a policy needed to address was extremely broad, and included the provision of modern social housing, collective childcare, national school lunches, modernist home furnishing, public health care, social security, the availability of sex education, contraception, abortion, and again, in a jarring five-page discussion, sterilization.

The place of sterilization in Swedish social democratic theory and practice became a subject of intense national—and indeed international—debate in 1997, when the

[21] William J Barber, *Gunnar Myrdal* (Palgrave Macmillan 2008) 53.
[22] Bok, *Alva Myrdal* (n 4) 126.
[23] Myrdal, *Nation and Family* (n 3).
[24] Daniel Patrick Moynihan, 'Foreword to the Paperback Edition', ibid vii.
[25] Myrdal, *Nation and Family* (n 3) 4.
[26] ibid.
[27] ibid 5.
[28] ibid 2.

journalist Maciej Zaremba published two major articles in *Dagens Nyheter*, Sweden's major morning newspaper, addressing the history of forced sterilization in Sweden. Those articles and an accompanying editorial reminded readers that Sweden had engaged in forced sterilization from 1935, when the practice was first provided for in legislation, through to 1976, when the laws allowing forced sterilization were repealed. More than 'four sterilisation operations were carried out every day for forty years, or as many in Sweden as in the whole of the USA', with 60,000 sterilization operations conducted during those four decades, a striking number in a country of between seven and nine million inhabitants.[29] Alva Myrdal was named as a principal advocate of sterilization policy during the debate that followed and 'denigrated for her support of that policy'.[30] One of the main controversies in that Swedish sterilization debate was whether forced sterilization was a specific product of social democracy or part of the broader milieu of the period.[31] According to Zaremba, 'purging the "inferior" was mainly a social democratic project' and 'Swedish sterilisation surgery formed an integral part of the very base of the construction of the welfare state'.[32]

Other participants in the Swedish debate, however, argued that while Swedish social democrats were complicit in continuing processes of coercive sterilization, the broader question remained whether this was a last remnant of conservative social thinking with which social democrats were wrestling in the 1930s and 40s or a more fundamental condition of the social democratic welfare state. The Myrdals, for example, had clearly not been fellow travellers with the Nazis. The couple had been outspoken anti-fascist activists during the Second World War, and publicly opposed the way that the Swedish coalition government had accommodated the demands of Nazi Germany. Alva Myrdal was a member of the Swedish Committee for International Aid and the Swedish Refugee Commission and worked with Count Folke Bernadotte to rescue prisoners from German concentration camps and find them jobs and schools in Sweden. Two refugee children lived with the Myrdals during the war, and a circle of socialist refugees including Willy Brandt and Bruno Kreisky met regularly in the Myrdals' house to discuss postwar plans for a democratic Europe.

The 1990s debate over whether the Swedish population policy espoused by the Myrdals was a form of genocidal authoritarianism was in part a proxy for a broader struggle. That struggle concerned the interpretation and legacies of the 'rationalistic futurism' that had been such a feature of Swedish social democratic politics.[33] By the mid-1990s that version of socialist modernism was being displaced by the rising tide of European neoliberalism that emerged triumphant with the end of the Cold War. Rather than establishing links between Nazism and the social democratic project in particular, the Swedish history of sterilization raised more foundational questions. It revealed the continuities between older forms of eugenics and modern government more generally. Those continuities extend beyond sterilization policies to include

[29] Ekerwald, 'The Modernist Manifesto (n 14) 540–41.
[30] ibid 541.
[31] ibid 542.
[32] ibid 542–43.
[33] On the 'rationalistic futurism' of Swedish social democrats, see Arne Ruth, 'The Second New Nation: The Mythology of Modern Sweden' (1984) 113 Daedalus 113, and on its demise, see Ole Wæver, 'Nordic Nostalgia: Northern Europe after the Cold War' (1992) 68 International Affairs 77.

the coercive biopolitical processes of 'normalization' through psychiatric and criminal interventions that underpin most liberal democracies, as well as the claim underpinning modern genetics that people's lives are limited by inherited biological characteristics.[34]

The United Nations and Global Population Policy

After the Second World War, Alva Myrdal's work began to take on a more internationalist focus. In 1946, Trygve Lie, the first Secretary-General of the newly created United Nations, offered Alva Myrdal the position of director of social affairs in the UN secretariat. Alva reluctantly turned the position down, explaining that although she would have found it rewarding, 'she could not put an ocean between the family and herself'.[35] In early 1947, she was invited by Julian Huxley to be the assistant director of the newly formed UNESCO. Gunnar, however, 'made it clear that he did not want to move to Paris' and leave Sweden.[36]

In March 1947, however, Gunnar was asked to head the UN Economic Commission for Europe (ECE), which was in the process of being set up in Geneva. At that point, his desire to stay in Sweden appears to have evaporated. Gunnar accepted the position, leaving Alva to pack up her work as principal of the experimental teacher training college she had established in Stockholm, set up a new home in Geneva, and find schools for the children. This ushered in a difficult period in Alva's life. Gunnar was absorbed in an intensive new position that took up long hours, while Alva had no possibility of work in Switzerland as a foreigner and a woman and was expected to act as hostess and housewife.

In the autumn of 1948, Alva was given another chance to take up a position at the United Nations, when she was asked by Trygve Lie to become head of the UN's Department of Social Affairs, the 'highest-placed woman in any international organization'[37]. She accepted, and on the day after her forty-seventh birthday she left Geneva and her family for New York, to take up a position in an organization for the first time after many years of creating her own possibilities for work. Her departure marked the moment when, in her words, she 'became a free person'.[38]

Alva made a significant contribution to developing the role of the Department within the UN Secretariat. Her daughter Sissela Bok comments of that new position: 'All the issues that she had dealt with earlier—the position of women and children, schooling, housing conditions, population—she could now consider with the whole world as a background.'[39] Alva was involved in the creation of a Social Welfare

[34] See Peter Weingart, 'Science and Political Culture: Eugenics in Comparative Perspective' (1999) 24 Scandinavian Journal of History 163; Thomas Etzemüller, 'Rationalizing the Individual—Engineering Society: The Case of Sweden' in Kerstin Brückweh and others (eds), *Engineering Society: The Role of the Human and Social Sciences in Modern Societies, 1880–1980* (Palgrave Macmillan 2012) 97; Martin Ericsson, 'What Happened to "Race" in Race Biology? The Swedish State Institute for Race Biology, 1936–1960' (2021) 46 Scandinavian Journal of History 125.

[35] Bok, *Alva Myrdal* (n 4) 194.

[36] ibid.

[37] ibid 207.

[38] ibid.

[39] ibid.

office with sections on housing, town planning, family policy, and child welfare. The Department provided research for the Commission on Human Rights and the Commission on the Status of Women. Alva pushed for social issues to be included within the new practice of providing technical assistance to developing states, and she argued that social questions must be at the heart of development, advocating a slow process of 'balanced modernization' in which men and women could keep up with the pace of change.[40]

International development experts at the time believed that population growth could erode any gains made through development aid, and there was some expectation that Alva as a population expert would make a statement on this issue. In 1949, Alva and Paul Vincent published a book called *Are We Too Many?: UNESCO, Food, and People*.[41] Despite its title, the book did not focus upon overpopulation or the limits to the earth's resources. Instead, it challenged Malthusian approaches, asking whether the idea of overpopulation in fact shielded rich nations and their citizens from recognizing the reality of preventable famine in the Third World. Myrdal and Vincent argued that people should not only be seen as 'consumers of natural resources', but also as 'creators of increased abundance'. In addition, they argued that with increasing opportunity and education, couples might choose to limit the size of their families.[42] The book cited Sweden's history as an example of this approach.

In 1950, Alva took up the Directorship of the Division of Social Sciences at UNESCO in Paris, where she stayed until 1955. She was again an innovator in the role, for example bringing the question of the education of girls and the importance of literacy more generally to the forefront. By as early as 1953, Alva had begun to voice her concerns that development under UN auspices had become a field for outsiders enforcing American-financed development projects that required large capital outlays and bore little relation to the values and knowledge of local communities.[43] She faced concerted conservative opposition to her attempts to develop a coordinated policy on questions of reproduction by UNESCO, the World Health Organization, and the United Nations Population Commission.[44] At the World Population Conference held in Rome in 1954, Soviet bloc and Catholic governments 'joined forces to block all efforts to address population problems', arguing 'that there was no real population problem anywhere in the world but only a need for huge social and economic reforms'.[45] Alva in contrast saw 'access to contraceptives and sexual education', along with literacy and healthcare, as basic requirements for empowering women and families, and in so doing ensuring 'the welfare of nations'. In her view, it was 'unconscionable simply to leave the poor and the illiterate to their fate'.[46]

[40] Sondra R Herman, 'Solidarity Abroad: Alva Myrdal's Campaign for the Developing Nations' in Peter Wallensteen (ed), *Alva Myrdal in International Affairs* (Uppsala Publishing House 2002) 23, 26–27.

[41] Alva Myrdal and Paul Vincent, *Are We Too Many?: UNESCO, Food, and People* (Bureau of Current Affairs 1949).

[42] Herman (n 40).

[43] Sunil Amrith and Glenda Sluga, 'New Histories of the United Nations' (2008) 19 Journal of World History 251, 265.

[44] Bok, *Alva Myrdal* (n 4) 216.

[45] ibid.

[46] ibid 216–27.

Social Democratic Diplomacy

In 1955, Alva left the United Nations and took up an appointment as Swedish Ambassador to India, Burma (now Myanmar), Ceylon (now Sri Lanka), and Nepal. She was only the second woman to be appointed as a Head of Mission by the Swedish Government.[47] While her arrival at the Delhi airport was greeted with an 'ovation-like whirl of women, garlands, and press photographers' organized by her friends in the women's movement, her welcome at the Swedish embassy the following morning was far more lukewarm, in large part because the first secretary who had been acting ambassador prior to her arrival made clear how inexperienced he found her.[48]

During that period, she became a close friend and political ally of the Indian Prime Minister Jawaharlal Nehru. This period represented the high point of Indian central planning, as manifested in India's second Five Year Plan with its focus upon rapid industrialization and family-planning as responses to rural 'underemployment'. Alva saw Sweden and India as two nations with shared issues and approaches. Both were neutral nations with large rural populations faced with the challenge of lifting themselves out of poverty, and both had been determined to do so through social democratic policies, egalitarian ideals, education, and cooperation rather than authoritarian rule. Throughout her time as ambassador, Alva travelled widely throughout the country, often accompanying Nehru to visit village projects or agricultural developments. She worked closely with women's groups in India, focused particularly on bringing about access to education for girls. She also worked with Ceylon's Minister of Health to establish a bilateral aid treaty for cooperation between Swedish and Ceylonese health workers to develop a pilot birth-control programme in Ceylon.

During her time in India, Alva was influenced by Nehru's approach to nonalignment, a term he had been using since the late 1940s.[49] Watching Nehru's skill at balancing the demands of the United States, the Soviet Union, and neighbouring China shaped Alva's approach to what she called Sweden's 'active neutrality'. It was an approach she would take up in her new role in the field of disarmament.

The Game of Disarmament

When Alva Myrdal returned from India in 1961, she became involved in a topic and a campaign that would absorb the rest of her working life. Swedish Foreign Minister Östen Undén, who was 'well-known for occasionally having promoted able women to high offices',[50] asked her to take up the question of disarmament. The growing arms race and the positions taken by the two Cold War superpowers on nuclear

[47] The first was Katrina Stopia, whose husband died while he was ambassador to Russia in 1632, and who served as ambassador in her husband's place until 1634.

[48] Bok, *Alva Myrdal* (n 4) 240.

[49] Lorenz M Lüthi, 'Non-Alignment, 1946–1965: Its Establishment and Struggle against Afro-Asianism' (2016) 7 Humanity 201.

[50] Jan Prawitz, 'Arms Controller Alva Myrdal—Word Power for World Politics' in Peter Wallensteen (ed), *Alva Myrdal in International Affairs* (Uppsala Publishing House 2002) 55, 57.

proliferation and testing were causing increasing tension, and Undén sought to facilitate a fresh start on the issue. One aspect of Alva's work became known as the 'Undén Proposal', which suggested that states possessing no nuclear weapons should form a 'Non-nuclear club' and declare that they refused to participate in nuclear armaments and did not intend to manufacture nuclear weapons or permit stockpiling of nuclear weapons on their territories.[51]

Alva was elected to the Swedish Parliament in 1961, headed Sweden's delegation to the UN Committee on Disarmament from 1962 to 1973, and in 1969 joined the Swedish Cabinet as Minister for Disarmament. She was a formidable negotiator, working with the nonaligned movement to oppose the push by the United States and the USSR to turn the issue of nuclear weapons into one that was controlled by the superpowers. She fought, amongst other things, for nuclear-weapons-free zones, a no-first-strike pledge from the nuclear powers, and a comprehensive ban on nuclear testing, and promoted the 1967 Treaty of Tlatelolco, which created the first nuclear-free zone in the world and was signed by all thirty-three Latin American states. In addition, as she set out in her prescient address to the Hague Academy of International Law, she pushed to prohibit military uses of the sea-bed and ocean floor, including through participating in the drafting of a treaty to prohibit the emplacement of nuclear weapons, weapons of mass destruction, or facilities designed to enable the launch of such weapons on the sea bed and ocean floor.[52]

After leaving the government in 1973, Alva became president of the Labour Movement's Peace Forum, which became the joint voice of the Swedish peace movement. Three years later, in 1976, she published *The Game of Disarmament*.[53] There she described her 'gradually increasing feeling of near despair after 12 years of participating in multilateral negotiations' and accused the world's superpowers of indulging 'in subterfuges and half-truths with their closest and most dependent allies following suit or keeping silent'. She considered however that 'the strength of the disarmers has been the allegiance of the non-aligned'. While she concluded that on balance there had been no real advance towards disarmament, she continued to insist that 'there were better futures to choose'.[54] For Alva, disarmament and development were two sides of the same coin. She remained convinced that the road to peace lay through nuclear disarmament and social democracy globally. The creation of large nuclear arsenals had 'been achieved at the sacrifice of social welfare'.[55] She believed that the trend towards more dangerous armaments could be reversed by educating peoples 'to recognize their true interests'.[56]

[51] Statement by the Minister for Foreign Affairs, Mr Östen Undén in the First Committee, 26 October 1961. The proposal was adopted in GA Resolution 1664, XVI, 4 December 1961. See further Katarina Brodin, 'The Undén Proposal' (1966) 1 Cooperation and Conflict 18.

[52] Alva Myrdal, 'Preserving the Oceans for Peaceful Purposes' (1971) 133 Collected Courses of the Hague Academy of International Law 1.

[53] Alva Myrdal, *The Game of Disarmament: How the United States and Russia Run the Arms Race* (Pantheon 1976).

[54] ibid xxii.

[55] ibid 6.

[56] ibid 113.

Alva Myrdal was nominated four times for the Nobel Peace Prize.[57] When she was overlooked for the third time in 1981, nineteen Norwegian political and pacificist organizations created and presented her with an alternative Norwegian People's Peace Prize. The next year in 1982 she was awarded the Nobel Peace Prize along with the Mexican diplomat Alfonso Garcia Robles for their work on nuclear disarmament. Gunnar had earlier been awarded the Nobel Memorial Prize in Economic Science in 1974. Alva and Gunnar Myrdal are to this date still the only couple in history to be awarded Nobel prizes independently of each other and in separate fields.

The Contested Legacies of Social Democracy

Alva Myrdal died in February 1986 on her eighty-fourth birthday. A memorial service was held in Storkyrkan, the medieval cathedral next to the Royal Palace in Stockholm's Gamla Stan. The event began with a massive torchlight parade through the streets of Stockholm, led by Alva's family and by Prime Minister and leader of the Social Democratic Party Olof Palme and his wife Lisbet. Crowds of people holding candles stood outside the cathedral in the dark, listening to a broadcast of the service. Palme presented the eulogy, speaking for what would turn out to be the last time in public before he was assassinated two weeks later.[58] In his tribute, Palme said: 'When you talk about Alva Myrdal, people become inspired. To them, she signifies happiness about life's potential, a bright faith in the future.'[59] For Palme, Alva Myrdal's 'unique perseverance and will to fight ... gave hope and confidence to those in despair over the madness of the arms race'.[60]

Alva's life and work challenges the worldview of those who envisage socialist politics only in the form of barricades or who privilege questions of production over reproduction. Perhaps for that reason, outside Sweden her name is less well known than that of her economist partner Gunnar. In international law and in many other fields, Gunnar's insights about international political economy are discussed outside the context of the work and thinking of his lifelong collaborator and intellectual sparring partner Alva. In her introduction to a collection entitled *The Essential Gunnar Myrdal*,[61] their daughter Sissela Bok implicitly rebuked the academic world more broadly when she wrote that no one who knew Gunnar 'could possibly conceive of what is essential about his life and work apart from his companionship, for nearly seventy years, with [my mother, Alva Myrdal]'.[62]

The question of how we should interpret the meaning and legacy of Alva Myrdal's life is a subject of heated public debate. In terms of her private life, that legacy has been contested publicly and painfully through competing memoirs published by her

[57] See generally Maj-Britt Theorin, 'Alva Myrdal and the Peace Movement' in Peter Wallensteen (ed), *Alva Myrdal in International Affairs* (Uppsala Publishing House 2002) 43.
[58] Bok, *Alva Myrdal* (n 4) 361.
[59] ibid.
[60] *New York Times* obituary.
[61] Sissela Bok, 'Introduction' in Örjan Appelqvist and Stellan Andersson (eds), *The Essential Gunnar Myrdal* (New Press 2005) xix.
[62] ibid xxi.

children—one by her son Jan Myrdal, which attacked his mother for being cold and uncaring, and one by her daughter Sissela Bok, which offers a profoundly generous reflection on her mother's legacy. The resulting public debate in Sweden over whether Alva was a good mother is more than simply an example of institutionalized misogyny (although it is that). At stake are her radical ideas about the place of families, the role of women, and the education of children within social democracies. The inability of her private life to live up to the high ideals she espoused was in part an effect of the 'social problem' that working women posed.[63] To be fair to Alva, it also seemed easier to invent the welfare state than to get Gunnar to do the vacuuming or care for his children. However in her struggle to make sense of the dilemmas she faced as a working mother, Alva diagnosed a problem that transcended her immediate situation—in particular, that the combination of continued patriarchal relations and capitalist modernization made it increasingly undesirable for women to have children.

Studying Alva Myrdal left me with a feeling of sadness about what happened to her optimistic dreams for the future of Sweden and of social democracy globally. I found myself going over the details of her life and work, trying to find the moment where she made the wrong choice or social democracy more generally took the wrong turn. Yet as McKenzie Wark reflected in the aftermath of Donald Trump's election in 2016:

> To be a socialist with any real clarity and honesty is to realize we are a defeated people ... But one can't linger in the melancholy embrace of defeat. One can't hold on to what's lost. Nor can one study the past simply to win the next time. There is no next time.[64]

Instead, Wark argues that we have 'to begin again'. Rather than searching the past for guides or programs, Wark calls on us to recognize that the counter-hegemonic forces we seek are imminent to our situation.

Alva Myrdal had already learnt that lesson. She never resigned herself to the melancholy embrace of defeat. Throughout her life, Alva saw clearly what had been lost, she mourned that loss, and then she moved on. She kept on working and organizing to make a better future. Perhaps that is why, despite the ongoing attacks on her legacy, Alva is still remembered with such admiration and affection by many Swedes today. Studying her life and work does not leave us with a program for action. Rather, the legacy she leaves those standing in the ruins of social democracy is her ability to begin again, her perseverance, her fighting spirit, and her commitment to 'laboring, planning, and dreaming' to bring a more egalitarian community into existence.[65]

[63] Bok, *Alva Myrdal* (n 4) 138–39.
[64] McKenzie Wark, 'The Spectacle of Disintegration', *Public Seminar*, 9 November 2016 <https://publicseminar.org/2016/11/disint/>.
[65] Myrdal, *Nation and Family* (n 3) xxi.

15
Ester Boserup
Women and Development on the Margins

Miriam Bak Mackenna

It is somewhat ironic that an individual despite being largely on the margins of discipline can, through their work, come to have a profound influence on its most fundamental tenets. Or, it could be said, it is not despite but rather because of this fact. Whatever the case, Ester Boserup, one of the world's first female economists, came to trigger a fundamental shift in international economic law and development; and yet her role in this process is virtually unknown in international legal circles.

Her pioneering book *Woman's Role in Economic Development* marked a key step in altering the understanding of women and gender in economic practice and international development policy and practices more generally. Positing the then radical idea that women made a significant economic contribution to both their households and the macro-economy, and were thus fundamental to national development, Boserup's book was amongst the first to document how women's economic role impacts women's subordinate position in many societies, particular, as well as the first to systematically investigate the sexual division of labour and its changing nature under conditions of modernization.[1] Equally groundbreaking were her observations of the largely negative consequences to women's power and roles that followed colonialism, urbanization, and mechanization, as well as the detrimental impact of Western development schemes on the status of and opportunities for women.

Her book heralded the start of a reassessment of international economic legal frameworks and activities, including helping to inspire the UN Decade for Women (1976–1985), ultimately providing the foundation for the Women in Development (WID) framework, and four world conferences on women from 1975 to 1995. Boserup's work also prompted the inclusion of the term 'invisible woman',[2] denoting the marginalization of women's activities in modernization processes which was the starting point of transnational gender development policies.[3] Women's equal right to development has emerged as one of the central elements of the international legal framework surrounding gender equality.[4] The right to development now encompasses

[1] Maria Patricia Fernandez Kelly, 'Development and the Sexual Division of Labor: An Introduction' (1981) 7(2) Signs 269.

[2] GLN Scott, *Recognizing the 'Invisible' Woman in Development: The World Bank's Experience* (World Bank 1979).

[3] Gudrun Lachenmann, 'Following Boserup's Traces: From Invisibility to Informalisation of Women's Economy to Engendering Development in Translocal Spaces' in Marina Fischer-Kowalski and others (eds), *Ester Boserup's Legacy on Sustainability* (Springer 2014).

[4] United Nations Development Programme (UNDP), *Human Development Report 1995: Gender and Human Development* (OUP 1995); World Bank, *Engendering Development:Through Gender, Equality in*

Miriam Bak Mackenna, *Ester Boserup* In: *Portraits of Women in International Law.* Edited by: Immi Tallgren,
Oxford University Press. © Miriam Bak Mackenna 2023. DOI: 10.1093/oso/9780198868453.003.0015

Figure 15.1 Ester Boserup.
Source: Courtesy of artist Diana Cristina Banciog.

not only issues of poverty reduction, but also the broader impact of human poverty, such as lack of agency and participation in decision-making, on the enjoyment of human rights and gender equality.[5]

Five decades later, Boserup's foundational insights into women's economic role in society continue to influence international political and legal policy and have paved the way for the integration of women into theories of development and social change.[6] This portrait is thus a picture of an outsider, both in her chosen field—economics—and in international law—whose refusal to be bound by disciplinary dogma and professional restraints, came to have a lasting impact on women's lives.

Rights, Resources, and Voice (OUP 2001) 100; Nicholas D Kristof and Sheryl WuDunn, *Half the Sky: Turning Oppression into Opportunity for Women Worldwide* (Virago 2010), xxi–xxii.

[5] See Marilyn Waring, 'Gender and International Law: Women and the Right to Development' (*Australian Year Book of International Law* 1988–1989) 12, 183; Bård A Andreassen and Stephen P Marks (eds), *Development as a Human Right: Legal, Political and Economic Dimensions*, 2nd edn (Intersentia 2010), 11; Hope Lewis, 'Women (under)development: The Relevance of 'the right to development' to Poor Women of Color in the United States'', *Law and Policy* (1996) 18(2–3) 281–313.

[6] See, eg, Marilyn Waring, *If Women Counted* (Harper and Row 1988); Amartya Sen, *Development as Freedom* (OUP 1989); Martha Nussbaum, *Women and the Human Right to Development: The Capabilities Approach* (Cambridge University Press 2000); Emmanuel Akyeampong and Hippolyte Fofack, *The Contribution of African Women to Economic Growth and Development in the Pre-Colonial and Colonial Periods: Historical Perspectives and Policy Implications* (World Bank 2013).

Introduction

Born in Copenhagen in 1910, Boserup was raised by her mother in relative poverty after the death of her father when she was two, leaving the family destitute. It is perhaps unsurprising therefore that Ester Boserup should dedicate a great deal of her scholarship to underlining the implications of economic hardship and the sexual division of labour on women. By her teenage years, Boserup had developed a keen interest in Marxist social theories and was active in leftist political groups, where she met her partner, Mogens Boserup, a fellow economist, whom she married in 1931. Encouraged by her mother, she began studying economics at the University of Copenhagen. Describing her decision to pursue economics as a career, she wrote:

> From the very beginning of my university study of economics, the structural problems of human societies had imposed themselves on me by the contemporary world conditions: I began the University in the autumn of 1929, when the New York stock market crashed, and when I left we were still in the middle of the Great Depression of the thirties. Against this background, the prevailing theories of equilibrium and marginal utility seemed irrelevant and—like many of my fellow students—I looked for alternatives.[7]

By 1935 she was a newly minted economist, a field dominated by men, in which women's concerns and activities were largely sidelined.[8] She took up employment at the Danish National bank's foreign exchange office, later at the Directorate for Commodity Supply, during which time she gave birth to three children. After spending several years working for the Danish government, she moved into the area of agricultural trade policy, relocating to Geneva to work for the newly formed United Nations Economic Commission of Europe (ECE) (1947–1957). This period had a profound impact on her work, and she began to consider the relationship between industrial and agricultural growth and population. She also began to express concerns about the impact of development aid and food subsidies on agricultural development, particularly in Africa.[9]

Her critical concerns about contemporary development policy were stoked during secondments to India (1957–1960) and Senegal (1964–1965). In India, she and her husband worked alongside Swedish ECE researcher Gunnar Myrdal on a project on Indian economic development. Boserup's field observations in India, however, did not fit with the prevailing Western development paradigm, particularly those concerning

[7] Ester Boserup, *My Professional Life and Publications 1929–1998,* (Copenhagen Museum Tuscularnum Press 1999) 9.

[8] This situation largely continues today. Academic economists are overwhelmingly male. According to information from university websites, about 20 per cent of Europe's senior economists are women. In the United States, only 13 per cent of full economics professors are women. See American Economic Association 'CSWEP Survey and Annual Report' available at <https://www.aeaweb.org/about-aea/committees/cswep/about/survey> accessed 3 October 2022.

[9] Irene Tinker, 'Utiziling Interdisciplinarity to Analyze Global Socio-Economic Change: A Tribute to Ester Boserup' in Lourdes Beneria and Savitri Bisnath (eds), *Global Tensions: Challenges and Opportunities in the World Economy* (Routledge 2004) 174–75.

agricultural production, population density, and migration.[10] These experiences provoked a sense of doubt about Myrdal's evaluations, later published as *Asian Drama* in 1965, and the development paradigm being applied to India as a whole. After completing their consultancies, she and her husband left the project and returned to Copenhagen, where Boserup began work on her first major book: *The Conditions of Agricultural Growth: The Economics of Agrarian Change Under Population Pressure.*[11]

The book, published in 1965, proposed a counter argument to neo-Malthusian ideas about population growth and subsistence *in the field of* agricultural development. Contrary to classical ideas about the negative relationship between population/production, which dominated development theory at the time, Boserup argued that population growth is the main stimulus to agricultural change and that the primary cause is the intensification of land use.[12]

Women in Economics

Based on her field experiences in India, Boserup began to turn her attention to the issue of the invisibility of women in development theory and the lack of systematic analysis of the differing impact of economic development and macroeconomic policies on men and women's lives. She began the process of collating extensive field research in Africa and Asia, noting 'knowing that this was a controversial issue, I wanted it to be a solid study, based on official statistics'.[13] This would become the foundation of *Woman's Role in Economic Development*, published in 1970.[14]

By its year of publication calls for a reappraisal of the global international economic and financial relationships had reached their peak, particularly as the dramatic increase in the price of crude petroleum made clear the inequities and imbalances of the international economic system. It was becoming increasingly evident that despite the efforts made during the First Development Decade (1961–1970) 'the gap between the standards of living in the developed and developing countries has widened instead of narrowing'.[15] While in 1950 Western Europe's real gross national product per capita was five times greater than that of Africa and Asia, by 1970 the gap had grown to about 8:1 for Africa and 8.5:1 for Asia.[16]

Despite the increasing focus on issues of international development, however, very little attention had been paid to the issue of gender, which was still considered a separate (and niche) concern. As economist Gudrun Lachenmann explains 'starting from structural adjustment programmes, where women were marginally considered, as well as in processes of democratisation and the decentralisation of services ... In

[10] ibid.

[11] Ester Boserup, *The Conditions of Agricultural Growth: The Economics of Agrarian Change under Population Pressure* (George Allen and Unwin 1965).

[12] Tinker, 'Utilizing Interdisciplinarity' (n 9) 175.

[13] Boserup, *My Professional Life* (n 8) 24.

[14] Ester Boserup, *Woman's Role in Economic Development* (George Allen and Unwin 1970).

[15] GA Resolution 2084 (xx) 'United Nations Development Decade' 1404th plenary meeting, 20 December 1965. See Susan Marks, 'Empire's Law' (2003) 10 Indiana Journal Global Legal Studies 449–66.

[16] Cited in A Westad, *The Global Cold War: Third World Interventions and the Making of Our Times* (Cambridge University Press 2007) 90.

conceptualisations of (good) governance, women and gender do not turn up. In poverty reduction programmes (PRSP), they are only regarded as "vulnerable" groups, not as agents of transformation and their links to the formal, liberalising mainstream economy are not established'.[17] Many development professionals and researchers began underlining the 'male-bias' in aid efforts, resulting in women being sidelined and disadvantaged.[18]

In broader feminist debates, economic inequality and its impact on women's social role was also high on the agenda, led by the socialist feminist movement. Following on from early interventions (eg Charlotte Perkins Gilman) the theoretical and policy implications of the sexual division of labour, women's role in the economy, and its impact on women's social, political, and economic status, the feminist debate started togain traction in the 1970s.[19]

The year prior to the publication of *Woman's Role in Economic Development*, Margaret Benston's seminal article 'The Political Economy of Women's Liberation' also emerged in print.[20] Frustrated with the marginalization of gender and the role of women in political economy theory, Benston sought to bring to light not only the invisibility of women's work in the home in the chain of production and accumulation, but to underline that this was also the source of women's subordination in social-economic relations.[21] Around this time, the concept of patriarchy—the 'manifestation and institutionalisation of male dominance over women and children in the family and the extension of male dominance over women in society in general'[22]—was also emerging as a theoretical framework to address the asymmetries in gender relations. Both radical feminists and socialist feminists proposed that patriarchy's relationship to capitalism was a defining aspect of women's oppression; however, they differed as to how they defined and understood this relationship. Some social reproduction theorists proposed a 'dual-system theory' in which capitalism and patriarchy are distinct systems that fused in the pre-industrial era to create the system of exploitation along

[17] Gudrun Lachenmann, 'Following Boserup's Traces: From Invisibility to Informalisation of Women's Economy to Engendering Development in Translocal Spaces' in Marina Fischer-Kowalski, Anette Reenberg, Anke Schaffartzik, and Andreas Mayer (eds), *Ester Boserup's Legacy on Sustainability* (Springer 2014), 142.

[18] Gina Koczberski, 'Women in Development: A Critical Analysis' (1998) 19(3) Third World Quarterly 395–409, 396.

[19] See, eg, especially Silvia Federici, *Wages Against Housework* (Power of Women Collective and Falling Wall Press 1975); Mariarosa Dalla Costa and Selma James, *The Power of Women and the Subversion of the Community* (Falling Wall Press 1972); Nicole Cox and Silvia Federici, *Counterplanning from the Kitchen: Wages for Housework, A Perspective on Capital and the Left* (Falling Wall Press 1975).

[20] Margaret Benston, 'The Political Economy of Women's Liberation' (1969) 21 Monthly Review 13.

[21] Benston was responding on the focus within the Marxist tradition of women's subordination as being linked to the productive sphere. For example, Frederick Engels argued that the 'first premise for the emancipation of women is the reintroduction of the entire female sex into public industry.… And this has become possible not only as a result of modern large-scale industry, which not only permits the participation of women in production in large numbers, but actually calls for it and, moreover, strives to convert private domestic work also into a public industry.' And later in the same passage: 'Here we see already that the emancipation of women and their equality with men are impossible and must remain so as long as women are excluded from socially productive work and restricted to housework, which is private.' Frederick Engels, *Origin of the Family, Private Property and the State* (Progress 1968) ch 9, 158.

[22] Gerda Lerner, *The Creation of Patriarchy* (OUP 1986) 239.

the lines of class and gender we see today.[23] Others developed a 'single-system theory' in which patriarchy and capitalism 'are not autonomous, nor even interconnected systems, but the same system'.[24]

Boserup's study with its data centred analysis make her observations less outwardly feminist; and indeed, she faced criticism for failing to centre a defined feminist theoretical framework in her text.[25] And yet, while Boserup was less focused on theorizing the social, political, and cultural origins of patriarchy and the sexual division of labour, her study dovetails neatly with the broader discourse of feminist economic theory both for its focus on the relationship between economic development and women's subordinate position in most societies, and her challenge to existing gender stereotypes. Her critical contribution, namely that the process of economic development widens rather than narrows the gap between men and women in terms of status, opportunity, and income level, issued a profound challenge to development theory, generating a great deal of focus amongst economists and social scientists alike.[26] In this sense her study is almost Trojan horse-like in its ability to infiltrate the ranks of a conservative economic field and raising a range of controversial topics including gender, population pressure, modernization of agriculture, colonization, and changing labour patterns.

Women's Role in Economic Development

Woman's Role in Economic Development examines the manner in which gender relations and the sexual division of labour plays out across three key settings relevant to the impact of modernization on developing economies: agricultural transformation, industrialization, and rural–urban migration. Emphasizing that gender is a basic factor in the division of labour across all economic settings, and across all cultures, she also underlines that there are significant differences in women's stereotypical work roles across countries and regions, associated with the particular environmental and social characteristics of the region.[27]

[23] Pat and Hugh Armstrong, 'Class is a Feminist Issue', in Silvia-Wayne Prince and Althea Vernon (eds), *Feminisms and Womanisms: A Women's Studies Reader* (Women's Press 1986) 317. See also Heidi Hartmann, 'The Unhappy Marriage of Marxism and Feminism: Towards a More Progressive Union', in Lydia Sargent (ed), *Women and Revolution: A Discussion of the Unhappy Marriage of Marxism and Feminism* (South End Press 1981) and Sylvia Walby, *Gender Segregation at Work* (Open University Press 1988).

[24] See, eg, Lisa Vogel, *Marxism and the Oppression of Women: Toward a Unitary Theory* (Rutgers University Press 1983); Iris Marion Young, 'Beyond the Unhappy Marriage: A Critique of Dual Systems Theory' in Lydia Sargent (ed), *Women and Revolution: A Discussion of the Unhappy Marriage of Marxism and Feminism* (South End Press 1981).

[25] Lourdes Beneria and Gits Sen, 'Accumulation, Reproduction, and Women's Role in Economic Development: Boserup Revisited' (1981) 7(2) Signs 282

[26] See, eg, the review essay by economist Norton Dodge, 'Women in Economic Development: A Review Essay' (1973)19(1) International Review of Education, 161–66 who sardonically began his review with the lines 'While the Kate Millets, Germaine Greers, Betty Friedans and Gloria Steinems grab the headlines and appear on popular television shows, much serious, objective, non-polemical work on the past, present, and future position of women is being done by other women (and men) who are less in the limelight but equally concerned with the abuse and misuse of women and their talents in various parts of the world.'

[27] As she notes 'Both in primitive and in more developed communities, the traditional division of labour within the family is usually considered 'natural' in the sense of being obviously and originally imposed by the sex difference itself'. Boserup *Woman's Role* (n 15) 15, 26.

Contrary to the belief that women are not active in food production and cultivation, Boserup presents an overview of the many economic activities women participate in the world over. In Africa, where shifting cultivation is practiced, for example, female farming is the dominant pattern. She also points to the fact that women make up 80 per cent of the labour force in trade in Ghana and 50 per cent of the labour force in trade in Burma, Thailand, Cambodia, Laos, the Philippines, and Vietnam; a fact she links to their participation in agriculture. In areas where women's participation in the labour force occurs it is generally accompanied by a higher status for women; however, they are still universally ranked below men in social and labour standing.[28]

Her observations about the socio-cultural dynamics that accompany women's participation in the workforce are particularly telling. Boserup underlines that across the world no matter what sector women dominate, women's work is generally ranked below men's work, and is subject to smaller remuneration. The main variant is the cultural rationalizations for this assessment. For example, in the Philippines it is argued that women are better traders because 'men are too sensitive for the coarse language and aggressive behavior necessary in a good tradesman'.[29] While in Vietnam trade is seen as 'debasing for men' while women are considered better suited to economic transactions.[30] The relationship between physical capacity and employment which also dominates many western constructions of labour and women is also a more variable factors in the rest of the world. Female labourers, load carriers, and dock workers are prevalent in many parts of the world.[31] Environmental factors such as population density and access to land, as well as social factors like class differentiation, also play a large part in the differences in male and female labour.[32] In the African system of shifting agriculture, for example, easy access to land, low population density, and less class differentiation led to a division of labour whereby men cleared land for cultivation, and women were in charge of subsistence crops.[33] In Asia, high population density, a more stratified class system, and a ready supply of low-class labourers and more technical agricultural methods discouraged female involvement in agriculture and reinforced the segregation of the sexes.[34] In underlining these differences, Boserup made an important departure from 'universal' and 'naturalistic' explanations of the division of labour, instead emphasizing the material and environmental determinants involved.

The varied picture on the nature of gender relations across a range of cultural settings that emerges provides a powerful counterpoint to many of the existing narratives on the 'backwards' nature of gender relations in developing nations, many of which have historically been used to justify Western colonial intervention.[35] While these are ground-breaking in themselves, it is her analysis of the impact of modernization and

[28] ibid 147–51.
[29] ibid 92.
[30] ibid 80.
[31] ibid 67.
[32] ibid 20-23.
[33] ibid 45–47.
[34] ibid 26.
[35] For a discussion of the role of gender in the civilizing mission see, eg, Jean Comaroff and John Comaroff, 'Home-Made Hegemony: Modernity, Domesticity and Colonialism in South Africa' in Karen Hansen (ed), *African Encounters with Domesticity* (Rutgers University Press 1997) 37–74.

industrialization on existing gender relations in the labour force that presents a particularly dramatic challenge to the discourse of modernization as beneficial to women. Observing that when economic modernization occurs 'a new sex pattern of productive work must emerge, for better or worse', the study makes it clear that this is generally for the worse.[36]

Boserup's analysis in particular underlines the fact that modernization takes a heavy toll on women both in the spheres of production and reproduction, by causing a widening and sharpening of the two spheres, with women increasingly confined to the home and excluded from industry and agriculture. Predicting the impact of the feminization of labour on patterns of work, Boserup demonstrates how women are looked upon as a source of low status, supplemental, and less remunerative types of work and responsibility[37] . In many traditional societies, women's dominance in agricultural work and handicraft production began to wane with the introduction of new technology, with attendant changes in family and production organization.[38] This trend continued with further modernization, resulting in a decrease in the status and importance of female activities which tend to be confined to the traditional sector. As Boserup notes: 'It is the men who do the modern things ... women perform the degrading manual jobs ... men represent modern farming in the village, women represent the old drudgery'.[39] This pattern emerges throughout the economy, including trade and industry, where male labour is associated with specialization and higher status; a trend reinforced with a broader social belief in male prestige. In societies where women's economic activities were already restricted, such as in North Africa and the Middle East, the economic opportunities of women were further reduced.[40] By providing this historical perspective on how the sexual division of labour operates and changes, Boserup underlines the multiple ways in which these relationships, both in the domestic and public domains, are highly responsive to broader shifts in relations of production more generally.

While many of these attitudes towards the sexual division of labour were present in pre-industrialized communities, Boserup highlights how it was exacerbated by the introduction of European concepts of land ownership, and stereotypical ideas of gendered labour activities.[41] Indeed, women emerge as some of the biggest losers in the colonial relationship. She points to the ideological and social pressure exerted by colonizers, particularly regarding ideas of sex-stereotypes divisions of labour, which led to the reduced status of women in many parts of Asia, Africa, and the Middle East. 'Europeans' she writes, 'showed little sympathy for the female farming systems which they found in many of their colonies'.[42] Moreover, many women lost their land rights as a result of 'land reforms introduced by European administrators', which were introduced on the basis that cultivation was 'man's work'.[43] The imposition of European

[36] ibid 5.
[37] ibid 66–69; 130–35.
[38] ibid 80–85.
[39] ibid 56.
[40] ibid 70, 108.
[41] ibid 53–66.
[42] ibid 19.
[43] ibid 60.

modes of education and vocational training, which also discriminated against women, further exacerbated the division of labour. Denied access to education and training it became much harder for women to transition from their (more central) role in an agriculturally based economy to an industrialized economy.[44] As Cynthia Epstein points out, 'this growing division is exacerbated by an often-total ban on female migration to towns, (where even in cases where they do migrate, they are almost entirely excluded from employment), by the refusal of authorities to teach them technical skills, and by assigning the men real property which is, by custom, shared by the women who are its cultivators'.[45]

Boserup was also groundbreaking in making clear the link between productive and reproductive labour, and the vast extent to which women's work both paid and unpaid have made a major impact on economic development. She also highlighted the underreporting of subsistence activities in economic statistics, which, she notes, 'are largely women's work'.[46] Documenting the labour intensive burden borne by women in carrying out domestic work, food gathering and preparation, the fetching of water and fuel, and unpaid family labour, Boserup's data highlights the enormous economic contribution to national accounts such activities represent.[47] In doing so, she reveals that conventional economic frameworks which exclude such activities are ideological biased towards female dominated activities and therefore maintain an undervaluation of women's work. Held up against Western standards of economic reporting, this undercounting of subsistence production also exaggerates the income gap among developing countries and between developing and industrialized countries. For example, data from South Africa suggested that the subsistence income not usually included in official income statistics accounted for more than 55 per cent of total income.[48] Were domestic labour included, the difference would have been even greater, while data from Malawi suggested that domestic labour accounted for 23 per cent of gross domestic product.[49]

Impact: Towards an Integrated Approach to Women in Development

The book had an immediate impact upon its publication. Coinciding with the general disenchantment with international development policy, it confirmed what many feminists had been arguing for years: that women were peripheral to economic policy, including development strategies pursued by major aid donors. In 1972 Boserup was appointed to the UN's Committee of Development Planning (1972–1980), and later as rapporteur for the first UN Experts Meeting concerning the role of women

[44] Cynthia Fuchs Epstein, 'Review of Woman's Role in Economic Development' (1973) 78(5) American Journal of Sociology 1309–11, 1312.
[45] ibid.
[46] ibid 163.
[47] ibid 160–72.
[48] ibid 162.
[49] ibid 162.

in development, co-sponsored by the UN Commission on the Status of Women (CWS).[50] The same year the UN also began preparations for the United Nations Decade for Women from 1976 to 1986, designating 1975 as International Women's Year, and highlighting the need to involve women in issues of economic development at the urging of the recommendations of the Experts Meeting.

During the first United Nations-sponsored women's conference, held in Mexico City in 1975, women's poverty was a leading area of debate, and the UN Development Program distributed a summary of Boserup's book to all delegates.[51] It provided an important scholarly basis for many of the demands, including the Plan of Action regarding women and development, lodged by delegates. Boserup's study, together with the work of other feminist activists, led to the development of several General Assembly resolutions,[52] international agreements, planning aids, and projects focused on women, under the *Women in Development* (WID) approach. The influence of the WID approach can be seen in the *Convention on the Elimination of All Forms of Discrimination against Women.*[53] The Convention's preamble states that a 'new international economic order based on equity and justice will contribute significantly towards the promotion of equality between men and women', and article 14 focuses on rural women and calls on states to ensure that women 'participate in and benefit from rural development' and also that they 'participate in the elaboration and implementation of development planning at all levels. However, WID and its productionist and market-centred underpinnings also faced critique for failing to challenge many of the gender-biased underpinnings of development work,[54] eventually leading to a shift towards *Gender and Development* (GAD) and later the adoption of gender mainstreaming in 1995.[55]

Despite these criticisms, Boserup's observations that women were excluded from new social and economic opportunities resulting from development efforts led to policy changes that aimed to provide employment for women in urban areas, as

[50] Since its founding in 1946 the CWS had primarily focused on women's civil and political rights, yet with the shifting demographics of the UN more generally due to decolonization, along with pressure applied by the Soviet bloc, it had begun to turn its attention to social and economic issues.

[51] With Christina Liljencrantz, *Integration of Women in Development: Why, When, How* (UNDP 1975).

[52] Resolutions 3522 (XXX) on the improvement of the economic status of women for their effective and speedy participation in the development of their countries; 3523 (XXX) on women in rural areas; 3524 (XXX) on measures for the integration of women in development.

[53] See Fareda Banda, 'Article 14' in Marsha Freeman, Christine Chinkin, and Beate Rudolf, (eds), *The UN Convention on the Elimination of All Forms of Discrimination Against Women: A Commentary* (OUP 2012) 357–85 and Lisa Pruitt, 'CEDAW and Rural Development: Empowering Women with Law from the Top Down, Activism from the Bottom Up' (2012) 41 Baltimore Law Review 263.

[54] See Nalia Kabeer, *Reversed Realities: Gender Hierarchies in Development Thought* (Verso 2003) 1–11; Eva M Rathgeber, 'WID, WAD, GAD: Trends in Research and Practice' (1990) 24(4) Journal of Developing Areas 489; Hope Lewis, 'Women (under)development: The Relevance of 'the right to development' to Poor Women of Color in the United States" (1996) 18(2–3) Law and Policy, 281–313, 288.

[55] Charlotte Bunch, 'Women and Gender: The Evolution of Women Specific Institutions and Gender Integration at the United Nations' in Thomas G Weiss and Sam Daws (eds), *The Oxford Handbook on the United Nations* (OUP 2007). For a discussion of gender mainstreaming see, eg, Sari Kuovo, *Making Just Rights? Mainstreaming Women's Human Rights and a Gender Perspective* (Uppsala, Iustus Forlag 2004), 310–11; Sari Kuovo, "The United Nations and gender mainstreaming: limits and possiblities", in D Buss and A Manji (eds), *International Law: Modern Feminist Approaches* (Hart 2005), 237–52. See also Hilary Charlesworth, 'Not Waving but Drowning: Gender Mainstreaming and Human Rights in the United Nations' (2005) 18 Harvard Human Rights Journal 1–18.

well as better access to education and training.[56] Her findings regarding female farming systems, as Christine Okali writes, 'were used to challenge the welfare approach to women's needs and to highlight women's customary role in the rural economy'.[57] This integrative economic approach to women's equality, one centred on women's lives and experiences, became the hallmark of development policy, along with broader economic policy, in the 1970s and early 1980s.[58] This led to several positive trends. For example, increased focused on access to education and training for women worked to narrow the gender gap in education, especially in Asia and South America.[59] It also encouraged jobs, training, and promotions for women in industry, and shined a spotlight on home-based work in both rural and urban areas.[60] Boserup's documentation of the time and labour intensive burden borne by women in carrying out domestic work and fetching water and fuel, and the negative impact that it could have on childcare and nutrition, and on women's health and well-being also led to policy changes.[61] As Boserup pointed out in the preface of a later edition of *Woman's Role in Economic Development*, since its publication 'access to jobs in large scale industries and modern-type services, the rapid spread of female education, and the access to health services and family planning have altered their life experiences'.[62]

And yet, as Boserup was also aware, the limitations of mainstream development also persisted, in part reinforced by the rigidity of economic models. Writing in 1999 she bemoaned the short sightedness of economists, who largely ignore the rapid changes in political and social systems arguing:

> long-term analysis must take into account the changes in those structures which economists usually leave to be studied by other scientific disciplines, for instance national cultures... Rapid technological change created conflicts with national culture through its radical influence on the way of life: Cultural attitudes and behavior, which may have been rational before, are no more so.... The importance of these problems for economic development is overlooked by economists, when they make the assumption that rational behavior is the rule whatever the circumstances.[63]

Ironically, given the criticism the WID paradigm has faced for being a 'neoclassical economic construct',[64] Boserup considered one of the biggest threats to women's

[56] Tinker 'Utilizing Interdisciplinarity' (n 10) 189.

[57] Christine Okali, 'Searching for new pathways towards achieving gender equity. Beyond Boserup and "Women's role in economic development"', ESA Working Paper No 11-09 (2011) 5

[58] Gina Koczberski, 'Women in Development: A Critical Analysis' (1998) 19(3) Third World Quarterly 395–409, 396.

[59] Shahrashoub Razavi Carol Miller, 'From WID to GAD: Conceptual Shifts in the Women and Development Discourse' United Nations Research Institute for Social Development, Geneva (1995) 9–12.

[60] Ibid.

[61] Julia Behrman, Ruth Meinzen-Dick, and Agnes R Quisumbing, 'An Interpretation of Large-Scale Land Deals Using Boserup's Theories of Agricultural Intensification, Gender and Rural Development' in Marina Fischer-Kowalski et al (eds) *Ester Boserup's Legacy on Sustainability* (Springer 2014) 189–202, 190.

[62] Cited in Tinker 'Utilizing Interdisciplinarity' (n 10) 180.

[63] Boserup, *My Professional Life* (n 8) 58–59, 60.

[64] Reham El Morally 'Women in Development: A Critique of Neo-classical Economic Theory as One of the Causes for Gender Inequality' (2020) 10(1) Open Journal of Political Science 1–14; see also S

well-being to be the global rise of neoliberalism. In a letter to Professor Irene Tinker in 1999 she wrote: 'I think that today the greatest threat to women comes from the US neoliberal campaign, which if it succeeds in privatizing schools, universities, child institutions, and culture, will also "reprivatize women in their homes". I wonder how long the European governments can keep up their resistance against the American pressure.'[65] And indeed, despite the numerous insights Boserup's provided into the limitations of the current development and economic reform models, particularly the link between productive and reproductive labour, as well as the negative impact of key policy strategies designed to encourage economic development on the labour market and social status of women, the development reforms adopted from the 1970s onwards did little to alter the sexual division of labour which was simply reconstituted in other settings.

The growth of women in the paid labour force have seen income inequalities increase both between and within countries, and the labour force and poverty have been feminized. The increase of women in the labour market has largely failed to disrupt the division of labour in the home, leading not only in an increase in the number of hours women work, but paving the way for the commodification of social reproduction outside the home, particularly exposing extra vulnerable workers such as non-white and immigrant workers to exploitation.[66] Reduction of state investment in social services and welfare programmes and the deregulation of labour markets have resulted in increases and intensification in women's unpaid household work to make up for the shortfalls in public services.[67]

Against the backdrop of changing social and environmental conditions in developing economies, moreover, in particular, climate change and the spread of HIV/AIDS, women's economic situation has further worsened.

Conclusion

While women continue to struggle for recognition of their economic and social contributions, Ester Boserup's efforts to include women's role in economic theory and development practice paved the way for future developments particularly at the international governance level. Her groundbreaking study finally made women visible in international development discourse, and more broadly in economic thinking. What her insights pointed to, but perhaps failed to establish in development policy, was that

Aikman and E Unterhalter (eds), *Beyond Access: Transforming Policy and Practice for Gender Equality in Education* (Oxfam 2005); AM Basu, Why Does Education Lead to Lower Fertility? A Critical Review of Some of the Possibilities (2002) 30(10) World Development 1779–90; L Benerîa, *Gender, Development, and Globalization: Economics as if All People Mattered* (Routledge 2003).

[65] Tinker 'Utilizing Interdisciplinarity' (n 10) 182.

[66] Kim Moody, *On New Terrain: How Capital is Reshaping the Battleground of Class War* (Haymarket 2017) 20.

[67] P Espinoza Revollo, 'Time to Care: Methodology' (Oxfam 2020): <https://dx.doi.org/10.21201/2020.5419> accessed 8 October 2022.

promoting women's equality required both a recognition of women's economic roles and contributions and their inclusion as active participants in the development process. But as the past decades have underlined, women's equality also demands not only a fundamental change in relations between men and women but of the economic system as a whole.

16
Helvi Sipilä
Advocating Women's Rights at the UN

Raimo Lintonen

Helvi Sipilä (1915–2009) was a prominent Finnish lawyer, women's rights activist, and international civil servant. She was a pioneering legal professional in Finland and the first woman senior officer in the UN Secretariat.[1]

Sipilä can be considered a normative and organizational entrepreneur. She promoted norms and practices to eliminate discrimination against women and to expand women's rights in law and practice. From the late 1960s until the mid-1970s, a critical period for the advancement of women's rights, Sipilä held pivotal positions in the UN as a member of the Commission on the Status of Women (CSW), the Special Rapporteur on Family Planning and the Status of Women, and the Assistant Secretary-General. Though often remembered in Finland, her role and contributions have largely been forgotten internationally and academically.[2]

Born into a well-off family, Sipilä enjoyed a relatively privileged and happy childhood. Both her parents acquired a commercial education. Uncommon at the time, Sipilä's mother had a professional life of her own. Although an only-child, Sipilä eventually went on to have four children herself.

As a young girl, she joined the Guides and Scouts of Finland, while later becoming active in three other organizations of mainly professional women: Women Lawyers' Association, a Zonta club, and the National Council of Women. She rose to national and international leadership positions in all four.[3]

[1] The main source for the portrait Helvi Sipilä's archive (HSA) is housed at the National Archives of Finland (NA).

[2] The remembrance has taken place in seminars and fundraising campaigns organized by internationally oriented and women's organizations; see ,eg, Helvi Sipilän työ ei unohdu, Suomen YK-liitto,<https://www.ykliitto.fi/uutiset-media/yk-blogi/helvi-sipilan-tyo-ei-unohdu-lasikattoja-rikkoneen-vaikuttajan-tyo-esilla-ykn> accessed 26 November 2020; 'Mitä Helvi tekisi?', Suomen Pakolaisapu, <https://pakolaisapu.fi/> accessed 26 November 2020. Internationally, the passages about Sipilä are short, often limited to mentioning her formal positions. In the landmark project on the intellectual history of the UN Sipilä is bypassed in its general overview volume, despite listing numerous other women who advanced women's ideas. See Richard Jolly and others, *UN Ideas That Changed the World* (Indiana University Press 2009) 72–73. Three scholars have written about the substance of her work; see Devaki Jain, *Women, Development, and the UN, A Sixty-Year Quest for Equality and Justice* (Indiana University Press 2005); Arvonne S Fraser, *The U.N. Decade for Women, Documents and Dialogue* (Westview Press 1987); John R Mathiason, 'The Long March to Beijing: The United Nations and the Women's Revolution' vol 1 The Vienna Period sa l 33–37, 45–49 <http://intlhum.cipa.cornell.edu/Readings/Long%20March%20Part%20One.pdf> accessed 16 February 2020.

[3] Helvi Sipilä was member of the World Committee of the World Association of Girl Guides and Girl Scouts in 1957–1966, president of the International Federation of Women Lawyers in 1954–1956, president of Zonta International from 1968–1970, and vice president of the International Council of Women in 1970–1972. All of these organizations were embedded in the extant social order in Finland and internationally.

Raimo Lintonen, *Helvi Sipilä* In: *Portraits of Women in International Law.* Edited by: Immi Tallgren, Oxford University Press.
 DOI: 10.1093/oso/9780198868453.003.0016

Figure 16.1 Helvi Sipilä, Assistant Secretary-General for Social Development and Humanitarian Affairs, displaying a press kit on the International Women's Year, during a meeting on the Women's Year Conference at the World Population Conference at Bucharest 19–30 August. Seated next to her is Mr. Rafael Salas, Executive Director of the UN Fund for Population Activities (UNFPA).
Source: UN Photo/ARA.

Sipilä graduated in 1939 as the 38th woman lawyer in Finland.[4] In 1943, she became the second woman to own a private law office, where she became known for employing other women lawyers. International assignments and duties soon followed. As a scout, Sipilä took part in the first international camp in Finland in 1931, and in 1939 she led the Finnish delegation to an international camp called 'Peace Ting' (peace assembly) in Hungary. From 1957 to 1966 Sipilä acted as an adviser for new national scouting organizations.

In 1959, the Finnish government announced its candidacy for the seat on the CSW, rotating among the Nordic countries. Finland was elected, and the Finnish government nominated Sipilä as its delegate.

The CSW became the principal policy-making body on women's issues at the UN. Its main objectives were to promote women's political rights, the status of women in private law, access to education, economic rights and opportunities, and improving UN assistance in the advancement of women's issues. Sipilä served three terms on the CSW (1960–1968), one term more than her Nordic predecessors. Later in 1972, she accepted a new extraordinary CSW term as a delegate, but it was cut short after she was appointed to the UN Secretariat.[5]

[4] Ritva Juntunen and Anneli Winter-Mäkinen, 90-vuotias Helvi Sipilä on tehnyt monta mahdotonta asiaa mahdolliseksi, Lakimiesuutiset 7.1.2014 <https://lakimiesuutiset.fi/90-vuotias-helvi-sipila-on-tehnyt-monta-mahdotonta-asiaa-mahdolliseksi/> accessed 17 October 2020.

[5] Letter of Helvi Sipilä 7 October 1973 to Saara Rantanen, HSA NA box 5.

Private Law: At the Roots of Inequality

Margaret Galey has argued that '[p]erhaps the most significant area in which the CSW worked ... concerned marriage and family law'.[6] For Sipilä, private law was of 'utmost importance' as 'equality begins at home'.[7] On the CSW's agenda, 'private law' comprised of, for example, dissolution of marriage, parental rights and duties, free choice of spouse, status of unmarried women, and status of children born out of wedlock—subjects which motivated Sipilä to specialize in civil family law and lobby for gender equality.

The relatively salient position given to private law at CSW, however, caused controversy in the Eastern bloc and some developing countries who prioritized economic and social rights, women's participation in community development, and world peace over civil family law. Sipilä noted the difficulties in finding common ground on these issues in an international legal regime due to the marked differences in legal (and political) systems. Nonetheless, she considered it possible to formulate common recommendations and standards at international forums, such as the UN and the CSW, and that in the long run national positions on these issues might shift with increasing international contact.[8]

Drafting the 'Declaration on the Elimination of Discrimination Against Women'

In the mid-1960s, Sipilä faced a more challenging demand at the CSW: the UN General Assembly requested the Commission to draft a Declaration on the Elimination of Discrimination Against Women (DEDAW). Initially Sipilä opposed the idea, for it could take time and resources away from carrying out the 'practical agenda' of the CSW.[9] Indeed, drafting the Declaration ultimately took three years (1965–1967). Nevertheless, Sipilä remained active at the CSW, exerting her influence on a number of issues. Besides being a member of the Commission during the DEDAW drafting process, she was Vice Chair in 1963 and 1965–1966, and Chair in 1967. Additionally, she belonged to a small drafting committee and actively took part in the Third Committee

6 Margaret E Galey, 'Women Find a Place' in Anne Winslow (ed), *Women, Politics, and the United Nations* (Greenwood Press 1995) 19.

7 Summing up of the XX Session of the Commission on the Status of Women, Chairman, Mrs Helvi Sipilä, 3 HSA NA box 34; likely date 6 March 1967.

8 Kertomus naisten asemaa käsittelevän toimikunnan kokouksesta ... 24. istunto Genevessä 14 February–3 March 1972, Helvi Sipilä and Helena Roos, HSA NA box 35; Commission on the Status of Women, Report on the Twentieth Session 13 February–6 March 1967, Economic and Social Council Official Records: Forty-Second Session, Supplement No 7, United Nations, New York 1967, 63; Commission on the Status of Women, Report on the Twenty-Fourth Session, 14 February–3 March 1972, Economic and Social Council Official Records: Fifty-Second Session, Supplement No 6, United Nations, New York, 1972, 21-–22. Helvi Sipilä, Behöver vi en internationell familjerätt? HSA NA Box 24; date: probably 1963.

9 Helvi Sipilä 5 October 1967 to Klaus Törnudd, HSA NA, box 1; Selonteko YK:n naisten asemaa käsittelevän toimikunnan kahdeksannestatoista istunnosta Teheranissa 1 March–19 March 1965, HSA NA box 34.

of the General Assembly meetings in autumn 1967 when it considered the draft. Sipilä influenced the drafting process *inter alia* by twice persuading adjourning the proceedings of the CSW in 1965 and the Third Committee in 1966 for a year. These actions kept the drafting process in the hands of the CSW and strengthened its commitment to DEDAW.[10] Successful, Sipilä assembled a small drafting group for an extended meeting on a public holiday in 1967 to finalize the Declaration.

However, numerous amendments, often aimed to weaken the draft, complicated its finalization. Sipilä and a group of like-minded CSW members, with their intimate knowledge of the draft, fought back hard and the CSW version of the Declaration largely survived.[11] The defence relied on the legitimacy of the CSW proposal: the diversity of the Commission membership, the unanimous adoption of the draft, and the reliance on basic and the widely shared UN norms (the Charter, the Universal Declaration of Human Rights (UDHR), the UN Declaration on the Elimination of All Forms of Racial Discrimination, and related ILO and UNESCO conventions). The Declaration ultimately proved its value through a comprehensive interpretation of the UDHR. Consequently, it almost wholly provided the basis for Convention on the Elimination of All Forms of Discrimination Against Women (CEDAW) adopted in 1979.

Family Planning Framed a Woman's Right

In the mid-1960s, Sipilä started a new project: promoting women's equality through family planning. In 1965, Sipilä, with the help of three other CSW delegates, submitted the first ever resolution to the Commission to deal with family planning (Resolution 7 (XVIII). The resolution welcomed and urged the promotion of family planning in the context of women's rights. Its final version was negotiated under Sipilä's leadership. Subsequently, Sipilä was appointed the UN Special Rapporteur on the Relationship Between the Status of Women and Family Planning in 1968.[12]

Around this time, family planning was receiving greater attention worldwide due to skyrocketing global population growth rates. Journalists, scholars, experts, Nobel laureates, and heads of government were all focusing in on the serious consequences

[10] Declaration on the elimination of discrimination against women—an instrument which unites women in the world, Historical notes of the development, HSA NA box 24, date probably 1968; United Nations General Assembly, Twenty-First Session, Third Committee, 1442nd Meeting, 1 December 1966 paras 5–7; 'Madam Chairman, The Draft Declaration on the elimination of discrimination against women now before us . . .', date: probably autumn 1966; HSA NA box 79; Helvi Sipilä 5 October 1967 to Klaus Törnudd, HSA NA box 1; Selonteko 1965 (n 9); Commission on the Status of Women, Report on the Eighteenth Session, 1–20 March 1965, Economic and Social Council Official Records: Thirty-Ninth Session, Supplement No 7, United Nations New York, 1965, 32–33; Commission on the Status of Women Report 1967 (n 8) 10; UNGA Third Committee, meeting 1422nd, 1 December 1966 paras 5–8; Note of the main points from the oral ex tempore statement of Helvi Sipilä, representative of Finland in the CSW, 17 March 1965, HSA NA box 79.

[11] Helvi Sipilä 5 October 1967 to Klaus Törnudd, HSA NA box 1; UN General Assembly, Third Committee, 1468th, 1473th, 1476th, 1477th, 1478th, and 1483rd meetings, 2–13 October 1967.

[12] Selonteko 1965 (n 9); Helvi Sipilä, Status of Women and Family Planning, Report of the Special Rapporteur appointed by the Economic and Social Council under resolution 1326 (XLIV), United Nations World Conference of the International Women's Year, Mexico City, 19 June to 2 July 1975, United Nations, New York, E/CONF.66/BP/9, 23 May 1975; Galey 1995 (n 6) 21.

of overpopulation, especially those of poverty and hunger. American foundations and the US government were especially involved in funding family planning efforts in part out of fear over the potential instabilities and communist insurgencies quick population growth could lead to.[13]

Sipilä shared this concern in the context of women's rights: frequent and unplanned pregnancies could have many negative consequences for mothers regarding, for example, their health, education, and economic opportunities. She saw family planning as a human right, entailing the right of spouses and individuals to decide freely and responsibly on the number and spacing of children, and their right to access relevant information. Thus, family planning aimed to not only curb overpopulation, it addressed issues relating to parental and sex education, access to maternal and childcare provisions, and treatment of sterility. Sipilä called this a preventative approach. She emphasized that family planning alone could not be successful without improving women's legal status and economic, social, and political rights. However, Sipilä found abortion unacceptable, except as a very last resort, as she believed it violates human dignity and indicates the failure of the preventative approach.[14]

Though these efforts raised concerns over Western dominance in family planning policy and methods, Sipilä pointed out that numerous developing countries had independently adopted family planning projects previously. Nonetheless, family planning remained controversial due to fears over foreign interference, violation of family privacy and autonomy, and its suspected promotion of birth control methods and abortion.[15] Sipilä lobbied for family planning policies at the 1968 UN Human Rights Conference in Teheran, which, for the first time, recognized family planning as a human right. Finland, with Sipilä as its delegate, in a group of ten other countries, all signatories to the World Leaders Declaration on Population (1966–1967) drafted the conference resolution Human Rights Aspects of Family Planning.[16]

[13] Rachel Sullivan Robinson, 'UNFPA in Context: An Institutional History', Background paper prepared for the Center for Global Development Working Group on UNFPA Leadership Transition (October 2010) available at <https://www.cgdev.org/sites/default/files/archive//doc/UNFPA-in-Context.pdf> accessed 13 October 2022, 4–5.

[14] Statement of Mrs Helvi L Sipilä, Assistant Secretary-General for Social Development and Humanitarian Affairs, Chairman, International Forum on the Role of Women in Population and Development, New York, 25 February 1974, 3, 5, HSA NA box 82; Selonteko 1965 (n 9); Jain 2005 (n 2) 61; Helvi Sipilä, Suomiko avainasemassa ylikansoittumisen ongelman ratkaisussa? Rejoinder, sent to magazine *Suomen Kuvalehti*, 1971, 7–8, HSA NA box 24; 'Mr Chairman, Family planning is a question . . .' 1968, (probably at UN human rights conference in Teheran); HSA NA box 25.

[15] Helvi Sipilä Suomiko avainasemassa 1971 (n 14); Roman Birke, UN Resolution on Human Rights Aspects of Family Planning (1968), December 2018, in *Quellen zur Geschichte der Menschenrechte*, Arbeitskreis Menschenrechte im 20. Jahrhundert (ed) available at <www.geschichte-menschenrechte.de/schluesseltextefamily-planning> accessed 23 July 2020; Final Act of the International Conference on Human Rights, Teheran, 22 April to 13 May 1968, United Nations, New York, 1968, resolution XVIII, Human rights aspects of family planning, para 3.

[16] Galey 1995 (n 6) 21;

New Senior Appointment with an Almost Impossible Assignment

In February 1972, Sipilä was unexpectedly offered a prominent position at the UN. At the time, and arguably still today, there existed a stark under-representation of women in senior positions in the UN system. The newly elected Secretary General Kurt Waldheim promised to change this and consequently invited Sipilä into the Secretariat to the delight of the Foreign Ministry of Finland, who saw her appointment as compensation for ambassador Max Jakobson's electoral defeat for Secretary General in 1971. However, Sipilä was not offered the position of Under-Secretary General, as envisaged by both Waldheim and the Finnish Foreign Ministry, as allegedly the position was not available at the time. Instead, Sipilä accepted the slightly lower rank of Assistant Secretary General (ASG), thus becoming the first ever woman in said position.[17] The post was specially tailored for Sipilä as she was to lead the Centre for Social Development and Humanitarian Affairs (CSDHA).

As the new ASG, Sipilä was quickly put to the test: she oversaw the World Conference of International Women's Year in 1975 and serving as its Secretary General. The UN General Assembly and ECOSOC made the assignment purposefully difficult as they were slow to endorse and authorize funds for the mandate for the Conference, hoping it would be delayed. Furthermore, the Conference had to unexpectedly change site from Colombia to Mexico. Sipilä travelled widely to increase publicity for the Conference and to mobilize female attendees as well as to raise voluntary funds.[18]

Despite such setbacks, Sipilä's efforts proved momentous: the historic Conference became the first ever conference of governments focusing solely on women. It was also a success in terms of its large number of participants, particularly with its unprecedented 73 per cent share of female attendees. The most significant achievement of the Conference, however, was the World Plan of Action (WPA), in the drafting of which Sipilä had a 'strong hand'.[19] The Conference decisions set the normative and organizational groundwork for the Decade for Women (1976–1985), two subsequent conferences, and the creation of the international women's regime.

[17] Personnel Questions, Composition of the Secretariat, Report of the Secretary-General, UNGA, A/8483, 1 November 1971, 17; Letter of Helvi Sipilä to Max Jakobson 17 February 1972; HSA NA box 4; Telex message, UN Mission of Finland 23 February 1972 to Helvi Sipilä, HSA NA box 4; Letter of Helvi Sipilä 25 February 1972 to Sauli Sipilä, HSA NA Box 4; Letter of Helvi Sipilä 8 March 1972 to Max Jakobson, HSA NA box 4; Telex from Max Jakobson, the UN Mission of Finland 16 March 1972 to Helvi Sipilä, HSA NA box 4; Vastauksia Valt tri Riitta Auvisen kysymyksiin kirjeessä, 5 October 1977 HSA NA box 3. See also Jaakko Iloniemi, Vallan käytävillä, WSOY, Porvoo-Helsinki-Juva 1999, 86.

[18] Mathiason 2006 (n 2) 36; Statement by Mrs Helvi Sipilä, Assistant Secretary-General for Social Development and Humanitarian Affairs, Secretary-General of the International Women's Year and the World Conference of the IWY at the Plenary Meeting of the 59th Session of the ECOSOC, on 24 July 1975, 7–8, HSA NA box 55 (Sipilä statement at ECOSOC 1975).

[19] US Center for IWY 1975, Washington DC, Newsletter No 4–75, 1 August 1975; Fraser 1987 (n 2) 22; Mathiason 2006 (n 2) 37, 45.

Champion of a 'New International Human and Social Order'

For Sipilä, the established view of development policies was askew due to its economic emphasis and focus on the macro, thus ignoring the individual and the human element. This also held true for the New International Economic Order (NIEO), a policy programme which envisaged a fundamental restructuring of the global economic system to strengthen the sovereignty of developing countries and reduce external dependences. It predominantly targeted economic aspects of development, such as trade, monetary reforms, and transfer of resources. According to Sipilä, this emphasis on the economic was one major reason the UN failed to implement effective policy to reduce poverty, malnutrition, and illiteracy, among other problems associated with global development.[20]

More appropriate, Sipilä argued, was the human and social development framework which had its roots in human rights, especially concerning gender equality, social progress, and globally bettering standards of living. Accordingly, developmental goals cannot be achieved through a singular focus on GNP or other economic growth indicators. In practice, economic development occurs when social issues pertaining to, for example, health, nutrition, employment, education, housing, social welfare, and institutional infrastructure are addressed.[21] Sipilä thus saw moral, intellectual, and cultural resources equally as important for global and social development as material resources.

To this end, Sipilä had a women-centric worldview: women were the source of life, energy, and labour upon which the success of development goals rest. Particularly in their role as mothers, women's activities are consequential in numerous respects including child rearing, family nutrition, population growth, informal education, and family well-being. All these contribute to a society's wider prospering and/or deterioration and therefore to related global problems. However, structures of gender inequality curtail women's possibilities to realize their full potentials and prevent them from disentangling oppressive structures.[22] A focus on women was therefore essential for global development, Sipilä believed.

Important groundwork for such human-centred social development was laid in the 1970s by UN Theme Years and Special Conferences (for example on human environment, settlements, population, and food) and their resolutions, final acts, and action plans. In Sipilä's mind, the 1975 Mexico Conference and the World Plan it adopted were turning points in including the human element in developmental planning.

[20] Sipilä statement at ECOSOC 1975 (n 18) 7–8.

[21] See UNGA Resolution 2542 (XXIV), Declaration on Social Progress and Development, 11 December 1969; Address of Mrs. Helvi Sipilä, United Nations Assistant Secretary-General for Social Development and Humanitarian Affairs, at the opening of the tenth international seminar of the conference for social activities of Yugoslav women, at Bled, Yugoslavia, on 10 October 1977, 'Women and Development', HSA NA box 82; Address of Mrs Helvi Sipilä, United Nations Assistant Secretary-General for Social Development and Humanitarian Affairs at the Western Regional Leadership Conference on 'Emerging World Economic Order', Los Angeles, California, USA, 10 September 1977, HSA NA Box 82.

[22] Helvi Sipilä, Nainen inhimillisen elämän lähteenä maailmassa—kotona ja työelämässä, IBM Katsaus no 3 1975, HSA NA box 6.

Sipilä as a Person

Sipilä was ambitious, indomitable, and independent, though hardly the 'heroine'[23] former UN official Bertrand Ramcharan nicknamed her. When Sipilä represented Finland at the UN, the personnel of the Finnish Permanent Mission in New York knew that her arrival into office meant 'the hustle would begin'.[24] She never considered assignments impossible: 'What is difficult can be done at once, what is impossible takes a little more time.'[25] She often emphasized early action: 'As time is not on our side, let us begin our actions today, as every tomorrow will make it more difficult to succeed.'[26] Recognizing the great challenges faced at the UN, she took comfort in an old saying: 'The first day dangling from the gallows is the worst.'[27] She never strayed away from taking on new assignments.

Sipilä once called herself a 'colporteur'[28] referring to her frequent travels to take part in meetings and delivering speeches and statements all around the world. She made numerous trips across the globe to promote the ideas of the UN and its norms and programmes for the benefit of women in bilateral meetings or international conferences, overall giving over 250 speeches and statements between 1972 and 1977.

Working at the UN: Constraints and Opportunities

The CSW had a relatively benign environment. It was a small body with a limited mandate and a membership composed of women with mostly an expert background. It was a safe place for women, offering dialogue and building trust in a co-operative working environment. Moreover, the CSW offered possibilities of exerting influence: the drafting of resolutions could be endorsed as decisions of the whole UN.[29] It was originally separated from the Commission on Human Rights (CHR), bringing it formally onto equal footing. The CSW was a more modest body compared to the CHR with respect to authority, resources, and instruments. Sipilä argued for CSW legitimacy as an independent organization based on gender discrimination faced by women; autonomous women's groups were essential for obtaining resources for women, building trust amongst them, and enabling more efficient use of resources—these would diminish if mainstreamed into male-dominated organizations.[30]

[23] Bertrand Ramcharan, Thank You, UN, for Protecting the Rights of Women, PassBlue, 28 February 2018<https://www.passblue.com/2018/02/28/thank-you-un-for-protecting-the-rights-of-women/≥ accessed 21 October 2019.

[24] Iloniemi 1999 (n 17) 86.

[25] The speech of Helvi Sipilä at the Opening Ceremony of the NGO Forum at the stadium in Beijing, China, Wednesday 30 August, 1995, HSA NA box 73.

[26] Address of Sipilä at the International Population Conference 'Since Bucharest—and the Future', Washington, 19 November 1975, HSA NA box 123.

[27] Hanne Alametsä, 'Helvi Sipilä: Oletko valmis?', Me Naiset 12, 1972, HSA NA box 6.

[28] Letter of Helvi Sipilä 7 March 1976 to Saara Rantanen, HSA NA box 123.

[29] The Third Committee was open to all UN member states; Selostus YK:n naisten asemaa käsittelevän toimikunnan 20. istunnosta New Yorkissa 13 February to 6 March 1967, 27, HSA NA box 34; 'Dear Friends', letter by Sipilä 13 February 1967, HSA NA box 34; Fraser 1995 (n 2) 81, 83.

[30] Lecture by Mrs Helvi Sipilä, Assistant Secretary-General, United Nations, Population and Women's Rights, Seminar on Law and Population, The Fletcher School of Law and Diplomacy, April 14, 1977, 3, HSA

Helvi Sipilä made important contributions to the CSW as member and on the Chair. She participated in drafting and sponsoring many resolutions on various subjects. She was actively involved in the steering and drafting of the 1967 Declaration on the Elimination of Discrimination against Women, the precursor to CEDAW. She helped to solidify family planning as a women's right. As the ASG, she was in charge of the 1975 Mexico Conference on women which endorsed the World Plan of Action and enlarged the international regime for women.[31] Sipilä's mission was ideationally grounded in a framework of human and social development through advancing women's rights—a legacy which changed the legal landscape of women everywhere.

NA box 83; Margaret Snyder, 'The Politics of Women and Development', in Anne Winslow (ed), *Women, Politics, and the United Nations* (Greenwood Press 1995), 110.

31 Myra Marx Ferree and Carol McClurg Mueller, 'Feminism and the Women's Movement: A Global Perspective' in David A Snow, Sarah A Soule, and Hanspeter Kriesi (eds), *The Blackwell Companion to Social Movements* (Blackwell 2004) 585–86.

PART VII
THE BREAKERS OF THE GLASS CEILING: THE 'FIRST AND ONLY' IN INTERNATIONAL INSTITUTIONS

17

Suzanne Bastid

The First of the 'Firsts'

*Immi Tallgren and Antoine Buchet**

Photography was elevated, by Roland Barthes, to the supreme way to authenticate the past, for photography 'does not invent... Every photograph certifies a presence'.[1] In this photograph taken before the neoclassical *Palais des Académies* in Brussels, twenty-five lawyers look into the camera to memorialize their gathering for the second post-war session of the *Institut de droit international* (IDI) in July–August 1948. The worst rubble of destruction from the Second World War has been cleared, but the new international community remains to be constructed. International law, the great failure of the pre-war years, is again expected to cement peace between nations.

Zooming in this image, it is impossible not to notice the only woman. In the third row on the far right appears the woman we are trying to portray: Suzanne Bastid (1906–1995). As if an iconic encounter of individual fate and collective narration *à la* Barthes' contemporary, cinematographer Luchino Visconti, the image appears to capture a crossroads, both in the path of Bastid and the histories—yet to be written—of 'women in international law'. What had led to that particular moment, and what happened afterwards?

To portray 'the only woman', but how? And why? The latter question is the easier one to answer. Bastid is today a leading symbolic figure, 'the first', impossible to bypass in a research effort to describe and analyse the late and slow entry of women as professionals and intellectuals in international law.[2] Nonetheless, she receives, at the maximum, a quick mention in the histories of international law in languages other than French.

The how question merits more reflection. A 2022 effort to understand who Bastid was, did, thought, and wrote, confronts layers of changes in discourses, representations, and interpretations of what Bastid may become to mean. The textual, visual, and oral sources and their previous analyses exceed what we could integrate for this short portrait. What became clear in the materials, even if it was never made explicit, were the three filters through which she appears: her family affiliations, her sex and gender,

* We recognize with gratitude the inspiring exchanges with Karen Knop. We thank Hilary Charlesworth, Martti Koskenniemi, and the participants of the authors' seminars 2020–2021 for comments and discussions. Dzovinar Kevonian helped us with access to a few sources in times of Covid-19 and Katariina Flinck provided diligent research assistance.

[1] Roland Barthes, *Camera Lucida: Reflections on Photography* (Hill & Wang 2010).

[2] See Immi Tallgren, 'Re-curating the Portrait Gallery of International Law: The Objectives, Process and Floorplan of the Exhibition', in this volume.

Immi Tallgren and Antoine Buchet, *Suzanne Bastid* In: *Portraits of Women in International Law*. Edited by: Immi Tallgren, Oxford University Press. © Immi Tallgren and Antoine Buchet 2023. DOI: 10.1093/oso/9780198868453.003.0017

Figure 17.1 Suzanne Bastid in the 1948 session of Institut de droit international in Brussels.
Source: Courtesy of Institut de Droit International (http://www.idi-iil.org/).

and her nationality. We have chosen to orientate our portrait to study the diverse effects of those filters, foregrounding the representer and the viewers.

We do not know the name of the photographer in Brussels in 1948, but it is probable it was a man, as most photographers at the time were. This is how Suzanne Bastid and other 'women in international law' have most times been seen and represented, in visual and textual portraits. In addition to the photograph, we focus on '*Notice sur la vie et les travaux de Suzanne Bastid*'.[3] It is a transcript of the solemn elocution presented in *Palais de l'Institut de France* in Paris on 4 February 1997 by Francois Terré, the professor of law who succeeded Suzanne Bastid as the occupant of chair number 7 in the *Académie des sciences morales et politiques*. The tradition has it that the new member praises his or her predecessor, in a presumptuous ritual of transfer of academic prestige celebrated in luxurious outfits.[4] Suzanne Bastid had likewise pronounced a eulogy of Gabriel Le Bras she replaced—as 'the first woman' in that chain of transmissions.

It is the qualification as 'the first' we are trying to grasp with its diverse connotations. Did sex and gender matter as greatly for Bastid's career in international law as they have imprinted its representations? Susan Sontag wrote that '(t)o photograph people is to violate them, by seeing them as they never see themselves, by having knowledge of them that they can never have; it turns people into objects that can be

[3] François Terré, 'Notice sur la vie et les travaux de Suzanne Bastid', (speech, Académie des sciences morales et politiques, 4 February 1997).

[4] 'Une des rares occasions dans notre société où un homme peut s'habiller en femme', Claude Levi-Strauss commented his own inauguration, Emmanuelle Loyer, *Lévi-Strauss* (Flammarion, 2015) at 636.

symbolically possessed'.[5] Was Suzanne Bastid 'the first' lonely, feeling different from other international lawyers, as the photograph might suggest to its viewers today? Or was her ascent rather an easy, natural succession inside 'the family', as Terré hints in his intimate 'notice'—disconcertingly as if entering Suzanne Bastid's privacy, making us follow his gaze?

Climbing the Steps and Taking Rank

A girl was born on 15 August 1906 in Rennes, French Brittany. Given the name Suzanne, she was the eldest of seven children from the marriage of Renée Mallarmé and Jules Basdevant, son of Dominique Basdevant, who was the mayor of a village called Anost, located in the Morvan massif, 'a poor and harsh region',[6] and a *juge de paix*. At the time of Suzanne's birth, Jules Basdevant was a professor of law, assigned to the Law Faculty of Rennes, then to Grenoble. In 1918 he started at the Law Faculty of Paris, where he taught international law and '*le droit des gens*'. Terré pictures 'a father who adored his daughter, serious as himself, very close intellectually'.[7] The mother also contributes, Terré writes, by complementing in terms of affectivity, 'her understanding of femininity, her strong sense of family and friendship, (…) and her kindness'.[8]

Suzanne (Basdevant, later Bastid) studied in the Lycée Fénelon, the first high school for girls in Paris. The school carried the name of François de Fénelon, a Catholic archbishop, poet, and author, also of '*Traité de l'éducation des filles*', published in 1687. After school, she decided to study law, unusual for a woman in the 1920s, but not a huge surprise for a brilliant pupil whose father was an already prominent figure in French legal academia.

In 1930, Suzanne Basdevant obtained the highest diploma, the *doctorat en droit*, after defending her thesis on international civil servants. The thesis was awarded the Goullencourt Prize[9] and is considered one of the first major works on this subject.[10] In 1932, Suzanne Basdevant became the first woman in France to obtain an *agrégation* in Public Law and Political Sciences.[11] In 1933, she was the first woman nominated as a professor of law, assigned to the Law Faculty of Lyon.

Before she turned thirty, Suzanne Basdevant had thus began her series of castings as the 'first woman' in France. We do not learn much, from Terré, about how she personally perceived those factual events.[12] How did she actually experience it,

[5] Susan Sontag, *On Photography* (Picador 2001) at (will add this)

[6] Terré, 'Notice' (n 3) 1.

[7] ibid. 3.

[8] ibid.

[9] Prize awarded to the best doctoral student at the Faculty of Law of Paris.

[10] Witold Zyss, 'The International Civil Servant' in EM Chossudovsky, Jacques Lemoine, and M. Boisard (eds), *Multilateral Diplomacy* (Kluwer Law International 1998) 58.

[11] The *agrégation* is a competitive examination for the civil service in the French public education system. A candidate who is admitted can become a *professeur agrégé* and is expected to teach at high schools and universities.

[12] We had no access to private archives. Thanks to Dzovinar Kevonian, we accessed an interview with one daughter, Geneviève Bastid-Burdeau by Kévonian and P Rygiel, 'Entretien audiovisuel avec Geneviève Bastid-Burdeau', *La contemporaine*, Projet AJII (2017) <https://argonnaute.parisnanterre.fr/ark:/14707/a011568126281VhxrfW> accessed 19 November 2021. See also Dzovinar Kevonian and Philippe

as a young woman, penetrating the segregated spaces of erudition and authority, with their gendered codes of habitus and traditions of professional conviviality? Even if such passages are typically given major symbolic importance in women's histories, the transitions have not been studied in detail in the sociology of professions or history of (international) law.

At the age of thirty-one, Suzanne Basdevant became Suzanne Bastid by marriage to Paul Bastid. The French Civil Code stated at that time that 'the husband owes protection to his wife, the wife obedience to her husband'. Her husband was a law professor, politician, and member of the French parliament. An eminent figure of the Radical-Socialist Party, Paul Bastid became Minister of Commerce in 1936 in the first government of the *Front Populaire*, the left-wing coalition led by Léon Blum that would not last more than a year. Suzanne Bastid became the Head of Cabinet of her husband. This was the first French government that included (three) women, although women were not allowed to vote or to be elected.[13] When the Second World War broke out and the German army invaded France, Paul Bastid was one of the few members of the parliament who refused to accept the end of hostilities in June 1940. The parliament outvoted the objectors, dissolved the Third Republic, and established the authoritarian regime of Marshal Philippe Pétain in July 1940. Paul Bastid became active in the French Resistance.

In 1941, Suzanne Bastid became the first woman to teach at the *Institut de Sciences Politiques*, '*Sciences Po*', and remained the only one for the next twenty-seven years. She started in *Sciences Po* at a time when the very Parisian institution had relocated to Lyon, in the 'Free Zone' created after the Armistice of June 1940. Michèle Cointet writes that Paul and Suzanne Bastid turned the Faculty of Law of Lyon during the war into 'a node of resistance forces'.[14] Suzanne Bastid would even have received 'a friendly warning from the dean of the faculty' for having named her daughter, born in November 1940, Marianne.[15] In 1943, Paul Bastid entered the *Conseil national de resistance française* (CNR), participating in the preparation of its programme of political reforms to be implemented after the war. According to Claire Andrieu, it was Paul Bastid 'who opposed the inclusion of the vote for women in the CNR's programme. According to the testimony of Jacques Debû-Bridel, he would have threatened to leave the CNR if the measure was recommended.'[16]

Rygiel, 'Archives of International Lawyers: Towards a Social History of International Legal Practice', Symposium: *Archives of International Law: Histories of International Lawyers between Trajectories, Practices, and Discourses*, Jus Gentium 2020.

[13] The women were appointed with the function of *sous-secrétaire d'État*, ie under the authority of a (male) member of the Government: Cécile Brunschvicg, for Education, Suzanne Lacore, for Public Health, and Irène Joliot-Curie, the daughter of Pierre and Marie Curie, for Research.

[14] Michèle Cointet, 'Les juristes sous l'occupation: la tentation du pétainisme et le choix de la résistance' in André Gueslin (ed), *Les Facs sous Vichy* (Publications de l'Institut d'Études du Massif Central 1993) 62.

[15] Cointet, 'Les juristes'. Marianne is the personification of the French Republic, replaced in 1940 by the authoritarian regime led by Marshal Philippe Pétain. See also, Maurice Agulhon, *Marianne au combat: L'imagerie et la symbolique republicaines de 1789 à 1880* (Flammarion 1979).

[16] Andrieu sees the programme as 'a conservative, even reactionary text', Claire Andrieu, 'Le programme du CNR dans la dynamique de construction de la nation résistante' (2014) Histoire@Politique 3, <www.cairn.info/revue-histoire-politique-2014-3-page-5.htm> accessed 19 November 2021.

The Reign of Suzanne the First in France

After the war, the career of Suzanne Bastid truly took off. She was appointed to the Law Faculty of Paris in 1946, to replace her father who had been elected judge at the International Court of Justice (ICJ) in The Hague.[17] She taught international law simultaneously at the university and at *Sciences Po*, relocated in Paris. Bastid soon became a prominent and respected figure among the French professors of international law, reigning as such until her retirement in 1977.

Suzanne Bastid is pictured, by international lawyers that succeeded her in France, as a great teacher who devoted more time to her students than publishing notable articles or books.[18] She appears to have prioritized co-ordination of international law as an academic discipline in France above her independent doctrinal or theoretical work. Was such a head-figure role more adapted to her gender and the expectations created by her ascendance of a father who 'exercised a direct influence on the destinies of the world'?[19] Or was she rather to confirm and enlarge a dominium she had inherited than to create, reform, lead independently? Would the latter behaviour have been tolerated?

There is so far little material available based on which to form an opinion on such questions. There are, in any case, repetitive insinuations to a dynasty, perhaps nepotism, in the way she is viewed and represented. When Bastid founded the review *L'Annuaire français de droit international* in 1955— 'her child, her creation',[20] Terré cherishes—it was professor Gilbert Gidel, supervisor of her thesis in 1930 who wrote the foreword to the first edition of the new review: 'Maintaining the high level of the *Annuaire* is guaranteed by the presence at the head of the Editorial Board of Professor Bastid-Basdevant, a worthy continuator of illustrious and respected family traditions.'[21]

In a similar assembling role, Bastid presided a colloquium in Strasbourg devoted to the problems of teaching and research of international law in France in 1967. As a result, the *Société française pour le droit international* (SFDI) was created to promote the study and progress in international law, under the presidency of Bastid. She remained president for twenty years, and then became honorary president.

The festive coronation of Bastid's reign took place in 1971: she was elected to the prestigious *Académie des sciences morales et politiques*,[22] as the first woman to receive such recognition. The members of the Academy are elected for life by their peers on account of their personal merits. The system of co-optation, a guarantor of independence from political influence, also favoured the reproduction of a masculine elite for

[17] Jules Basdevant had his pension rights admitted on 30 September 1945.

[18] Alain Pellet, 'Suzanne Bastid (1906–1995)' <www.sfdi.org/internationalistes/bastid>accessed 19 November 2021; Daniel Vignes, 'Madame Bastid' <www.persee.fr/doc/afdi_0066-3085_1994_num_40_1_3179> accessed 19 November 2021.

[19] Terré, 'Notice' (n 3) 3. On 'academic household' positions, see Tallgren, 'Re-curating' (n 2).

[20] Terré, 'Notice' (n 3) 7.

[21] Gilbert Gidel, 'Preface' (1995) 1 Annuaire français de droit international 9.

[22] Academy of Moral and Political Sciences, divided in six sections: Philosophy, Moral and Sociology, Legislation, Public Law and Jurisprudence (the section where Bastid was assigned), Political Economy, Statistics and Finances, History and Geography, and a General Section.

centuries. 'The improvement and influence of letters, the sciences, and the arts', the missions assigned to the French Academies placed in 1795 under the umbrella of the *Institut de France,* were until recently exclusively allocated to men.

What had changed, to explain the selection of Suzanne Bastid? Victor Tapié, who presided over the *Académie des Sciences Morales et Politiques* in 1971, cherished her election as follows:

> Juste hommage à une œuvre d'exceptionnel mérite, mais aussi une conquête du féminisme et peut-être dépassement d'un préjuge qu'on a parfois prêté aux académiciens … On dit qu'une hirondelle ne fait pas le printemps… mais comment méconnaître que la première hirondelle est pourtant signe irréfutable de l'approche des plus beaux jours?[23]

Terré comments on Suzanne Bastid's entry by stating that there are two ways of being a feminist: 'by protectionism or merit'. Bastid was, for Terré, an example of the right kind: 'There is nothing in her behavior and … in her expressions, that could bring to mind images of those bullied women who should be protected by a quota system; nothing that can militate in favour of the success of a woman because she is a woman'.[24] Even if glad to save Bastid from the stable of a 'quota woman', Terré is proud that 'our *Académie* was not late compared to the others'.[25] As all comparisons, his is relative to the samples compared. The *Académie Française*, created to defend the French language, waited nine more years—until 1980—to elect its first female member, the novelist and essayist Marguerite Yourcenar.

In contrast to the ever-discreet Bastid, who in 1982 continued the series of 'firsts' by becoming the president of *Académie des sciences morales et politiques*, Yourcenar was explicit about the gendered politics of merit. In her first address to *Académie Francaise* in January 1981, Yourcenar stated how she felt 'surrounded, accompanied by an invisible troop of women who should, perhaps, have received this honour much earlier, to the point that I am tempted to step aside to let their shadows pass'.[26]

Suzanne Bastid and the 'Rayonnement' of France in International Law

Already well-established in France, Bastid emerged on the international scene in 1948, in the meeting where the photograph on our second page was taken. The IDI accepted Bastid's election as an *associate member*, the starting rank. Eight years later, the IDI made her the first female full member. Also from 1948 on, she became a regular member of the French delegation to the General Assembly of the United Nations (UNGA). One year later, the UNGA adopted the Statute of the United Nations

[23] A quote from Victor Tapié: quoted by Terré, 'Notice' (n 3) 4.

[24] ibid.

[25] ibid.

[26] Marguerite Yourcenar, '*Discours de reception à l'Académie française*', (Académie Francaise 1981)< www.academie-francaise.fr/les-immortels/discours-et-travaux-academiques > accessed 19 November 2021 (our translation).

Administrative Tribunal (UNAT),[27] charged with resolving employment-related disputes between UN staff and the UN administration. The Assembly also appointed 'Madame Paul Bastid'[28] as one of its first seven members, ie international judges. Bastid later presided the UNAT for ten years (1953–1963) and remained a member of this jurisdiction for thirty-two years. The extensive scope of jurisdiction of UNAT gave Bastid the opportunity to contribute to the development of a particular international civil service law, already a key interest in her doctoral thesis of 1930. Diverse legal issues passed through her hands: education allowances for children, pensions for widows, non-renewal of temporary contracts, abolition of posts, disciplinary sanctions, dismissals.

Simultaneous were the years of her father's, Jules Basdevant's, presidency of the ICJ (1949–1963), described by Terré as a 'happy epoque when the French vision of international law illuminated the world', the objective he sees Suzanne Bastid as 'always fighting for'.[29] Counterintuitive at first, if international law is expected by definition not to depend on nations, the remark reflects today's understanding of 'comparative international law'.[30] What was the universal illumination Terré refers to, the vision of France soon engaged in the war in Algeria? Apparently not that of René Cassin, who contributed to the elaboration of the *Universal Declaration of Human Rights* and presided the European Court of Human Rights until 1968, while France declined to ratify the *European Convention of Human Rights* (until 1974). The defence of French as the language of international law is more likely to make part of the vision, as an objective that the family continues to defend.[31]

Terré does not offer much detail of the functions Bastid occupied as an international judge. Yet among the numerous judgments in which Bastid participated—over 200—there were hard cases, judgments rendered under Cold War pressures and lack of legal clarity. The most famous concerned the situation of UN officials of United States nationality in the early 1950s prosecuted by the authorities of the Host State, the United States. Summoned to appear before the bodies empowered to investigate 'anti-American activities', inspired by Senator Joseph McCarthy, some United States citizens employed by the UN refused to answer questions concerning their political orientations, invoking the Fifth Amendment to the United States Constitution, which enshrines the protection against self-incrimination. Infuriated, the United States Department of State rushed to Trygve Lie, UN Secretary General (SG), to obtain the heads of the recalcitrant officials.[32] Several were suspended and their contracts were eventually terminated.

[27] General Assembly, 'Establishment of a United Nations Administrative Tribunal' RES 351/A, 1949. Statute entered into force on 1 January 1950.

[28] She often appears as 'Madame Paul Bastid' in the composition of the UNAT, but the judgments are signed 'Suzanne Bastid'.

[29] Terré, 'Notice' (n 3) 3.

[30] See, eg, Anthea Roberts, *Is International Law International?* (OUP 2017).

[31] Interview with G Burdeau (n 12).

[32] The United States would eventually transform their demarche into an official procedure for the acquisition of information by investigation and for its transmission to the UNSG in order to assist the SG in the exercise of his responsibility for determining whether any United States citizen employed or being considered for employment on the Secretariat has been, is, or is likely to be, engaged in espionage or subversive activities against the United States, through the executive order 10422 of 9 January 1953.

Some of the sacked officials turned to the UNAT. The tribunal, under the presidency of Bastid, declared illegal the decisions terminating the employment of the applicants, and awarded them with financial compensation. They found themselves in despair to find employment in the United States, stigmatized by their dismissal. The UNAT rejected the arguments put forward by the SG and considered, in particular, that 'taking the Fifth' could not be qualified as a 'serious misconduct' within the meaning of the UN Staff Rules and Regulations.[33] The UNAT's judgments were indirectly challenged before the International Court of Justice (ICJ), but in substance the outcome remained untouched.[34]

The UNAT was Bastid's most important conquest, her home base. But she also broke the glass ceiling of the most prestigious courtroom in the world, becoming the first woman to plead at the ICJ, in the Peace Palace in 1964. Bastid was one of the legal representatives of Belgium seeking to make Spain bear the responsibility for losses of Belgian nationals in the bankruptcy of the Barcelona Traction, Light and Power Company.[35] She focused on the applicability of a treaty concluded in 1927 between Spain and Belgium, which would in her opinion constitute a valid legal basis for the ICJ jurisdiction.

In 1985, Suzanne Bastid became the first woman on the bench of the same jurisdiction, as an *ad hoc* judge in the Continental Shelf case, chosen by the Tunisian Government.[36] This was the first time an application for revision came before the ICJ. In its Judgment of 10 December 1985, the Court rejected the application for revision as inadmissible. This sentence was rendered unanimously. Judge Bastid, as another first, voted against the State that had chosen her as an *ad hoc* judge.

Having entered the IDI in 1948, as discussed above, Bastid rapidly became an indispensable part of its functioning. For a woman in IDI, recognition, not to mention promotion, was not a given.[37] Female names did appear sometimes in the yearbooks of IDI, but as the beneficiaries of dinners, excursions, or artistic programmes.[38] That tide turned in 1963, for a while. The Belgian capital, again, was that of the consecration for Suzanne Bastid, who became, at the 51st session, the first—and unique until now—female Secretary General of the IDI. She held this position until 1969. She was

[33] See, eg, *Harris v The Secretary-General of the United Nations* [1953] Judgment No 31, <https://untreaty.un.org/unat/UNAT_Judgements/Judgements_E/UNAT_00031_E.pdf> accessed 19 November 2021.

[34] The United States government opposed to financing the GA appropriations required to satisfy the UNAT awards. The GA presented two questions to the ICJ for an advisory opinion, with a clear intention to refuse to give effect to the award of compensation made by the UNAT. The ICJ answered that the GA has not the right on any grounds to refuse to give effect to an award of compensation such as that in the UNAT judgments. See ICJ, 'Effects of Awards of Compensation Made by the United Nations Administrative Tribunal', Advisory Opinion [1954] ICJ Rep 47, 62. The father of Suzanne Bastid, Jules Basdevant, judge of the ICJ, was not part of the composition that issued this opinion.

[35] *Belgium v Spain*, Case Concerning the Barcelona Traction, Light and Power Company [1962] < www.icj-cij.org/public/files/case-related/50/050-19640311-ORA-01-00-BI.pdf> 453 accessed 19 November 2021. Bastid appeared to defend the position of the Kingdom of Belgium.

[36] *Tunisia v Libyan Arab Jamahiriya*, Application for Revision and Interpretation of the Judgment of 24 February 1982 in the Case Concerning the Continental Shelf, [1984] <www.icj-cij.org/en/case/71> accessed 19 November 2021.

[37] See also Hilary Charlesworth, 'L'IDI dans le monde d'aujourd'hui', *Livre du Sesquicentenaire de l'Institut de Droit international 1873–2023* (forthcoming).

[38] See, eg, Hans Wehberg, 'Avant-Propos' (1954) Institute of International Law 49 <www.idi-iil.org/app/uploads/2017/05/4025-45B-OCR-min.pdf> accessed 19 November 2021.

also active in The Hague Academy of International Law, giving a course in 1951, 1957, and 1962.[39]

All these activities did not mean an absence of publications. Bastid devoted attention to the legal analysis of geopolitical actualities of her time,[40] decolonization, the 'Third World',[41] and the relations between the West and the East.[42] The emergence and the following erratic international recognition of the People's Republic of China interested her. Encouraged by her daughter Marianne Bastid-Bruguière, a French academic on Chinese history, Bastid visited China several times and gave lectures.[43]

The Art of Being (the First) Woman

'Ai-je su, grâce à tant de conseils, évoquer aujourd'hui fidèlement son image et son destin?', asks François Terré at the end of his Notice. Similarly, our portrait of Suzanne Bastid's ascent and reign unfolded, its readers are likely to be in search for replies to the questions we started with. What counted most for Terré was that 'she continued the paternal tradition' and served her family and nation, successful as expected.[44] For a viewer vested in feminist histories observing the photograph today, in contrast, the narratives of 'otherness' and transition may overwhelm.

Yet Suzanne Bastid was not amongst strangers. She was not only a white and educated citizen of a powerful old European nation, but part of the intimate family of international law elites. Her father stands in the first row, the third from right. Before Suzanne Bastid, Jules Basdevant had occupied the same or similar roles. He was a professor of international law at the Law Faculty of Paris, as well as at *Sciences Po*; he was elected to *Académie des sciences morales et politiques* twenty-seven years before her, in 1944, and became a full member of the IDI in 1928. In addition to having a prominent and well-connected father whom she followed, Bastid was married to a professor of law and a celebrated member of the French Resistance. This was an asset, precious social capital, in the post-war France of her quick ascension in the hierarchies of the French academy and international law.

Such a reading of Bastid's 'firstness', implied by Terré and others, may seem to disgracefully cast doubts on her individual qualities or belittle her accomplishments. At the same time, attention to her family of birth, social class, and marriage are part of the social context where Bastid was able to exceed all women before her, in so many

[39] Suzanne Bastid, 'La jurisprudence de la Cour internationale de justice', (1951) Collected Courses of The Hague Academy of International Law 78 575–702; Suzanne Bastid, 'Les tribunaux administratifs internationaux et leur jurisprudence' (1957) 92 Collected Courses of The Hague Academy of International Law 343–489; Suzanne Bastid, 'Les problèmes territoriaux dans la jurisprudence de la Cour internationale de justice' (1962) 107 Collected Courses of The Hague Academy of International Law 361–495.

[40] See, eg, Suzanne Bastid, 'Le droit international de 1955 à 1985' (1984) 30 Annuaire français de droit international 9.

[41] Maurice Flory and Suzanne Bastid, *Pays en voie de développement et transformation du droit international* (Pedone 1974).

[42] Suzanne Bastid, 'Les conditions juridiques de la "coexistence"', (1955) 1 Politique étrangère 9.

[43] Suzanne Bastid, *Les mutations politiques et traités: le cas de la Chine*, in *La communauté internationale: mélanges offerts à Charles Rousseau* (Pedone 1974) 1.

[44] ibid.

ways. For there had been other 'firsts': Julie-Victoire Daubié, the first woman to obtain a *Baccalauréat* in 1861; Sarmiza Bilcescu, admitted to take courses at the Faculty of Law of Paris in 1887; Jeanne Chauvin, to obtain a doctorate in law in 1890; Sophie Balachowsky-Petit, to take the oath of lawyers in 1900, preceding by a few days Jeanne Chauvin, who became the first to plead before a court in 1901.[45] When Bastid was born, five years later, a narrow path for women was open. The explicit legal impediments on women's way to the professions of (international) law receded at the pace of her growth to adulthood.[46]

Bastid overcame the remaining social, cultural, and political obstacles through the combined effects of perseverance, talent, and family emulation. She soon became an emblem of progress for women's access to the legal professions, but was she a feminist? These two different inflections are not always kept separate in the representations of her. Much depends on the understanding given to 'feminism(s)'. Both Alain Pellet and Francois Terré enter into the questions of the sex and gender marking on Bastid's career, turning it into a site of struggle for representation.

For Alain Pellet, '(w)ithout being a feminist in the militant meaning of that word, [Bastid] has done a lot for the cause of women'.[47] Bastid was, however, cautious to engage in public activism against discrimination based on sex and gender. Some sources suggest she rather abhorred it.[48] Did Bastid try to avoid becoming a role model, not to risk being associated with Pellet's 'militant' feminism?[49] Or was it simply because she generally resisted all personal attention to herself?[50] Was she a '*garçon manqué*', and as such the perfect '*fils à papa*'—and was the low-key approach on sex and gender questions a condition of her successes? Terré hints in that direction, praising Bastid's resilient behaviour and the absence of claims for (other) women's ascent. Whereas she appears to have conformed, externally, to the heteronormative expectations towards married women and mothers of her social class, up to the often-mentioned confitures she cooked, her everyday choices differed from the norm underneath: she worked ambitiously and persistently, and travelled abroad frequently even if a wife and mother of young children. She did not shy away from using help for secretarial and household chores.[51]

Paradoxically, with time, the attention to Suzanne Bastid seems to increasingly turn to employ the sex and gender filter, omitting the dynastic and nationalistic filters. It is in her own temporal context, however, that sex and gender mattered so much more than today, beyond personal choices to manifestly address it or not. The peculiarities

[45] Dzovinar Kévonian, 'Histoire des femmes juristes en France' in E Tourme Jouannet and. others (eds), *Féminisme et droit international. Etudes francophones du réseau Olympe* (2016) Société de législation comparée 323–46 presents a broad review of sources on French women in legal professions.

[46] For example, women were authorized to become judges or prosecutors in France by a law adopted in 1946 (Law no 46-643 of 11 April 1946).

[47] A Pellet, 'Suzanne Bastid' (n 18).

[48] See commentaries in the 1930s, cited by Kevonian, Histoire (n 12) at 331, fn 32.

[49] See Fiona M Kay and Elizabeth Gorman (eds), 'Women in the Legal Professions' (2008) 4 Annual Review of Law and Social Science 299–332, regretting that Suzanne Bastid had chosen not to communicate with them.

[50] Bastid is often described as having always refused to put herself forward, A Pellet, 'Suzanne Bastid' (n 18); Terré, 'Notice' (n 3), at 4.

[51] Dzovinar Kévonian and Philippe Rygiel, 'Entretien audiovisuel avec Geneviève Bastid-Burdeau' (n 12).

or shadows of ambiguity of her ascent underline it. She was, for example, teaching constitutional law of a country where she herself could not vote. She took decisions as an international judge, by international law expected to be independent and impartial, whereas French law subordinated her to her husband.[52] Tellingly, her family name as a judge oscillates between that of her father and her husband: a woman lacks a name of her own. In her professional successes, her husband's or father's influences were never far. Sometimes the proximity was so tight that it might raise eyebrows, today. She wrote, for example, a case analysis of the Nottebohm case of the ICJ that her father was deciding on.[53]

What do we learn, by Terré's notice, of Suzanne Bastid as an intellectual and an international lawyer? She is described as pragmatic, hardworking, austere, and rigorous—male-gendered qualifications at the first sight, but also frequent clichés attached to Protestants in France. When Terré tries to define the individual, he soon slips back to evoking a certain 'spirit of resistance that animates the family'.[54] What is meant by that spirit? Not resistance to the discriminating structures of the French law and society, but resistance in the sense of resisting those who denied the rule of law during the Second World War. Resistance also to various ideologies, new schools of thought, probably. Bastid was faithful to traditions, and those traditions may have cemented her conceptions of international law, conservative when compared to Monique Chemillier-Gendreau, for example—another French international lawyer, almost her contemporary.[55]

The Image that Remains

Suzanne Bastid the professor, judge, legal counsel, editor-in-chief, leader of academic and professional associations, daughter, wife, mother, and grand-mother defies simple characterizations. Notwithstanding Barthes' confidence, the photograph of Brussels might mislead and requires an explanation. Bastid's life was hardly that of a lonely woman. She was not fighting against patriarchy. Her sex and gender intersected with her family's standing, her ethnicity and nationality, and her access to education in a manner which made her a highly privileged lawyer. She acceded to posts and responsibilities through her networks, not feminist or female but male and French. As many other histories of successful women show, the importance of the support by a father, husband, or academic supervisor is relative to their socio-economic and cultural capital. Mothers most times strongly support their talented and studious daughters, as well. But as long as women were powerless by law, without degrees, profession, or property, that made less difference.

[52] Until the reform of matrimonial property regimes in 1965 (law 65-570 of 13 July 1965), a married woman was unable to work or open a bank account without the consent of her husband.

[53] Suzanne Bastid, *L'affaire Nottebohm devant la Cour Internationale de Justice*, (comment) (1956) 45 Revue critique de droit international privé 607.

[54] Terré, 'Notice' (n 3) at 7.

[55] Monique Chemillier-Gendreau is professor emeritus of international law and author of, for example, *Humanité et souverainetés* (La Découverte 1995), *L'injustifiable: Les politiques françaises de l'immigration* (Éditions du Centurion 1998), and *Pour un Conseil mondial de la Résistance* (Textuel 2020).

Naming a particular 'legacy' of Bastid is not possible for us, nor do we find it necessary. We are impressed by the tenacity of her orientation in the diverse contexts of her exceptional career which seems, in our eyes, to speak for a genuine commitment to the ideas, perhaps an ideal, of international law. Bastid chose international law as her vocation in a temporal context of violence and hatred in Europe and globally. She grew into her profession in the turbulences of the Second World War, where she also lost two of her brothers.[56] Examples show that when totalitarianism and nationalistic hubris threaten to prevail, some lawyers choose to follow the powerful, perhaps even encourage excess—women just as men, as the portrait of Leah Meriggi[57] suggests—while others cling to what they in their context consider the rule of law.

Bastid belonged to the second category, as she demonstrated in many ways, perhaps most notably during the crisis that shook the young UN at the time of McCarthyism. With pragmatism, without taking the risk—or the guilty pleasure—to give a moral lecture to the UNSG, Bastid destroyed one by one the fallacious arguments which had led to the dismissal of loyal civil servants of the UN. With these judgments, did Bastid again follow in the footsteps of her father? Jules Basdevant resigned from his duties as legal adviser to the French Ministry of Foreign Affairs during the Vichy regime. In his letter of 29 May 1941, informing Marshal Philippe Pétain of his resignation, Basdevant wrote that 'respect for the law and the sentiment of honour are among the moral forces France should always support'.[58] Did this sentence linger in Bastid's mind when she placed respect for the law above the political considerations favoured by the UNSG, too mortified to confront the powerful Americans?

Faced with the other pole of the Cold War, the Soviet Union and its satellites, Bastid's pragmatism and the confidence she placed in the search for negotiated international legal solutions led her to reject a confrontational approach: 'Achieving peaceful coexistence requires abandoning the idea that one system must prevail over the other, if necessary by force; it requires putting an end to the crusade'.[59] Later, she paid tribute to Michel Virally by insisting on the efforts that he made to give international law the prominent place it deserves, including in the resolution of so-called 'civilization conflicts', such as that which opposed the United States to the Islamic Republic of Iran after the 1979 Revolution.[60]

Suzanne Bastid, the first of the 'firsts', appears to us as a courageous conservative, loyal to her family and nation but an independent mind. She has come to symbolize—perhaps '*malgré elle*', as some evidence suggests—a transition in international law after which sex and gender no longer absolutely hinder women from conquering positions of authority and leadership. Are we suggesting that her sex and gender did not matter, after all? That would be a hasty conclusion, to start with scant remembrance and interest she receives in scholarship. No proper biography has been written about her—a

[56] Interview with G Burdeau (n 12).

[57] Serena Forlati, 'Lea Meriggi: A Fighter—For the Wrong Cause', ch.28 of this volume.

[58] Jules Basdevant, Letter to the Marshal (29 May 1941)<www.sfdi.org/wp-content/uploads/2014/03/SFDI_Galerie_Basdevant_lettre_Demission.pdf> accessed 19 November 2021.

[59] S Bastid, 'Les conditions' (n 42).

[60] Suzanne Bastid, 'Adaptation du droit international aux relations nouvelles entre Etats' in Mélanges Michel Virally (ed), *Le droit international au service de la paix, de la justice et du développement* (Pedone 1991) 79.

regrettable lack in international law history. We would rather ask whether Bastid ever got as high as she could have or should have. Terré comments, misleadingly, that 'her career unfolds, no less brilliant, in the wake of that of her father'.[61] Suzanne Bastid presided the UNAT, an administrative tribunal, while her father had presided the ICJ. She was never chosen by her home state to be appointed in any of the major European or international courts, nor to the International Law Commission of the UN. She may have been loyal to her nation, but was her nation loyal to her? France was and remains notorious for its gendered policy of nominations: its authorities have never submitted the candidature of a woman to become a judge or a comparable prominent judicial figure at the ICJ, the International Criminal Court, or the Court of Justice of the European Union.[62]

In this exhibition, the sight of Suzanne Bastid alone amidst her eminent male colleagues in 1948 flags not more but also not less than a starting point of new traditions, different genealogies. When the twenty-eight students of the 'Suzanne Bastid promotion'[63] of Master in Arbitration and International Trade, University of Paris-Saclay, line up for their formal group photograph, no woman poses with an eminent father, nor is she the only one.

[61] Terré, 'Notice' (n 3) at 5.

[62] Women have been included in the short list of candidates by France in the European Court of Human Rights elections, but not chosen by the Parliamentary Assembly of the Council of Europe. See also, Delphine Placidi, 'Les femmes francaises a l'Onu: l'influence ambigue du multilateralisme' in Yves Denéchère (ed), *Femmes et relations internationales au XXe siècle* (Presses Sorbonne Nouvelle 2007) 213–24; See also Stéphanie Hennete-Vauchez, 'Les femmes juges à la Cour Européenne des Droits de l'Homme' in O Bui Xuan (ed), *Représentation et Représentativité dans les institutions*, (LGDJ/Varenne 2016); Stéphanie Hennete-Vauchez, 'Gender Balance in International Adjudicatory Bodies' in H Ruiz Fabri (ed), *Max Planck Encyclopedia of International Procedural Law* (OUP 2019).

[63] Maci-Saclay, 'Suzanne Bastid (2017–2018)'≤http://maci-saclay.fr/promotion-suzanne-bastid-2017-2018≥ accessed 31 January 2022.

18
Marguerite Frick-Cramer
A Life Spent Shaping the Geneva Conventions

Boyd van Dijk

At the start of the twentieth century Marguerite Frick-Cramer became the first woman to receive a professorial title from the University of Geneva, having previously won two major awards for her scholarship. She was the first woman to write for the world-renowned journal of the International Committee of the Red Cross (ICRC). She was among the first women to lead a major department of the ICRC's International Prisoners-of-War Agency. As a leading member of the ICRC, she was the first woman to accede to the highest governing body of a non-Communist international organization. She was the first woman to provide advice to ICRC legal experts and act as drafter of the Geneva Conventions.

Yet the history of these Conventions—the most important treaties concerning armed conflict ever formulated—is populated by 'great men'. Indeed, in received accounts, the archetypical drafter remains a white bourgeois man from Geneva, such as Gustave Moynier or Jean Pictet. What this obscures, however, is the modest but significant role played by women in the formulation of this body of international law—Cramer centrally among them. In seeking to remedy this oversight, this chapter recovers Cramer's international legal thought, emphasizing how she shaped key legal principles and practices on the global stage. Although scarcely remembered outside of Geneva today,[1] her work as an ICRC legal expert was arguably more significant than that of many of her male compatriots. Among other achievements, she attained international legal prominence while simultaneously breaking a number of gender barriers at a range of different institutions.

Despite the significance of women's contributions to humanitarian law, the sequence of events held in 2019 to mark the seventieth anniversary of the 1949 Geneva Conventions failed to recognize their efforts. Whereas some observers simply assume that women played no role in the drafting process (save that of typing out the Conventions' final texts), others have suggested that Cramer either behaved in a too 'cautious and legalistic' manner,[2] or failed to make any historically significant impact

[1] The main exception to this rule is the groundbreaking scholarship of feminist Genevan historians such as Irène Herrmann, Silvia Cadei, Camille Meyre, and Daniel Palmieri. Their work has recently fostered a new initiative naming one avenue in Geneva after Cramer herself.

[2] James Crossland, *Britain and the International Committee of the Red Cross, 1939–1945* (Palgrave Macmillan 2014) 40. For the opposite view complimenting Cramer's 'courage', see Cédric Cotter, *(s')Aider Pour Survivre: Action Humanitaire et Neutralité Suisse Pendant la Première Guerre Mondiale* (PhD thesis, University of Geneva 2017) 141, 340. Georg Editeur published his excellent PhD one year later.

Boyd van Dijk, *Marguerite Frick-Cramer* In: *Portraits of Women in International Law.* Edited by: Immi Tallgren, Oxford University Press. © Boyd van Dijk 2023. DOI: 10.1093/oso/9780198868453.003.0018

Figure 18.1 Marguerite Frick-Cramer at the Rath Museum, ICRC POW Agency (First World War).
Source: ICRC Audiovisual Archives, V-P-HIST-03557-05.

at all.[3] This mischaracterization of Cramer's work serves less to exclude her from the literature than to accord her a subordinate position within an overarching narrative of male international legal action. My aim in analyzing Cramer's work, then, is to restore women's agency to the story of the Geneva Conventions. Recovering her ideas and interventions (successful or not) aligns neatly with the volume's larger objective of giving women in international law a voice.[4]

Women in Humanitarian Law

After finishing degrees in history and constitutional law at the University of Geneva, Cramer began an international legal career at the International Prisoners-of-War Agency. Established in August 1914, immediately after the outbreak of the First World War, this new ICRC institution pioneered the idea of reconnecting isolated prisoners of war (POWs) with their families. She began working as co-director of the Agency's Entente department on behalf of Allied POWs. More women would follow her example in joining the Agency: of its 3,000 employees, two-thirds were (often unpaid)

[3] David Forsythe, *The Humanitarians: The International Committee of the Red Cross* (Cambridge University Press 2005) 204.
[4] This aim is inspired by the work of Patricia Owens, 'Women and the History of International Thought' (2018) 62 International Studies Quarterly 467–81, 469.

women and often served in subservient roles.[5] Their shared objective was to monitor the lives of millions of military and civilian prisoners held captive in enemy territory, often in poor conditions. Many prisoners of war and civilian internees were forced to work in harsh environments; others suffered starvation or other forms of ill-treatment.

During the First World War, numerous reports circulated of prisoners being exposed to brutal reprisals. Moreover, thousands of sick or wounded POWs would only receive proper medical treatment if repatriated to neutral countries.[6] Cramer's attempts to alleviate their suffering were hindered by the fact that the existing Geneva and Hague Conventions did not sufficiently protect these prisoners.[7] Given these shortcomings, she had no choice but to develop new legal methods through which she could help those suffering behind barbed wire.

Compelled to alleviate human suffering, in large part out of a sense of noblesse oblige, Cramer helped to develop new groundbreaking international legal standards that sought to ensure the right of humane treatment and strengthen international supervision. In seeking to improve the conditions of soldiers in captivity, she put considerable pressure on states to abide by the new norms that she had co-designed. When they failed to live up to these standards, she was not afraid to criticize them directly, which speaks to her outspoken character. More remarkably still, Cramer was the first to call for a new network of permanent ICRC delegations so as to better coordinate the organization's actions globally. To foster these initiatives, she went on foreign missions to meet heads of state, including the French president George Clemenceau.[8]

What explains Cramer's rapid rise to prominence within the ICRC? The outbreak of the First World War created unique opportunities for women with similar levels of expertise and class backgrounds. Despite prohibiting them from taking up arms, states mobilized women as humanitarian actors.[9] This allowed Cramer to participate in the world's most important international organization in wartime. Beyond the gender trouble created by war, she also benefitted from her Genevan upper-middle-class background, through which she had direct access to powerful voices in the ICRC's highest echelons. Indeed, her grandfather served on the Committee and three of her cousins acted as delegates. Being related to these men enabled Cramer to rise quickly through the organization's ranks. Making use of her privilege and family connections, she began reimagining existing international law in ways that would prove historically significant.[10]

One important example of Cramer's important legal work was the important part she played in developing the Bern Agreements (1918). During the war, the ICRC participated in inter-belligerent conferences, at which states discussed the repatriation

[5] Daniel Palmieri, 'The International Committee of the Red Cross in the First World War' Website ICRC (2014), available at <https://www.icrc.org/en/document/international-committee-red-cross-first-world-war-0>.

[6] Cédric Cotter, 'The 1918 Bern Agreements: Repatriating Prisoners in a Total War' (2018) Website Humanitarian Law & Policy, available at <https://blogs.icrc.org/law-and-policy/2018/03/29/1918-bern-agreements-repatriating-prisoners-of-war/>.

[7] Gradimir Djurovic, *The Central Tracing Agency of the International Committee of the Red Cross* (Henry Dunant Institute 1986) 35.

[8] Cotter, *(s')Aider Pour Survivre* (n 2) 141, 340.

[9] Cotter, 'The 1918 Bern Agreements' (n 6).

[10] Cotter, *(s')Aider Pour Survivre* (n 2) 339, 247.

of sick and wounded POWs to neutral countries. As part of this effort, by acting as representative of the ICRC and the Swiss government, and by mediating between both parties, Cramer successfully convinced Germany and France to sign the Bern Agreements, which dramatically expanded the potential number of POW repatriates.[11] In the end, these wartime initiatives prompted the emergence of new international legal standards, emboldening Cramer's organization to undertake further initiatives. Indeed, the agreements established a precedent, which the ICRC used to develop a new POW code.

Some of its experts had already begun working on this question in the last phase of the war. In June 1918, the ICRC's governing Committee instructed Cramer and Alfred Gautier, another legal expert from Geneva, to start drafting a new code for the treatment of POWs as part of its broader attempt to reimagine the laws of war. Gautier was something of an intellectual mentor to Cramer, stimulating her interest in international law and advocating her interests at the Committee.[12] Despite their collaboration, it took Cramer and Gautier more time to draft a new POW code from scratch, not least because the task proved infinitely more complex than they had originally expected. The end of hostilities in Western Europe, however, meant that they could work longer on developing their (Eurocentric) proposals, which they finally presented at the Red Cross Conference in 1921.

Creating a Prisoners' Code

At this meeting, Cramer and Gautier reported on their new plans in the hope of triggering a wider debate about the future of the POW code. Although they noted the insufficiency of existing international law, they also drew upon the wartime agreements in developing a set of general principles on which the future treaty was to be based. Among other principles, they placed special emphasis on the importance of stigmatizing the internment of women and children during armed conflict.[13] To this end, they proposed a gendered definition of POWs, according to which only mobilizable adult men could be interned.[14] In line with this view, Cramer later wrote that 'to make war less terrible, one must first strictly adhere to the principle of limiting the fight against the armed forces alone; without that, all efforts at regulation will collapse like a house of cards'.[15] Although it was intended to keep women out of war, this proposal still undermined the foundational principle of discriminating between civilians and

[11] Neville Wylie, 'The 1929 Prisoner of War Convention and the Building of the Inter-war Prisoner of War Regime' in Sibylle Scheipers (ed), *Prisoners in War* (OUP 2010) 91–108, 94; and Cotter, 'The 1918 Bern Agreements' (n 6).

[12] Daniel Palmieri, *Les Procès-Verbaux de l'Agence internationale des Prisonniers de Guerre (AIPG)* (ICRC 2014) 234–35, 240–41.

[13] ICRC Report 1921, No CI_1921_022_FRE_016_HD, ICRC Library, Geneva.

[14] For more details, see Boyd van Dijk, *Preparing for War: The Making of the 1949 Geneva Conventions* (Oxford University Press 2022).

[15] Marguerite Frick-Cramer, 'A propos des projets de conventions internationales réglant le sort des prisonniers' (1925) Revue Internationale de la Croix-Rouge et Bulletin Internationale des Société de la Croix-Rouge 73–84, 80.

soldiers. This is significant, because Cramer's argument for a single treaty for predominantly male prisoners was based on her own version of distinction.

An equally striking aspect of Cramer's vision for the code was her stress on the importance of promoting elementary human rights thinking.[16] She claimed a number of '*droits elementaires*' for future POWs, including the right to life, dignity, social rights (eg relating to labour conditions), humane treatment, and immunity from reprisals.[17] Whereas other proposals from this period were reluctant to fully endorse that last principle, Cramer advocated prohibiting reprisals against prisoners.[18] What is more, she participated in international women's advocacy to protect children's rights on the global stage. Her most important contribution to this campaign was her role in convincing the ICRC to support the International Save the Children Union. The collaboration between these two institutions would go on to facilitate Eglantyne Jebb's groundbreaking campaign for a new Declaration of the Rights of the Child.[19]

These different initiatives attest to the breadth of Cramer's engagement with the various ongoing international rights' debates in Geneva, the seat of the League of Nations. Beyond being the locus of legal discussions, the League was directly implicated in Cramer's proposals for the future Conventions, despite its own scepticism towards this body of law. In case of alleged violations of the POW code, for example, the League was expected to facilitate an investigation and could impose sanctions on those found responsible for them. Furthermore, in the event that a suspect was to face trial, the League could help sponsor an international tribunal to decide upon his fate (the male sex is mentioned intentionally here, for women were not seen as potential war criminals). In designing this new system of enforcement and garnering international recognition for the International Prisoners-of-War Agency, Cramer hoped to strengthen the principles of the new treaty and thus better protect prisoners incarcerated in future wars.[20]

When she put these proposals to Red Cross delegates meeting in Geneva in 1921, Cramer convinced many of her male colleagues of their importance. After some discussion of her co-written report, the representatives eventually endorsed a broader code covering POWs and various civilian categories. Moreover, they banned reprisals against POWs, just as Cramer had demanded. In response to the rise of communist violence in Central and Eastern Europe—another matter which had her close attention as a child of Geneva's bourgeoisie, they also endorsed ICRC intervention in civil wars. To turn these proposals into actual draft texts, delegates instructed the ICRC to establish a special committee, which would prepare a new code for discussion at a future diplomatic conference.[21]

16 For a definition for the concept of elementary human rights thinking, see Boyd van Dijk, 'Human Rights in War: On the Entangled Foundations of the 1949 Geneva Conventions' (2018) 112(4) AJIL 553–82.

17 Frick-Cramer, 'A propos des projets de conventions internationales' (n 15) 82.

18 Wylie, 'The 1929 Prisoner of War Convention' (n 11) 97.

19 Zoe Moody, *Les Droits de l'Enfant: Genèse, Institutionnalisation et Diffusion (1924–1989)* (Éditions Alphil-Presse 2016) 100–101; and Cotter, *(s')Aider Pour Survivre* (n 2) 133.

20 ICRC Report 1921, No CI_1921_022_FRE_016_HD, ICRC Library, Geneva.

21 ICRC Report 1921, No CI_1921_002_FRE_002, ICRC Library, Geneva.

Breaking the ICRC Gender Barriers

Despite her prominence at the 1921 Red Cross Conference, Cramer was not asked to join the new committee tasked with preparing drafts for the future Conventions. That body was to be composed only of men. What happened? Why was she not invited? What explains her absence from a committee whose existence she was so instrumental in creating?

Answers to these questions can be found by attending to a short but traumatic period of Cramer's membership of the ICRC's governing Committee, between 1918 and 1922. Before this time, several male colleagues had opposed a proposal to appoint her to the Committee, as its first ever woman member. Cramer had been nominated for the first time in June 1918 by ICRC president, Edouard Naville, presumably because of her successful role during the First World War in co-managing the Agency.[22] Some argued that allowing women to enter the ICRC's highest institution would directly undermine the nineteenth-century principles on which it was originally founded. A Committee member named Adolphe Moynier, to give one example, argued that the decision required extended debate in light of the Committee's historical 'traditions'.[23] Not long before this, his father, Gustave Moynier, had expressed a similar misogynist trope, suggesting that women lacked the capacity for leadership. They had no role to play in the ICRC, he argued, except for that of nursing the wounded during wartime.[24]

Other members of the Committee worried that Cramer's potential appointment might be opposed by powerful states. In particular, it feared that allowing Cramer to join its ranks might open a Pandora's Box, encouraging states to push through the appointment of their own favoured candidates. They were especially concerned about the United States authorities' response in this regard. The Committee was aware that Cramer's assertiveness when engaging with male American officials during the First World War had generated personal enmity against her. German officials had similarly decried her 'outspokenness'—another familiar misogynist trope.[25] Their animosity towards her as a woman with agency, combined with internal opposition at the Agency itself, made it very difficult for Cramer to continue her work. In early 1918, she even resigned as a result of these impediments. The ICRC rejected this request, however, compelling her to continue working towards its interests.[26]

At length, the Committee left Cramer in suspense, postponing its decision as to her appointment. Only after the war in Western Europe had finished, as Gautier urged for his protégée's appointment,[27] did Cramer finally break through this gender barrier. In November 1918, she became the first woman on the Committee thereby opening the door to other women in the future. Indeed, six years later, Suzanne Ferrière became

[22] Irène Herrmann, 'Marguerite Cramer: "Appréciée Même des Antiféministes"' in François Bugnion, Françoise Dubosson, and Irène Herrmann (eds), *Humanitaire et Paix* (Georg 2018): 149–61, 151.

[23] Palmieri, *Les Procès-Verbaux de l'Agence* (n 12) 242–43.

[24] Silvia Cadei, 'Le Comité du CICR: Une Affaire d'Hommes?' (2017) (2) Histoire & Genre 74–83, 76.

[25] Palmieri, *Les Procès-Verbaux de l'Agence* (n 12) 266; and Herrmann, 'Marguerite Cramer' (n 22) 156.

[26] Palmieri, *Les Procès-Verbaux de l'Agence* (n 12) 226; and Herrmann, 'Marguerite Cramer' (n 22) 153.

[27] Palmieri, *Les Procès-Verbaux de l'Agence* (n 12) 273–74.

the second woman to sit on the ICRC's Committee, acting on behalf of the interests of civilians in international law.

Despite this apparent sea change, the ICRC remained a hostile environment for women, even for those in the highest position. Persistently treated differently, women realized that their male colleagues would never accept them as equals. The Committee's decision to admit some women while maintaining structural gender inequalities in place indicates a longstanding gap between rhetoric and daily reality, and between exclusion and inclusion. Just as the Swiss denied women the right to vote in the years after 1919, the ICRC did little to protect them against unequal treatment in the 'humanitarian' workplace. Cramer learned this painful lesson at a particularly difficult time: just as she began working at the Committee, she had to face a marital crisis.

In 1922, she felt forced to resign from her position because, in part, her husband, Edouard Frick, had been 'wrongly accused of embezzling funds from the ICRC'.[28] Having previously been an ICRC representative in revolutionary Petrograd, he served as Fridtjof Nansen's deputy, in which capacity he temporarily worked from Geneva on behalf of Russian victims of famine—and marrying Cramer there in 1920. Frick also came up with the revolutionary idea of a special travel document for stateless refugees ('the Nansen passport'). This innovation would be important to the 'other' Geneva Convention, from 1951, concerning the protection of refugees.[29] None of these achievements, however, would protect his wife from having her position challenged from within the ICRC. As a result of the accusation levelled against her husband and having followed him to Weimar Germany, she stepped back from Geneva's Committee.[30] By including women in this body, the ICRC had been able to present itself to the outside world as modern, at least on the face of things. Nevertheless its misogyny ultimately proved stronger, as evidenced by Cramer's marginalization from the process of drafting the Conventions.

Dangerous Woman

In the mid-1920s, after her reputation had been restored, Cramer returned on the ICRC's legal stage as an 'honorary member'.[31] Although she did not take up her seat on the Committee again until 1939, Cramer played a significant role in the 1929 Conventions' history by giving ICRC legal experts advice on a more informal basis. More significantly, the organization invited her to participate in the diplomatic conference of 1929, making Cramer the first woman drafter of the Geneva Conventions. Her attendance indicated not just how her fortunes at the ICRC had changed substantially. It also suggests that women experts such as Cramer were increasingly seen as

[28] Cadei, 'Le Comité du CICR' (n 24) 77; and Daniel Palmieri, 'Marguerite Frick-Cramer' in Erica Deuber Ziegler and Natalia Tikhonov (eds), *Les Femmes Dans la Mémoire de Gèneve: Du XVe au XXe Siècle* (Éditions Suzanne Hurter 2005) 183.

[29] Charlotte Mohr, 'Fridtjof Nansen,' ICRC Website (2019), available at <https://blogs.icrc.org/cross-files/fridtjof-nansen/>.

[30] Camille Meyre, 'Renée-Marguerite Frick-Cramer,' ICRC Website (2020), available at <https://blogs.icrc.org/cross-files/fr/renee-marguerite-frick-cramer/#_ftnref33>.

[31] Palmieri, 'Marguerite Frick-Cramer' (n 28) 183.

able to handle complex international legal questions, at a time when women could not even vote (Switzerland would not grant full suffrage until the 1970s).

While attending the 1929 conference, Cramer's delegation proved 'uniquely successful' in reshaping the Conventions' principles.[32] Among other things, it established the world's first codified law prohibiting reprisals against POWs, the principle of third-party supervision, and international legal recognition for the Agency. Cramer already grasped the crucial significance of each of these questions from the very start of the long drafting process. Despite its achievements, Cramer's delegation was ultimately unable to persuade states to widen the Conventions' scope to encompass civilians, a significant failure in her international legal career. Still, Cramer and Ferrière kept pushing this issue to the fore. Eventually, in 1934, it led the ICRC to present a draft treaty concerning civilians at the Red Cross Conference in Tokyo, which Cramer attended.[33] Most strikingly, however, she believed humanitarian law did not apply equally to every part of the world since 'Arabs [and] negroes followed quite different principles'.[34] Although Cramer and her male colleagues at the ICRC argued that they were acting on a universal basis, few if any ever questioned the shocking racial hierarchies underpinning their legal work.

Returning to the Tokyo Draft, no state signed this text, fatally undermining its potential to support Ferrière and Cramer's efforts on behalf of Jewish civilians during the Second World War.[35] As a consequence of this lack of legal backing, the ICRC acted only extremely cautiously when other actors invoked this document as a means of stopping the Nazi genocide. Still, Cramer pressured the Committee to break its silence regarding the Holocaust, calling for the ICRC to take a principal stand and approach the Nazi leadership.[36] (This refutes the notion suggested earlier by those who have presented her as overly 'legalistic and cautious'.[37]) Regardless of Cramer's resistance, which was shared by a majority of members including all four women, the Committee decided to refrain from denouncing the genocide. This was the most tragic episode in its history. Time and time again, ICRC women would be marginalized or sidelined if they challenged their male leaders' views, with crucial consequences for how the organization was being managed and for those who suffered from this.[38]

Despite this hostility towards women, Cramer contributed to reinventing the Conventions after the Second World War. In addition to attending preliminary drafting meetings, she also actively sought to influence the ICRC's internal debates with regard to key questions, such as partisan warfare. She even developed her own drafts concerning this and various other issues to become the basis for the future Conventions, whose main objective she understood in gendered terms as placing a

[32] Wylie, 'The 1929 Prisoner of War Convention' (n 11) 96.

[33] Letter Cramer to president, 29 October 1929, no CR-119-2, Les Archives du Comité international de la Croix Rouge (ACICR), Geneva.

[34] The original quote in French: '... pour des Arabes ou des nègres il y aurait des principes tout différents à suivre'. Quote is cited from Wylie, 'The 1929 Prisoner of War Convention' (n 11) 104.

[35] Van Dijk, 'Human Rights in War' (n 16) 563–66.

[36] Meyre, 'Renée-Marguerite Frick-Cramer'(n 30).

[37] Crossland, *Britain and the International Committee of the Red Cross* (n 2) 40.

[38] Deborah Stienstra, *Women's Movements and International Organizations* (The Macmillan Press 1994) 53.

barrier on 'the primitive instincts of man [and his] love of power'.[39] Building upon her experience and maturing human rights thinking, these drafts also suggested that the Conventions be fused so as to cover civilian and military prisoners under a single treaty pertaining to wars both within and between states. In addition to this, she invoked the Nuremberg principle of individual criminal responsibility as a means of strengthening the law's enforcement mechanisms, as she had tried to do before the war. Though they were far from perfect, Jean Pictet (the ICRC's leading drafter) called her proposals '*remarquable*', acknowledging that they were of '*grande utilité*' for his own drafting project.[40]

Although he gave Cramer credit internally, Pictet declined to circulate her proposals at the meeting held for Allied government experts in Geneva in April 1947. In fact, he wished to ban their presentation outside of the organization, initially preventing their publication in the ICRC's journal. He feared that disseminating Cramer's proposals before the meeting might make his own project vulnerable to external criticism and undermine the ICRC's united image to the outside world. One prominent ICRC expert, Max Huber, even called some of her ideas, such as creating a single Convention for both civilian and military prisoners, 'very dangerous'.[41] Although her article was eventually published, and Cramer did influence the ICRC's positioning on some key imprisonment issues, it is methodologically difficult to determine the extent of her influence.[42] What is certain, though, is that she broke several gender barriers, thereby enabling other women to contribute to the drafting process. At the 1949 conference, an unprecedented number of women served as official representatives engaged in global lawmaking for armed conflict. Their presence was politically significant for the ICRC in that it presented its idea of universality to the outside world. Further research is needed to establish a fuller account of how the organization approached gender, how those women shaped the Conventions, and how their position of privilege reflected upon that of rank-and-file sisters whose work enabled this.

Conclusion

Focusing on the legal thought and politics of women serves to render histories of humanitarian law more inclusive and less one-dimensional. This chapter has shown how women played important roles in developing the most important rules for armed conflict ever designed. Although the ICRC preached universality—if not inclusivity, this lawmaking process rested on acute gender and racial inequalities.[43] The drafting table represented a space of hierarchies and differences, which constantly influenced both legal debate and the shifting positions of men and women. Though unable to overturn this resilient hegemonic gender order (as the ICRC lacked a woman president in its

[39] Marguerite Frick-Cramer, 'Contribution à l'élaboration d'une Convention sur les prisonniers, militaires ou civils, tombés au pouvoir de l'ennemi ou d'une autorité non reconnue par eux' (1947) Revue Internationale de la Croix-Rouge et Bulletin Internationale des Société de la Croix-Rouge 228–47, 230.

[40] Minutes of Commission Juridique, 19 February 1947 No A PV JUR.1, ACICR.

[41] Minutes of Commission Juridique, 17 April 1945 No A PV JUR.1, ACICR.

[42] Frick-Cramer, 'Contribution à l'élaboration d'une Convention' (n 39).

[43] Inspired by Joan Scott, *Gender and the Politics of History* (Columbia University Press 1988) 186.

history until September 2022), Cramer created lasting change by developing new legal thought and blazing a trail for other women to serve as drafters of the Conventions. In response to the violent upheavals of the twentieth century and in accordance with her own conceptions of rights and humanity seeking to ensure the protection of both civilian and military prisoners in armed conflict, she helped reshape the future of these historic treaties.

19
Vijayalakshmi Pandit
Gendering and Racing against the Postcolonial Predicament

*Parvathi Menon**

International law portrays the year 1945 as the beginning of the discipline's success story, culminating in the San Francisco Conference, also known as the United Nations Conference on International Organization (UNCIO). Often, while highlighting the role played by the representatives of the Great Powers and Allied nations of the Second World War, one forgets that dependent states like India played an influential, but ambivalent, part in the United Nation's founding. Although India was represented at the conference by three cabinet members of the British Indian government (or the Viceroy's Executive Council), one unofficial member of the Indian delegation became the lone radical voice to represent the state's presence as the 'pivot of the whole system of imperialism and colonialism'. It was the voice of Indian diplomat, Vijayalakshmi Pandit (1900–1990), born Swarupa Kumari Nehru. Calling the other representatives 'the three stooges' of the British government, Pandit used the opportunity at San Francisco to put the UN to what she called an 'acid test' of its principles.[1] Willing to detract from the official Indian (British) course of action, Pandit projected the Indian example to pressure the UN to adopt a categorical stance on the independence of colonial territories.[2] What was the outlier voice in 1945, of the British Indian delegation, later became the common voice of the anticolonial pursuit at the UN and outside. Pandit became independent India's lead representative to the UN until 1968.

Against the background of a growing polarization in the geopolitics of the Cold War, Pandit's work in steering India into 'non-alignment', already prior to the Bandung conference of 1955 and thereafter, is often overshadowed by the prowess of her famous brother and India's first Prime Minister, Jawaharlal Nehru (1889–1964), albeit sometimes of her own choosing.[3] Following her years as Indian Ambassador to the Soviet Union from a newly independent India in 1947 and later to the United States in 1949,

* * I thank Immi Tallgren for guiding me towards choosing Pandit, and for her helpful comments after I wrote the chapter. I also thank Vasuki Nesiah for her insightful feedback during the author seminar. Thanks are also due to Rohit De, Christopher Gevers, Alexandra Kemmerer, and Karen Knop for their comments and suggestions. Lastly, I thank all the contributors and participants of the several author seminars for their presentations and discussions, which helped refine my own thoughts about this chapter.

[1] Manu Bhagavan, *The Peacemakers: India and the Quest for One World* (HarperCollins 2012) 52.

[2] Julie Laut, 'The Woman Who Swayed America': Vijayalakshmi Pandit, 1945, DEP: Deportate, esuli, profughe (Deported, Exiles, Refugees—Journal of Women's Memory Studies) 10 July 2018.

[3] Vijayalakshmi Pandit, *The Scope of Happiness: A Personal Memoir* (Speaking Tiger Books 2018). On the Bandung Conference as the first big milestone for Asian and African nations coming together, both newly independent and on the cusp of independence, see Luis Eslava, Michael Fakhri, and Vasuki Nesiah (eds),

Parvathi Menon, *Vijayalakshmi Pandit* In: *Portraits of Women in International Law.* Edited by: Immi Tallgren, Oxford University Press. © Parvathi Menon 2023. DOI: 10.1093/oso/9780198868453.003.0019

Figure 19.1 Vijayalakshmi Pandit during a visit in the Netherlands, 1965.
Source: Photograph by Ron Kroon, Anefo. National Archives of the Netherlands.

she became the United Nations General Assembly's first female President in 1953. The 'first female' label inevitably projected her as a feminist icon. However, her feminism was mostly non-confrontational, and sometimes accused of elitism.[4] If redistribution (the economy), recognition (culture), and representation (politics) are the three pillars of the modern feminist manifesto,[5] one could look back at Pandit as enjoying the luxury of caring mainly about representational or identity politics. Her worldview was perhaps a consequence of her upper class and caste status, as many Indian Marxist feminists begrudged her for at the time. Yet, there were a few notable instances of her championing revolutionary causes of the left.

Much like her feminism, Pandit felt she could rise above the distributional differences that subjugated many postcolonial states by focusing on political equality. From struggling to placate the East and the West in the initial years of free India and trying to forge a South-East Asian alliance, Pandit later championed a precarious neutrality for newly independent states like India. Exalting the burgeoning internationalism on the one hand, Pandit also denigrated the absence of a strong Asian presence in the UN Security Council. Her efforts allow us to re-examine the pre-Bandung era less as

Bandung, Global History, and International Law: Critical Pasts and Pending Futures (Cambridge University Press 2017).

[4] Geraldine Forbes, *Women in Modern India* (Cambridge University Press 1996).
[5] Cinzia Arruzza, Tithi Bhattacharya, and Nancy Fraser, *Feminism for the 99%: A Manifesto* (Verso Books 2019).

heralding the Third World as a force to reckon with, and more as a complex tactical measure during the Cold War. The complexity of India's role in what later became the 'Non-Aligned Movement', when studied through Pandit's associations and dissociations, tells us a story of various shifting alignments that led to such a stance. Whether as a consciously laid path towards neutrality or as a path of least resistance, Pandit's voice can help us appreciate a nuance in the early developments of the Third World.

In this chapter, I examine different approaches to reading and understanding Pandit by reclaiming her role in postcolonial politics and, in turn, the development of international law. The archival materials and scholarship distil her memory as the innocuous sister, feminist visionary, privileged Indian elite, freedom fighter, staunch anti-imperialist, South-East Asian integrationist, and a Cold War neutral imbued with a liberal and left internationalism. Her multi-faceted appearances, at times seemingly contradictory, allow us to examine the spirit of the postcolonial state, while engaging with the intricacy of its contingencies in the international legal order.

(En)Gendering a Path to the United Nations

When international law scholars confront the inequalities facing the Global South, whether through its participation or resistance, they often mark them by the Bandung moment in 1955.[6] United in their stance against European imperialism, delegates from twenty-nine Asian and African states, either newly independent or on the cusp of independence, attended a conference in Bandung, Indonesia. The images from the conference with faces of top delegates—Jawaharlal Nehru, Kwame Nkrumah, Josip Broz 'Tito', Gamal Abdel Nasser, Sukarno —allow us to imagine an all-male cast of crucial actors who propelled into limelight what the Third World alliance meant for the rest. In the face of racism, sexism seemed a non-issue. At Bandung, sexism was subsumed in the rhetoric of social and economic freedoms and progress. If the fight was against the Western, imperialist foundation upon which institutions and other world structures were built to propagate inequality, Bandung signified a win. However, as Aziza Ahmed notes, 'the Final Communiqué [spoke] to human rights, [but] it [made] no mention of women, gender, or women's rights'.[7]

Almost ten years prior, in 1946, as a leading member of the Indian delegation to the United Nations, Pandit encouraged its members to fight racial inequalities, no doubt, but also discriminations against women. In her first speech at the United Nations, Pandit took the opportunity to highlight the work of two leading Indian women—Hansa Mehta[8] and Lakshmi Menon[9]— and their worthy contributions to the various Committees' work in connection with the United Nations Organization.

[6] Eslava, Fakhri, and Nesiah, *Bandung* (n 3).

[7] Aziza Ahmed, 'Bandung's Legacy Solidarity and Contestation in Global Women's Rights', in Eslava, Fakhri, and Nesiah, *Bandung, Global History* (n 5) 450.

[8] Hansa Mehta represented India on the Nuclear Sub-Committee on the status of women in 1946. As the Indian delegate on the UN Human Rights Commission in 1947–48, she was responsible for the gendered changes in the language of the Universal Declaration of Human Rights from 'all men are created equal' to 'all human beings'.

[9] Lakshmi Menon was India's delegate to the Third Committee, argued in favour of non-discrimination based on sex and 'the equal rights of men and women' in the Universal Declaration of Human Rights.

Putting 'gender' on the table, she expressed her hope that 'women of all countries will have the occasion to participate more fully with men in all departments of life, including the world of this Assembly'.[10] Projecting Indian women to the forefront was in itself a powerful statement, which focused on the inequalities of race and sex, whether Pandit intended it like that or not.

However, Pandit's early years demonstrated a more conflicting view and experience regarding the role of women. Growing up as the daughter of a top Indian lawyer and political leader of British India, Motilal Nehru, and sister of a leading Indian nationalist, Jawaharlal Nehru, Pandit felt early on that she would always play a secondary role to the men in her family. Praising her father's 'championship of women's rights', she notes the paradoxical disregard for his own daughter's education.[11] Home-schooled by an English governess and a slew of tutors, Pandit's education was in line with the 'foreign-oriented' way of living that was accessible only to the privileged classes in India. Yet she was not allowed the access her brother availed by attending Harrow, a premier boy's school in London. The Anglophile education worked to create a favourable international persona for her, while her Indian attire often kept her under an 'orientalist gaze'.[12] Furthermore, it also signalled, in the postcolonial, a narrative of 'self' and 'other', marginalizing non-English speakers in India.[13]

Accustomed to Western ways and manners, Pandit's notions surrounding progressiveness constituted equal rights for men and women, since advocating for women's rights was considered a signpost of modernity among Third World feminists.[14] However, she often related her 'modernity' to the British lifestyle, even though the participation of Indian (and Pakistani) women in the drafting of the Indian Constitution was something even most of her Western counterparts could not boast of having done.[15] Calling her family a touch arrogant, she ascribed it to being 'different' from other Indians, more British than them. Nevertheless, offended by the restrictions imposed upon Indians by the British, Pandit separated her appreciation for the British from the antagonism she felt towards British colonialism.

While known for many conspicuous utterances in favour of women at the United Nations, Pandit often shrugged off any relevance or impact from being the first female President of the UNGA, stressing that 'she would like to consider it as an honour to India rather than as an honour to women'.[16] Whether as a sign of privilege or a

[10] Speech delivered by Vijaya Lakshmi Pandit, leader of the Indian Delegation, at the General Assembly of the United Nations, on 25 October 1946. South Asian American Digital Archive.

[11] Pandit (n 3) ch 8.

[12] Julie Laut (n 2). The Chicago Tribune praised her 'dazzling white robe [...] alluring curves [...] Oxonian accent', quoted in Bhagavan (n 1) 52.

[13] In a letter from Nehru to Pandit, he wrote about another Indian representative sent to the United States, Amarnath Jha. Calling him unimpressive on the basis of his 'affected way of speaking English' that would 'get on the nerves of Americans' in Nayantara Sehgal (ed), *Before Freedom: Nehru's Letters to his Sister 1909–1947* (The Lotus Collection, Roli Books 2004). Elsewhere I refer to the postcolonial's reproduction of self-other dichotomy as 'internal othering' Parvathi Menon, *Self-Referral to the ICC: A Continuation of War by Other Means* (2016) 106 AJIL Unbound.

[14] I thank Vasuki Nesiah for highlighting the link between feminism and nationalism as modernity in the pre-independent Global South.

[15] Rebecca Adami, *Women and the Universal Declaration of Human Rights* (Routledge 2018) 118.

[16] Lady Hartog, *India: New Pattern* (George Allen & Unwin Ltd 1955) 150. See also Chronoscope, Madame Vijaya Lakshmi Pandit, interview by Larry Le Sueur and Edward P Morgan (Columbia Broadcasting System 1953).

testament to her sense of self, Pandit's engagement with women's issues adopted a liberal stance, which later became visible in her foreign policies. However, this was not unlike the suffragists and other liberal feminists all over the world, whose focus was often on women's autonomy and equality of the sexes, undermining the complexity and fluidity of identity. In furthering such agenda, Indian women like Hansa Mehta, Lakshmi Menon, Begum Hamid Ali, and Rajkumari Amrit Kaur were responsible for bringing about the gendered perspective in the international through their work for women in India.[17]

Mehta, Menon, and Amrit Kaur together authored the 'Draft of Indian Woman's Charter of Rights and Duties' ('Draft'), prepared under the aegis of the All India Women's Conference (AIWC) and submitted to the United Nations Economic and Social Council (ECOSOC) on 1 May 1946. AIWC was a non-governmental organization founded by an Irish woman, Margaret Cousins, in India in 1927. Almost all the Indian women who were delegates to the UN had ties to AIWC, which Pandit joined in 1946. AIWC held several conferences across India, presided by female heads of Princely States like the Maharani Chimnabai Saheb Gaekwar of Baroda, Her Highness Jahan Begum of Bhopal, and others. The working class and rural members supported many of AIWC's political goals and ideologies, even if shunning its liaisons with the higher echelons of society.[18] Renu Chakravartty and other Marxist feminists did not treat Gandhians like Pandit as an ally, considering them representatives of the Indian power elite.[19] Despite the animosities, they all came together for the causes AIWC put forward as its goals. The AIWC Draft was wide-ranging in the issues it addressed, even if much of it did not go beyond the tenets of liberal feminism: from women's education, health, property ownership, and the right to work. Positioning women's oppression within the larger context of economic exploitation, the Draft also demanded that housework by women be recognized as labour entitled for compensation.[20]

Although AIWC presented their ambitious Draft before the ECOSOC at the UN, they were never given a seat on the dais of the Commission on the Status of Women, chaired by the Danish activist and diplomat, Bodil Begtrup. Nor was their mandate adopted in the Convention on the Political Rights of Women in 1953, drafted mainly by members of the Commission on the Status of Women.[21] What followed in the international arena was equally a feminism sanitized of any revolutionary fervour. ECOSOC along with the UN General Assembly's Third Committee (dealing with social, humanitarian, and human rights issues) diluted any goals beyond 'equality

[17] E/HR/ST/5, Draft of Indian Woman's Charter of Rights and Duties Prepared by India by all India Women's Conference and Submitted by Mrs. Hansa-Mehta for Information of Sub-Commission, New York, UN ECOSOC 1 May 1946.

[18] Elisabeth Armstrong, *Gender and Neoliberalism: The All India Democratic Women's Association and Globalization Politics* (Routledge 2014) 32.

[19] Malini Bhattacharya, 'Communist Party and Indian Women's Movement' (1982) 17(1/2) Economic and Political Weekly 20–22. Ashoka Gupta, *In the Path of Service: Memories of a Changing Century* (Sipra Bhattacharya with Ranjana Dasgupta trs, STREE Publications 2005) 77. Gupta was also a member of the AIWC. On Gandhianism as liberalism see Bidyut Chakrabarty, *Confluence of Thought: Mohandas Karamchand Gandhi and Martin Luther King, Jr* (OUP 2013).

[20] Draft of Indian Woman's Charter of Rights and Duties prepared in India by All Women's Conference and submitted by Mrs Hansa Mehta for information of Sub-Commission, United Nations Economic and Social Council, E/HR/ST/5 1 May 1946.

[21] Convention on the Political Rights of Women, 193 UNTS 135, *entered into force* 7 July 1954.

between the sexes'. Albeit sharing Begtrup's liberal ideologies, during the twenty-third meeting of the UNGA, Pandit veritably pushed against a garden-variety feminism. When the Danish delegation introduced a resolution for political equality of women at the UNGA in 1946, Pandit was one of the few members to disagree with the resolution. 'She feared that if the words "political rights" were mentioned in the resolution, they would imply, in fact, a limitation of the rights of women.'[22] Pandit took issue with the 'political rights' angle because she was an ardent believer in 'equal rights' for women in all arenas, including allowing them to inherit property just like men could. It was also probably a reflection of the already existing political rights for women in India, which encouraged her to urge the UN to go beyond it. Countering Eleanor Roosevelt's fear that women were 'perhaps not yet ready to assume the responsibilities which it was proposed to give them', Pandit fittingly questioned how one could know if women were ready or not, without first conferring on them those responsibilities.[23]

Pandit's brand of feminism may have borne the burden of her British-influenced upbringing, showing less faith in working-class movements and more in the establishment's frameworks, but she found her foot (and support) among the left mainly owing to her approach towards colonialism. As a part of the group of 'notorious anti-colonials',[24] as the British referred to Pandit, Nehru, and VK Krishna Menon (the Indian representative to the UN from 1949–62), Pandit and many other Indian elites suffered severe hardships in their fight for India's independence from Britain. Therefore, it was predictable that she would carry the torch for other subjugated groups around the world when she represented India at the UN. She implicated a Wilsonian, liberal international law with radical anti-colonial pursuits.

Of Racial Allegiances and a Tactical Neutrality

In the early years of the UN, a newly Independent India became the voice of all oppressed people in the world. With Pandit at the helm of the Indian affairs, a multitude of resolutions and interventions on her part allow us insights into the role India played in shaping the Third World alliances. At the same time, the impressions she created upon foreign relations, not merely in Britain, the Soviet Union, and the United States, but also African countries, go a long way in assessing Third World neutrality and its ignored trajectories.

After gaining independence, the British closely evaluated Indian policies to safeguard their own. It was clear to the British, quite early on, that India's international stature was steadily increasing, for which they credited Pandit and the success of the Indian delegation at the UN under her leadership.[25] At times, the British thought her more moderate than her compatriot, Krishna Menon, and preferred to negotiate with

[22] Continuation of the discussion of the draft resolution regarding the political rights of women submitted by the delegation of Denmark, United Nations General Assembly, Twenty-Third Meeting, 15 November 1946, A/C.3/SR/23.

[23] ibid, Draft Resolution regarding Political Rights.

[24] The National Archives (TNA) Foreign Office (FO) 371/112214, Indian Government Policy towards British Colonialism, 1954 ff 109.

[25] TNA FO 371/63528/204 Folder 1, Transfer of Power to India.

her as opposed to him to foster goodwill between the UK and India.[26] At other times, they attributed her desire to create a neutral Third front to her friendliness with the Communists and hoped she would not influence her brother, Nehru.[27]

Britain's aim in the initial years after letting go of its crown jewel, India, was to steer her away from Russian policy and the belief that the capitalist world must be disrupted.[28] Any information they received regarding alliances built in the South was a potential interference they were intent on quelling. Pandit became the Indian Ambassador to Russia a week before India became independent on 15 August 1947. In such capacity, she spoke with United States Secretary of State, Dean Acheson, regarding her wishes for a regional alliance between India, Pakistan, Ceylon, Burma, Siam, and Indo-China, alluding to USSR's interest in helping them.[29] Therefore, the impression that the Soviets would help build India's neutrality or create a regional group of Eastern nations was a crisis the West wanted to avert.[30] As evidence of this fear, the United States delegate to UNGA, John Foster Dulles, remarked during a speech that 'communism exercises a strong influence through the Interim Hindu Government' in India.[31] After his comment made headlines in all the national daily newspapers, it was incumbent upon Pandit to respond. In her response, she made it very clear that India only espoused the cause of the 'dependent peoples' during the workings of the Trusteeship Committee, where Dulles and Pandit represented their respective countries. She went on to clarify that simply because India and USSR strove hard to 'liberalise the trusteeship agreements' did not imply that India was under Communist influence, since 'India will evolve her own policy according to her own interests'.[32] At the same time, to improve relations with the Soviets, she was instructed (by her brother) 'to speak frankly to Molotov, Vyshinsky, and other important functionaries in the Soviet Foreign Office, and tell them that it is quite absurd for anyone to think that we are tied to the apron-strings of England or that we attach ourselves to the USA'.[33]

Staying clear of any suggestion that India was hand in glove with the Soviets on the one hand, while ensuring that the Soviets did not think India was an extension of its former colonial power or the USA, on the other hand, the pre-Bandung era of 'neutrality' was a complex tactical positioning. It was not merely 'the delegates step[ping] out of the dynamics of the Cold War that was producing such conflicts into a free space of neutrality'.[34] Although there is evidence to suggest that India did champion the causes of many dependent peoples, it began as a case of extending support to Indians who entered Mauritius, Fiji, West Indies, Natal Colony (and other parts of

26 This was discussed in reference to Indian representation at the Suez Conference in 1956. TNA FO 371/123590/2 ff 24.

27 TNA Dominions Office (DO) 133/101, ff 61, India's Cooperation with other Countries in Asia and Pacific.

28 TNA DO 133/99 ff 4, India's attitude towards the USSR.

29 TNA DO 133/101, ff 49, India Cooperation with other Countries in Asia and Pacific.

30 ibid.

31 TNA FO 371/63529 ff 164.

32 ibid.

33 BR Nanda, *Jawaharlal Nehru: Rebel and Statesman* (OUP 1998) 228.

34 Robert Young, 'Postcolonialism: From Bandung to the Tricontinental' (2005) 5 Historein 11, 14, quoted in The Spirit of Bandung, in Eslava, Fakhri, and Nesiah, *Bandung* (n 3) 13.

modern South Africa), and Malaya as indentured labourers in the 1870s, and East Africa as small traders and railway labourers.[35] It is against the background of India's support for other Indians that Pandit's assertion of neutrality and the reiteration of unity amongst 'dependent people' must be understood.

The allegiance India manifested towards its migrated populations played an important role in Pandit's case against South Africa's discrimination against its Indian inhabitants. It is here that her battle for the cause of oppressed peoples, much like her feminist aspirations, demonstrates her renewed faith in the internationalism heralded by the UN. At its inaugural session in 1946, UNGA passed a resolution initiated at Pandit's behest,[36] regarding the treatment of Indians in South Africa, urging both governments to abide by their bilateral agreements and the UN Charter.[37] When the resolution was discussed in 1947 at UNGA, the South African representative, HG Lawrence, relied on Article 2(7) of the UN Charter to support non-intervention by the international organization.[38] Citing the South African Prime Minister, Field Marshall Jan Smuts' irreverence for the UN, Pandit attacked South African land tenure laws' racial discrimination against Indians as being repugnant to the Charter.[39] The UNGA voted in favour of Pandit and The Asiatic Land Tenure and Indian Representation Act, 1946, 'became apartheid'.[40] Therefore, her attack won her praise from many, including one of the founding figures of America's National Association for the Advancement of Colored People (NCAAP), WEB Du Bois, who called it the 'successful assault upon the color line in the UN Assembly', while noting the deafening silence from the rest of the 'colored world'.[41] Later, the NCAAP extensively engaged with Pandit for her support in their petitions to the UN and other conferences.

For someone who was an Indian nationalist and freedom fighter like Pandit, the state was a pivotal terrain for anti-colonial struggle. Therefore, it was unsurprising that she was also an ardent believer in the international's support for causes that had local impact and vice versa. Later, in the early-1950s, India extended support to all subjugated races, especially Africans, going as far as defending Jomo Kenyatta in the killing of the Kenyan Chief Waruhiu in 1952, for protecting British presence in Kenya.[42] Along with Krishna Menon and Nehru, Pandit supported the 'African Students Conference' and the initiative to start an Indian Institute in African Studies in Delhi. By locking-in its foreign policies in domestic initiatives, both in India and in British

[35] TNA FO 371/112214, Indian Government Policy Towards British Colonialism ff 102.

[36] 'General Assembly of the United Nations: Indian Complaint Against South Africa', Memorandum by Secretary of State for Foreign Affairs, 17 October 1946, CP(46)373, CAB 129/13.

[37] A/RES/44(1), 8 December 1946.

[38] A/C.1/SR.111, Summary record of the 111th meeting: 1st Committee, 17 November 1947, Lake Success, New York, General Assembly, 2nd session.

[39] ibid.

[40] Bhagavan (n 1) 81.

[41] WEB Du Bois *The Winds of Time*, WEB Du Bois Papers (MS 312) 30 December 1946, Special Collections and University Archives, University of Massachusetts Amherst Libraries . See also Letter from Walter White to Indian Delegation to the United Nations, 18 September 1947 (ibid).

[42] ibid ff 105. Indian-born lawyers who had recently made Kenya their home—Ajeet Singh, Achhroo Ram Kapila, and Fitz de Souza—were a part of Kenyatta's legal defence team. See David Anderson, *Histories of the Hanged: The Dirty War in Kenya and the End of Empire* (WW Norton 2005).

colonies, Pandit encouraged Indian participation in a left-internationalism that in many ways co-opted the UN.[43]

Conclusion

Anti-colonial histories of international law rarely put the spotlight on Pandit's efforts in the postcolonial shaping of what became the Third World, often highlighting the known names of Nehru and VK Krishna Menon.[44] For those who did, like Abdul Majid Khan, his biography on Pandit is perhaps a poignant reminder of her relegation to a 'relational status', evident in the title: 'The Great Daughter of India: An Appreciative Study of Mrs. Vijaya Lakshmi Pandit and Her Ideas in the Background of Nehru Family's Heroic Struggle for the Political Emancipation of India'.[45] That she remained in the background, despite holding eminent positions, seemed an inevitable eventuality for the sister of Jawaharlal Nehru. 'I have a mind of my own and have always been able to use it whether in small or larger decisions. But gradually I found myself accepting *Bhai's* [brother's] views without any questioning',[46] Pandit curiously remarks in her autobiography.

On the contrary, it was clear that she asserted her own place in the workings of an independent India and its role in the international. Whether appearing to the British more radical than Nehru in her anti-imperialism, or instrumentalizing the international in her pursuit to defend subjugated races all over the world, Pandit owned her politics and carved her own niche. Although the Bandung conference remains a milestone in the resistance by the Third World, it is worth recognizing through Pandit's work that the path to that moment is studded with efforts to invoke (even if naively) the international and its legal frameworks.

[43] Bhagavan (n 1) 34.

[44] There are exceptions among historians: Bhagavan (n 1); Annie Devenish, *Debating Women's Citizenship in India 1930–1960* (Bloomsbury 2019), where the author devotes a chapter to Pandit's role in the international sphere; Rakesh Ankit, 'Between Vanity and Sensitiveness: Indo–British Relations During Vijayalakshmi Pandit's High-Commissionership (1954–61)' (2016) 30(1) Contemporary British History 20–39; Laut (n 2).

[45] See also Mark Mazower, *No Enchanted Palace: The End of Empire and the Ideological Origins of the United Nations* (Princeton University Press 2009) 175.

[46] Pandit (n 3).

20
The Timing of Felice Morgenstern

*Jan Klabbers**

Introduction

There is a picture in circulation, taken in 1952, of Hersch Lauterpacht with six research students: four young men and two young women.[1] The young men look self-assured and confident, and all would go on to become successful practicing lawyers and academics. The women, by contrast, look different. One of them is caught with her eyes closed, giving a dreamy impression. She is, mistakenly it seems, identified as Ruth Goldstein. The other woman in the picture looks more alert, but is equally caught off-guard: standing next to Lauterpacht, Felice Morgenstern has her head turned to the left and is looking behind Lauterpacht, as if she has just picked up a noise or spotted a speck on his winter coat. Morgenstern was not 'in the moment', and it is arguable that for much of her career, her timing was just a little off. She made significant contributions to international law, often pioneering the treatment of a particular topic, but typically did so before the discipline was ready to receive her insights and give them their due recognition.

That Morgenstern stood in the picture next to Lauterpacht was perhaps no coincidence: she was, at the time, Whewell scholar at Cambridge (the first female Whewell scholar[2]), and in the process of joining the legal service of the International Labour Organization, partly based on Lauterpacht's ringing endorsement. Comparing her to another of his former students, who had applied to the same position, Lauterpacht wrote: 'I have no doubt that from the long-range point of view she is by far the better candidate.' He added, however, that this other candidate, himself a rather well-known international lawyer, would be the more socially adept of the two. Still, Lauterpacht clearly recommended Morgenstern—he was very impressed.[3]

The ILO's legal advisers have over the years made deep and serious academic contributions. Lawyers worth their salt will recognize the relevance of the work of the likes of Nicholas Valticos, Ebere Osieke, Francis Maupain, and one-time ILO Director-General C Wilfred Jenks. And even in the non-legal discipline of International Relations (former) ILO staff have made a mark. One example is Robert

* I am indebted to Riikka Koskenmäki, Sarah Nouwen, and the ILO's archivists for their help in accessing material, and to Karen Knop for insightful comments.

[1] It is reproduced in Elihu Lauterpacht, *The Life of Hersch Lauterpacht* (Cambridge University Press 2010) plate 20.

[2] It is only since the turn of the century that women have become regular Whewell scholars. Besides Morgenstern, only three women received the scholarship until the 2000s.

[3] This was, in fact, the second letter concerning Morgenstern, dated 21 May 1951, probably precisely for purposes of comparison. The first had been sent two months earlier. See further (n 12) below.

Jan Klabbers, *The Timing of Felice Morgenstern* In: *Portraits of Women in International Law*. Edited by: Immi Tallgren, Oxford University Press. © Jan Klabbers 2023. DOI: 10.1093/oso/9780198868453.003.0020

Figure 20.1 The picture shows Hersch Lauterpacht with some of his research students in Cambridge in 1952, with Felice Morgenstern in the middle, standing to the right of Lauterpacht.
Source: Courtesy of Sir Elihu Lauterpacht's private collection.

Cox, who became a leading voice in the neo-Gramscian approach to the study of international relations.[4] While the work of Jenks in particular has recently been subjected to academic scrutiny, also in light of his relevance for the law of international organizations,[5] considerably less attention has been paid to Felice Morgenstern. Perhaps this is partly so for practical reasons. Where Jenks wrote two handfuls of monographs and an astonishing amount of other contributions (and did so while occupying high office within the ILO), Morgenstern has written considerably less. There is also the awkward circumstance that her main work is out of print, despite its considerable significance for the law of international organizations.[6] But possibly the main reason for the relative neglect of her work resides in its advanced nature. She was often far ahead of her times, so much so that some of her work must have bewildered less far-sighted colleagues. One can just imagine audiences from the 1950s to the 1980s sighing that they 'just don't see the problem' she analyzed and discussed with great sophistication.

She was also, as a scholar, difficult to categorize. For a public international lawyer, she came close to discussing issues of private international law or conflict of laws. For an international lawyer, she devoted much energy to its connection to domestic law.

[4] Robert W Cox, *Production, Power, and World Order: Social Forces in the Making of History* (Columbia University Press 1987).

[5] Guy Fiti Sinclair, 'Wilfred Jenks and the Futures of International Organizations Law' (2020) 31 EJIL 525–42.

[6] This refers to Felice Morgenstern, *Legal Problems of International Organizations* (Grotius1986).

And while some may say her most important work was in international organizations law, others may instead refer to her work in labour law.[7] Moreover, while her early years do not display any obvious feminist sympathies, her writings nonetheless mark some sensitivity to what may have been considered more or less as 'women's issues', and an argument can be made that she 'radicalized' a little over the years. Having paid some isolated attention to problems of family law as they relate to international officials in the 1960s (what do terms like 'marriage', 'adoption', and 'residence' mean in international civil service law?),[8] half a decade later she devoted a short article to women workers before the courts.[9] And another decade later she ended her Lauterpacht lectures with a sneering comparison between the status of international organizations in international law, and women in domestic law—a comparison she is unlikely to have made earlier in her career, even if she had occasionally demonstrated some spikiness in the past.[10]

Morgenstern was not a leading theorist by any standards, but made her mark mostly as a transitional figure, in various ways. She spoke of 'legality' in international organizations long before the rule of law was thought to apply in international affairs. She posited the autonomy of international organizations long before autonomy become a popular lens. She discussed the extraterritorial application of labour law long before the topic became topical; and she wrote about the relationship between international and domestic law just before this topic took a novel turn with the creation of what is now the European Union. In all these cases, her writings depart from then-prevailing opinion and received wisdom, though without settling on new definitive insights. And as is so often the case with transitional figures, in their own time they are viewed with some bemusement, and perhaps it did not help either to have worked for decades in the shadow of one of the giants of the field, Wilfred Jenks. It seems doubtful, as is sometimes off-the-cuff suggested, that she did the hard work in Geneva while Jenks was lecturing all over the world and writing his gigantic output. Morgenstern herself never made such a suggestion, not even between the lines. In fact, in her obituary of Jenks, she notes that his voluminous output owed much to the 'unity of thought' in his work for the ILO and his academic work: they cover much the same ground and discuss much the same topics.[11] There is no sign of bitterness or jealousy here, and she was a good enough writer subtly to insert bitterness or jealousy had she felt any.

In what follows, I provide a brief sketch of Morgenstern's biographical details, but this will be brief by necessity: very little is known about her private life ('A very private person'). Thereafter, I will devote some attention to her scholarly work.

[7] Felice Morgenstern, *International Conflicts of Labor Law* (ILO 1984).

[8] Felice Morgenstern, 'The Law Applicable to International Officials' (1969) 18 International and Comparative Law Quarterly 739–56.

[9] Felice Morgenstern, 'Women Workers and the Courts' (1975) 112 International Labour Review 15–28.

[10] 'In some ways the position of international organizations is reminiscent of the status of women in international law. It is accepted—with varying degrees of enthusiasm—that they are subjects of the law with a claim to rights and obligations… Inertia, far more than active resistance, is an obstacle to adaptation of the law even where particular needs are identified.' Morgenstern, *Legal Problems* (n 6) 135.

[11] Felice Morgenstern, 'Wilfred Jenks in the I.L.O.' (1972–73) 46 British Yearbook of International Law xvi–xxx, at xvii.

A Very Private Person

Little is known about the early life of Felice Morgenstern.[12] She was born into a Jewish family on 23 October 1926, in the Austrian capital Vienna, and died in 2000. The family moved to the United Kingdom when she was twelve or thirteen years old, in 1939, and settled in Cambridge, where she attended the Perse school for Girls. Upon graduation, Morgenstern obtained a scholarship and entered Newnham College at Cambridge in 1944, while the war was still ongoing. At Cambridge, she read history and obtained a first class degree in 1947.[13] She was awarded the Whewell scholarship in international law in 1948, and finished her master's studies with a dissertation on the right to asylum, a topic on which she would also publish several articles. Her doctoral studies involved the relationship between international and domestic law, with a dissertation dated 1954. In addition, she started to work towards legal qualifications, passing several examinations of the Council of Legal Education,[14] and in the late 1940s was part of the editorial team of the *Annual Digest*, that unsurpassed repertory of judicial decisions involving international law, later renamed *International Law Reports*.

In 1951, she applied for a position at the ILO and was eventually appointed on 1 February 1952. By all accounts, she performed her tasks very well. Usually, especially later on during her career, her supervisors ticked all the boxes marked 'excellent' on her performance reports.[15] In her earlier days, those performance reports suggested that there was still some room for improvement, not so much intellectually, but rather socially: it usually concerned categories such as aptitude to collaborate, to adapt, or to direct the work of others. This confirms the impression already given by Lauterpacht in his original letter of recommendation, calling her 'rather shy and retiring', but also 'the ablest student I have had so far'.[16]

Morgenstern's intellectual abilities were never in doubt. If Lauterpacht referred to her as his 'ablest student', Robbie Jennings recommended her to Jenks as being 'fairly easily the best international lawyer Cambridge has produced in recent years'.[17] Arnold McNair, somewhat less effusively and writing from the bench (he was a judge at the ICJ at the time and probably knew her less well), nonetheless reported that 'she has got really good intellectual abilities', and referred to her academic publications as 'thoroughly competent and scholarly pieces of work'.[18]

12 This section is to a large extent culled from her personnel files, accessed on 18 June 2019 in the ILO's archives. Her file comes in two dossiers, marked P.5278/A (originally marked 'confidential') and P.5278/B ('highly confidential').

13 Some of the general Cambridge atmosphere in these days is nicely captured in Christine Jennings, *Robbie: The Life of Sir Robert Jennings 1913–2004* (Matador 2019).

14 In those days, one could become a legal practitioner in the United Kingdom without a university degree in law. One notable example is classicist HLA Hart receiving his legal credentials by passing the required bar exams. See Nicola Lacey, *A Life of H.L.A. Hart: The Nightmare and the Noble Dream* (OUP 2004) 40.

15 eg, a 1977 performance appraisal by Francis Wolf, the legal adviser of the ILO from 1956 to 1987, lists only 'excellent' scores.

16 Hersch Lauterpacht to Wilfred Jenks, 21 March 1951.

17 Robert Jennings to Wilfred Jenks, 23 March 1951.

18 Arnold McNair to Wilfred Jenks, 23 March 1951.

Of Morgenstern's private life, little is known. Having joined the ILO, she lived for many years in the pleasant Eaux-Vives district of Geneva, in the Rue Viollier, and in 1970 she drove a Simca 1100, but little additional information is available. There never was a husband or other spouse in the picture. Instead, in the late 1950s, she applied to her employer for a family allowance with the specific purpose of supporting her mother, who lived with her. Later, she lists as emergency contacts a cousin living in London, and a female friend living in Geneva. The latter is named as E Johnstone, which may refer to Elizabeth Johnstone, whom she had first met, it seems, in 1964, in connection with the Committee on Women's Work of the Second African Regional Conference, a bi-annual events organized by the FAO which she attended as ILO representative.

In the end, the general picture that emerges is that of a dedicated, somewhat introverted international civil servant, much appreciated by her colleagues and superiors—legal adviser Wolf already left her in charge of the Legal Division during his annual leave in the summer of 1957, when she had yet to turn thirty-one.[19] Both Jenks and Wolf praised her analytical powers. Jenks recalled how correct the assessment of her referees had been, and praised her lucidity.[20] Wolf, in a performance appraisal from 1981, listed among her strengths a 'perfect knowledge of her trade', and heralded her rigour and loyalty.[21] On the occasion of her (early) retirement, moreover, Francis Blanchard, the ILO's Director-General at the time, praised her 'unswerving devotion' and her 'remarkable memory and intelligence', combined with the 'unhesitating acceptance' of her responsibilities.[22]

Much later, a letter from the ILO to Sir Elihu Lauterpacht (curiously misnamed Sir Eliah) suggests that it was only her early retirement which prevented her from climbing to the top of her profession to become the ILO's Legal Adviser. She was nonetheless promoted to the D2 grade 'in testimony of the exceptional contribution she had made'. This was confirmed, in a manner, in a note by Francis Wolf, sent to the Director-General, once Morgenstern her announced her retirement. Wolf noted that he had envisaged her as his successor, and urged the Director-General to find a way to keep her involved in one way or another.[23]

The letter to Sir Elihu further recalls her 'technical competence, her moral integrity and authority and the brightness of her analytical mind', and observed that other international organizations often turned to her for advice. Moreover, and despite her 'gut aversion to any form of militancy in this field', the note concludes by suggesting that she may have contributed more than anybody else 'to the promotion of gender equality in the secretariat of international organizations'.[24]

[19] Francis Wolf to Personnel Office, 12 July 1957.

[20] Note by Wilfred Jenks, 20 March 1973.

[21] He wrote in French: '*Parfaite connaissance de son métier*'. Francis Wolf, 30 September 1981. The United States had withdrawn from the ILO in 1977, citing the need for organizational reform, only to return to the fold in 1980; the episode is briefly discussed in Jan Klabbers, 'The EJIL Foreword: The Transformation of International Organizations Law' (2015) 26 EJIL 9–82.

[22] Francis Blanchard to Felice Morgenstern, 8 February 1982.

[23] Francis Wolf to Francis Blanchard, 29 June 1981. Wolf further said, somewhat tongue in cheek perhaps but speaking volumes of his appreciation, that he would have been tempted to reject her request for early retirement.

[24] Unsigned letter to Elihu Lauterpacht, 17 July 2001.

Wolf's wish to keep her involved also after her retirement met with mutual approval. In her request for retirement, she had flagged that the main reason was to devote herself to a study that could be of interest to the ILO (this must refer to her Lauterpacht lectures, given in 1985), but that she would also be 'glad to consider any specific tasks' that the ILO might have for her.[25] In addition to some short-term research work,[26] probably the most important of these was that she represented the ILO in February and March 1986 during the Vienna Conference on the Law of Treaties between States and International Organizations or Between International Organizations. Characteristically, she did not say much during the Vienna Conference: occasionally the representatives of other international organizations also spoke on behalf of the ILO.[27] But equally characteristically, the one time she spoke, her words were well-heard.[28] She averred that it was too early to insert a provision into the 1986 Convention concerning the effects of treaties concluded by international organizations on their member states, and a draft provision to that effect was duly deleted.[29]

It seems reasonably clear that Morgenstern was somewhat introverted ('shy and retiring', in Lauterpacht's evocative phrase), and hardly prone to exaggerating her qualities. It is surprising to note, for example, that when applying to the ILO, she reports that does not speak French well (although she also notes that she reads it fluently), and merely has a 'good working knowledge' of German—the latter in particular is surprising, given that she lived in the German-speaking world for much of her childhood. And yet, she could also demonstrate a certain spikiness. Quite lovely is how she despairs at the ILO's request to specify the costs she makes on behalf of her mother, who had moved in with her a few months earlier. In a note oozing exasperation, she writes: '. . . I am unable to give you any definite financial figure of the cost of the support of my mother, since my duties at the Office do not permit me to spend the time on the detailed break-down of household and other expenses that would be necessary to arrive at such a result'.[30] And some spikiness is also apparent from some of her writings.

Morgenstern the Scholar

Prior to her career at the ILO, Morgenstern spent a few years in the academy, writing a handful of articles, doing some editorial work for the *Annual Digest*, and writing a number of brief but excellent book reviews for *International Affairs*, the journal associated with the Royal Institute of International Affairs. These book reviews, usually some two or three paragraphs long, show her versatility, in various ways: she was able

[25] Felice Morgenstern to Francis Wolf and Francis Blanchard, 25 June 1981.

[26] There is mention, eg, of a contract for two weeks in November 1983 to conduct various studies for the legal service, and another for two weeks in March 1986—this overlapped partly with the 1986 Vienna Conference.

[27] See UN Doc A/CONF/129.16 (vol I). Daniel Vignes, representing the WHO, did so, as did Mr Noll (ITU), introducing a joint amendment proposal.

[28] ibid 142.

[29] Seminal is Catherine Brölmann, 'The 1986 Vienna Convention on the Law of Treaties: The History of Draft Article 36*BIS*' in Jan Klabbers and René Lefeber (eds), *Essays on the Law of Treaties* (Martinus Nijhoff 1998) 121–40.

[30] Felice Morgenstern to ILO, 2 May 1957.

to review works written in French and German (in addition to English), and could review works on various aspects of international law, but also works on constitutional law or public law more broadly. She was also, while always polite,[31] occasionally witty,[32] and always brutally honest. One fine example is how she held that a work on neutrality by Judge Fabela, the Mexican judge at the International Court of Justice at the time, was 'disappointing'. While it contained some 'potentially valuable material... there could usefully be more discussion of that material'.[33] Of a work on sociological aspects of law it is said that there is 'nothing strikingly novel', but well-written and serving an informative purpose[34], and a study of advisory opinions, she holds, is 'not very satisfactory, as it cannot be said that [the author] adequately proves' his proposition.[35]

The latter review is suggestive of her general jurisprudential outlook: its author, she insists, went much too far in his assumption that all matters should be subjected to judicial procedure. Instead, for her, it was important that with international political institutions being 'in their infancy', legal concepts should be 'developed by the practice of political organs'.[36] There is a faint echo here of her mentor Lauterpacht as well as of Schwarzenberger. Indeed, she seems intrigued by the latter's work, and her own preferred methodology comes perhaps closest to Schwarzenberger's inductive approach.[37]

Some of Morgenstern's early works were devoted to questions related to asylum, while others discussed sometimes highly intricate aspects of the ever-problematic relationship between international and domestic law. They have in common that they are all extremely skillful doctrinal studies, with their author showing a sophistication and finesse to do Lauterpacht proud. She proved capable of making fine distinctions, and of introducing even finer nuances. Moreover, her historical training served her well: she could plausibly cite Foreign Office archives if and when appropriate. But none of the papers suggested a budding interest in the law of international organizations or the work of the international civil service. Instead, those early articles show an author very much at home in the world of classical inter-state law, where international law was still mostly a matter of what states said and did, without a very pronounced role for international institutions.

What those articles also have in common to a greater or lesser extent—and this is a characteristic of pretty much all her work—is that they tend to pick up issues not

[31] She pointedly chides LC Green, contributing to a volume she reviews, for casting ridicule on scholars with different views. Felice Morgenstern, 'Review of George Keeton and Georg Schwarzenberger (eds.), *Current Legal Problems 1951*' (1952) 28 International Affairs 209.

[32] Two articles on German public law are described as 'full of meat'—and one immediately knows what she means. Felice Morgenstern, 'Review of Gerhard Leibholz (ed.), *Jahrbuch des öffentlichen Rechts der Gegenwart 1954*' (1956) 32 International Affairs 80. At this point in time, she was already based in Geneva; this was the only review written for *International Affairs* after leaving the academy.

[33] Felice Morgenstern, 'Review of Isidro Fabela, *Neutralité*' (1949) 25 International Affairs 510.

[34] Felice Morgenstern, 'Review of Charles Boasson, *Sociological Aspects of Law and International Adjustment*' (1951) 27 International Affairs 485.

[35] Felice Morgenstern, 'Review of Louis Wehle, *The U.N. By-Passes the International Court as the Council's Adviser: A Study in Contrived Frustration*' (1950) 26 International Affairs 541.

[36] ibid.

[37] Felice Morgenstern, 'Review of Georg Schwarzenberger, *International Law Vol. 1*' (1950) 26 International Affairs 100.

often picked up by others. Where, for instance, many discussions on the relationship between national and international law focus on the reception of treaties or custom in domestic legal orders, she devoted a very thoughtful article to recognition and enforcement of foreign official acts, both judicial and legislative, that are contrary to international law.[38] The topic is still, to this day, left largely unexplored by public international lawyers, despite touching on real life problems of real people of flesh and blood.

It cannot seriously be claimed that her early work has been influential, though where a topic has been picked up later, her work tends to be referred to.[39] Perhaps the greatest obstacle was her unique talent for being ahead of her time, and while this comes to the fore specifically in reference to her work on international organizations law, it also afflicts some of her other writings. It was novel, for example, to discuss the law relating to dispatched workers as early as the 1970s.[40] And it was unorthodox, in the early 1950s, to frame an argument on the validity of exercises of jurisdiction by states in violation of international law, in terms of the principle of legality.[41] If 'legality' had a meaning in those days, it was by and large confined to criminal law. Morgenstern, however, imbued it with a sense coming much closer to what is nowadays commonly referred to as the Rule of Law, a notion that itself had only recently started to gain some currency when she was writing, and even then was rarely, if ever, associated with international law. And yet, this is precisely what she did, suggesting that while prosecuting suspects upon seizing them in violation of international law may appeal to some sense of justice, there is a 'requirement of justice of overriding importance', embedded in 'higher considerations of legality'.[42] The article ends with a notable Rule of Law flourish: 'There is merit in upholding the authority of the international community—and of its law—as the guarantor of the rights of the individual.'[43]

The notion of legality would find a central place in her writings on international organizations during the 1970s and 1980s. Those writings were not voluminous, but they were invariably thoughtful and thought-provoking if also, again, ahead of her time. The notion of legality played a key role here, and did so in two ways. First, and most obvious, one of her articles was explicitly devoted to legality in international organizations.[44] Second though, and intellectually more significant, is that her conception of the international organization as a site of legality has serious theoretical consequences. Viewing organizations as spaces for legality isolates them—at least to some extent—from member state influences, and in doing so stresses their relative autonomy, at least

[38] Felice Morgenstern, 'Recognition and Enforcement of Foreign Legislative Administrative and Judicial Acts Which Are Contrary to International Law' (1951) 4 International Law Quarterly 326–44.

[39] eg, one of her early works dealt with belligerent occupation, and is duly referred to in the leading recent study on the law of occupation. See Felice Morgenstern, 'Validity of the Acts of the Belligerent Occupant' (1951) 28 British Yearbook of International Law 291–322; Eyal Benvenisti, *The International Law of Occupation* (2nd edn, OUP 2012) 309.

[40] Felice Morgenstern and Blaise Knapp, 'Multinational Enterprises and the Extraterritorial Application of Labour Law' (1978) 27 International and Comparative Law Quarterly 769–93.

[41] Felice Morgenstern, 'Jurisdiction in Seizures Effected in Violation of International Law' (1952) 29 British Yearbook of International Law 265–82.

[42] ibid 281.

[43] ibid 282.

[44] Felice Morgenstern, 'Legality in International Organizations' (1976–77) 48 British Yearbook of International Law 241–57.

vis-à-vis those member states.[45] In other words, through her conceptualization of international organizations as venues for legality, she utilized a distinct focus on organizations. To her, they were not solely, as is so often the case, vehicles for their member states (although her work also contains traces of such a conception[46]), but also actors in their own right, doing things (or not doing things) on their own initiative and in their own name. And whenever she tapped into this latter sense, her work proved to be far ahead of her time.

The great merit of Morgenstern's work then resides in its identification of salient legal issues. This was already the case with her early academic work, and would continue to be the case. In 1969 she devoted an article to issues arising in relations between organizations and their staff, discussing the need to come to terms with the precise meaning of notions such as 'marriage' or 'adoption'. Much the same applies to *Legal Problems*, where in particular her discussion of relations between international organizations *inter se*, is decades ahead of its time.

This may have owed much to her practical experiences. One example concerns relations between international organizations, where she loudly wonders whether the adoption of a convention within another organization could deprive an ILO Convention of some of its effects.[47] The standard functionalist approach would be to analyze both instruments in light of the functions of their respective sponsoring organizations and in light of their respective powers, but doing so would merely shift the problem. It is much to her credit that she recognized such problems long before anyone else did, and while she does not offer a solution in this case (she merely notes that comparative study had found that there were no conflicting provisions in the example discussed), the mere spotting of the issue and taking it seriously is suggestive of deeper reflection. And it seems clear that if she were to have advanced a possible solution, it would not be based on the functions of the respective organizations. For she realized all too well that the problem resided precisely in overlapping or competing functions. Astutely, she noted with respect to issues affecting private persons that as 'the action of the organization may affect persons which are in direct relationship to it, it is not as free as it would be in a matter falling wholly within its internal law to draw upon other legal sources'.[48]

Conclusion

Having retired in the early 1980s, Morgenstern eventually died in 2000. In the years of her retirement, she held her Lauterpacht lectures and did some freelance work for the

[45] Autonomy is a relative concept: it pays to ask in relation to whom an agent or entity can be considered autonomous. See Jan Klabbers and Panos Koutrakos, 'Introduction: An Anatomy of Autonomy' (2019) 88 Nordic Journal of International Law 1–8.

[46] This is no surprise, in that most work on international organizations taps into two opposed conceptualizations: the organization as forum, and the organization as vehicle. See Jan Klabbers, 'Two Concepts of International Organizations' (2005) 2 International Organizations Law Review 277–93.

[47] Morgenstern, *Legal Problems* (n 6) 27.

[48] Morgenstern, *Legal Problems* (n 6) 45. This is a conclusion others were reluctant to draw: see, eg, Jan Klabbers, 'Schermers' Dilemma' (2020) 31 EJIL 565–82.

ILO, including representing the ILO at the 1986 Vienna Conference and, a few years later, writing a brief evaluation thereof.[49] Beyond this, little is known about her final years. She seems to have spent these in full anonymity, either in Geneva or elsewhere.

It is possible that Morgenstern was heading for a stellar academic career when she decided to move to Geneva, and one can only speculate why she moved. Perhaps she felt that as a woman in a men's world (and the British international law scene at the time was strongly male-dominated),[50] she lacked confidence that her career would ever take off. Or then perhaps personal reasons drove her to Geneva, or away from Cambridge. What is clear, though, is that her work merits a re-appraisal: she personifies Friedmann's law of co-existence as well as the law of co-operation,[51] and made original and significant contributions to both.

[49] Felice Morgenstern, 'The Convention on the Law of Treaties between States and International Organizations or between International Organizations' in Yoram Dinstein (ed), *International Law at a Time of Perplexity* (Martinus Nijhoff 1989) 435–47.

[50] Luíza Leao Soares Pereira and Niccolò Ridi, 'Mapping the "Invisible College of International Lawyers" Through Obituaries' (2021) 34 Leiden Journal of International Law 67–91.

[51] Wolfgang Friedmann, *The Changing Structure of international Law* (Stevens and Sons 1964).

21
Paula Escarameia
Envisioning the Humane Face of International Law in the Twenty-first Century

Ana Caldeira Fouto, António Pedro Barbas Homem, and Pedro Caridade de Freitas

Paula Ventura de Carvalho Escarameia (1960–2010) had an international career as an academic and a legal expert in international institutions that continuously shaped her views on the evolution of international law. She exercised a role in major international legal developments such as the independence of East Timor and the creation of the International Criminal Court (ICC). These experiences made her a firm believer in the power of new actors in international relations, inducing a change of the traditionally state-centred legal system. Her reflections on international legal thought were developed in several publications[1] throughout her career, shortened by her premature death.

If international law exists in a 'slippery zone'[2] between principles and the realistic deference to power as Martti Koskenniemi describes, it is remarkable that so many of Escarameia's colleagues repeatedly identified kindness as one of her driving strengths as an internationalist—one who matched 'heart with reason'.[3] The 1990s were a golden age of international law-making, driven by an overall optimistic atmosphere which enabled the achievement of compromise—and, as her friend and current member of the ILC Marja Lehto recalled from their shared experience in the establishment of the ICC, Escarameia thrived in this environment. Hers was not an empty optimism, as her role as a member of the Portuguese delegation in the negotiations of the Rome Statute and thereafter in the implementation of international criminal law demonstrate.[4] She

[1] Paula Escarameia, 'Timor-Leste—Aspectos jurídicos do problema', in O Direito, Maio 1991; *Paula Escarameia, Formation of Concepts in International Law: Subsumption under Self-Determination in the Case of East Timor* (Fundação Oriente: Centro de Estudos Orientais 1993); Paula Escarameia, *Reflexões sobre temas de Direito Internacional Público: Timor, a ONU e o Tribunal Penal Internacional*, (Instituto Superior de Ciências Sociais e Políticas 2001); *Paula Escarameia, O Direito Internacional Público nos princípios do século XXI* (Almedina 2003).

[2] Martti Koskenniemi, 'Imagining the Rule of Law: Rereading the Grotian "Tradition"' (2019) 30 EJIL 17–52 10.1093/ejil/chz017.

[3] Borrowing the expression from Georg Nolte's recollection of Paula Escarameia; *Yearbook of the International Law Commission* vol 1, A/CN.4/3081 *Summary Record of the 3081st Meeting*, 8.

[4] Paula Escarameia, 'Notes on the Implementation of the Rome Statute in Portugal' in Claus Kreß and Flavia Lattanzi (eds), *The Rome Statute and Domestic Legal Orders*, vol I: *General Aspects and Constitutional Issues* (Nomos 2000) 184–201; Paula Escarameia, 'Quando o Mundo das Soberanias se Transforma no Mundo das Pessoas: o Estatuto do Tribunal Penal Internacional e as Constituições Nacionais', in *Themis*, Revista da Faculdade de Direito da UNL, A.2, no 3, 2001, 143–82; Paula Escarameia, 'The Implementation of the ICC Statute: Problems of a Constitutional Order', in Stelios E Perrakis (ed), *International Criminal Court—A New Dimension in International Justice. Questions and Prospects for a New Humanitarian Order*

Ana Caldeira Fouto, António Pedro Barbas Homem, and Pedro Caridade de Freitas, *Paula Escarameia*
In: *Portraits of Women in International Law*. Edited by: Immi Tallgren, Oxford University Press.

DOI: 10.1093/oso/9780198868453.003.0021

Figure 21.1 Paula Escarameia.
Source: Instituto de Ciências Sociais e Políticas, Universidade de Lisboa.

saw it as a jurist's duty to act keeping in mind that 'the law was not some abstract game but a tool for justice and progress'.[5]

Escarameia presented her PhD thesis on *Formation of Concepts in International Law, subsumption under self-determination in the case of East Timor* at Harvard in 1988. She was one the main forces behind the creation of the 1991 International Platform of Jurists for East Timor which provided decisive legal support to the independence process on the international stage. An honorary member of the Portuguese Association of Women Jurists, she was also Vice President of the International Centre for Economic, Social and Cultural Rights, based in Lisbon, and Director of the Centre for International Institutions in Lisbon.

From 1995 to 1998 she served as legal counsel to the Permanent Mission of Portugal to the UN. She was particularly active in matters of international terrorism and law of the sea, as well as the international protection of victims of international crimes. In 2001, she was one of the two first women ever elected as a member of the International Law Commission (ILC) since its creation in 1947, along with Xue Hanquin in 2001.[6] In 2005, she was listed as member of the Permanent Court of Arbitration in The Hague.

(Ant N Sakkoupas 2002); Paula Escarameia, 'The ICC and the Security Council on Aggression: Overlapping Competencies?' in Mauro Politi and Giuseppe Nesi (eds), *The Rome Statute of the International Criminal Court*, vol II (Ashgate Publishing Co 2004).

[5] Alain Pellet on Paula Escarameia; *Yearbook of the International Law Commission*, vol 1, A/CN.4/3081 *Summary Record of the 3081st Meeting*, 7.

[6] Escarameia was Portugal's first representative in the ILC, re-elected in 2006.

Paula Escarameia's Observations on International Law in the Making

Paula Escarameia was a member of the Portuguese delegation to the UN negotiations for the creation of an ICC since 1995. She considered that the negotiations for the set-up of this Court represented the creation of a new model of international law. It was brought about by a change in the actors of the international order, which ranged from multinational companies and international organizations to international conflicts mediators, and international and regional courts. However, for Escarameia 'the profound change is not merely reflected in the appearance and role of new entities but, more substantively, in the basic structure on which International Law is based, such as the relative importance of its sources, with a recent increase in authority stemming from jurisprudence and the emergence of guiding principles, especially in areas such as the environment or human rights'.[7]

The arguments of her doctoral thesis were revisited and put to the test in 2003, in her book *O Direito Internacional Público nos Princípios do Século XXI* (*Public International Law in the Early 21st Century*). In this work, Escarameia set out from the events of 9/11 and the following wars in Afghanistan and Iraq to highlight two confronting aspects of international law as a legal order in transition: the remaining role of the sovereign state, heir to the Westphalian system, and the growing defence of human dignity and rights.

Escarameia's introductory note to the book, is revealing:

> The two cases [the attacks of September 11 and the Iraq war] thus reinforce the idea of a period of transition, where the characteristics of a Westphalian model, based almost exclusively on state sovereignty, anchored in the sacredness of borders and the internal domination of the sovereign, come face to face with those of a different model, in which considerations relating to human dignity take on a prominent role and which will be built on the actions, compromise, innovations and creations that we have today.[8]

The protection of human dignity, human rights, and the peoples' right of self-determination played a key role in Escarameia's international legal thought. These were the central subjects addressed in her last book, *The Status of International Public Law Today*,[9] in which she presented her vision on the UN and advocated for the need to revise the Charter. She offered an analysis of an international law that she believed to be in a phase of transition, considering the two great engines of such transition to be the concept of self-determination and the protection of human rights through criminal law.

[7] Paula Escarameia, *O Direito Internacional Público* (n 1) 231.

[8] ibid 9.

[9] Paula Escarameia, 'Que Direito Internacional Público Temos nos Nossos Dias?', in ibid, translated into 'The Status of International Public Law Today' in Katherine G Young (ed), *Globalization and the Future of Economic, Social and Cultural Rights* (Kentigern Publishing 2006).

Escarameia acknowledged the interpretation of the historical process of transition in the international order proposed by Richard Falk,[10] focusing on the decline of territorial sovereignty and the rise of new actors[11] as having introduced the almost consensual interpretation of the decline of the Westphalian order in contemporary international law. This perspective is in line with the broader influence, in her work, of the 'new approaches in international law', inspired by Critical Legal Studies: the re-assessment of international law grounded on methodological internal critique and structuralist technique, such as Koskenniemi's thesis of the 'rise and fall' of international law,[12] and David Kennedy's take on the conceptual possibilities of structure in international law.[13]

In her view, the first decade of the third millennium witnessed a gradual, sometimes silent change in the paradigm of international law. The changes were brought about, in her assessment, by the 'inadequacy of the existing structures (basic principles, existing institutions, concepts used, explanatory theories) but not by their total substitution by other realities',[14] as she considered this to be a gradual and often 'silent' substitution, disguised by the continued use of the previous conceptual model, even if inadequate and incoherent.

Escarameia argued that the beginning of the millennium with genocides, new forms of war, and terrorism violently disrupted the previous international order, and defied the structuring principles of contemporary international law and international organizations that support it. Even if such phenomena had always existed, their increase presented a different problem to the international order built in the second half of the twentieth century, revealing structural inefficiencies that required substantial changes in international law to accommodate effective solutions.

One challenging aspect of this change in international order that was close to Escarameia's heart was the right of peoples to self-determination. The support of the East Timorese people's claim was the most important example for her and a life-defining cause.[15] She witnessed the arrival of Timorese refugees in Lisbon in the aftermath of the Indonesian invasion in 1975—the constant fear in their eyes—that led her to devote her master's[16] and doctoral theses to the case of East Timor, even against the indifference of some professors she approached at Harvard.[17]

[10] Paula Escarameia, 'The Structure of Transitions in International Law' in Augusto de Athayde, João Caupers, Maria da Glória Dias, and FPD Garcia, *Em Homenagem ao Professor Doutor Diogo Freitas do Amaral*, Comis org (Almedina 2010) 619–41, at 621.

[11] Richard Falk, *Revitalizing International Law* (Iowa State University Press 1989); Richard Falk and Andrew Strauss, *Toward Global Parliament* (January/February 2001) 80(1) Foreign Affairs 212–20.

[12] Martti Koskenniemi, *The Gentle Civilizer of Nations: The Rise and Fall of International Law* (Cambridge University Press 2001); Martti Koskenniemi, *From Apology to Utopia: The Structure of International Legal Argument* (Cambridge University Press 1989, reissued 2006).

[13] David Kennedy, *International Legal Structures* (Nomos 1987); David Kennedy, 'When Renewal Repeats: Thinking Against the Box' (Winter 2000) 32(2) Journal of International Law and Politics, New York University 335–500.

[14] Paula Escarameia, *O Direito Internacional Público* (n 1) 13.

[15] Paula Escarameia, *Formation of Concepts* (n 1); Paula Escarameia, 'The Meaning of Self-Determination and the Case of East Timor' in Pedro Pinto Leite (ed), *International Law and the Question of East Timor*, (CIIR/IPJET 1995).

[16] Paula Escarameia, *The Limitations of International Law: The Case of East Timor* (Harvard 1986).

[17] Edda Kristjansdottir, 'Profile —Paula Escarameia' in (2004) 6(1) International Law FORUM du droit international 27–31, at 28.

Escarameia's work was not driven by a critical approach to the legal status of East Timor during the Portuguese colonial period, but focused on the legal imperative of achieving self-determination—even when the concept itself was considered part of the problem, and against a hostile, or at best indifferent, international political environment.

East Timor's example was useful to point out the limitations of international law in a time of structural change. Escarameia criticized the negative effects of the predominant conceptual connotation of self-determination with anti-colonialism. She believed ideological contamination associated to anti-colonial movements and to the East Timorese political events in 1975 had greatly contributed to harm East Timorese claims, creating political and legal limitations to effecting self-determination. Yet, the conceptual ambiguity of self-determination revealed a fundamental characteristic of the changing legal order—there was a new meaning to the word, brought by its context—in this case, legal solutions primarily prescribed for individuals or unidentified groups, along with the vagueness of the concept of 'people'.[18]

Escarameia pointed particularly at the risks of adopting an inadequate legal vocabulary—that maintains a traditional theoretical apparatus not in line with the recent evolution of international relations: 'The change of our legal language is a real necessity and not just a theoretical one. It was partly because of our legal vocabulary that genocide was committed in East Timor. The noblest task of Law is precisely that contribution to a society in which the best characteristic of human beings, the ability to dream, is not frustrated by a hostile reality.'[19]

Human Rights in a Shifting International Order

In the context of human rights, Escarameia highlighted the fight against poverty and the preservation of the environment.[20] In her view, their gradual recognition at the institutional level—as the 'Millennium Declaration' did—reflected the new model of international law in the making, supporting her theoretical proposals. She pointed out twelve characteristics of the international legal order that led her to identify a transitional moment between what she called the 'classical model' (based on territorial sovereignty) and a future model, that 'would be characterized by a greater institutional recognition of human rights and would reflect a more interconnected world'.[21]

These twelve characteristics, perceived by Escarameia in contemporary international law, are: (i) the demise of the traditional paradigm of state sovereignty with reserved internal dominion; (ii) the erosion of the notion of territory; (iii) the strength of new actors; (iv) a surge of institutional creativity; (v) an increased adoption of

[18] Referring to the inclusion of the right to self-determination in article 1 of both UN Covenants on Civic and Political Rights and on Economic, Social and Cultural Rights; Paula Escarameia, 'O Que É a Autodeterminação?—Análise Crítica do Conceito' in (1993) 1 Política Internacional 7–8.

[19] ibid.

[20] Paula Escarameia, 'Self-Administration and the Politics of Ethnic Accommodation in China—Commentary' in Wolfgang Danspeckgruber and Sir Arthur Watts (eds), *Self-Determination and Self-Administration: A Sourcebook* (Lynne Rienner Publishers 1997).

[21] Paula Escarameia, 'The Structure of Transitions' (n 10) 621.

universal jurisdiction at the domestic level; (vi) the change in importance of sources of international law; (vii) the activity of the Security Council; (viii) the reform of international institutions, especially the UN; (ix) the transformation of self-determination into preferential forms of autonomy with the guarantee of human rights; (x) the growing inability to find adequate vocabulary; (xi) the use of constructive ambiguity; (xii) and the fragmentation of explanatory theories.[22]

The connection between these elements is illustrated as follows. The erosion of the traditional state sovereignty paradigm is caused by the emergence of other subjects of international law—such as international organizations, multinational companies, individuals. Furthermore, 'the defence of the rights of human beings which makes territorial divisions and sovereign powers irrelevant, leading to recent phenomena such as armed interventions of a humanitarian nature, the establishment of international criminal courts and the growing acceptance of international jurisdiction for national courts'[23] show the erosion of the notions of territorial sovereignty and reserved internal dominion.

'Institutional creativity' and the 'increased adoption of universal jurisdiction at the domestic level' is reflected in the increased creation of international institutions, many of them ad hoc, which apply and enforce the law, such as international commissions and courts. The transition is also marked by the evolution and reform of the existing prominent international institutions—such as the revitalization of the Security Council after the end of the Cold War and the reform pressures in the UN. A further example of the shift is the emergence of new international legal mechanisms, such as large-scale investment agreements among private companies and states.

Resulting from this process of change, the uncertainty of the explanatory theories introduced by world doctrines (in the past referred to as 'schools' of internationalist thought, but more recently as 'methods' or 'styles') demonstrates the difficulty of translating a changing reality to the language of the old order: it underlines how diverse the understandings of the international phenomenon have become.[24]

The future of international law, according to Escarameia, is marked by the growing importance of 'non-traditional actors' such as individuals, the media, multinational companies, interest groups and movements, and the roles international law takes in regulating the relations among these various actors.[25] What difference can legal theory and doctrine make in understanding the reality of a world order in the making? For Escarameia,

> [t]heories will naturally follow as events unfold, with the intention of giving them coherence, organisation and explanation so that the future can fit into relatively predictable schemes. At present, there is a noticeable fragmentation of theories in the field of International Law, a consequence, in my opinion, of the fragmentation of an evolving reality whose basic traits are still difficult to capture. In fact, the tendency is to point out that different visions are nothing more than methods of capturing reality

[22] ibid fn 6.
[23] Paula Escarameia, *O Direito Internacional Público* (n 1) 18.
[24] ibid 39–43.
[25] ibid 52.

> and not elaborate constructions that aim at a global explanation of the international legal reality. It seems to me that, in a relativistic world, future theories are not so much concerned with knowing what the law is as with a pragmatic and functionalist view of knowing what it can serve for.[26]

Essential to Escarameia's vision of the transition is how the renewal takes place by weakening previous legal system. The ICC was one of her favourite examples of that process. She referred to a 'shift from marginality to centrality', to express how previously marginalized elements[27] gain gradually in importance to the point of contesting formerly central aspects. The international protection of human rights by means of a permanent Court created to judge individuals for grave crimes questions the traditional state sovereignty model over a specific territory and population.[28] In addition to the creation of the ICC as such, Escarameia mentions as an example of the shift from marginality to centrality the protection of women under the Statute of the ICC[29].

As a consequence of the weakening of the former model, an increase in the legislative and judicial production follows. Not only in quantitative terms, but qualitatively, with more space given to the margin for creative solutions, as the previous conceptual framework is fading. In this context, the implementation of law takes more influence and leads the transition.[30] While identifying precursors of the transition with regard to the model based on the territorial state sovereignty which no longer secured 'the final satisfactory answer to our problems',[31] Escarameia acknowledged it was not overcome yet.

Teaching International Law

Paula Escarameia was a teacher with a soul and with a very particular idea of public service. To be a professor is to be a scholar who studies, researches, reflects on subjects; an actor who captures and entertains an audience; a psychologist, who perceives the reactions of students; a judge, who has to evaluate and decide if someone passes or fails; a counsellor, who tries to 'shape the way others look at the world, whether this is done through the selection of subjects (…) method of exposing them (…) from the incitement that is provided for certain characteristics of the audience (…) up to the more personalized advice that is given in individual works under the guidance of the teacher or even in situations where the student asks for guidance from the teacher for his future life';[32] a missionary, who is happy to share knowledge, discuss points of view,

[26] ibid 52–53.

[27] Escarameia explains the meaning of 'marginal' as in the sense of 'being merely tolerated', sometimes 'disregarded because they did not fit the prevailing framework'; and when they were 'mentioned they were often presented as deviations, as "the exception that confirms the rule"'. Escarameia, 'The Structure of Transitions' (n 10) 623.

[28] ibid 624.

[29] ibid 624.

[30] ibid 625–26, 632–34.

[31] ibid 634.

[32] Paula Escarameia, *O Direito Internacional Público* (n 10) 330–31.

discover new solutions or other means of argumentation. As Escarameia expressly stated that 'this enthusiasm for the subject to be taught and for the act of conveying it to others requires a liking that one can only have for the vicissitudes of what one loves. It is this attitude that provides life and soul to a lesson and that manages to draw the attention of so many people with such different interests and circumstances of life in a single undertaking.'[33]

Escarameia saw university education through two lenses: the communication of knowledge and methods to students, and research, as a necessity for teaching and as a contribution to society.[34] As regards teaching international law, she valued the dynamics of the Socratic maieutic's dialogical method. Following this method, international law was taught through questions posed to the student, aiming at 'producing in the latter the realization that only knowledge that already belonged to the interlocutor is being revealed'.[35] With this method she intended to develop the reflexive, analytical, and critical spirit of her students. As the analysis of primary sources of international law, be it conventions, judicial decisions, preparatory work documents, etc, takes a central role in this form of teaching, she published two collections of primary sources in Portuguese.[36]

Conclusion

Despite Paula Escarameia's awareness of her position as a female jurist in male-dominated international law structures, feminist concerns or methods in international law were seldom evoked in Escarameia's work.[37] We did not find examples of the use of gender relations as a 'category of analysis' nor as a cause for the limitations of international law.[38] She acknowledged the methodological trend, but did not adopt the stance herself. Though she wrote about the international protection of women and the development of international legal instruments to effectively achieve it, she did so within the framework of international human rights.

Escarameia's legal thought drew from her experience and participation as an active advocate for human rights in key international processes such as the East Timorese independence process or the creation of the ICC. These contributed to her analysis of the methodological contexts in which concepts evolve in international law and shaped, more particularly, her understanding of the new legal possibilities of *self-determination* in the late twentieth-century world order.

Her perception of the transformation of the international order was not merely theoretical, even if it was optimistic. One could wonder how her optimism would fare in

[33] ibid 331.

[34] ibid 315.

[35] ibid 327.

[36] Paula Escarameia, *Colectânea de Jurisprudência de Direito Internacional* (Almedina 1992); Paula Escarameia, *Colectânea de Leis de Direito Internacional* (ISCSP 1994).

[37] Paula Escarameia's only text dedicated to the subject is 'Integração da Perspectiva de Género no Estatuto do Tribunal Penal Internacional' in *Direitos Humanos* (Coimbra Editora/Ius Gentium da Faculdade de Direito de Coimbra 2001).

[38] We are using the characterization of feminist methods by Hilary Charlesworth, 'Feminist Methods in International Law', in (April 1999) 9(2) AJIL 379–94.

light of the legal developments of the past decade. Reading Paula Escarameia today, we trust that her enthusiasm for a new international law would prevail. As Georg Nolte, her colleague in the ILC, recalled, 'she had been the Commission's conscience. With her capacity to be critically constructive and a civilized fighter for her ideals, she had seen the bad but had projected the good.'[39]

[39] Georg Nolte's recollection of Paula Escarameia; *Yearbook of the International Law Commission*, vol 1, A/CN.4/3081 *Summary Record of the 3081st Meeting*, 8.

PART VIII
THE OTHER GROUP PICTURES IN INTERNATIONAL LAW

22

Forgotten Female Actors in Private International Law

The International Social Service

*Roxana Banu**

Introduction

At the end of the First World War, the American Young Women Christian Association (YWCA) vouched to provide 'a special type of assistance for women and children who had come to [U.S.] shores from half around the world'.[1] By 1921 experimental services in France, Belgium, Czechoslovakia, Greece, Poland, Turkey, and the United States were sponsored by the YWCA. This network of female social workers and volunteers initially helped migrants with purchasing steamship tickets, translation services, or securing temporary lodgment throughout their transit.[2] Yet within a few years the services involved increasingly complex socio-legal questions relating to transnational marriages, divorces, custody disputes, property and inheritance claims, cross-border maintenance claims, and adoptions. By 1924, when the war funds of the YWCA were running low, a handful of women social workers dubbing themselves 'The Committee on the Universe' met in a small New York City apartment to map out a bold vision for an independent worldwide network of social service branches meant to offer socio-legal assistance to migrants and refugees, regardless of their gender, race, ethnicity, or religious denomination.[3]

Today the International Social Service (ISS) forms a vast network of international social workers present in over 120 countries and helping approximately 75,000 families in the world each year. Nearing its 100-year anniversary, the ISS can trace its involvement in a staggering range of transnational socio-legal projects including offering socio-legal assistance to displaced persons and unaccompanied minors following the Second World War, reuniting Greek families after the civil war, providing legal and social support to refugees fleeing dictatorship in Latin America, offering assistance

* The archival research was generously facilitated by the research funds of Western University Faculty of Law. Linnea Anderson has offered invaluable assistance at the archives of ISS–USA at the University of Minnesota, Social Welfare History Archives. For very helpful comments and discussions I am grateful to Veronica Ruiz Abou-Nigm, Nicole Stybnarova, Alexandra Kemmerer, and all the participants to the workshop on my chapter.

[1] Jus Sufragii, July 1922, i.

[2] Jus Sufragii, December 1924, Supplement of the Young Women's Christian Association, 4.

[3] International Social Service American Branch (ISSAB) Archives (hereafter, ISSAB), Box 5, World News, June 1957.

Roxana Banu, *Forgotten Female Actors in Private International Law* In: *Portraits of Women in International Law*. Edited by: Immi Tallgren, Oxford University Press. © Roxana Banu 2023. DOI: 10.1093/oso/9780198868453.003.0022

Figure 22.1 Photo of ISS staff members at the 1959 meeting in Geneva, Switzerland (22 countries are represented). Published in the ISS Newsletter, 1960.
Source: ISS Headquarters Archive, Geneva.

to Vietnamese refugees and Korean adoptees. The conventional historiographies of public and private international law (PrIL) fail to record both the ISS's unique perspective in the international law arena as a social work organization and the pioneering work of its female actors in many transnational socio-legal projects. This chapter starts to fill that void by uncovering the role of the ISS in the history of PrIL. It briefly catalogues the engagement of the ISS with questions of the nationality of married women and with cross-border family maintenance claims in the 1920s and 1930s as well as its engagement with cross-border adoptions from the 1940s onwards. It unpacks these examples from the ISS's much larger portfolio of PrIL projects against the complex set of aspirations as well as contradictions that defined the ISS's socio-legal work.

The Women of the ISS

When the ISS got off the ground three women in particular set the vision.

Mary Hurlbutt (1888–1980), American social worker and daughter of a prominent American doctor, was YWCA's first Migration Secretary. Based on extensive research of incoming migration from Czechoslovakia and Poland, her report 'The Welfare of Migrants' gained ISS widespread recognition in various international circles and marked the beginning of a long-standing collaboration between the ISS and the

International Labour Organization.[4] Hurlbutt served as ISS–USA's first director from 1924 to 1928 and returned to the organization in the 1950s after retiring from her position as professor of social work at the Columbia University School of Social Work. She wrote extensively on social work history, theory, and methods, and was involved in various projects to train both American and foreign social workers.

Ruth Larned (1890–1974), an American trained social worker, was the organization's first international director from 1924 to 1926, director of the United States branch until 1928, and then Associate General Director until 1954. Before joining the ISS, Larned worked in an institution for delinquent girls and in the settlement house movement as the director of the Madison House in New York. She organized the ISS's Greek branch in Constantinople to help Greeks, Armenians, and Russians after the First World War and the Smyrna disaster.[5]

Suzanne Ferrière (1886–1970) worked in the Civilians Section of the Central Prisoners of War Agency from 1914 to 1915 and later in the International Committee of the Red Cross (ICRC) Relief Section. She replaced her uncle Frederic Ferrière, a Swiss doctor and long-standing member of the ICRC. She was one of only three women on the ICRC during the Second World War.[6] Her advice was valuable in drafting the four Geneva Conventions as well as the Draft Tokyo Convention. She was a frequent contributor to the International Review of the Red Cross. In 1919 she played an important role in the founding of the International Union of Child Welfare with Eglantyne Jebb and became its Secretary-General. Ferrière was the ISS's Secretary-General until 1945 and thereafter its assistant director.[7]

A few years into its founding, the ISS had opened branches across Europe and collaborated with correspondents in virtually every corner of the world. Like the vast majority of social work organizations at the time, the American branch of the ISS was staffed primarily by women, generally white middle class, highly educated, and multilingual, aided by a wide network of volunteers. Most of the women of the ISS had social work degrees and some had pursued doctoral degrees in their fields. Based on a general ethos of liberal multiculturalism, the ISS was keen to recruit women who had extensive international experience and were ethnically diverse. For example, Eugenie Hochfeld was a supervisor in the ISS–USA branch. She had received her law degree in Prague, where her family relocated during the civil war in Russia. During the Second World War, she worked with the refugee programme of the American Friends Service Committee in the South of France. Upon immigration to the United States she obtained a graduate degree in social work from the Columbia University School of Social Work.[8]

Some of the women were joining the ISS after extensive postings abroad within a whole range of international organizations and social work offices, which meant that

[4] Ruth Larned, 'International Social Service, A History 1921–1955' ISSAB, Case 3, Folder 23 (hereafter, Larned, 'A History'); Jus Sufragii, July 1922, ii.

[5] Newscast from the American Christian Committee for Refugees, no 2, vol VI, May–June 1945, 3.

[6] See the contribution by Boyd van Dijk in this volume.

[7] For a brief biography of Suzanne Ferrière see 'Death of Miss S. Ferrière, Honorary Member of the ICRC' (1970) 109 IRRC 210.

[8] ISSAB, Box 14, Eugenie Hochfeld, 'Problems of International Adoption, Dependency and Custody' (October 1963) 14 Juvenile Court Judges Journal Fall Issue 3.

the ISS could tap into the lived experiences of their staff in war-torn cities throughout the world. For example, Susan Pettiss, Assistant Director of the ISS–USA branch from the mid-1950s to the mid-1960s, joined the United Nations Relief and Rehabilitation Administration (UNRRA) in 1945 and was sent to Germany where she helped concentration camp survivors find lost relatives. She was also responsible for the search, repatriation, or migration of unaccompanied displaced minors. After obtaining a degree in social work from the Columbia School of Social Work, she worked as a settlement officer with the International Refugee Organization. In Washington she helped locate sponsors for handicapped refugees from Latvia, Poland, and Lithuania; in Shanghai she assisted Russian and Jewish refugees after the Communist Revolution and later in Vietnam she supported Amerasian children.[9]

The ISS also relied on prominent women in the position of international president to serve as spokespersons and international representatives of the organization. Amongst the international presidents until 1960 were Viscountess Gladstone, wife of first Governor General of South Africa and daughter-in-law of UK prime minister William Edward Gladstone; Madame Revilliod-Masaryk, daughter of the first president of Czechoslovakia; Margaret Curtis, American golf and tennis champion, lifelong social worker, and for three years head of the Red Cross Bureau for Refugees after the First World War; Madame Edouard Long-Landry, member of a prominent French family of radical socialist intellectuals, whose sister was the head of the UN Commission on the Status of Women; and Marchesa Iris Origo, English-born biographer and writer living in Italy, who sheltered many refugee children and escapees in defiance of the fascist and Nazi regime.[10]

Private International Law and Migration Policy

Much of the socio-legal work of the ISS started with very detailed research studies showing that migration laws and uncoordinated national private laws facilitated, if not encouraged, family desertion and a denial of financial support obligations towards the family left behind.

Acknowledging this stark denial of justice, Suzanne Ferrière led the ISS through a concerted effort, over many decades, to push for an international socio-legal mechanism to ensure cross-border family maintenance. In an attempt to show the value of the ISS as 'a tool of reform for private international law', Ferrière encouraged the ISS to follow its cases to the 'bitter end' and to be 'very methodical and quite precise about what doesn't work and why' in securing family support across borders.[11] With this goal in mind, the ISS pursued a number of unprecedented avenues, until then untested by social work organizations. In stark contrast to many other American social work agencies, it encouraged its members to combine legal and social work methods.

[9] For an interview with Susan Pettiss on her life and career see 'Caseworker to History's Victims' (*The Times*, 23 May 1982) s1, 56. For her autobiography of her years at the UNRRA see Susan Pettiss and Lynne Taylor, *After the Shooting Stopped* (Trafford Publishing 2004).

[10] An Introduction to the International Social Service, ISSAB, Box 3, Folder 25, Annex 3.

[11] ISSAB, Box 15, Letter from Ferrière to all branches, 4 March 1928.

At the start of the cross-border maintenance project, an internal memorandum was circulated amongst all branches advising ISS members that 'legal work in our cases is undoubtedly pioneering work. We will face many challenges [...] It is, therefore, essential that all of us are convinced that this is an important and necessary part of our function'.[12] Unlike many social work organizations, which saw their role merely as providing social support before or after legal proceedings, the ISS took an active role in socio-legal experimentation. It helped bring petitions on behalf of foreign children for family support[13] and pressed United States courts to assume jurisdiction in cross-border maintenance cases by arguing that the 'crime' of non-support was localized in the United States.[14] The American branch also collaborated with the 'Friends of the Court' to inform women residing abroad when men in the United States attempted to obtain a divorce based on false allegations of the women's infidelity or desertion and thus sought to avoid family support obligations.[15] The ISS believed that ensuring adequate cross-border family maintenance should be the concern of a whole range of actors. Therefore, it conducted interviews with employers from various industries to understand whether the business sector could become an indirect avenue of enforcing cross-border maintenance claims and pressed consulates to offer legal assistance to women trying to test different legal avenues in the United States while residing abroad.[16]

The project was only a partial success from the ISS's point of view. Following the ISS's long-standing efforts, the topic of cross-border maintenance obligations finally made it on the agenda of the Child Welfare Commission of the League of Nations, the ECOSOC, and the Hague Conference.[17] However, the ISS had mixed views about the success of the international conventions being drafted. To the ISS the UN Convention on the Recovery of Maintenance Abroad showed a 'definite lack of social consideration'[18] and by framing the issue of cross-border maintenance as one of 'recognition of foreign judgments', the Child Welfare Committee was 'putting the cart before the horse'.[19]

Only a few years after the League of Nations took on the question of family maintenance, in 1930 the first Conference on the Codification of International Law held under the auspices of the League of Nations took on the question of the nationality of married women. Due to conflicting national rules, a woman marrying a foreigner could lose her nationality and, if she could not obtain the nationality of her husband,

[12] ISSAB, Box 15, 'The Legal Work of the IMS (write-up of the 1931 report to the staff conference)', 4.

[13] ibid Box 15, file 5.

[14] ibid Box 15, letter from Weiss (Geneva) to Warren (United States) on 21 December 1931 asking whether it was possible, for jurisdictional purposes to say that the 'crime' of not paying support was committed in the United States because United States laws were violated and seeing whether they could find a lawyer to bring a 'test case'. 'I do not think we should miss this opportunity.'

[15] David Wainhouse, 'Protecting the Absent Spouse in International Divorce: The Detroit Experiment' (1935) 2(3) Law and Contemporary Problems 360.

[16] ISSAB, Box 15, especially files 1, 2, 5.

[17] Statement sent by the ISS to ECOSOC E/AC.39/1/Add.1, ISSAB Box 14. ISS Report submitted to the Legal Sub-Committee of the Child Welfare Commission of the League of Nations, Document CPE 252, 1930.

[18] Memorandum by Dr Ursula Mende, 9 November 1962, ISSAB, Box 15.

[19] Reply from Suzanne Ferrière on 9 June 1931 in response to Letter sent from International Labour Office, Geneva, 8 June 1931, ISSAB, Box 15.

was rendered stateless. The League of Nations aimed to enact an international convention that sought to solve the problem by eliminating the conflict between different national laws. Although the debates on the nationality of married women in the Hague quickly exposed a big divide between liberal and social feminists, most believed that the League attempted to 'minimize' the issue of dependent nationality by framing it as a conflict of laws question.[20]

The ISS took a fundamentally different position. In a report sent by Suzanne Ferrière to the League of Nations, the ISS argued that the danger was not in framing the question of dependent nationality as a conflict of laws question, but rather in failing to appreciate the full range of problems faced by women because of conflicting private laws. The ISS offered an overview of twenty-one of its cases, showing the different ways in which women were impacted by an uncoordinated overlap of private laws and laws on nationality. Ferrière cautioned the League that conflicting national civil laws and PrIL norms form 'a very dense and little understood legislative network, often contradictory, always subject to complicated interpretations, which requires the intervention of highly qualified jurists, who sometimes have different opinions among themselves on the same question'.[21] ISS therefore argued that the convention should neither force women to acquire the nationality of their husbands, nor merely allow them to keep their own, but rather enable women to 'to keep, acquire or reacquire more easily the citizenship of the place where, because of her personal circumstances, she is obliged to reside, whether that is her place of birth or that of her husband'.[22]

The ISS's engagement with pressing questions of family support and gender equality gained the organization widespread recognition and respect in international circles in the interwar period. By the start of the Second World War, the ISS was therefore routinely called upon to help with a new crisis, that of temporarily relocating European children facing the horrors of the impending war. At the request of the German Jewish Children's Aid, Ruth Larned, Mary Hurlbutt, and Eleanor Blackman were responsible for the urgent transfer of young Jewish children fleeing the Nazi regime to the United States in 1939.[23] In 1945 and 1946, the ISS managed to locate five hundred Polish children and reunite them with their families in France and was responsible for the resettlement of 1,700 refugee unaccompanied minors. In the aftermath of the Hungarian Revolution of 1946, it assisted in the resettlement of unattached Hungarian youths with their American relatives.[24]

The ISS collaborated with the Office of Foreign Relief and Rehabilitation of the United States Department of State, the United Nations Relief and Rehabilitation Administration, the International Refugee Organization, UNHCR, the Intergovernmental Committee for European Migration, and the United States Escapee

[20] Linda Guerry, *La nationalité des femmes mariées sur la scène international* (1918–1935) (2016) 43 Clio. Femmes, Genre, Histoire 74, 80.

[21] Memorandum on the Nationality of Married Women. 'Examples illustrating the problem of the nationality of married women drawn from the experience of the International Migration Service and in particular the German, Czechoslovak and American branches", June 1932, sent to the League of Nations, Codification of International Law, League of Nations Archives, R2076, 3E/38182, 1.

[22] ibid 2.

[23] Judith Tydor Baumel, 'The Transfer and Resettlement in the United States of Young Jewish Refugees from Nazism, 1934–1945' (1988) 77(3) American Jewish History 413.

[24] Larned, 'A History' (n 4) 54.

Program, as well as many other national and international organizations, academics, philanthropists, and government and legal officials. Several of the ISS's personnel had previously served in these organizations.

In their work on the resettlement of unaccompanied minors, Susan Pettiss and many other ISS social workers were travelling an unchartered PrIL domain. They had to ascertain what should be done about the children whose nationality could not be established or who were stateless, who could serve as their guardian during cross-border migration, whether these children could be adopted, and whether the adoption would be recognized in Germany as well as the country of future residence of the child and adoptive parents.[25] During the Korean conflict of the early 1950s, the ISS was also heavily involved in adoption programmes involving Korean, often bi-racial children. By 1955, the ISS branches and cooperating agencies in fourteen countries had united to make the inter-country adoption programme possible.[26]

Refocusing Private International Law's Geopolitical Imaginations

Although the ISS's PrIL projects span over the entirety of the network, many of these projects were co-ordinated or spearheaded by the American branch especially between the 1930s and 1960s. Incidentally, over the same period, American PrIL scholars were developing an entirely new and still unique theory known as the 'state interest analysis'. According to this theory, states would apply their laws to regulate transnational inter-personal legal matters if they had an interest in protecting one of the parties as their constituents, leaving open whether 'constituents' were understood as citizens, domiciliaries, or mere residents.[27] It is unclear whether the ISS was engaged in those academic debates just as there is no clear evidence that the ISS's role in PrIL was fully acknowledged by American scholars at the time. Yet, the ISS's approach to PrIL questions, viewed against the background of the state interest analysis theory, intersects with but also departs from the interest analysis theory in many important ways.

Like American interest analysis theorists, the ISS pushed for a pragmatic perspective and believed that transnational legal matters should be analysed from a broader point of view than the legal technical one. However, while American scholars were anchoring PrIL in state regulatory policies, the ISS was arguing that transnational legal matters should be analysed 'from the point of view of social psychology, world outlook, political geography, and world economy, and, I might add, human economy and family welfare'.[28]

Furthermore, while American interest analysis theory focused on the pursuit of regulatory policies of individual states, the ISS showed that a focus on individual state interests was bound to create injustices for individuals and families as well as

[25] Lynne Taylor, *In the Children's Best Interests: Unaccompanied Children in American-Occupied Germany, 1945–1952* (Toronto University Press 2017) ch 4.

[26] Larned, 'A History' (n 4).

[27] Brainerd Currie, *Selected Essays on the Conflict of Laws* (Duke University Press 1963).

[28] Ruth Larned, 'International Aspects of Work with the Foreign Born. The Tangled Threads of Migrant Family Problems' 469 Official Proceedings of the Annual Meeting on Social Welfare, 1930 at 477.

an unequal division of responsibility among states. ISS believed that a strict focus on state interests meant condoning protectionist and exclusionary interests that were designed to protect United States citizens to the detriment of foreigners. For example, a combination of rules of civil procedure, PrIL and migration policies allowed foreign men living in the United States to escape any financial responsibility to families left behind especially if they had formed new family ties with United States citizens.[29] Furthermore, until as late as 1963, it was still federal military policy that for 'enlisted personnel in the lower grades, their wives are not authorized government transportation back to the United States'.[30] Combined with a lack of cross-border maintenance instruments, this blunt expression of American state interests ensured that American soldiers bore no responsibility for the women and children they had formed ties with during overseas deployment.

Focusing on state interests therefore left entirely unexposed the interests of individuals and families. For example, in an interview conducted by the ISS, the German Consul in the United States admitted that 'the American public will never be willing to bear the burden of the cost of men who are imprisoned because of non-support of families abroad' and 'Germany might prefer non-support of [German] wives and children rather than deportation of able-bodied men, who could earn a living over here'.[31]

At the time PrIL scholars often displayed a naïve and nationalistic conceptualization of state interests in their PrIL theory. By contrast, the ISS's view was strikingly, insisting that focusing on state interests ultimately fostered an unequal global distribution of wealth and of state responsibility for the fate of individuals and families in the transnational realm. The ISS's firm belief was that 'without recognition that there is an international obligation, the entire financial burden falls on the countries that happen to be the theater of war or of troop concentration, as well as areas of foreign occupation'.[32] In a heartfelt speech before the National Conference on Social Welfare the director of the American Branch argued in 1931 that in fact PrIL should not tap into states' interests to 'immediately disclaim all responsibility for the social care of those forced to travel from one to the other' but instead to create a mechanism for the 'protection of their fundamental human rights wherever they may go'.[33]

Layered Context

Because of its deep engagement with cross-border family issues on the ground, the ISS was acutely aware of the geopolitical context of PrIL matters. In 1954, for example Mrs Burns, the ISS President at the time, offered the following overview of the geopolitical context of inter-country adoptions and the lack of cross-border maintenance mechanisms when speaking at the Saturday Morning Club:

[29] ISSAB, Box 15, Letter sent from International Labour Office, Geneva, 8 June 1931 reproducing a passage by Edith Abbott.

[30] ISSAB, Box 15, Folder Maintenance Obligations 1960, 1961, 1961, file 2.

[31] Interview with Mr von Lewinski, German Consul in the US, 11 July 1929, ISSAB, Box 15.

[32] Larned, 'A History' (n 4) 55.

[33] George Warren, 'International Aspects of Immigration' (1931) Official Proceedings of the Annual Meeting of the National Conference of Social Welfare 451, 461.

> Most of the children available for adoption are the children of men in our armed forces. In Great Britain, after the comparatively short sojourn of comparatively few Americans, the estimates of illegitimate children vary, but are in the thousands. In Germany the official estimate in 1952 was 94000 over half of them in the US zone. Perhaps if we ever again found ourselves in the role of an occupying army, we would be wiser in our efforts at control. Perhaps we would not begin with unenforceable rules against fraternization, followed by laws against marriage with women of the country. Perhaps when we found we had not prevented various sorts of alliances, and finally recognized brides and fiancées, we would have set up less red tape about their admission to the law of their husbands. Perhaps another time we would succeed in breaking earlier the deadlock between the military authorities and the local courts which control adoptions, so that such might have been possible, at least by a father of his own child. By the time some of these difficulties had been ironed out in the occupations of Germany and Japan, the marriages had been under long strain, children had grown too old to transplant easily; the father's interest had reached the vanishing point.[34]

Yet, the complex context in which the ISS was operating in the first half of the twentieth century did not make it easy for the ISS to always be upfront about its geopolitical diagnosis of most PrIL issues it was working on.

On the one hand, the ISS was operating in the typical gendered and class context of social work at the time. Although many of the women of the ISS had remarkable educational and professional backgrounds, the type of service that the ISS was developing at the intersection of PrIL and social work made a whole range of other skills seem valuable. From the 1930s, the ISS recruited men in the highest echelons of the organization, often for their prized expertise in law and foreign relations and their connections in academia and government. They were more heavily involved in lobbying, fostering relationships with government officials, and engaging in debates on foreign relations and geopolitical issues. Most of these men had a much higher professional mobility than their female colleagues. For example, David Wainhouse, member of the Maine and NY Bars and author of several foreign relations book, was director of the ISS for only two years before becoming Assistant United States Attorney in 1934. Similarly, after more than a decade as a director of the ISS, George L Warren was Adviser on Refugees and Displaced Persons in the Department of State (1944–1968) and the United States Representative to the Intergovernmental Committee for European Migration (1953–1966). This gendered staffing pattern was likely a pragmatic adaptation to the male-dominated fields of law, foreign relations, and humanitarian policy, in which ISS was operating. For example, while the cross-border maintenance project was Ferrière's brainchild, George Warren and Hans Weiss were the ones who lobbied Ernst Rabel and other 'university men' for their support.[35] Similarly, although Susan Pettiss spoke before the men of the American Bar Association about ISS's cross-border

[34] ISSAB, Box 3.
[35] Letter From Weiss to Warren, 1 July 1931, ISSAB Archive, Box 15.

adoption projects, she urged William Kirk to 'help strengthen the relationship' with the ABA to enable ISS to 'lobby for real legislative reform in the US'.[36]

On the other hand, the ISS, like the vast majority of social work organizations, was operating in the context of the intense professionalization of social work in the first half of the twentieth century. This professionalization was a symbol of how female social workers 'organized and defined themselves'.[37] In 1926, Ruth Larned, for example, stressed that ISS staff and social workers generally should aim for 'more scientific interest, more precision and more knowledge' to ensure that 'scientists and legislators would finally see the significance of our work'.[38] For the ISS, professionalization was meant to provide not only credibility for a female-dominated field of work. It was a necessary benchmark to pursue reform while routinely lobbying high profile national and international organizations, academics, and diplomats. Being overtly political could make the entire mission of the ISS unworkable. When making submissions before the United States Congress, the ISS was keen to plead for increased quotas for family members and adoptees while clarifying that it had no political agenda of open borders.[39] When lobbying Ernst Rabel for his support on cross-border maintenance, the ISS clarified that it had no global liberal project of increased harmonization of private international law, but simply wanted to 'study' the issue.[40] Similarly in a memo sent to Susan Perkins, Secretary of Labour in 1933, following a meeting at the Women's University Club between Perkins and various social workers, Hurblutt attempted to forge a relationship with the Labour Department by clarifying that the ISS 'criticizes no government and engages in no propaganda for changes in laws or procedures. Its sole objective is to establish the facts of human experience and to present these facts in temperate scientific manner whenever called upon to do so.'[41]

Whether purely strategic or not, this focus on professionalization and political neutrality viewed against the background of ISS's work on progressive causes to better the lives of foreigners and minorities caused a range of tensions. For example, when working on massive projects of cross-border adoption of illegitimate and/or orphaned, often bi-racial, children fathered by American soldiers posted in Korea, Japan, Greece, or Germany, the ISS insisted on best adoption practices to maximize the integration of bi-racial children. It refused to openly discuss or compare racial relationships and prejudices in different countries, although it openly criticized the geo-political context, which explained the humanitarian crisis of the illegitimate children of American soldiers. Its insistence on following 'scientific' guidelines for the placement of bi-racial children, whom the ISS perceived as a special category of children facing discrimination both in the receiving and sending country, was perceived both as resistant to

[36] Letter from Susan Pettiss to William Kirk, 22 March 1961, ISSAB, Box 19, Folder ISS Relationship with the ABA.

[37] Daniel Walkowitz, *Working with Class: Social Workers and the Politics of Middle-Class Identity* (University of North Carolina Press 1999) xii.

[38] Cited in Joseph Krakes, Social Consequences of Migration (1928) at 74 (ISSAB).

[39] ISSAB, Box 15, Memorandum by Joseph Chamberlain, Hearing Before the United States Senate, Immigration Committee, 18 March 1926.

[40] ISSAB, Box 15, Letter from Hans Weiss to George Warren on the Interview with Ernst Rabel, 1931.

[41] ISSAB, Box 3, File 26.

social change and relying on racial stereotypes,[42] and as a pragmatic and thoughtful engagement with questions of race and migration.[43]

Furthermore, in trying to identify the causes of socio-legal problems for migrants, the ISS sometimes relied on broad ethnical stereotypes while constantly underscoring the background context of systemic socio-economic and legal injustices. For example, in one of her books, Mary Hurlbutt decried ethnical prejudice, yet she encouraged social workers to correlate individual and group attitudes to broader cultural patterns of each nationality. She insisted that cases should be handled by social workers who shared the ethnicity of the client, but she cautioned against relying on social workers who resented their own cultural and ethnical background, such that the optimal social workers were described as those who achieved 'a serene acceptance of their own cultural background'.[44] She warned of the danger of American life tending to undermine the foreigner's 'resourcefulness' while being clear about the fact that 'economic security—in fact a margin above mere subsistence—is a factor directly affecting assimilation'.[45]

Almost a century after its establishment, exploring the role of the ISS's female social workers in the theory and practice of PrIL achieves more than a long overdue portrait. It reveals a surprising joined history of international social work and PrIL. It presses both public and private international law scholars to examine the role of women who were lobbying the League of Nations and other organizations for transnational social issues. Most timely, it helps recover a way of thinking about PrIL questions alongside issues of migration and the status of foreigners.

[42] Heide Fehrenbach, *Race After Hitler: Black Occupation Children in Postwar Germany and America* (Princeton University Press 2005) ch 5.

[43] Catherine Cheniza Choy, *Global Families: A History of Asian International Adoption in America* (New York University Press 2013).

[44] Ruth Larned, *New Americans in Allegheny County—A Cultural Study* (New York School of Social Work 1937) 73. This resulted in what Franca Iacovetta and Erica Toffoli called a 'double-edged pluralism'. See Franca Iacovetta and Erica Toffoli, 'A Double-Edged Pluralism: Paradoxes of Diversity in the International Institute Movement, 1945–1965' (2020) 53 Journal of Social History 1.

[45] Larned, *New Americans* (n 44) 75.

23

Female Staff in the Legal Section of the League of Nations

Benjamin Auberer

Introduction

This photograph taken from the photo collection of the Geneva based archive of the League of Nations points out a major discrepancy between the historiography on the Legal Section of the League of Nations and its visual representation: according to Article 7 of the Covenant of the League, all positions within the League were open equally for men and women, making the League theoretically one of the world's first equal opportunity employers.[1] The photograph is a visual symbolic representation of how the League aimed to make women a key part in its administrative work on international law.[2] However, historical research on the Legal Section rarely mentions women.

It is the contention of this portrait that making these women visible advances a fair evaluation of the Legal Section and the role of the League of Nations in the democratization of international relations and international law. The advancement of international law is in this context understood in a very broad sense: the female employees of the Legal Section are considered as part of a structural change in international relations influencing the practices of international law beyond the dissolution of the League in 1946. Thus, this portrait contributes to an actor-centred and globalized history of the League of Nations, considering its employees not only as vehicles but as pacemakers of change. In this regard, the League and its Secretariat are not read as a utopian community of progressive libertarian diplomats, on the contrary, the League was in many ways a continuation of nineteenth-century imperialism. However, as the only permanent institution of the League, the Secretariat served as a social hub for internationalism, evolving into an assemblage of multinational cosmopolitan lifestyles which subsequently exercised an everlasting influence on the post-war international system.

Methodologically this paper combines macro and micro perspectives. First using data from the database project 'League of Nations Search Engine' (LONSEA), which provides professional biographical information for every employee of the League of

[1] The Covenant of the League of Nations, Article 7 <https://avalon.law.yale.edu/20th_century/leagcov.asp> accessed 1 May 2021.

[2] Madeleine Herren, 'Gender and International Relations through the Lens of the League of Nations (1919–1945)' in Glenda Sluga and Carolyn James (eds), *Women, Diplomacy and International Politics since 1500* (Routledge 2012) 182, hereafter Herren, *Gender and International*.

Benjamin Auberer, *Female Staff in the Legal Section of the League of Nations* In: *Portraits of Women in International Law*. Edited by: Immi Tallgren, Oxford University Press. © Benjamin Auberer 2023. DOI: 10.1093/oso/9780198868453.003.0023

Figure 23.1 The Legal Section of the League of Nations Secretariat in 1924–1925.
Source: United Nations Archives at Geneva.

Nations, a prosopographical bird's eye view on the personnel of the Legal Section is provided. The database LONSEA contains the digitalized personnel sheets of the League of Nations and thus allows a reconstruction of the professional trajectories of its personnel.[3]. Thus, in line with current debates on the application of micro-historical approaches to international history,[4] a closer look on individual achievements within the international administration can contribute to an actual understanding on the significance of the League and the role that women played in its functioning.

Placing the Legal Section in the League's Cosmos

The establishment of the League of Nations in the aftermath of the First World War was a key moment in international history.[5] As the first international governmental organization with a truly global scope, the founding of the League was a major step in the development of long-lasting structures of global governance until today.[6] The fundamental claim of the League was to advance the international system beyond the

[3] See Christiane Sibille, 'LONSEA—Der Völkerbund in neuer Sicht. Eine Netzwerkanalyse zur Geschichte internationaler Organisationen' (2011) 8(3) Zeithistorische Forschungen/Studies in Contemporary History 475.

[4] Francesca Trivellato, 'Is There a Future for Italian Microhistory in the Age of Global History?' (2011) 2(1) California Italian Studies, available at<http://escholarship.org/uc/item/0z94n9hq> accessed 1 May 2021, hereafter Trivellato, *Future for Italian Microhistory.*

[5] Madeleine Herren, Martin Rüesch, and Christiane Sibille, *Transcultural History: Theories, Methods, Sources* (Springer 2012) 1.

[6] Madeleine Herren, *Internationale Organisationen seit 1865: Eine Globalgeschichte der internationalen Ordnung* (WBG 2009) 55.

nineteenth century great power diplomacy to a public and open diplomacy in order to prevent future world wars. Even though the League system was, underneath its idealistic claims, in many ways a (sometimes barely veiled) continuation of imperialist structures and finally failed in its ambition to prevent the outbreak of the Second World War. Susan Pedersen has shown how the League system nevertheless fundamentally changed not necessarily the content but form, language, and mode of global governance, enabling new actors and groups to articulate their voices on a global diplomatic stage.[7] The Legal Section, with its main task to register and publish every international treaty, became one of the fundamental expressions of the League's claim to put an end to clandestine diplomacy. Article 18 of the Covenant of the League of Nations stated

> Every treaty or international engagement entered into hereafter by any Member of the League shall be forthwith registered with the Secretariat and shall as soon as possible be published by it. No such treaty or international engagement shall be binding until so registered.[8]

To fulfil this task, the Legal Section was created with the objective and resources to collect, register, and publish all international treaties, making its famous Treaty Series a centrepiece not only in the development of public diplomacy but also in the development and codification of international law. Before 1943 more than 202 volumes of international treaties were published. A second function of the Legal Section was the more general task of supplying the different organs of the League of Nations with legal aid and advice.[9]

Despite being one of the core Sections of the League of Nations and, from the beginning, one of the largest single services, the actual workings of this Section have been relatively unmoored by historical research until today. This trend already began immediately after the dissolution of the League: former League employee Francis Paul Walters, who published a two-volumes comprehensive history of the League of Nations, only mentioned the Legal Section on three occasions without elaborating on its actual significance.[10]

In recent years historiography has shown more interest in the legal work of the League of Nations. In 2006, Susan Pedersen emphasized the necessity to go 'back to the League of Nations'[11] and to investigate its history beyond simplistic narratives of decline and failure.[12] In order to fully evaluate the actual significance of the League of Nations for a global history of international organizations, she highlights the necessity to contextualize the League and to investigate the ramifications and actual

[7] Susan Pedersen, 'The Meaning of the Mandates System: An Argument' (2006) 32(4) Geschichte und Gesellschaft 560.

[8] The Covenant of the League of Nations, Article 18 <https://avalon.law.yale.edu/20th_century/leagcov.asp> accessed 1 May 2021.

[9] Egon F Ranshofen-Wertheimer, *The International Secretariat: A Great Experiment in International Administration* (Carnegie Endowment for International Peace 1945), hereafter Ranshofen-Wertheimer, *International Secretariat*.

[10] Francis P Walters, *A History of the League of Nations* (OUP 1960).

[11] Susan Pedersen, Back to the League of Nations (2007) 112(4) The American Historical Review 1091.

[12] ibid.

contributions to the genesis of the modern world: on different fields from intellectual cooperation and disarmament to global healthcare and the channelling of worldwide finances. This trend in international history falls together with a shift of interest in the history of law: away from exegetic intellectual approaches towards praxeological approaches to the history of international law. Important works by Stephen Wertheim and Megan Donaldson investigate the mechanisms of international law that originated in the League of Nations.[13] Other works study the metamorphosis of international law: since 2019 the research project 'Laying the Foundations—The League of Nations and International Law 1919 to 1945' at the university of Copenhagen aims to systematically uncover the practices of international law that were shaped by and fostered through international networks.[14]

Together with this shift, interest into the Geneva Secretariat of the League moved closer in the historical interest of researchers: it was in the bureaucratic institutions with its multinational employees of the League where the actual practices of internationalization were shaped. The international civil servants of the League are considered major actors in the construction of the international order.[15] However, until now, research has focused mainly on the higher-ranking positions: secretary-generals, directors, and members of Sections.[16] These studies provide us with insights into the inner workings of the Secretariats but tend to focus on the male perspective of international administration. A few works point out how the League of Nations, as one of the world's first equal opportunity employers,[17] opened up new career possibilities for women in the field of internationalism and diplomacy.[18]

A Prosopographical Perspective on the Legal Section

Existing research on the League's Secretariat and biographical data from the League of Nations Search engine (LONSEA) makes it possible to work out similarities in the lives of the female staff and thus to take a prosopographical look at their careers and analyse some of their common characteristics such as education, age, or length of employment.[19]

[13] Stephen Wertheim, 'The League of Nations: A Retreat from International Law?' (2012) 7(2) Journal of Global History 210; Megan Donaldson, 'The Survival of the Secret Treaty: Publicity, Secrecy, and Legality in the International Order' (2017) 1111(3) AJIL 575

[14] Laying the Foundations—The League of Nations and International Law, 1919 to 1945 <https://internationallaw.ku.dk/about/>accessed 1 May 2021.

[15] Karen Gram-Skjoldager and Haakon A Ikonomou, 'Making Sense of the League of Nations Secretariat—Historiographical and Conceptual Reflections on Early International Public Administration' (2019) 49(3) European History Quarterly 420.

[16] Torsten Kahlert, 'Pioneers in International Administration: A Prosopography of the Directors of the League of Nations Secretariat' (2019) 13(2) New Global Studies 190.

[17] One of the first is Carol Miller, *Lobbying the League: Women's International Organizations and the League of Nations* (DPhil Thesis, University of Oxford 1992) 77, hereafter Miller, *Lobbying the League*.

[18] Myriam Piguet, 'Gender Distribution in the League of Nations: The Start of a Revolution?' in Karen Gram-Skjoldager and Haakon Ikonomou (eds), *The League of Nations: Perspective from the Present* (Aarhus University Press 2019) 60.

[19] In this regard, this article contributes to a recent wave of prosopographical research on the League of Nations personnel, cf Torsten Kahlert, 'Prosopography—Unlocking the Social World of International Organizations' in Karen Gram-Skjoldager, Haakon Ikonomou, and Torsten Kahlert (eds), *Organizing the*

The multinational staff of the international Secretariat of the League was generally organized into three groups according to their specific responsibilities: the so called First, Second, and Third Divisions. The personnel of the Legal Section came from the First and Second Division. The First Division was assigned the staff that was referred to in the narrower sense as international officials. As Members of this Section they were responsible for the content-related work in the Sections, be it in the political or technical field. The First Section was throughout the history of the League heavily male dominated. The available data shows that the number of women in the First Division Secretariat increased at the beginning of the 1920s, stagnated over the course of the 1930s, and then fell.[20] This development reflects how many women were frustrated by the career prospects within the Secretariat and subsequently left Geneva.

Although there were a number of female figures in the First Division, such as Mary McGeachy or Rachel Crowdy, the career prospects of women in the First Division were limited. Most of the open positions in the First Division were given to men. Crowdy, a trained nurse active in the Voluntary Aid Detachments remained the only female Chief of Section. After she left the Secretariat, she was succeeded by male colleague Erik Ekstrand who was raised to the higher-ranking position of a Director.[21] When women's organizations criticized the lack of representation of female Secretariat members, the Secretariat stoically replied that the obligation to have a multinational composition would already lead to such severe restrictions on the filling of vacancies that adequate representation of women could no longer be taken into account and pointed out that the Second Division was dominated by women.[22] The Second Division was responsible for secretarial and routine administrative duties and was heavily dependent on temporarily employed and therefore fluctuating workers during the Assemblies and Council meetings. It is hard to quantify the actual extent of the Second Division. In general, it can be said that this Division comprised the largest part of the League of Nations' personnel: according to LONSEA data up to 57 per cent of all employees belonged to the Second Division most of whom were women. So far there have been no systematic studies focussing on the Second Division, which is why the social backgrounds of the employees from this Division have not yet been adequately examined. As far as nationalities were concerned, the commitment to a multinational composition was only valid to a certain extent for the Second Division, as those positions were not considered as representative or diplomatic, unlike their colleagues in the First Division.

The Legal Section consisted during most of the time of its existence of a Director and about five Members of Section, all of whom were members of the First Division. They were supported by a fluctuating number of clerical staff from the Second Division.

World: International Organization and the Emergence of International Public Administration 1920–1960 (Bloomsbury Publishing 2020) 49, (hereafter Kahlert, *Prosopography*). For an detailed analysis of the First and Second Division cf Benjamin Auberer, From the International Bush to the International Jungle. Internationale Karrieren und der Völkerbund (Heidelberg University Publishing 2023 (forthcoming)) (hereafter Auberer, International Jungle).

[20] This was the result of an analysis of the workforce by LONSEA and Ranshofen-Wertheimer. cf Ranshofen-Wertheimer, *International Secretariat* (n 9) 369.

[21] Available at <http://www.lonsea.de/pub/person/5463> accessed 1 May 2021.

[22] Henry R Cummings to Helen A Archdale, 11 October 1922, LONSEA 29/23987/18166.

Since 1932, the Director of the Legal Section had the rank of Under-Secretary General. Filling positions (especially of higher positions) in the International Secretariat was usually the result of complex negotiation processes between different member states.[23] The protocols in the League's archive show how important the distribution of the key positions in the Secretariat between the member states was considered.[24] Two of the three heads of Section of the Legal Section were Latin-American, and one was Dutch. Ranshofen-Wertheimer highlights that 'a number of jurists of world-wide repute' served at the Legal Section of the League such as: American lawyer Manley Hudson, Belgian law Professor Georges Kaeckenbeeck, and Swedish-born Registrar of the Permanent Court of International Law Åke Hammarskjöld. Neither Ranshofen-Wertheimer nor Walters mention any women in the staff of the Legal Section. However, LONSEA assigns fifty-two persons to the Legal Section of the Secretariat of the League of Nations. Out of these fifty-two, about twenty could be identified as female and all of them can be assigned to the League's Second Division.

Women employed by the Legal Section worked either as a shorthand typists, clerk secretaries, proofreaders, or assistants to one of the male members of the Sections or the Directors. While many other Sections of the League had at least one or two women from the First Division, the Legal Section only employed Second Division women. The field of international law remained strongly male dominated and it was easier for women to progress into areas of work which were considered 'female' such as social services or childcare.[25] When in such positions, however, the official job description did not always represent the tasks the personnel would actually fulfil from day to day: as many women—especially in the Legal Section—were educated, it seems possible, if not probable, that they took on responsibilities beyond their actual pay level. Regularly prepared evaluations of the employees indicate this, as many women of the Legal Section were praised for their capacities and willingness to facilitate the work of the Section.[26]

In addition, one should keep in mind that these positions had a specific meaning in the context of women's history in the 1920s and 1930s.[27] The job description of secretaries and shorthand typists only emerged in the late 1880s and opened up new perspectives for educated women with middle- and lower-middle-class backgrounds. The typist also became the embodiment of an alternative lifestyle that enabled women not only to have a (limited) professional career, but also a life outside of traditional ideas of marriage, family, and gender roles.[28]

Looking at the nationality of the women in the Legal Section, British (six) and French (five) clearly dominated, followed by women with Dutch origins (three). Furthermore, there were one Swiss, one Russian, one Spanish, one Belgium, and two

[23] Klaas Dykmann, 'How International Was the Secretariat of the League of Nations' (2015) 37(4) The International History Review 721, 743.

[24] ibid.

[25] Kahlert, *Prosopography* (n 19) 61.

[26] Madeleine Herren emphasizes the involvement of women in specialized areas of work played for their overall representation. Herren, *Gender and International* (n 2) 183.

[27] Teresa Davy, 'A Cissy Job for Men, A Nice Job for Girls. Women Shorthand Typists in London, 1900–39' in Leonore Davidoff and Belinda Westover (eds), *Our Work, Our Lives, Our Words: Women's History and Women's Work* (Rowman & Littlefield 1986) 124.

[28] Christopher, Keep, 'The Cultural Work of the Type-Writer Girl' (1997) 40(3) Victorian Studies 401, 404.

Austrians of the Secretariat. The fact that the majority of women were either British or French can easily be explained by looking at the official languages of the League of Nations, English and French. Fluency in at least one of these two languages was required for every employee.[29] And it is probably not by chance that three Dutch women were recruited in a Section headed by Dutch Director van Hameln.

Most of the women were in their mid- or late-twenties when they were first hired by the League.[30] This is common for the personnel of the League of Nations: the newly founded organization attracted young personnel. This contributed—as the photograph above underlines—to the self-staging of the League of Nations as young and modernist.

They all contributed to an important feature of Geneva's internationalism, as American journalist Clive Holland pointed out as early as 1927: Geneva's internationality hardly came from the city itself, its history, or international organizations, but from 'an army of shorthand typists and clerks, as well as high officials, 'who played a leading role in creating' a new atmosphere and [...] a more serious air'.[31] The international organizations—and other actors in the same context—had a steadily growing need for staff that could not be met by the Geneva city population. The specific work environment created a job market for people who had the skills and knowledge to work in an international environment. This included, above all, foreign language skills, but also an understanding of the complex world of international organizations and international politics.[32]

Ludovica Marchet—A Micro Perspective

In this last part, one single biography will be examined in depth to investigate the ramifications of working as a woman in the Legal Section: that of former calligrapher and shorthand typist Ludovica Marchet. Marchet was selected out of the female staff of the Legal Section because she worked for a comparatively long time for the Legal Section and because the source material on her life is comprehensive, allowing us to follow her actions and her career thoroughly. Her case is not meant as a general example of women in the Legal Section but it is this chapter's contention that in the 'uniqueness' of her life lies (in the micro-historical sense) an element of 'normality' incorporating elements of the international system and allowing thus to draw conclusions about the significance of the League.[33]

The personnel file of Ludovica Marchet tells that she was born in June 1901 as the daughter of Gustav Marchet, former Minister of Public Education of Austria.[34] In 1917 she obtained her A levels in Vienna and subsequently passed the University Examinations for French instructors and the entry Examination for French Interpreters, both with honours. She taught French in Sweden and worked as an interpreter for the Interparliamentary Union.[35] According to her application, Marchet rated

29 Miller, *Lobbying the League* (n 17) 84.

30 cf LONSEA.

31 Clive Holland, 'Cameos of European Cities: Seat of the League of Nations': *The Christian Science Monitor* (7 August 1927) 7.

32 Miller, *Lobbying the League* (n 17) 88–89.

33 cf Trivellato, *Future for Italian Microhistory* (n 4).

34 Particulars of Miss Marchet, LoN S826/131/2309.

35 Ludovica Marchet to Eric Drummond, 22 May 1924, LoN S826/131/2309.

her proficiency in French, English, and Swedish as 'perfect', was able to take shorthand in German and French, and could typewrite in all the four languages she spoke; in addition acquired a proficiency in Esperanto.[36] Marchet's 1922 shorthand-typist application, was forwarded to the Secretary-General of the League by Austrian diplomat Egon Pfügl, a friend of her late father,[37] an informal mode of recruitment typical for the early secretariat.[38] Pfügl had heard that the secretary of the Administrative Commission Section was leaving and hoped that the post would be eligible for Marchet. But Eric Colban, as Chairman of the Appointments Sub-Committee, decided that twenty-one-year-old Marchet was too young for a post 'where greater experience [was] required'.[39]

The League at that time required typists to speak either French or English as a mother tongue. Despite this setback, Marchet stayed keen to start work at the League. In January 1923, she managed to enter on a temporary basis in the calligraphical service of the Legal Section, for six months.[40] Working samples of calligraphical work within her personnel files show that her main task was to provide readable and representative accounts of important documents[41]—definitely a more manual than political job.[42] Marchet found the calligraphical work monotonous and in her evaluations, her subordinates mentioned that she tended to neglect the calligraphical work for her other tasks.[43]

This position was changed into a Junior Assistant contract and prolonged twice, each for another six months at a time, before being converted into a permanent appointment.[44] As Junior Assistant, Marchet's main duties were to support the work in the Treaty Registry in English and French translations of Scandinavian Treaties and to correct mistakes before the Treaties were published.[45] The willingness of the highly qualified and polyglot Marchet to accept a temporary position as a calligrapher in the Legal Section demonstrates the appeal that the League had as an employer, particularly for women. As Junior Assistant, she earned about 7.800 Swiss Francs a year which was about a quarter of what an employee in the First Division made,[46] but which was still more than women would earn in comparable positions in their home countries.[47] A glimpse of the popular culture of the 1920s and 1930s shows numerous poems,

[36] ibid.

[37] Egon Pflügl to Eric Drummond, 10 June 1922, LoN S826/131/2309.

[38] Haakon Ikonomou, 'He used to give me Turkish lessons in Constantinople:' How to get a job in the League Secretariat' <http://projects.au.dk/inventingbureaucracy/blog/show/artikel/he-used-to-give-me-turkish-lessons-in-constantinople-how-to-get-a-job-in-the-league-secretariat> accessed 1 May 2021.

[39] Sub-Appointments Committee, 17 January 1923, LoN S826/131/2309.

[40] ibid. Howard Huston to Joost van Hamel, 26 January 1923, LoN S826/131/2309; Herbert Ames 9.

[41] Le Nouvel an à Rome, 4 January 1923, LoN S826/131/2309.

[42] According to LONSEA there were only two calligraphers within the service of the League. The other one, the Swiss artist and author Willy Aeschlimann had the position between 1922 and 1940. cf <http://www.lonsea.de/pub/person/8531> accessed 1 May 2021.

[43] Certificate as to grant of annual increment, 8 March 1927, LoN S826/131/2309.

[44] Joost van Hamel to Ludovica Marchet, 13 March 11923, LoN S826/131/2309. During this time she was still doing calligraphical work for the section.

[45] Ludovica Marchet to Eric Drummond, 22 May 1924, LoN S826/131/2309.

[46] Various Lists, LoN S696/1/3.

[47] In newspaper articles many women accentuated how working for the League allowed them to have a comparatively high standard of living. cf Fight Still on For Equal Pay, *The Sun*, (Sydney 8 February 1940) 29.

songs, comics, and even musicals featuring the League.[48] International Geneva with its cosmopolitan flair became a cultural hotspot. Research has pointed out how Geneva evolved at the same time to a place where political and civil society actors began to manifest their international political claims.[49]

The opportunity to be close to international Geneva, where global politics were being rethought, was obviously so attractive that Marchet was willing to accept a position for which she was overqualified, as a stepping stone into the International Secretariat. A look at the social background of her colleagues shows that Marchet was by no means an isolated case.[50]

As a junior assistant, she was able to familiarize herself with the technical work of the Legal Section and thus acquire a working knowledge of the day-to-day of international legal administration. Furthermore, it also clearly shows that the League of Nations became a point of contact for women interested in international politics. Several applications of Marchet for different positions in the Registry and the Minorities Section were not accepted but Marchet decided to stay in Geneva with the League nonetheless.[51]

Marchet resigned in February 1929 without giving a reason. Many women in the Second Division eventually left as an advancement to other posts or a promotion to the First Division turned out impossible. Marchet may have decided to return to university instead: in any case, she studied German and French at Vienna University[52] and began a long career as an educator and international women's rights activist in Germany and Austria. Throughout her life, she remained interested in topics of internationalism, international understanding, nonviolence, and education and evolved to an active pan-Europeanist. From 1934 she was editor of the monthly *Europa Echo, das Blatt für zwischenstaatliche Verständigung* (Echo of Europe, an International Politics and Humanitarian Journal)[53] and in 1935 she became head of the Austrian Women Club Call.[54] During the Second World War, she emigrated to Sweden before returning to Austria after the war. To her network belonged activists such as Nobel laureate Nelly Sachs and educationists Paulus und Edith Geheeb.[55] Her interest in the League remained unbroken as correspondence in her personnel files in the 1930s demonstrates: she tried, for example, to place an Austrian colleague of herself within the Secretariat.[56] During her political work the idea of the direct democracy remained guiding. Publications such as *Ehrfurcht vor dem Leben als Staatsgrundgesetz*[57] (Awe

[48] Benjamin Auberer, 'Murder, Intrigue, Sex and Internationalism—Novels about the League of Nations' in Karen Gram-Skjoldager and Haakon Ikonomou (eds), *The League of Nations: Perspective from the Present* (Aarhus University Press 2019) 211.

[49] cf, eg, Leila J Rupp, *World of Women: The Making of an International Women's Movement* (Princeton University Press 1997).

[50] Auberer, International Jungle.

[51] Ludovica Marchet to Eric Drummond, 22 May 1924, LoN S826/131/2309.

[52] Ludovica Marchet to Eric Drummond, 20 February 1929, LoN S826/131/2309.

[53] Elsa Koss, 'Hainisch-Marchet, Ludovica' in Ilse Koroton (ed), *biografiA* (Böhlau 2016) 11, hereafter Koss, *Hainisch-Marchet*.

[54] ibid 12.

[55] ibid 11.

[56] AS to Ludovica Marchet, 13 February 1937, LoN S826/131/2309.

[57] Ludovica Marchet, *Ehrfurcht vor dem Leben als Staatsgrundgesetz*, (Forum Humanum 1952).

for Life as a Constitutional Law) underline Marchet's continuing interest and engagement in democratic citizen education. Eventually she became the first (albeit unsuccessful) female candidate for the position of President of Austria in 1951.[58]

This reconstruction of Ludovica Marchet's life is not suggesting an *ipso facto* argument that she would not have had a career without the League or that her later life was a direct cause of her time in Geneva. Nevertheless, Marchet's biography shows that the League became pivotal for people interested in international relations and diplomacy. In Geneva, women could network and take their first steps on the international stage, familiarize themselves with topics and terms of diplomacy, and learn strategies with which to advance female representation at the global level. Marchet became an advocate for women's rights, education, and international cooperation. Her activism and career path cannot be understood without acknowledging her time at the League.

Conclusion

The examination of female biographies in the Legal Section of the League of Nations gives an insight into the internationalization of law, away from codification and the history of ideas. The women of the Legal Section were all employed in subordinate ranks and had no direct part in the reconceptualization and development of international law, even though the League was heralded for their inclusion of women. The newfound inclusion of women onto the global stage and the struggles they faced are exemplified by the life and career of Ludovica Marchet.

Looking at the lives of female staff members of the League provides an insight into the historical social context where women were beginning to gain a foothold in international cooperation, diplomacy, and the internationalization of law. Although women were not employed in leadership positions, they made their mark as typists or secretaries for leading men. The lack of opportunities to progress and other gendered obstacles at the time, such as family and marital expectations, saw female staff alternate frequently. Marchet, despite owning the qualifications, experienced this and thus transitioned into more relevant domestic positions. The League of Nations can nonetheless be understood as not only a key player in the development and internationalization of law and diplomacy, but also in its democratization. Although the historical and spatial social contexts restricted their options, the League introduced an unprecedented opportunity for women to enter the global stage.

[58] Koss, *Hainisch-Marchet* (n 53) 12.

24
The 'Indigenous Women' behind the 'Other' Beijing Declaration

*Bérénice K Schramm**

> We stand in unity behind this '1995 Beijing Declaration of Indigenous Women' which is the fruit of our collective efforts to understand the world and our situation as Indigenous women, critique the Draft Platform for Action, and articulate our demands to the international community, the governments, and the NGO's.
>
> Beijing Declaration of Indigenous Women (1995) para 5.

Two years ago, I was looking for material on Indigenous women's rights for one session of my 'Women's Rights' course. As I was browsing through a few references online, I stumbled upon a webpage with a 1990s feel where a lengthy text entitled the 'Beijing Declaration of Indigenous Women' was reproduced against a cerulean background.[1] While I was familiar with the famous 1995 Beijing Declaration *tout court*, I had never heard about this 'other' declaration. But its first paragraph has stayed with me ever since:

> 'The Earth is our mother. From her we get our life, and our ability to live. It is our responsibility to care for our mother and in caring for our mother, we care for ourselves. Women, all females are a manifestation of Mother Earth in human form.

As I continued reading the 'Other' Declaration, I took in the raw portrait its authors, the group of Indigenous women present in Beijing in 1995, make of the world in which they have lived: a place where the land is simultaneously the sacred origin of everything yet remains exploited and many of its inhabitants oppressed. Perhaps, I pondered, was it in fact this Declaration, and not the official one, that said it all about what was, and still is, wrong with the way our world is governed.

Yet, then and still now, it is the *official* Beijing Declaration (and more specifically the Platform for Action appended to it) that is dubbed, at least by the relevant institutions,

* I wish to extend my sincere thanks to Immi Tallgren, Sarah Riley Case (formerly Mason-Case), and Anne-Charlotte Martineau for their extremely generous and stimulating comments and Katariina Flinck for her editing work on the previous versions of this chapter.

[1] 'Beijing Declaration of Indigenous Women Declaration of Indigenous Women' <www.ipcb.org/resolutions/htmls/dec_beijing.html> accessed 3 October 2022.

Bérénice K Schramm, *The 'Indigenous Women' behind the 'Other' Beijing Declaration* In: *Portraits of Women in International Law.* Edited by: Immi Tallgren, Oxford University Press. © Bérénice K. Schramm 2023. DOI: 10.1093/oso/9780198868453.003.0024

to be 'the most progressive blueprint ever for advancing women's rights and a powerful source of guidance and inspiration'.[2] On the one hand, it is true that at the time of their unanimous adoption by the 189 states attending the Fourth UN Conference on Women in China, both the official Beijing Declaration and the Platform's content crystallized policy orientations more progressive than most of the domestic legal frameworks in force at the time[3] and contributed to important progress for the latter's promotion and protection globally.[4] On the other hand, such progressive vision is not without limitations[5] and has come under scrutiny ever since. Some critiques have unearthed the global, neoliberal, patriarchal, and colonial paradigms framing this vision: through these documents, the world becomes a place where empowered women are economic agents working in the name of 'structurally adjusted' progress[6] and where sustainable development replaces more radical ways to live on and with the earth.[7]

In light of these critiques, the 'Other' Declaration seems to offer a more encompassing and radical 'blueprint for advancing women's rights' and, correlatedly, for taking care of the land. This is why I chose to write about the 'Other Declaration' and its collective authors, the 'Indigenous Women', as part of this volume as they provide a unique window into overlooked institutional aspects of global governance both then and now. The 1990s were indeed a fruitful decade for multilateral conferences across the board—eg on matters pertaining to the environment and development (Rio 1992), human rights (Vienna 1993), population (Cairo 1994), women's rights (Beijing 1995), international trade (Marrakesh 1995), and criminal law (Rome 1998). These conferences became spaces where civil society, through the integrated or parallel participation of non-governmental organizations (NGOs), pioneered interventions within inter-state conversations, introducing a 'new dynamic of embryonic participatory democracy to the global community and to the shaping of international law'.[8]

The 'Indigenous Women' behind the 'Other' Beijing Declaration met in this dual context, that of a decade where the post-Cold War New World Order was being built in the international arena, and that of the Beijing conference itself where women's rights organizations, including Indigenous women's ones, were trying to 'turn grassroots concerns into UN policies to be implemented over the next ten years at the local, national, and global levels'.[9] The Beijing Declaration of Indigenous Women can

[2] 'The Beijing Platform for Action: Inspiration Then And Now' (*UN Women|The Beijing Platform for Action
Turns 20*) <https://beijing20.unwomen.org/en/about> accessed 3 October 2022.

[3] Rhonda Copelon, 'Introduction: Bringing Beijing Home Symposium: Women's Rights Are Human Rights: Selected Articles Dedicated to Women in the International Human Rights Arena' (1995) 21 Brooklyn Journal of International Law 599, 602.

[4] Pascale Allotey and Fatima Denton, 'Challenges and Priorities for Delivering on the Beijing Declaration and Platform for Action 25 Years On' (2020) 396 The Lancet 1053.

[5] Copelon (n 3) 601–02.

[6] Sarah Ahmed, 'Close Encounters—Feminism and/in "the Globe"' in Sarah Ahmed, *Strange Encounters: Embodied Others in Postcoloniality* (Routledge 2000) 174 and 176.

[7] Lliane Loots and Harald Witt, 'Beijing +10: Women and the Environment—How Close Are We to Earth Democracy?' (2005) 19–64 Agenda 52–62.

[8] Dianne Otto, 'Nongovernmental Organizations in the United Nations System: The Emerging Role of International Civil Society' (1996) 18 Human Rights Quarterly 107, 120.

[9] Marian Doub, 'Reflections on the NGO Forum on Women '95' (1995) 27 Bulletin of Concerned Asian Scholars 80, 80.

therefore be appraised as one piece of the (so far) un-obtained radical legacy of this period, including all that it could have engendered if realized. It can further be read as the outcome of an exercise in world-making and institutional portraiture on the part of Indigenous women: with it, they paint themselves as global actors to be reckoned with. With Kankana-ey Igorot activist Victoria Corpuz's unyielding words: 'They should have to look at us in the face when they make those decisions.'[10]

Because I am a non-Indigenous white French international legal scholar, I can only wish, with the present chapter, to introduce such portraiture to a new readership.[11] My own country and part of my own family have benefitted from colonialism, including settler colonialism. I therefore write this chapter from a very epistemologically disadvantaged position,[12] all the more so as I was unable to secure interviews or co-authorship with some of the Declaration's authors. Yet, I decided to write it in order to avoid using silence as a (privileged) coping mechanism for the rage that stems out of what should be[13]—namely, a more just international legal order. My research is first and foremost informed by first-hand written accounts and scholarly analyses published at the time of the Conference or later by Indigenous women, and in some cases, by non-Indigenous women. I rely in particular on Anishinaabe activist Winona LaDuke's account and address as well as Inuit activist Mary Sillett's exposition of their experience as participants in Beijing 1995.[14] LaDuke, Sillett, and their peers' accounts help to understand how Indigenous women became a collective in their own right and how they produced their very own Declaration.

'Indigenous Women' as a Collective: 'Finding Common Ground' from Adelaide to Beijing and Beyond

With their unique intersectional positionality, Indigenous women as political subjects have historically been illegible to both the women's rights and the Indigenous rights movements.[15] Indeed, Indigenous feminist scholarship has shown how Indigenous womanhood as a site of oppression pits against the whiteness of mainstream feminism

[10] Winona LaDuke, 'I Fight Like a Woman: The UN Conference on Women in China', and 'Mothers of Our Nations: Indigenous Women Address the World' in W LaDuke, *The Winona LaDuke Reader: A Collection of Essential Writings* (Theytus Books 2002) 231–32.

[11] This chapter does not contribute to the decolonization of international law. In fact, it remains a move to settler innocence on my part (*conscientiszation*), and on the part of the discipline (which I take part in; *a(s)t(e)risking peoples*); Eve Tuck and K Wayne Yang, 'Decolonization Is Not a Metaphor' (2012) 1 Decolonization: Indigeneity, Education & Society 2–4 and 19–23.

[12] Sandra Harding, 'Rethinking Standpoint Epistemology: What Is "Strong Objectivity"?' in K Brad Wray (ed), *Knowledge and Inquiry: Readings in Epistemology* (Broadview Press 2002) 357.

[13] Ahmed (n 6) 166–67.

[14] LaDuke 'I Fight' (n 10); Mary Sillett, 'Ensuring Indigenous Women's Voices Are Heard' (1996) 16 Canadian Woman Studies/Les Cahiers de la femme 62. I have been unable to identify Sillett's specific First Nation.

[15] Finding Common Ground. First International Indigenous Womens Conference, 7–18 July 1989, Adelaide, Australia, Conference Report, <www.samemory.sa.gov.au/webdata/resources/files/zpamb1177 1665ocr.pdf>.

and the maleness of historical decolonial struggles.[16] To be recognized,[17] Indigenous women have to choose gender over indigeneity or indigeneity over gender[18] in the way they portray themselves and frame their claims. Such a choice is one they refuse to make, or rather one they do not have the luxury to make: in Goenpul (Quandamooka nation) scholar Aileen Moreton-Robinson's words, '[a]ll Indigenous women share the common experience of living in a society that deprecates us'.[19] Only by owning one's image, that is engaging in self-representation (instead of being represented)[20] can Indigenous women adequately express the challenges produced by such an intersectional experience of marginalization. To do so, they 'create[d] new diplomatic spaces at the global, regional, state, and local levels to pursue simultaneous negotiations for both their individual rights as women and collective rights as members of Indigenous nations'.[21] As Indigenous Peoples institutionalized their presence at the United Nations[22] and the women's movement's leadership auspiciously shifted, during the UN Decade for Women, from women in the North to women in the South,[23] Indigenous women forged their own transnational alliances in order to become who they were in Beijing.

As a matter of fact, the 'Indigenous Women' behind the 'Other' Beijing Declaration realized who they had to become, namely a collective, ten years before, at the Third UN Conference on Women held in Nairobi. Although only twelve Indigenous women attended,[24] one of them, Wakka Wakka activist Jo Willmot recalls how powerful an experience it was to meet 'a group of people who understood'. She explains, 'Indigenous women came to formulate the idea that we should have our own international Indigenous women's conference'.[25] Four years later, in 1989, the dream came true and Willmot convened the First International Indigenous Women's Conference in Adelaide (settler state of Australia) on the befitting theme of 'Finding Common

[16] Rauna Kuokkanen, 'Self-Determination and Indigenous Women's Rights at the Intersection of International Human Rights' (2012) 34 Human Rights Quarterly 225, 225–27. See also the telling silence on Indigenous women's position and contribution to international law in all the pieces making up the recent AJIL Symposium on 'The Impact of Indigenous Peoples on International Law'; S James Anaya and Antony Anghie, 'Introduction to the Symposium on the Impact of Indigenous Peoples on International Law' (2021) 115 AJIL 116.

[17] Paddy McQueen, 'The Politics of Recognition' in P McQueen, *Subjectivity, Gender and the Struggle for Recognition* (Palgrave Macmillan UK 2015).

[18] Laura Parisi and Jeff Corntassel, 'A "Revolution within a Revolution"' in J Marshall Beier (ed), *Indigenous Diplomacies* (Palgrave Macmillan US 2009) 79.

[19] Aileen Moreton-Robinson, *Talkin' Up to the White Woman: Aboriginal Women and Feminism* (University of Queensland Press 2000) 163 and xvi.

[20] ibid xxii. See also Parisi and Corntassel (n 18) 94.

[21] Parisi and Corntassel (n 18) 80.

[22] See, eg, 'Indigenous Peoples at the United Nations | United Nations For Indigenous Peoples' (5 June 2015) <www.un.org/development/desa/indigenouspeoples/about-us.html> accessed 3 October 2022. That said, Indigenous diplomacies have existed before and after the colonial encounter, see J Beier, *Indigenous Diplomacies* (Palgrave Macmillan US 2009).

[23] Doub (n 9) 83.

[24] According to Quechua activist Tarcila Rivera Zea, referenced in FIMI—IIWF, 'The Global Study on the Situation of Indigenous Women and Girls In the Framework of the 25th Anniversary of the Beijing Declaration and Platform for Action' (2020) <www.fimi-iiwf.org/the-global-study-on-the-situation-of-indigenous-women-and-girls/?lang=en> accessed 3 October 2022.

[25] 'Finding Common Ground' (n 15) 3.

Ground'. Attended by 1,500 Indigenous women hailing from fifteen states,[26] this first international conference was a success and, according to its official greetings, the beginning of 'a unique chapter in the history of Indigenous women's lives'.[27] It led to the adoption of several resolutions and a Declaration of Unity.[28] The second edition took place in 1990 in Samiland (Kárášjohka, settler state of Norway),[29] and the third in 1993 in Aotearoa (settler state of New Zealand).[30] Before and following these singular events, Indigenous women created several regional networks and conferences.[31]

Hence, in Beijing old and new friends met, as transpires from LaDuke's lively account,[32] in numbers and diversity never before attained by Indigenous women in a non-Indigenous global space. As a result, 'Beijing 1995' has been described in Indigenous feminist scholarship as a 'milestone in the creation of the global Indigenous Women's movement'.[33] There and then, were its existence and claims formally introduced to the rest of the world through the Beijing Declaration of Indigenous Women.

The 'Other' Beijing Declaration: 'Indigenous Women Address the World' from Amidst the 'Other' Forum

As much as its first paragraph is striking with its land-based address that already complicates what women's rights are, the Beijing Declaration of Indigenous Women's signature line—'*Approved And Signed On 7 September 1995 At The Indigenous Women's Tent, Huairou, Beijing, China*'—further conjures up a complex space-time as it illuminates the multi-layered topography of 'the' Beijing Conference.[34] As with other multilateral conferences in the 1990s and previous UN Women Conferences, 'Beijing 1995' was not only an inter-state event but also, and most importantly, a civil society forum. On the one hand, located in the centre of the Chinese capital, the 'official' UN Conference was where state delegations—17,000 people—negotiated the final text of the official Beijing Declaration and Platform for action from 4 to 15 September 1995. On the other hand, in Huairou, a suburban town approximatively fifty kilometres north of the site of the UN Conference, was where the NGO Forum on Women 95[35] met with women's organisations—between 30,000 and 35,000 people, among them

[26] International Indigenous Women's Conference, Letter to Ms Teresa Aparicio, Executive Director of International Work Group for Indigenous Affairs, 31 July 1989, <https://cendoc.docip.org/collect/cendocdo/index/assoc/HASH7e50/13411333.dir/WGIP%2089%20IIWC.pdf>. See also, FIMI (n 23) 21 n 17 and 18.

[27] Finding Common Ground (n 24). See also Jackie Huggins, 'International Indigenous Women's Conference' (1990) 5 Australian Feminist Studies 113.

[28] 'Declaration of Unity of the First International Indigenous Women's Conference', annexed to Letter (n 25).

[29] Letter (n 25).

[30] No documents of the 1990 and the 1993 conferences are available; FIMI (n 25) 21 n18.

[31] For an overview of said networks and conferences, see ibid 21–22.

[32] As transpires from LaDuke, 'I Fight' (n 10).

[33] FIMI (n 23) 21.

[34] LaDuke, 'Mothers' (n 10) title.

[35] Doub (n 9) 87. Unfortunately, the few pictures I was able to find of the Indigenous women in Beijing were either too incomplete or of low quality to be chosen as illustration. For said pictures and other from the Forum, see ibid 82 and 85; International Work Group on Indigenous Affairs, Indigenous Affairs, 'Indigenous Women' 3/2000, No 3 July–August–September 2000, 6–9 <www.iwgia.org/images/publications/IA_3-00.pdf> accessed 3 October 2022; NGO Committee on the Status of Women, 'NGO CSW64 Handbook 2020', 18–20 <https://ngocsw.org/ngocsw64/ accessed 3 October 2022.

150[36] Indigenous women—demonstrating, workshopping, building, and strengthening their networks from 30 August to 8 September 1995. While these were two distinct events and travelling between sites was not easy,[37] about 8,750 of the NGO participants were actually members of state delegations attending the Conference while others participated in both the Conference and the Forum.[38]

Figure 24.1 The Indigenous Women Caucus gathers under the Indigenous Women's Tent at the Huairou's 'NGO Forum on Women 95' between 30 August and 8 September 1995.
Source: Item S03 United Nations Archives at Geneva.

Huairou's International Convention Centre, as well as nearby schools, hotels, and inflatable tents became a lively site where hundreds of events and activities took place every day.[39] Amidst this maze, LaDuke recounts meeting with Corpuz thus: 'We sit talking in the Indigenous Woman's Tent #49 at the conference.' Based on the Declaration's signature and Sillett's corroborative account,[40] and as shown in the picture above,[41] 'the Indigenous

[36] LaDuke 'I Fight' (n 10), 228; Sillett (n 14) 63. Quechua activist Tarcila Rivera Zea recalls 'almost' 100 in total; 'We Want to Be Actors in Our Own Futures with Full Rights' (*UN Women | The Beijing Platform for Action Turns 20*) <https://beijing20.unwomen.org/en/news-and-events/stories/2014/5/we-want-to-be-actors> accessed 3 October 2022.

[37] The NGO Forum's peripheral location was strategically chosen by the Chinese government to hamper NGOs' activities; see Ruth P Dawson, 'When Women Gather: The NGO Forum of the Fourth World Conference on Women, Beijing 1995' (1996) 10 International Journal of Politics, Culture, and Society 8; Doub (n 9) 81; Ahmed (n 6) 163.

[38] Doub (n 9) 82.

[39] Doub (n 9) 80 and 82. Dawson talks about more than 4,000 events in total; Dawson (n 36) 11.

[40] Sillett (n 14) 63.

[41] The Tebtebba Foundation (Indigenous Peoples' International Centre for Policy Research and Education) to whom the picture is credited was founded in 1996 by Corpuz herself; she has been its executive director

Women's Tent' appears to be the place where the 150 Indigenous women who could travel to Huairou met daily and worked on their radical text. To the rest of world, amidst the Forum and in the Declaration's title, Indigenous women are 'Indigenous Women'. However, Sillett's account seems to complicate this self-presentation from within: she reports the existence of two distinct (yet possibly interlapping) groups of Indigenous women in Beijing-including-Huairou.[42] The first group is the 'Indigenous Women Caucus' which drafted, under the 'Indigenous Women's Tent' in Huairou, the 'Other' Beijing Declaration before approving and signing it on 7 September 1995.[43] The Caucus then handed it to Kehewin Cree activist Madeleine Dion-Stout, attending as an observer on the Canadian delegation and a member of the 'Indigenous Working Group'. Based on Dion-Stout's affiliation and Sillett's synecdochical description, said group appears to have been located in Beijing proper. Its creation, exact mandate, and membership however remain unspecified by the latter author.[44] Yet, she does explain that the transmission of the Declaration was accompanied by a discussion between the two groups so that the Working Group can adequately represent the positions developed by the Caucus or, in other words, still Sillett's, so that Dion-Stout 'could use it in attempts to influence the drafting sessions of the Platform for Action'.[45]

Such discussion must have highlighted differences and commonalities, in particular across the politico-institutional divide.[46] Indeed, although they now presented themselves as a collective, Indigenous women remain a collection of individuals hailing from extremely diverse backgrounds and foregrounding various issues. To find common ground, since 1989, has required numerous conversations, and at times disagreements, at the local, regional, and transnational levels.[47] That said, from these varied stances and previous conversations and earlier declarations,[48] emerged in 1995, from under the 'Indigenous Women's tent', a unitary text constituting 'the basis of Indigenous women's claims as Indigenous and as women'.[49] The first of its

to this day. For more pictures of Indigenous women participants and of the Forum as a whole, see Doub (n 9), 82 and 85; International Work Group on Indigenous Affairs, Indigenous Affairs, `Indigenous Women' 3/2000, No.3 July-August-September 2000, <HYPERLINK "C:\Users\kflin\Downloads\www.iwgia.org\images\publications\IA_3-00.pdf"www.iwgia.org/images/publications/IA_3-00.pdf> accessed 23 May 2021, 6-9; NGO Committee on the Status of Women, `NGO CSW64 Handbook 2020', <HYPERLINK "C:\Users\kflin\Downloads\www.ngocsw.org\ngocsw64\"www.ngocsw.org/ngocsw64/> accessed 23 May 2021, 18-20.

[42] ibid.

[43] Sillett further mentions the drafting by the Caucus of a message to the G7 states; she however does not reference it; ibid. I have been unable to find such a document.

[44] 'The UN Conference also had an Indigenous Working Group (...)' ibid 62–63. I have been unable to find more information on the Indigenous Working Group.

[45] ibid 62–63.

[46] ibid 62.

[47] On the disagreements experienced at the 1989 Conference, see 'Finding Common Ground' (n 24) 1 and 5. On specific issues raised in Huairou, see, eg, Sillett (n 14) 62–63; Maria Fernanda Espinosa, 'Indigenous Women on Stage: Retracing the Beijing Conference from Below' (1997) 18 Frontiers: A Journal of Women Studies 237; LaDuke 'I Fight' (n 10) 227f, including Kanak activist Susanna Ounei who used Huairou as a platform to raise awareness about and to build solidarity against the nuclear tests France was concurrently conducting in the Pacific waters under its settler jurisdiction.

[48] See Beijing Declaration of Indigenous Women, para 2. Specifically mentioned are the 1990 Declaration of the Second International Indigenous Women's Conference and the 1992 Kari-Oca Declaration.

[49] FIMI (n 23) 21.

fifty paragraphs which is reproduced in introduction already distils a crucial epistemological common ground: the spiritual dimension of Indigenous Women's diplomatic efforts and of their relationship to their lands.[50] Recalling the foundational truth according to which, '[t]he Earth is our mother', Indigenous Women proclaim their responsibility in caring for her. They extend such responsibility to all women who, according to them, are also 'daughters of the Earth'. This is the first way in which, Indigenous Women are, according to LaDuke's formulation,[51] 'addressing our world', that is all women. And they do so by speaking as women addressing other women.

But the second way in which Indigenous Women are 'addressing our world' is even more all-encompassing. They start the sixth paragraph of their Declaration by pointing to the 'New World Order' which, under the guise of globalization and trade liberalization, is in fact responsible for recolonisation. Indigenous Women posit that behind the New World Order stand 'rich industrialised nation-states, their transnational corporations, financial institutions', those who have already 'abused and raped Mother Earth, colonised, marginalised, and discriminated against us' (para 6). As such, the Indigenous Women's address provides an uncompromising portrait of who makes the world as it stands today, and who can possibly contribute to remedy the past and current destruction of it. In the meantime—and here Indigenous Women speak as Indigenous— '[i]t is an imperative for us, as Indigenous peoples, to stand in their way, because it means more ethnocide and genocide for us' (para 9).

Indigenous Women therefore challenge the Beijing (then Draft) Platform for action (para 10) because of its in-built New World Order bias (paras 11–12). The Declaration lifts the veil on the ill-logic behind the Platform's focus on achieving 'equality, development and peace'[52] within a system that itself produces the inequalities, underdevelopment, and conflict it wishes to assuage. The Declaration further unpacks the colonial Western-centric nature of education, health, and media tools and programmes fostered by the Platform (para 13) as well as the violence imposed on Indigenous women's bodies and lands by extractive and labour-intensive economic policies that underlie the Platform's agenda (paras 13–15). Last but not least, by being a gender-obsessed narrative only, the Platform ends up depoliticizing Indigenous women's issues (para 16), that is sustaining, if not promoting, the colonial and racist ethos that have sought to erase them in the first place.

Against such problematic agenda, Indigenous Women made a list of demands and proposals addressed to governments, international non-governmental and governmental organizations (paras 19–49). Reflecting the Declaration's authors' unique positionality, said demands and proposals can be classified in two categories: the first set stems from their claims as members of Indigenous nations while the other arises from the challenges faced as Indigenous *women*. As to the first set, Indigenous

[50] Parisi and Corntassel (n 17) 83–84. Moreton-Robinson (n 18) 162. For another example of spiritual wording in a similar declaration, see the 1992 Kari-Oca Declaration and Indigenous Peoples' Earth Charter's introduction and first paragraphs.

[51] The passage is in fact identical to a portion of the first paragraph of LaDuke's (individual) address delivered at Huairou; LaDuke, 'Mothers' (n 14) 234. This could be evidence of LaDuke's intense involvement in the drafting of the Declaration.

[52] Or even more of it, according to superlative mottos seen on banners or heard in rallies throughout the NGO Forum; Doub (n 9) 80.

Women's demands and proposals revolved around the recognition and respect by the aforementioned entities of Indigenous peoples' rights to self-determination, to their territories, development, education, health, intellectual and cultural heritage, and to control the biological diversity in their territories.

The second category of demands regards the human rights violations and violence experienced by Indigenous women, including their murder, forced disappearances, and the historical and systemic lack of adequate monitoring, investigation, protection, and enforcement of Indigenous laws and cultural representations. This second set further aims to ensure Indigenous women's political participation, and enhance their capabilities and access to resources, including by collaborating with non-Indigenous women's organizations and formations as well as with the NGOs working with them. The Indigenous Women conclude their Declaration by returning full circle to the land as they thank the Chinese authorities and people for their hospitality.

So, what has changed in twenty-eight years? Not much perhaps if one looks at the ongoing ecological disasters and rising economic disparities whose impact is felt first and foremost by the most marginalized peoples. Among them, Indigenous women who continue to disappear inexplicably while their abducted children are found in mass graves. Does that mean that settler futurity[53] shall remain the only (deadly) horizon in sight? Hopefully not. In this regard, it is important to take stock of the numerous battles won by Indigenous peoples in favour of their right to self-determination.[54] Besides, Indigenous Women have furthered, as announced in their Declaration, their use of international institutions including those dedicated to women's rights,[55] as the recent adoption of a General Recommendation for Indigenous Women and Girls (no 39) within the CEDAW framework.[56] So much so, in fact, that the CEDAW Committee's Concept Note spoke of how the '*Beijing Declaration of Indigenous Women* and the *Beijing Declaration and Platform for Action* paved the way to [their] international visibility' and other declarations afterwards.[57] Yet, these institutional successes have visibly failed to completely destabilize the very order denounced in the 'Other' Declaration, thereby pointing at the limits inherent to a liberal politics of recognition.[58] But as the overlooked radical blueprint it is in many aspects General Recommendation No. 39 still only refers to the official Beijing Declaration, the Beijing Declaration of Indigenous Women could remind us now, more than ever, of 'what decolonisation wants'.[59]

[53] Tuck and Wayne Yang (n 11) 36.

[54] 'Self-Determination as Anti-Extractivism: How Indigenous Resistance Challenges IR' (E-International Relations, 21 May 2014) <www.e-ir.info/2014/05/21/self-determination-as-anti-extractivism-how-indigenous-resistance-challenges-ir> accessed 3 October 2022.

[55] See FIMI (n 23) 26ff.

[56] General Recommendation No. 39 (2022) on the rights of Indigenous women and girls, 31 October 2022, CEDAW/C/GC/39 <www.ohchr.org/en/documents/general-comments-and-recommendation-no39-2022-rights-indigeneous> accessed 27 January 2023.

[57] CEDAW, 'Concept Note for a General Recommendation on the Rights of Indigenous Women', para 4 <www.ohchr.org/Documents/HRBodies/CEDAW/CN_IndigenousWomen_EN.docx> accessed 3 October 2022. The posterior declarations are: the Beijing Declaration as the Declaration of the International Forum of Indigenous Women—Beijing + 5 (New York 2000), Abya Yala's Continental Declarations of Indigenous Women of the Americas, the Conference on Indigenous Women and Gender Relations (Denmark 2004), the Declaration of the Indigenous Women's Network on Biodiversity (Malaysia 2004), and the document on Political Positioning and Plan of Action of Indigenous Women of the World (Peru 2013).

[58] Glen Sean Coulthard, *Red Skin, White Masks: Rejecting the Colonial Politics of Recognition* (University of Minnesota Press 2014) 6. Coulthard's critique could also serve as a framework to examine the language of recognition used in the Indigenous Women's Declaration itself.

[59] Tuck and Wayne Yang (n 11) 3.

25

The Women's Caucus for Gender Justice

Writing Gender into International Criminal Law

*Anna van der Velde**

Introduction

The 1990s marked a period of feminist contestation of patriarchal norms imbued in international law. According to Costa Rican lawyer and Women's Caucus member Ana Elena Obando, '[f]or the feminist movement there were so many things to do that you moved from one thing to the other because one needed to be on all the fronts'.[1] One of these fronts was the negotiations preceding the adoption of the Rome Statute on 17 July 1998, which established the first permanent International Criminal Court (ICC) to prosecute individuals for war crimes, crimes against humanity, and genocide. Besides codifying and broadening 'traditional prohibitions in humanitarian law', it inscribed for the first time also gender into 'hard' international law. Previously vaguely framed gendered crimes such as rape, sexual slavery, forced pregnancy, and other forms of sexual violence were defined as grave and universally punishable crimes.[2] The Women's Caucus for Gender Justice (WCGJ/Caucus), a transnational network of more than 300 women's organizations that formed in response to the lack of gender justice considerations in the first ICC Draft Statute, contributed to this inclusion of gender justice concerns in the new Statute through their advocacy work nationally and at the negotiation sites.[3]

Its members combined feminist (human rights) activist strategies with the force of a global feminist lobbyist network, that had formed at the World Conferences on Human Rights in Vienna (1993) and Beijing (1995),[4] and in-depth legal analysis

* I thank Immi Tallgren, Parvathi Menon, and Freek van der Vet for their comments and encouragement, and Katariina Flinck and Marta Paricio Montesinos for their transcription assistance.

[1] Interview with Ana Elena Obando.

[2] See Rome Statute Articles 8[2][b][xxii], 8[2][e][vi], and 7[1][c, g, h], and 7[2][c], further specified in the Elements of Crime; Pam Spees, 'Women's Advocacy in the Creation of the International Criminal Court: Changing the Landscapes of Justice and Power' (2003) 28(4) Signs 1233, 1245.

[3] State delegates negotiated the Draft Statute, with among others representatives from Canada, New Zealand, Switzerland, France, and the Nordic states already early on arguing for the inclusion of gendered crimes and procedural concerns. WCGJ members could not directly negotiate or vote on drafts but were lobbying and discussing draft proposals with state representatives outside the negotiation rooms. See Janet Halley, 'Rape at Rome: Feminist Interventions in the Criminalization of Sex-Related Violence in Positive International Criminal Law' (2008) 30(1) Michigan Journal of International Law 22–23; Cate Steains, 'Gender Issues' in Roy SK Lee (ed), *The International Criminal Court: The Making of the Rome Statute—Issues, Negotiations, Results* (Kluwer Law International 1999) 357, 365.

[4] There, feminist human rights advocates sought the reframing of international human rights law as inclusive of women's rights, shifting these from the private to the public sphere. Barbara Frey, 'A Fair Representation: Advocating for Women's Rights in the International Criminal Court' (2004) Case Studies

Anna van der Velde, *The Women's Caucus for Gender Justice* In: *Portraits of Women in International Law*.
Edited by: Immi Tallgren, Oxford University Press. © Anna van der Velde 2023. DOI: 10.1093/oso/9780198868453.003.0025

Figure 25.1 The Colosseum Demonstration at the 1998 Rome Conference. Protest organised by the Women's Caucus for Gender Justice.

Source: Courtesy of Tebtebba Foundation (Indigenous Peoples' International Centre for Policy Research and Education.

skills to advocate for the criminalization of violence against women in conflict and a gender-just procedural reform of international criminal law (ICL) institutions. They supported the transposing of gender justice from a niche topic recognized in specialized soft law documents to a binding mainstream international treaty, by providing detailed legal expertise 'on the corridors of power' outside the negotiation halls and continuously upholding the visibility of women's concerns in the public.[5] Yet, twenty-five years after its formation, the Caucus' work as a social movement and its broader agenda that addressed the Court's 'positioning [...]—its independence, its fairness, and its associations with peace',[6] the persons behind the network and their working processes have faded into the shadows.

This portrait builds on interviews with eight members of the WCGJ[7] and their writings to examine how the WCGJ advocated for a feminist agenda at the Rome Statute negotiations. The following analysis reflects on the interviewees' understandings of

on Women and Public Policy, University of Minnesota 5–6, available at <https://www.academia.edu/826971/A_Fair_Representation_Advocating_for_Womens_Rights_in_the_International_Criminal_Court> accessed 6 October 2022.

[5] Louise Chappell, *The Politics of Gender Justice at the International Criminal Court* (OUP 2015) 1.

[6] Spees (n 2) 1233–34.

[7] I am grateful to Alda Facio, Ana Elena Obando, Aurora Parong, Eleanor Conda, Lorena Fries, Pam Spees, Teresa Ulloa Ziaurriz, and Indai Sajor for their support and willingness to share their experiences. All interviews were conducted between January and April 2021 via Zoom (transcripts on file with author).

their formation, agenda, experiences, and encountered challenges lobbying for the inclusion of gender-based crimes in the ICC Statute. It shows that without a deeper understanding of how the WCGJ operated and coped with obstacles, we risk undervaluing how a global network of social and feminist movements' contributions to international (criminal) law are often only remembered by the end results while the movements are forgotten.

Forming the Women's Caucus for Gender Justice

The WCGJ's formation built on multiple parallel transformations in international law in the 1990s. The 1993 and 1994 International Law Commission draft statute for a permanent international criminal court followed the creation of ad hoc international tribunals to adjudicate war crimes in Rwanda (ICTR) and the Former Yugoslavia (ICTY).[8] These tribunals' statutes and initial proceedings only limitedly 'address[ed] sexual and gender violence', mirroring the lack of recognition of gender crimes in international humanitarian law treaties, which were framed as violations of a woman's honour or dignity but did not give rise to separate charges or universal jurisdiction.[9] This changed partially, with sexual violence crimes being for the first time prosecuted at the ICTY and ICTR following concerted civil society pressure.[10]

Meanwhile, negotiations on the ICC Draft Statute commenced culminating in the treaty in July 1998. For the first time civil society, organized under the Coalition for an International Criminal Court (CICC) umbrella, were welcomed at the preparatory committee meetings.[11] Though civil society was lobbying state delegates since the mid-1990s, also raising gender concerns, women's NGOs were mostly absent focusing instead on preparations for the Beijing World Conference.[12] United States feminist human rights lawyers and activists Rhonda Copelon, Charlotte Bunch,

[8] See United Nations, 'Draft Statute for an International Criminal Court 1994' <https://legal.un.org/ilc/texts/instruments/english/draft_articles/7_4_1994.pdf> accessed 5 December 2020; Anne-Marie de Brouwer, *Supranational Criminal Prosecution of Sexual Violence* (Intersentia 2005).

[9] See, eg, Art 27 of the IV Geneva Conventions and the 1977 Additional Protocol, Barbara Bedont and Katherine Hall-Martinez, 'Ending Impunity for Gender Crimes under the International Criminal Court' (1999) 6(1) Brown Journal of World Affairs 65, 70; Kelly D Askin, 'Prosecuting Wartime Rape and Other Gender-Related Crimes under International Law: Extraordinary Advances, Enduring Obstacles' (2003) 21 Berkeley Journal of International Law 288; Interview with Alda Facio (n 7); see Keina Yoshida, 'Yaori Matsui: Challenging the Silences of International Law through Pan Asian Feminist Solidarity' in this volume.

[10] Heidi Nichols Haddad, 'Mobilizing the Will to Prosecute: Crimes of Rape at the Yugoslav and Rwandan Tribunals' (2011) 12 Human Rights Review 109–32.

[11] Alda Facio, 'All Roads Lead to Rome, But Some Are Bumpier Than Others' in Sharon Pickering and Caroline Lambert (eds), *Global Issues: Women and Justice* (Federation Press 2004). The coalition included human rights monitoring and advocacy groups, faith-based groups, victim/survivor advocacy groups, and others. Eleanor Conda, 'International Human Rights, Humanitarian & Criminal Laws: An Insider's View of Tough Women's Lobby for the ICC' (1998) 2(4) Women in Politics Newsletter in Asia and the Pacific; Ma Lourdes Veneracion-Rallonza, Reconstructing the Narrative of Transnational Feminist Agency: The Women's Caucus for Gender Justice in the International Criminal Court' in S Köngeter and W Smith (eds), *Transnational Agency and Migration: Actors, Movements and Social Support* (Routledge 2015) 109–29 at 111–12.

[12] Interview with CICC's director Bill Pace on 8 June 2000, 'If Hope Were Enough', Box 3114, documentary footage E008981, accessed via the University Library of Texas on 4 December 2020.

and Dorothy Thomas acknowledged the need for a more structured and permanent women's advocacy presence at the meeting sites. They used their personal and global feminist networks to recruit members to establish a permanent Women's Caucus.[13] The WCGJ commenced working under the CICC by mid-1997, nearly a year after the negotiations on the Draft Statute began. As the WCGJ's first director Alda Facio, a Costa Rican lawyer and feminist activist, recalls, the 'idea [was] to bring women from around the world, so that not only the voices of women in New York were heard'.[14] The WCGJ based their arguments with a particular focus on women's inclusion on the Beijing Programme, structural-bias feminist demands and their members own legal work.[15]

Facio points out that by the time of the Rome conference in 1998, the Caucus had more than 300 member organizations worldwide with 'a regionally diverse pool of advocates and experts with experience advocating in national systems [and] international forums'.[16] A three to five persons secretariat based in New York was present throughout the conference. Core members were among others head of the legal team Rhonda Copelon, founding director Alda Facio, co-director Eleanor Conda, a Philippine lawyer and director of the Asian Centre for Women's Human Rights, and Copelon's law student and later programme director Pam Spees. Other board members included Chilean lawyer Lorena Fries, Indian social activist Vahida Nainar, and Kenyan lawyer Betty Kaari Murungi.[17] They were supported by a rotating group of fifteen to twenty women, invited and sponsored by the secretariat to lobby delegates and write legal position papers during the five weeks meeting in Rome.[18]

The cornerstone of the WCGJ were national member organizations who monitored local policies and social justice projects, lobbied national officials and informed the secretariat of national law practices.[19] Maintaining local networks and regional responses allowed WCGJ members in Rome to draft detailed analyses and commentaries for revising the Draft Statute that were then used to lobby delegates nationally and at the negotiation site. Conda argues that 'we would not have achieved what we did without those strong movements and networks. It was not only women's rights and feminist organisations that helped build our networks in the different regions but also other social justice groups working for an independent, effective international mechanism for universal justice.'

13 Interview with Alda Facio (n 7).

14 Facio 'All Roads' (n 11).

15 The Beijing Programme for action 'identified rape as a war crime and an act of genocide' and called for a 'gender balance in the nomination and promotion of candidates for judicial positions and other staff positions in international bodies'. Frey (n 4) 5–6; Spees (n 2) 1236; Rhonda Copelon, 'Surfacing Gender: Re-Engraving Crimes Against Women in Humanitarian Law' (1994) 5 Hastings Women's Law Journal 243.

16 Facio in Spees (n 2) 1237; Facio 'All Roads' (n 11).

17 These names were repeatedly mentioned by interviewees. See also the Caucus' agenda,<www.iccwomen.org/wigjdraft1/Archives/oldWCGJ/aboutcaucus.html> accessed 3 December 2020.

18 Interview with Eleanor Conda (n 7).

19 Facio in Spees (n 2) 1237.

Framing the Caucus' Agenda and Lobbying Strategies

The Caucus challenged prevailing international humanitarian and criminal law framings and practices. The Vienna and Beijing World Conference conclusions, emerging jurisprudence from the ICTY and ICTR, and information exchanges with gender advisers at both courts gave the Women's Caucus authority for many of its positions.[20] Additionally, there were significant law reforms on violence against women ongoing in several states worldwide revealing 'gaps [in the] criminal justice systems'.[21] Though the Caucus did not invent new laws on gender-based violence, their arguments combined international law, especially human rights law, with national precedents to show the pitfalls in the prevailing ICL framework.

Facio explains that initial divisions on the Caucus' agenda were caused by 'diverse experiences and conceptions of the law' and bridged in long discussions.[22] Overall, the agenda followed structural-bias feminist's argumentations on the need to acknowledge the violation of women in conflicts as separate crimes not solely by adding women to existing patriarchal structures but substantially reforming institutions and underlying power constructions.[23] Articulated at Vienna and Beijing within the human rights framework, Spees stresses that these '[f]eminist critiques and theories of justice and power underlay the Women's Caucus's advocacy for broader conceptualizations of justice, a more empowered role for victims, [... and], the insistence on the independence of the Court from traditional power structures'.[24] Key elements were the 'international legal recognition of the effects of armed conflict on women' through the removal of sexual violence as honour crime framings dominant in international humanitarian law and the codification of gendered crimes in a binding international treaty as self-standing grave violations defined as genocide, war crimes and crimes against humanity under the new court's jurisdiction.[25] Within these the particular emphasis lay on the criminalization of sexual violence against women as means to achieve justice.[26] Moreover, on the Caucus' agenda were provisions to 'remove gender-based discrimination in the application of law', ensure sufficient 'personnel and resources to effectively and respectfully address the gendered dimensions of prosecuting these crimes', and granting civil society 'access to the Court'.[27]

[20] Bedont and Martinez (n 9) 67; Veneracion-Rallonza (n 11) 115–16.

[21] Veneracion-Rallonza (n 11) 118–19.

[22] Facio (n 7) recalls that the level of punishments, including the death penalty, and the definition of forced pregnancy with linkages to abortion were among the most contentious discussions. Other issues of dissent were only hinted at.

[23] Interview with Aurora Parong, Philippine doctor and director of the Medical Action group treating torture victims (n 7). On the feminist debate see Karen Engle, *The Grip of Sexual Violence in Conflict* (Stanford University Press 2020) 23–25.

[24] Spees (n 2) 1249; Obando (n 1). See the Caucus agenda (n 17).

[25] Frey (n 4) 9.

[26] Halley (n 3) 39, 63; see Engle (n 23) for a critical discussion of the framing.

[27] Facio 'All Roads' (n 11).

Choosing Strategies

To implement their agenda, the Caucus used a dual strategy of preparing legal expert statements and lobbying, particularly at the Rome conference. A group of Caucus experts in humanitarian and human rights led by Rhonda Copelon, provided daily in-depth legal analyses and rewritings of the Statute draft proposals as one-page position papers detailing suggested changes and their impact.[28] WCGJ lobbyists presented these documents then to delegates and national officials outside meeting rooms and in personal discussions.[29] Obando describes that 'we would go around to the delegations to explain to them our position and see what their reactions were'. Interviewees identify nationality and language skills as central elements that facilitated access to and established working relationships with delegates. Further key strategies were concentrating on text passages in brackets indicating disagreement and approaching female or like-minded delegates first.[30] Another was to 'focus on the smaller delegations, those that are usually ignored' but have formally equal voting power.[31]

Organizing panel debates[32], inviting gender experts, but also hearings with victims of sexual violence in the vicinity of the negotiation site enabled the Caucus to increase their visibility. Here, victim narratives and experiences served as basis for the WCGJ's positioning. Facio stressed that 'we presented testimonies from indigenous women, from afro-descendant women, about what was done to them in conflicts, which helped humanise the law because it showed that it is people, it's not articles and commas in our hands'.[33] Intertwining formalistic negotiation procedures with locally informed advocacy practices, Spees describes the rift between a 'quiet legal body that did not see a lot of activism and this constituent formation of this international women's human rights movement that had been forming up to the Beijing and Cairo meetings'.[34] Fries gives an example of the Caucus' activists' lobbying strategies that included demonstrations in front of the FAO Headquarters in Rome 'showing how many women had died during internal conflicts and wars'.

Though the core of the Women's Caucus was predominantly legally trained, the secretariat aimed for a diverse group of women representatives. Conda emphasized that we 'knew that the expertise of each one in their respective areas in their country or region would be vital for the collective's positioning and understanding the rationality of the issues under negotiation'. The equality and multidisciplinarity principle in

[28] Conda (n 11).

[29] Veneracion-Rallonza (n 11) 118.

[30] Obando (n 1), interview with Teresa Ulloa Ziaurriz (n 7).

[31] Frey (n 4) 8; Conda (n 7).

[32] The panel debates illustrate the WCGJ's wide network of allies, spanning for example from NGO representatives such as Rwanda Women's Community Network's Mary Balikungeri, President of the Jordanian MIZAN project Asma Khadaer, co-founder of Medica Mondiale Gabriela Mischkowski, Yaori Matsui (see Yoshida (n 10)) to representatives from international organizations such as Madeleine Rees from the Office of the High Commissioner for Human Rights, former ICTY judge Elizabeth Odio Benito, Donald Piragoff from the Canadian Department of Justice, and Jan Perlin from the Guatemalan Truth Commission. See description of unedited footage on WCGJ documentary at <https://legacy.lib.utexas.edu/taro/hrdi/00005/hrdi-00005.html> accessed 4 December 2020.

[33] Facio (n 7).

[34] Interview with Pam Spees, US feminist lawyer (n 7).

representation and advocacy were a distinct feature of the Caucus, attempting to have an equal number of representatives from each region at Rome, encouraging particularly non-lawyer activists to join.[35] The backgrounds of rotating participants varied from social work, health care to economists and historians, including also conflict-related sexual violence survivors.[36] Within national member organizations the educational spectrum was even broader and many members had personal or community experiences of marginalization or violence.[37]

Mentoring relationships developed between active Caucus members to bridge the experience gap.[38] Trainings prior to preparatory committee (PrepCom) meetings and retreats including workshops to discuss the Caucus's agenda and toolkit served to prepare Caucus members for lobbying.[39] The wider availability of and extensive online communication facilitated and accelerated information dissemination with member organizations worldwide, and helped to develop and approve positions for the Caucus' briefing papers and national lobbying strategies.[40]

Coping with Challenges

Over a series of PrepCom meetings, the Caucus' lobbying efforts had gained them a support basis among delegations.[41] Yet, by the time of the Rome Conference, Arab states and the Vatican boycotted the negotiations on the gender policy positions the WCGJ had advocated for, specifically the definitions of gender and forced pregnancy. This opposition nearly stalled the negotiations on gender provisions.[42] Among activist circles these states were supported by an anti-choice organization from North America. Facio holds that the 'presence of these groups in the CICC meetings deprived the Caucus of a safe place to discuss problems and strategies'.[43]

Challenging in Conda's words was that 'the status quo of the law was used by these state negotiators against expanding the scope of crimes to other forms of violations against women with references to existing international agreements recognising these violations being dismissed as merely non-binding soft law'. Relying on this argument, she continues, 'even the concept of gender which had been recognised by the international community and was already being mainstreamed within the UN system was questioned'.[44] Consequently, advances on women's human rights made for example at

[35] Interview with Lorena Fries (n 7).

[36] The diversity was also visible in terms of background knowledge on gender theories as 'some of the women didn't even know what gender was, so it was difficult for them to lobby for a gender perspective'. Facio (n 7).

[37] Parong (n 23).

[38] Legal advisor Copelon and director Facio were repeatedly mentioned as influential mentors.

[39] See, eg, the Caucus's documentary footage on the Sag Harbor retreat on 2–4 December 1999 (n 32).

[40] Veneracion-Rallonza (n 11) 114; ICTR gender adviser Francoise Ngendahayo in an interview on 8 April 2000 describes the support she received from the WCGJ for her work on furthering victim recognition (n 32) box 3214 folder E008976.

[41] Key allies were, eg, Canada, with a WCGJ member as delegate, France, Germany, the Nordic countries, Mexico, and Trinidad and Tobago. Facio (n 7) and Ziaurriz (n 30).

[42] Steains (n 3) 364–75.

[43] Facio 'All Roads' (n 11).

[44] Conda (n 11).

Vienna and Beijing had to be repeatedly reiterated. For the Draft Statute, the gender term was not struck out but re-defined by state delegates as a compromise in terms of binary sex categories despite the WCGJ's lobbying efforts to broaden the definition to acknowledge the societal impact on gender.[45]

Additionally, resource inequalities affected whose voice was heard at the conference. Though by 1998, the Caucus had received external funding, only two groups of fifteen to twenty women divided over five weeks could attend the Rome conference.[46] Finding a regional representational balance was challenging as Obando points out that 'it was voluntary work, covering only the hotel and food. We were all doing everything and it was very tiring.'[47] WCGJ members describe a regular day in Rome as commencing with an early morning assembly to discuss the day's schedule and divide assignments, balancing participation in regional, thematic, and the CICC assembly meetings, monitoring the conference and lobbying delegates before ending the day with a collective debriefing and a group drafting position papers for the next day at night.[48] This required strategic planning on a daily basis which meetings to follow as at times proposals were quickly adopted thereby ending all discussions.[49] Teresa Ulloa Ziaurriz, a Mexican lawyer, describes the intensity of the work: 'I learned in three weeks three times what I learned in six years at university.'

Within the Caucus, but also between state delegates and WCGJ's members, the heterogeneity of the network and collaborative but diverse working approaches contributed to power struggles and frictions. Some Caucus members were familiar with the UN negotiation procedures having previously been involved in the Beijing preparatory work, other UN legal drafting processes, and national political or judicial processes with connections to national political elites.[50] A few Caucus members acted as national delegates during the ICC negotiations taking on a dual role. Others had little experience with international law or came from countries where the feminist agenda and organizations developed only in the late 1980s following political and justice sector reforms.[51] Nonetheless, Spees contends that even for experienced feminist advocates 'in the highly technical and legal arena of the ICC, we were feeling our way in the dark.'[52]

One of the largest divides within the Caucus was between lawyers and non-lawyers. Though diversity in the selection of WCGJ representatives was a conscious strategy, women were faced with a dual power dynamic. Spees emphasizes that 'in the legal negotiations, lawyers had to be relied on in ways that were not always comfortable.

[45] Rome Statute Article 7(2); Frey (n 4) 11–12.

[46] Private donors such as the Ford Foundation, Global Fund for Women, John D and Katherine MacArthur Foundation, UNIFEM, Shaler Adams Foundations, Urgent Action Fund, United Methodists, and the governments of Canada, Germany, Netherlands, and the UK. <http://iccwomen.org/wigjdraft1/Archives/oldWCGJ/index.html> accessed 5 April 2021.

[47] Obando (n 1).

[48] Ziaurriz (n 7); Facio 'All Roads' (n 11); Conda (n 7).

[49] Facio 'All Roads' (n 11).

[50] For example, Copelon, Conda, and Facio were involved in the Beijing Conference and the Committee on the Elimination of Discrimination against Women (CEDAW) Optional Protocol negotiations among others as official state delegates. Spees (n 2), Conda (n 11).

[51] Conda (n 7).

[52] Spees (n 2) 1243.

People are imbued with all this privilege and power that comes with being a lawyer that changes the dynamic.' She further adds that at the negotiation table women's 'voices were not as respected as a white male speaking to these issues who would be heralded as an expert'. Fries describes the atmosphere as

> intimidating, because again it was a legal instance and therefore very formal. When it comes to human rights things are more relaxed. I asked myself 'do we have to transform ourselves to become serious professionals?' I had to buy a suit, little heels and whatever to look like a professional lawyer that allowed me to initiate a dialogue with a lot of men.

Subsequently, some women were unwilling to return to the negotiation sites, instead sending lawyer colleagues, as Facio recalls, who would be involved in discussions over the legal text whereas non-lawyers would 'gather separately to discuss non-legal issues such as a media campaign or how to get more women involved', deepening the imbalance.[53] Nonetheless, due to the focused agenda, tight timeline, and strong outside opposition, Facio maintains that 'issues relating to the balancing of our commonalities with our ethnic, sexual, generational or other diversities did not surface as much as in other conferences'.[54]

The challenges translated also to the communication with the local level, how to make the relevance of the Rome Statute understandable to women on the ground living under different national legal systems. To address the latter issue, the Caucus commissioned a documentary 'If Hope Were Enough' on the WCGJ and the ICC's goals, and a study on regional criminal codes' definitions of rape, genocide, or sexual violence. Also, 'preparing a publication on gender in truth commissions in Latin America helped to model definitions that afterwards were part of different national law reforms'.[55]

Other power dynamics concerned the North–South division and the negotiation language. These affected in Obando's words particularly women from areas with less resources or less familiarity with the UN system, whose work has remained less visible.[56] Legal advocacy in English was reportedly challenging particularly for activists from Latin America, Asia, and francophone countries, hampered further by the lack of resources to hire translators.[57] While tensions within the North–South dynamics are particular of many women movements inside and outside the UN, Obando stressed the importance of openly pinpointing these dynamics despite them remaining undercurrents.

Lobbying efforts did not end post-Rome, though the focus shifted to the Elements of Crime and the Rules of Procedure and Evidence negotiations, the election of judges, and the ratification process on the national level. The WCGJ re-organized as the Women's Initiative for Gender Justice, which continues to monitor and lobby

[53] Facio 'All Roads' (n 11).
[54] ibid.
[55] Parong (n 23); Fries (n 35).
[56] Obando (n 1).
[57] Fries (n 35).

the ICC's work with a narrower mandate.[58] This narrowing of the agenda was a disappointment to members envisioning to carry the transnational movement further to impact women's lives on the ground.[59] However, due to the involvement of most WCGJ members in multiple causes, the majority returned to working at the national level. Nonetheless, specifically Latin American and Asian members continued their collaboration locally to further national law reforms processes.[60] Given the return to the domestic context, and the fact that few Caucus members remained in academia or continued to publish, few WCGJ members have remained part of the global public discourse.

Conclusion

The WCGJ was not the first civil society movement to advocate for women's inclusion in the male-defined field of international criminal law but distinct in creatively connecting human rights and criminal law by using a window of opportunity and structural-bias feminist visions combining activist strategies with legal analysis. Despite organizing only in mid-1997, and access to formal negotiations being limited to state delegates, its persistent activism emphasized not only the inclusion of women's concerns on the substantial but also procedural level in international law. Though not all the WCGJ's demands or wordings were adopted, its activism contributed to the writing of gender crimes into a binding international treaty, opening new spaces for victim inclusion and reparations, civil society involvement, and institutionalizing a role for gender expertise in international criminal institutions.[61]

The Caucus' strategy of providing skilled legal analysis utilizing the language and practices of the field to advocate for their agenda in the centre of international law was informed by national dialogues and the multidisciplinary skills of its members. This approach sought not only to question the prevailing power dynamics in international law but translate the Rome Statute's relevance and make international criminal law accessible to local contexts. Many Caucus members ventured afterwards into other social justice projects using international law. Yet, their marginal visibility post-Rome reflects broader challenges of women's movements in international law that remain unresolved. These included overlapping causes and multiple fronts, a need for highly specialized legal skills to be heard, and the often voluntary nature, limited resources, and thus short time-span of women's movements' work in the background of international law negotiation sites, restraining still the access of many women to these spaces.

[58] See the Initiative's agenda at <https://4genderjustice.org/who-are-we/> accessed 7 December 2020.
[59] Facio 'All Roads' (n 11).
[60] ibid; Fries (n 35); Parong (n 23).
[61] Chappell (n 5) 2.

PART IX
THE MISSING FACES OF THE FACULTY CORRIDORS

26
Sarah Wambaugh
Life at the Frontiers of International Law

Imogen Saunders

In 1934, *Time* magazine announced 'The most expert woman in the world on plebiscites is a US citizen and her name is Sarah Wambaugh.'[1] Wambaugh worked on frontiers, both literal and metaphorical, throughout her life, carving out a position of international expertise acknowledged by her peers and reported on by international press. I stumbled across Wambaugh by chance when exploring my university library. Amidst the 100-year-old records of the establishment of the League of Nations (written by James Brown Scott, a mentor of Wambaugh) stood out a tall and unusually fat book: *A Monograph on Plebiscites*, Sarah Wambaugh, 1920. I realized that in the entire time I had been researching international law works from the early twentieth century, I had never come across one obviously written by a woman.

A trailblazing scholar of international law, a realist, and an optimist, Wambaugh was always aware of the inherently divisive subject matter she specialized in. Frontiers, she wrote, are 'very unhappy places. All of them, unless they are oceans or the highest mountains, are artificial boundaries. They cut across the web of human life and the pulse beats more slowly.'[2] Despite, or perhaps because of, this unhappiness, Wambaugh was an unrelenting globalist, pushing collective action and cooperation as the solution to division and conflict. In this portrait sketch I explore the frontiers on which she lived, wrote, and worked. The chapter starts with a biographical sketch of Wambaugh's career, then sets out some of the challenges she faced, followed by an examination of Wambaugh's advocacy for the international law project. It concludes by looking at the concepts of margins and frontiers in Wambaugh's life and work.

Much of the material is drawn from archival research I undertook in 2019 from two collections held by the Schlesinger Library at Radcliffe College: one donated by the Sarah Wambaugh Estate in 1956,[3] the other from an unknown donor 'discovered in the basement of the Harvard Law Library in 1970'.[4] Many of the papers are in English, but others are in French, Spanish, and German—a reflection of Wambaugh's multilingual skills. The collection contains the physical medals and degrees, as well as an array of newspaper clippings, notebooks, sketches, business cards, receipts, letters,

[1] 'Foreign News: Saar Umpires' (1923) 20 *Time Magazine* 21.
[2] Sarah Wambaugh, 'A New Kind of Frontier' (1923) 108 The Annals of the American Academy of Political and Social Science 174, 174.
[3] Papers of Sarah Wambaugh 1902–1949 A-93, held at the Schlesinger Library ('Papers of Sarah Wambaugh').
[4] The Sarah Wambaugh Papers, 1919–1948 86-M64, held at the Schlesinger Library ('Sarah Wambaugh Papers').

Imogen Saunders, *Sarah Wambaugh* In: *Portraits of Women in International Law.* Edited by: Immi Tallgren, Oxford University Press. © Imogen Saunders 2023. DOI: 10.1093/oso/9780198868453.003.0026

speeches, telegrams, and notes. The collections focus mostly on Wambaugh's various roles in observing and advising on plebiscites pre-Second World War, as well as her speaking tours and academic writings. The focus of this sketch follows these lines. There is very little in the collection of a personal nature—the most that can be gleaned is that Wambaugh remained close to her parents throughout her life and never married. 'Plebiscites', she once quipped in a letter, 'like matrimony, are not to be undertaken lightly or informally.'[5] It appears she followed her own advice well.

Biography

Sarah Wambaugh was born in 1882 Cincinnati, Ohio, moving to Cambridge, Massachusetts, in 1892 when her father, Eugene Wambaugh, was appointed Professor of Law at Harvard University. Wambaugh undertook her Bachelor of Arts at Radcliffe College, graduating in 1902. After graduation she held various positions including with the Women's Education and Industrial Union and the Woman's Peace Party.[6] In 1916 Wambaugh returned to Radcliffe and undertook a Master's in International Law. At the conclusion of her studies, Wambaugh suggested to James Brown Scott, then the Director of the Carnegie Endowment for International Peace, a monograph on all proposed or established plebiscites since the French Revolution. Wambaugh explained that her studies had lit an interest in the struggle 'between the two conflicting doctrines of popular sovereignty and of the right of conquest' but took pains to reassure Scott although she was 'a believer in nationality and the right of people to dispose of themselves in questions of transfer of territory', she would present the facts in the monograph as 'fairly and impartially as possible'.[7] This ambitious proposal was ultimately approved: Wambaugh later recounted Scott entrusting 'me, an untried historian, the job of writing my first book on international plebiscites'.[8] That book became the 1,000-plus page tome that first intrigued me, and kick-started Wambaugh's career in international law.

Wambaugh started working in the League of Nations Secretariat in 1920,[9] and was the representative of various periodicals at the Assemblies in 1922, 1923, and 1924.[10] However, it was in 1925 when Wambaugh was appointed an expert advisor to the Peruvian Government on the proposed Tacna-Arica plebiscite (1925–1926), that her career on the physical frontiers began. Following her time in Peru, Wambaugh was appointed one of three experts to draft regulations for the Saar Plebiscite a member

[5] Letter, S Wambaugh to A Sweetser dated 12 February 1934, contained in Sarah Wambaugh Papers (n 4) 5–4 'Folders on the Saar Question . . .'.

[6] Radcliffe College, *Half a Hundred Radcliffe Women: What They Have Given to the World* (Radcliffe College 1922) 8.

[7] Letter, Sarah Wambaugh to James Brown Scott, 18 September 1917, contained in Papers of Sarah Wambaugh (n 3) A-93.

[8] American Society of International Law, 'Address by Miss Sarah Wambaugh' (1946) 40 American Society of International Law Proceedings 149, 149.

[9] Sarah Wambaugh, 'Why the League Succeeds' [1934] The Civic Pilot 9.

[10] Representative of the *Woman Citizen* in 1922, the *Atlantic Monthly* in 1923 and the *Century Magazine* in 1923: 'Sarah Wambaugh—Biographical Note' contained in the Papers of Sarah Wambaugh (n 3) 1–4 'Folders and Scrapbooks on the Tacna-Arica Question 1925, International Papers'.

Figure 26.1 Photo taken of archival material contained in the Papers of Sarah Wambaugh, 1919–1948. Reading Room, Schlesinger Library, 25 October 2019.
Source: Courtesy of Imogen Saunders with permission from Schlesinger Library.

of the Saar Plebiscite Commission (1934–1935), an advisor to the chief United States Mission to observe elections in Greece (1945–1946), and to the UN Plebiscite Commission to Jammu and Kashmir (1949). Her work was well publicized and highly regarded: she was the first woman to lecture at the Académie de Droit International,[11] she published three more books on plebiscites,[12] received six honorary degrees,[13]

[11] In 1928.

[12] Sarah Wambaugh, *La Pratique Des Plébiscites Internationaux* (Librairie Hachette 1928); Sarah Wambaugh, *Plebiscites since the World War, with a Collection of Official Documents* (Carnegie endowment for international peace 1933); Sarah Wambaugh, *The Saar Plebiscite, with a Collection of Official Documents* (Harvard University Press 1940).

[13] Ohio State University (1935), Western Reserve University (1935), Tufts College (1935), University of Geneva (1935), Columbia University (1936), and Russell Sage College (1938).

various memberships,[14] and five medals/honours.[15] Contemporaneous reviews of her books[16] describe them as 'unique and invaluable',[17] 'intelligently and conscientiously executed',[18] and 'a detailed and authoritative account'.[19] A review in the American Journal of International Law described Wambaugh as 'the leading authority on international plebiscites'.[20] During this time, Wambaugh was a regular on the lecture circuit in the United States, represented by William B Feakins, a New York agent who organized speaking tours for 'notables'.[21] This activity saw Wambaugh become something of a minor celebrity, featuring in newspapers and magazines across the Anglophone world.[22]

Challenges

Wambaugh's success was not easily gained, and her gender often exacerbated the difficulties. When first considered for the Saar plebiscite, Wambaugh was approached to take on a secretarial role, which she rejected, arguing instead to Arthur Sweetser, the inaugural president of the League of Nations, that she should be a fully-fledged Commissioner: 'the position which I have enjoyed for years as the chief and almost the only writer on international plebiscites (it is a time for truth rather than modesty) would make such an appointment appear fitting . . . '.[23] Sweetser agreed, although warned the Council may prefer to appoint Wambaugh as an advisor rather than a

[14] Member of the Honour Society of the University of Lima (1926), Members of the Sociedad de Geografica de Lima (1926), Honorary Diploma from La Sociedad Patriotica Tacna, Arica y Tarapaca de Arequipa (1926), Fellow of the American Academy of Arts and Sciences (1944).

[15] Gold Decoration of the City of Arequipa (1925), Knight Cross, first class, Austrian Order of Merit (1935), Officer, Order of the Sun, Peru (1937), Heraldic Order of Christopher Columbus of the Dominican Republic (1939), Knight, Royal Order of the Phoenix, Greece (1949).

[16] In addition to those set out in (nn 17–20) below, Wambaugh's books received reviews in many other top journals including *American Historical Review*, *American Political Science Review*, *Cambridge Law Journal*, *Harvard Law Review*, *Journal of Comparative Legislation and International Law*, *Political Science Quarterly*, and *The Journal of International Relations*.

[17] Carlton JH Hayes, 'Reviewed Works: A Monograph on Plebiscites, with a Collection of Official Documents by Sarah Wambaugh, James Brown Scott; The Employment of the Plebiscite in the Determination of Sovereignty. by Johannes Mattern' (1921) 15(2) AJIL 337, 338.

[18] David Jayne Hill, 'Reviewed Work: A Monograph on Plebiscites, with a Collection of Official Documents by Sarah Wambaugh' (1921) 21(4) Columbia Law Review 398, 401.

[19] Frank M Russell, 'Review: The Saar Plebiscite, with a Collection of Official Documents by Sarah Wambaugh' (1941) 13(1) The Journal of Modern History 126, 127.

[20] Hans J Morgenthau, 'Review: *The Saar Plebiscite*. With a Collection of Official Documents. By Sarah Wambaugh.' (1940) 34(3) AJIL 541, 541.

[21] 'W.B. Feakins, Head of Lecture Bureau; Founder of Agency Here Dies at 74—Arranged Tours for Many Notables' *The New York Times* (26 March 1946) 23.

[22] See eg 'Plebiscite Expert' *The Maitland Daily Mercury* (New South Wales) (26 September 1934) 3; 'Women in the World' *The Australian Women's Mirror* (5 February 1935) 20; 'Clever American who is Widely Recognised as Plebiscite Authority' *The Daily News* (Western Australia) 9 April 1936, 9; Sarah Wambaugh, 'Poland and Danzig: Balanced Claims to Freedom—A Just Compromise' *The Times* (11 July 1939) 15; 'Equal Opportunity for All' *Northern Whig* (Ireland) (29 December 1934) 11; 'Saarlanders Plump for Return to Reich' *Gloucester Citizen* (England) (15 January 1935) 1; 'World Judgment' *Shields Daily News* (England) (12 July 1939) 4.

[23] Letter, S Wambaugh to A Sweetser dated 12 February 1934, contained in Sarah Wambaugh Papers (n 4) 5–4 'Folders on the Saar Question . . . '.

Commissioner.[24] This is indeed what happened—the League of Nations Council voted to appoint Wambaugh as the technical advisor attached to the Commission (alongside three men from Switzerland, the Netherlands, and Sweden).[25] While not attracting the title of Commissioner, this was a paid, non-secretarial position (albeit paid less than the male Commissioners).[26]

At other times, modifications were made to Wambaugh's travel plans on account of her gender: for example, on being dispatched to Peru for the proposed Tacna-Arica plebiscite, Wambaugh learned she was to arrive separately and several days after the rest of the Commission for the 'sake of (her) comfort'.[27] Wambaugh protested, asking instead to 'take what chance there may be of discomfort' in order to meet with General Pershing, the United States appointed arbitrator to the dispute, as soon as possible.[28]

Even when Wambaugh achieved success, the reporting of it was almost inevitably gendered.[29] This ranged from the innocuous to the dismissive: in *The New York Times*, Harold B Hinton opened a story on Wambaugh in 1946 with the words 'If you are looking for a life work involving agreeable working hours, little competition and a good deal of distinction, you might take up plebiscites', later referring to her 'soft brown eyes'.[30] It should be noted that Hinton's assessment of the agreeableness of plebiscites was not shared by those involved in the process. General Pershing, writing to Wambaugh to commend her on an article she had published in *The New York Times* following their work on the Tacna-Arica plebiscite, commented that 'I feel quite as fit as ever, but under no circumstances would I like to undertake another Tacna-Arica job.'[31]

Although faced with these gendered challenges, as the educated, multilingual child of a Harvard professor, Wambaugh undoubtedly benefitted from her class and background. Indeed, her father's position was used to smooth her travel and research, with his friends writing to introduce Wambaugh to contacts on the ground.[32] Wambaugh sometimes struggled to escape her father's shadow: even when she gave her address to

[24] Letter, A Sweetser to S Wambaugh dated 13 March 1934, contained in Sarah Wambaugh Papers (n 4) 5–4 'Folders on the Saar Question ... '.

[25] League of Nations 'Saar Territory: Preparatory Measures in View of the Plebiscite. Appointment of the Plebiscite Commission Note by the Secretary General' Doc No C 313.1934.VII 17 July 1934 copy contained in Sarah Wambaugh Papers (n 4) 5–3 'Folders on the Saar Question ... '.

[26] The salary for Commissioners was set at 16,900 French francs a month, while Wambaugh received initially 10,000 francs per month which was raised to 11,500 francs a month in September 1934 due to her acting as a Deputy Commissioner 'more frequently than had been anticipated': League of Nations, 'Saar Territory: Salary of the Technical Advisor attached to the Plebiscite Commission' Doc No C.414.1934.VII 18 September 1934 copy contained in Sarah Wambaugh Papers (n 4) 5–3 'Folders on the Saar Question ... '.

[27] Letter from S Wambaugh to Manual de Freyre y Santander dated 17 July 1925, contained in Sarah Wambaugh Papers (n 4) 1–8 'Folders and Scrapbooks on the Tacna-Arica question, 1925'.

[28] ibid.

[29] See, eg, Dorothy G Wayman, 'Cambridge Woman Has Flair for Clothes and Plebiscites' *The Boston Globe* (1 October 1938) 11.

[30] Harold B Hinton, 'She Specialises in Plebiscites' *The New York Times* (17 February 1946) 95.

[31] Letter, John J Pershing to S Wambaugh dated 14 October 1926, contained in Sarah Wambaugh Papers (n 4) 2–2 'Folders and Scrapbooks on the Tacna-Arica question, 1925'.

[32] See, eg, letter from Thomas W Palmer Jnr to E Pombo dated 27 May 1928 contained in Sarah Wambaugh Papers (n 4) 2–2 'Folders and Scrapbooks on the Tacna-Arica question, 1925'.

the American Society of International Law, she was introduced in the context of her father's prior address.[33]

In addition to challenges posed by being a woman working in the international sphere in the early twentieth century, Wambaugh's work on politically divisive frontiers carried inherent danger. While working for the Peruvian Government on the Tacna-Arica plebiscite, Wambaugh detailed the political violence and intimidation surrounding the vote.[34] Her notes reveal that she became aware she was being followed by the Chilean secret police.[35] Wambaugh met with the Chilean intendent of Tacna, Luis Barceló Lira, to determine 'the Chilean explanation of their own attitude'. Wambaugh asked Barceló Lira why the secret police were following her. The response was, in her words, delivered in a humorous vein: 'You must have done something. But you are mistaken. They could not be secret police. When I was a young man I too followed the ladies.'[36] Wambaugh does not detail in her notes whether she was convinced by this explanation, but reading between the lines it would seem not.[37]

During her work on the Saar plebiscite, Wambaugh stayed in Saarbrücken, the capital of Saar territory. The plebiscite question was whether Saar would remain with France or return to Germany, which, in 1934, was under the Nazi party. A division quickly emerged between the Nazi party and an opposing union of American anti-Nazi and anti-Fascist bodies called the Committee of the Status Quo.[38] The Gemeindeausschüsse (community committees) pulled together to observe the plebiscite were heavily dominated by the Deustche Arbeitsfront (the Nazi Labour organization) although Wambaugh observed that all was not as it seemed: 'It is true that the great number of the members of the Gemeindeausschüsse belong to the Deutsche Front, but that does not mean that some of these very men do not support the Status quo.'[39]

Nazi attempts at intimidation during this period are well documented,[40] and Wambaugh herself was targeted by anti-Semitic, pro-Nazi papers (erroneously) describing her as Jewish.[41] Nonetheless, Wambaugh saw the conduct of the Saar plebiscite as an ultimate success, due to the presence of the League of Nations. When asked whether Germany had been successful in intimidating voters, Wambaugh replied

[33] Remarks by President Hyde, Proceedings of the Annual Meeting (1946) 141 American Society of International Law Proceedings 149.

[34] Newspaper clipping titled 'Chile Severely Criticized by a Woman Investigator: Sarah Wambaugh, Counsel for Peru, Discusses Bitter Tacna-Arica Dispute' contained in Sarah Wambaugh Papers (n 4) 2–1 'Folders and Scrapbooks on the Tacna-Arica question, 1925'.

[35] Draft Cable by S Wambaugh dated 7 August 1925, contained in Sarah Wambaugh Papers (n 4) 1–8 'Folders and Scrapbooks on the Tacna-Arica question, 1925'.

[36] S Wambaugh, 'Memorandum on Conversation with the Intendente Barcelo Lira September 30th 1925' contained in Sarah Wambaugh Papers (n 4) 1–4 'Folders and Scrapbooks on the Tacna-Arica question, 1925'.

[37] William E Skuban, 'Lines in the Sand: Nationalism and Identity on the Peruvian-Chilean Frontier' (University of New Mexico Press 2007) 176.

[38] 'Nazi Foes Unite to Keep Saar in Status Quo' 20 September 1934 *Jewish Daily Bulletin* 8.

[39] Letter, S Wambaugh to Emily G Balch dated 20 October 1934, contained in Sarah Wambaugh Papers (n 4) 5–2 'Folders on the Saar question'.

[40] See eg 'Nazi Intimidation in Saar Increases: Commission Informs League It Feels Obliged to Adopt Extraordinary Measures' 12 November 1933 *The New York Times* 2.

[41] 'Streicher Assails U.S. Saar Official: Anti-Semite's Paper Finds Miss Wambaugh, a Protestant, Is a 'Member of the Jewish Race' 2 July 1934 *The New York Times* 2.

'They certainly tried in the Saar, but they didn't really succeed there. The answer to them in the Saar was chiefly absolute confidence that we inspired in our voters in the secrecy of the casting and the counting of the ballot, plus the fact that we got in an international police force.'[42] This belief in the necessity of international cooperation and an overarching international institution can be seen throughout Wambaugh's life.

The International Law Project

Wambaugh was committed to the international law project, first as a passionate advocate for the League of Nations, and subsequently for the United Nations. Wambaugh's involvement with the League of Nations began early: although she did not attend the Paris Peace Conference, when President Wilson attended in 1919, 'he carried with him advance sheets of a part of Miss Wambaugh's work, which had been in preparation during the preceding year'.[43] Wambaugh arrived at the League of Nations in 1920. There are few papers from this period in the archives,[44] however it is clear from later correspondence that it left an ongoing deep impression on her. Wambaugh regularly corresponded with Erik Colban, the Director of the League of Nations Minorities' section.[45] Their letters show a clear, mutual, and explicit plan to advance the ideals of peace, and the auspices of the League specifically.[46] Colban lauded Wambaugh's advocacy in the United States: 'We could hardly overestimate the value of having in important American intellectual centres such friends of our Organisation as you are.'[47]

In fulfilling this role, Wambaugh advocated to United States politicians. She met with President Coolidge in 1925 and took the opportunity to advance the case of the League of Nations. Wambaugh believed, following her speaking tour around the United States, that domestic antagonism to the League was dying and the United States was 'ripe for leadership'.[48] According to Wambaugh, Coolidge was supportive of United States membership of the League but saw it as premature.[49] Wambaugh, however, saw the opportunity 'to sow a seed which may come to some useful fruition in the future'.[50]

[42] S Wambaugh, 'New Tools for Peaceful Settlement' 31. Manuscript of article with questions and answers contained in the contained in Sarah Wambaugh Papers (n 4) 7–6 'New Tools for Peaceful Settlement'.

[43] Hayes (n 17) 337.

[44] One exception is a letter written to Wambaugh in 1920 by a representative from the Northern Epirotes community in America: Letter, Constant Patos to S Wambaugh dated 14 November 1920, contained in Sarah Wambaugh Papers (n 4) 4–2 'Folder of Notes concerned with the League of Nations and Territorial Questions 1920–26'.

[45] There is correspondence between Wambaugh and Huntington Gilchrist in the archived papers.

[46] Letters between S Wambaugh and E Colban contained in Sarah Wambaugh Papers (n 4) 4–2 'Folder of Notes concerned with the League of Nations and Territorial questions 1920–26'.

[47] Letter, E Colban to S Wambaugh dated 19 June 1921 contained in Sarah Wambaugh Papers (n 4) 4–2 'Folder of Notes concerned with the League of Nations and Territorial questions 1920–26'.

[48] S Wambaugh, 'Memorandum, Interview with President Coolidge' dated 24 March 1925, contained in Sarah Wambaugh Papers (n 4) 3–1 'Folder of material on U.S. adherence to the League of Nations and the Irish Mandate for Armenia, 1919–1925'.

[49] For an overview of the general divide in the United States between 'legalists' and 'institutionalists', see Gary B Ostrower, 'Review: Historical Studies in American Internationalism' (1971) 25(4) International Organization 899.

[50] ibid.

In 1932 she wrote to then Governor Franklin D Roosevelt, lamenting his lack of support for the League or for any international political cooperation beyond trade goals.[51] Judging by Roosevelt's response, her pleas were unsuccessful,[52] although it is rumoured he later considered her for the post of Ambassador to Austria.[53]

Margins and Frontiers

Wambaugh's scholarly works were received with great acclaim. Wambaugh's works have been consistently cited in works on plebiscites and self-determination.[54] However, her role in the development of international law and its institutions is not widely known. Wambaugh is mentioned briefly in some histories of international law[55] but excluded from others.[56]

While Wambaugh's marginalization seems inevitably gender-based, the concept of marginalization in the context of self-determination requires discussion of another ground as well—that of race. Wambaugh did not often explicitly speak of race or comment upon the somewhat inconsistent application of the principles of self-determination. For instance, it appears she never publicly wrote or commented on the League of Nations (and then UN) mandate over Southwest Africa which operated throughout her international career, and when questioned about India, she prevaricated 'I am going to dodge it!'.[57] However, reported extracts from a speech to the Bowdoin Institute of Social Sciences in 1929 did address racial minorities, giving her perspective on the difference between European and United States approaches:

[51] Letter, S Wambaugh to FD Roosevelt dated 31 March 1932, contained in Sarah Wambaugh Papers (n 4) 3-1 'Folder of material on U.S. adherence to the League of Nations and the Irish Mandate for Armenia, 1919–1925'.

[52] Letter, FD Roosevelt to S Wambaugh dated 22 April 1932, contained in Sarah Wambaugh Papers (n 4) 3-1 'Folder of material on U.S. adherence to the League of Nations and the Irish Mandate for Armenia, 1919–1925'.

[53] 'Plebiscite Expert' *The Maitland Daily Mercury* (26 September 1934) 4.

[54] See eg MK Nawaz, 'The Meaning and Range of the Principle of Self-Determination' 1965 Duke Law Journal 82; Nathaniel Berman, 'But the Alternative Is Despair: European Nationalism and the Modernist Renewal of International Law' (1993) 106(8) Harvard Law Review 1792; Hurst Hannum, 'Self-Determination in the Post-Colonial Era' in Donald Clark and Robert Williamson, *Self Determination: International Perspectives* (Palgrave Macmillan 1996) 12; Karen Knop, 'Of the Male Persuasion: The Power of Liberal Internationalism for Women' (1999) 93 American Society of International Law Proceedings 177; Emmanuel Vianes, 'What Is an International Post-Belligerent Administration?' (2015) 25(3) Indiana International and Comparative Law Review 421; Karen Knop, 'A Market for Sovereignty: The Roles of Other States in Self-Determination' (2017) 54 Osgoode Hall Law Journal 491.

[55] See, eg, Dorothy Jones, *Toward a Just World: The Critical Years in the Search for International Justice* (University of Chicago Press 2002); Paolo Amorosa, 'The American Project and the Politics of History: James Brown Scott and the Origins of International Law' (Doctoral Dissertation presented for examination at the University of Helsinki, 14 April 2018).

[56] See, eg, Stephen C Neff, *Justice among Nations: A History of International Law* (Harvard University Press 2014). Heff at ibid 371–72 gives examples of 'prominent liberal figures in international law who pressed for increased cooperation with the leagues of Nations' including Wambaugh's contemporary Manly Hudson.

[57] Transcript of lecture and questions and answers given by Wambaugh titled 'New Tools for Peaceful Settlement', 36 contained in Sarah Wambaugh papers (n 4) 7-6 'New Tools for Peaceful Settlement'.

> Where Europe for the most part has tried assimilation of racial minority, through persecution and force, forbidding them their own language and religion and attempting to cripple them economically, we have depended on tolerance of language and religion, good wages, and the public school.[58]

While Wambaugh recognized the links between race and self-determination—in the same speech she noted approvingly that 'far fewer minorities' were 'under alien rule than before the world war' and that those minorities were now 'guaranteed far greater rights'[59]—she did not view this link as necessary in all cases.[60]

It is tempting to further examine Wambaugh's attitudes to race and gender from the suffrage of the plebiscites she advised upon. All included equal voting rights for women—a fact that, as Karen Knop points out, is remarkable 'given that the treaties were negotiated when women's suffrage was still the exception'.[61] I was unable to glean from her papers what influence Wambaugh had on this. However, it is clear she supported universal suffrage. In speaking of the Treaty of Versailles, Wambaugh noted 'the franchise was provided, the requirements, in the Treaty, and everybody was to vote regardless of sex, I am glad to say, over twenty'.[62]

Certainly, Wambaugh was aware of the impact of her gender and indeed the role of women in international law. Wambaugh corresponded with key women's institutions[63] and other women working in international law and relations.[64] Wambaugh also exchanged letters with Dorothy Kenyon on the suffrage of women in Greece.[65] It is fair to say, though, that Wambaugh's public work mostly (and I venture carefully) had no overt feminist agenda. There is one exception to this in her papers: 'The New Frontiers of Diplomacy'.[66] It is undated, but contextual paragraphs suggest it was written sometime in 1941. Wambaugh writes:

> The stake of women in peace and international goodwill has been at least as a great as that of men. Their contribution has been far less, and for a reason. Women, disenfranchised, did not, save in exceptional cases, possess a world horizon [...] This simple concept the World War shattered at one blow. [...] Ever since then they have been

[58] 'Holds We Could Aid in League Problem: Miss Sarah Wambaugh, in Talk at Bowdoin, Discusses Protection of Minorities' *The New York Times* (8 May 1929) 2.

[59] ibid.

[60] S Wambaugh, *The Saar Plebiscite* (n 12) v.

[61] Karen Knop, *Diversity and Self Determination in International Law* (Cambridge University Press 2002) 284.

[62] S Wambaugh, 'New Tools for Peaceful Settlement' (n 57) 46.

[63] See eg the Women's International League for Peace and Freedom: see letters between Emily Belch and S Wambaugh contained in Sarah Wambaugh Papers (n 4) 5–2 'Folders on the Saar Question'. Wambaugh also corresponded with the Joint Standing Committee of Women's International Organizations, the Women's Advisory Council of the League of Nations Union, the Swiss Association of University Women, and the Women's Department of the National Civic Federation. Correspondence contained in Sarah Wambaugh Papers (n 4) 5–4 'Folders on the Saar Question'.

[64] Including Elizabeth Wiksemann: Letter, S Wambaugh to Elizabeth Wiskemann dated 6 October (no year) contained in Sarah Wambaugh Papers (n 4) 5–4 'Folders on the Saar Question'.

[65] Letter, Dorothy Kenyon to S Wambaugh dated 30 August 1934 and draft letter, S Wambaugh to Dorothy Kenyon (undated) contained in Sarah Wambaugh Papers (n 4) 4–3 'Folders of Notes on the Dismemberment of the Turkish Empire ...'.

[66] Contained in Papers of Sarah Wambaugh (n 3) A-93–4.

> attempting to make up for lost time, by informing themselves, formulating programs and by circulating petitions in their support.[67]

Possibly Wambaugh viewed herself in this same situation. Her post-First World War life was extraordinarily committed to advancing, communicating, and educating the ideals of peace, international cooperation, and collective security, even though her country for much of her career was resistant. In 1923, she wrote 'There is still a frontier—not on our map, but in the world of international relations—and the pioneers in Geneva are trying to work out paths in the wilderness. They are working at great odds, and alas, we are not with them.'[68]

Under the threatening clouds of the forthcoming Second World War, Wambaugh maintained her belief that peace could only be achieved through the rule of law:

> Only by banding tougher of the pacific minded nations, great and small, to protect each other against attack by another can democracy wipe out the frontier between chaos and law, and establish orderly relations between nations.[69]

Wambaugh died in 1955,[70] when the modern international law project and the age of the UN was still in its infancy. Before her death, however, she acted as advisor to the UN mission to observe elections in Greece as well as to the UN Plebiscite on Jammu and Kashmir. In comments made hours after her return from Greece, Wambaugh's deep pleasure that her own country was finally contributing to international law was clear: 'As Americans we may well take pride in this first venture of ours in international cooperation.'[71]

67 S Wambaugh, 'The New Frontier of Diplomacy' contained in Papers of Sarah Wambaugh (n 3) A-93–4.
68 S Wambaugh (n 2) 177.
69 S Wambaugh, 'The New Frontier of Diplomacy' (n 67).
70 'Dr. Sarah Wambaugh, Plebiscite Expert Who Advised League and U. N., Is Dead' *The New York Times* (13 November 1955) 88.
71 Remarks by S Wambaugh, Proceedings of the Annual Meeting (1946) 141 American Society of International Law Proceedings 149.

27

Exile and Access

Lilly Melchior Roberts and the Infrastructures of International Law

*Alexandra Kemmerer**

Introduction

Lilly Melchior Roberts was a master of systematic classification. Meticulously accurate and conceptually precise, it seems very unlikely that she would ever have introduced herself as an 'international lawyer'. However, in her two consecutive and yet closely interwoven legal careers, as a young corporate lawyer in one of Berlin's premier transnational law firms in the years of the decline of the Weimar Republic and as a law librarian and bibliographer in one of the world's leading law libraries at the height of the Cold War, she was involved in the construction of international order. And part of an intellectual project of international legal studies that encompassed the disciplinary fields of international law, comparative law, and the emerging field of European legal integration, inspired by conceptual frameworks and perspectives of transnational law.

Was her contribution just an auxiliary one? The complementary and supportive work of a 'law school aide', as the local newspaper titled her obituary?[1] Was Lilly Melchior Roberts a 'counterpart in law librarianship' to the 'corps of distinguished German émigré academic lawyers'?[2] In this chapter, on a biographical journey from Hamburg and Berlin to Ann Arbor, challenging well-worn distinctions between content and infrastructures, scholarship and practice, academia and administration, Lilly Melchior Roberts is portrayed as a transformative actor in her own right, an intellectual protagonist in the emerging field of transnational (and, in particular, European) legal studies as well as in the disciplines of comparative and international law.

* I would like to thank David Armitage, Jochen Abraham Frowein, Karen Knop, and Immi Tallgren for their thoughtful engagement with, and helpful comments on draft versions of this chapter. Thanks also to Dorothea Hauser for providing access to the files of the Stiftung Warburg Archiv/Warburg Archive Foundation (SWA) and introducing me to Kösterberg, and grateful thanks to the archivists at Bentley Historical Library, University of Michigan, for their always excellent support. I learned about Lilly Melchior Roberts in conversations with Eric Stein and Virginia Rhine Stein during my first visit in Ann Arbor, but it was Immi Tallgren who encouraged me to write about her life and work some years later. Elsa Roberts Auerbach and William Melchior Roberts generously shared memories of their mother. I am grateful to them all.

[1] 'Law School Aide, Mrs. Roberts, Dies', *Ann Arbor News* (29 June 1966).

[2] Michael Taggart, 'Gardens or Graveyards of Scholarship? Festschriften in the Literature of the Common Law' (2002) 22 Oxford Journal of Legal Studies 227–52, 244 (fn 85).

Alexandra Kemmerer, *Exile and Access* In: *Portraits of Women in International Law.* Edited by: Immi Tallgren, Oxford University Press. © Alexandra Kemmerer 2023. DOI: 10.1093/oso/9780198868453.003.0027

Networks

Lilly Melchior Roberts was born on 19 April 1903 in Hamburg, Germany, as daughter of the merchant Willy Morris Elkan and Elsa Warburg, a scion of the prominent German-Jewish banking family. Following the death of her father in 1914, she acquired the name of her stepfather, Sally George Melchior, a noted arbitrator and expert on private international law and conflict of laws.[3] 'Her childhood and youth might have come from a chapter in Thomas Mann's *Buddenbrooks*: a sheltered, even a spoiled life against the background of a wealthy Hanseatic city, surrounded by the cultural and intellectual traditions of an old family', her Michigan colleague and fellow émigrée scholar Vera Bolgár would later write in an obituary.[4] Yet, the horizon of Melchior's cosmopolitan family network widely transcended the narrow worlds of the declining Hanseatic bourgeoisie portrayed in Mann's 1901 novel that won him a Nobel Prize in 1929.

M. M. Warburg & Co., founded in 1798 by the brothers Moses Marcus and Gerson, emerged in the Golden Wilhelmine Era of the Second German Empire and the Weimar Republic as 'the largest and most prestigious private bank in Germany'.[5] The 'fourth generation' that Melchior's mother had been born into marked the peak of the family's wealth, reputation, and influence—and the era of the Warburg Bank as a global player: Elsa Warburg's cousin Max led the banking empire as senior partner, his brothers Felix and Paul moved to the United States (where Paul became the main initiator of the Federal Reserve System, and director of the Council on Foreign Relations at its founding in 1921), and their eldest brother Aby established the legendary *Kulturwissenschaftliche Bibliothek Warburg*, transforming art history with his new method of iconography. The Warburgs were noted for accomplishments in biochemistry, botany, political activism, economics, investment banking, law, physics, classical music, art history, pharmacology, physiology, finance, private equity, and philanthropy—and they were held together by strong family traditions.[6]

When women were finally admitted to the legal professions in Germany in July 1922,[7] Melchior had just begun her legal studies at the University of Freiburg, as one of

[3] Marion Röwekamp, Melchior-Roberts, Lilly, in Marion Röwekamp, *Juristinnen. Lexikon zu Leben und* Werk (Nomos 2005) 258–60, at 258. In this chapter, names reflect biographical ruptures and transformations. In the following, I will, in biographical contexts, use the name which the protagonist herself used during the respective period, but refer to her as Lilly Melchior Roberts when I write about her substantive contributions on a more abstract level (in accordance with the author's name as provided in her posthumous book).

[4] Vera Bolgár, 'In Memory of Lilly Melchior Roberts', *International Law Library Review*, Ann Arbor 1967, 44–46, SWA, attachment to letter Gerald Roberts to Eric M Warburg, 9 April 1967 (EMW Correspondence Ro-Ry 1967–1970; F-10309).

[5] Ron Chernow, *The Warburgs: The Twentieth Century Odyssey of a Remarkable Jewish Family* (Random House 1993) 322.

[6] See, eg, Eduard Rosenbaum and Ari J Sherman, *M.M. Warburg & Co., 1798–1938: Merchant Bankers of Hamburg* (C Hurst 1979); Chernow, *The Warburgs* (n 5). On the Warburgs' political role and agenda, see also Alfred Vagts, 'M. M. Warburg & Co. Ein Bankhaus in der deutschen Weltpolitik 1905–1933' (1958) 45 Vierteljahresschrift für Sozial- und Wirtschaftsgeschichte 289–388.

[7] Marion Röwekamp, *Die ersten deutschen Juristinnen. Eine Geschichte ihrer Professionalisierung und Emanzipation (1900–1945)* (Böhlau Verlag 2011).

only a handful of female law students. She went on to Hamburg and Berlin, passed her first state examination in Hamburg 'with distinction' ('*gut*') on 1 March 1928, and her bar exam on 18 December 1931 'with distinction' ('*fast gut*'), trained by fellow pioneer lawyer Cläre Meyer.[8] Formally accepting a position as an associate judge (assessor), she immediately applied for leave, joined the prestigious law firm Dr hc Albert Pinner, Dres Walter Schmidt II, Wilhelm Beutner, Friedrich Kempner in Berlin and lived at Matthäikirchplatz 8–10 in Berlin's 'posh Tiergartenviertel'.[9]

Lilly Melchior belonged to a first cohort of formally educated 'professional women' in her family, with her older stepsister Emilie excelling as an outstanding lawyer.[10] Yet, while Warburg women of previous generations had not worked in paid professional positions, there was in fact a long tradition of female leadership in the family (bank).[11] Lilly Melchior's preeminent mentors and professional role models were, however, her stepfather 'Sally' George Melchior and his brother Carl Melchior, a lawyer, banker, Warburg partner, and expert adviser to the German government.[12]

When George Melchior, a leading proponent of inter-war German private international law, wrote his seminal treatise on the foundations of the field, Lilly Melchior was part of a remarkable group of (otherwise only male) young law clerks and academic assistants who helped prepare and edit the volume, among them Walter Julius Derenberg and Konrad Duden. The contribution of the *Rechtsreferendarin* (law clerk) Melchior stood out as 'particularly extensive and profound' ('*besonders lange und eingehend*').[13]

George Melchior's brother Carl had been appointed as head of the German financial policy delegation for the Versailles Peace Treaty, and became friends with the British negotiator John Maynard Keynes.[14] For the next fourteen years, he played 'a role at every major reparations conference'.[15] In 1930, he had been named Vice-President of the newly established Bank for International Settlements in Basel.[16] As an excellent corporate lawyer, Lilly Melchior collaborated with Carl Melchior and Max M Warburg on the complex details of the German standstill agreement (*Stillhalteabkommen*)

[8] Röwekamp, Melchior-Roberts, Lilly (n 3) 259.

[9] For a colourful sketch of the Tiergarten area, see Jeremy Adelman, *Worldly Philosopher. The Odyssey of Albert O. Hirschman* (Princeton University Press 2014) 27–28. Another rising German lawyer, FA Mann, had spent a stage of his practical legal training ('Referendariat') with Pinner, Kempner, Beutner in 1931, see Frederick Alexander Mann, *Life and Cases. Manuscript of an Autobiography* (Wolfgang Ernst ed, Bonn University Press 2021) 37.

[10] Marion Röwekamp, Melchior-Braun, Emilie, in Röwekamp (n 3) 254–57.

[11] Lilly Roberts' great-grandmother Sara Warburg (1805–1884) led the bank for nine years as sole director (alleinige Geschäftsführerin, see Referendariat (n 9)) following the death of her husband in 1854, see Chernow, *The Warburgs* (n 5) 3–20; Gabriele Hoffmann, *Max. M. Warburg* (Ellert und Richter 2009) 21–23.

[12] On Carl Melchior, see now: Dorothea Hauser and Christoph Kreutzmüller, *Carl Melchior. Ein jüdischer Vorkämpfer eines europäischen Friedens*, Stiftung Warburg Archiv, Hamburg 2019 (Booklet documenting an exhibition at the Jewish Museum Berlin, 18 January–30 June 2019); Verein für Hamburgische Geschichte (ed), *Carl Melchior—Ein Buch des Gedenkens und der Freundschaft*, JCB (Mohr Siebeck 1967).

[13] George Melchior, *Die Grundlagen des Deutschen Internationalen Privatrechts* (Walter de Gruyter 1932, reprinted 1971 and 2016) III–IV, at IV; conversation with Elsa Roberts Auerbach, 14 June 2021.

[14] Carl Melchior, *Der Friedensvertrag und die deutschen Finanzen* (Ackermann & Wulff 1919); John Maynard Keynes, *Two Memoirs: Dr. Melchior: A Defeated Enemy* and *My Early Beliefs* (August M Kelley 1949) 32–33.

[15] Chernow, *The Warburgs* (n 5) 211.

[16] Hauser and Kreutzmüller, *Carl Melchior* (n 12) 44–47.

concluded between foreign creditors and German bank debtors in August 1931 in Basel, and on subsequent standstill agreements.[17] Later, she kept Carl Melchior's picture on her desk in Ann Arbor.[18] In the last year of her life, weakened by illness, she worked hard co-editing his *Gedächtnisschrift*, and corresponded intensely with the lead editors, discussing the substantive quality of various contributions.[19] In the book, her name is not mentioned.

As the fragile Weimar democracy collapsed, Max Warburg and Carl Melchior were among those leading the Jewish community's nationwide self-help efforts, and developed sophisticated financial schemes enabling the transfer of capital abroad, under rapidly worsening conditions and mounting pressures.[20] In early summer 1933, growing anxiety could be felt in Warburg's Hamburg offices, but also within the wider family network. Arrests and suicides, intimidation, and harassment had become everyday realities.

On 30 June 1933, Lilly Melchior was dismissed from her 'frozen' position as an associate judge in Hamburg according to §3 of the infamous Law for the Restoration of the Professional Civil Service (*Gesetz zur Wiederherstellung des Berufsbeamtentums*). When the family and the bank's senior leadership consulted about her professional prospects and reached out to former partners in Belgium and the Netherlands, it quickly became apparent that the influence, reputation, and social capital of the house of Warburg was rapidly melting away in Europe.[21] Melchior continued to practice as a lawyer until 1935.[22] In 1936, she worked as legal adviser for Swedish Match in Stockholm, then in The Hague, and after November 1936 as paralegal with Dr Alfred Kauffmann in London.[23]

On 24 January 1939, shortly before her emigration to the United States, Lilly Melchior married the German–Jewish banker Gerhardt Richard Rosenthal in London, of the Berlin Kuczynski bank which had been founded by his grandfather Wilhelm in 1869, and 'aryanised' in 1938 (Gerhardt changed their surname to 'Roberts' when arriving in the US, and his first name into Gerald in 1942).[24] In March 1939, she prepared her immediate emigration, boarding for New York on 15 May 1939.[25]

[17] SWA, Max Warburg to Albert Palache, 24 July 1933 (Auswandererakten 1933 Me; Laufende Nr 10.867).

[18] SWA, Lilly Melchior Roberts to Eric M Warburg, 6 February 1957 (EMW Korrespondenz Me—Mz bis 31. März 1965).

[19] Verein für Hamburgische Geschichte (ed), *Carl Melchior*; SWA, Gerald Roberts to Eric M Warburg, 11 February 1967 (EMW Correspondence Ro-Ry 1967–1970; F-10309).

[20] Dorothea Hauser, 'Banking on Emigration: Reconsidering the Warburg Bank's Late Surrender, Schacht's Protective Hand, and other Myths about Jewish Banks in the "Third Reich"' in Christoph Kreutzmüller and Jonathan R Zatlin (eds), *Dispossession: Plundering German Jewry, 1933–1953*, University of Michigan Press 2020) 148–66, 148.

[21] SWA, Elsa Warburg to Max Warburg, 14 July 1933; Hans Meyer to Carl Melchior, 22 July 1933; Carl Melchior to Frits Fentener van Vlissingen, 30 July 1933; Frits Fentener van Vlissingen to Carl Melchior, 2 August 1933; Max Warburg to Albert Palache, 24 July 1933 (Auswandererakten 1933 Me; Laufende Nr 10.867).

[22] Röwekamp, 'Melchior-Roberts, Lilly'(n 3) 259.

[23] ibid; Bolgár, 'Lilly Melchior Roberts'(n 4) 44–46, 44.

[24] Röwekamp, 'Melchior-Roberts, Lilly'(n 3) 259; Bolgár, 'Lilly Melchior Roberts'(n 4) 44–46, 44.

[25] SWA, Lilly Sara Melchior to MM Warburg & Co, 5 March 1939 and 9 March 1939, Lilly Sara Rosenthal to MM Warburg & C, 2 May 1939 (Auswandererakten 1939 Me-Mer; 53-III-1).

Exile

In New York, Lilly Roberts briefly worked as a secretary and translator, then studied library science at Columbia University.[26] For a female German Jewish lawyer in her late thirties, arriving at the peak of Jewish emigration from Europe, a law firm career was entirely out of reach.[27] Even for highly qualified male professionals who had worked and lived in various European countries, prospects on the United States labour market were bleak. Many German émigré lawyers set out on new careers as law librarians.[28]

In March 1940, upon recommendation of Yale international law professor Edwin Borchard, Roberts was appointed research assistant at the University of Michigan Law School where just two major comparative legal projects had taken off under the aegis of Hessel Yntema: Ernst Rabel's monumental treatise on the conflict of laws—and an analytical concordance of the negotiable instruments laws of the Latin-American countries. Roberts was 'eminently qualified to give assistance to both projects. Her European legal background, combined with the complete mastery of the German, French, English, and Spanish languages and the classical bases of her education proved to be of invaluable help to the two great comparatists (…)'.[29]

The German-Jewish émigré Ernst Rabel, founding director of the Kaiser Wilhelm Institute for Foreign and International Private Law in Berlin who had found refuge at the University of Michigan Law School in 1939, credited Lilly Melchior Roberts' 'devoted services' in the preface to the first volume of *The Conflict of Laws: A Comparative Study*.[30] In 1942, she was appointed research associate in international law, and continued her work for Rabel and Yntema until summer 1945, when she took up the position of legal bibliographer and counsellor for the acquisition of foreign legal materials that she held until the end of her life, substantially contributing to the emerging field of transnational (and, in particular, European) legal studies as well as to the disciplines of comparative and international law.

In Ann Arbor, Michigan, the independent lawyer from Weimar-Era Berlin settled into a new life as scholar–librarian, and working mum—and only took short unpaid leaves when her son William Melchior (Mel) was born in November 1942, and her daughter Elsa Ann in November 1945.[31] In the small worlds of a traditional and, in the

[26] Röwekamp, 'Lilly Melchior Roberts' (n 3) 259.

[27] Ernst C Stiefel and Frank Mecklenburg, *Deutsche Juristen im amerikanischen Exil (1933–1950)* (Mohr Siebeck 1991) 1–8; Frank Mecklenburg, 'The Occupation of Women Emigrées: Women Lawyers in the United States' in Sibylle Quack (ed), *Between Sorrow and Strength: Women Refugees of the Nazi Period* (Cambridge University Press 1995) 289–99.

[28] Stiefel and Mecklenburg, *Deutsche Juristen* (n 27) 11–13; Melchior Roberts is mentioned in Mecklenburg, 'Occupation of Women Emigrées' (n 27) 291.

[29] Bolgár, 'Lilly Melchior Roberts' (n 4) 44–46, 46.

[30] Ernst Rabel, *The Conflict of Laws: A Comparative Study. Volume One. Introduction: Family Law*, Preface (University of Michigan Press 1945) XIV. On Rabel's productive, but—also due to his outsider position in the Law School and his precarious financial situation—isolated and depressing exile in the Midwest: Bernhard Grossfeld and Peter Winship, 'The Law Professor Refugee' (1992) 18 Syracuse Journal of International Law and Commerce 4–20, 8–11; Rolf-Ulrich Kunze, *Ernst Rabel und das Kaiser-Wilhelm-Institut für ausländisches und internationales Privatrecht 1926–1945* (Wallstein 2004) 231–33. On Yntema, see Mathias Reimann, 'Hessel E. Yntema', in Roger K Newman (ed), *The Yale Biographical Dictionary of American Law* (Yale University Press 2009) 608.

[31] Röwekamp, 'Melchior-Roberts, Lilly' (n 3) 259.

1940s and 1950s, still somewhat provincial Midwestern Law School, a world of stay-home faculty wives organizing tea parties with sponge cakes, potluck dinners on home game weekends, and barbecues for the closely-knit faculty community built by their men,[32] female scholar–professionals like Roberts and Bolgár were rare appearances in an (almost) all-male academic environment.[33] And so they remained in post-war Western legal academia and its professional circles.

Roberts excelled not only as legal information expert, but also proved herself a networker in the best Warburg traditions.[34] Her hospitality, first in a small furnished apartment at 1917 Geddes Avenue and later in the welcoming Roberts house at 11 Ridgeway Street, overlooking the Arboretum, became proverbial among friends and colleagues.[35]

Access

A close reading of Lilly Melchior Roberts' publications takes her reader back into the distant pasts and strange materialities of the pre-digital era, when law libraries were still cathedrals of books, filled with voluminous treatises, precious manuscripts, and long display shelves showcasing the colourful covers of law journals in many languages. But her writings also resonate with today's worlds of citations, metrics, scores, reputation measurement, and rankings where access is everything—and where expert librarians and bibliographers are still important architects of (now entirely digital) information structures, and intermediaries, scouts, and gatekeepers in the factories of law and legal knowledge production.[36]

Lilly Melchior Roberts' work was much appreciated by those who benefitted from it, both at Michigan Law and in the wider professional networks of United States law librarians. She was honorary member of the Kappa Beta Pi legal sorority, of the American Association of Law Libraries, of the Committee on Foreign Legal Periodicals, served with distinction on the Committee on Foreign Law Indexing of the American Association of Law Libraries, and played a leading role in the establishment of the *Index to Foreign Legal Periodicals*.[37] In 1957, she was granted sabbatical research leave.[38]

[32] Conversation with Virginia E Rhine Stein, Ann Arbor, July 2016. Virginia Rhine Stein (1922–2020), an alumna of Columbia's Russian Studies Program, communications expert, and art historian, came to Ann Arbor in 1956 with her husband, Eric Stein, who had left the State Department for a professorship at the Law School. See also her self-authored obituary: 'Obituary Virginia E Stein' (*Dignity Memorial*, February 2020) <https://www.dignitymemorial.com/obituaries/ann-arbor-mi/virginia-stein-9033356> accessed 15 January 2021.

[33] Vera Bolgár served as research assistant and associate at the University of Michigan Law School from 1949 until 1987, and as the Executive Secretary and Associate Editor of the *American Journal of Comparative Law* from its founding in 1949 until 1971. She had been the first woman to receive a doctorate in legal science from the University of Budapest. See also Alfred F Conard, 'Vera Bolgar (1913–2003)' (2004) 52 American Journal of Comparative Law 5–7.

[34] Her address is listed in Alberto Dines, Israel Beloch, and Kristina Michahelles (eds), *A rede de amigos de Stefan Zweig: sua última agenda (1940–1942)* (Memória Brasil 2014).

[35] Bolgár, 'Lilly Melchior Roberts' (n 4) 44–46, 46. See also Beverly J Pooley, 'In Memory of Lilly Melchior Roberts' American Law Library Journal (May 1967) 162–63, 163.

[36] See Michael Chiorazzi (ed), The Role of Citation in the Law: A Yale Law School Symposium (AALL Publication Series No. 86, William S. Hein & Co., Inc. 2022).

[37] Bolgár, 'Lilly Melchior Roberts' (n 4) 44–46, 45. See also Pooley (n 35) 'Lilly Melchior Roberts' 163.

[38] Röwekamp, 'Melchior-Roberts, Lilly' (n 3) 260.

Her *Bibliography of Legal Festschriften*, posthumously published in 1972, and the preceding shorter contributions on the somewhat obscure genre of *Festschriften* (and the bibliographical challenges it poses)[39] became 'classics' among law librarians and scholars interested in legal knowledge production and methodologies.[40] While legal *Festschriften*— 'collections of legal essays by different writers, issued to honour an individual, an institution (eg a code or a court) or an event (such as the founding of a law school, a lawyers meeting)'[41]—might today be a genre of rapidly declining relevance, Lilly Melchior Roberts' agenda is as timely today as it was half a century ago: making valuable sources of information accessible to a wide readership, even (and in particular) if they are 'buried' in marginal(ized) publications, written in 'lesser-used' languages, overlooked by reviewers, and inconsistently referenced and catalogued.[42] She also had a keen sense of the symbolic relevance of *Festschriften* as commemorative venues, as legal landmarks of ritualized professional celebration—and would not have been surprised by their potential to build and strengthen a transnational judicial community strongly committed to European legal integration.[43]

As a legal-cultural broker, she introduced foreign legal thought and scholarship to America, and the intricacies of United States law to visiting scholars and interlocutors from Europe and beyond. Melchior Roberts' review of the German Association of Comparative Law's 1965 *Bibliography of German Law* is an example of scholarly craftmanship, prudent judgement, and reflexive situatedness.[44] It mirrors a dialogical, conversational hermeneutics which not only accepts, but cultivates the plurality of the law and its interpretative communities.[45]

When Roberts arrived at the University of Michigan in March 1940, the Law Library was in the midst of a transformation that developed a modest, primarily American collection (of about 80,000 volumes in 1928) into one of the foremost foreign, comparative, and international law collections in the United States, and globally (with about 350,000 volumes in 1965).[46] The collaborative efforts of Dean Henry Bates and Law

39 Lilly Melchior Roberts, *A Bibliography of Legal Festschriften* (Martinus Nijhoff 1972) (posthumously completed by Herbert L Bernstein); Lilly Melchior Roberts, 'The Importance of Legal Festschriften for Work in International and Comparative Law' (1962) 11 American Journal of Comparative Law 403–11; Lilly Melchior Roberts, 'Legal Festschriften' (1963) 56 Law Library Journal 47–60.

40 Peter Macalister-Smith and Joachim Schwietzke, 'Festschriften in Public International Law: An Annotated Bibliographical Compilation of Titles, 1930-2000/2001' (2002) 71 Nordic Journal of International Law 349–430, 358–99; Taggart, *Gardens or Graveyards* (n 2) 244, fn 85. Only her systematic bibliographical work is mentioned in Helmuth Schulze-Fielitz, 'Festschriften im Dienst der Wissenschaft', in Helmuth Schulze-Fielitz, *Staatsrechtslehre als Mikrokosmos* (Mohr Siebeck 2013) 204–15, 10, fn 41.

41 Melchior Roberts, *A Bibliography of Legal Festschriften* (n 39) VIII.

42 Melchior Roberts, 'The Importance of Legal Festschriften' (n 39).

43 Antoine Vauchez, *Keeping the Dream Alive: The European Court of Justice and the Transnational Fabric of Integrationist Jurisprudence* (2012) 4 European Political Science Review 51–71.

44 Lilly Melchior Roberts, 'Review (of German Association of Comparative Law, ed, Bibliography of German Law, Karlsruhe 1964)' (1965) 63 Michigan Law Review 1121–26. See also Lilly Melchior Roberts, 'Building up a Small Foreign Law Collection for Small and Medium-Sized Libraries' (1960) 53 Law Library Journal 379–85.

45 On a Gadamerian concept of conversational hermeneutics, see Alexandra Kemmerer, 'Sources in the Meta-Theory of International Law: Hermeneutical Conversations' in Samantha Besson and Jean d'Aspremont (eds), *Oxford Handbook on the Sources of International Law* (OUP 2017) 469–90.

46 Margret A Leary, 'Building a Foreign Law Collection at the University of Michigan Law Library, 1910–1960' (2002) 94 Law Library Journal 395–425; Elizabeth Gaspar Brown, *Legal Education at Michigan, 1859–1959* (University of Michigan Law School 1959) 359–87, 920–30.

Library director Hobart R Coffey were part of a larger project: Michigan's Program in International Legal Studies that had commenced in 1919. The Legal Research Building with its striking architecture and decorative splendour opened its doors in 1931, providing space and atmosphere for a 'lawyer's laboratory'.[47] Coffey—a true Renaissance person, well-travelled and fluent in six languages, tirelessly working to identify and acquire books, primary sources, and the documents of international organizations—was the perfect role model of an entrepreneurial scholar–librarian.[48]

The spirit of Coffey's Law Library resonated well with Roberts' personality, habitus, and social capital. As the Law Library's bibliographer (since 1945), she could build on her work as research assistant to Rabel and Yntema. Her Latin-American legal bibliography 'became the basis of the now famous Latin-American collection of the University of Michigan'.[49] She also 'made a number of valuable compilations of the legal materials available for teaching and research of various countries, including a preliminary survey of Latin-American legal materials, comprising roughly 2,000 pages; also surveys of the laws of Turkey (1956); Lebanon (1956); Egypt (1956); Greece (1958); surveys of the laws of the Balkan countries and those in the Middle-East; two surveys of the Japanese and Dutch collections of the University of Michigan Law Library, both concluding with desiderata of further necessary acquisitions, and a compilation of current foreign legal periodicals received by the University of Michigan Law Library (1958)'.[50]

When retrospective collection building was nearing its completion in 1960, 'gradually the primary responsibility for selecting individual titles shifted to reference librarians who were assigned collection development responsibilities for areas of the world congruent with their reference work duties'.[51] For Lilly Roberts, this organizational shift created an opportunity to engage even more actively with emerging structures of transnational legal integration in (Western) Europe, and to integrate these into the Law Library's collection.

She worked closely with Eric Stein, a Czech-Jewish émigré lawyer who had joined the Law School in 1955 from the State Department, hired by Dean E Blythe Stason to direct and coordinate Michigan's Program of International Legal Studies. The Program, initiated by Dean Bates in 1919, had been boosted by a major (and unexpectedly generous) Ford Foundation grant, enabling profound internationalization of teaching and research on foreign, international, and comparative law, and in the new field of the law of European integration. Stein designed classes, seminars, and cutting-edge research projects involving a number of faculty members, established networks for exchange and collaboration and brought European students, faculty, and eminent practitioners to the Law Quadrangle.[52]

[47] *Law Students' Handbook 1957–58* (University of Michigan Law School 1957) (cited in Brown, *Legal Education* (n 46) 382).
[48] Leary, 'Foreign Law Collection' (n 46) 40325.
[49] Bolgár, 'Lilly Melchior Roberts' (n 4) 44–46, 45.
[50] ibid 44–46, 45–46.
[51] Leary, 'Foreign Law Collection' (n 46) 423.
[52] On Michigan's Program in International Legal Studies, the Ford Foundation's International Legal Studies, and on Eric Stein and his *American Enterprise in the European Market*, see my forthcoming book *Law, Exile, and the Making of a Transnational Constitution: A Life of Eric Stein* (in progress). For a concise profile of Stein, see also Anne Boerger, 'At the Cradle of Legal Scholarship on the European Union: The Life and Early Work of Eric Stein' (2014) 62 American Journal of Comparative Law 859–92.

Roberts helped create and expand the research infrastructures which fostered Michigan's leadership as a centre for European, international, and comparative law during the Cold War and beyond.[53] As an intermediary and networker, she opened new avenues to obtain access to legal documents and materials, published and unpublished, including brand-new Court decisions from Karlsruhe or Luxemburg, draft directives, press communications, policy papers, teaching materials, grey think tank publications. In 1957, the Michigan Law Library became the first library in the United States to be designated a depository for publications of the European Coal and Steel Community.[54]

Whenever Stein and other faculty members travelled in Europe, mapping new legal developments and meeting scholars and practitioners, diplomats, and politicians, Roberts was an indispensable interlocutor in the background. She helped canvassing evolving areas of law (and their protagonists), sought to discover the best means to acquire books on the want lists and to set up reliable methods to acquire material in the future. Roberts visited courts, universities, and libraries, contacted former students and visiting scholars, instructed travelling faculty on how to set up contacts and curate networks.

The law school and its library benefitted from her old friendships and renewed professional contacts, particularly in Germany. One of her correspondents, Walter Strauß (1900–1976), the architect of the post-war reorganization of the judicial system and its personnel in the Federal Republic and one of the very few German-Jewish lawyers in high public office,[55] had worked closely with Carl Melchior as a legal adviser at the *Reichswirtschaftsministerium*. From 1963 until 1970, he served as German judge at the European Court of Justice.[56]

Throughout her life, Roberts remained in close contact with the two key protagonists of her family's 'fifth generation' with whom she also openly discussed the strange dynamics of public silence in post-war (and post-holocaust) Germany: the great networker and transatlanticist Eric Warburg, a confidant of former United States High Commissioner John Jay McCloy who had returned to Hamburg in 1956, and his cousin Siegmund George Warburg, a firm supporter of European economic integration who played an influential role in the development of merchant banking and the rise of the City of London in global finance. Roberts introduced friends and colleagues to them both, and to the legendary Warburg estate on Hamburg's Kösterberg.[57] She

[53] Lilly Roberts joined Stein's and Alfred Conard's first explorative research trip to Europe; she connected them to her former colleague Friedrich Kempner in Paris und corresponded regularly about acquisitions. See, eg, Eric Stein to Lilly Melchior Roberts, 16 July 1958, Eric Stein Papers, Bentley Historical Library, University of Michigan.

[54] Leary, 'Foreign Law Collection' (n 46) 422, with further reference.

[55] Markus Apostolow, *Der 'immerwährende Staatssekretär'. Walter Strauß und die Personalpolitik im Bundesministerium der Justiz 1949–1963* (Vandenhoeck & Ruprecht 2019). On Strauß and his connections to the Warburg firm and family, see also Friedemann Utz, *Preuße, Protestant, Pragmatiker. Der Staatssekretär Walter Strauß und sein Staat* (Mohr Siebeck 2003) 36–37.

[56] Vera Fritz, 'Walter Strauss (1900–1976)', in Vera Fritz, *Juges et avocats généraux de la Cour de Justice de l'Union européenne (1952–1972)* (Vittorio Klostermann 2018) 317–324.

[57] SWA, Lilly M Roberts to Eric M Warburg, 16 January 1961[sic] (1962, ak); Eric M Warburg to Lilly Melchior Roberts, 18 June 18 1963, and 23 August 23 1963 (EMW Correspondence Me—Mz bis 31. März 1965).

also brought her family's legacy to Michigan: 148 volumes from the library of her stepfather George Melchior, 'distinguished author and international lawyer in The Hague', were accepted as a gift by the Law Library in 1950, including five 'Treaties of Peace with Germany, 1919–1920'.[58]

Acquisitions and Desiderata

When Lilly Roberts died, after months of severe illness, on 27 June 1966, her death, though not unexpected, came as a shock to friends and colleagues.[59] Obituaries and epitaphs tell us about her vitality and responsiveness, her professional discipline and sense of duty, her creativity and affection, and her firm determination to build a new life 'in the country that had adopted her and that she had adopted'.[60]

Konrad Zweigert, the comparatist, paid tribute to the 'scholar of comparative law, and librarian', but above all to the daughter and law firm associate, to the research assistant, student, mother, and wife, 'an extraordinary woman, (…) a harmonious master of understanding people, things, destinies and factual problems, (…) a helpful guide to all the foreign lawyers who came to Ann Arbor to further their education, their teaching and learning at this ideal study site in the cloistered atmosphere of the idyllic university town'.[61]

After the catastrophe of the *Zivilisationsbruch*, Lilly Melchior Roberts, the sharp legal mind who had begun her career at the height of Weimar 'interwar feminism', had rebuilt a life in which she could realize her personal talents and values.[62] She had remained true to her humanist and emancipatory ideals, to her commitment to law as a means to achieve justice and equality. Her closest friends included women scholars who were directly discriminated against because they were women, among them the Swiss astronomer Edith Alice Müller who was long denied a faculty appointment despite her achievements. 'My mother was the object of innumerable micro-aggressions because she was a woman', her daughter told me, and I have seen traces, and sometimes explicit manifestations of such aggressions in letters, notes, and protocols of the men Melchior Roberts worked with, and for. One of the 'life lessons' she taught to her daughter was a pointed admonition: 'Never learn to type, because if you are a good typist, you will end up typing things that men have written.'[63]

Her substantial contribution to international law scholarship and the legacy of her reflexive approach to legal knowledge production in a world of multiple and

[58] Law Library Reports, cited in Leary, 'Foreign Law Collection' (n 46) 419.

[59] Bolgár, 'Lilly Melchior Roberts'(n 4) 44.

[60] SWA, Peter Fleck, 'In Memory of Lilly Melchior Roberts. From the Memorial Service held at the First Unitarian Church, Ann Arbor, Michigan, on Thursday, June 30, 1966', 2 (EMW Correspondence Ro-Ry 1967–1970; F-10309).

[61] Konrad Zweigert, 'Lilly Melchior Roberts (1903–1966)' (1967) 31 Rabels Zeitschrift für ausländisches und internationales Privatrecht 77 (my translation).

[62] On Weimar-era feminism and 'new women', see Jan Bürger and Petra Gehring (eds), *Feminismus zwischen zwei Kriegen* (Zeitschrift für Ideengeschichte XIV/Winter 2020)(CH Beck 2020).

[63] e-mail Elsa Roberts Auerbach to Alexandra Kemmerer, 11 June 2021, on file with the author; conversation with Elsa Roberts Auerbach, 14 June 2021.

Figure 27.1 Lilly Melchior Roberts at Lake Lucerne, Switzerland, 1937.
Source: Collections of Leo Baeck Institute.

competing cultures and imaginations of (international) law remains to be explored and acknowledged, as well as her 'rooted cosmopolitanism', firmly grounded in traditions and habitus of an immensely fruitful, yet ever precarious and ultimately failed German–Jewish symbiosis.[64]

[64] The notion 'rooted cosmopolitanism' is borrowed from James Loeffler, *Rooted Cosmopolitans. Jews and Human Rights in the Twentieth Century* (Yale University Press 2018).

28
Lea Meriggi
A Fighter—For the Wrong Cause

Serena Forlati

Introduction

Lea Meriggi was the first—for several decades the only[1]—woman to hold a chair of International Law in Italy, and among the first in Europe.[2] Meriggi was born in Liège in 1902 and graduated in Law at the University of Genoa on 14 December 1924.[3] At a time when Italian women could not vote and faced several restrictions in access to legal professions—with the judiciary totally precluded[4]—she pursued a career in International Law, travelling throughout Europe for teaching and research, earning a scholarship from the Carnegie Foundation in 1931 and a prize from the Accademia d'Italia.[5] She authored several books and articles on private and public international law, in line with the Italian scholarly tradition in which they are part of the same discipline. Her works were published in several languages—Italian of course, but also German,[6] French,[7] and English[8]—which she all spoke (she could also read Spanish).[9]

[1] Only in 1979, two other women (Maria Rita Saulle and Maria Laura Picchio Forlati) qualified as professors in international law.

[2] The precursor was Suzanne Bastid, who earned a chair in International Law at the University of Lyon in 1933 (see above, Chapter 17).

[3] Information kindly provided by Ms Gaia Riitano, of the Archives Office of the University of Milan, where Meriggi enrolled as a student in humanities in 1925 and later taught Private International Law (her teaching programmes 1930–31 and 1934–35 are still archived: see https://archivi.unimi.it/oggetti/IT-UNIMI-ST0035-006360_meriggi-lea/ accessed 19 January 2021.

[4] Admission to the judiciary was possible only in 1963.

[5] Founded by Mussolini in 1929 as a 'fascist' replacement of the prestigious Accademia dei Lincei, which regained its autonomy only at the end of the Second World War.

[6] 'Das Wesen des internationales Rechts und seine Beziehungen zum inneren Recht der Staaten', (1932) XVI *Zeitschrift für Völkerrecht*; *Faschismus und Recht: Vortrag, gehalten in der 2. Vollsitzung der Akademie für Deutsches Recht am 29 January 1934* (reviewed by Hans-Helmut Dietze in 1935(1) *Archiv für Rechts- und Sozialphilosophie*); Lea Meriggi, 'Recht und Philosophischer Gedanke nach der Philosophie Francesco Orestanos' (1939) 32 Archiv für Rechts- und Sozialphilosophie.

[7] Lea Meriggi, 'Les qualifications en droit international privé' (1933) 28 Revue de droit international privé 212; Lea Meriggi, 'Considérations sur le problème des sources du droit des gens' (1934) III-15 Revue de droit international et de législation comparée 492–529.

[8] Lea Meriggi, 'Conflicts of Law—A Theoretical Approach' (1934) 14 Boston University Law Review.

[9] See the matriculation sheet filed with the Ministry of National Education.

Serena Forlati, *Lea Meriggi* In: *Portraits of Women in International Law*. Edited by: Immi Tallgren, Oxford University Press.
 DOI: 10.1093/oso/9780198868453.003.0028

Figure 28.1 Lea Meriggi. Courtesy of Donata Kalliany von Kallian, private archive.

Lea Meriggi was appointed as '*professore straordinario*'[10] at the University of Ferrara in 1940[11] and led a rather extraordinary life for the time in many other respects. Reportedly a charismatic and fascinating woman, she faced several personal, financial, and professional struggles also due to her unconventional choices—and to her being a woman in a profession then dominated by men.[12]

This notwithstanding, she is far from being an iconic figure; she is mentioned in surveys on Italian International Law scholarship in the inter-war period—but not in

[10] Newly appointed professors who had not been confirmed in their role (a step that typically came after three years in office) were titled 'extraordinary'. Meriggi's teaching activities in Germany were recognized in Germany so she was treated as '*professore ordinario*' from her first appointment in Ferrara (decree of the Rector of the University of Ferrara, 23 July 1942).

[11] The appointment was with effect from 16 November 1940.

[12] Her only contemporary colleague was Luisa Riva Sanseverino, a prominent labour lawyer: see P Passaniti, 'Luisa Riva Sanseverino', available at www.treccani.it/enciclopedia/luisa-riva-sanseverino_(Dizionario-Biografico)/accessed 19 January 2021. Teresa Labriola, a well-known women's rights activist and later a fascist acolyte, earned a '*libera docenza*' in Philosophy of Law in 1900 but never obtained a tenured position: see M Tesoro, 'Labriola, MT', available at www.treccani.it/enciclopedia/teresa-labriola_%28Dizionario-Biografico%29/ accessed 19 January 2021. Other women were part of the Italian intellectual establishment of the time: the main example is probably Margherita Sarfatti, journalist, renowned art critic, Mussolini's longtime lover, and first biographer: see PV Cannistraro, BR Sullivan, *Il Duce's Other Woman* (William Morrow & Co 1993).

a positive light nor for the value of her writings, but rather for her political affiliation.[13] In a context where being a member of the Fascist Party was a must for every civil servant and the few professors who refused to take the oath to faithfully serve the king and that party were expelled from Italian universities,[14] the mainstream attitude among international lawyers was not one of open opposition:[15] nonetheless, Lea Meriggi stood out as one of the few staunch supporters of the fascist regime among the international law academic community.[16]

An Unconventional Life

Lea Meriggi shared this political faith with her lifetime companion, Count Cesare Vernarecci di Fossombrone. Originally a family friend, he was a university professor too, ran a successful law firm and later worked as legal advisor to the Italian embassy in Berlin, and as de facto diplomatic representative in Cracow. He was also a married man, who never separated from his wife at a time when divorce was hardly conceivable in Italy. Unsurprisingly, Meriggi's family of origin strongly opposed this bond. Lea also struggled to earn financial independence, teaching at different universities in Italy and Germany. In 1934 she wrote Vernarecci: 'The motto of my life could be "fight". Not a single event was easy, not a single achievement came for free. Everything was paid for, deserved, labelled by the most bitter tears.'[17] Challenges came also in the following years: in May 1940 she sought a marriage of convenience with Eugen Kalliany von Kallian, Hungarian aristocrat and friend of Vernarecci, to 'give a name' to the baby she was expecting—the daughter of the latter, whose birth in December 1940 prompted Meriggi to seek a postponement of her inaugural lecture in Ferrara. Kalliany disappeared immediately after the wedding.

Lea Meriggi then became a single mother: never accepting any financial support from Vernarecci, she entrusted her baby to a nanny when commuting to work, struggling to make ends meet and to be treated on an equal footing with her male colleagues in terms of revenue. In several exchanges with the Ministry for National Education she sought the reinstatement of a family allowance as the sole support for her daughter,

[13] G Bartolini, 'The Impact of Fascism on the Italian Doctrine of Public International Law' (2012) Journal of International Legal History 237; Alessandro Somma, *I giuristi e l'asse culturale Roma-Berlino* (Klostermann 2005) 412; Giulio Bartolini, 'Italian Legal Scholarship of International Law in the Early Decades of the Twentieth Century' in Bartolini (ed), *A History of International Law in Italy* (OUP 2020) 127, 163. Other international lawyers took refuge in silence (as Anzilotti) or in strictly positivist approaches as a way to avoid publicly criticizing the regime: see Francesco Salerno, 'La *Rivista* e gli studi di diritto internazionale nel periodo 1906–1943' (2007 vol. 90) Rivista di diritto internazionale 305–43, fn 23.

[14] In 1931, twelve of approximately 1200 university professors refused to take the oath. The Catholic Church and the Communist Party encouraged their affiliates to comply to oppose the regime from the inside.

[15] While Dionisio Anzilotti was never a member of the Fascist Party (see Salerno, 'La *Rivista*' (n 13) fn 23), other international lawyers endorsed fascism, including professors of Jewish descent who were nonetheless expelled from the Universities in 1938, such as Angelo Piero Sereni: see Francesco Salerno, 'Gli anni ferraresi di Angelo Piero Sereni', in Angela Di Stasi et al, *Liber Amicorum per Massimo Panebianco* (Editoriale Scientifica 2020) 653–67 at 656.

[16] Salerno, 'La *Rivista*' (n 13).

[17] Letter to Cesare Vernarecci di Fossombrone, Frankfurt am Main, 4 December 1934. Courtesy of Ms Donata Kalliany von Kallian. Here and elsewhere, translations are by this author.

noting that her husband was 'absent for reasons of war' and that her male colleagues could obtain this allowance without difficulty.[18] Differently, she was asked to prove that her spouse did not earn an income; the Ministry also sought information in this regard from the Royal Commissioner (Rector) of the University of Ferrara.

The '*assegno di famiglia*' (family allowance) was eventually confirmed by Vallerini, Director-General of the Ministry of Education of the Republic of Salò,[19] with a decree of 23 September 1944 which also records Meriggi's death. The disruptions of the war had affected her life as one of so many others. While she lived in Bologna during the first years of the conflict, she had resettled with her daughter to Lonato, a village near Lake Garda, to avoid allied bombings which targeted the bigger cities of Northern Italy. Having contracted typhus, and with no appropriate medication, she died there on 14 July 1944.

Teaching and Writings: A 'Positivist' Approach Permeated by Ideology

Lea Meriggi obtained her '*libera docenza*' (that is, was entitled to teach) by unanimous deliberation in 1930.[20] Thereafter, she taught International Law, Italian Law, and Italian Legal Terminology at the University of Frankfurt from 1930—when she held her inaugural lecture on 'The essence of international law and its relationship to States' domestic law'—to 1936,[21] while also lecturing in Private International Law at the University of Milan between 1931 and 1934. Moreover, she taught Italian Law in Berlin (1932–34).[22] Her programme for the courses of Italian Law covered topics such as 'Mussolini and the fascist revolution', 'class struggle', 'social democracy and revolutionary industrial relations', 'the principle of corporativism', 'the national fascist party', 'value of the fascist party and its relationship to the State'.

Her work was apparently valued by her superiors,[23] but in 1935 she was denied permission for a contract renewal,[24] possibly as part of the more general Nazi policy towards women which ultimately led to the expulsion of women academics from universities.[25] Lea Meriggi then moved to Modena, where she taught International Law between 1935 and 1940. She sought a career advancement by participating in competitive selection processes in Cagliari, Catania, and Urbino[26] before obtaining the Chair

[18] Meriggi to Director General Vallerini, on 18 April 1944, complaining that the family allowance had been suspended since 1942 as her husband was not mentioned in the family record.

[19] Formally headed by Mussolini and backed by the Nazi occupying forces, the Republic of Salò ruled Northern Italy between 1943 and 1945.

[20] See her application for teaching international law in Ferrara of 3 November 1939.

[21] Meriggi taught in Frankfurt from 1931 to at least 1935.

[22] The course outlines and their translation are in Meriggi's personal files in Ferrara and Rome.

[23] In a letter of 6 July 1934, Professor Heymann, Director of the Berlin Institute for Foreign Law and Law and Economics described her teaching as 'fully successful'.

[24] Mr Matthias Lorenz, Goethe University Frankfurt Archives Service, kindly reported: 'On 24 September 1935, the Reich and Prussian Ministry of education denied to extend her permission of holding lectures in Frankfurt and Berlin' (letter of 10 February 2020, on file with the author).

[25] Claudia Koonz, *Mothers in the Fatherland—Women, the Family and Nazi Politics* (Routledge 2014).

[26] See Salerno (n 15) 658, fn 34.

in Ferrara—where she replaced Angelo Piero Sereni, who had been expelled in 1938 due to the infamous 'racial laws'.[27]

Lea Meriggi was a fairly prolific writer: she lists around forty works by 1940, on different issues of public and private international law. An early essay, *Stati Uniti d'Europa* (United States of Europe), discusses the legacy of Giuseppe Mazzini and Carlo Cattaneo—as well as Immanuel Kant—to advocate the idea of a federation of European states, led by the United States of America and built around the League of Nations, expressly commending the admission of Germany to the League.[28] Later works dealt in a more critical perspective with the League of Nations and its reform,[29] as well as with several other topics: recognition of states;[30] the Lithuanian-Polish conflict;[31] the advisory competence of the Permanent Court of International Justice;[32] the relationship between domestic and international law;[33] the sources of international law;[34] the effects of treaties on third states;[35] nationality;[36] the theory of private international law[37] and, in the same field, characterization[38] and bankruptcy.[39]

Meriggi defined herself as a positivist and her writings are at least formally anchored in the positivist tradition typical of Italian scholarship of the time,[40] with frequent references to the official fascist stances. For instance, her entry on nationality in the *Nuovo Digesto Italiano* accepted a definition of nationality 'in line with a sociological concept of similarity or affinity in a given human aggregation'[41] which reflects the Mancinian tradition and was also endorsed by German contemporary scholarship, underpinning the expansionistic aspirations of the Third Reich.[42] The entry nonetheless closes by highlighting that 'in the fascist doctrine of the State a people acquires the status of a nation insofar as is organized as a State. There are neither "people" nor "nation" outside the State'—quoting a speech of Mussolini in support.[43]

[27] See again Bartolini (n 15); Salerno (n 15). In Ferrara Meriggi also taught Church law.

[28] Lea Meriggi, *Stati Uniti d'Europa* (Casa editrice Imperia 1926). This early essay (dated October 1924) could be her final dissertation at university. The language is rhetoric, but the tone is very different from her later works. No reference is specifically made to fascism.

[29] Lea Meriggi, 'Reform des Völkerbundes und Philosophie des Völkerrechts' (1936) 16 Zeitschrift für öffentliches Recht.

[30] Lea Meriggi, *Il riconoscimento di Stati nella pratica dei più recenti avvenimenti internazionali* (Edizioni del Circolo di cultura giuridica 1929).

[31] Lea Meriggi, *Il conflitto lituano-polacco e la questione di Vilna* (Istituto editoriale scientifico 1930).

[32] Lea Meriggi, *Le funzioni consultive della Corte permanente di giustizia internazionale* (Athenaeum 1930).

[33] Meriggi, 'Das Wesen' (n 4).

[34] Meriggi, 'Considérations' (n 5).

[35] Lea Meriggi, *I trattati ed i terzi* (UTET 1938).

[36] Lea Meriggi, Nazionalità, in *Nuovo Digesto Italiano*, vol VIII (UTET 1939) 962.

[37] Meriggi, 'Conflict of Law' (n 5).

[38] Lea Meriggi, 'Saggio critico sulle qualificazioni' (1932) Rivista italiana di diritto internazionale privato e processuale 189–308, which she was invited to republish in French (see n 8).

[39] Lea Meriggi, *Contributo alla dottrina del fallimento nel diritto internazionale privato* (Società editrice del nuovo Stato 1936).

[40] See for instance Meriggi, 'Le problème' (n 7) 501.

[41] 'Nazionalità' (n 36) 959.

[42] cf Salerno, La *Rivista* (n 13) fn 114.

[43] ibid 962.

Neither in this entry nor in her other writings did I find any express or indirect endorsement of Nazi-fascist racial theories or hate speech.[44] Specifically her monograph on treaties and third states, published in 1938, is conceived as a critique of Hans Kelsen's 'Contribution à la théorie du traité international',[45] but it would not seem that this choice was politically motivated. Her critique—based on a private law analogy and a reading of contemporary literature and practice through a traditional lens enhancing the role of state's will as the source of international legal rules—was framed as a normal scholarly disagreement, where she also quoted Sereni's theses, as well as those of Balladore Pallieri and several other—mainly Italian—scholars, in support of her own conclusions. More generally, she tried to emphasize the role of Italian scholarship in her writings (with Anzilotti being often invoked as an authority, alongside other authors such as Ago, Cavaglieri, Diena, Fedozzi, Gemma, or Morelli) She also discussed and relied upon the work of European authors including Kelsen, Niboyet, and Rabel. While she often advocated theoretical stances that were also used to underpin fascist legal policies (eg, when emphasizing the role of nationality as the main element upon which to base her 'universalist' approach to characterization), this was always presented as a 'neutral', apparently non-politicized choice.

This said, Meriggi's political orientations most clearly emerged when she dealt with issues other than international law. She devoted an essay (in German) to the prominent fascist philosopher Francesco Orestano;[46] her most striking title, *Faschismus und Recht* [Fascism and the Law], published in 1934, is the written version of the speech delivered at the second meeting of the Academy of German Law. The Academy had been founded in 1933 by Hitler's trusted lawyer, Hans Frank (later sentenced to death at Nuremberg), who also appears to have been instrumental in establishing the courses of Italian Law in Frankfurt and Berlin.[47] She might have gotten in touch with him through Vernarecci di Fossombrone, who helped her find employment in Germany and regularly met her there;[48] he was also in contact with Frank for official reasons.[49] *Faschismus und Recht*, whose table of contents in part reflects the structure of Meriggi's courses on Italian law, opens with a chilling eulogy of Fascism in all its forms, including Nazism. The booklet rhetorically hails to the fascist revolution, built upon the sacrifices of those who lost their lives in the (first) World War: thus, 'Fascism is a child of the battle, the battle for an ideal Fatherland, Justice, Human Value and Human

[44] cf C Costamagna, 'Razza e diritto' in (1939) 10 *Lo Stato* 136. See further P Pollice, 'Giuristi ebrei tra la seconda metà dell'ottocento e la prima metà del novecento, con un richiamo alla figura di Alessandro Graziani' (2015) 64 Accademia pontaniana 191 at 215.

[45] Meriggi (1936) X *Revue internationale de la théorie du droit* 253–92.

[46] Meriggi, 'Recht und Philosophischer Gedanke' (n 4).

[47] The then Rector of Ferrara, Calzolari, mentions this in a speech prepared for the conferral of the honorary degree to Frank.

[48] Information provided by Ms Donata Kalliany von Kallian.

[49] He sent diplomatic communications from Germany to the Ministry of Foreign Affairs in the years 1935–38 (see Ministero degli Affari esteri, *Indici dell'Archivio Storico*, vol XI (P Pastorelli ed) (Istituto Poligrafico e Zecca dello Stato 1999): the Index' entry No 683 mentions reports by Vernarecci on his contacts with Frank in the 'Busta 165' (Gab 366). Vernarecci was later posted to Poland, where he acted as 'legal advisor' and de facto diplomatic representative upon appointment by Hans Frank (see Stefania Ruggeri, 'Ambasciata d'Italia in Varsavia (1945–1971)' in (2014) 2 Storia & Diplomazia—Rassegna dell'Archivio Storico del Ministero degli Affari Esteri 145.

Dignity ...'.[50] Rather than plunging countries into crisis and loss of influence—as the French and Soviet revolutions—Fascism reacted to a 'spiritual disorder' and brought back order and stability for the state and for the freedoms of its citizens ...'correctly understood'.[51] This Revolution, as a 'synthesis of thought and deed', would never have succeeded without a single guide (*Führer*), an interpreter (*Dolmetscher*) of the feelings of all those involved, a catalyzer of their energies: Mussolini in Italy, Hitler in Germany.[52]

In the last part of the book, Meriggi discusses the influence of fascism and its corporativist theories could have on the development of international law, expressing the hope that the limits of the League of Nations would be overcome by the Four Powers Pact proposed by Mussolini—the apex of his diplomatic success as 'forger' of a new European order which, however, never entered into force.[53] Meriggi also argued that smaller states should not be concerned by the idea of an 'European concert' of strong states, and that strong states (notably those organized around fascist principles, such as Italy and Germany) would be more peace-loving than weak ones ...

Defining Moments: The Honorary Degrees to Hans Frank

Upon returning in Italy, Lea Meriggi strived to promote ties between Italian Universities and Nazi Germany. She encouraged the Modena Faculty of Law to confer an honorary degree to Hans Frank—then Minister of the Reich and *Generalgouverneur* in the occupied Polish territories.[54] A delegation of the University travelled to Berlin in April 1940 for the formal conferral ceremony. Meriggi could not attend due to 'health problems' (she was in fact pregnant), but Frank thanked her, the 'pioneer of Italian-German legal relations', in his acceptance speech.[55]

After moving to Ferrara—where she helped in obtaining the University's change of status from private to public institution[56]—Meriggi replicated her efforts to honour Frank. At a time when he was already implementing the 'final solution' decided at Wannsee, a minute of a Faculty meeting of 12 March 1943 records the unanimous approval of the Rector's proposal to award an honorary degree to this

[50] Meriggi, *Faschismus und Recht*, 10.

[51] ibid 13.

[52] ibid 16: This approach was in line with the anti-individualist approach of Fascism (cf Rose Parfitt, 'Fascism, Imperialism and International Law: An Arch Met a Motorway and the Rest is History ... ' 31 (2018) Leiden Journal of International Law 509–38, fn 103 and corresponding text).

[53] The Pact was signed by Germany, Italy, the United Kingdom, and France in 1933. France eventually declined to ratify it.

[54] See the booklet of the Regia Università di Modena, *In occasione della solenne consegna della laurea honoris causa in Giurisprudenza al Presidente dell'Accademia per il diritto germanico Dr Hans Frank, Ministro del Reich (Berlino—Palazzo dell'Accademia per il Diritto Germanico—28 aprile 1940)* (Premiata Società Tipografica Modenese 1940). See further Giovanni Cazzetta, 'La Facoltà di Giurisprudenza nella Libera Università di Ferrara (1860–1942)' (2004) Annali di storia delle università italiane; Elio Tavilla, 'La Facoltà modenese di Giurisprudenza: dalle leggi razziali al rinascimento repubblicano' in Marco Cavina (ed), *Giuristi al bivio. Le Facoltà di Giurisprudenza tra regime fascista e età repubblicana* (CLUEB 2014) 141–57.

[55] 'Discorso del Ministro del Reich dottor Hans Frank', *In occasione* (n 54) 23.

[56] Salerno, 'Gli anni ferraresi' (n 15).

> highly esteemed Jurist and eminent Statesman ... [who] raised Italian Legal science to renewed fame in his Homeland, inspiring his thoughts and deed to humanistic ideals, and reinforcing with his noble feelings and brilliant mind the cultural ties between the two allied Countries.[57]

The feeling of shame in reading this document is in no way limited by the fact that it is not as such valid, since it is not signed by the Dean, nor by the circumstance that the honorary degree was never awarded, due to a decision by the Government that the honour should rather come from the University of Bologna (which was more prestigious) on 3 April 1943.[58] Frank would nonetheless come to Ferrara two days later, and be appointed as honorary member of the Ferrara Academy of Sciences (whose President at the time was Professor Gaetano Boschi, a prominent neurologist and a friend of Meriggi's); the diploma was prepared, but Frank's name does not feature among the honorary members of the Academy, nor is there any record of the Academy's meetings formalizing such a status[59]—since Frank never actually came to Ferrara.[60] On 1 April Meriggi received a telegram signed by Frank himself, explaining that he was forced to postpone his trip due to 'unforeseen circumstances related to [his] office that urgently required [him] to remain in the *Generalgovernment* and in Germany'.

Conclusion

An endorser of the 'revolutionary limb' of Fascism, Lea Meriggi strived to change a society whose rules she did not always accept; she was a cultivated, independent, passionate woman, who refused the traditional role of '*angelo del focolare*' ('fireside angel') but was at the same time a loving mother; she paid for her choices with personal difficulties which, in a different context, would bring many to sympathize with her. She had a keen interest in her work and pursued her academic career with determination; her international legal scholarship covered a wide range of topics with sound technical bases. She was valued by students and colleagues, not only because she used her connections in Rome to the advantage of the University and its staff.[61] In the framework of the tenure track procedure, the Dean of the Ferrara Law Faculty Leopoldo Tumiati

[57] Draft verbatim record, sitting of 12 March 1943.

[58] On 25 March the Minister of National Education notified that the award of the honorary degree was suspended.

[59] I am grateful to Counsellor Francesco Scutellari, current President of the Ferrara Academy of Sciences, in 2019–21 for his kind efforts in clarifying the status of Hans Frank within the Academy.

[60] This is my reading of the available documents. In January 2001 Professor Giovanni Cazzetta, then Dean of the Law Faculty, gave a partly different account of the events in a letter to a local newspaper, whose readers had invited the Faculty to 'revoke' the honorary degree. Cazzetta reported that the Faculty refused to do so, not only because it did not fall within its competences but also because a 'revocation' would be a merely formal gesture, which would risk appearing as a denial of what had happened. On the tendency in Italy to 'forget' the memory of racial persecution cf Claudio Fogu, '*Italiani brava gente:* The Legacy of Fascist Historical Culture on Italian Politics of Memory' in RN Lebow, W Kansteiner, and C Fogu, *The Politics of Memory in Post-War Europe* (Duke University Press 2006) 147–75 at 170.

[61] Besides helping with the transformation of the University of Ferrara into a public institution, she also supported staff members for issues relating to their position (see unsigned letter, probably by Mr Malagù, Administrative Secretary, of 4 January 1943, warmly thanking her for her help).

described her as 'a lively mind, deeply engaged in teaching, with excellent results at exams and who has earned the esteem of colleagues and students. Her scientific outputs are remarkable.' While the language is bureaucratic, nuances seem to speak of real appreciation. After her death Tumiati (who was not a fascist zealot[62] and had just lost his son at the hand of the occupying Nazi forces) commemorated her twice in Faculty meetings, both before *and after* the liberation of Ferrara.[63]

If, therefore, Lea Meriggi's character is more nuanced than the common depiction as a faithful 'loudspeaker' of a dictatorial regime, why was she so keen to honour one of the worst Nazi criminals, at the very time in which he was perpetrating his direst crimes? Was it gratitude for helping her find a professional status? Sheer intellectual admiration? Did anybody press her to do so for political or other reasons? Was she aware of the nature of the 'official tasks' that kept Frank from travelling to Italy in April 1943?[64] Did the other Faculty members voting in favour of the honorary degree know? Did she ever reconsider her faith in the regime?

There can be only conjectures here, and not much purpose in making them. It is quite clear, in any case, that she had all the means of understanding the essence of Fascism—and specifically of Nazism, having been a privileged observer of its seizing power in Germany.[65] In the best hypothesis, she did not question what she saw, nor was she capable to look beyond ideology and acknowledge the actual nature of the events unfolding before her eyes.

A Personal Post-Scriptum

The scholarly work of Lea Meriggi is sparsely available in university libraries and other research institutions, including the Peace Palace Library (with most of her works present in the collection of the University of Milan '*Statale*'). I mainly drew information about her academic career from the personal files stored with the archives of the Ministry of National Education[66] and of the University of Ferrara.[67] I also used materials on file with professor Giovanni Cazzetta (whom I warmly thank) as regards the honorary degrees to Hans Frank by the Universities of Modena and Ferrara. However, I could never have gathered the personal information that allowed me to fill in many blank spots and read these materials in the right perspective without the help of Lea Meriggi's daughter, Donata Kalliany von Kallian. When I tentatively reached out through her Linkedin account she immediately telephoned me, deeply moved at the idea that somebody would wish to write about her mother, to whose memory

[62] See Salerno, 'Gli anni ferraresi' (n 15) 666.

[63] The first commemoration was on 25 October 1944, the second on 22 May 1945 (almost a month after Ferrara was freed by partisans and the Allied forces). See Salerno (n 15) 659 and 664.

[64] Vernarecci was in Poland in 1943 and could not be unaware of the Holocaust, but I have no information about the nature of his contacts with Meriggi at the time.

[65] See Meriggi, *Faschismus und Recht* (n 50) 7–8.

[66] File No I-123. The Italian Ministry of Education, University, and Research has stored the relevant files with the National Central Archive in Rome.

[67] File No 144. This file also includes some materials connected to Hans Frank's 'missed' honorary degree.

she is fondly attached although she has no direct recollection of her. She knew about Meriggi's fascist ideology but had no idea of her involvement with Nazism, nor specifically of her links to Hans Frank. A journalist by profession, she did not pull back after I told her that these events would be a key part of my essay; on the contrary, she accepted to meet me. It was a moving experience to hear this bright lady talk about her mother over a cup of hot chocolate at the Milan Royal Palace's cafeteria. I also received a copy of the autobiographical book *Coda senza lucertola* [Tail without a Lizard] (Vertigo 2016), where Donata Kalliany wrote much of what she knows about her mother, albeit in an anonymized way. At the end of our meeting she looked straight into my eyes and asked why I wanted to dig up 'such ugly things'. I explained that I felt bound to shed light on the choices made in 1943 by the institution I now work for. She understood and encouraged me to 'write all the evil possible' about her mother's political faith. I am indebted for this support and grateful that she did not turn away from disturbing truths.

29
Isabella Diederiks-Verschoor
(A Life) Creating Spaces

Christiaan Verwer and Anna van der Velde

Introduction

Isabella Diederiks-Verschoor was a pioneer in the field of air and space law. Among the first women in academia in the Netherlands and worldwide, she furthered and popularized the research of air and particularly space law among others as a co-founder of the International Institute of Space Law (IISL) in Vienna and the International Institute of Air and Space Law (IIASL) in Leiden. As a passionate teacher and advocate for her area of research, known for her hospitability and personally invested teaching style, she was driven to make the field accessible to students and professionals, particularly from developing countries. Though a highly productive scholar, with the exception of two textbooks, which have become standard reading in air and space law courses, little of her other work is widely known. This partially speaks to the male-dominated field and gendered prejudices that she encountered throughout her career. She became a vocal advocate in the Dutch women's movement for female academics also partially in response to the gendered barriers that she faced.

Yet, what motivated her to continue pushing against the personal and professional barriers placed in the way of female academics? And what prompted her to pursue her career path in an emerging, highly specialized field of law and promote it beyond the Dutch academic context? What personal characteristics were required to build a network that allowed her to significantly shape the next generation of air and space law lawyers?

This portrait reflects upon these questions through the eyes of her friend Christiaan Verwer, who met Isabella (Isa) Diederiks-Verschoor during his law studies at the University of Amsterdam in 1971. Writing his final thesis on air law, he was advised by his supervisor to contact the leading teacher in the field at the time, Diederiks-Verschoor. She continued to assist him also with his PhD thesis and they remained in close contact thereafter. Since 2005, he accompanied her once a month to friends or relatives, and became her personal assistant for the last nine years of her life, supporting her among others with her international correspondence. After 2010, their contact intensified even further as Verwer became her caretaker manager and drafted a, to date, unpublished biography.

Christiaan Verwer and Anna van der Velde, *Isabella Diederiks-Verschoor* In: *Portraits of Women in International Law*.
Edited by: Immi Tallgren, Oxford University Press.
DOI: 10.1093/oso/9780198868453.003.0029

Figure 29.1 Isabella Diederiks-Verschoor.
Source: Photograph by Jochmann Disco. Archive of Isabella Henrietta Phileppina Diederiks-Verschoor (1476, 82) at Het Utrechts Archief.

Private Life

Isa Verschoor was born on 29 July 1915 in Amersfoort in the Netherlands as the daughter of a grenadier in the Dutch army and a teacher. Upon completion of her high school exam, she studied Dutch law at the University of Leiden from 1935 to 1940. There she came in contact with aviation law for the first time in a course given by Professor Goedhuis in 1938. The course sparked her interest and she became his research assistant. As a result of her passion for aviation law nurtured by her research work for Professor Goedhuis and following a suggestion by one of her father's friends, the Director-General of the Dutch Civil Aviation Authority, K van Ede van der Pals, Isa Verschoor went on to pursue her doctoral studies in aviation law at the University of Utrecht, while at the same time working full-time as an attorney in Amsterdam.[1] She defended her doctoral thesis on the Brussels Treaty of 1938 on the search and rescue at sea of or by aircraft in 1943.[2]

Around the same time, she also met Boy de Rode, a fellow lawyer, whom she married in 1943, and had a daughter with. However, their shared time remained short-lived. Following the passing of her husband in 1953, she brought up her daughter by herself. In 1966, Isa de Rode-Verschoor married an old classmate, Cees Diederiks. She died on 17 October 2017 at the age of 102 in her own house in Baarn.

Professional Life—A Passionate Teacher and Networker

After six years as a practicing lawyer, Isa de Rode-Verschoor got a temporary position as an assistant private secretary of Queen Juliana of the Netherlands in 1952.[3] In October that year she returned to academia joining Utrecht University as the first and only female university lecturer in the field of aviation law. Her return to academia was not easy. As a woman in Dutch academia she had to fight resistance on multiple levels: she had to present a triple recommendation to get her position and had to accept an unsalaried position as a private lecturer for air law that she held for eight years.[4] Only in 1961 was she offered a paid position and became a staff member of Utrecht University. This, however, did not discourage her from expanding her initial focus on teaching her preferred subject aviation law to space law, and as the first to do so in the Netherlands in 1957.[5] That only four students attended her first lectures may be telling of the novelty of the subject. By 1973, she was appointed senior lecturer in air and space law at Utrecht University, which was transformed into a full professorship in 1980, a position she held until her retirement in 1984.

Teaching and Interest in Her Students' Work

Her former students' accounts speak of an enthusiastic and highly engaged teacher, who was deeply invested in the learning experience and career development of her students.[6] As a lecturer she challenged her students with the goal to actively involve them

[1] Tanja Masson-Zwaan, 'In Memoriam Professor Dr. Isabella H. Ph. Diederiks-Verschoor (1915–2017)' (2017) 4 Ruimtevaart: Orgaan van de Nederlandse Vereniging voor Ruimtevaart (NVR) 16 <https://scholarlypublications.universiteitleiden.nl/access/item%3A2949701/view> accessed 5 March 2021.

[2] Isabella H Ph Verschoor, *Het Verdrag van Brussel van 1938 betreffende hulp en berging van of door luchtvaartuigen op zee* (Nijhoff 1943).

[3] See proof of this employment in the letter of the secretary of Queen Juliana in 1952.

[4] This appears in an unsigned declaration by one of her two referees, Professor A van Oven.

[5] In the Australian newspaper *The Age* of 22 September 1965, she stated that 'Air law is so concrete; there are many written conventions. But Space law—it is necessary to think about it. There's so much fantastic talk about it—but I like things to be concrete.' Diederiks-Veschoor's take on this did not changed throughout her life.

[6] See, eg, entries in her condolence registry <https://avanpijpen.provider.aggeloo.com/profile/isabella-henrietta-philepina-verschoor> accessed 2 November 2022.

in class and introduce new teaching methods. For example, she tasked her students to write papers on different air and space law subjects and coached them to publish their essays in professional legal journals. Yet, her teaching engagement was not limited to the classroom. She supported foreign doctoral students, especially from developing countries, by utilizing her vast professional network. She either forwarded their documents or connected students with professionals in the different sectors within the Dutch aviation industry as well as with international institutions like the International Court of Justice (ICJ), the Permanent Court of Arbitration, or the International Civil Aviation Organization.[7]

Diederiks-Verschoor used for example her close relationship with ICJ judge Manfred Lachs to promote Chinese students' studies at the Academy of International Law in The Hague and the IIASL, among others by organizing funding and lodgings for them.[8] Many of her students went on to well-known research institutes and remained in contact with Diederiks-Verschoor after their studies.[9] One of these students, Yuwen Li, with whom Diederiks-Verschoor engaged in an intensive correspondence since the late 1980s, became Professor of Chinese Law at Erasmus University Rotterdam.[10] Their friendship helped Diederiks-Verschoor to maintain her contacts and support her students in China. Another form of letting foreign students profit from her network was by inviting them to accompany her to different meetings of international air and space law institutes for networking purposes.

In general, Isa Diederiks-Verschoor was a very hospitable and caring person for colleagues, students, and other law practitioners, blurring the lines between her professional and private life.[11] Her personal involvement in her teaching is best pictured by her tradition to invite her international air law LLM classes to an annual lunch in her home in Baarn to discuss current topics with them. Her efforts to support her students increased even further after her retirement in 1984. As with her LLM classes, she encouraged both Dutch and foreign students who liked to study at IIASL in Leiden by inviting them to Baarn for discussions, providing them with access to her extensive library and a home-cooked meal.[12]

The impact of her efforts for her students especially from developing countries is reflected not only in their career paths. In 1999, former students of Diederiks-Verschoor's founded the International Society for Air and Space Law to collect funds for foreign students to participate in an IIASL air and space law course. Additionally,

[7] Such as KLM, Martinair, Fokker Aviation Industries, Airport Schiphol, the Ministry of Transport, Civil Aviation Authority, Air Traffic Control, Dutch Aviation and Space Laboratory. See also Masson-Zwaan (n 1).

[8] eg Fu Yong Jun, Ting Wang, Zhao Yang, Wu Zenghlan, and Li Zhaojie.

[9] Such as Li Zhaoije, who continues at the Max Planck Institute in Germany, or Fu Yong Jun and Ma Li.

[10] See Professor Li's University profile at <www.eur.nl/en/people/yuwen-li> accessed 31 March 2021.

[11] The warm relations exude from a letter from early 2001 by Zhao Yun, the first PhD student to win the Diederiks-Verschoor award and later international law professor at the University of Hong Kong: 'I had a really nice time with you during Christmas. I would say that I really relaxed in Baarn. With the snow, with the nice cat, I felt the cozy atmosphere. Thanks, grandma, while relaxing you have been busy preparing foods for me. But I am happy we really had a great time together.'

[12] Masson-Zwaan (n 1). In a letter to the Bahar family in Indonesia dated 15 June 2000, Diederiks-Verschoor describes that 'My days are filled with ad hoc work. I have several foreign students, who study at the Leiden University for LLM examination or write a thesis, who come to my home.'

the society organized yearly meetings for former students and friends of Diederiks-Verschoor to keep them informed on aviation and space law developments.[13]

Teaching Abroad

Diederiks-Verschoor's teaching activities were not limited to the Netherlands as she was deeply invested in international cooperation and development efforts. Since re-entering academia at Utrecht University, Isa de Rode-Verschoor developed an expansive network of both national and international contacts in the field of air and space law. Her charm and expertise but also language skills, which she constantly tried to improve, were greatly valued, leading to a vast number of guest lectures worldwide.[14] She gave her first lecture abroad at the Higher School of Industrial Studies in Athens in 1957. Uncommon for a woman with family at the time, she continued to lecture extensively abroad for more than forty years. Facilitated by her networks, she taught particularly in areas that were at the time not known for being centres of air and space law research. She gave lectures on aviation and space law (among other topics) in France, Australia, the United States, Indonesia, China, Taiwan, Qatar, Malaysia, Israel, South Korea, and Canada, touring these areas for weeks at a time, sometimes under the most arduous conditions.[15]

The impact of these lecture tours and her expanding personal networks is visible in a depiction of her engagement in China. In 1984, Isa Diederiks-Verschoor was invited to support the preparations for an international law congress in China as part of the Aviation Expo. Though the Expo did not take place, she was subsequently invited to lecture at universities in Xian and Guangzhou. To facilitate her travelling, Diederiks-Verschoor was granted a diplomatic passport for this trip by her former student Hans van den Broek, the then Minister of Foreign Affairs in the Netherlands. Her Chinese colleague Professor Wang Tieya received her in his private home emphasizing the importance of the personal contacts she used to develop. This trip was also the beginning of a very long period of intense correspondence with Chinese professors and students.

Parallel to her lecture tours, she fostered these networks by organizing numerous air and space law courses for foreign professionals in the Netherlands. She taught aviation and space law courses at the Peace Palace in The Hague for professionals in the aviation industry from the United Arab Emirates, Iraq, Yemen, the Kingdom of Saudi Arabia, and Bahrain.[16] The selection of professionals from these states was inspired by the success of earlier courses in air law for French speaking African lawyers,

[13] In total, eight meetings took place covering subjects such as the investigation report on the crash at Bijlmermeer, unruly passengers (2000), the task and position of the *Nationaal Lucht en Ruimtevaart laboratorium* (2001), from JAA to EASA (2003), the fusion of Air France and KLM (2004), the offer of the second Liber Amicorum (2005), rules for experimenting in the Aviation Act, and the position of the Committee for Regional Consultation of Schiphol Airport (2006). Due to difficulties to raise sufficient funds, the Society was dissolved in 2008.

[14] To communicate with friends in Africa and Indonesia, she studied Swahili and Bahasa. She was eager to learn throughout her life, taking up Spanish studies at the age of seventy-five.

[15] Masson-Zwaan (n 1).

[16] From 9–20 September 1985, organized by the *Nederlands Vervoerswetenschappelijk Instituut* in Rijswijk.

which Diederiks-Verschoor had developed on the request of the United Nations.[17] The courses contained not only lectures but also organized visits to the aeronautical industry and other organizations, such as the ICJ and to the Royal Palace with His Highness Prince Bernhard, whom Diederiks-Verschoor had met while assisting Queen Juliana. Yet, her activities to make air and space law widely known and accessible were not limited to teaching.

Publications

Isa Diederiks-Verschoor published widely in scientific journals and engaged with the wider public through radio and television, commenting for example on important technical achievements like the landing of men on the moon. In addition to her written work, Diederiks-Verschoor established and contributed to the *Air and Space Law* journal as an advisory board member since 1975.[18]

Isa Diederiks-Verschoor published a total of 260 articles, books, commentaries, and other texts from 1943 until 2008. Of her long publication list, she is most well-known for her two textbooks '*Introduction to Air Law*' and '*Introduction to Space Law*'. Her first textbook '*Introduction to Air Law*' was published in Dutch in 1960. Though translated into English only two years later, the English version was not published until 1982. It became an international standard textbook for beginners' courses in air law and was commended for achieving what Diederiks-Verschoor set out to do, namely provide an easily accessible but compact summary of a quickly expanding field.[19] It has since been translated into 37 languages often by her former students.[20]

Also her second textbook '*Introduction to Space Law*' was published to positive reviews in 1992. Lauded for the clarity of analysis and the '[l]ucid explanations of the basic principles of space law', '[l]ike the perfect teacher, she leads the reader through difficult areas of the subject-matter and leaves it for the reader to further explore deeper into the interesting field of space law'.[21] Additional updated editions and translations to multiple other languages followed.[22]

[17] These courses took place in the years 1975–1977, 1979, and 1981, with participants from Upper-Volta, the Republic of Zaïre, Mali, Morocco, Tunisia, Madagascar, and Cameroon.

[18] In 1995, the Board of Editors of Air and Space Law composed a unique Liber Amicorum in her honour. Only two copies exist composed of sometimes handwritten pages of colleagues. These are available in the Museum of Utrecht and in Verwer's private collection.

[19] See eg Stanley B Rosenfield, Review of 'An Introduction to Air Law by I.H.P Diederiks-Verschoor, Kluwer Law and Taxation Publisher, 1983, pp.185' (1984) 12(1–2) International Journal of Legal Information 70, 71.

[20] The first translation was to Chinese by Professor Zhao Weitian, followed by among others Bahasa, Russian, and Korean. By now the eighth updated English edition by Professor Mendes de Leon has been published.

[21] Nandasiri Jasentuliyana, Book Review 'I.H.Ph. Diederiks-Verschoor, An Introduction to Space Law. Kluwer Law and Taxation Publishers, 1993, 238 pp' (1995) XX(1) Air and Space Law 40, 42.

[22] The third edition was reworked in cooperation with Vladimir Kopal. Diederiks-Verschoor had worked with him for a long time on the UN Committee on the Peaceful Uses of Outer Space. The fourth edition was edited by her former student Assistant Professor Tanja Masson-Zwaan and Kopal's student Professor Mahulena Hofmann.

Even after her retirement, Diederiks-Verschoor continued her research and her last article entitled 'Some Observations on the Air Transport of Animals' was published in 2010.[23] Her publications and extensive book collection continued to be accessible to the wider public as she supported the library of the Académie de Droit International in The Hague with a yearly donation and with gifts of books and foreign publications. After her death, Christiaan Verwer handed over a substantial part of her private library to the Académie and transferred her Air and Space Law library to the IIASL. However, this is not the only trace left of her.

Involvement in Air and Space Law Institutions

In addition to her teaching and publication activities, Diederiks-Verschoor co-founded and engaged in several international air and space law institutions. In 1958, as one of the few space law experts in the Netherlands, she participated in the First Juridical Colloquium of the Ninth International Congress on space activities in Amsterdam. As a Dutch delegate speaking on the liability question for damages caused by space vehicles, she was introduced as the 'beauty with brains' by the president of the Congress Dr Haley.[24] Her skillful presentation was noted as soon thereafter she became the Vice-President of a working group on damages caused by spacecrafts within the International Astronautical Federation. Simultaneously, she was also active in establishing the International Academy of Astronautics in 1960, generating support for the creation of 'Section 4' on social sciences[25] together with another female space law pioneer Eileen Galloway (United States), Vladimir Kopal (Czech Republic), and Vladlen Vereshchetin (USSR), with whom she would continue to cooperate throughout her career. This cooperation in politically difficult times was facilitated among others by her attitude towards politics, which she generally did not consider important for the development of air and space law.

With Eileen Galloway, she also inspired the founding of the International Institute for Space Law in 1960, and was elected its President in 1974.[26] Upon her election, she received a laudatory introduction by her mentor, the leading French air and space law professor Eugèn Pépin, stating that '*On ne présente pas Mrs. Diederiks-Verschoor car tous les juristes de droit aérien et de droit spatial la connaissent et savent*

[23] Chapter in Budislav Vukas and Trpimir M Šošić (eds), *International Law: New Actors, New Concepts, Continuing Dilemmas: Liber Amicorum Božidar Bakotić* (Brill Nijhoff 2010) 221–29.

[24] Andrew G Haley and Dr Welf Heinrich Prince of Hanover (eds), *First Colloquium on the Law of Outer Space, The Hague 1958, Proceedings* (Springer 1959); Het Haagsch Dagblad referred on 29 August 1958 to her speech as follows: 'The Netherlands were sharp-wittedly represented by Ms Dr. I.H.Ph. de Rode-Verschoor. She believed that the primary and continued responsibility should be placed on those countries that launch cosmic projectiles and that these countries remain liable for any damage caused by their satellites.'

[25] Smith and Galloway explain that the 'other three sections are for space science, space engineering and space life sciences'. Marcia S Smith and Jonathan F Galloway, 'Eilene M. Galloway (4.5.1906–2.5.2009)' in Stephan Hobe (ed), *Pioneers of Space Law: A Publication of the International Institute of Space Law* (Brill Nijhoff 2013) 126–48, 138.

[26] Except for 1965, Diederiks-Verschoor attended all yearly conferences until 2006.

avec quelle autorité elle saura conduire vos travaux.'[27] For Diederiks-Verschoor, the chairwomanship, which she held until 1990, meant a recognition of her work by the international space law community where she—next to Professor Galloway—was the only well-known woman. She was valued for her diplomacy skills and 'warm and upbeat' as well as firm but consensus-driven personality.[28] Commenting on her chairing approach she stated that 'the great value and advantage of the IISL is that it is an unofficial scientific forum, where the speakers are not representing governments but are giving their own scientific opinions. [. . .] We are here as colleagues and friends'.[29]

She adopted this human-focused leadership style also in her other institutional work. Despite Utrecht University having no intention to keep air and space law in its programme after her retirement in 1984, she was adamant to continue the teaching and research of air and space law. Subsequently, Diederiks-Verschoor co-founded the International Institute of Air and Space Law at the Leiden Law Faculty together with her friend Professor Wassenbergh and served as its Vice-President until 2004, and Honorary President thereafter.

Supporting the Women's Movement

At Utrecht University Isa Verschoor was one of the few female teaching staff in an environment hostile towards female academics. Her own supervisors' description of Verschoor as '*een indringerige bemoeizieke dame*' (an intrusive nosy and meddlesome lady) reflects this atmosphere. Rather than discouraging her, it strengthened her to fight for women in academia. On a personal level she was joined in this fight by two fellow female space law pioneers, her close friends Professor Eileen Galloway, with whom she corresponded frequently (if they did not meet at conferences) and Professor Elisabeth Back Impallomeni from Padua.

Aware of her unusual position within academia, Diederiks-Verschoor engaged in several women's networks seeking to advance the position of women in academia and society. Already during her studies, Isa Verschoor was an active member in a sorority (*Vereniging van Vrouwelijke Studenten*). Returning to academia in the early 1950s, she engaged in the 'Association for women with a higher education'[30] and joined the Soroptimists, which sought to empower women through education thereby increasing their economic opportunities.[31] In Utrecht, Verschoor was elected the club's governor for the term 1964–1968. In this capacity she continued her outreach work also outside of the Netherlands, travelling, for example, to Australia to give a lecture to

[27] 'Ouverture du Colloque E. Pepin' IISL Proceedings, 'Report of the 17th (1974) Colloquium on the Law of Outer Space' 1. Personal testimony to the author in 2009.

[28] See statement by Ambassadeur Eugene Wyzner, former chair of the COPUOS Legal Subcommittee in Masson-Zwaan (n 1), 17 and Dato Mahadev Shankar's condolence register entry of 23 November 2017 <https://avanpijpen.provider.aggeloo.com/profile/isabella-henrietta-philepina-verschoor> accessed 2 October 2022.

[29] IISL Proceedings, 'Report of the 19th (1976) Colloquium on the Law of Outer Space' 419.

[30] She joined its board in 1962 and acted as President from 1963 to 1968.

[31] Soroptimist Utrecht Association report part 1 (1929–1969), (2nd ed, 1991) 54.

fellow Soroptimists in Canberra in 1966.[32] As with her teaching work, she utilized her personal contacts also within Soroptimist circles to connect members. Exemplary thereof, as the 1974–1975 President of the Utrecht-circle, she invited Queen Juliana to the 50th anniversary of the Dutch Soroptimists.

Her engagement for women was generally well-received by fellow Soroptimists. In a report on a lecture given by Diederiks-Verschoor for the Utrecht-circle in 1983, speaking 'about her activities as President of the International Institute of Space Law and the difficulties arising for peaceful use of space', she was described by an attendee as 'impress[ive] as an enthusiastic lawyer, teacher, mediator for aviation jobs, diplomat and so forth. (Isa, does your twenty-four-hours period really count 24 hours?)'.[33] Her friendship with some of her Soroptimist-sisters lasted until her death.

Diederiks-Verschoor was very outspoken about the role of women in educational circles and more broadly in the labour market. She utilized public media and broadcasts to discuss, for example, gender discrimination in the labour market, pointing at differences in performance requirements, the prioritization of men's career prospects but also acknowledging some advances in terms of the increase in the number of women appointed to the Dutch benches.[34] Not afraid to publicly raise awareness of discriminatory practices, she was described as always acting in a vividly friendly but also vigorous way.[35]

For her work and expertise she was honoured with the life-time award of the International Astronautical Federation in 1999 and the Hugo de Groot Prize in 2001. In the same year, the IISL's 'Prof. Dr. I. H. Ph. Diederiks-Verschoor Award' was established for the best publication by an author under thirty years of age.[36] Other forms of recognition were a Liber Amicorum under the title 'Airworthy' presented to her at the Peace Palace in 1985, and a second Liber Amicorum presented to her on her ninetieth birthday in 2005, both composed by former students and close friends.[37]

Conclusion

Christiaan Verwer's portrait of Diederiks-Verschoor paints a picture of a bright and energetic teacher, with exceptional networking skills that she put to the service of her students and colleagues. She not only advanced the research and teaching of air and space law worldwide through her textbooks, extensive lecturing tours, especially to developing economies with a rising interest in air and space law, but also vividly fought for the recognition of female academic expertise for more than fifty years. As a teacher she went above and beyond to support and encourage her students through challenging them as scholars and connecting them to professionals in the field. As a

[32] Short summary in the Association report '*de Nederlandse Soroptimist*', December 1966. The lecture was part of a five weeks trip to different Australian universities lecturing on air and space law.

[33] Soroptimists Utrecht, agenda item III of the meeting on 21 September 1983.

[34] See, eg, a Dutch Radio broadcast programme in February 1968.

[35] Interview on the Hugo de Groot award in Moscow in the Newsletter of the Association in 2001.

[36] 'The Isa Diederiks-Verschoor Award 2001', (2001) 26(3) *Air and Space Law* 135–36.

[37] JWE Storm van 's Gravesande and A van der Veen Vonk (eds), 'Liber Amicorum honouring Professor Dr Isabella H. Ph. Diederiks-Verschoor', (Kluwer 1985).

result of her ability to create new spaces for research and growth, many had successful careers and remained in close contact. As Verwer describes, during her last years, her international correspondence seemed never-ending and covered all parts of the world.

Studying law at a time when the subject choice was not common for women, even less so in an emerging field of international law, her choice of pursuing a career in academia was met with resistance and belittling all along the way. In 1952, salaried positions for female teachers were not easily available and the acceptance of her presence in the Utrecht Law Faculty was minimal among the staff. This was still clearly visible at her retirement by the refusal of the faculty to continue the position for air and space law, despite rising interest in the field. Diederiks-Verschoor showed determination to continue developing the field by co-founding the IIASL in Leiden and taking on multiple leadership positions within professional air and space law institutions. Her relentless energy and optimism is also visible within her work with the Soroptimists and Dutch female professionals' associations furthering the women's cause to equality and economic independence. Thereby her special skills as a unifier on the international stage and her conciliatory and consensus-driven leadership style seem to have been key elements to her success and public recognition.

At a time when society positioned women predominantly in the private sphere, Diederiks-Verschoor's atypical working approach crossed gender barriers. She combined traditionally female-associated traits of caring, loyalty, dedication, and empathy in her teaching and leadership with male-ascribed characteristics such as a willpower, outspokenness, and enjoyment of public speaking. This is not only reflected in her interactions within her personal and professional relationships but also her development-focused approach to furthering the spreading of knowledge and research skills in areas outside of the dominant air and space law geopolitical arena. This unwillingness to conform to prevailing societal and academic norms combined with her approachability, expertise, and charisma, enabled her thus to gain public positions of power and trust showing that these are not gender-specific.

30

Gezina van der Molen

A Journey from Universalism to Pluralism

Sarah MH Nouwen and Wouter Werner

A Recognized International Lawyer

From a professional international law perspective, Gezina van de Molen (1892–1978) is an easily justifiable choice for a portrait gallery of women in the field.[1] In many of her roles, she was the pioneering first: in 1937, at the Free University of Amsterdam, she was the first woman to obtain a doctorate in international law, indeed the first woman to obtain a doctorate, full stop. In 1949, at that same university, she became not just the first female professor in international law, but the first female professor—again, full stop. In 1966, she was the first woman to be appointed as a member of the Permanent Court of Arbitration. And she attended several of the profession's highlight events: meetings of the League of Nations in Geneva, the first sessions of the United Nations in New York, and the Eichmann trial in Jerusalem.

Contrary to many of the women discussed in this book, she was already recognized as a significant actor in the world of international law and relations in her day. Her PhD and the revised version that appeared in book form thirty years later, *Alberico Gentili and the Development of International Law: His Life Work and Times*, were discussed in, among others, the American Journal of International Law,[2] the London Quarterly Review,[3] the Nordic Journal of International Law,[4] and the University of Toronto Law Journal (according to which 'many readers will be grateful to *him* for having written

[1] Our wish to study the life and work of Gezina van de Molen has been greatly facilitated by Gert van Klinken's biography, on which we gratefully rely in this piece. See Gert van Klinken, *Strijdbaar & Omstreden: Een Biografie van de Calvinistische Verzetsvrouw Gezina van der Molen [Combative & Controversial: A Biography of Calvinist Resistance Fighter Gezina van der Molen]* (Boom 2006) (hereafter Van Klinken, *Strijdbaar & Omstreden*). For a documentary on our protagonist (in Dutch), see *Gezina van der Molen (1892–1978)*, Brandpunt Profiel, KRO-NCRV (2 May 2007) <https://www.npostart.nl/profiel/02-05-2007/POW_00117927> accessed 1 June 2021.

[2] Percy T Fenn, 'Alberico Gentili and the Development of International Law. By Dr. Gezina H. J. van der Molen. (Amsterdam: H. J. Paris, 1937. pp. xii, 342. Fl. 4.50.)' (1938) 32 AJIL 209; Edward Dumbauld, 'Alberico Gentili and the Development of International Law. 2nd Revised Edition. By Gesina H. J. Van Der Molen. (Leyden: A. W. Sijthoff, 1968. Pp. Xviii, 348. Index. FI. 35.)' (1969) 63 AJIL 180.

[3] Elizabeth Thorneycroft, 'Alberico Gentili and the Development of International Law. His Life Work and Times. By Dr. G. H. J. van der Molen. Amsterdam: H. J. Paris. 1937.:142 pp.' (1938) 54 London Quarterly Review 609.

[4] Anon, 'Dr. Gesina H. J. van der Molen: Alberico Gentili and the development of international law, 2nd revised edition. A. W. Sijthoff, Leyden, 1968' (1968) 38 Nordisk Tidsskrift for International Ret 187.

Sarah MH Nouwen and Wouter Werner, *Gezina van der Molen* In: *Portraits of Women in International Law.*
Edited by: Immi Tallgren, Oxford University Press.
DOI: 10.1093/oso/9780198868453.003.0030

Figure 30.1 Painting by Roeland Koning (1962), oil on canvas.
Source: Collection Vrije Universiteit, Amsterdam, photo by René den Engelsman (2009).

his book in the English language').[5] Van der Molen interacted with, among many others, Bert Röling, Martin Buber, Charles Henry Alexandrowicz, and Max Huber. Her best-known research assistant and PhD supervisee was Peter Kooijmans, who would make it to the position of judge of the International Court of Justice.

Her name is no longer generally known among international lawyers today—the same applies to most of her male colleagues—but among Gentili scholars, her book

[5] HA Smith, 'Alberico Gentili and the Development of International Law: His Life and Times. By *G. H. J. van der Molen*. Amsterdam: H. J. Paris. 1937. Pp. xii, 342. (4.50frs.)' (1939) 3 University of Toronto Law Journal 178, 179. (emphasis added).

continues to be referred to. In her 2020 book, Valentina Vadi writes of Van der Molen's as 'one of the best available monographs on Alberico Gentili', explaining that '[h]er lucid writing coupled with an in-depth knowledge of international law has made her monograph among the best starting points for approaching Gentili's contribution to international law for decades'. Vadi also cites Arthur Nussbaum who had, in 1954, praised Van der Molen's book as 'perhaps the best biography ever written on an author in the field of international law'.[6]

And yet, while she played a significant role in international law, it would be wrong to portray her primarily and only as a career international lawyer. Van der Molen was not interested in international law for the sake of international law, but as an instrument to order the world to realize certain universal values. She pursued these values in *all* the roles she fulfilled in Dutch society and in international circles. Among those roles, that of international law expert came relatively late, due to the social and cultural inhibitions preventing women engaging in study and paid work in The Netherlands, and especially in the part of society to which she belonged. But even when she had become an expert in international law, this role was just one among many. In 1946 she would be knighted in The Netherlands not for her role in international law, but for leadership in the Dutch resistance against the Nazis.[7] Similarly, Van der Molen would be posthumously recognized by Yad Vashem as 'righteous among the nations', not for a contribution to international law, but for having saved dozens of Jewish children from the Germans.

The values she promoted corresponded for most of her life with those of a specific branch of the Dutch Protestantism, but towards the end of her life this symbiosis weakened and there was more space for alternative visions of the good life. Throughout her life, Van der Molen was confronted with a dilemma that continues to challenge international lawyers today: how to reconcile a belief in pre-given moral categories with the experience of plurality? Given that there are many different readings of what justice requires, who determines its meaning in concrete circumstances?

Coming 'too late' to International Law

While her friends and relatives were celebrating her success, Van der Molen's own comment on being awarded a doctorate was: 'too late'.[8] Aged forty-five and a woman, she doubted she would ever get to do something professionally with the degree.

The societal context made it difficult to have been any faster.[9] Until the 1960s, Dutch society was divided into three 'pillars' (Protestant, Catholic, and social-democratic; those who did not feel they belonged in any of these were 'the liberals',

[6] Valentina Vadi, *War and Peace: Alberico Gentili and the Early Modern Law of Nations* (Brill 2020) 30, citing Arthur Nussbaum, *A Concise History of the Law of Nations* (rev edn, Macmillan 1954) 101.

[7] Marijke Waalkens, 'Molen, Gezina van der (1892–1978)' (*Het Digitaal Vrouwenlexicon van Nederland*, 4 July 2016). <http://resources.huygens.knaw.nl/vrouwenlexicon/lemmata/data/Van_der_Molen> accessed 1 June 2021.

[8] Van Klinken, *Strijdbaar & Omstreden* (n 1) 129.

[9] See, more elaborately, Janne E Nijman, 'Marked Absences: Locating Gender and Race in International Legal History' (2020) 31 EJIL 1025, 1035ff.

essentially a non-pillar). This 'pillarization' was a kind of Westphalian order within The Netherlands: the political parties representing the pillars collaborated at the top (which Arend Lijphart has famously theorized as 'consociationalism'), and each pillar was 'sovereign' in a wide range of aspects of social life. Each pillar had its own political parties, its own trade unions, employers' organizations, newspapers, schools, universities, sport clubs, and hospitals. The pillarization went as far as people shopping only at the baker, butcher, and greengrocer who belonged to their own pillar.

Van der Molen was born Protestant, and her father played a prominent role in one of the more conservative groups within that pillar: the Neo-Calvinist. To her own frustration, she was not allowed to go to grammar school (which would prepare her for university) on the ground that the calling of a good Protestant woman was marriage and family life. The only respectable paid jobs to be fulfilled by a woman were that of a teacher and nurse. Not interested in marriage, she tried both, but found satisfaction in neither. A turning point came when her mother organized for her to live in the house of a befriended family within the same pillar, headed by a professor of law and prominent member of the political party in which father Van der Molen was also active. Anne Anema recognized Gezina's intellectual talents, sharpened her writing skills, and encouraged her to apply for a position as a journalist at a Dutch newspaper. She started as editor of the 'women's pages', covering both housekeeping (how to remove stains, how to cook cabbage soup), and the role of women in society.[10] But her reach expanded: four years later she was sent to Geneva to cover the meetings of the League of Nations, including the adoption of the *Protocole pour le règlement pacifique des différends internationaux*. Encouraged by Anema, she decided, aged thirty-two, to study law and to focus, inspired by this Geneva experience, on the law of nations. During all those years, she was also active in her church, in the women's movement, and in the peace movement.

Throughout her life, Van der Molen operated within and was committed to the Neo-Calvinist branch of the Protestant pillar. According to the descriptions of people who knew her, she also embodied some of the characteristics ascribed to people belonging to that branch: firm on principles, hard-working, sober, stubborn, polemic, and moralistic. At the same time, Van der Molen was in many ways exceptional. She lived together with a Catholic woman, thus breaking two taboos for Neo-Calvinist women at the same time. On top of that, she made a career, published political brochures, and was not afraid openly to take issue with the male-dominated elite of her pillar. Yet, at least initially, this was not because she believed in gender equality. In the 1920s and 1930s, Van der Molen even went further than her party (which was cautious about state interference) by advocating for legislation that would force married women to stay home. Invoking God's will, natural law, and 'the strength of the Dutch people', Van der Molen argued that the natural role for married women was that of taking care of the family—and that it is up to the state to enforce this. The situation was different, so Van der Molen argued, for unmarried women: they should be able to participate freely in economic, social, and political life.[11] Van der Molen would change her view

[10] Van Klinken, *Strijdbaar & Omstreden* (n 1) 73–74.

[11] Van Klinken, *Strijdbaar & Omstreden* (n 1) 118–23. Original: Gezina HJ van der Molen, *De beroepsarbeid van de gehuwde vrouw* (Edecea 1938).

regarding married women after the Second World War, but her pre-war stance already reveals the complexity of her position. Her polemic style, her invocation of the Bible, and her conservative take on the duties of married women all fitted the Neo-Calvinist tradition. And yet, they were presented by a woman living together with a Catholic woman who took issue with the male elite because she was so convinced of her own reading of God's will, natural law, and the nature of the Dutch people that she propagated intrusion by the state into the private life of citizens. At the same time, she advocated and claimed more freedom for women such as herself who chose not to follow the traditional path of marriage.

Her commitment to the principles of the Calvinist Church as universal ones was visible in her dissertation. Its first thesis was: 'Alberico Gentili should be considered among the Calvinist lawyers of his time, some deviations in his doctrine notwithstanding.'[12] This was controversial: at some point Gentili had joined the Anglican Church and he had been legal counsel for the Catholic Spanish Crown (in cases against the Protestant Netherlands, that is). Van der Molen expresses her surprise that Gentili accepted that job, given his opposition to the Catholic Church and his characterization of the Pontificate as the Antichrist. At the end of the day, however, she downplays the importance of his aid to the Catholic empire as follows:

> That he did not refuse this flattering commission, may be attributed to a weakness in his character, but does not imply a denial of his faith. For he was only concerned with pure lawsuits and it is merely the pronounced religious conviction of his client which surprises us in this connection.[13]

For her it was important that Gentili was recognized not just a Christian thinker, but a *Calvinist* Christian thinker: unlike Christian Grotius, Gentili had not separated natural law and natural reason (*ratio naturalis*) from God.[14] Natural reason according to Gentili is, so Van der Molen writes, 'God's gift after the fall, and manifests itself in the voice of our conscience'.[15]

This, then, was Van der Molen's initial answer to the question that would accompany her throughout her adult life: how to reconcile a belief in pre-given moral categories with the experience of plurality? In her dissertation, she grounds the idea of a legal order between a plurality of communities on a firm, pre-given basis: the *ratio naturalis* as God's gift to a sinful humanity. International law is thus both specifically Christian and pluralistic as it allows one to be a legal counsel irrespective of one's own belief, even for a Crown that uses its power to spread a Church recognizing the 'Antichrist' as its spiritual leader.

After her doctorate, Van der Molen obtained a research grant from a Calvinist research foundation to write a biography of the sixteenth-century Calvinist

[12] Gezina HJ van der Molen, *Alberico Gentili and the Development of International Law: His Life Work and Times* (HJ Paris 1937), preliminaries (hereafter Van der Molen, *Alberico Gentili*). While the body of the text was in English, the preceding list of 'theses' was written in Dutch; this is our translation.

[13] ibid 265.

[14] ibid 203. For contrast with Grotius see ibid 205.

[15] Van Klinken, *Strijdbaar & Omstreden* (n 1) 203.

monarchomach Théodore de Bèze. He had written on a question that was again topical in the late 1930s: under which circumstances was a Calvinist allowed to stop obeying a tyrannical government? When the war broke out in 1939, Van der Molen criticized the generally shared desire in the Netherlands to stay neutral: one had to fight for justice and take up the struggle against an anti-Semitic country.[16] Putting her money where her mouth was, Van der Molen abandoned the research into Bèze and instead did the work that she would become most famous for, as well as the work that made her internationally notorious. Neither work was in international law.

The Second World War and Aftermath: Defining Choices

Not long after the German occupation, Van der Molen assumed a leading position in the Dutch resistance movement, again as one of very few women in a male-dominated underground world. She called for resistance in a brochure she wrote on the law of occupation, published in 1941, in which she took issue with some leading figures in the Calvinist movement who had argued that citizens had to obey orders from the occupying power. She also publicly objected to the so-called 'Aryan declaration' and those who had signed it: a declaration to certify one was not Jewish, which the Nazis required Dutch civil servants to sign if they wanted to keep their jobs. Van der Molen also established, organized, and wrote for clandestine press (a role for which some of her colleagues were assassinated).[17] Finally, she helped Jewish children escape the Nazis by finding them families with whom they could hide. It was for her role in the Dutch resistance that she would later be decorated.

However, it was her role *after* the war that made her notorious and in which context she is mostly remembered today.[18] While the occupation was still ongoing, Van der Molen had been concerned about the future guardianship of children who had been with *de facto* foster families during the war. Together with other leading figures of the resistance movement, she proposed the creation of a national committee that should decide on their fate. The proposal was accepted by the government in exile and the *Commissie voor Oorlogspleegkinderen* ('Committee for War Foster Children'; OPK) was formed, with Van der Molen as chair, and tasked with deciding on a case-by-case basis where children who had been with foster parents would go after the war.

From Van der Molen's perspective, her work after the war was a natural continuation of that during the war: she had taken responsibility for finding Jewish children foster families during the war; after the war she had the responsibility to ensure their care. As one commentator has observed, her approach to the children was also consistent: 'If these children were little warm bodies first and Jewish only after that, she acted in a similar vein after the war, in her capacity as head of the OPK.'[19] Van der

[16] ibid 147.

[17] The newspaper she co-founded, *Trouw*, still exists: <https://www.trouw.nl/> accessed 1 June 2021.

[18] It is, for instance, in this context that she makes an appearance in the best-selling 2018 Costa Book of the Year: Bart van Es, *The Cut Out Girl: A Story of War and Family, Lost and Found* (Penguin Books 2019) 196–97.

[19] Bela Ruth Samuel-Tenenholtz, 'Define Saving: Gezina van der Molen and Anneke Beekman: History and Identity after WWII' (2009) 14 Shaanan E23, E37.

Molen's guiding principle, and subsequently that of the majority of the Commission, was that the children were first and foremost *Dutch* and not to be regarded as belonging to a special group within Dutch society.

This guiding principle had implications for who was to decide on the children's future and what to decide on their future. As to who was to decide, Van der Molen's reasoning was that because this was a national affair regarding Dutch citizens, it was up to a national commission; the Dutch did not follow, for instance, the French or Belgian approach, which left decisions on the placement of orphans to Jewish organizations. As to what was to be decided, the Commission considered that it had to act as much as possible in the spirit of the parents, but it was the Commission that decided what would have mattered for the parents. To the Commission, and in particular its chairwoman, Jewishness per se was not a relevant factor in deciding on the children's future. In Bela Ruth Samuel-Tannenholtz's words, Van der Molen was 'unable (or unwilling) to understand Jewish identity in the secular sense'.[20] The decimated Jewish community in the Netherlands experienced her and the Commission's approach as 'a denial of a right to exist of a Jewish community in The Netherlands'.[21]

The approach adopted by the Commission followed from the moral principles that had inspired the resistance movement during the war. To set apart a group of society as different, as 'Jewish', was unacceptable, Van der Molen argued, also because it would replicate what the Nuremberg laws had tried before:

> Who thinks these children are a purely Jewish affair is mistaken. When our common enemy and suppressor started to persecute our Jewish compatriots vehemently, the best part of Dutch people did not regard this as a Jewish matter. They felt it was a Dutch problem, which regards all of us because of humanitarian considerations.[22]

In this lecture on the Dutch radio, Van der Molen moved seemingly smoothly from a universalistic logic ('humanitarian considerations') to the national level ('a Dutch problem') to an elite ('the best part of Dutch people') that knows best how to determine what universalism and the Dutch nation require. What complicated this picture even further is that often only a thin line separated 'Dutch' and 'Christian'. The spirit of the Dutch people, as Van der Molen had already argued in the 1920s and 1930s in relation to the position of women, was a Christian one. The result of the decisions of the Commission was that hundreds of Jewish children were placed in Christian homes. This was supposedly done in the name of a Dutch nation, acting through its 'best people', in order to realize humanitarian aspirations.

Commentators have accepted that, in the circumstances after the Second World War, 'determining the best interests of the child was not only highly fraught and political but in fact may have constituted an epistemological impossibility' due to 'the

[20] ibid E30.

[21] Maurice Swirc, 'Gezina redde en roofde kinderen' ['Gezina saved and stole children'] *Trouw* (Amsterdam, 15 February 2014) <https://www.trouw.nl/nieuws/gezina-redde-en-roofde-kinderen~b06759ee/> accessed 1 June 2021.

[22] Van Klinken, *Strijdbaar & Omstreden* (n 1) 202, citing 'Radiotoespraak voor Herrijzend Nederland 17-9-1945', HDC AGM inv.nr.43.

irreparable damage to families created by war and genocide'.[23] More than anything else, though, they criticize Van der Molen for her self-righteous and exclusive way of decision-making on this hugely complex issue. In order to deal with this impossible and tragic situation, Van der Molen fell back to the modes of operation and thinking that guided her during the war: in her view, it was up to an elite of 'righteous people' acting on clear moral principles to settle the situation. But the characteristics that had made her a hero during the war became the source of the greatest criticism of her in peace time.

A Thinning Universalism and a Thickening Pluralism

Van der Molen's post-OPK writings on international law demonstrate a relativization of her belief in firm moral and God-given principles. In a brochure that she wrote for her pillar's political party in 1950 on the ambitious topic of 'Christendom and International Ordering',[24] we again see her grapple with the tension between universality and plurality, but the universality is becoming thinner. She still argues that the ultimate foundation of international law is the fact that God has created men after his image, and that humankind sprang from this divine creation. The starting point, in other words, is the deep unity of mankind under God. However, the unity of mankind was spoiled when Adam and Eve sinned, resulting in God's command to spread around the earth. This was reinforced by the curse after mankind tried to build the tower of Babylon: mankind was divided into different linguistic communities, who do not live together in a single world community. The political message Van der Molen distills from these stories is that attempts to undo the plurality of mankind are vain and dangerous. To strive for a world state, she argues, is a dangerous utopia, comparable to the Leviathan, the beast arising from sea in the Book of Revelation. Christians should cherish the nation state as a way to deal with the consequences of the fall, to restrain and protect sinful human beings through law. Instead of a world state, they should strive for a stronger rule of law among nations, especially in a time when 'God's world plan' has made nations more interdependent than ever before. Again, what starts out from primordial creation and a single, Christian foundation of international law, ends up in a pluralist world, where law serves to keep the peace and to bring nations closer together. As this world is made up of Christian and non-Christian nations (and Van der Molen strongly opposes privileging Christian nations), the rule of law can do its job only if it transcends its Christian foundations. She thus ends up arguing that the unity of mankind is embodied in the unity of a legal order that applies between independent—and diverse—nations. Almost a decade later, Van der Molen would even explicitly distance herself from her earlier reading of Gentili's *societas humana* as a Western world society, a reading that, she admitted, betrayed a 'fatal exclusivity'.[25]

[23] Diane L Wolf, 'Child Withholding as Child Transfer: Hidden Jewish Children and the State in Postwar Netherlands' (2013) 12 Journal of Human Rights 296, 306.

[24] Gezina HJ van der Molen, *Christendom en Internationale Ordening* (Antirevolutionaire Partijstichting 1951).

[25] Van Klinken, *Strijdbaar & Omstreden* (n 1) 254, citing 'Some remarks on overseas student in Europe (lecture for the Fondation Européenne de la Culture, Vienna, 20 November 1959)', HCD AGM inv.nr.66.

Foreign journeys, almost always work-related, were key to the broadening of Van der Molen's normative horizons. Abroad, she experienced a sense of freedom to think and say things that she did not feel in the confines of the Dutch Calvinist society. As one of the twenty women among the thousand delegates to the United Nations General Assembly in 1946, she stated: '[W]e can hardly understand that after two world wars, which have certainly done as much harm to women as to men, there are still countries in which only men are fully responsible for state politics'.[26] And three months earlier she had written during a conference in Zurich that she felt 'vraiment libre,—libre d'aller où je veux, libre de dire que je pense'.[27]

Travelling made Van der Molen's thinking more flexible and shifted her priorities. In Palestine, in 1945–46, she was more open to the idea of letting Dutch Jewish foster children go to Palestine than when she had been in the Netherlands, or indeed, than she would be upon return.[28] In 1961, at the age of sixty-nine, she used her sabbatical to visit, research, and give lectures in New Delhi, Thailand, Ceylon, Syria, Egypt and, once again, Israel. Officially, she was going to search norms common to all people that could be the foundation for international law, in part to argue against fellow international lawyer Bert Röling, who had emphasized the West-European character of international law.[29] But the encounter with the realities of the street—poverty, racism, and the caste system—made her change her research agenda. In her Valedictorian a year later, she argued that as long as the majority of the world's population lacked livelihoods, international law would remain paralysed.[30] After her retirement, the struggle against racism and apartheid became among her primary causes. She saw this work as a natural extension of that of the resistance in the Second World War:

> We as Christians and as Europeans should be deeply ashamed instead of feeling superior on the ground that we are 'white', considering how in this Christian Europe six million Jews were insidiously murdered. And all of this resulted from a foolish and criminal racial awareness.[31]

In her view, the fight against racism was more important than the Cold War.[32]

Little was left of Van der Molen's universalization of Calvinist principles as the basis for international law. In the beginning of her academic international law career, she had promoted Gentili's work as a system of international law grounded in Protestant articles of faith and had argued for using the scriptures as the basis for international law to deal with an imperfect world after the original sin. In later life she moved from a Christian foundation of international law to a set of norms that could be found in religions and cultures around the world. Instead of Gentili's *ratio naturalis*, she looked

[26] ibid 237, citing 'Speech G.H.J. van der Molen, Lake Success 11-12-1946', HDC AGM inv.nr.57.
[27] ibid 230, citing 'Discours au Troisième Congrès Feminin Suisse le 23 septembre 1946 à Zürich', AGM inv.nr.65.
[28] ibid 212.
[29] ibid 277.
[30] ibid 281, citing Gezina JH van der Molen, *Norm en Praktijk in de Internationale Samenleving* 19.
[31] ibid 284, citing Gezina HJ van der Molen, *Recht op de Naaste Af* (Keesing BV 1976) 39 (hereafter Van der Molen, *Recht op de Naaste Af*) (our translation).
[32] ibid 274.

for a natural sense of justice shared by humankind at large. More importantly, she concluded that it would not be fitting to pass judgement on peoples, religions, and cultures that were foreign to her. Partly as a result of changing times, but also because of her travels, her belief in moral superiority had waned, and was eventually replaced by embarrassment and a sense of guilt. What she had held to be universal, objective truths now appeared to be culturally biased opinions. While she took pride and comfort in being a Christian, she also realized how Christianity had been implicated in the Holocaust.[33] She kept searching for principles that apply across the world, but by the end of her academic career she tried to develop them from the bottom up, through dialogue with other cultures.

And yet, this did not mean that she gave up on Christianity as the moral basis for international cooperation. She accused Christendom for complicity in racism, anti-Semitism, and imperialism, but she could not let go of her moral anchor. Meeting foreign cultures and religions, Van der Molen stated, 'has only strengthened my own Christian belief'.[34]

A Recognized International Lawyer who Cannot Be Celebrated

In 1992, Jeanne de Bruijn, the newly appointed professor of 'women's studies' at the Free University of Amsterdam proposed the creation of a Gezina van der Molen Chair. To mark what would have been her 100th birthday, the inter-faculty study group on 'women's studies' also organized an open seminar.[35] The turnout was low, and a prominent Dutch novelist and emeritus professor of criminology was offended just to be invited: 'What were you thinking? How could I, as a Jewish woman, participate in such a seminar?'[36] The Van der Molen Chair would never materialize. Instead, some two decades later the law faculty created a (rather modest) Gezina van der Molen Fund, which provides research support for women academics. The website of the fund contains no information on Van der Molen herself and most recipients have no idea who she was.

Another controversy emerged in 2013 when the municipality of Bloemendaal, where Van der Molen had lived until her death in 1978, proposed to name a street after her. This proposal, too, spurred fierce opposition from a variety of groups, including the Association of Jewish War Children and the Association of the Postwar Jewish Generation.[37] This time the criticism did not abort the initiative: one can now visit the Van der Molenstraat in Aerdenhout, Bloemendaal.

[33] After attending the opening of the Eichmann trial in 1961, she observed: 'This trial made me realize, that we all as Christians and Europeans are co-responsible for the catastrophe that we did not try to prevent.' Van der Molen, *Recht op de Naaste Af* (n 31) 78.

[34] ibid 117.

[35] See Van Klinken, *Strijdbaar & Omstreden* (n 1) 311.

[36] ibid 312. See also Elma Verhey, *Om het Joodse Kind* (Nijgh & Van Ditmar 1991).

[37] See Gert van Klinken, 'Herinneren aan de Vrije Universiteit. Gezina van der Molen en de "affaire Bloemendaal"' in Wim Berkelaar and others (eds), *Een oorlogsplaquette ontrafeld. Het herdenkingsmonument 1940–1945 van de Vrije Universiteit Amsterdam* (Boom 2020) 35–46.

These two episodes illustrate how initiatives to commemorate Gezina van der Molen turn into controversies. Whereas her supporters and admirers emphasize her pioneering role in Dutch society and her courage as a resistance fighter, opponents highlight her responsibility for the treatment of Jewish children, and by extension the Jewish community, after the war. For us as authors, too, there was no way around these controversies. While the international law focus of this book seemed to make it logical to foreground Gezina van der Molen as an international lawyer, it would be a misrepresentation *not* to discuss the roles that came to define her in eyes of the wider public.

And yet, as always, it is impossible to reduce a person to some of the roles she performed during her life, however influential these may have been. There are more stories to tell, and this chapter is an attempt to do so. We have argued that although the explicit reference to Christian articles of faith is far removed from the language of international law practised today, Van der Molen's writing in this area stands for a struggle in international law that continues: the struggle between universalism and pluralism.

Throughout her professional life, Van der Molen maintained that international law rests on two pillars: positive law and transcendental justice. Positive law is relative to time and place: different times, different places, different rules. Justice, by contrast, functions as an anchor. It provides a universally applicable scheme to assess the validity of positive rules and to ground directly applicable rules. In her early work, Van der Molen grounded 'justice' primarily in the Calvinism she grew up with. Later in life, her notion of justice became torn between universality and pluralism. She tried to distill it from values shared by Christianity, Islam, Hinduism, and Buddhism. Despite the undeniable differences between the four worldviews, Van der Molen found enough commonalities to conclude that a sound basis for international cooperation did exist. However, what she found was a set of positive values, dependent on the actual acceptance by the four worldviews or religions she studied. If this was all there is to it, the set of core values would be vulnerable to change, while it remained yet to be seen whether other worldviews would buy into them. While her experiences with others (and 'the other') made her less dogmatic about the ultimate foundation of law, she still maintained that the ethics of Christianity rose above that of other religions.[38] At the end of her journey she returned to where she came from, albeit more aware of its shortcomings and the promises held by other worldviews.

[38] Van der Molen, *Recht op de Naaste Af* (n 31) 117.

31

Elisabeth Mann Borgese

Ecology, Relationality, and Law of the Sea

*Sara Seck**

Introduction

Elisabeth Mann Borgese is recognized today for her contributions to oceans advocacy and governance, and often referred to as the 'Mother of the Oceans'.[1] She advocated for the inclusion of the principle of common heritage of mankind (CHM) in the deep seabed mining regime under the UN Convention on the Law of the Sea (UNCLOS).[2] Mann Borgese viewed this principle as vital to the global world order, and ocean governance as an opportunity to test its application.[3] She was also the author of over a dozen books, and editor of diverse texts from short stories to children's literature to academic writings .[4] Philosopher, aestheticist, and friend Peter Serracino Inglott describes her work as ranging 'from musicology to surrealist fiction to experiments with animal communication to an odd manifesto of idiosyncratic feminism to the economics of self-management in productive organisations'.[5] These eclectic contributions partly reflect her unique life experience as the daughter of Thomas Mann, Nobel Prize for literature laureate, and Katia Pringsheim, the granddaughter of Hedwig Dohm who has been described as 'one of the greatest exponents of feminism in the nineteenth

* I would like to thank Immi Tallgren for inviting me to contribute to this volume, and participants in a virtual workshop who commented on a first draft. I am also grateful to Sarah MacLeod, JD, for research assistance and to Tahnee Prior, post-doctoral fellow, for research support funded by an Ocean Frontiers Institute seed fund grant, and for sharing my enthusiasm for the remarkable EMB.

1 The following websites all make the same claim: Dalhousie University—Dalhousie Originals—Elisabeth Mann Borgese: <https://www.dal.ca/about-dal/dalhousie-originals/elisabeth-mann-borgese.html>, accessed 7 October 2022; So German—Mother of the Oceans: <https://sogerman.ca/story/mother-of-the-oceans/>, accessed 7 October 2022; <International Ocean Institute—Elisabeth Mann Borgese—The Founder of IOI: <https://www.ioinst.org/elisabeth-mann-borgese/>, accessed 7 October 2022.

2 United Nations Convention on the Law of the Sea (UNCLOS) (adopted 10 December 1982, entered into force 16 November 1994) 1833 UNTS 397, Part XI, and especially Article 136.

3 Elisabeth Mann Borgese, 'The Years of My Life' in Chircop and others (eds), *Ocean Yearbook* (Vol 18, University of Chicago Press 2004) 1–21 at 12 [Nexus Lecture]. This lecture was originally presented at the Nexus Institute in 1999 in Tilburg, the Netherlands, and published at that time in Dutch. See also EM Borgese, 'Caird Medal address' (2001) 25 Marine Policy 391–97 at 391.

4 An archive of Elisabeth Mann Borgese's contributions is available through Dalhousie University Libraries: <https://findingaids.library.dal.ca/elisabeth-mann-borgese-fonds> accessed 7 October 2022 (Fonds MS-2-744).

5 Peter Serrancino Inglott, 'Elisabeth Mann Borgese: Metaphysician by Birth' in Chircop and others (eds), *Ocean Yearbook* (Vol 18, University of Chicago Press 2004) 22–74 at 23. Most of her writings are in English, with some in German.

Sara Seck, *Elisabeth Mann Borgese* In: *Portraits of Women in International Law.* Edited by: Immi Tallgren, Oxford University Press.
 DOI: 10.1093/oso/9780198868453.003.0031

Figure 31.1 Elisabeth Mann Borgese, IOI-Canada, photographer/date unknown.
Source: Dirk Werle, International Ocean Institute.

century'.[6] Yet, even Mann Borgese's early writings reveal an underlying ecological worldview that is expressed in her work as a 'philosophy of continuity between the individual, society, and nature'.[7] Julia Poertner suggests that Mann Borgese's mission was to change the dominant Western narrative of uncooperative individualism that underlies contemporary capitalism and related societal subsystems, including gender norms. She sought to replace it with a narrative of humans as caring, co-operative, and a part of nature.[8] In 2002, Mann Borgese was nominated for the Nobel Peace Prize jointly with the International Ocean Institute (IOI), which she founded.[9] The IOI has been described as her 'most enduring and endearing legacy'.[10]

The life and legacy of Elisabeth Mann Borgese have become of increasing interest to me since I was invited to research this portrait. First, like Mann Borgese, I am a professor (of law) at Dalhousie University in Halifax, Nova Scotia, Canada, where she was

[6] Patricia Mallia and David Testa, 'Elisabeth Mann Borgese, Gender and the Law of the Sea' in Irini Papanicolopulu (ed), *Gender and the Law of the Sea* (Brill Nijhoff 2019) 106–121, at 107.

[7] Julia Poertner, *Narratives of Nature and Culture: The Cultural Ecology of Elisabeth Mann Borgese* (PhD thesis, Dalhousie University, March 2020) at 270, https://dalspace.library.dal.ca/handle/10222/78028accessed 7 October 2022.

[8] Poertner (n 7) at 270–71.

[9] 'Nomination for Elisabeth Mann Borgese and the International Ocean Institute for the Joint Award of the Nobel Peace Prize' (PDF) *Dalhousie Library*, January 2001https://findingaids.library.dal.ca/uploads/r/dalhousie-university-archives/5/1/3/513e40ae8524bb09c932cb523e96c7c5bf4e30fc15b13c9637f5d1c77aa06bff/ms-2-744_361-24_access.pdf accessed 7 October 2022 [Nobel Prize Nomination]. See also Betsy Baker, 'Uncommon Heritage: Elisabeth Mann Borgese, *Pacem in Maribus*, the International Ocean Institute and Preparations for UNCLOS III' in A Chircop and others (eds), *Ocean Yearbook* (Vol 26, Martinus Nijhoff Publishers 2012) 11–34.

[10] Mallia and Testa (n 6) at 114.

a professor (of political science, and, for a shorter period, adjunct professor of law) between 1980 and 2002. I did not have the opportunity to meet her, although several of my colleagues at Dalhousie's Marine & Environmental Law Institute worked closely with her. They continue her legacy through support for IOI and publication of the *Ocean Yearbook*, described by Shastri as IOI's flagship publication, and 'another EMB brainchild'.[11] Her approach and vision to overcome narratives of Western individualism intrigue me because it coincides with some of my own work. I advocate for the necessity to reimagine humans (including workers and investors) and states as ecologically embedded relational beings, even as each is differentially situated.[12] Moreover, as a legal scholar who started her career as a professional musician, I was curious to learn that Mann Borgese observed that her only academic training was in music.[13] In her writings on cultural perspectives on the ocean, notably in *The Oceanic Circle*, she offers musical analysis while also observing how the sea and music influenced her father's writings.[14]

In this portrait, I first describe Mann Borgese's life and contribution to international law, drawing primarily on her own words. I then turn to the views of others to shed light on her legacy. In the third part, I reflect on how her other contributions reveal a common theme of ecological relational thinking that influenced her contributions to the development of international law, including oceans governance. I conclude with reflections on why her legacy, beyond the usual focus on CHM, law of the sea, and the establishment of the IOI, might merit closer attention in our time of global ecological crisis.

Life Sketch and Law of the Sea

Elisabeth Mann Borgese was born in 1918 in Germany, and escaped with her family to France, then Switzerland, and finally the United States when Hitler came to power.[15] She read Sicilian Guiseppe Antonio Borgese's writings on fascist totalitarianism when she was eighteen years old, met him in Princeton in 1938, and married him in 1939 when he was fifty-seven and she twenty-one.[16] In her 1999 Nexus lecture, she describes Borgese as 'not only my husband and the father of my children but also my teacher, whose influence on the development of my thinking matched that of my parents'.[17]

[11] Sunil M Shastri, 'Elisabeth Mann Borgese: A Life Dedicated to Pacem in Maribus' in A Chircop and others (eds), *Ocean Yearbook* (Vol 18, University of Chicago Press 2004) 75–87 at 81. And, I have myself agreed to become one of the co-editors as of July 2021.

[12] See, eg, Sara L Seck, 'A Relational Analysis of Enterprise Obligations and Carbon Majors for Climate Justice' (2021) 11(1) Oñati Socio-Legal Series 254–84: Climate Justice in the Anthropocene; Sara L Seck, 'Relational Law: Re-imagining Tools for Environmental and Climate Justice' (2019) 31(1) Canadian Journal of Women and the Law 151–77.

[13] Inglott (n 5) at 46.

[14] Elisabeth Mann Borgese, *The Oceanic Circle: Governing the Seas as a Global Resource* (United Nations University Press 1998) 51–54.

[15] Nexus lecture (n 3) at 1, 4.

[16] ibid 4. Inglott (n 5) at 37.

[17] ibid 5.

Between 1945 and 1952, the Borgeses and others founded the multidisciplinary Chicago Committee to Frame a World Constitution along with its journal *Common Cause*.[18] The initiative was encouraged by Robert M Hutchinson, then President of the University of Chicago.[19] As much work on the development of the nuclear bomb was done at the University, 'profound feeling of guilt gripped Chicago as the mushroom clouds rose over Hiroshima and Nagasaki'.[20] Borgese believed that this placed a moral responsibility upon the university to unite the world.[21] According to Mann Borgese, the Chicago Committee was distinct from other world government movements at the time as its focus went beyond the usual goals of preventing international violence and the maintenance of peace.[22] Instead, the Committee approached 'government or governance in an interdisciplinary and holistic mode' that viewed peace as 'more than the absence of war', and that peace could only be attained through social and economic justice, nationally and internationally.[23]

The drafters maintained that transcending existing economic systems and particularly the Roman law concept of ownership was essential for economic justice.[24] A new system was needed, which 'declares that the four elements of life—earth, water, air, and energy—are the common property of the human race'.[25] While aware that the immediate adoption of the Constitution by the international community was unrealistic, the intention was to provide a 'blueprint pointing in the direction of a desirable, or probably, ineluctable future'.[26]

The work of the Chicago Committee came to a halt during McCarthysim as '[a]nyone who dared to speak out for peace, was branded as a Communist, condemned to silence and fired from his job'.[27] Hutchinson and many exiles, including Mann Borgese's family, returned to Europe.[28] However, Borgese died suddenly in 1952 in Italy leaving Mann Borgese with two children. She stayed in Italy for fourteen years.[29]

In 1964, Mann Borgese was invited by Hutchins to become a fellow with the Center for the Study of Democratic Institutions to resume work on the world constitution and she relocated to California.[30] In November 1967, Arvid Pardo, the Maltese Ambassador to the United Nations delivered an 'epoch-making ocean address to the United Nations' in which he proposed the CHM principle to transcend 'both

[18] ibid 6. Mann Borgese notes that while hundreds of world constitutions were produced around this time by 'escapist, blasphemous, and constructive utopians' and analyzed in the *Common Cause* journal, the Chicago Committee's constitution, dedicated to Gandhi, 'was certainly the most successful'. ibid 10.

[19] ibid 6.

[20] ibid 6.

[21] ibid 6.

[22] ibid 8.

[23] ibid 8.

[24] ibid 9.

[25] ibid 9.

[26] ibid 8–9. Nevertheless, Mann Borgese observes these ideas did find their way into UNCLOS 1982.

[27] ibid 10–11.

[28] ibid 10–11.

[29] Inglott (n 5) at 37; Tirza Meyer, *Elisabeth Mann Borgese: Deep Ideology* Dissertation (Norwegian University of Science and Technology 2018) 58–59.

[30] Nexus lecture (n 3) at 11. Mann Borgese observes, however, that the Constitution 'still looked to me like a very great piece of work. It did not need improving. It was the world that needed improving!'.

sovereignty and freedom' of the high seas and address mounting perils such as pollution, armed conflict, and the extinction of marine living resources.[31] Believing that the Cold War made progress on the world constitution unlikely, Mann Borgese proposed to Hutchins that the ocean could serve as 'our great laboratory for the making of a new world order'.[32] Joining forces with Pardo, she organized a three-year project leading to the 1970 *Pacem in Maribus* conference ('Peace on the Oceans').[33] Over thirty *Pacem in Maribus* international conferences were held between 1970 and 2013 as a forum for the consideration of the challenges of ocean space 'in their interconnectedness'.[34] Mann Borgese established the International Ocean Institute (IOI) in 1972 to 'enhance a broad interdisciplinary dialogue on ocean law and development' with its headquarters in Malta.[35]

The IOI was actively involved in the third UN Conference on the Law of the Sea, which culminated in the adoption of the UN Convention on the Law of the Sea in 1982.[36] The President of IOI's Governing Board, who was also the President of UNCLOS III, described UNCLOS as 'A Constitution for the Oceans'.[37] According to Mann Borgese, all major actors participated in the *Pacem in Maribus* conferences and the UNCLOS III process.[38] Mann Borgese herself contributed in many ways, including through her association with Pardo, on behalf of IOI, and later as a member of the Austrian delegation.

Mann Borgese's Social Capital and Influence

The previous part draws heavily on a biographical lecture given by Mann Borgese in 1999 in which she reflects on her life and engagement with oceans governance. But what might others who have assessed her contributions to the development of the law of the sea have to say about her influence? To what extent was her ability to participate and influence enabled by her family history?

Tirza Meyer has taken an historical and biographical approach to Mann Borgese's role prior to, during, and after UNCLOS.[39] According to Meyer, Mann Borgese developed her ideal of internationalism through her work with the Chicago Committee, and was able to apply it to UNCLOS through the CHM principle by utilizing her experiences in Chicago and Santa Barbara to stage her own conferences and design the IOI. Mann Borgese's privileged background led to her meeting Borgese, and her relationship with him enabled her participation in the world constitutionalism project where

[31] ibid 11–12.
[32] ibid 12.
[33] ibid 12. Mann Borgese describes Malta as 'a small county without big vested interests, in the middle of the Mediterranean Sea, at the confluence of European, African and Asian cultures, and with the historic merit of having triggered the whole contemporary Law of the Sea development'.
[34] 'Pacum in Maribus (PIM) Conferences', online: IOI https://www.ioinst.org/about-1/pacem-in-maribus-pim-conferences/accessed 7 October 2022.
[35] Nexus lecture (n 3) at 13.
[36] ibid.
[37] ibid.
[38] ibid.
[39] Meyer (n 29).

she contributed as a research assistant to the Committee and as editor of *Common Concern*, ultimately writing twelve articles closely related to the Committee's work.[40] According to Mann Borgese, while Borgese was the key author of the constitution, she 'very actively assisted'.[41] Following Borgese's death, Mann Borgese undertook a wide range of activities while based in Italy, from editing, writing, and teaching to travel 'to India to interview Nehru and conduct behavioural experiments on elephants'.[42] During the time, she kept in touch with Hutchins and others from the Chicago circle.[43]

Mann Borgese describes Pardo as having an influence 'on my thinking and on my life [that] is commensurate only to that of my parents and my husband'.[44] Yet, while she clearly attributes the CHM principle to him, Pardo's was not the first introduction of the concept of CHM to the deep seabed context.[45] While Pardo and Mann Borgese viewed the CHM principle as able to reinforce developing countries' goals in the New International Economic Order (NIEO),[46] Mann Borgese's vision of CHM was broader. She saw the ocean regime as akin to world governance, while Pardo limited his vision to the area outside national jurisdiction.[47] Yet both Mann Borgese and Pardo identified multiple ways in which UNCLOS and the NIEO could be mutually reinforcing beyond CHM, including through the establishment of exclusive economic zones, South-South cooperation and regional organization, capacity building at multiple levels, protection of the interests of land-locked states, and the establishment of regional centres for co-operation, development, and transfer of technology.[48] Mann Borgese was able to bring concrete proposals forward for the negotiations and gained influence by affiliating herself with high profile people like Pardo and key delegations including the Group of Landlocked and Geographically Disadvantaged States, the Evensen Group, and the Austrian Delegation.[49] While some were unwilling to work with her, such as the Neptune Group,[50] Mann Borgese was able to

[40] ibid 54–56. Meyer notes that Mann Borgese started out as a personal secretary to Borgese, as her mother had been to her father. ibid 46. Further, Meyer observes that while Mann Borgese described herself as a co-founder of the Chicago committee, Borgese was unlikely to have seen it that way and in 1949 was said to have struggled with her professional independence. ibid 54, citing Holzer, *Elisabeth Mann Borgese*, 129.

[41] Elisabeth Mann Borgese, 'Arvid Pardo: Retrospect and Prospect' (1999) at 1, online: <https://findingaids.library.dal.ca/arvid-pardo-retrospect-and-prospect-by-elisabeth-mann-borgese> accessed 7 October 2022 [File MS-2-744, Box 3, Folder 4]. See also Mallia and Testa (n 6) at 108.

[42] Meyer (n 29) at 58–59.

[43] ibid 59.

[44] Nexus lecture (n 3) 11.

[45] Meyer (n 29) 102–06, citing Ranganathan, 'Global Commons', 704, 707. Ranganathan suggests that 'As early as 1963, a corporate executive suggested the UN assume title to the international seabed and allocate exploitation rights generating revenue for itself.' Meyer (n 29) 106.

[46] *Oceanic Circle* (n 14) 7. See further Arvid Pardo and Elisabeth Mann Borgese, 'The New International Economic Order and Law of the Sea' in Jan Tinbergen (ed), *Reshaping the International Order (RIO): A Report to the Club of Rome* (Pergamon 1976); Arvid Pardo and Elisabeth Mann Borgese, *The New International Economic Order and the Law of the Sea*, Occasional Paper No 4 (International Ocean Institute, Malta 1976).

[47] Meyer (n 29) 33, 131–32. See further Mann Borgese's first draft of 'The Ocean Regime', described by Meyer as 'an attempt to extend ocean governance to world governance'. ibid 132.

[48] *Oceanic Circle* (n 14) 7.

[49] Meyer (n 29) 179–96. See further ibid 216–25, noting that the Austrian delegation as a landlocked state was interested in CHM, and that Austrian contributions at the time reflected the NIEO vision of the ISA as a joint venture and single system, despite negotiations having moved on from these ideas.

[50] ibid 196, fn 950, citing Miriam Levering in Levering and Levering, *Citizen Action*, 33, who saw Mann Borgese as both tactless and ineffective.

adapt to changing situations, and was not an 'ivory tower idealist' as suggested by some.[51]

Despite Mann Borgese's extensive efforts to promote an international oceans organization equivalent to the World Bank, this idea never gained traction.[52] Her written statement on behalf of IOI to UNCLOS III advocating for 'an ocean space authority' was met with a complaint from the Russian delegation and was 'ruled out of order'.[53] As a member of the Austrian delegation, she actively developed earlier work on joint venture models of the exploitation of the deep seabed that could successfully bring together entities from differing economic systems.[54] Yet while her work leading to UNCLOS III may ultimately have had little lasting influence given the 1994 Agreement on implementation of Part XI,[55] her primary influence may have been 'to bring together people interested in shaping the new regime for the oceans'.[56] Without Mann Borgese having 'devoted her career to the cause of the oceans' neither IOI nor *Pacem in Maribus* would exist, and many of those who gathered for the UNCLOS III negotiations in 1974 would have had access to less information and less understanding of the issues and their significance.[57] Mann Borgese noted the importance of IOI supporting smaller nations in Africa and Asia at UNCLOS III and included a collection of their statements in IOI's earliest publications.[58] Her colleagues at Dalhousie considered her 'genuine connection to colleagues in the "Third World"' as one of her most substantial contributions, including the launch of IOI training programmes for ocean professionals from the developing world,[59] which continue to this day.

Mann Borgese's commitment to developing countries is also evident in her involvement with the founding of the Independent World Commission for the Oceans (IWCO), modelled on the Brundtland Commission.[60] Though Mann Borgese's purpose was to promote the CHM narrative, it officially sought to draw attention to sustainable development in marine areas and to prepare a report with recommendations for the international community in celebration of the 1998 United Nations Oceans Year.[61] On receiving the draft volume of background papers for the report, Mann Borgese complained that there were not enough papers from developing countries.[62] In her letter of resignation of 1998, she 'accused the Commission of discriminating against developing countries and representatives of the South'.[63]

[51] ibid 296.
[52] Baker (n 9) 25–26.
[53] ibid 29.
[54] ibid 31–33.
[55] ibid 33. See Agreement relating to the implementation of Part XI of the United Nations Convention on the Law of the Sea of 10 December 1982, UN Doc A/RES/48/263, 17 August 1994, especially amendment to Article 153.
[56] Baker (n 9) 33.
[57] ibid 34.
[58] ibid 28–29.
[59] ibid 30.
[60] Poertner (n 7) 164. Indeed, in a letter threatening resignation in 1996, Mann Borgese suggests it was her hard work and her own $50,000 donation that led to the establishment of the Commission in the first place. ibid 165.
[61] ibid 165.
[62] ibid 167–68.
[63] ibid 168–69. Mann Borgese's letter states in part: 'I have had many occasions to object against the 'Northern' orientation of the work of the Commission.... One of the purposes of our Commission was

Mann Borgese's Ecological Relational Worldview and UNCLOS

Mann Borgese's contributions to the development of the law of the sea have received much attention. This part illuminates how her diverse writings and related activities reveal a common theme of ecological relational thought according to which everything is interconnected.[64] How does this vision reflect Mann Borgese's understanding of the legacy of UNCLOS?

Both Borgese's political writings and his realistic-mythic writings inspired Mann Borgese. In Borgese's short story 'The Sea', a bureaucratic employee dreams he is a fish caught in a fisher's net which is his firm—Mann Borgese was deeply impressed by Borgese's ability to identify with the fish and his depiction of its escape back into the ocean.[65] Her fascination with non-human animals is also evident in her own writing including a collection of short stories written after her husband died.[66] The first story concerns an ape being induced by humans to conduct an orchestra made up of human players.[67] In reality, Mann Borgese taught her dog to type on a specially designed typewriter, and to play the piano with his nose on a piano with enlarged keys.[68] Her book, *The White Snake*, contributes to the understanding of animal learning and communication.[69]

Influenced by her feminist grandmother Hedwig Dohm, Mann Borgese wrote about the challenges facing women.[70] The epilogue of her 1963 book *The Ascent of Woman*,[71] entitled 'My Own Utopia', was inspired by transformations in some snails and fish. In it, babies are born without a sex, then all become women in their early twenties, and transform into men in their mid-forties.[72] Meyer describes *Ascent of Woman* as not feminist; arguing it illustrates the rise of Mann Borgese to male acceptance in a male dominated family and society.[73] However, Poertner suggests that throughout *Ascent of Women*, Mann Borgese is 'testing the hypothesis that there is an affinity between the feminine and the collective, on the one hand, and the masculine and the individualistic

to help bridging the gap between North and South. It has miserably failed to fulfill this mandate.' ibid 169, citing Elisabeth Mann Borgese in a letter to Mario Soares from 24 February 1998. MS-2-744_244-3.

64 ibid 270. This part is greatly influenced by ibid. See also François Bailet, 'The Capacity Development Imperative: Elisabeth Mann Borgese's Legacy' in International Ocean Institute (ed), *The Future of Ocean Governance and Capacity Building: Essays in Honor of Elisabeth Mann Borgese* (Brill Nijhoff 2018) 71–76.

65 Inglott (n 5) 40.

66 ibid 47–48. Elisabeth Mann Borgese, *To Whom It May Concern* (Braziller 1959).

67 ibid 49.

68 ibid 49, 51, 64, 66.

69 ibid 51, 62–63. See Elisabeth Mann Borgese, *The White Snake* (Macgibbon and Kee 1966) at p149 as cited in Inglott (n 5) 62. See also *The Language Barrier* (1967) and *Sea Farm: The Story of Aquaculture* (1982).

70 The epitaph on Hedwig Dohm's gravestone repeats one of her most famous statements: 'Human rights have no gender' (English translation). It has been said to exemplify Mann Borgese's life's work. See Richard Samuel Deese, *Climate Change and the Future of Democracy* (Springer 2019) ch 5, 'Transcending the Tragedy of the Commons' 71–85 at 74.

71 Elisabeth Mann Borgese, *Ascent of Woman* (MacGibbon & Kee 1963).

72 ibid 213–23; Inglott (n 5) 44.

73 Meyer (n 40) 44.

on the other, by looking at the social organization in the animal world, the behaviour of crowds, and grammatically gendered language'.[74] While competitive natural selection has led to individuation and physically stronger men, cultural evolution has led to higher socialization in humans. Equality for women will only be possible through the integration of the individual and the social.[75] Mann Borgese believed that 'the history of the development of the individual' led to both the collapse of the unity of nature and culture, and 'the inferiority of women': '[i]n pre-individualistic times, "the essence of this unity, of this collective, was women... and man was marginal" '.[76]

Mann Borgese also wrote many books about the oceans, including the 1970s best seller *The Drama of the Oceans*,[77] which expresses ideas of interconnection and ecological grounding.[78] For example, she describes the ocean system as indivisible where '[e]verything in the oceans interacts with everything else, and the oceans themselves interact with the atmosphere and the land'.[79] To then divide ocean and land, or man and nature, makes no sense, as these concepts are in 'dynamic continuum, each part of the other'.[80]

This ecological relational worldview is reflected in how Mann Borgese describes the legacy of UNCLOS III. Beyond the CHM principle, Mann Borgese noted that UNCLOS introduced a valuable relational concept: that the problems of the ocean space must be considered as one, where change in one part affects the system as a whole.[81] Moreover, she suggests that UNCLOS 'limits, transforms, and transcends the concept of 'sovereignty' in an interdependent world'.[82] Without UNCLOS, subsequent international environmental law initiatives such as the Rio Earth Summit in 1992 would not have taken place, or would have been ineffective, due to a lack of framework. Specifically:

> The Convention has created what still today [1999] is the only existing comprehensive, binding international environmental law, covering all kinds of pollution from all sources, whether oceanic, land-based or atmospheric, and on a global basis: a framework which can and must be filled by more specific geographically or functionally limited agreements and conventions, of which there are already several hundreds ...[83]

Beyond this, UNCLOS includes extensive provisions on marine scientific research, cooperative technology development, and 'the most comprehensive, binding yet flexible system for the peaceful settlement of disputes ever accepted by the international community'.[84]

[74] Poertner (n 7) 82.
[75] ibid 82–83.
[76] Ibid 83, citing *Ascent of Woman* (n 71) 55.
[77] Elisabeth Mann Borgese, *The Drama of the Oceans*, (Harry N Abrams Inc Publishers 1975).
[78] Poertner (n 7) 42–43.
[79] ibid, citing *The Drama of the Oceans* (n 77) 230.
[80] ibid, citing *The Drama of the Oceans* (n 77) 230.
[81] Nexus lecture (n 3) 13.
[82] Ibid 13.
[83] Ibid 14.
[84] ibid 14.

Mann Borgese saw the relationality of UNCLOS and the CHM principle as fundamentally important not only for oceans, but also as for sustainable development.[85] For Mann Borgese, the term sustainable development is 'the new name, the new form of "humanistic socialism" or "social humanism" that we need for the next century'.[86] Development that is not sustainable cannot be development.

Ultimately,

> Mann Borgese's utopia transcends the boundaries that for centuries have characterized modern conceptualizations of human identity, including the foundational assumptions of humanism and social and global orders. It finds its most profound formulation in her understanding and advancement of the common heritage of mankind. Without denying the value and agency of human beings, Mann Borgese's continuous[ly] dismantle[s] strict boundaries and dualisms between human and nonhuman forms of life, the artificial and the natural, the past, present and the future.[87]

Conclusion

This portrait has touched upon the surface of the many inspiring contributions and insights that emerge from the work of Elisabeth Mann Borgese. Another theme to explore is her commitment to interdisciplinarity, which emerges from her cultural ecology, and is evident in practice in the structure, workings, and contributions of the IOI as an example.[88] Yet another is Mann Borgese's proposal for 'a web of interconnected world communities' that would serve as the 'organizational pattern of the global order', overlapping with nation states, with the international regime of the ocean serving as one community, while others include universities (learning society, managing science and technology as CHM), energy, land-based resources, and communications.[89] This vision of transnational law beyond sovereignty and property clearly merits further attention.

Mann Borgese's work appears highly relevant to the current global ecological challenges. At the very least, her thinking on CHM including its application to marine living resources is of importance to the ongoing BBNJ negotiations (the Intergovernmental Conference on an international legally binding instrument under

[85] Ibid 13.

[86] ibid 13. See further Poertner (n 7) 144–65, exploring Mann Borgese's serious concerns over the emergence and dominance of sustainable development, something that is addressed in part by Mann Borgese in her 1995 monograph: Elisabeth Mann Borgese, *Ocean Governance and the United Nations* (Centre for Foreign Policy Studies, Dalhousie University 1995).

[87] Poertner (n 7) 7–8. Poertner suggests that this positions Mann Borgese's work 'on the spectrum of posthumanism or post-anthropocentrism'.

[88] ibid 253, 263.

[89] Ibid 232–39. The idea was inspired in part by her studies of the Yugoslav constitutional model of nonownership and self-management.

UNCLOS on the conservation and sustainable use of marine biological diversity of areas beyond national jurisdiction).[90] But it would appear there is much more on offer that might inform 'our' need to reimagine systems across scales, perhaps including the nature of the humans who design them.

[90] See eg Vito De Lucia, 'The Question of the Common Heritage of Mankind and the Negotiations towards a Global Treaty on Marine Biodiversity in Areas Beyond National Jurisdiction: No End in Sight?' (2020) 16(2) McGill Journal of Sustainable Development Law 140–57, available at <https://static1.squarespace.com/static/610855af3be40c6cab4ff38e/t/616dd11f8ba87b5cedcfb47b/1634586911526/mjsdl_16.2-vito_de_lucia-common_heritage_of_mankind.pdf>, accessed 7 October 2022..

32
Marie Theres Fögen
The Universalization of a Rotten Deal

Reut Yael Paz

Introduction: *La femme n'existe pas*

Marie Theres Fögen was an exceptional legal historian.[1] Her premature death ended both her professorship at the University of Zurich and her directorship at the Max Planck Institute for European Legal History in Frankfurt (MPIeR, 2001–2008).[2] That she was the first woman to be entrusted with such directorship dedicated to *Rechtswissenschaft*, legal science, as it is called in Germany, was well-deserved.[3] As Dieter Simon, Fögen's mentor and *Doktorvater*, describes her: 'She was the only one who was knowledgeable enough to cover legal history from Greece through Rome, the Byzantium, Charlemagne all the way to Hitler.'[4] That her scholarship remains overlooked, particularly by English language readerships, is poignant and informative about the profession. On the one hand international audiences have become more and more monolingual, no matter how 'comparative', 'historical', and/or 'international' the purpose of the research is.[5] On the other hand, the insularity of the German legal culture which sustains a conservative, if not reactionary, status quo in terms of a constant reproduction of an exclusive and elitist class of jurists also plays a role.[6] This implicates obvious gender biases too. After all, during Fögen's time 'women in German

[1] Lacan, *Seminar XX* (New York: WW Norton & Co 1998).

[2] Marie Theres Fögen died in 2008 of cancer in Zürich.

[3] Lorraine Daston, the American historian of science, was the first woman to head the Max Planck Institute in 1994, Fögen was the first to receive a directorship of a research institute dedicated to legal history.

[4] Much of the biographical information used in this contribution comes from an interview between the author and Dieter Simons on 30 July 2019. (Henceforth 'Interview'). It can be problematic to rely on the oral narrative of someone close to your protagonist, and involved in her biography on many levels. Yet, it is an indispensable testimony of Fögen's academic context. Simon's recognition that 'what I tell is purely subjective', is as important as his acknowledgment that his 'work would not have been possible without Fögen'. I have done my utmost to uncover her voice from his narrative and tried to avoid 'gossip-like' details. (The transcript of the interview is in my possession.)

[5] For a full list of Fögen's publications see Available at <https://www.ius.uzh.ch/de/staff/professorships/former-profs/foegen/mtf/publikationen.html> accessed 8 October 2022.

[6] That German legal academics remain content with their own almost self-sufficient community of readers, reinforces the importance of law for the construction of a national heart versus its Others. On the introspective habitus of German legal academia, see the 2011 report of the Wissenschaftsrat (Prospects of Legal Scholarship in Germany) available at https://wissenschaftsrat.de/download/archiv/Jahresbericht_2011.pdf;jsessionid=C4DA3626E70CADBF89C039830AFDCE92.delivery2-master?__blob=publicationFile&v=4) accessed 8 October 2022.

Reut Yael Paz, *Marie Theres Fögen* In: *Portraits of Women in International Law*. Edited by: Immi Tallgren, Oxford University Press.
 DOI: 10.1093/oso/9780198868453.003.0032

Figure 32.1 Marie Theres Fögen.
Source: Jos Schmid, University of Zurich.

law faculties could at best be professor's assistances or their lovers, but would not be accepted as equal colleagues'.[7]

Such structural patriarchy, sexism, and/or misogyny remain both particular and universal experiences. This includes the legal academic field and labour with its generated specific *habitus* and *cultural capital*.[8] Focusing on Fögen highlights the troubles and limitations of the profession as a whole and the slow and painful integration of women into the legal discipline. Linking Fögen's work to her social context is

[7] As Simon continued: 'Often after it was made clear that Fögen wrote something that was previously anonymous the response was often "really? Fögen wrote this?"'. 'Interview' (n 4). Only in 1965, (forty-five years after women were first accepted to law faculties) did the first woman became a public law professor in Germany. In 1970, the year of Fögen's completion of her *Erstes Staatsexamen* (First State Examination), only 15 per cent of law students in Germany were women. Today half the students are women, and about 15 per cent of law professors. See Ute Sacksofsky and Carolin Stix, 'Daten und Fakten zur Repräsentanz von Frauen in der Rechtswissenschaft' (Goethe-Universität 2018) available at <www.jura.uni-frankfurt.de/73356125/Daten_und_Fakten_zur_Repräsentanz_von_Frauen_in_der_Rechtswissenschaft_Sacksofsky_Stix_2018.pdf> accessed 8 October 2022.

[8] On how the world of law lives off and within the hybrid world of the social see Pierre Bourdieu, *Distinction: A Social Critique of the Judgment of Taste* (Harvard University Press, 1987); Pierre Bourdieu, *Masculine Domination* (Polity Press, 2001); 'The Force of Law: Towards a Sociology of the Juridical Field' (1987) 38 *The Hastings Law Review* 805 Available at <https://repository.uchastings.edu/hastings_law_journal/vol38/iss5/3> accessed 9 October 2022; Pierre Bourdieu, *Other Words: Essays toward a Reflective Sociology*, Stanford University Press, (1990).

important because it enables us to examine how and why certain choices, problems, and solutions were available—and/or unavailable—to the legal profession and professionals in a specific historical period.[9] Moreover, legal history will remain incomplete and distorted as long as the academic endeavours undertaken by the 'supressed Others' is neglected and/or ignored by the traditional disciplinary corpus.[10] Apart from unpacking Fögen's subtle and highly artistic examination of the almost invisible beginning of law as a social system and the manner in which it 'irritates' gender, this contribution also features Fögen's academic biographical context as well as the important correlation between Roman law, German law, and international law.

Reading Law through Witchery, Poetry, and Miracles: Fögen's Academic Biography

Fögen received her licence to practice law in 1975 after completing her PhD entitled *The Struggle for Judicial Publicity* (*Der Kampf um Gerichtsöffentlichkeit*) with Dieter Simon in 1974.[11] After briefly representing Turkish and Italian 'Gastarbeiter'— 'disappointed with the limitations imbedded in the bureaucracy of 'justice'— Fögen returned to academia as Simon's research assistant.[12] After quickly mastering Greek,[13] Fögen embarked, with Simon, on a Roman and Byzantine history of law project at the MPIeR.[14] They founded and co-edited the *Rechtshistorisches Journal.*[15] In 1993 she habilitated with *The Expropriation of the Seers: Studies Regarding the Monopoly of Knowledge in Late Antiquity*. This was 'well-received',[16] and mentioned in the *Juristenzeitung*'s list of reading recommendations of 1995.[17] Alas it got little attention elsewhere. Perhaps because the book's nonconformist topic remained 'too demanding for German legal circles'.[18]

[9] See China Miéville on the need to question the 'inhering' legal ideologies with a why: 'One is left no sense of why this "idea" of international law should have arisen at a certain time and political-economic context'. China Miéville, *Between Equal Rights: a Marxist Theory of International Law* (Haymarket Books, 2005), at 81.

[10] See more in Reut Yael Paz, 'A Forgotten Kelsenian? The Story of Helen Silving-Ryu (1906–1993)' (2015) 25(4) *EJIL* 1123–146, available at <http://www.ejil.org/article.php?article=2550&issue=123>, accessed 9 October 2022.

[11] Marie Theres Fögen, *Der Kampf um Gerichtsöffentlichkeit* (Duncker und Humblot 1974).

[12] 'Interview' (n 4).

[13] ibid. In a year Fögen became proficient enough in Greek 'to read the New Testament as quickly as we read the newspaper'.

[14] Resulting in the *Lexica Iuridica Byzantina (Fontes Minores VIII)* Ludwig Burgmann, Marie Theres Fögen and others (eds), Forschungen zur Byzantinischen Rechtsgeschichte (Löwenklau Gesellschaft 1990).

[15] Fögen does not appear as an editor of the journal from the start. Simon explained that Fögen 'today would have been considered the *Redaktörin*' while I was the *Herausgeber.* (In German the former is closer to editor and the latter editor in chief.) Either they carried the load equally or Fögen did most of the work. 'Interview' (n 4).

[16] See Heinrich Honsell, Marie Theres Fögen † zum Gedenken, available at <www.ius.uzh.ch/de/staff/women-in-academia/former-profs/foegen/obituary.html> accessed 8 October 2022 and Michael Stolleis, *In Commemoration of Marie Theres Fögen (1946–2008)* available at WWW.RG.MPG.DE/1432291/NOTICE-18-01-18-COMMEMORATION-FOEGEN accessed 8 October 2022.

[17] See Gerhard Dilcher, *Eine Leseempfehlung—die juristischen Bücher des Jahres 1995.* JuristenZeitung 50 (Mohr Siebeck Nr 23, 1 Dezember 1995) 1165–168.

[18] According to Simon, the book should have gotten more attention but the title already made her colleagues 'lose their consciousness'. 'Interview' (n 4).

The book unearths, in Fögen's original, elegant, and critical style, relevant debates by lawyers, historians, and 'miracle workers' who were entirely omitted from the victory of Christianity over the old Roman state religion. Constructing her argument, Fögen draws from the works of forgotten miracle workers like Apollonios and Apuleius together with classical jurists, imperial laws by Constantin and his successors, as well as historians such as Tacitus and Sueton.[19] Claiming that together with Christianity—and the complete certainty that Jesus was not like (*Gott ähnlich*) but identical to god (*Gott gleich*) —the Roman Emperor could become the only one akin to God and hence achieve monopoly of truth, which in turn assists in the consolidation of powers.

The completion of this *Habilitation* (after fifteen years as a research assistant!) finally enabled her to become a full professor. Thus, when Regina Ogorek, a colleague from Zurich and former research assistant to Simon, was called back to Frankfurt, she made sure her professorship for Roman law at the University of Zurich was given to Fögen. As a dedicated and passionate teacher this resulted in a vigorous return to Roman law,[20] characterized also in *The Song of Law* (*Das Lied vom Gesetz*) first published in 2007.[21] Her leitmotif here was taken from Cicero, who mentions in passing how in school he learnt the Twelve Tables by heart as a '*carmen necessarium*', (a necessary song). Recognizing Cicero's politicization of 'a necessary song' and understanding the normativity it carries, Fögen unpacked the 'necessary' creativity and fiction at the origin of law.

With retrospective irony that breathes a sigh of relief—Fögen eruditely links the tendency of fascist and communist dictatorships with palatable legal prominences to the works of Kelsen, Kafka, Luhmann, and Derrida. From Kelsen and Kafka she draws the insistence on the singularity, purity, the distance, and even inaccessibility of the law because it makes law autonomous, which in turn 'protects' it from all political and ideological challenges.[22] Fögen links this concept of singularity of the law to Derrida's ideal of justice as an unattainable goal. She then adds Luhmann's 'contingency formula' where legal practice must always know and simultaneously forget that the law is neither impossible nor necessary. Fögen relies on this sophisticated 'theoretical formula' in her later contributions.

Fögen's Approach: From Ancient Mythology to Modern Legal Facts

Fögen did not consider Roman law indispensable. Instead it was a part of the curriculum and a fascinating object of knowledge.[23] For Fögen, the historical analysis of

[19] See more in Dilcher, *Eine Leseempfehlung* (n 17) at 1166.

[20] In his obituary of her, Heinrich Honsell writes how it was not uncommon for Fögen to have more than 500 students attend her classes (n 16).

[21] The book is an elaboration of a lecture held in March 2006. Marie Theres Fögen, *Das Lied vom Gesetz* (Carl Friedrich von Siemens Stiftung 2007).

[22] While Kelsen's legal positivism expresses the desire 'to cleanse the law of everything that has been slipped to it in the course of history', with Kafka's novels, all gates to the law—all para-textures and all 'songs'—remain closed. (See Hans Ulrich Gumbrecht, 'Die schöne Unvollständigkeit des Gesetzes', *Neue Bücher Zeitung* 2008.)

[23] Honsell (n 16).

Roman law was the history of stories, where the theory of legal evolution began. And in the beginning of (written) Roman law there is a 'maiden, in the bloom of youth, and of extraordinary beauty'.[24] The beauty of this virgin, Virginia,[25] only brought grief: a very premature death by her own father, Lucius Virginius. The father stabbed his only daughter in the chest, to free her from (sexual) slavery to Appius Claudius, who was 'the worst of all the ten decemvirates'.[26] What we know of Virginia, and the trial preceding her death—the first recorded trial—reaches us through orators, writing in dialogue form. We receive Virginia from Cicero, Livy, and Dionysius who exhibit altered styles and details, for each had diverging goals and audiences.[27] The law was not central to their stories but just a part of the social experience. Whatever its lacking preciseness and other deficiencies 'we are all at some level the "*heredes necessarii*" of Roman law'.[28]

Instead of questioning the impact of Roman law, as a professional, ingenious, and singular law, Fögen started with its enormous impact in Europe during the Middle Ages and the modern era.[29] For her it was essential to critically examine the all too 'natural' metaphorical use of Roman legal texts/law as the 'roots', 'influence', and 'source' of the Western legal system.[30] How, has the law—of a specific time and place—become Roman law as we know it today?[31] This opens up further questions about historical contingencies and conditions for the development of other structural possibilities. Such questions, as Fögen wrote, are mostly answered implicitly (if at all) particularly by nineteenth-century legal historians who re-created or re-invented Roman law for their own purposes.[32] After all, the history of ancient Rome—written by Livy, Dionysius, Tacitus, Cicero etc—does not know of us, our historical views, and requirements.[33] We, however, have particular historical demands and needs from this history.

That the Twelve Tables—a virtual text already during BC 60 (neither Livy, Dionysius, Tacitus or Cicero had ever seen the Twelve Tables)—are still recognized as 'the basis of the later legal developments' remains an important albeit curious phenomenon.[34]

[24] Most sources use Verginia or Virginia unsystematically. I mostly rely on Livy (Titus Livius BC 59–AD 17) *History of Rome. The History of Appius and Virginia* (BC 447) in George Baker (tr), *The History of Rome by Titus Livius* (E. P. Dutton and Co. 1823) Vol I (of VI) [Widener Lo 16 412].

[25] As Sandra R Roshel describes in ancient Rome 'the "good" woman's threatening element is her attractiveness','The Body Female and the Body Politic: Livy's Lucretia and Verginia' in Amy Richlin (ed), *Pornography and Representation in Greece and Rome* (OUP 1992) 112–30 at 120.

[26] On the sexual economy of the Roman Empire see Kyle Harper, *From Shame to Sin: The Christian Transformation of Sexual Morality in Late Antiquity* (Harvard University Press 2013).

[27] Cicero (BC 106–BC 43) was a generation older than both Dionysius (BC 60–BC 7) and Livy (BC 64–12 AD).

[28] On *heredes necessarius* see K Sriram, 'Roman Impact on Common Law: Legend or Legacy?' 16 Student Bar Review (2004) 25–45 at 25.

[29] Marie Theres Fögen, *Römische Rechtsgeschichten. Über Ursprung und Evolution eines sozialen Systems* (Vandenhoeck & Ruprecht 2002), and 'Verginia: Von der Tyrannei einer Unterscheidung' (*Wissenschaftskabinett*), in: Gegenworte, 6. Heft Herbst 2000, 64–68.

[30] Fögen (n 30).

[31] ibid.

[32] Fögen lists editors of the newly discovered Veronese Gaius' texts, eg, Friedrich Carl von Savigny (1779–1861); Johann Friedrich Ludwig Göschen (1778–1837); Christian Gottlieb Haubold, (1766–1824). See ibid 72, and Cornelia Vismann, *Das Recht und seine Mittel. Ausgewählte Schriften*, (Marcus Krajewski, Fabian Steinhauer, eds, Fischer Verlag 2012).

[33] ibid 13–14.

[34] Fögen quotes from Gerhard Dulckeit, Fritz Schwarz, and Wolfgang Waldstein, *Römische Rechtsgeschichte: Ein Studienbuch*, Munich, 1995 at 59, see more in ibid at 15–16.

Equally intriguing is that European civil law developed further out of this virtual text.[35] The unfounded boldness of nineteenth-century legal historians to make the argument that the Twelve Tables eventually became a *secular* private legal science infuriated Fögen.[36] She therefore reversed the argument 'that the history of Roman legal science knows no sensational moments'.[37] Fögen read Roman history to be the exact opposite: the Romans mostly describe sensational miracles, not roots or sources (*Wunder statt Wurzeln*).[38] Roman law was spectacular. It has never been the slow rationally and systematically developing law that modern German legal historians envisioned it to be.

Through this paradigm Fögen read Virginia but also Appius.[39] Appius represents 'a climactic moment in Roman tyranny'.[40] Fögen briefly mentioned how Appius could not control his desire for this extraordinary beautiful virgin, the daughter of an honest Plebeian Roman citizen and the fiancé of a people's tribune clerk After he failed to win her in an 'acceptable' fashion (ie sweet talk, bribery, subordination, and gifts), Appius instigates a legal process: Appius sends a strawman to declare Virginia his slave instead of a free woman. That he 'speaks as a judge to his own dependent/strawman indicates an access for Appius to take ownership over Virginia'.[41]

No Roman doubted that Appius's verdict was a clear breach of the legal principle *in favorem libertatis* ('in case of doubt in favour of liberty'). Not only was this a central legal principle, it was the addition to the Ten Tables created by Appius![42] Just before Appius gets what he desires, Virginia's father manages to sacrifice her dramatically declaring: 'In this manner, my child, the only one in my power, do I secure your liberty.' Virginia's death led to a revolt; the people freed themselves from tyranny; Appius committed suicide in prison; the republic was re-established and *Vaterhand rettete das Vaterland*.[43] This is, Fögen writes, what inspires art. But as it turns out also law: it is then and there that we are told the Twelve Tables were attractively set up in bronze.

Virginia—and Roman legal history—became part and parcel of the imagery of the European enlightenment. Together with the birth of factual-truth seeking 'scientism' modern historians were challenged with such legendary, mythological, poetic, and artistic sources. The existence of which were simply ignored. Clear separation between art and 'science, truth, regularities and facts' was imposed.[44] Historian Barthold Georg

[35] ibid.

[36] Here she refers Fritz Schultz (1879–1957), s *Geschichte der römischen Rechtswissenschaft*, Weimar, 1961, 11.

[37] ibid, and Schultz, Geschichte der römischen Rechtswissenschaft 13.

[38] The real challenge lies in the need to accept that ancient historians wrote about the phenomenal, the marvellous, the thrilling; here Fögen paraphrases Wittgenstein's famous sentence 'that which could not be understood, needs to be told' (ibid).

[39] Fögen's *Römische Rechtsgeschichten* first chapter is dedicated to Lucretia, 'the death of a matron', who symbolizes the origins of the Roman Republic. The second chapter discusses the death of Virginia who signifies the birth of law, the Twelve Tables. See also Marie Theres Fögen, 'Verginia: Von der Tyrannei einer Unterscheidung, *Wissenschaftskabinnett*, Gegenworte' (2000) 6 Heft Herbst 64–68.

[40] ibid.

[41] ibid.

[42] It was during Appius's Second Decemvirate rule, that the Ten Tables was completed with two extra Tables. Arguably apart for the law related to *favorem libertatis*, intermarriages between plebs and patricians were now banned.

[43] Marie Theres Fögen, 'Verginia' (n 39) 65.

[44] Fögen, *Römische Rechtsgeschichten* (n 39) 63.

Niebuhr (1776–1831), Theodor Mommsen (1817–1903), or Eugene Täubler (1879–1953), all knew with conviction and clarity that in BC 450 the Romans contracted ten men to write the law on Twelve bronze Tables. '*Punkt und basta*. The rest is implausible.'[45] These modernists according to Fögen therefore managed to 'sacrifice Virginia a second time'.[46] Moreover, the insistence on the separation between fact and fiction also sacrificed the beauty and brilliance of the ancient predecessors.[47] Fögen painstakingly vindicated these scientific distinctions to be nothing less than 'intellectual tyranny'.[48]

But what about the law? More specifically: 'Why do Romans assign such an irritating problematic figure that signifies both the law-giver and law-breaker simultaneously at the top of their greatest cultural achievement, especially at their law's very beginning?'[49] Fögen asked and then answered: '"Lawful" as such is meaningless. "Unlawful" must come in addition, for the law to have any meaning. *A legal system, like all social systems, can come into being only when it is codified through binaries*.'[50] It is clear that Livy and his contemporaries did not question the law and its functionality. For them it was a given. How exactly it began remains unknown. But that is exactly where the legal system's importance lies. Here Fögen quoted Luhmann directly: 'for the operational. . . . there is never a beginning, because the system had to have already started, in order for its effectivity to be reproduced'.[51] For law to remain functional it must be a mystified given that is repeated.

Virginia's importance, according to Fögen, is in the price that she becomes. Perhaps Virginia was the necessary atonement to the Gods to excuse the violent birth of the law? Either way, Virginia became the muted and dispensable object and symbol of the too powerfully abusive (and abused) judicial process, especially its affront on women: together with the birth of law women lose their subjectivity, their birth rights, *and* become legalized property. It is no coincidence that Virginia symbolizes the socio-juridical-economical construction of property. Jean-Jacque Rousseau description of masculine ownership fits perfectly:

> The first man who, having fenced off a plot of land, thought of saying 'This is mine' and found people simple enough to believe him was the real founder of civil society. How many crimes, wars, murders, how many miseries and horrors might the human race have been spared by the one who, upon pulling up the stakes or filling in the ditch, had shouted to his fellow men, 'Beware of listening to this imposter; you are lost, if you forget that the fruits of the earth belong to all and that the earth belongs to no one.'[52]

[45] Only at the beginning of the twentieth century Ettore Pais and Edouard Lambert began to doubt the existence of the Twelve Tables, Fögen, 'Verginia (n 39) 64.
[46] ibid.
[47] ibid.
[48] ibid 66.
[49] ibid.
[50] ibid.
[51] ibid 78.
[52] Jean-Jacque Rousseau, 'Discourse on the Origin and Foundations of Inequality Among Men' in Alan Ritter and Julia Conaway Bondanella (eds), *Rousseau's Political Writings* (WW Norton & Co 1988) 3–57 at 34.

Virginia belonged to her father and was promised to her fiancé. Virginia's trial is also the only evidence, or rather myth, that we receive of the Twelve Tables, the first chronicled written law. Virginia's symbolic importance lies in her historical context for she exemplifies an important revolutionary moment in human history: the formal patriarchal legalization of property, land, slaves, and women alike.

Virginia symbolizes a specific story that emerged from the struggle for freedom and equality. While it is a reaction against serious social exclusion, injustice, and economic constraints, it only functions based on the 'hidden' marginalization of women. '*Die Republik ist nicht paternalistisch, sondern "egalitär" und "brüderlich"*'.[53] Such reconfiguration of the freedom and equality excludes women in a resilient and persistent formula to this very day, delivering a perpetual narrative of a rotten and universal deal.

Encroaching Gender from its Irritation with the Law

Fögen drew her refreshing approach to the foundational myth behind Roman law from Luhmann, even if his approach remains silent on gender.[54] For Fögen, law as a social system entailed reconsidering the context of the conditions availing the possibilities, variations, selection, and re-stabilization of the law.[55] Enlightenment's idea of a patriarchal 'subject' who is the creator, modifier, and often even the improver of the world, makes self-overestimation more feasible.[56] Therefore, it is clear that modern enlightened 'historians cleaned up the chaos left by the Greeks and Romans "arranging" history as they pleased, straightforward and consistent'.[57] Given that 'antiquity does not know us', or our legal needs, Fögen contextualized the modern legal historian as an observer who assisted in uncovering possible intentions in the 'rediscovery' of these texts and legal sources.[58] Fögen urged us to criticize the conventional and 'linear' development of Roman law, which remains—in theory and practice—the shared foundation of most European legal traditions.[59]

Whereas this avails a more nuanced view of law and gender,[60] her primary goal remained to prove that European law is rooted in our enlightened and modern perceptions of Roman law, which actually goes back to the pre-Enlightened age that created its own mythology, one that excluded the sensational wonder; the whimsical escapades of the evolution of Roman law as it was.[61] It is as if Fögen asks us to leave aside

[53] Fögen, *Römische Rechtsgeschichten* (n 39) 59.

[54] Aside from mentioning that gender is an aspect that 'typecasts' people Luhmann does not discuss gender-related issues in general, and/or a social system specifically. Niklas Luhmann, 'Allgemeine Theorie organisierter Sozialsysteme' in Soziologische Aufklärung 2. Aufsätze zur Theorie der Gesellschaft (Westdeutscher Verlag 1975) 44.

[55] Fögen, *Römische Rechtsgeschichten* (n 39) 17.

[56] ibid.

[57] ibid 13.

[58] ibid 14.

[59] ibid 183.

[60] Her approach is reminiscent of Nicola Lacey's feminist legal critique emerging from within the law: the need is 'to question, unsettle and expose to careful scrutiny not only current laws and their organization but also the claims to authority and legitimacy which officials, law-makers, legal practices and theories express *on law's behalf*. Nicola Lacey, *Unspeakable Subjects: Feminist Essays in Legal and Social Theory* (Hart Publishing 1998) 168.

[61] Fögen, *Römische Rechtsgeschichten* (n 39) 19.

our presumed knowledge of Roman law so that we get to appreciate it the way Romans themselves experienced it in their singular, dramatic, and artistic way.

There is much to be said about Fögen's subtle approach. It did not resemble other contemporary feminist legal historians,[62] as none have ever gone as far back into Roman law with a new Luhmannian theoretical legal apparatus that produces a fresh reading of it altogether. Without explicitly stating it, Fögen who spoke to a very specific legal audience, gently confirmed both law and gender as social systems because these two systems—or semantic codes—do not consciously deal with 'the particular sensitivities of one system to its designated as-other'.[63] Instead gender *irritates* the law as a social system and vice versa, law irritates gender. This irritation confirms each other's independent and overlapping existence.

Virginia, Fögen, and Public International Law

Virginia's timeless and international significance lies in her perpetual enslavement that she symbolizes. If Roman law is considered *ratio scripta*—the 'expression of a timeless and universal law'[64]—then detaching the matter of women's inequality to men, or indeed their enslavement to men, was made possible because it was part and parcel of *ius gentium* (the law applicable to non-citizens as well) and not *ius naturale* or *ius civile*.[65] Thus, Roman law begins by an affirmation of the paternalistic hierarchy of Rome as the applier of a universal (*ius gentium*) law of women's enslavement.[66] In other words, that women's subjugation to men was a *ius gentium* issue from law's inception assisted in removing it from the specific history of Rome and attaching it in subsequent centuries to the universal truth of human beings twice divided: as men and women, and freemen and slaves.[67] Although Fögen's main goal was to disparage one of the main projects of German legal 'science' altogether: the rediscovery/reinvention of Roman law by nineteenth century legal historians' approaches to the Twelve Tablets, her fresh paradigmatic approach to Roman legal history altogether advanced a gender and an international legal critique.[68]

[62] See Tracy A Thomas and Tracey Jean Boisseau (eds), *Feminist Legal History: Essays on Women and Law* (NYU Press 2011).

[63] See Anders La Cour and Andreas Philippopoulos, *Luhmann Observed: Radical Theoretical Encounters* (Palgrave Macmillan 2013).

[64] Randel Lesaffer, 'Argument from Roman Law in Current International Law: Occupation and Acquisitive Prescription' (2005) 16(1) EJIL 25–58 at 25, 33.

[65] That slavery falls under *ius gentium* expressed the main distinction between *ius naturale* and *ius gentium*. At least according to Ulpian *ius gentium* enables slavery whereas 'everyone would be born free by natural law'. Lloyd L Weinreb, *Natural Law and Justice* (Harvard University Press) 1987 45–46.

[66] *Ius gentium* goes back to the customary legal principle that presupposes that natural reason is shared among all people.

[67] Nancy Demand concludes: 'in the end, the difference (between the treatment of female and slave bodies) is overridden, because although used differently, the bodies of both women and slaves were instruments... with a single purpose—work in the case of slaves and reproduction in the case of women'. 'Women and Slaves as Hippocratic Patients' in Sandra R Joshel and Sheila Murnaghan (eds), *Women and Slaves in Greco-Roman Culture: Differential Equations* (Routledge 1998) 69–84 at 83.

[68] See the manner in which Carl Friedrich von Savigny (1779–1861) constructed *jus gentium* solely on the basis of private law discussed in Reut Yael Paz, 'Legalizing Antisemitism? The Legacy of Savigny's Roman(tic) Law' in Pamela Slotte and John H Haskell (eds), *Christianity and International Law: An Introduction* (Cambridge University Press 2021).

Conclusion: Fögen as a Sharp Observer

Fögen's idiosyncratic reading of Roman law through a historian's lens while reflecting what it actually means to be an observing legal historian in the first place is capturing. Although the focus here was primarily her analysis of the Twelve Tables and the story of Virginia most specifically, it is this story that symbolizes the centrality of patriarchy in Roman law, European law, and thus also public international law.

Fögen criticized the 'discovery' and/or 're-invention' of Roman law by nineteenth-century German men and their weighty contribution to sustaining the violent silencing and exclusion of both women and 'the unknown'—the mysterious, the artistic, and the magnificent—from and/or of the law as a theoretical system. She redressed the fathers and grandfathers of her *Doktorvater* by relying on a formal theory of observation that links the minds of Romans to our minds through law. But also the power relationship between law and gender. Fögen successfully salvaged women from being a footnote in Roman legal history. And because she wished her critique to penetrate the mainstream her gendered approach remains abstract. In other words, Fögen observed and addressed her own German legal patriarchal community by constructing a complex and beautifully fabricated theoretical approach with the hope that her critique is not footnoted as well.

After all, Fögen was very familiar with how power is channeled through different social systems: from her upbringing in a conservative, bourgeois, Catholic, and very patriarchal family in Frankfurt, to her brief practice as a lawyer and her research and teaching in German-speaking law faculties. Situating Fögen's work within the larger context of her historical conditions is representative of her desire to observe the manner in which legal/political institutions were 'made and shaped by gendered subjects who in turn were made and shaped by those gendered institutions'.[69]

The patriarchal social system behind the foundational myth of the Twelve Tablets that marginalizes Virginia but also the miracle-based aspect of the law are still resilient. Fögen therefore attempted to crack open our misconceived perception of law from its very inception. Her work takes us back to the beginning: the very birth of Roman law. It is hardly coincidental that this birth is attached to a story of a missing mother—*Virginia's biological mother remains unknown*—and while the legal structure should have found out who this mother is, at least for the sake of justice, it falls short of doing so. Law, just like Virginia's mother, remains an unknown mystery. A myth. A miracle or a poem. A pure ideal, a perpetual goal, to be reached.

The attempt to disinherit this aspect of Roman law reaches modern law through its functionality and symbolical communication used by patriarchal scholars who interacted with the law as a social system. Fögen's agency, as an observer and a female legal historian, prompts us to retain this aspect of the law, which became more detrimental

[69] Anna Becker, 'Gender in History of Early Modern Political Thought', (2017) The Historical Journal 60(4), 1–21 at 2. Also available at <https://www.cambridge.org/core/journals/historical-journal/article/gender-in-the-history-of-early-modern-political-thought/3DCF0ACEB0159770786BB275157D7FA7/share/41bbb0fefe58326b8de013589676ecd17675b11e> accessed 9 October 2022.

and universal because of the way it re-creates the rotten deal that objectifies and enslaves women. However, even if traditionally law attempts to protect scientifically stale formulas that confine us women to be enslaved mothers or martyred maidens, Fögen's authorship and experience shows that at least now women can also be creative, brilliant, and extraordinary jurists.

33

Kalliopi Koufa

First Greek Female Academic of Public International Law

Marilena Papadaki

On a sunny day in August 2014, I met for the first time Mrs Koufa in her large living room having a splendid view of the Thermaic gulf of Thessaloniki, her beloved hometown. A strict and austere figure, but at the same time very approachable, she immediately gained the respect of her interlocutor. She discussed with passion international law science and international politics as well as expressed her concern for the future generation of scientists living in a country in a full-blown economic crisis. In the coming years, both her efforts to promote international law and to gather new scientists from all over the world in her hometown around a private institution founded and financed by her personal fortune in order to revive the program and goals of the well-known Institute of IL of Thessaloniki, will certainly be appreciated.

Kalliopi Koufa, born in 1936, was the first Greek female Professor of Public International Law (1989), who engaged in multiple academic and political institutions on both national and international levels. During her long career, she dealt with a wide range of contemporary theoretical and practical international problems linked to the international legal system and the legal organization of international society: the relation between regional and international organization, law-making issues, the diversification of international dispute settlement, and the use of force in international relations, terrorism, and international human rights law, among others.[1]

This chapter tries to cover the general gap of bibliography related to women's involvement as international lawyers and legal theorists and practitioners in the twentieth century.[2] At the same, it is a contribution to the general absence of bibliography on the role of Greek international lawyers in shaping international law during the same period.

Kalliopi Koufa was born in Thessaloniki (Greece) and was the second child of surgeon Konstantinos Koufas, and dentist, of Austrian origin, Anna Frenkel. Due to her parents' different nationalities and their high professional and social status, Koufa benefited from an open-minded and cosmopolitan environment. She graduated from Anatolia High School.[3] After graduation, she expressed strongly a desire to study

[1] Useful information about Kalliopi Koufa's life and the many topics she dealt with is provided in Aristotle Constantinides and Nikos Zaikos (eds), *The Diversity of International Law, Essays in Honour of Professor Kalliopi Koufa* (Martinus Nijhoff Publishers 2009).

[2] Immi Tallgren, 'Absent or Invisible?, "Women" Intellectuals and Professionals at the Dawn of a Discipline' in Frédéric Mégret and Immi Tallgren (eds), *The Dawn of a Discipline: International Criminal Justice and Its Early Exponents* (Cambridge University Press 2020) 381.

[3] For the history of Anatolia College, see William McGrew, *Education across Cultures: Anatolia College in Turkey and Greece* (Rowman & Littlefield Publishers 2015).

Marilena Papadaki, *Kalliopi Koufa* In: *Portraits of Women in International Law.* Edited by: Immi Tallgren, Oxford University Press.
 DOI: 10.1093/oso/9780198868453.003.0033

Figure 33.1 Kalliopi Koufa in the UN Sub-Commission on the Promotion and Protection of Human Rights (formerly Sub-Commission on Prevention of Discrimination and Protection of Minorities). Koufa is the third from the left, front row.
Source: Courtesy of Kalliopi Koufa's private collection.

abroad. Her love for English literature and her good knowledge of the English language (a result of completing her education mostly in English) led her to pursue further studies in Great Britain.[4] Between 1954 and 1956, she studied at the Royal Polytechnic Institution, today a part of the department of the University of Westminster. While in London, she discovered a brochure of the Graduate Institute for International Studies in Geneva which led her to leave Great Britain and pursue her studies in Switzerland.

In 1956, she began studying at both the Department of Economic and Social Sciences of the University of Geneva and the Graduate Institute for International Studies. The Institute was founded in 1927, as part of several new international law institutions of the interwar period funded by American Foundations in an effort to ensure international peace and cooperation.[5] During Kalliopi Koufa's studies, the Institute attracted students from wealthy families across all continents, creating an international elite of experts specialized in multilateral institutions. Its roster included well-known jurists such as Maurice Bourquin, Paul Guggenheim, and Hans Wehberg. Koufa also had the opportunity to learn from other renowned theorists of international law, such as Hans Kelsen.[6]

[4] According to Kalliopi Koufa, she also had some knowledge of German, because of her mother's origin, but never spoke it, due to discrimination issues related to the German occupation of Greece during the Second World War (Kalliopi Koufa interview 25 September 2020).

[5] Guillaume, Sacriste, Antoine Vauchez, 'La guerre hors-la-loi, 1919–1930, Les origines de la définition d'un ordre politique international' (2004) Actes de la recherche en sciences sociales 151–52.

[6] Constantinides and Zaikos (n 1) XVII–XXV.

The environment, structure, and curriculum of the studies within the Institute deeply influenced Kalliopi Koufa, who showed a particular interest in international law. Consequently, she was eager to begin her post-graduate studies on international humanitarian law under the supervision of one of Paul Guggenheim's formers students and the first female professor of the Institute, Denise Marcelle Bindschedler-Robert, wife of internationalist Rudolf Bindschedler.[7] However, her PhD studies were interrupted due to her mother's illness that forced her to return to Greece, after receiving her Political Science degree (*Licence des sciences politiques*) in 1960.

Koufa's desire to continue her studies in international law led her to the realization that a law degree would be a necessary asset to her future career.[8] She therefore decided to study law at the Faculty of Law of the Aristotle University of Thessaloniki, where she excelled at both the undergraduate and postgraduate levels. In 1970, she became assistant to Dimitrios S Constantopoulos,[9] who held the Chair of public international law, and five years later Koufa defended her doctoral thesis titled 'On Regional Organization of International Society'.[10]

During this period, as Constantopoulos' assistant, Koufa participated actively in the academic life of the Faculty of Law and of the Institute of International Public Law and International Relations of Thessaloniki founded by Constantopoulos in 1966, as a training and research institution to advance international studies in Greece.[11] In 1993, Koufa became director of the Institute, playing a vital role in attracting distinguished scholars from all over the world, in organizing the annual courses and keeping up and increasing the various scholarly activities of the Institute. While being an assistant, she was also a doctoral fellow at the Hague Academy of International Law and visiting scholar in various universities of the United States as a Fullbright

[7] From 1956, Bindschedler-Robert Denise Marcell taught international humanitarian law, Geneva Conventions, and Human Rights at the Institute, where she became an Associate Professor in 1964<https://www.bindschedler.name/personen/personen-ab-20-jahrhundert/bindschedler-robert-denise-marcelle/>.

[8] Kalliopi Koufa interview (n 4).

[9] DS Constantopoulos (1917–2008) held the Chair of Public International Law of the Aristotle University of Thessaloniki from 1960–1989. He was the founder and President for many years of the 'Institute of Public International Law, European Law and International Relations of Thessaloniki'. For his legal theory of international law see Antonio Truyol y Serra, Robert Kolb, *Doctrines sur le fondement du droit des gens* (A Pedone 2007) 72–75. See also *Modern Problems of International Law and the Philosophy of Law: Miscellanea in Honour of Professor D.S. Constantopoulos* (Institut of International Public Law and International Relations of Thessaloniki 1980).

[10] Kalliopi Koufa, *On Regional Organization of International Society* (in Greek) Doctoral Thesis, AUTH 1975.

[11] The 'Institute of International Public Law and International Relations of Thessaloniki' was founded in 1966. It consisted of four departments (Public International Law, International Relations and Diplomacy, International and European Organization, and Greek Foreign Policy). It also provided Tribunals, law preparing commissions of the Ministry of Justice, and Parliamentary Committees with legal counsel on questions of international law. Its series of publications (in their majority in English) consist of a rich source for international law studies covering a great scale of matters related to international law and international relations. Since 1973 the Institute organized annual summer sessions of courses on different matters of international relations, with the participation of eminent academics, diplomats, experts, international judges, and officers of international organizations. In recognition of its significant contribution to the promotion of peace as set forth by the General Assembly of the United Nations in the Proclamation of the International Year of Peace, the Secretary-General of UN designated the Institute as a 'Peace Messenger'. (Introduction in published series 'Thesaurus Acroasium', 36 volumes of the Institute, containing lectures delivered during the annual sessions of courses organized by the Institute, as well as research papers by participants in these courses.)

scholarship fellow. In 1989, she was elected Professor in Public International Law and International Organizations at the Law Faculty of Aristotle University of Thessaloniki, thus becoming the first female Greek jurist to hold this position, in her country. Over more than three consecutive decades, she has taught mainly Public International Law, but also Law of International Organizations, and other specialized subjects related to the law of the United Nations and European Union, the peaceful settlement of international disputes, the sources of international law and the international protection of human rights. In 2004, to honor her contribution to the discipline of law, she was elected Emeritus Professor.[12]

Legal Theory

Koufa's approach to international law is deeply influenced by her studies at the Graduate Institute for International Studies where she received a thorough education on international legal theory. This most likely influenced her work addressing major and demanding doctrinal questions of general international law and international organization law. Kalliopi Koufa chose to follow the legal positivist school of thought.[13] Nevertheless, she very often takes into account in her approaches the social reality of international relations and the political aspects of the question, a practice that distances her thought from rigid positivism and is certainly connected to her experience in international organizations and political fora where she participated in international law-making. Moreover, Koufa considers international law a decentralized legal system. The majority of her work is written in Greek, with some of her works/articles translated to many other languages. Her first major monograph 'On Regional Organisation of International Society' (1975) deals with the phenomenon of the legal relationship between universal and regional attempts of international organization. In her monograph 'The Function of the Phenomenon of Acts of State in International Relations' (1983) she studies sovereign governmental acts as an expression of government policy in relation to the rule of law in international relations. She concludes that international practice shows a tendency towards the gradual elimination of domestic jurisdiction of states to the benefit of international law rule. After a certain point, Koufa's work begin to gradually reflect the political situation and the issues she dealt with as a member and adviser of Greek delegations in international organizations and conferences.[14]

Expertise/Political Engagement

In order to explain Koufa's non-academic engagement, as an expert and member of different political and international institutions of her time, it is important to place it

[12] Constantinides and Zaikos (n 1) XVIII.

[13] Legal positivism refers to a legal system based on predetermined legal rules without reference to social considerations.

[14] Constantinides and Zaikos (n 1) XIX–XX.

within its historical context. Koufa was born in the northern part of Greece (in the region called Macedonia) and belonged to the first generation born after the First World War. The later led to the creation of various minority issues in the region of Macedonia as a result of the dissolution of the Ottoman Empire. However, the compulsory exchange of populations between Greece and Turkey, following the Greek-Turkish war of 1919–1922, resulted to the establishment of a compact Greek element promoting the Greek national homogeneity in the region. Koufa grew up in post-Second World War Greece, a country that was struggling to recover from both an international and a civil war, which resulted (contrary to many of its neighbors) in placing Greece under the Western block influence. Greece's external politics and vision after the Second World War were steadily oriented towards its traditional allies (the West). Greece was the first and only country of Southeastern Europe to join the European Economic Community (EEC, now EU) since its establishment. It is also a member of the North Atlantic Treaty Organization (NATO) since 1952.

Minorities

Koufa's interest in minorities' issues began in 1967–1968, when she worked as a legal advisor at the Center of Emigrant Macedonians of the Society for Macedonian Studies in Thessaloniki. Koufa was one of the first internationalists who examined minorities' problems through a legal perspective. In 1987, she became a member of the European team of scholars and academics involved in a major research program of the 'European Science Foundation' concerning minorities in Europe, which resulted in the publication of a series of eight volumes under the general title 'Comparative Studies on Governments and Non-Dominant Ethnic Groups in Europe 1850–1940'.[15] Koufa contributed in this publication along with renowned historian Constaninos Svolopoulos with a paper on 'The Compulsory Exchange of Populations between Greece and Turkey' (1991) that examines and evaluates this unprecedented inter-war legal arrangement (a subject traditionally addressed by historians) for the first time from both a historic and a legal point of view and especially from the perspective of international law regarding contemporary human rights standards. Koufa and Svolopoulos argued that the obligatory exchange of populations between Greece and Turkey was a radical means of restricting the centrifugal tendencies caused by ethnic minorities and was driven by pure realistic politics without any humanistic considerations.[16]

Between 1991 and 1993, in a climate of resurgent Balkan nationalism, the Macedonian issue arose around the recognition of the name of Former Yugoslav Republic of Macedonia (FYROM), today North Macedonia. The issue raised awareness and caused the intense involvement of Greek society and Greek diaspora in a foreign policy issue, for the first time since the mass demonstrations of the Cypriot

[15] ibid XXIII.

[16] Kalliopi Koufa and Constantinos Svolopoulos, 'The Compulsory Exchange of Populations between Greece and Turkey: The Settlement of Minority Questions and the Conference of Lausanne, 1912 and its Impact on Greek-Turkish Relations' in P Smith in collaboration with K Koufa and A Suppan (eds), *Ethnic Groups in International Relations* (Dartmouth/European Science Foundation, 1991) Comparative Studies on Governments and Non-Dominant Ethnic Groups in Europe, 1850–1940, Vol V) 275.

anti-colonial struggle in the 1950s. Koufa joined the hundreds of concerned individuals of more conservative political views, feeling 'personally affected by their sense of identity and their perception of heritage'.[17] She was a part of a group of academics that lobbied to influence the perceptions of the government. In 1991, Koufa replaced E Kofos, Greece's Foreign Ministry Special Advisor on Balkan Affairs, as member and adviser to the Greek delegations in various meetings such as the Conference on Security and Cooperation in Europe (CSCE), the Human Dimension Meeting in Copenhagen and Moscow, and the CSCE Meeting of Experts in National Minorities in Geneva. These meetings dealt with the international commitment of post-Cold War states to build democratic societies based on free elections, rule of law, and full respect for human rights and fundamental freedoms.[18] During this period (1990–1992) Koufa also directed the Institute for Balkan Studies in Thessaloniki.

United Nations

In 1985, which marked the fortieth anniversary of the United Nations, Koufa published a study ('The United Nations Organisation Forty Years after their Creation'), providing a historical overview of the current status of the international organization. In 1990, she published 'Evolution of International Law: 'International Legislation' through the United Nations', which examined the involvement of the General Assembly of the UN in the global law-making process, by referring to the theory of the sources of international law.[19] In a different study, 'International Conflictual Situations and their Peaceful Adjustment' (1990), she analysed the legal distinction between 'disputes' and 'conflictual situations' in the United Nations' Charter, the International Court of Justice, and the work of the political bodies of the United Nations charged with the task to ensure peaceful settlement or adjustment.[20]

Her academic interest in international organizations (specially the United Nations) combined with her engagement in the 'Macedonian issue' as an expert and representative of the Greek government, led to her active engagement in the United Nations.

In the UN, she participated as a Greek delegate in the drafting of the 'Declaration on the Rights of Persons Belonging to National or Ethnic, Religious and Linguistic Minorities', adopted by the General Assembly resolution 4/135 of 18 December 1992.[21] She was also a member of the Greek delegations to the Third (Human Rights), the Sixth (Legal) Committees of the General Assembly of the United Nations in

[17] Evangelos Kofos, 'Greece's Macedonian Adventure: The Controversy over FYROM's Independence and Recognition', Greece and the New Balkans: Challenges and Opportunities', in James Pettifer, *The New Macedonian Question* (Macmillan Press Ltd 1999). See also Harald Kopping, Joris Korbee, Ioannis Moraitis, and Stephanie Vertongen, 'What's a Name?: The Macedonian Question':<https://www.academia.edu/28145142/Whats_in_a_Name_Theoretical_Perspective_on_State_and_Nation_building>.

[18] Available at <https://www.osce.org/files/f/documents/9/c/14304.pdf>.

[19] Kalliopi Koufa, 'Evolution of International Law: International Legislation through the United Nations' (1990) v XVI Thesaurus Acroasium of the Institute of Public International 263–87.

[20] Constantinides and Zaikos (n 1) XXI.

[21] A/RES/47/135,<https://www.refworld.org/docid/3ae6b38d0.html>.

New York, the Commission of Human Rights in Geneva, and the World Conference on Human Rights in Vienna (1993). In 1994, Kalliopi Koufa was elected alternate member to the United Nations Sub-Commission on the Promotion and Protection of Human Rights (formerly Sub-Commission on Prevention of Discrimination and Protection of Minorities). In 2002, she became a member of the Sub-Commission, a post she held until its final session in 2006.

In this context, she was appointed Special Rapporteur on Terrorism and Human Rights (1998–2004).[22] Following the attack of 11 September 2001 in the USA and the worldwide outbreak of acts of terrorism, Koufa's reports focused on Counter-Terrorism measures and the protection of human rights, as the subject became more relevant and urgent given the circumstances. Thanks to her active role in this field during this period, according to her, she was known by the nickname 'the terrorism lady' in the circles of the United Nations. She also states that her reports on terrorism received comments of disapproval from some European states' representatives, who considered her views 'too internationalist' and not completely in line with the European Union interests.[23]

In 2005 and 2006, she was Chairperson of the UN Sub-Commission's Working Group on the Elaboration of Principles and Guidelines Concerning the Promotion and Protection of Human Rights When Combating Terrorism. She has also acted as a Vice-President of the Sub-Commission (2003) and a member of the Working Group on Contemporary Forms of Slavery (2004). Counterterrorism and Human Rights are the subject of numerous publications by Koufa and were also among the many issues she dealt with while a member of the European Commission for Democracy through Law, better known as the Venice Commission.[24]

In 2012, Koufa founded a private institution named 'Kalliopi Koufa Foundation for the Promotion of International Law and the Protection of Human Rights Law', aiming to continue the work of the Institute of International Relations of Thessaloniki that had gradually reduced its activities until its official closure in 2014. The mission of the Foundation is the theoretical and applied research and cultivation of international law in all of its aspects, and in particular the promotion of the multidisciplinary study of human rights protection and of humanitarian law, at the international and national levels.[25]

[22] At its forty-ninth session (1997) the 'Sub-Commission on Prevention of Discrimination and Protection of Minorities' recommended that the 'Commission on Human Rights' authorized Kalliopi Koufa's appointment as Special Rapporteur to conduct 'a comprehensive study on terrorism and human rights on the basis of her working paper (E/CN.4/Sub.2/1997/28). The 'Commission on Human Rights' at its fifty-fourth session (1998) approved her appointment as a Special Rapporteur and she submitted her preliminary report in 1999 (E/CN.4/Sub.2/1999/27) containing an historical overview of the evolution of the question of terrorism within the United Nations system and analysis of the major areas in which terrorism affects, directly and indirectly, the full enjoyment of human rights. She also presented two progress reports (E/CN/4/Sub.2/2001/31 and E/CN.4/Sub.2/2002/35), the second one written in the wake of 11 September 2001.

[23] Kalliopi Koufa interview (n 4).

[24] CDL-AD (2010) 022 Study no 500/2008 European Commission for Democracy through law, Report on counter-terrorism measures and Human Rights adopted by the Venice Commission at its 83rd Plenary Session (Venice, 4 June 2010) on the basis of comments by Iain Cameron, Pieter van DIJK, Kalliopi Koufa, Guido Neppi Modona

[25] Available at <*www.koufafoundation.org*>.

Conclusion

Although she claims the opposite, it is clear that Kalliopi Koufa had to overcome many difficulties to progress in multiple male-dominated environments, such as the Greek Law Faculties of her time, the CSCE meetings, or the United Nations' various commissions.[26] It seems, she has not been particularly engaged in the Greek feminist movement that was mostly promoted by leftist women.[27] In reality, she does not feel the need to highlight the feminist claims because she thinks everyone has to go through the same path to succeed in the professional world.

Koufa's family was royalist, and she has always been politically conservative, even though she defines herself as an apolitical person 'interested only in the science of international law'.[28] This position maybe explains why she remained in her political posts (as an expert) for many years, through different political regimes. Her career must be analysed and understood by taking into account her class background. It was also the case for other Greek women at the time who showed a strong desire to offer to the country and contribute to its modernization.[29] Among these women, Koufa constitutes a special case because of her academic excellence in a traditionally male discipline.[30] These choices, combined with her hard-working and strong character led to significant contributions both in legal theory and practice in a period of general intensification of international relations and a consequent increasing need for legal expertise in both national and international law. However, the fact that most of her work is written in Greek, along with the low-profile she prefers to keep have surely affected her national and international visibility. It is important to note though that she has multiple connections and an extensive influence among international law experts, as shown in the great number of contributions from all around the world in a collection of essays published in her honour in 2009.[31] These connections can partially be attributed to her active involvement for many years at the Institute of International Law of Thessaloniki.

Koufa's life and work and multiple engagement as an academic, theorist, and practitioner can be considered an example of the expansion and diversification of international law, as a result of the intensification and complexity of international relations after the Second World War: the diversification of subject matters, the different

[26] Hilary Charlesworth, 'The Gender of International Institutions' in Anne-Marie Slaughter and Hilary Charlesworth (eds), *Proceedings of the Annual Meeting ASIL*, vol 89, Structures of World Order, 5–8 April 79–85.

[27] Efi Avdela and Aggeliki Psara, *Feminism in Greece in the Interwar Period: An Anthology* (in Greek) (Gnosi 1985). Maria Repousi, 'Womens' Space: Political Parties, Women Organizations and Groups', pt 3, (2003) *History of New Hellenism* 1770–2000 (in Greek),TA NEA 121–44.

[28] Kalliopi Koufa interview (n 4).

[29] Efi Avdela, '*Youth in Danger*'. *Surveillance, Reformation and Juvenile Justice after the War* (Polis 2013) 197–98.

[30] Up until the late 1970s law school university teachers were inclusively men (see list of law school professors in Kostas Gavroglou, Vaggelis Karamanolakis, and Haido Mparkoula (eds), *University of Athens and its History (1837–1937)* (in Greek) (Panepistimiakes Ekdoseis Kritis 2014) 352.

[31] See Constantinides and Zaikos (n 1).

functions, the various approaches and visions of international scholars, and its multiple applications in international practices. She is an engaged scholar who often supports the dominant discourses at both national and international levels even though sometimes she chooses to promote international law and justice over political guidelines and decisions.

PART X

THE ROOF-TOP GALLERY OF DIPLOMACY AND INTERNATIONAL RELATIONS

34
Thomas Baty in Japan
Seeing through the Twilight

Shinya Murase[*]

Introduction

An enigmatic and controversial figure at home because of his undeviating support for Imperial Japan, Dr Thomas Baty (1869–1954) had been educated at both Oxford and Cambridge. He was an authority on international law, on which he had published many books. From 1916 to 1941, he served as a legal adviser to the Imperial Japanese Foreign Ministry. When war between Japan and Great Britain came in 1941, Baty decided that he could not continue to serve the Japanese government without compromising his loyalty to his own country, and tendered his resignation. Following the outbreak of hostilities, other British and allied nationals were detained, and were later returned to their home countries through the reciprocal exchange of enemy nationals. Baty, exceptionally, stayed in Japan throughout the war. After the defeat of Japan in 1945, the country came under allied occupation. With the conclusion of the San Francisco Peace Treaty in 1952, Baty was once again able to return to his post and to offer his advice to the Foreign Ministry. Yet he continued to meet with cold and unsympathetic treatment from the British Embassy in Tokyo. This meant that right up to his death, he was prevented from travelling overseas.

It is also clear that, in pre-war Japan, Baty made an immense contribution, both in the field of diplomacy and in his own field of international law. The aim of this chapter is to provide some indication of that contribution. He was a scholar of the first rank, and his overall academic achievements in international law should be properly examined and valued before he becomes entirely forgotten. It has also been revealed in recent years that 'Irene Clyde', known as a radical feminist writer in the first few decades of the twentieth century, was the pseudonym of Thomas Baty. 'Irene Clyde' fiercely attacked conventional distinctions of sex, but at the same time longed for a peaceful world which would value feminine ideals of behaviour. Thomas Baty was an outstanding international lawyer, an extraordinary literary persona, and also a loyal and honourable Englishman. By writing this chapter, the present writer hopes to do something to restore his reputation.

Indeed, any discussion of Baty's career involves consideration of the problematic relationship between professionalism and loyalty. This was an issue that must have been

[*] [*] This chapter is a shortened and slightly edited version of Shinya Murase, 'Thomas Baty in Japan: Seeing through the Twilight' (2003) 73(1) British Yearbook of International Law 315–42, published with the permission of the author, editors of the BYIL and the OUP.

Shinya Murase, *Thomas Baty in Japan* In: *Portraits of Women in International Law*. Edited by: Immi Tallgren, Oxford University Press. © Shinya Murase 2023. DOI: 10.1093/oso/9780198868453.003.0034

Figure 34.1 Thomas Baty (between ca. 1915 and ca. 1920).
Source: Library of Congress, Prints & Photographs Division, [LC-DIG-ggbain-22216], George Grantham Bain Collection.

a constant preoccupation for Dr Baty in the course of his duties as legal adviser to the Imperial Japanese government throughout the pre-war period. A number of questions can be asked about Baty's life and work, and what relationship they had to his views on international law. First of all, why did he choose to come to Japan, or to put it differently, what position did he assign to Japan in his framework of international law? How did he conceive of his role as a legal adviser to the Japanese government, especially from the 1930s onwards, when Japanese foreign policy became ever more imperialist and extreme? If Baty was an erudite and intelligent man, it follows that he should have been quite capable of understanding where Japan was going. Did he fail to understand the implications of his work for the Japanese government, or was he actually unconcerned about them?

Through his writings, one could at least understand what made him think that he should stay on board. He was not a man to jump ship to avoid a collision, even when it looked as though a collision was about to happen. It seems that his reasons for working for Japan, and for continuing to do so in those difficult days, were closely connected to his views on international law. These views were undoubtedly highly unusual for a man of Baty's background, originating as he did in the English academic establishment. Clearly, Baty had his limitations as well as his merits, and both need to be taken into account. It may be appropriate here to offer a brief sketch of his early life.

Brief Biographical Note

Dr Thomas Baty DCL, LLD, was born on 8 February 1869. He was the eldest child of William Thomas Baty and his wife Mary of Stanwix, near Carlisle in the county of Cumberland. His father, who was a cabinet-maker, died when he was seven. He was educated at Carlisle Grammar School. As an undergraduate, he read law at Queen's College, Oxford. He then came up to Trinity College, Cambridge, in 1894 on a Whewell Scholarship, and began to devote himself to international law. He was later appointed to the Stowell Civil Law Fellowship at University College, Oxford. On leaving Oxford, he read in the chambers of the future Lord Justice Romer, and also spent some time in the office of Messrs Field, Roscoe & Co, the well-known solicitors' firm of Lincoln's Inn. He was admitted by the Inner Temple in 1896, called to the Bar in 1898, and later practised in Chancery and Admiralty (in the Prize Courts).

In 1901, he obtained the degree of Doctor of Civil Law from the University of Oxford; in 1907, Cambridge awarded him the degree of Legum Doctor. In 1906, he became Joint Honorary Secretary of the International Law Association, and organized its conferences at Christiana, Berlin, Portland (Maine), Budapest, London, Paris, and Madrid. He was also named Associate Member of the Institute of International Law in 1922. He served as Examiner at Oxford, London, and Liverpool Universities.

From 1900 to 1916, before he began his work in Japan, Baty was a prolific scholar. The anonymous author of Dr Baty's obituary in *The Times* stated as follows:

> 'It is ... as a writer of international law that he will be remembered. His views cannot always be accepted without qualification, and his conclusions have by no means met with universal assent, but his writing was always alive and vigorous and his books, if they differ from more conventional works on the subject, make all the more interesting reading.[1]

These remarks give a flavour of Baty's style and characteristic approach as a writer. His works were unique, stimulating, and even provocative, and challenged the orthodoxies and conventional legal thinking on the subject.

What is especially striking is the fierce hostility Baty expresses towards what he sees as the arrogant and chauvinistic attitudes behind the way the great powers deal with international law. This is apparent in one of his first books, *International Law in South Africa*, which was based on lectures he gave at Oxford and was published in 1900. The work discussed the position of the Boer Republics of the Transvaal and the Orange Free State under British suzerainty, which, in Baty's view, was tantamount to the mere subjugation of small states to a great power. At the time of the Anglo-Boer War, this subject was both controversial and topical. The book also severely criticized the British

[1] *The Times* (10 February 1954).

doctrine on continuous voyage regarding neutral vessels' trade in time of war, by demonstrating how unfair many of the British Prize Courts' decisions had been for smaller countries.

In many of his early writings, Baty doggedly and persistently attacked what he saw as the self-interested application of superior force that lay behind the way Britain made, applied, and enforced maritime law, and international law in general.[2] He made no attempt to conceal how much he detested the infringement of the sovereignty of small states which the great powers perpetrated to satisfy their own selfish ambitions.

Thomas Baty at the start of the twentieth century might have believed that Japan's international conduct presented something of a contrast to the behaviour of the European great powers. Japan had worked hard to convince the rest of the world that she was a civilized, law-abiding country which respected international conventions, and this aspiration was evident in the restraint she showed in the way she prosecuted her wars against China (1894–1895) and against Russia (1904–1905).[3] For Baty, to serve as a legal adviser to the Japanese government would certainly have seemed much less in conflict with his ideas about international law than, for instance, performing a similar role at the British Foreign Office. Indeed, Baty might well have pictured Japan even as Asia's rising star, despite Japan's shadowy history of subjugating Korea since 1875 and China since 1894. In this period, on the international stage, Japan was engaged in a steady effort to contest the Western great powers' chauvinistic dominance of the region. Japan's approach to international relations at the time when Baty took up his post at the Imperial Foreign Ministry would still have appeared to be one of championing the rights and claims of small states, a cause she was only to betray a few decades later.

Baty's enthusiasm for Japan was rather one-sided. The fact that Japan was a young and vigorous imperialist power appeared to have made little impact on him, and it is surprising that Japan's continental enterprises in Korea and Manchuria should not have worried a man who was so critical of the imperialist attitudes of his own country. He seems to have over-looked the political realities: in the early twentieth century, the two island empires were allies which took care of each other's imperial interests in East Asia. Baty failed to balance Japan's internationalist achievements against her expansionist achievements.

Thomas Baty was a liberal-minded progressivist, but the catastrophe of the First World War was a blow to many of the optimistic hopes of the Edwardian period. Since Japan's involvement in the First World War was very limited, a post in Japan gave Baty an opportunity to exercise his talents that Britain in 1916 could not provide. Japan looked like she would continue to build on her internationalist legacy; no one in 1916 could have imagined that Japan would instead cast that inheritance to the winds.

Baty had long had a fascination for Japan. Even as a child, he searched for books about Japan and read them avidly. The press confirmed that 'for everything Japanese, he had an unbounded admiration'.[4] This assertion may appear exaggerated, and therefore rather dubious, but Baty's attachment was to a country which he felt had much

2 See the Report of the International Law Association (ILA), 26th Conference, 2–5 August 1910, 115–19.
3 Shinya Murase, 'Japan and International Law' (1997) XXV(4) The Japan Foundation Newsletter, 1–5.
4 Obituary, *The Times* (n 1).

in common with Britain, and from which he thought Britain could learn. As he explained in his memoirs, he expected that he would find 'another Britain with none but superficial differences—, of a delightfully pictorial character'.[5] His interest in Japan was already apparent during his career in England. In 1910, he became a member of the Japan Society in London, and his decision to take up a position in Tokyo six years later was perhaps a natural way of satisfying his curiosity and personal tastes.[6]

Baty's Appointment as Legal Adviser

After the Meiji Restoration in 1868, the Japanese State embarked on a far-reaching programme to modernize, that is to say, Westernize, the country. For this purpose the Meiji government employed hundreds of foreign advisers to assist it in their particular field of expertise. One important aim of the Meiji State was to be able to conduct diplomacy according to Western practices, and it was to this end that the Imperial Foreign Ministry began to make use of foreign legal specialists. Prior to Baty's appointment, the Foreign Ministry had already employed various legal advisers.

Thomas Baty seemed like the natural and obvious candidate for the position. Not only did he enjoy a high professional reputation as a scholar of international law, but he was also known to possess a deep understanding of Japanese culture. His initial annual salary was set at (Japanese yen) 15,000, and was later doubled. This meant that he came to earn three times as much as the Prime Minister of Japan (and fifty times as much as the present writer's father was then earning, at a point in his life when he was just starting out as a school teacher!). The government also undertook to provide Baty with a fine official residence, which was located near the Foreign Ministry. These terms of employment appeared satisfactory, and so, at the age of forty-seven, Thomas Baty embarked for Japan, accompanied by his sister, Anne, and his seventy-five-year-old mother. Having rounded the Cape of Good Hope, their ship landed at Kobe on 29 May 1916.

Baty's employment contract also contained a clause which stated that, should he decide to leave Japan, the Japanese government would undertake to defray his and his family's travel expenses. On the basis of this evidence, one might infer that Baty planned to work in Japan for five or ten years at the most before returning with his relatives to England. It is not clear that at this point Baty seriously imagined that he would be devoting so long a period of his career as thirty-eight years to the service of the Imperial Foreign Ministry, or that he intended to remain in Japan until his death. His mother passed away in August 1916, in less than three months after arrival; his sister died during the Second World War.

[5] Thomas Baty, *Alone in Japan* (Maruzen 1959) 91.

[6] It should be mentioned that Baty was a spokesman for vegetarianism. He became vice-president of the Vegetarian Society, a British organization. Baty adopted a strict vegetarian diet at the age of nineteen primarily for reasons of health, because in his youth he had a delicate constitution. He did permit himself eggs, cream, and honey. Yet his vegetarianism came to be an expression of his personal tastes and outlook. His was an aesthetic which valued plainness and simplicity. These virtues are especially prized in traditional Japanese culture, and are evident in Japanese cuisine.

Having taken up his post, he recorded that he 'led a quiet life in Tokyo'. Of his early days in Japan, he wrote: 'My duties were light—one might say nominal. I never saw the Minister or Under-Secretary, and only occasionally received a formal 'Case for Opinion'.[7] Such a situation must have been a disappointing one for Baty. His appointment coincided with a change in the practices of the Foreign Ministry. Communications were now written in Japanese, and only translated into English on occasions when Baty's opinions were sought. For this reason, Baty's role as legal adviser was a different one from that of his predecessor. Such tasks as Baty was called upon to perform for the Ministry, in addition to drawing up legal opinions and preparing briefs, appear to have included the more menial work of correcting and improving English in diplomatic documents. Nonetheless, he took a professional approach to whatever assignment he was given.

An exception to this pattern came in 1927, when Baty accompanied the Japanese delegation to the Geneva Naval Conference. Although he described the conference in very modest terms as one 'which I (unofficially) attended, to give what minor help I could',[8] the assistance he rendered the Foreign Ministry on that occasion was obviously substantive and significant. The proposals made by the Japanese at the Conference are said to have been unusually detailed and comprehensive as a result of Baty's thoughtful suggestions. He took part in all the preparatory meetings of the delegation, which is an indication of how much he enjoyed the confidence of its members.

Apart from this conference, however, Baty did not take a particularly prominent part in the Ministry's activities. It appears, indeed, as will be described later, that for the first ten years of his work there he concentrated more on his academic activities than on practical services for the Ministry.

Baty's Contribution to International Law Studies in Japan

Japan's international law community owed a great deal to Dr Thomas Baty. Two of his many important contributions deserve special mention: one was the establishment of the Japan Branch of the International Law Association (ILA) in 1920, and the other, beginning in 1925, was the organization of study groups based in Japan for the codification of inter-national law, a project which had been requested by the League of Nations' Preparatory Committee for the Codification Conference to be held at The Hague in 1930.

As was already mentioned, Baty had been closely associated with the ILA in England, having served as its Honorary Secretary since 1905 until his departure for Japan in 1916. After his arrival in Japan, he gradually came into contact with the scholars and experts in international law, and it was natural for him to encourage them to establish a national branch of ILA in Japan. A domestic association already existed in the form of the Japanese Society of International Law (JSIL) which had been established in 1897. Baty himself joined this association in 1919. However, he eagerly

[7] Baty, *Alone* (n 5) 93. It should be remembered that he was always guardedly modest when he spoke of his own activities as legal adviser.

[8] ibid 132.

stressed the importance of Japanese involvement in the worldwide dimension of academic developments in international law. He gave a talk on ILA at the JSIL annual meeting in 1919, and encouraged its members to join the efforts for the creation of a branch in Japan. In consequence, an ILA Japan Branch was established in 1920.[9] Baty was named an Executive Council member of the Branch, and was actively involved in its activities.

The ILA became inactive during the war years, and similarly, the activities of the Japan Branch were at a standstill during the same period. The Japan Branch, however, was re-established in 1955, in the year following Baty's death. In 1964, the ILA's 51st Conference was held in Tokyo, the first ever to be held in Asia. The 79th ILA Conference was held online at Kyoto, Japan, in 2020. The Japan Branch has now grown to become one of the largest of ILA's national branches, with 342 members (in May 2021). Thomas Baty has been, and will long be, remembered by the Japan Branch as its real founder.[10]

Baty's second major contribution to international law studies in pre-war Japan was the vigorous assistance he gave to the Japanese scholars who participated in the project for the codification of international law, the League of Nations' initiative that began in 1924. Under the combined auspices of JSIL and the ILA Japan Branch, a committee was formed for the codification of international law, which eventually elaborated nine separate draft conventions. Baty volunteered to correct and improve the English of these drafts. When completed, they were sent to the League, and at its Assembly meeting in 1928, Professor Henri Rolin, as rapporteur of the codification project, expressed his particular appreciation for the contributions made by the Japanese study team, and also for those of the Harvard research group.[11] Having won this recognition from the world organization, the whole Japanese community of international lawyers was immensely proud of its achievements, and was deeply grateful for the assistance of Dr Baty, without whose efforts the project would not have been so successful.[12]

Baty spent much of his time with international law scholars during his thirty-eight years in Japan. He continued to attend the JSIL annual meetings until the early 1950s, his last years. People recall him as 'sitting quietly at the back of the conference room and listening attentively to the speakers with his hands always placed on his lap'.[13] His presence meant a great deal to the Japanese members.

Thus for the first ten or fifteen years, Baty's life in Tokyo was probably an enjoyable time for him. That period of modern Japanese history is known as the era of 'Taisho Democracy', when the Japanese people enjoyed political and cultural freedom under a relatively democratic government. Baty formed a social salon called Kohakubaikai

[9] The Japan Branch is the third oldest of all the ILA branches after the Netherlands Branch (1910), and the German Branch (1912), and its foundation was followed by the establishment of branches in the United States (1921), Sweden (1922), and Poland (1923).

[10] See Shinya Murase, 'One Hundred Years of the ILA Japan Branch' in Catherine Kassedjian and Olivier Descamps (eds), *ILA 150 Years* (tentative title) Brill/Nijhoff (forthcoming 2023).

[11] Societe des Nations, Resolutions et voeux adopté par l'Assemblee au cours de sa neusneme session ordinaire, du 3 au 26 septembre 1928, 9.

[12] Baty also made a significant contribution to the project to provide an English translation of the Japanese civil and commercial codes in the 1930s.

[13] Masao Ichimata, 'Ko Thomas Baty Hakusi no Shogai to Gyoseki' (Life and Work of the late Dr Thomas Baty) (1954) 53 (1–2) Kokusaiho Gaiko Zasshi (The Journal of International Law and Diplomacy) 89–90.

(literally, the Red and White Plum-Blossoms Society): he would give parties for his wide circle of friends from the diplomatic and academic communities, and would sometimes take them on pleasure tours. He also took home leave four or five times, including periods in 1922, 1927, and 1933–34. He spent his leave not only in Britain, but would also visit his friends in Spain, Switzerland, and Sweden.

Baty's Double Identity

Baty led a rather simple and quiet life in Tokyo with his sister Anne. His apparent satisfaction with the modest role given him at the Foreign Ministry seems curious. One might also wonder how he spent his large earnings. It was not until 1993 that an answer was supplied to these questions. In an article published that year, two American feminist scholars unveiled Baty's double identity,[14] and demonstrated that his life's work had been dedicated to another important agenda, besides international law. This was his personal project for a radical feminist movement.

Baty was a self-confessed 'feminist'. He admired the feminine virtues and desired to emulate them. In his 'Autobiographical Sketch', he explains that from his 'earliest days' he had 'longed passionately to be a lady—and have continued to do so'. In adulthood, he showed a pronounced hostility towards sex distinctions and towards the institution of marriage. He himself never married. Neither was he a homosexual. He was what would be called today a 'transgendered' person.[15] In a pamphlet which was published in 1926, titled 'On Love and Marriage', Baty affirmed that 'beauty and sweetness' were his ideals in life.[16] He also stated elsewhere that he 'was desirous of forming an extreme feminist organization, to abolish or eliminate the consciousness of sex—and to advocate an identical ideal for "men" and "women" alike', adding that he had 'so far had no success'.[17] Feminine delicacy was at once the essence of his own personality and the quality he most valued, and so it is not surprising that 'feminist principles' should have been at the centre of his conception of international law.

As Thomas Baty's father died when he was only seven, his childhood was in the tender hands of his mother, Mary. Baty's mother appears to have been a typical Victorian lady; her sweetness, delicacy, tenacity, perseverance, and courage were qualities which Baty saw as the basis for a fully developed humanity. The example of his mother must have been a formative influence on his 'feminine' character and outlook. His sister Anne was his lifelong companion and able collaborator. It should be noted that he and his sister jointly translated from the original German George Jellinek's brief monograph, *The Rights of Minorities*, in 1912. While it is regrettable that very

[14] Daphne Patai and Angela Ingram, 'Fantasy and Identity: The Double Life of a Victorian Sexual Radical' in Angela Ingram and Daphne Patai (eds), *Rediscovering Forgotten Radicals, British Women Writers*, 1889–1939 (University of North Carolina Press 1993) 265–304.

[15] Alison Oram, '"Sex is an Accident": Feminism, Science and the Radical Sexual Theory of Urania, 1915–1940' in Lucy Bland and Laura Doan (eds), Sexology in Culture: Labelling Bodies and Desires (Polity Press 1998) 216.

[16] Reproduced in Thomas Baty, 'A Letter on Love and Marriage', in Baty, *Alone* (n 5) 188–92.

[17] Thomas Baty, 'An Autobiographical Sketch' in Baty, *Alone* (n 5) 185–87.

little is known about Anne, clearly, she was not just a housekeeper, and her intellectual collaboration must have meant a great deal to Baty in shaping his ideas on gender.

In the meantime, the name of Irene Clyde had been known in England as the author of a novel, Beatrice the Sixteenth published in London (George Bell 1909), and later, of a book of essays, also published in London *Eve's Sour Apples* (Eric Partridge 1934). She was also a frequent contributor to a feminist journal called *Urania*. Nobody, however, was aware of her identity and background, and the search for them was begun in the late 1980s by Patai and Ingram. They were finally able to identify Irene Clyde as the pseudonym of Thomas Baty, mainly through a comparative textual analysis of the writings. It can now be fairly assumed that Baty was one of those who founded and financed *Urania*.[18] The journal was published six and, later, three times a year between 1915 and 1940. It was privately printed and circulated, which suggests that it was almost an underground publication, as its printers' addresses changed from one city to another, and included Bombay, London, Seattle, and Tokyo.

It was in his last book, *International Law in Twilight*, published posthumously in 1954, that Baty finally acknowledged his pseudonym. A lone footnote on page 14 of the book stated in a nonchalant manner: 'Reference may perhaps ... be allowed to two books published under the name of I. Clyde, *Eve's Sour Apples*... and *Beatrice the Sixteenth* ..., which the curious may care to consult'. With no 'curious' readers around, this footnote remained largely unnoticed for some forty years since it was written. So did the identity of Irene Clyde, for more than eighty years since her name first appeared in the literary world.

Baty tirelessly assaulted conventional gender distinctions, because he observed that they only served to justify domination and submission. Baty's opposition to the gender hierarchy in human relations was consonant with his condemnation of great powers' domination over small nations in international relations. What is important here from the international law perspective is that he tried to establish an intrinsic link between feminism and pacifism (which he spelled 'pacificism'). In an article published in 1939 in the *Contemporary Review*, Baty discussed the time-honoured distinction between men and women, and asserted that the masculine character retained a predisposition towards struggle, and accordingly, war, while the feminine character would repudiate struggle and thus eliminate war. In his view, 'the conclusion must surely be that if war is to be brought to a permanent end, the feminine type of character must be cultivated to the exclusion of the masculine'.[19]

A lifelong radical feminist, Baty was indeed radical, in the sense that he assailed the very distinction of sex, the radix of the human existence. He maintained this position right up to his last book, *International Law in Twilight*, where he tried to develop his concepts of feminism into certain legal principles which would be applicable in international relations.[20] While the 'feminist approach to international law' has attained a certain popularity since the 1980s, Baty's theories, which he developed in the 1950s, should be deemed extraordinary in that he placed his ultimate goal on the abolition

[18] Oram, Sex (n 15) 214–30.

[19] Thomas Baty, 'Feminism and Pacificism' (July–December 1939) CLVI The Contemporary Review 95–100 at 99.

[20] Thomas Baty, *International Law in Twilight* (Maruzen 1954) 299–300.

of the gender distinction itself, rather than on achieving equality between both sexes or securing special protection for women as primary targets while recognizing such a distinction. This seems to be the main reason why Baty's feminist principles may be considered significantly different from those advocated in the field of international law today.[21]

Conclusion

Baty was a person who faced squarely, and struggled to overcome, the inconsistencies, discrepancies, paradoxes, and gaps of the times: the gaps between the west and the east, old and new, theory and practice, great powers and small nations, peace and war, and finally, men and women. He took all these problems seriously but he was not always successful in handling them. Looking at his last book, *Twilight in International Law*, one would notice that in the photograph of him at the start of the book he looks very sorrowful, and that his views in the rest of the book sound very pessimistic.

Since his boyhood, he had been deeply interested in Japan. Though he wanted to serve as a bridge between Japan and Britain through his profession, access to the bridge was closed off at both ends. He wished to be of assistance to Japan in her effort through international law to resist the domination of the great powers, but in fact, by the 1930s if not before, Japan was clearly the victimizer rather than the victim. As a 'pacificist', he wanted peace, but paradoxically, he became caught up in Japan's descent into war.

Baty's view of international law was anachronistic and even irremediably conservative. He retained a classical atomistic view of the international community, which he regarded exclusively in terms of the relations between the independent sovereign states of which it was composed. While he admitted that any law must have a foundation in the conscience of the general public, he nonetheless relied on a traditional elitist view on the function of international law that it operates basically upon the minds of influential statesmen and publicists.[22] This limited his intellectual horizons, and led him to take a dim view of many new developments in the twentieth century, such as, for instance, the importance that international organizations like the League and the UN were coming to hold. He never believed in the arbitral and judicial settlement of international disputes, because he thought they tended to be manipulated and abused by lawyers. In spite of his extremely learned presentation of legal theories, he

[21] Hilary Charlesworth, Christine Chinkin, and Shelley Wright, 'Feminist Approaches to International Law' (1991) 85(4) AJIL 613–45; Hilary Charlesworth, 'Feminist Methods of International Law' (1999) 93(2) AJIL 379–94; see also, Hilary Charlesworth and Christine Chinkin, *The Boundaries of International Law: A Feminist Analysis* (Manchester University Press 2000). The book contains no mention of Thomas Baty, nor are his works listed in its bibliography.

[22] For a more favourable evaluation of Baty's theoretical contributions toward restructuring international law, see Anthony Carty, 'Changing Models of the International System' in WE Butler (ed), *Perestroika and International Law* (Kluwer Academic Publishers 1990) 22–27. For an interesting account on the exchange of views that Baty had before the war with some American scholars of international law such as Edwin O Borchard and Quincy Wright, see Hatsue Shinohara, *Senso no Ho kara Heiwa no Ho e: Senkanki no Amerika Kokusaiho Gakusha* (Forgotten Crusade: The American Scholars of International Law in the Interwar Period) (University of Tokyo Press 2003).

seems somehow to have lacked a historical sense of the direction in which the world was moving, and perhaps was also unable to appreciate the political dimension of the theories he was putting forward.

One thing in his exposition of international law doctrines is remarkably striking. That is his theory of feminism in international law. Baty had been a strong supporter of women's suffrage. His association with the leaders of the women's liberation movement in Japan was well known. It is particularly significant that Baty in the late 1930s tried to clarify an intrinsic linkage between feminism and pacifism, and in the early 1950s tried to develop his concepts of feminism into certain legal principles which would be the basic norms of the international community. In his twilight years, he believed he could see the dawn of a new age, where 'flows serenely the eternal tide of Loveliness'.[23]

[23] Baty, *Alone* (n 5) 300.

35
Zheng Yuxiu and the Diplomacy of Nationalism and Feminism

Margaret Kuo

Introduction and Historical Overview

Zheng Yuxiu (1896–1959) is best remembered as China's first woman lawyer and judge.[1] Her pioneering career in international law and diplomacy encompassed important developments in Chinese feminism, nationalism, and constitutionalism. Zheng made notable contributions to the revolutionary movement in late Qing China, the constitutional movement in the 1920s, diplomatic efforts to restore China's sovereignty and to abrogate its unequal treaties under international law, the women's rights movement that sought equality for women under Chinese law, and wartime efforts to enlist international support for the Chinese struggle against the Japanese.

Her accomplishments were all the more remarkable given the considerable array of problems confronting China in the first half of the twentieth century, including the major upheavals wrought by war and revolution, like the 1911 Revolution that toppled the dynastic system of government, civil war during the successive warlord governments of the Beiyang period (1912–1928), the Nationalist Revolution of 1928 that brought the Guomindang to power, Japanese invasion and occupation during the War of Resistance (1937–1945), civil war between the Nationalists and the Communists, and the 1949 Revolution.[2] Although her commitment to gender equality and political equality remained steadfast, these crises largely set the boundaries of Zheng's professional work. Her work was hampered not only by political fragmentation, but it was also constrained by the culturally conservative elite male legal and diplomatic circles in which she was often the sole woman. Despite these obstacles, her persistent legal and diplomatic efforts eventually helped bring about gender equality under law for Chinese women and an abrogation of the unequal treaties for the Chinese nation.

[1] I use the pinyin system of Romanization and refer to the subject of this chapter as Zheng Yuxiu 鄭毓秀 (Zheng being her surname). In previous publications, her name appeared as Soumay Tcheng, Soumè Tcheng, and Soumi Tcheng. After her marriage to Wei Daoming in 1927, the Western press most often referred to her as Madame Wei Tao-ming. Her date of birth is listed as 1891 in some sources, 1896 in others. There is one book-length Chinese biography on Zheng, Tang Dongmei's *Chuanyue shiji cangmang: Zheng Yuxiu zhuan* [*Across the Vastness of a Century: Biography of Zheng Yuxiu*] (Zhongguo shehui chubanshe 2013). After decades of obscurity, Zheng appears to be enjoying a revival of interest in China as short articles and translations of her English-language memoirs have appeared.

[2] For additional historical context for the transformations in Chinese politics and society during the Republican period, see Diana Lary, China's Republic (Cambridge University Press 2007) and Rana Mitter, A Bitter Revolution: China's Struggle with the Modern World (Oxford University Press 2004).

Margaret Kuo, *Zheng Yuxiu and the Diplomacy of Nationalism and Feminism* In: *Portraits of Women in International Law*. Edited by: Immi Tallgren, Oxford University Press. © Margaret Kuo 2023. DOI: 10.1093/oso/9780198868453.003.0035

Figure 35.1 Zheng Yuxiu.
Source: Photograph by Fu Bingchang. Courtesy of Y.W. Foo and Special Collections, University of Bristol Library (www.hpcbristol.net).

Youthful Rebellions

In the crisis-ridden period of the late Qing, the twinned emergence of modern feminism and nationalism profoundly shaped Zheng's eventual revolutionary path. Zheng viewed feminism and nationalism as closely tied together. Zheng likened the weakness of Chinese women to China's weakness as a nation. To strengthen Chinese women, by means of education for example, meant to strengthen the Chinese nation.[3]

[3] Lydia H Liu, Rebecca E Karl, and Dorothy Ko, 'The Historical Context: Chinese Feminist Worlds at the Turn of the Twentieth Century' in *The Birth of Chinese Feminism: Essential Texts in Transnational Theory* (Columbia University Press 2013) discusses the context of late Qing feminist discourse. The classic study by Mary Backus Rankin, 'The Emergence of Women at the End of the Ch'ing: The Case of Ch'iu Chin' in Margery Wolf (ed), *Women in Chinese Society* (Stanford University Press 1975) examines late Qing feminism through the experiences of the female revolutionary Qiu Jin.

Zheng's feminist beginnings were forged in the radical anti-traditionalism of the late Qing dynasty, when a nascent Chinese women's movement emerged that led to gradual improvements to the status of women. Zheng was the beneficiary of this transitional period in which the re-examination of longstanding Confucian values led reformers to denounce the custom of foot-binding, promote girls' education, and establish women's associations and a women's press.[4] During childhood, Zheng valorized the legendary woman warrior Mulan for her circumvention of traditional gender norms. Inspired by Mulan, Zheng strenuously rebelled against the traditional practices of foot-binding, arranged marriage, and patriarchal family authority.[5] Growing up in the Canton region of China in an elite gentry–literati family, Zheng received her initial education from private tutors. Later, with her reform-minded father's support, she attended a new-style girls' school in Beijing. Like other female activists who grew up in the late Qing, education served as the path of her independence from the gender expectations that limited female roles to within the family.[6] Breaking even further with conventional gender expectations at the age of twelve, Zheng escaped from an arranged marriage betrothal and left her family compound to attend an American missionary school in Tianjin. At the missionary school, she learned English, adopted a Western hairstyle and clothing, and took classes in physical education for the first time. Aided by sympathetic family members, she then travelled abroad to Japan for a few months and onto France for several years where she continued to pursue her independence through education and political activism.

Japan and France: From Student Radicalism to Legal Professionalism

Zheng's nationalism first found expression in her activities as a student radical and late Qing revolutionary. Travel and study not only served as ways for Zheng to cast off traditional family expectations, but they also opened up new paths, like fostering her political radicalization. Her travels overseas to Japan, for example, brought her into contact with early Chinese revolutionaries, like Liao Zhongkai and his wife He Xiangning, who were dedicated to overthrowing the Manchus and creating a Chinese

[4] On efforts to abolish foot-binding, the importance of women's education, and the emergence of a women's press, see Dorothy Ko, *Cinderella's Sisters: A Revisionist History of Footbinding* (University of California Press 2005); Paul J Bailey, *Gender and Education in China: Gender Discourses and Women's Schooling in the Early Twentieth Century* (Routledge 2006); Charlotte L Beahan, 'Feminism and Nationalism in the Chinese Women's Press, 1911' (October 1975) 1(4) Modern China 379–416; and Yuxin Ma, *Women Journalists and Feminism in China, 1898–1937* (Cambria Press 2010).

[5] Much of what is known about Zheng's early life comes from her autobiography, *My Revolutionary Years: The Autobiography of Madame Wei Tao-ming* (Charles Scribner's Sons 1943). She also published an earlier memoir in France with the help of her friend Bessie Van Vorst, as Soumé Tcheng, *Souvenirs d'Enfance et de Révolution* (Payot & Cie 1920). This work was later published in English as Soumay Tcheng, *A Girl from China* (Frederick A. Stokes Company 1926). On Mulan as a cultural icon, see Lan Dong, *Mulan's Legend and Legacy in China and the United States* (Temple University Press 2011) especially chs 2–3, and Louise Edwards, 'Transformations of the Woman Warrior Hua Mulan: From Defender of the Family to Servant of the State' (2010) 12 Nan Nü: Men, Women and Gender in China 175–214.

[6] Weikun Cheng, 'Going Public Through Education: Female Reformers and Girls' Schools in Late Qing Beijing' (June 2000) 21(1) Late Imperial China 104–44.

republic. Stirred by anti-Manchu nationalist sentiment herself, she joined forces with the Revolutionary Alliance (*Tongmenghui*, precursor to the Guomindang or Chinese Nationalist Party), in Tokyo, the revolutionary group founded by Sun Yat-sen that opposed the Manchu emperor in favour of popular sovereignty. Back in China, Zheng mobilized for the revolution by carrying out several daring missions smuggling weapons from Tianjin to Beijing, relying upon her friends in the foreign diplomatic corps to ease her way past train station inspections. That was how she first gained renown. Later in Paris, her associates included the anarchist founder of the work–study movement, Li Shizeng, with whom she worked on the monthly *La Chine Nouvelle*.[7]

Ultimately, though, Zheng was most closely aligned with a cohort of legal and diplomatic elites in the Foreign Ministry, Shanghai Mixed Court, and foreign embassies that represented one of China's earliest generations of international lawyers.[8] United by the desire to save and strengthen China, this group of Western-educated figures like Wang Chonghui, Wu Tingfang, VK Wellington Koo, Wang Shijie, and many others systematically engaged with international law to elevate China's status in the world order.[9] In retrospect, this group of professional lawyers, diplomats, and intellectuals represented a form of legal gradualism that continued throughout the various regime changes.

After the 1911 Revolution, Zheng celebrated the collapse of the Qing dynasty, but soon thereafter, the GMD (Guomindang, also referred to as Kuomintang or KMT), was forced to retreat as warlord militarists seized power and political fragmentation thwarted the nationalist cause. Even as Zheng sought refuge in Europe, she continued to pursue activities to advance the nationalist cause. Zheng dedicated her studies in international law and her political organizing to the struggle against domestic warlordism and foreign imperialism. International law represented a relatively new field of knowledge in China whose origins were deeply connected to a set of trade and military conflicts with modern European powers.[10] Foreign powers had encroached upon Chinese territory since the Treaty of Nanjing in 1842. Chinese inexperience with modern European notions of international law in the mid-nineteenth century led to a series of disastrous unequal treaties.

[7] For an examination of the ideological differences among the various youth groups in France, see Nagatomi Hirayama, '"Young China" in Europe: The Lives and Politics of the May Fourth Youth in France, 1919–23' (2018) 91(252) Historical Research 353–74.

[8] Pasha L Hsieh, 'The Discipline of International Law in Republican China and Contemporary Taiwan' (2015) 14(1) Washington University Global Studies Law Review 87–129.

[9] Her male contemporaries became the subject of many more biographies and accolade, see Ole Spiermann, 'Judge Wang Chung-hui at the Permanent Court of International Justice' (2006) 5(1) Chinese Journal of International Law 115–28; Pao-chin Chu, *V.K. Wellington Koo and a Case Study of China's Diplomat and Diplomacy of Nationalism, 1912–1966* (Chinese University Press 1981); David Strand, *An Unfinished Republic: Leading by Word and Deed in Modern China* (University of California Press 2011) ch 5. See also Lu Zhengxiang, *Souvenirs et Pensées* (Desclee de Brouwer 1945).

[10] Yongjin Zhang, *China in the International System, 1918–20: The Middle Kingdom at the Periphery* (Palgrave Macmillan 1991). On Western perceptions of Qing law, see Li Chen, *Chinese Law in Imperial Eyes: Sovereignty, Justice, and Transcultural Politics* (Columbia University Press 2015). For an overview of China's struggles to attain equal status in the system of international law, see David Scott, *China and the International System, 1840–1949: Power, Presence, and Perceptions in a Century of Humiliation* (State University of New York Press 2008) and Phil CW Chan, 'China's Approaches to International Law since the Opium War' (December 2014) 27(4) Leiden Journal of International Law 859–92.

The main goal of Chinese nationalists, like Zheng, was to establish China as an equal nation, in other words to gain recognition for Chinese sovereignty and overturn the system of unequal treaties that had marked Chinese foreign relations since the Opium War. Beginning in the late Qing when a commission on the abolition of extraterritoriality was formed that championed adopting international law, international law continued to be viewed as an essential means to modernize China and salvage its sovereignty. Abolishing the system of unequal treaties necessitated that Chinese laws undergo a fundamental reorganization along modern Western lines. The unequal treaties contained humiliating provisions like the right of extraterritoriality which granted foreigners immunity from Chinese law. Zheng embarked on her legal education with the determination that international law was the path to protect China's national sovereignty and gain equal legal status.

Zheng's first official foray into international diplomacy was as an attaché to the sixty-person Chinese delegation at the 1919 Paris Peace Conference. Many conventional narratives characterize Chinese diplomatic efforts there as obstructed by failure, disappointment, and even betrayal, while other accounts emphasize that the conference served somewhat paradoxically to mark the transformation of Chinese diplomacy from an isolationist to an internationalist orientation.[11] The young Chinese republic in 1919 was perceived as weak and fragile inheriting a string of military defeats, financial burdens of indemnity payments and foreign loans, and regional divisions. Although inexperienced on the international stage, Zheng, like the rest of the Chinese delegation represented a group of young, enthusiastic, reform-minded individuals inspired by United States President Woodrow Wilson's principle of national self-determination.

Zheng's job was to gain sympathy for China's post-war interests among the foreign press. She worked to restore Chinese territorial integrity over Jiaozhou Bay in Shandong Province, which was formerly leased to Germany and seized by the Japanese during the war. The Chinese position on the Shandong question stressed that China was a loyal ally that contributed to the Allied victory. Having declared war against Germany in August 1917, China sent around 140,000 labourers to alleviate the British and French labour shortage.[12] For these reasons the Chinese delegation and populace expected the German concession in Shandong to be returned to China. Despite strenuous efforts and high hopes, instead of restitution, the Treaty of Versailles awarded the territory to Japan. After a massive public outcry, the Chinese delegation refused to sign in protest over infringements on Chinese sovereignty. In her autobiography, Zheng claims she personally stopped the head of the Chinese delegation Lu Zhengxiang from signing the treaty and betraying the Chinese people by pretending to wield a gun

[11] See Chi-Hua Tang, 'China-Europe' in Bardo Fassbender and others (eds), *The Oxford Handbook of the History of International Law* (OUP 2012) 701–23; Rosemary Foot, 'Remembering the Past to Secure the Present: Versailles Legacies in a Resurgent China' (January 2019) 95(1) International Affairs 143–60; Erez Manela, *The Wilsonian Moment: Self-Determination and the International Origins of Anticolonial Nationalism* (OUP 2007) ch 5; Bruce A Elleman, *Wilson and China: A Revised History of the Shandong Question* (ME Sharpe 2002); and Guoqi Xu, *China and the Great War: New National Identity and Internationalism* (Cambridge University Press 2005).

[12] Guoqi Xu, *Strangers on the Western Front: Chinese Workers in the Great War* (Harvard University Press 2011).

(actually a rosebush under a piece of cloth) at him. Outrage and controversy ensued back in China, and the unjust treatment of China at the peace conference touched off the seminal nationalist movement known as the May Fourth/New Culture movement. Western diplomats' perceived hypocrisy hastened an outpouring of Chinese nationalist protest with the first mass demonstrations in Chinese history and the birth of modern Chinese nationalism.[13]

Zheng's disappointment with the outcome of the Paris Peace Conference convinced her that understanding international law was a great national imperative and she embarked on a programme of doctoral studies in law at the University of Paris where she graduated in 1924.[14] Zheng wrote her doctoral thesis, 'The New Draft Chinese Constitution,' on the newly-promulgated 1923 Constitution and the constitutional movement in China. Constitutionalism was a central problem to the Chinese revolution in which leaders hoped to replace the dynastic system with the establishment of a constitutional government, and the underlying premise of her thesis was to promote constitutionalism as the best means of bringing about the rule of law in China.[15] Chinese elites hoped that constitutionalism could greatly improve China's international standing, just as Meiji Japan had successfully rid itself of unequal treaties after adopting a Western-style constitution. The constitutional movement began in the late Qing with a constitutional commission tasked with studying and investigating the constitutions of other countries. Efforts continued with the drafting of a provisional constitution, convening constitutional conferences, and promulgating a permanent constitution.

Zheng's thesis first compared the Anglo-American constitutional model which placed more emphasis on individual rights to the Continental European model that she deemed more statist. Zheng then examined the reasoning by which drafters shaped the Chinese constitution to embody the highest legal authority (in contrast to the emperor of old) and grappled with defining government powers, including the separation of powers, limits on government power, and the distribution of power among the central and local governments, and incorporating democratic and liberal ideas about rights to the extent deemed suitable for China. Zheng's explanation of the complicated history of the constitutional movement in China, including several draft and provisional constitutions, was published in China and in France as *Le mouvement constitutionnel en Chine*. The publication of her thesis brought recognition that she was one of the elite Western-educated legal experts shaping China's political future.[16]

[13] Rana Mitter, *A Bitter Revolution: China's Struggle with the Modern World* (OUP 2005), chs 1–5.

[14] Marilyn A Levine, *The Found Generation: Chinese Communists in Europe during the Twenties* (University of Washington Press 1993) sheds light on the experiences of Chinese students in France around the same time as Zheng, though it focuses on those students who gravitated toward the Chinese Communist Party.

[15] Shuping Hua, *Chinese Legal Culture and Constitutional Reform* (Routledge 2019); Suisheng Zhao, *Power by Design: Constitution-Making in Nationalist China* (University of Hawaii Press 1996); Peng Chengyi, *Chinese Constitutionalism in a Global Context* (Routledge 2019); and Jerome A Cohen, 'China's Changing Constitution' (December 1978) 76 China Quarterly 794–841 provide useful overviews of the ongoing process of constitutional reform in China.

[16] Detractors, like Hu Shi, however, later claimed that she performed poorly at her thesis defence and that her close male friend, the prominent jurist Wang Chonghui, was the actual author of her thesis.

Shanghai and Nanjing: Lawyer, Judge, Legislator, Law Professor

Zheng returned to China in 1926 and for the next decade embarked on a remarkably productive phase of her life. Her varied career included stints as a lawyer, judge, diplomat, government administrator, lawmaker, and educator. The wide-ranging set of responsibilities she held reflected a period of rapid changes in Chinese society and politics. By the late 1920s and 1930s, attitudes toward women had undergone dramatic changes since the feminist tide of the New Culture movement.[17] Opportunities for educated career women to participate in public life grew considerably especially in urban areas like Shanghai, where Zheng chose to open her law practice in the French Concession. Her partner in this endeavour was Wei Daoming, a fellow law student in France, whom she later married (Zheng had remained steadfastly unmarried since her broken childhood betrothal, and it is not clear why she chose to marry in her thirties). Their law practice thrived even amidst Shanghai's convoluted legal jurisdiction with the conflicting authority of Chinese courts, mixed courts, and consular courts over Chinese and foreign residents. In addition to practicing law, Zheng and Wei continued to work underground for the GMD in conjunction with the Northern Expedition. The pair closed their law practice in 1928 when called upon to work for the party after the GMD reunified the country and established a new government based in Nanjing.

Zheng made her most important professional contributions during the Nanjing decade (1928–1937), a watershed period in Chinese modernization efforts.[18] Her long-standing affiliation with the now-ruling Nationalist Party opened up opportunities and led to a series of prominent appointments in 1927–1928, including to the Shanghai District Court (thereby becoming the first female judge in Chinese history), to the nine-member Jiangsu Provincial Council (the governing body for the province), and service as a special envoy to France to drum up international support for the newly-formed government. Perhaps most significantly, she played a highly visible role as one of only two women appointed to the Legislative Yuan (*Li fa yuan*立法院) (the other being Song Meiling, the wife of Chiang Kai-shek). In this prestigious body, she served as the only female member of the five-person Civil Codification Commission in 1928–1930.[19] The commission sought to introduce modern legal principles while preserving Chinese cultural characteristics and implementing Nationalist Party social values.[20] In this role, Zheng advocated for the principle of gender equality as a modern value in civil law. Not without controversy, the final version of the code provided for gender equality with respect to marriage and divorce, contract, property, and

[17] Wang Zheng, *Women in the Chinese Enlightenment* (University of California Press 1999) examines New Culture feminism and the lives of urban career women, including a lawyer, educator, and magazine editor. Hua R Lan and Vanessa L Fong (eds), *Women in Republican China: A Sourcebook* (ME Sharpe 1999) provides sources on the debates over New Women.

[18] John Fitzgerald, *Awakening China: Politics, Culture, and Class in the Nationalist Revolution* (Stanford University Press 1996).

[19] Foo Ping-sheung [Fu Bingchang], 'Introduction', *The Civil Code of the Republic of China* (Kelly and Walsh 1930).

[20] Hu Hanmin, 'Preface', *The Civil Code of the Republic of China* (Kelly and Walsh 1930) v–vi.

inheritance rights. Her place as a legislator enabled her to stamp China's new civil code with the principle of gender equality. As she reflected years later, 'The Constitution guaranteed absolute equality for women, but I wanted to be sure.'[21] The Republican Civil Code went into effect in 1930–1931 and is still the law of the land in the Republic of China.[22] Shortly thereafter Zheng left government to return to the private practice of law in Shanghai and to serve as President of the University of Shanghai's school of law and politics for seven years.[23] The promise of the Nanjing decade meanwhile was abruptly halted by the Japanese invasion of China in 1937.

Wartime and Exile

Zheng's next major assignment was to serve as a diplomatic wife after her husband was appointed Chinese ambassador to the United States in 1941. During the Second World War, Zheng worked tirelessly to promote the Chinese war effort, to mobilize American public opinion to support China, and to raise money for China relief. In 1942–1943 she also accompanied her friend Song Meiling, the wife of Generalissimo Chiang Kai-shek, during her famous tour of the United States and speech before the United States Congress enlisting American aid to China. These efforts paid off in 1943 when China finally achieved its steadfast pursuit of the abrogation of China's unequal treaties and the restoration of its national sovereignty. In the international arena, these wartime years proved to be crucial to Chinese efforts to abolish extraterritoriality, the loathsome clause that had granted foreigners immunity from Chinese law. Thus, the Second World War marked a turning point in China's international standing with a rare triumph after decades of disappointment.

After the Japanese surrender in 1945, a civil war between the Nationalists and the Communists broke out and ended in the Communist Revolution of 1949. On the wrong side of the 1949 Revolution, Zheng and her husband fled to the United States where she remained largely out of the limelight and lived in exile until her death in 1959. Although she spent her final years in relative obscurity, in her heyday she played a central role in the evolution of Chinese nationalism and feminism as the first Chinese woman lawyer and judge and one of the strongest advocates for gender equality under the law.

[21] 'Lady from China,' *The New York Times* (8 November 1942) SM11.

[22] Margaret Kuo, *Intolerable Cruelty: Marriage, Law, and Society in Early Twentieth-Century China* (Rowman & Littlefield 2012).

[23] One possible reason for Zheng's retreat from politics to education was the allegation of corruption that was raised against her. On legal training in Republican China, see Alison W Conner, 'Legal Education During the Republican Period: Soochow University Law School' (1994) 19(1) Republican China 84–112 and 'Anglo-American Law at Soochow University,' in *China's Christian Colleges* (Stanford University Press 2020) 147–72.

36
Marjorie M Whiteman
Not Flowers but a Medal

Hatsue Shinohara

As a major contributor to the birth and development of international law, and among the first women to ever work in the field, Marjorie Millace Whiteman was deeply concerned with uncovering and documenting the changing nature of international law.[*] Her major contributions to legal scholarship, the so-called Whiteman *Digest* and her dissertation-based trilogy, *Damages in International Law,* are invaluable sources to the international lawyer, who Whiteman herself noted to struggle with 'the extreme dearth of collated material [. . .] in international cases'.[1] Moreover, her work in several major international projects, like the League of Nations Codification Conference of 1930 and the first United Nations Conference on the Laws of Sea 1958 as an Assistant Legal Advisor at the United States Department of State, has contributed to the development of international law and indirectly aided in women's inclusion in this process.

Despite her extraordinary impact, Whiteman is often overlooked and her contributions seem near forgotten in its scholarship. In this profile, this neglect is remedied by an examination of Whiteman's contributions to the development of international law in conjunction with an historical examination of her personal career.

Early Career

Marjorie M Whiteman graduated from Yale Law School, where she obtained two law degrees: LLB in 1927 and JD in 1928. At Yale, she received her academic training primarily from Edwin O Borchard, a specialist of diplomatic protection and one of the most prominent scholars of international law at the time, which likely guided Whiteman's interest in state responsibility in international law.[2] Following Yale, Whiteman specialized in international law as a grantee of a Carnegie Fellowship. She began her professional career as a high school history teacher before becoming a temporary member of staff at the United States Department of State in 1929 as an assistant to the then Legal Advisor, Green H Hackworth.[3] In July 1930, she became a full staff member and one of only three female lawyers to assist the Legal Advisor.[4]

* * My special thanks go to Immi Tallgren, Linda Lee, and Katariina Flinck for making this work possible, substantial, and refined.

1 Marjorie M Whiteman, *Damages in International Law* (vol 1, US Government Publishing Office 1937) v.

2 Machian Nash Leich, 'Marjorie M. Whiteman (1898–1986)' (1986) 80 AJIL 933–40.

3 ibid.

4 ibid; Ellery Stowell, *The Legal Adviser of the Department of State* (The Digest Press 1936) 6, (fn 18), 28–29.

Hatsue Shinohara, *Marjorie M Whiteman* In: *Portraits of Women in International Law.* Edited by: Immi Tallgren,
Oxford University Press. © Hatsue Shinohara 2023. DOI: 10.1093/oso/9780198868453.003.0036

Figure 36.1 Whiteman in her office in Washington D.C.
Source: Courtesy of Linda Lee, niece of Marjorie Whiteman.

The Hague Codification Conference

Whiteman participated in the League of Nations Codification Conference of International Law (hereafter the Hague Codification Conference) in 1930 as a member of the American delegation under David H Miller and Green H Hackworth. The Conference dealt with three issues, each with its own committee: nationality, territorial sea, and state responsibility. With the official title of Research Assistant of the Delegation to the United States at the First Conference of the Codification of International Law,[5] Whiteman was assigned to the committee on state responsibility alongside Borchard and Hackworth.

[5] Marjorie M Whiteman, 'Codification of the State Responsibility of States' (1930) 8 New York University Law Quarterly Review 188.

Whiteman published an article reflecting on the Conference shortly after. As a whole, it reads rather like a proceeding of meetings, noting details of who said what. Yet, she pointed out the difficulties the Conference encountered, writing that 'it is possible that each of the three Committees approached the problem of codification differently'.[6] One such difficulty concerned how codification should be defined and practised. Citing one of the most active scholars of international law at the time and a fellow committee member, she noted that 'codification of international law can be imagined in several forms'.[7]

Whiteman also mentioned problems raised in the committee regarding the definition of an international obligation and the division created between member states over the treatment of foreigners. On the latter topic, Whiteman wrote that 'the Committee's work became stranded'.[8] She observed that during the Conference, many non-Western states argued that aliens should be treated in the same manner as nationals, while Western states had assumed that 'international' standards would be applied.[9]

Attending the Conference was a valuable experience and fortunate opportunity for Whiteman to learn about various views from different parts of the world. She wrote that the Conference did not bring out any tangible results but that the publication of the minutes of the Committee and Reports by the League would give some influence on international law.[10] She seemed positive, quoting the statement addressed by a member, Chao-Chu Wu of China, 'I do not think that the work of the Committee has been in vain ... we have elucidated certain complicated points'.[11] Whiteman had grasped the difficulties involved in codification and the value of considering and singling out differences of opinions and later availability of official records in print.

Post-war Years

Legal Advisor to Mrs Franklin D Roosevelt, Universal Declaration of Human Rights

Following her first assignment with the State Department at the Hague Codification Conference, a request by First Lady Eleanor Roosevelt to assign Whiteman to assist in the drafting of the UN Declaration of Human Rights 'came by surprise' to Whiteman in 1946.[12] Whiteman later recalled that Roosevelt, as Chairman of the Human Rights Commission at the time, wanted to make the Declaration something of a '"ringing declaration", to be committed to memory with ease and recited by school children the world over as we in America recite the opening clauses of our Declaration of

6 ibid 188.
7 ibid 186.
8 ibid 206.
9 ibid.
10 ibid.
11 ibid 216–17.
12 Marjorie M Whiteman, 'Mrs. Franklin D. Roosevelt and the Human Rights Commission' (1968) 62 AJIL 918–21, 918.

Independence or the Pre-amble to the Constitution of the United States'.[13] Roosevelt felt that the Declaration should neither be a simple international agreement nor a legal statement. Instead, 'it is a declaration of basic principles of human rights' whose 'initial impetus' Whiteman credits to Roosevelt.[14] Whiteman exchanged several letters throughout the years with Roosevelt, who came to count on Whiteman's professional expertise in international law in her various projects, thus placing Whiteman to effectively play the role of liaison between Roosevelt and the State Department.[15]

The Law of the Sea and the Convention on the Territorial Shelf

In the immediate years after the establishment of the UN, it sought to continue the codification project of international law initiated by the League of Nations. On 3 October 1946, Yuen-Li Liang, Director of the Division of Development and Codification of International Law of the UN, conversed with State Department officials regarding a draft resolution the UN Secretariat planned to submit for the General Assembly.[16] On the topic, Whiteman wrote a memorandum to John Maktos, the Associate Chief of the Division of International Organization Affairs, stating that if the Secretariat got involved in codification directly, it might be 'discharging its functions under Article 13 of the Charter'.[17] Instead, Whiteman suggested, the Committee on Procedure should be established to discuss the scope of codification, and the Secretariat should not take the lead.[18] Drawing on her experience at the Hague Codification Conference, Whiteman suggested that specially appointed international lawyers from the Committee of Experts for the Progressive Codification of International Law should take the lead. Whiteman was thus an essential communicator between the State Department and representatives at the UN at a crucial moment in time for the UN and the codification of international law.

Similarly, Whiteman's role in the codification of international law of the sea was essential to its development and saw her become an expert in inter-American affairs. At a time of decolonization and rapid globalization, smaller countries sought to defend and expand their fishery rights and resources. In particular, Chile, Peru, and Ecuador proposed a minimum of 200 miles for their territorial waters. In February 1956, when the Inter-American Council of Jurists met in Mexico to discuss, the participatory states adopted a resolution in favour of the suggestion, claiming that the 'distance of three miles as a limit of territorial waters is insufficient' and 'does not constitute the rule of general international law'.[19] Recording the events of the conference, Whiteman

[13] ibid 919.

[14] ibid.

[15] *Letters Between Whiteman and Eleanor Roosevelt 1949–1951*,<www.hollisarchives.lib.harvard.edu/repositories/8/archival_objects/3361307> accessed 3 February 2021.

[16] 'Memorandum by Miss Marjorie M. Whiteman of the Office of the Legal Advisor to the Associate Chief of the Division of International Affairs (Maktos)' (October 4 1946) The Foreign Relations of the United States 532–33.

[17] ibid 533.

[18] ibid 534.

[19] Richard R Baxter, Marjorie M Whiteman, and Herbert W Briggs, 'The Territorial Sea' (1956) 50 Proceedings of the American Society of International Law at its Annual Meeting 116–36, 130.

observed that the Principles of Mexico on the Juridical Regime of the Seas were thus adopted by a vote of 15:1.[20] The United States was the only country that distinctly opposed major coastal states' claims in the Americas.

At the State Department, Whiteman's regional expertise in inter-American affairs saw her participate in the Council of Jurists in Mexico and Specialized Conference on the Continental Shelf and Oceanic Waters at Ciudad Trujillo in March 1956. The United States opposed the propositional claim of 200 miles and contended that the issue had to be instead discussed at the UN rather than at a regional conference.

Naturally, the issue of territorial sea drew the attention of American international lawyers. When the American Society of International Law[21] held its fiftieth annual meeting in April 1956, Whiteman was invited to speak at a session entitled International Law Commission on Regime of the Territorial Sea.

In her speech, Whiteman quoted John Bassett Moore's statement at the Hague Codification Conference: 'the subject of territorial waters is among those that are least susceptible of codification'.[22] Bringing up Moore's account, she reminded the audience how complicated the issue is and the problems faced at The Hague with the codification of such complex matters. When Whiteman described the impression left at the Santiago Conferences, interestingly and unusually for the annual meetings, she quoted a part of a poem by Lewis Carroll, 'The Hunting of the Snark'.[23] She implied that if countries raised the claim repeatedly, however unreasonable the request might be, it might begin to sound right. Whiteman thus asserted that the American Republics should reconsider their positions even though the result of the Ciudad Trujillo Conference showed that there had existed a diversity of positions among them on the breadth of the territorial sea.[24]

Two years later, from 24 February to 27 April 1958, the first United Nations Conference on the Laws of Sea (UNCLOS) was held in Geneva. Whiteman was again involved which marked a significant and distinct achievement in her career. Whiteman, who had known the difficulties involved in codification at the Hague Codification Conference in 1930, bore a heavy responsibility as the chief United States delegate of Committee IV of UNCLOS. With Whiteman's knowledge on and experience with conference discussions and the positions of coastal states in Latin America, her task was to find the point where the interests of the United States and the international community intersect. She acted professionally with expert handling of legal terms and inter alia managed the wording of proposed articles.[25]

She claimed that the principle of the freedom of seas should be applied to superjacent waters' legal status as high seas. The United States delegates argued that 'the regime of the continental shelf' should be 'subject to and within the orbit of the paramount principle of the freedom of seas and the air space above them'.[26] Sensing the

[20] ibid 130.

[21] For the ASIL and women, see Alona E Evans and Carol Per Lee Plumb, 'Women and the American Society of International Law' (1974) 68 AJIL 290–99.

[22] Baxter and others (n 19) 125.

[23] ibid 130.

[24] ibid 125–35.

[25] Marjorie M Whiteman, 'Conference on the Law of the Sea: Convention on the Continental Shelf' (1958) 52 AJIL 629–40.

[26] ibid 641.

political tensions at the Conference, she observed that some representatives believed the United States wanted a separate Convention on the Continental Shelf, and that 'by holding off on their assent to a separate convention with reference to the shelf, something was to be gained from the United States'.[27] Evaluating the Conference, Whiteman concluded that the Convention would have a considerable effect on the development of international law even though 'the drafting in such a comparatively new field was difficult [because] the Conference was tinged with politics'.[28]

With her profound knowledge of international law and the competences of a skilled negotiator, Whiteman succeeded in the difficult task of reaching an agreement. This author can only speculate on Whiteman's undoubtedly deep feelings and sense of accomplishment.

The Legal Scholar

Damages in International Law (1937–1943)

One of Whiteman's greatest academic contributions to legal scholarship was published between 1937 and 1943 in three volumes deriving from her doctoral dissertation: *Damages in International Law*. The volumes cover numerous cases regarding, as the title would suggest, damages in international law such as personal injury and concessions. To preface, Whiteman recalls how at the Hague Conference, the committee of state responsibility agreed that there existed no crystallized principles to measure damages.[29] In these volumes, the cases presented are 'representative of the cases settled diplomatically and of those settled by international arbitration'.[30] Accordingly, 'the cases are indicative of how reasonable men have measured damages in a variety of circumstances'.[31] At the outset of Chapter 1, she writes that 'the methods in the measurement of damages' had practical importance in the study of international law, defining the term 'damage' as 'the existence of an international claim based upon the wrongful act or omission of one State toward another State'.[32] These volumes effectively made Whiteman the first lawyer and scholar not only to collate cases concerning damages in international law but also to give the concept a working definition and define its parameters. Whiteman's contribution to the scholarship of international law is therefore significant through her massive 1600-page legal trilogy in addition to her work as a legal research assistant at the Hague Conference.

Hackworth echoes these sentiments in his foreword in Volume 1 of *Damages*. He wrote that Whiteman's 'monumental' work is 'of inestimable value to lawyers, jurists, and claimants alike'.[33] He points out that in *Damages,* Whiteman 'has held the mirror up to the legal processes by which damages are measured and international claims

[27] ibid 657.
[28] ibid 659.
[29] Whiteman *Damages* (n 1) v.
[30] ibid.
[31] ibid.
[32] ibid 5–6.
[33] Green H Hackworth, 'Foreword' in ibid iii.

are decided' despite the 'lack of science in our law' 'where diverse and faulty methods abound'.[34]

Similarly, Whiteman's *Damages* was recognized as an essential addition to the scholarship of international law by Charles Cheney Hyde, a professor at Columbia University and predecessor of Hackworth's at the State Department, who for one acknowledged Whiteman's comprehensive collection of documents of court decisions and judgments on damages in international law; Hyde wished 'to acknowledge his indebtedness to the author and to say it with flowers'.[35]

Whiteman *Digest of International Law* (1963–1973)

Some years later, Whiteman began building upon Moore's and Hackworth's famous *Digests of International Law*,[36] creating the 'long-awaited' and 'remarkable'[37] Whiteman *Digest of International Law*. An official publication of the Department of State, the Whiteman *Digest* brought together 'an invaluable selection of the published decisions and documents and views of commentators'[38] including 'judicial decisions (American, foreign, and international), extracts from books and articles (both American and foreign), documents of the UN and other International Organisations, and whatever else might be useful in painting a picture of current developments in international law'.[39] Consisting of a whopping fifteen volumes, the Whiteman *Digest* offers not only a collection of important primary sources of international law, but a guide to its usage and development.

In preparation for the *Digest*, Whiteman utilized her practical experience and expertise gained from the Office of the Legal Adviser at the State Department and her previous works (most notably *Damages*) in order to locate and synthesize 'scattered materials, selecting those which would be most useful'.[40] This massive task Whiteman undertook all the while working at the State Department, which likely added to her sentiments that preparing 'a digest of international law is a prodigious undertaking'.[41]

In its substance, the *Digest* departs from its predecessors in scope in 'considerable measure […] because of new subject matter in the period dealt with and the changing emphasis on numerous concepts of international law'.[42] In doing so, the Whiteman *Digest* highlights the growing internationalization of law at a time when the United Nations, the International Court of Justice, the European Court of Justice,

[34] ibid iii.

[35] Charles Cheney Hyde, 'Review of *Damages in International Law* by Marjorie M. Whiteman' (1938) 32 AJIL 191–95.

[36] John B Moore, *A Digest of International Law* (US Government Printing Office 1906); Green H Hackworth, *Digest of International Law* (US Government Printing Office 1940–1941).

[37] Oliver J Lissitzyn 'Whiteman: Digest of International Law (Book Review)' (1964) 64 Columbia Law Review 1171–73, 1171.

[38] William W Bishop Jr, 'Whiteman: Digest of International Law' (1965) 63 Michigan Law Review1317–20, 1320.

[39] ibid 1317.

[40] ibid 1318.

[41] Marjorie M Whiteman, 'Preface' in *Digest of International Law* (US Department of State 1963–1973) iv.

[42] ibid iv.

and other multinational and transnational organizations were in their early stages of becoming major world players of international law. With the publication of the *Digest*, Whiteman wanted to emphasize the changing nature of both law and the international order, stating that 'To reflect the status of international law in this our time is to reveal considerable evolution in both its range and content. The volumes reflect a moving scene.'[43] Indeed, as 'international law reflects the distillation of man's experience through the ages in the conduct of relations between politically organised peoples', so too must such changes be reflected in the scholarship of international law.

The impact of the Whiteman *Digest* was great in its time but has recently been seemingly forgotten, except among legal historians. However, what remains important in these volumes for contemporary legal research and the practice of international law is its 'copious excerpts' and 'vast storehouse of information'[44] of raw legal material and how they demonstrate the changing face of international law—'Publications of this type are among the most needed working tools of international law.'[45] It is therefore unsurprising that the preserver of local history, the Ohio History Connection, and the Law Book Exchange both describe the *Digest* as 'Whiteman's greatest contribution to international law'.[46]

Memories of Hackworth

When her original chief, and perhaps a personal mentor, Hackworth, passed away in 1973, Whiteman published an obituary in the *American Journal of International Law* (AJIL).[47] It was a lengthy four-page obituary covering his accomplishments and career. From Whiteman's writing, one can quickly grasp how much she respected him, noting that he had 'an amazingly accurate memory'[48] and that he was 'a skilled legal draftsman'.[49] She also noted his devotion to the United States government, writing that he regarded his government position as having 'far outweighed any incentive for a more lucrative position in any large international law firm'.[50] The editorial board of the AJIL rightly recognized Whiteman's capacity to give a respectful tribute to a former Legal Advisor and judge of the International Court of Justice.

Jus Cogens

In 1977, despite having retired from public life, Whiteman published an article regarding *jus cogens* of international law. In the article, Whiteman introduced many

[43] ibid v.
[44] Lissitzyn (n 37) 1172.
[45] Bishop Jr (n 38) 1320.
[46] Ohio History Central Online, 'Marjorie M. Whiteman',<www.ohiohistorycentral.org/w/Marjorie_M._Whiteman> accessed 19 September 2021; Law Book Exchange, 'Digest of International Law Vols. 1–15, Marjorie M. Whiteman'.
[47] Marjorie M Whiteman, 'Green Haywood Hackworth' (1974) 68 AJIL 91–94.
[48] ibid 92.
[49] ibid 91.
[50] ibid 94.

scholars', such as Lord McNair and Gerald FitzMaurice, views on the concept in addition to examining discussions held at the ILC on the Law of Treaties in 1968 and 1969. Reflecting on these records, Whiteman recounted that most members of the ILC had agreed on the need for *jus cogens* in international law, but that there did not exist a satisfactory working definition or, quoting the First Session directly, 'no criteria for identifying the rules of *jus cogens*'.[51] Several delegations were concerned about the possibility that the idea might be used politically in the future.

At the end of the piece, she provided a proposition for the substantive contents of *jus cogens*. 'After all', she wrote, 'the identification and listing of human rights in the Declaration of Human Rights of the United Nations gave considerable impetus to world progress in that direction'.[52] Thus, she argued that listing possible items for *jus cogens* might help develop the concept and enable its practical use in international law. She hoped that 'considerable progress' in international law would be made and that this concept would be greatly strengthened 'by the year 2000 A.D. and in the years beyond', concluding that 'International law has 'miles and miles to go'.[53] This piece showcases Whiteman's future-oriented and optimistic view of international law.

Conclusion

During Whiteman's public life from 1929 to 1970, she served ten Secretaries of State; Whiteman published a three-volume doctoral dissertation and the so-called Whiteman *Digest* continuing her renowned predecessors; and played decisive roles at numerous international conferences. .

Presumably, because her debut to the actual practice of international law had been the Hague Codification Conference, she came to learn the importance of international legislation thoroughly, which signified the development of international law. As discussed in this paper, her last work in 1977 addressed the prospect of *jus cogens,* and her tone of writing was filled with positivity towards the future advancements for international law. Unlike Moore and Borchard, she appeared an optimistic follower and advocate of *lex ferenda,* consistently emphasizing what international law should look like and highlighting its changing nature. She was not a theorist of international law and her published works did not engage in heavy theoretical discussions. Instead, covering treatises and analysing discussions at conferences, she sought to point out the problems and difficulties regarding reaching agreements and the overall development of international law. In this regard, she was a pragmatic reformist.

In 1985, a year before her passing, she received the Manley O Hudson medal from the American Society of International Law—the first American woman to receive such an honour. The Announcement of Awards indicated her long service at the State

[51] United Nations, *Conference on the Law of Treaties*, 1st Sess., Vienna, 26 March–24 May 1968, Official Records, at 323, UN Doc. A/Conf. 39/11, quoted in Marjorie Whiteman, 'Jus Cogens in International Law, with a Projected List' (1977) 7(2) Georgia Journal of International and Comparative Law 609–27, 624.

[52] Whiteman (n 51) 625.

[53] ibid 626.

Department, including her participation in the Law of the Sea Conference in 1958, and referred to her works—*Damages in International Law* and *Digest of International Law*. In particular, the latter was hailed as 'a monumental work of scholarship which all international lawyers constantly refer to'.[54] As such, her imprint in international law will never fade like the shine of the medal.

[54] *American Society of International Law Proceedings* (n 19) 79, 144–45.

37
Aleksandra Kollontai
'New Woman'

Sergey Vasiliev[*]

> [W]omen can become truly free and equal only in a world organised along new social and productive lines.[1]

Prologue

Between 1935 and 1939, the Soviet Union's delegation to the League of Nations Assembly included a venerable woman diplomat who played a visible role in its work. Aleksandra Kollontai, USSR Envoy Extraordinary and Minister Plenipotentiary in Stockholm was highly regarded amongst the European diplomatic circles at a time when diplomacy was not just a male-dominated but entirely male profession.

Kollontai's missions abroad were preceded by decades-long prominence in the European and Russian socialist movements. The only woman in the Bolsheviks' 1917 Central Committee, she was elevated to Lenin's government as the first-ever People's Commissar of Social Welfare. Subsequently she led the Party's Women's Department (*Zhenotdel*) but was removed over her involvement in the Workers' Opposition. The political conflict with the leadership converged with its patriarchal rejection of her Marxist-feminist views on sexual morality.

The marginalization within the Party ensued, and in October 1922 Kollontai was reassigned to the Soviet trade delegation in Norway. This marked the start of an illustrious diplomatic career. The initial stint as an attaché and a plenipotentiary envoy was followed by posts in Mexico (1926–27), Norway again (1927–30), and Sweden (1930–1946; ambassadress from 1943). Kollontai is credited with ensuring Norway's *de jure* recognition of the USSR, brokering an agreement to end the Soviet–Finnish War (1939–40), and helping secure Swedish neutrality and bring Finland out of the Second World War. These efforts earned her the Nobel Peace Prize nominations in 1946 and 1947.

[*] Many thanks to Immi Tallgren for the inspiration and moral support and to Isabella Poewe for excellent research assistance.

[1] Alexandra Kollontai, 'The Social Bases of the Woman Question' in Alix Holt, *Selected Writings of Alexandra Kollontai* (Lawrence Hill & Co 1977) 58.

Sergey Vasiliev, *Aleksandra Kollontai* In: *Portraits of Women in International Law*. Edited by: Immi Tallgren, Oxford University Press. © Sergey Vasiliev 2023. DOI: 10.1093/oso/9780198868453.003.0037

Figure 37.1 Aleksandra Mikhailovna Kollontai (1872–1952), a Russian Communist revolutionary, 29 March 1927.

Source: Library of Congress Prints and Photographs Division Washington, [LC-DIG-ggbain-25077], George Grantham Bain Collection.

Kollontai lived multiple lives in one lifetime: a grassroots agitator, a female icon of the Revolution, a women's rights champion, a Marxist-feminist publicist, a foreign trade technocrat, and a diplomat of the highest caliber. A prominent presence in Russian/Soviet and Scandinavian history of the first half of the twentieth century, book-length biographies have been dedicated to her.[2] Besides countless traces in contemporaries' memoirs,[3] she left behind an extensive oeuvre: treatises on the woman

[2] Isabel de Palencia, *Alexandra Kollontay, Ambassadress from Russia* (Longmans, Green & Co 1947); Barbara E Clements, *Bolshevik Feminist: The Life of Aleksandra Kollontai* (Indiana University Press 1979); Beatrice Farnsworth, *Aleksandra Kollontai: Socialism, Feminism, and the Bolshevik Revolution* (Stanford University Press 1980); Cathy Porter, *Alexandra Kollontai: A Biography* (Virago 1980); Yngvild Sørbye (ed), *Revolusjon, Kjaerlighet, Diplomati: Aleksandra Kollontaj og Norden* (Unipub 2008); AI Itkina, *Revolutsioner, tribun, diplomat: Stranitsy Zhizni Aleksandry Mikhailovny Kollontai* [*Революционер, трибун, дипломат: Страницы жизни Александры Михайловны Коллонтай*] (Isdatel'stvo politicheskoi literatury 1970); Leonid Mlechin, *Kollontai* [*Коллонтай*] (Molodaya Gvardija 2013).

[3] Gabriel Gorodetsky (ed), *The Maisky Diaries: Red Ambassador to the Court of St James 1932–1943* (Yale University Press 2015); AM Aleksandrov-Agentov, *Ot Kollontai do Gorbachyova* [*От Коллонтай до Горбачёва*] (Mezhdunarodnyje otnoshenija 1994); GA Gripenberg, *Finland and the Great Powers. Memoirs of a Diplomat* (University of Nebraska Press 1965).

question,[4] political essays and speeches,[5] novels,[6] an autobiography completed twenty-five years before her death,[7] and posthumously published diaries.[8]

Yet, her name will not ring a bell to modern-day international lawyers. Albeit not a lawyer, Kollontai made lasting contributions to the advancement of gender equality as a women's rights champion. Her role in shaping international affairs as a top Soviet diplomat between the 1920s and 1940s secures her a place in this book's portrait gallery. But taking a reductive view of her *only* as a diplomat would reinforce the silencing she was subjected to during her life and after her death, reproducing the patterns of erasure of women's intellectual history. A dissident in the Party, Kollontai was written out of officialized histories of Marxism in the twentieth century. A radical Marxist–feminist advocate of women's liberation, she was opposed to liberal feminism and omitted from its 'herstories'.

Historians should read Kollontai for clues on paths not taken: the aftermath of 1917 could have been entirely different had her critiques of the Party's anti-democratic tendencies been heard. Feminist international and human rights lawyers in turn will be inspired by her eloquent advocacy and bold efforts to promote women's rights domestically and internationally. Kollontai's ideas about women's role in effecting socio-economic change were ahead of her time. She not only exposed how patriarchal institutions, cultural patterns, and legal modalities coalesce in perpetuating the economic, social, and psychosexual oppression of women, but also showed how obstacles to their full emancipation can be dismantled in practice.

Rebel

Aleksandra Kollontai (*née* Domontovich) was born into an aristocratic land-owning family in 1872 in St Petersburg and grew up spending summers at her maternal grandfather's estate in Finland. She received excellent private education at home, learning foreign languages, and traveling abroad. Despite her class privilege, Aleksandra developed an acute sense of social justice and political leanings toward the left from early on.

In 1893 Aleksandra married her distant cousin, engineer Vladimir Kollontai, and gave birth to son Mikhail the following year. When accompanying her husband to a factory inspection, Kollontai became radicalized by the utter misery, prison-like regime, and deplorable working conditions there. Determined to improve workers' lives, she started agitating among women in textile factories, distributing leaflets and raising strike funds. In 1898 Kollontai left her family to pursue an education in

[4] Aleksandra Kollontai, *Sotsialnyje osnovy zhenskogo voprosa* [*Социальные основы женского вопроса*] (Znanie 1909); Aleksandra Kollontai, *Obschestvo i materinstvo* [*Общество и материнство*] (Zhizn' i znanie 1916).

[5] Holt (n 1).

[6] Alexandra Kollontai, *Love of Worker Bees* (Cathy Porter tr, Academy Press Ltd 1978).

[7] Alexandra Kollontai, *The Autobiography of a Sexually Emancipated Communist Woman* (Schocken Books 1975).

[8] Aleksandra M Kollontai, *Iz mojei zhizni i raboty* [*Из моей жизни и работы*] (Sovetskaya Rossiya 1974); Aleksandra M Kollontai, *Letopis' mojei zhizni* [*Летопись моей жизни*] (Academia 2004); Aleksandra M Kollontai, *Diplomaticheskie dnevnikii* [*Дипломатические дневники*] 1922–1940, 2 vols (Academia 2001).

political economy and Marxist theory in Zurich and London. The research on Finnish workers she started then led to publications which earned her a name among social democrats.[9]

From the early 1900s onward Kollontai actively participated in Marxist revolutionary and women's groups in Europe. Following the 1903 split in the Russian Socialist Party, she collaborated with both the Mensheviks led by Julius Martov and the Bolsheviks led by Vladimir Lenin. In 1906, she joined the former—which would come to haunt her later. It was the concern for women's liberation that pushed Kollontai towards socialism. The 'woman question' was at the heart of her campaigning. A gifted orator, Kollontai sought to move it front and centre in the socialist agenda. She promoted working women's involvement in the revolutionary movement while turning them away from 'bourgeois' feminist organizations. In her view, liberal feminism distracted proletarian women from the class struggle, playing into the hands of the bourgeoisie.

Charged with the crime of calling for an armed uprising in Finland, Kollontai fled to Germany in 1908 and became active in the German Socialist Democratic Party (*SPD*). In 1910, she was elected to the International Women's Secretariat and, jointly with Clara Zetkin, ensured the passing of a resolution on the celebration of International Women's Day that year. Kollontai lectured across Europe and the United States and published works on maternity welfare and family legislation. These issues formed the thrust of social insurance legislation she would pursue in the revolutionary government.[10]

When the First World War broke out, the *SPD* was swayed by warmongering and nationalism incompatible with international solidarity among workers. Kollontai's search for anti-war internationalist allies drew her to Lenin. She endorsed his 'revolutionary defeatist' thesis that the imperialist war must be turned into a class war of the international proletariat against the bourgeoisie.[11] Joining the Bolshevik Party in 1915, Kollontai actively co-operated with Lenin by translating pamphlets and helping smuggle them to Petrograd with the assistance of Alexander Shlyapnikov, her partner at the time. Lenin made generous use of her talents. Yet, his letters evince an occasionally patronizing tone and a habit of mansplaining her 'serious political mistakes'.[12] Kollontai's revolutionary life was coloured by gender: she had to reckon not only with the patriarchal mentality of Russian society but also the party leadership's casual sexism.

Reformer

Amnestied by the Provisional Government, Kollontai returned to Petrograd after the February Revolution and threw herself into the cause of the uprising by the working class. When Bolsheviks seized power in October, Kollontai—a foremost Bolshevik

[9] Aleksandra Kollontai, 'Zemel'nyj vopros v Finlandii' ['Земельный вопрос в Финляндии'] (1902) 2 *Nauchnoye obozrenie*; Aleksandra M Kollontai, Zhizn' finlyandskikh rabochikh [*Жизнь финляндских рабочих*] (1903); Aleksandra M Kollontai, *Finlyandija i Sozializm* [*Финляндия и Социализм*] (1907).

[10] Kollontai, *Obschestvo i materinstvo* (n 4); Kollontai (n 7) 20.

[11] Aleksandra Kollontai, *Komu nuzhna voina?* [*Кому нужна война?*] (RSDRP 1916).

[12] Porter (n 2) 213–14.

and Lenin-loyalist—was the only woman in the Central Committee. Appointed as the People's Commissar of Social Welfare, she became the first and only female minister in Lenin's government.

In translating her progressive ideas on women's liberation into the policies of the young state, Commissar Kollontai initiated a family law reform to end Church rule in this domain and replace religious matrimony with civil marriage. Divorces were liberalized, and women were no longer property or dependants of male family members. They could now exercise control over their earnings and receive alimony when unable to work. Free maternity and infant care were to be provided by the state. Ground-breaking at the time, many of those reforms could not be completed due to an economic collapse while some backfired and were reversed. Thus, the new divorce legislation led to the widespread phenomenon of single mothers abandoned by husbands and unable to support children due to low wages and non-enforcement of alimonies.

In 1921 Kollontai fell out of favour with Lenin given her role in the Workers' Opposition (1920–22). Led by Shlyapnikov, this trade unionists' fraction rallied for returning control over the workplace in factories to working-class representatives and alerted against growing bureaucratization. Alarmed by the Party's anti-democratic creep, Kollontai expressed workers' grievances thus:

> Fear of criticism and of freedom of thought, by combining together with bureaucracy, often produce ridiculous results. . . .We give no freedom to class activity, we are afraid of criticism, we have ceased to rely on the masses: hence we have bureaucracy with us. . . .[B]ureaucracy is our enemy, our scourge, and the greatest danger to the future existence of the communist party itself.[13]

The statement was condemned by the Party but well-received abroad. Left without other recourse, Kollontai brought an (unsuccessful) appeal before the Comintern's Executive Committee. The Opposition was found in breach of Party discipline. Kollontai's was an act of courage: she knew 'disloyalty' would not be forgiven. Comrades had long been scandalized by her 'feminist' work and theories on sexual morality, and she now faced full-scale reprisals. The Central Control Commission recommended the Oppositionists' expulsion. Put on probation, Kollontai was crushed politically and subjected to a barrage of sexist remarks from its leaders, including Lenin. The patriarchal power resorted to misogyny to suppress a woman it saw as deviant.

Liberationist

Kollontai's views on the 'woman question' were interweaved with her Marxist convictions and informed by the teachings of August Bebel, Rosa Luxemburg, and Lily Braun. She saw in socialist revolution the only way towards gender equality. Typically

[13] Alexandra Kollontai, 'The Workers' Opposition' in Holt (n 1) 192.

labelled 'feminist', Kollontai would have been uncomfortable with this term. To her, liberal feminism's emancipatory promise was illusory:

> The feminists seek equality in the framework of the existing class society; in no way do they attack the basis of this society. They fight for prerogatives for themselves, without challenging the existing prerogatives and privileges.... However apparently radical the[ir] demands ...the feminists cannot, on account of their class position, fight for that fundamental transformation of the contemporary economic and social structure of society without which the liberation of women cannot be complete.[14]

In Kollontai's view, equality between sexes sought by bourgeois feminists would never translate into class equality: 'The woman and her male comrade are enslaved by the same social conditions; the same hated chains of capitalism oppress their will and deprive them of the joys and charms of life.'[15] Proletarian woman, she argued, should stand alongside her brother in the class struggle, not feminists claiming to be above class.

The path to emancipation lay through women's economic autonomy and participation in the workforce, which was impeded by gendered division of labour.[16] No equality among sexes was possible as long as traditional family and private property existed. Deprived of means of production and economic agency, women were a commodity sold to men either as prostitutes or as wives encaged by unpaid domestic labour and childbearing and childrearing duties.[17] Whereas the unholy union of capitalism and patriarchy corrupted relations among sexes, in an ideal communist society they would be unburdened of distortive contractual and monetary aspects and rest on love, affection, and respect. The patriarchal family would wither away, putting an end to gender oppression and enabling a profound transformation of sexual morality in line with human aspirations.[18]

Kollontai famously considered open marriages based on sexual freedom more fulfilling for women labouring under the double burden of domestic work and employment. Thus her name came to be associated with the erosion of traditional morality and family values, making her an object of ridicule for prudish comrades all too willing to misrepresent her views. The 'glass of water' theory that satisfying one's sexual needs under communism would be as easy as drinking a glass of water was wrongly attributed to her, while being at odds with the consistent emphasis on love and comradeship as the bases for sexual relations in her writings.[19]

Upon resigning as Commissar in March 1918, Kollontai continued in the Party line of work promoting women's literacy, labour rights, and political participation. Her efforts to carve out space for discussions about the 'woman question', culminated in the establishment of the women's departments in the Central Committee and at lower Party levels. The purpose of *Zhenotdel* was to create practical conditions and

[14] Kollontai (n 1)59–60.
[15] ibid 60.
[16] Ibid 64.
[17] Ibid 64–65.
[18] Alexandra Kollontai, *Communism and the Family* (Contemporary Publishing Association 1920) 9.
[19] Alexandra Kollontai, 'Make Way for Winged Eros: A Letter to Working Youth' in Holt (n 1) 276–92.

infrastructure—free day-care, dining rooms, laundry, and mending services—to disburden proletarian women of the drudgery of housekeeping and to free them up for socially useful work.[20] The Party, however, saw in it a mere tool to activate female labour force for the war effort and post-war reconstruction. Open debates about gender and sexuality were unwelcome: dwelling on private life undermined the unity of the working class. *Zhenotdel*'s work of advancing women's liberation was undercut by severe underfunding, persistent sexism, and patriarchal suspicion about its 'feminist' proclivities.

Despite her removal in 1922 and ensuing erasure from *Zhenotdel*'s institutional memory, Kollontai continued exploring the tabooed theme of proletarian sexuality in semi-autobiographical prose. She faced a backlash for it in the Soviet press and had to abandon unfitting literary pursuits. In 1926 she spoke out against the marriage law reform and advocated for a general insurance fund to finance maternity and childcare costs through a graduated tax on all citizens—the idea summarily dismissed as promoting decadent 'free love'.[21]

Kollontai went silent but never disowned her 'despised and rejected political credo'.[22] In the 1926 autobiography, she declared 'the complete liberation of the working woman and the creation of the foundation of a new sexual morality' to be her highest calling.[23] During the next decade, she saw the regime she served as a diplomat roll back the revolutionary years' achievements. As Stalin's propaganda foregrounded women's gendered responsibilities in the nuclear family, Kollontai was reduced to singing praises to Soviet progress in the matter of women's emancipation.

Diplomat

In 1922 Kollontai pleaded Stalin to give her a party assignment in the Far East or abroad. This presented a convenient opportunity to neutralize a troublemaker, and she was unexpectedly offered a post at the trade mission in Norway. Later that year, she became an advisor and afterwards a Soviet trade representative and plenipotentiary in Kristiania. When Norway recognized the USSR in 1924, Kollontai was promoted to a *chargée d'affaires* and an extraordinary and plenipotentiary envoy.

Despite inexperience, Kollontai quickly grew into her new role. Her international exposure, knowledge of Norwegian, and familiarity with the country she had stayed in during the First World War, made her uniquely qualified for it.[24] She already had contacts in the large pro-USSR Norwegian Labour Party (*DnA*). Although it was imperative for her as a diplomat not to meddle in domestic politics, Kollontai was a notable figure in the Comintern and could not stay aloof in the face of a crisis within the

20 Clements (n 2) 210–14.

21 Anne Bobroff, 'Alexandra Kollontai: Feminism, Workers' Democracy & Internationalism' (1979) 13(6) Radical America 51, 67.

22 Germaine Greer, 'Foreword' in Kollontai (n 7) ix.

23 Kollontai (n 7) 47–48.

24 Åsmund Egge, 'Soviet Diplomacy in Norway and Sweden in the Interwar Years: The Role of Alexandra Kollontai' in Kari Aga Myklebost and others (eds), *The Russian Revolutions of 1917: The Northern Impact and Beyond* (Academic Studies Press 2020) 80, 83–84.

DnA. On Moscow's instructions she privately consulted with the *DnA*, trying to prevent an internal split.[25] Following the 1923 breakaway of the (Comintern) Norwegian Communist Party, she maintained relations with both parties and received classified information through their members in the Norwegian Parliament (*Storting*).[26]

Kollontai's focus during the first years in Norway was attaining *de jure* recognition and related accommodation on Norwegian sovereignty over Spitsbergen. In February 1924, Norway became the third state (after the UK and Italy) to recognize the USSR. Kollontai's understanding of Norwegian politics, broad connections, and 'influence unusual for a diplomat' were decisive.[27] Nonetheless, the limits of her influence back home were all too evident. She was reprimanded for exceeding instructions and forced to seek a retroactive amendment of the 'favourable treatment' formula for the future trade agreement between the two nations, causing her major embarrassment.[28]

In April 1930, Kollontai became interim *chargée d'affaires* and subsequently Soviet minister in Sweden, where the 1914 expulsion order against her was still standing.[29] This duty station was challenging due to the cool attitude of the Swedish establishment towards the USSR. By the mid-1930s, her efforts to cultivate sympathies bore fruit among the left-leaning *intelligentsia*, who were alarmed by the rise of Nazi Germany. Yet, bilateral relations never quite thawed, reaching their nadir during the Soviet–Finnish Winter War (1939–1940): Swedish sympathies lay with the Finns. The conclusion of the August 1939 Molotov–Ribbentrop pact placed Kollontai in an unenviable position of having to justify it to the liberal–leftist circles.

In 1935, the Soviet envoy in Stockholm became the first woman to serve as Ambassador Plenipotentiary in the League of Nations. In the League Kollontai saw the world arena where the USSR could assert its position while promoting women's rights internationally. One year after the USSR joined the League, Kollontai addressed the XVI Assembly on women's rights in relation to the 1933 Montevideo Equal Nationality and Equal Rights treaties and partook in committees on health, drugs, and humanitarian questions.

During the Winter War and the Second World War, Kollontai devoted herself to securing Sweden's neutrality for as long as her age and deteriorating health permitted.[30] In 1940, she served as the contact point in negotiations to end the Winter War. From late 1943 onwards, she played a key role in helping Finland out of the Second World War, which was required to break off relations with Nazi Germany and disarm and intern German troops in the Finnish territory.[31] Reassuring the Finnish side of the USSR's peaceful intentions, Kollontai repeatedly declared fondness for her mother's country of birth. On 17 September 1944, with Swedish mediation, the USSR and Finland concluded the armistice ending the Soviet–Finnish Continuation War (1941–1944), sparing Finland from unconditional surrender and occupation and

[25] Kollontai, *Diplomaticheskie dnevnikii I* (n 8) 83 and 173.
[26] Egge (n 24) 82.
[27] ibid 84–86.
[28] Kollontai, *Diplomaticheskie dnevnikii I* (n 8) 197–203.
[29] ibid 439–40, 472.
[30] In August 1942 Kollontai suffered a stroke and became partially paralysed. Aleksandrov-Agentov (n 3) 25–28.
[31] For the Finnish perspective: Gripenberg (n 3) 281–317, 328, 336–44, 350.

preserving its independence. This was a triumph for Kollontai but tough negotiations had taken a toll as she suffered another stroke.

Alongside Commissar Maxim Litvinov and Ivan Maisky, her long-time friend and Ambassador to London, Kollontai belonged to the pre-Molotov school of Soviet diplomacy. The 'best-informed member of the diplomatic corps in Stockholm', she was an 'insightful, cold-blooded analyst'[32] who personally cultivated key connections, kept the most important tasks for herself, and weaved bits of information into insightful reports. Interlocutors in governments and in financial–industrial circles valued her constructive attitude, sensitivity about their difficulties, abstention from propaganda, and her human touch.[33] Despite unflinching loyalty to the State, Kollontai preserved independent thinking and agency in serving it the way she thought best. She took matters in her own hands and at times pre-empted instructions while stopping short of breaching them. On consequential matters, she provided advice she knew would not be well-received, occasionally winning superiors over to her side.

The revolutionary Kollontai's notoriety preceded her wherever she went. Bourgeois politicians and conservative press regarded her with hostility, although her aristocratic origins facilitated acceptance. Ultimately, she won respect and even a degree of broader popularity. Attitudes swung once she revealed herself not as an uncouth Bolshevik,[34] but a witty elegant socialite versed in court etiquette and fluent in seven foreign languages. An avid art lover, Kollontai cultivated contacts with writers, academics, and artists, turning Soviet missions into venues for diplomatic receptions and cultural events.

Kollontai's trailblazing ambassadorship required myriad adjustments to diplomatic protocol, leading to (at times amusing) complications she navigated with grace. Her arrival in Stockholm caused commotion at the royal court. It took special effort to negotiate a suitable outfit for the presentation of credentials: should a lady diplomat don an evening dress in the morning and may she wear a hat when appearing before the king whereas other ambassadors (men by default) do so bareheaded? After the ceremony—the chief of protocol instructed—, the King and (male) envoys converse while standing. But when receiving Kollontai, oblivious of the custom and 'twitching in obvious embarrassment', King Gustav V met her halfway and they continued conversation while seated.[35]

A long career was never Kollontai's goal. Pleased with professional successes, she enjoyed her status as it showcased what Soviet women could achieve.[36] This made true her ideal of an independent, accomplished 'new woman'.[37] Still, she wanted to leave the government and become a writer, repeatedly pleading Moscow to let her return home.

[32] Aleksandrov-Agentov (n 3) 25; 26–27.

[33] Gerard Aalders, *Swedish Neutrality and the Cold War 1945–1949* (PhD Thesis, Amsterdam 1989) 26–27; Kaare Hauge, *Alexandra Mikhailovna Kollontai: The Scandinavian Period 1922–1945* (University of Minnesota 1971) 163; Gripenberg (n 3) 300.

[34] On 'rumours about this bloodthirsty, coarse, cruel, amoral Bolshevik woman who dressed like a man, drank vodka, smoked day and night, and knew not the most elementary human decency': Porter (n 2) 410–11.

[35] *The Maisky Diaries* (n 3) 69–70; Kollontai, *Diplomaticheskie dnevnikii II* (n 8) 6–8.

[36] Kollontai, *Diplomaticheskie dnevnikii I* (n 8) 218–19; Kollontai (n 7) 6 ('the example of my life can…serve to dispel the old goblin of the double standard…from the lives of other women').

[37] Alexandra Kollontai, 'New Woman' in Kollontai (n 7) 51–103.

But she made herself oddly indispensable. This was one but not the only reason for her survival.

Survivor

The Party purges of 1936–38 consumed Kollontai's countless friends, including former lovers Satkevich and Shlyapnikov and former husband Dybenko. She suffered greatly from these personal losses. The same morbid fate could befall her as the notorious ex-Menshevik and Oppositionist: people had been destroyed for lesser misdeeds. Yet, Kollontai miraculously endured—one of only two Old Bolsheviks and 1917 Central Committee members besides Stalin himself.

By 1927 Kollontai had vacated the position of Party maverick and abandoned her radical-left revolutionary politics. Never again did she disagree with the 'general line'. In a decisive power struggle, she endorsed Stalin and publicly denounced the Trotsky bloc in *Pravda*. The belief that opposition was pernicious and her dislike of Trotsky provide a partial explanation. Her precarity on account of past 'missteps' also tipped calculus towards self-preservation. The extent of self-censorship performed on her 1926 autobiography evinces as much. Kollontai mercilessly edited out every single word, however innocuous, which might appear self-aggrandizing or critical of the party policies past or present. When appointed to Stockholm, she requested a Norwegian friend to place her personal archive in the care of *DnA* should she suddenly die.[38]

Just why Kollontai did not 'fall under the wheel of history' is a matter of speculation. One theory goes that women qualified for milder treatment.[39] Old-fashioned 'chivalry' was the flipside of Stalin's profound contempt for women: the view of female comrades as too dependent and gullible to deserve execution—for as long as they complied with that stereotype. Kollontai grasped these dynamics and skilfully played the gender card.[40] During rare encounters, Stalin treated her with playful condescension to which she responded abjectly, in a 'feminine' way. She flattered him unabashedly for showing 'sensitivity'—he was peeved with his reputation, courtesy of Lenin, as being 'too rude' to colleagues. Stalin spared Kollontai as Lenin's erstwhile closest comrade and as a living proof that *he* was a true Leninist, unlike the destroyed 'enemies of people'.

Moscow's dependence on Stockholm reports also afforded protection. Throughout the Great Terror and the Second World War only Kollontai and Maisky remained in their posts. Most other diplomats were recalled and executed.[41] Kollontai was under constant NKVD surveillance and feared for her life and family. When summoned in 1937 and 1938, she entrusted her friend Ada Nilsson with personal diaries and letters.[42]

[38] Egge (n 24) 82–83.

[39] Porter (n 2) 401.

[40] Beatrice Farnsworth, 'Conversing with Stalin, Surviving the Terror: The Diaries of Aleksandra Kollontai and the Internal Life of Politics' (2010) 69(4) Slavic Review 944, 949–51, 969.

[41] In 1930s, 163 diplomats including forty-four plenipotentiaries perished, and some of the recalled diplomats refused to return: MM Mukhamedzhanov, 'Exelenz madam Kollontay' in Kollontai, *Diplomaticheskie dnevnikii I* (n 8) 22–23.

[42] *The Maisky Diaries* (n 3) 112 (fn 24); Egge (n 24) 94.

She excelled in self-preservation during these summons. Her July 1937 trip 'coincided' with the Swedish Foreign Minister's official visit to Moscow. Stalin could not afford an international scandal the arrest of the plenipotentiary would have caused.[43]

Paranoid about Kollontai's sympathies towards Finland and Sweden, Stalin and Molotov increasingly distrusted her.[44] Reported on by fellow diplomats for running the Stockholm mission as her own realm, she was nearly removed in June 1941, but 'saved' by the start of Operation Barbarossa. The NKVD was after her diaries, and in 1942 agents broke into her safe.[45] Nothing incriminatory was found. Next year her personal archive was seized and shipped to Moscow. Once back in the USSR in 1945, she inquired about its fate and petitioned Stalin for its return. Two suitcases of documents were delivered to her flat.[46]

Enforced silence and capitulation to the 'apparatus' were a hefty price to pay for survival, but terror did not consume Kollontai entirely. She had a heart for others living in fear and intervened to help wherever she could. In 1946 she reassured the distressed mother of the disappeared Raoul Wallenberg that he was safe in Moscow and would be coming back. She promised Raoul's uncle, Marcus, to assist but was recalled shortly thereafter, being no longer able to *arranger les affaires*.[47] A wheelchair-ridden pensioner in Moscow and nominally a living legend, Kollontai kept inquiring about the fate of those 'repressed' until roughly ordered to desist.[48] Those desperate interventions made at personal risk show her genuine humaneness those who knew Kollontai personally noted was integral to her character.[49]

Postscript

Kollontai's character is organic yet not free of contradictions: a member of Soviet political elite *and* an unresentful revolutionary of radical democratic convictions; a bold critic of the Party *and* an obedient promoter of its policies internationally; a tame servant of a cannibalistic State *and* a close friend of the many victims it devoured. A herald of the Revolution's emancipating potential, Kollontai prophetically resisted the Party's drift towards dictatorship not of the proletariat but of one person, which made the liberation of women, or anyone for that matter, impossible. Defeated and muted by the terror, Kollontai tragically surrendered to the apparatus. She powerlessly observed this cancer metastasize and exterminate her fellow citizens in millions, while mimicking her own vocabulary to cynically proclaim women's liberation under socialism.

Kollontai's articulate critiques of patriarchal orthodoxy and the oppressive entanglement of traditional family and capitalism paved the way for the more equitable and humane alternatives both in the socialist camp and in the West. Her radical politics

[43] Farnsworth (n 40) 963–64; Mukhamedzhanov (n 41) 23.
[44] Aleksandrov-Agentov (n 3) 25 and 36–37.
[45] ibid 37.
[46] Mukhamedzhanov (n 41) 18.
[47] Elenore Lester, *Wallenberg: The Main in the Iron Web* (Prentice-Hall 1982) 13, 132, 153.
[48] Mukhamedzhanov (n 93) 23–24 (the last visit from MFA caused the fatal stroke).
[49] Aleksandrov-Agentov (n 3) 35.

and passionate advocacy for women's rights and sexual and economic autonomy will continue to energize feminist legal scholars and advocates. The early Soviet reforms provided a rich intellectual and experiential ground in respect of liberalized divorce and abortion legislation, paid parental leaves and day-care, and socialized domestic work—which are now mainstream and taken for granted in many countries.

38
The Role of International Law in Paulina Luisi's Activism

Andrei Mamolea

Considered the 'mother' of Latin American feminism, Paulina Luisi (1875–1950) is known for her efforts to build a more inclusive international feminism after the First World War. Less well known is the role that domestic and international law played in this project. Very early in her activism Luisi identified knowledge acquired through lived experience as indispensable for good government. She therefore advocated for greater representation of women, social workers, and marginalized peoples, in the making of domestic and international law. To this end she constructed a transatlantic network of activists and amplified its voice as an expert at the League of Nations, which she argued could be used to create new international norms which could then be incorporated into domestic law. Placing great value on the possibilities provided by international organizations, Luisi sharply criticized those that blocked reform and provided cover for authoritarianism, attributes she associated with Pan-American organizations. During the 1930s, Luisi's dissatisfaction with Pan-Americanism increasingly led her to emphasize the need for a constant transnational grassroots mobilization. This chapter examines the forgotten role of international law in Luisi's activism and thought.

Upbringing

Paulina Luisi was born on 22 September 1875 in Colón, Argentina, as the first child of recent immigrants from Europe. Her father, Angel Luisi, was a liberal Italian freemason and a supporter of Giuseppe Garibaldi. Her mother, Maria Teresa Josefina Janicki, was involved in the Dijon's first campaigns for women's suffrage. In 1872, the couple migrated to Colón and later across the Rio Plata to the Uruguayan town of Paysandú. Over the next four decades Angel and Josefina promoted democracy, secular education, and associational life in Uruguay and Argentina. Their influence on Paulina cannot be overstated. Luisi's early writings contain evidence of her attachment to moral and scientific progress, her father's Garibaldian ideals, and her mother's feminism. Josefina was a particularly strong influence, guiding Paulina to medicine and feminist activism.[1] In 1899 Paulina became the first Uruguayan woman to earn a bachelor degree and in 1908 the first Uruguayan woman doctor. With her mother, she

[1] María Castro Bustos de Elia, 'Conversando con Paulina Luisi' *El Hogar*, (18 November 1938) Archivo Centro Republicano Español (ACRE).

Andrei Mamolea, *The Role of International Law in Paulina Luisi's Activism* In: *Portraits of Women in International Law*. Edited by: Immi Tallgren, Oxford University Press. © Andrei Mamolea 2023. DOI: 10.1093/oso/9780198868453.003.0038

Figure 38.1 Paulina Luisi, the first Uruguayan woman doctor and PhD.
Source: Archivo Literario, Biblioteca Nacional de Uruguay.

was a founding member of the Asociación de Damas Liberales Uruguayas in 1906. In 1910 they were delegates at the Congreso Femenino Internacional in Buenos Aires.

Luisi had no mentors but drew inspiration from the work of Spanish women's rights advocate Concepción Arenal (1820–1890) and British feminist Josephine Butler (1828–1906), who dedicated her life to the abolition of human trafficking and prostitution. The most important influence on Luisi and her family, however, was Giuseppe Garibaldi (1807–1882). Garibaldi imparted a particular approach to international politics that, according to Luisi, included the idea that all nations are sisters, that war between them is inadmissible, and that disputes should be resolved through international institutions created and administered by people appointed, not by states, but by democratic associations from each nation.[2] This last point was very important for Luisi. The aim was not just to democratize foreign policy but to directly link local associational activism and international politics, circumventing the gatekeeping power of states in the pursuit of a world federation based on democratic representation. To

[2] Paulina Luisi, 'Paginas Garibaldinas: El Segundo Congreso Internacional por La Paz' (undated) Caja 4 ACRE.

achieve this aim Luisi devoted much of her activism to two separate but related endeavours: amplifying the voices of Hispanic women in international organizations and organizing a constant domestic political mobilization that stretched beyond state institutions.

Luisi was enmeshed in international networks from the outset, first through contacts to Argentinian activists, later through ties to French activists, and after 1919, through sustained participation in international organizations. Her political, intellectual, and social bonds during this period demonstrate that she was a transatlantic activist.

Initial Transatlantic Activism

Believing that Europe was an important source of ideas, the government of José Batlle y Ordoñez provided young leaders and activists, including Luisi, with the means to visit the continent. In 1913 Luisi met with Jules Siegfried and Avril de Sainte-Croix, two prominent members of the International Council of Women (ICW).[3] They encouraged her to establish a national branch of the organization, which Luisi did upon returning to Montevideo. The influence of France, its ideas, and people is visible in her speeches from the period. Like many activists and intellectuals from the Southern Cone, she spoke French, Spanish, Italian, and Portuguese fluently, but never mastered English. Luisi's intellectual, political, and emotional world spanned the Atlantic. It was a world where freemasons, freethinkers, republicans, liberals, socialists, and early human rights advocates carried ideas from Europe to the Americas and back. Luisi watched closely the reforms of the First Portuguese Republic (1910–1926) and later those of the Second Spanish Republic (1931–1936). The longest and most important relationship of her life was also transatlantic. Her partner, Sebastião de Magalhães Lima, was a Portuguese champion of secularism and republicanism who in 1921 founded the Liga Portuguesa dos Direitos do Homem. How extensive were Luisi's transatlantic ties? At the 1920 congress of the ICW in Christiana, Norway, Luisi represented Uruguay and Portugal. She described these two countries as 'spiritual daughters of France' and characterized the feminist movements in both as 'inspired by the women of France'.[4] Luisi lived for many months in Paris during the following decade, and during the 1930s, in Madrid. Her feminist thought and activism reflected these important transatlantic connections, especially in its emphasis on social rights.

Central to Luisi's early thought was the belief that women's participation in lawmaking was indispensable to good government. Already in her earliest writings she emphasized the importance of knowledge acquired through lived experience. She argued, for instance, that 'we women are familiar with the ulcers of our societies, because it is almost always our hands which apply the balm. Social assistance and beneficence are our patrimony, and this work, like nothing else, has opened our eyes to the horrors

[3] On Sainte-Croix see Frédéric Mégret, 'Ghénia Avril de Sainte-Croix: Abolitionism and the League of Nations', in this volume.

[4] Paulina Luisi, 'Discurso pronunciado en la sesión pública de la inauguración del Congreso de Cristiania' (1920) 4(34) Acción Femenina 162, 164.

that entrap our current civilization.'[5] Luisi argued that legislative reform should provide universal suffrage, expand women's access to education, work, and equal pay, and produce uniform moral and legal standards.[6] She also advocated for economic support for pregnant women, comprehensive sexual education, and negative eugenics.[7] Starting in 1919, and likely under the influence of Sainte-Croix, Luisi helped rescue victims of human trafficking and campaigned for the abolition of prostitution and the criminalization of pimping.

Luisi's efforts resulted in several legislative achievements, including laws that expanded the rights of illegitimate children, but the pursuit of universal suffrage proved elusive. In 1917, a new constitutional provision granting women the right to vote and hold office was approved by Uruguayan voters but failed to obtain the two-thirds support in both chambers of Uruguay's General Assembly necessary to become law. Following this setback, Luisi established a national branch of the International Alliance for Women's Suffrage (IWSA) and began to more seriously explore the advantages of international feminism. It was with this aim that Luisi set off for Europe in 1920 as a delegate to the IWSA congress in Geneva, the ICW congress in Christiania, and, as a Uruguayan delegate to the League of Nation's first General Assembly.

Disenchantment with International Feminism

Luisi's second encounter with international feminism was very different from her experience seven years earlier. Luisi and other activists from 'Latin countries' felt marginalized and humiliated by activists from countries with universal suffrage.[8] This scornful attitude prompted an open revolt led by Argentina, and joined by delegates from Uruguay, Italy, Spain, and Romania, who collectively demanded a genuine demonstration of international feminist solidarity.[9] Smarting from the mistreatment, Luisi used her speech at the ICW conference in Christiana to showcase Uruguay's achievements.

The negative experiences at these two conferences did not diminish Luisi's commitment to international feminism but they opened her eyes to the prejudice of self-styled 'Anglo-Saxon' activists and perhaps reinforced her sense of belonging to a wider group of unjustly marginalized 'Latin' women that spanned the Americas and southern Europe. Already before departing Uruguay she had invoked the concept of 'la raza' in correspondence with Hermila Galindo, the Mexican feminist, revolutionary, and proponent of an 'Indo-Latin' approach to international politics.[10] Luisi's experience reinforced her commitment to this type of solidarity. During this period, she began to

[5] Christine Ehrick, *The Shield of the Weak: Feminism and the State in Uruguay, 1903–1933* (New Mexico University Press 2005) 91.

[6] Paulina Luisi, 'Una Gestión Importante: Los Derechos Civiles de la Mujer' (18 June 1918) Caja 3 ACRE.

[7] On Luisi's eugenics, see Andrei Mamolea, 'Race, Eugenics, Civilization, and the Law in Paulina Luisi's Thought' (forthcoming).

[8] 'Informaciones de la Delegada del Gobierno doctora señorita Paulina Luisi' *Boletín del Ministerio de Relaciones Exteriores* 9 (Imprenta Nacional 1921) 1102–31, 1104.

[9] Magda Donato, 'Al margen del feminismo. La conspiración de los países latinos' (1920) 6(283) España 762–63.

[10] See Hermila Galindo to Paulina Luisi (23 December 1919) Carpeta G Biblioteca Nacional de Uruguay (BNU).

argue that Hispanic women would have to speak with a single voice to make an impact and that the League of Nations was the ideal site for this political solidary.[11]

Unlike with the IWSA and the ICW meetings, Luisi was instantly drawn to the League. Positions at the new organization were supposed to be 'open equally to men and women.' Luisi considered this the first 'great victory' of international feminism.[12] The organization's mandate also explicitly addressed problems which Luisi considered central to women's rights and required an international solutions, such as the trafficking of women and children.[13] Luisi also identified the League, along with the Permanent Court of International Justice, as the embodiment of human solidarity and Garibaldian ideals.[14] In her correspondence with other Latin American feminists she repeatedly emphasized the importance of having a voice in Geneva 'because it is in Geneva where the center is located'.[15]

Over the next two decades, Luisi dedicated herself to building an international network of activists, amplifying their voices through the League of Nations, developing a critique of Pan-American organizations, and mobilizing people across the Americas in support of political, social, and economic rights, and against imperialism, authoritarianism, and fascism. These endeavors shaped her thinking about the possibilities and limits of international law.

Representation and Lawmaking at the League of Nations

Luisi's activism on behalf of Hispanic women involved joining the *Liga Internacional de mujeres ibéricas e hispanoamericanas* as a vice-president in 1923. This network of activists attracted considerable social capital in subsequent years but was excluded from international lawmaking. Luisi's work at the League of Nations was a conscious attempt 'to force open the doors' of the League's umbrella Committee of Women's International Organizations to delegates from the *Liga Internacional*.[16] She believed that the League could be used to incorporate new international norms into domestic law and therefore repeatedly stressed the need for representation on committees dealing with problems ranging from disarmament to human trafficking. It was in this latter area that Luisi made some of her most important contributions as a delegate on the Advisory Committee on the Traffic in Women and Children.

Luisi's interest in the problem of human trafficking emerged, not from some imagined moral panic, but from first-hand experience helping working class women in Montevideo. As a result, her approach distinguished between the female victims and the male perpetrators. Regarding the victims, Luisi emphasized the importance

[11] Paulina Luisi to Julieta Lanteri, (5 November 1921) Carpeta L BNU.

[12] See art 7 of the League of Nations Treaty; Paulina Luisi, 'La Mujer en la Democracia' (19 October 1938) Caja 3 ACRE. cf Katherine Marino, *Feminism for the Americas: The Making of an International Human Rights Movement* (UNC Press 2019), 56–57.

[13] Art 23 of the League of Nations Treaty.

[14] See Paulina Luisi, 'Derecho o fuerza: lucha o sumisión' (1 December 1939) Caja 1 ACRE.

[15] Paulina Luisi to Celia Álvarez de Molina, (7 January 1932) Caja 256 Carpeta 6, Fondo Paulina Luisi, Archivo General de la Nación (AGN). On Luisi's rejection of Pan-American feminism see my forthcoming article on her activism.

[16] ibid.

of rehabilitation, and long-term solutions to the social and economic problems that made women vulnerable to trafficking.[17] With respect to the perpetrators, Luisi emphasized the need for a uniform body of international criminal law that would prevent traffickers from escaping justice.[18] In both her emphasis on the root causes of international crime and the need for uniform legal standards, Luisi consciously echoed the ideas of a progressive movement that formed around the *Bureau international pour l'unification du droit pénal*.[19]

Like many other advocates for unification, Luisi envisioned a body of criminal law founded on social science and administered primarily by social workers, not the police. Luisi argued that experience in social work provided important insights inaccessible to those from a purely legislative or police background. It followed, that the success of anti-trafficking laws depended on those tasked with designing and enforcing them.[20] Even those who approached the problem in good faith were often hamstrung by a narrow mindset.[21] Luisi argued that police work, in particular, distorted the understanding of the problem. But efforts to prevent trafficking were hampered not just by the inclusion of the police but also by the exclusion of women from the making and enforcement of law. One consequence, according to Luisi, was the failure to abolish prostitution.[22]

Luisi argued that the failure to abolish prostitution created a veneer behind which trafficking thrived.[23] International law allowed licensed houses which, she claimed, were the main channels through which women were trafficked.[24] The regulatory regime was also another example of laws made by men for the benefit of men. It policed the female prostitute, but not the male client, and granted the pimp legal authority over the woman in matters with the police.[25] Worse still, the international regime failed to provide support for the vulnerable and instead focused narrowly on deportation. The result was a cycle where foreign prostitutes were 'hounded by the police, expelled, deported, and abandoned at the border' only to be forced by the prevailing economic misery to secretly return to the country from which they had been expelled.[26] Luisi lamented that only private organizations were directly engaged in the process of rescue and rehabilitation. International organizations, meanwhile, strove to maintain an appearance of liberalism even as they relied on heavy handed police measures.[27]

[17] Paulina Luisi, *Otra Voz Clamando en el desierto* vol 2 (Montevideo 1948) 33.

[18] ibid vol 1, 43–44; ibid vol 2, 11–47.

[19] Luisi participated at the Bureau's 1933 meeting in Madrid, which addressed trafficking, ibid, vol 1, 186. On the Bureau, the unification movement, and its leading exponent, see Andrei Mamolea, 'Vespasian V. Pella: International Criminal Justice as a Safeguard of Peace' in Frédéric Mégret and Immi Tallgren (eds), *The Dawn of a Discipline: International Criminal Justice and Its Early Exponents* (Cambridge University Press 2020) 49–92.

[20] Luisi, *Otra Voz* (n 17) 11. On implementation: ibid 53.

[21] ibid 27, 32, 43.

[22] ibid 12.

[23] 'Proces-Verbal de la Deuxieme Session' (31 March 1923) 25 in R647/12/13720/27391, League of Nations Archive (LNA).

[24] According to Luisi, the findings of the commission on trafficking in the Orient demonstrated that states regulating prostitution were complicit in trafficking. Luisi, *Otra Voz* (n 17) 29.

[25] ibid 45.

[26] ibid 63, 70.

[27] ibid 42.

National prejudice was another problem Luisi identified with the anti-trafficking regime. She had initially encountered this phenomenon at the 1920 IWSA Conference, where she was forced to dispel rumours in the feminist press that Uruguayan feminism had emerged in response to massive human trafficking. The problem was 'no greater than in your big cities' Luisi responded, 'and perhaps considerably less'.[28] During her time on the Committee of Experts, Luisi encountered the same stereotypes on a vaster scale. The Committee was funded, led, and largely controlled by North American experts backed by John D Rockefeller. To Luisi's dismay, they downplayed the seriousness of trafficking in the United States, while exaggerating its scale in South America.[29] According to Luisi, the investigators sent to do fieldwork had a poor grasp of Spanish and spent only a few days in Rio de Janeiro and Buenos Aires, ignoring the rest of South America.[30] Their investigation was simplistic, superficial, and suffered from limited knowledge. Luisi declared the resulting report 'absolutely inaccurate' and refused to sign it.[31] In retaliation, she was sidelined by the North Americans.[32] In the report, they falsely claimed that she had been unable to attend the final session and fabricated a statement in which she was said to have praised the Committee's chairman.[33]

Despite these indignities, Luisi persisted in working with the Committee and gradually re-oriented its policy from regulation to abolition. Yet, Luisi's broader strategy failed. The emergence of new international norms did not produce domestic reform, as painfully illustrated by Uruguay, where Gabriel Terra reversed the country's anti-trafficking reforms after making himself dictator in 1933. The experience highlighted for Luisi that a victory at the international stage was meaningless without lasting political victories at the domestic level.[34]

Democratic Mobilization and the Problems of Pan-Americanism

Luisi responded to Terra's coup, which she regarded as fascist, by resigning from her diplomatic posts and, after a brief stay in Republican Spain, continuing the struggle against the dictatorship from within Uruguay.[35] Her thoughts on resistance are best captured in a 1936 speech where she argued that vibrant phrases and shaking passions would have to make way for the difficult work of organized resistance.[36] She asked activists to focus on the long-term political education of the public so that it learned to differentiate substance from sham and not fall prey to demagoguery. Much of the

[28] Paulina Luisi, 'Discurso pronunciado en el VIII Congreso de la Alianza Uruguaya para el Sufragio de las Mujeres' (1920) 4(34) Acción Femenina 169, 170.
[29] Luisi, *Otra Voz* (n 17) 28.
[30] ibid 111, 116; S49/4/5 at 35, LNA.
[31] See S149/4/1 at 13–14; S149bis/4/18 at 42–44, 50; S149bis/4/20 at 11, LNA. Luisi, *Otra Voz* (n 17) 29.
[32] Luisi, *Otra Voz* (n 17) 111–13.
[33] ibid 113, 115.
[34] ibid 271; 217–48.
[35] See Paulina Luisi, 'Derechos Civiles de la Mujer' (20 November 1938) Caja 3 ACRE.
[36] Paulina Luisi, 'Bajo el látigo de la dictadura Marzista: Homenaje a Baltasar Brum, defensor de los derechos de la mujer' (30 March 1936),Caja 3 ACRE.

speech was dedicated to the political education of working-class women, which Luisi believed would eventually overcome the influence of the church to support the left, as they had done in Republican Spain.

The Second Republic remained a powerful source of inspiration during this period. In 1937, Luisi wrote to the Spanish President Manuel Azaña that 'for the children of America' whose democratic aspirations were crushed under 'petty cacique dictatorships', the 'triumph of the Spanish republican left [...] represents a wonderful lesson in civics'.[37] At a time when most Latin American states had already slipped into authoritarianism and either tacitly or openly supported Franco's insurrection, the Republic remained a source of inspiration to the Latin American left. United States-dominated Pan-American feminism, meanwhile, remained a source of discontent. Luisi's emphasis on democracy and substance in politics increasingly brought her into conflict with the movement, which had long been characterized by a proclivity for empty rhetoric, a tolerance for authoritarian government, and a matching indifference to the implementation of public international norms.

Luisi argued that Pan-American conferences were used by authoritarian states to ostentatiously publicize their support for women's rights, sign treaties, never to ratify them, and never incur the opprobrium of having said one thing and done another. She considered the 1933 Montevideo Equal Rights Treaty a perfect example and Uruguay's conduct especially galling. At the same time that he signed the treaty, Terra was busy dismantling the legislative reforms made by previous governments.[38] In a 1936 pamphlet, Luisi contrasted the Uruguayan government's 'ostentatious publicity' on behalf of a promised new code for children with its abject failure to legislate anything on the subject.[39] Luisi then turned to the Equal Rights Treaty and pointed out that after having signed it, the Uruguayan government implemented a new constitution which provided that women's work will be 'regulated and limited.' She invited readers to drawn their own conclusions about the treaty's effectiveness.[40]

Two years later, in a pair of articles written before and after the 1938 Pan-American conference in Lima, Luisi more fully expressed her contempt for the Equal Rights Treaty and Pan-Americanism's complicity in covering for authoritarian governments. In the first article, Luisi observed that, five years after the Montevideo conference, the Treaty still lay dormant 'in the peace of the archives'.[41] In the second article, she indicted the hollow democratic rhetoric in Lima by highlighting the authoritarian nature of the participating and hosting governments.[42] Emphasizing the cognitive dissonance, Luisi juxtaposed the rhetoric of 'liberty and democracy that resounded in the great hall' with the reality of numerous Peruvians 'imprisoned for the crime of thinking freely'. She noted that while Unites States Secretary of State Cordell Hull spoke of 'American solidarity' and the 'good neighbor doctrine', his delegation included one of the chief oppressors of Puerto Rico. What's more, the Pan-American

37 Paulina Luisi to Manuel Azaña(1937) Caja 2 ACRE.

38 Paulina Luisi, 'El Tratado de Montevideo' (undated), Caja 3 ACRE. Cuban feminist Ofelia Dominguez argued that Pan-Americanism was based on 'insincerity, lies, demagoguery.' Marino, *Feminism* (n 12) 93.

39 Paulina Luisi, *Condiciones del trabajo femenino* (Open Door 1936) 20.

40 ibid 24.

41 Luisi, 'Derechos Civiles' (n 35).

42 Paulina Luisi, 'La VIIa Conferencia Pan-Americana de Lima' (December 1938) Caja 1 ACRE.

conference, once again, failed to address the political questions that were central to Latin American liberty. 'What countries in *nuestra América*', Luisi pointedly asked, 'enjoy true independence?' Which ones freely controlled their own economies? 'Could the common people, those who knew the cloth from which their clothes were made, sincerely believe in the benefits of the Lima Conference?' Luisi herself did not. The proletariat, she noted, paid huge sums in taxes for delegates to spend on 'sterile and inconsequential' meetings. And for what? 'The projects of the Montevideo Conference, collected in the realm of the "uncreated" as Faust says, can give us the measure of what the people can expect from the conference [in Lima]', Luisi suggested.[43] This was her assessment of the Equal Rights Treaty, five years later.

Pan-American officials made no effort to ensure that states complied with the promises made at Pan-American conferences. The Inter-American Commission of Women (IACW) was especially unconcerned with translating talk into law and law into practice. It helped legitimate many of the most reactionary and undemocratic states in the Americas.[44] During the early years of the IACW, its leader, Doris Stevens, praised the Cuban dictator Gerardo Machado as a 'feminist president.'[45] Later, the IACW provided Dominican dictator Rafael Trujillo with what historians have called 'a low-risk opportunity to appear progressive on an international stage.'[46] Stevens was not alone in relying on authoritarians. Her main rival for the IACW leadership, Bertha Lutz, relied on support from Brazilian dictator Getúlio Vargas.[47] Within the IACW little thought was devoted to the political implementation of norms, the subject that concerned Luisi the most during this period.

Luisi underscored these problems a few months later in a keynote address before the Garibaldian-inspired Congreso Internacional de las Democracies de America, which she organized in 1939. She noted that the Pan-American 'conferences and the commitments that they established were made by the governments, among which were vulgar personal dictatorships, cliques raised to power by betrayal or violence'. She contrasted these state-led projects with her own grassroots conference attended by hundreds of activists from across the Americas which would provide 'the authentic opinion of the people regarding the same problems'.[48]

Anti-Fascism and Anti-Totalitarianism

Luisi's efforts mobilizing democratic resistance to authoritarianism in Uruguay during this period had an international and anti-fascist dimension. She led rallies against the

[43] ibid.

[44] Unsurprisingly, it was these governments that gravitated most closely to the United States and to Pan-Americanism. See Andrei Mamolea, 'The Myth of Legalism in US Foreign Relations' (PhD Dissertation: IHEID 2018), ch 5.

[45] On Stevens' friendship with dictators see Marino, *Feminism* (n 12) 149–50.

[46] Ellen DuBois and Lauren Derby, 'The Strange Case of Minerva Bernardino: Pan American and United Nations Women's Right Activist' (2009) 32 Women's Studies International Forum 47.

[47] See Cassia Roth and Ellen Dubois, 'Feminism, Frogs and Fascism: The Transnational Activism of Brazil's Bertha Lutz' (2020) 32(1) Gender & History 208–26 at 214.

[48] Paulina Luisi, 'Congreso de las Democracias de América: Derechos de la mujer y tratado de derechos iguales' (12 March1939) Caja 3 ACRE.

Italian invasion of Ethiopia, denounced the Japanese aggression in Manchuria, protested against restrictions on immigration, and assisted refugees fleeing the Spanish Civil War. In her writings, Luisi warned of a 'terrible fire that is going to engulf the whole world in insatiable flames!'[49] The destruction of international norms provided fuel for further aggression.[50]

Luisi was an early adopter of the term 'totalitarian', initially applying it to Fascist Italy and Nazi Germany, but later also the USSR.[51] The Soviet Union's collaboration with Nazi Germany during the early months of the Second World War did much to dispel her initial admiration for that government. In December 1939, she denounced Japanese, Italian, German, and Soviet aggression, and cast doubt on the USSR's supposed commitment to female emancipation.[52] Later, after the USSR joined the war against Germany, Luisi paid tribute to the heroism and sacrifices of the Soviet people, without obscuring the Soviet Union's aggression or apologizing for the nature of its government. In this respect, Luisi followed a broad current of socialist thought that challenged Soviet totalitarianism.

Luisi's vision for a post-war international order drew on her commitments to social justice and human rights.[53] She argued that the class distinctions between workers and capitalists would have to be abolished and the workplace should remain open to women. Turning to international matters, Luisi argued against hierarchy and inequality in international organization, renouncing her earlier embrace of civilizational rhetoric and the Mandates Commission.[54] Any new international order would have to correct 'the grave constitutional error of the League of Nations, which was established on the basis of hierarchies between the different Member States'. According to Luisi, a new organization 'must be a great family in which all the brothers are equal, with the same rights and duties, despite differences in political, economic and other development that exist between them, so that all children within the family, whether younger or older, have the same rights'. Throughout this period Luisi identified as a socialist and believer in 'democratic political ideology', distancing herself from communism and totalitarianism.[55] At the same time she believed that 'each nation has the right to decide on its form of government without outside interference'. She also denounced claims of hegemony. In a nutshell, Luisi's views were socialist, internationalist, anti-totalitarian, anti-interventionist, and anti-hegemonic.

The war reinforced Luisi's conviction that 'there is an undeniable interdependence between all people' and that imbalances would sooner or later have repercussions for all.[56] Luisi believed that competition over primary resources was the primary cause of war and advocated for the control of the distribution of resources and arms production by an international organization. She also continued to promote the Garibaldian idea

[49] Paulina Luisi, 'Contra la Guerra Italo-Etiope' (22 September 1935) Caja 1 ACRE.
[50] Luisi, 'Derecho o fuerza' (n 14).
[51] Paulina Luisi, 'El Trabajo de la Mujer' (October 1937) Caja 3 ACRE.
[52] Paulina Luisi, 'Derecho o fuerza' (n 14).
[53] Paulina Luisi, 'La Neutralidad es Complicidad o Suicidio' (20 May 1940) Caja 1 ACRE.
[54] On this shift see Mamolea (n 7).
[55] Paulina Luisi, 'Cuestionario del Bureau of Latin American Research de Washington' (8 January 1943) 'Secundo Cuestionario del Bureau of Latin American Research' March 1943, both in Caja 1 ACRE.
[56] Paulina Luisi, 'Secundo Cuestionario' (n 55).

of a world federation founded on grassroot democratic political associations. The success of the 1939 Congreso de las Democracias in Montevideo was followed by the 1947 Congreso Interamericano de Mujeres in Guatemala City. Yet, despite these achievements, her postwar correspondence was pessimistic. In June 1945, the British feminist Katherine Bompas replied in agreement with Luisi that conditions were not promising for 'a truly new world, one more just, more democratic, and more fraternal'.[57] Luisi's project for a more inclusive international politics remained incomplete.

57 Katherine Bompas to Paulina Luisi (7 June 1945) Carpeta B BNU.

39

Working from 'Rooms of Their Own'

For a Realistic Portrait of Joyce Gutteridge CBE and Other Trailblazing Women

Luiza Leão Soares Pereira

'The personal is political' is a slogan of the feminist movement encapsulating how the women's struggles for power in the private realm—for control of their bodies, finances, jobs—are not individual experiences, but symptomatic collective systems of oppression.[1] Seemingly counter-intuitively, the private can also exist as facilitators, rather than hurdles, for women occupying places in the public realm. In other words, personal circumstances can be the very factors that enable *certain* women to overcome structural barriers that exist for *all* women. Wealth, social networks, whiteness, freedom from marriage and children, are all elements that determine women's individual experiences of the public, and that mediate their access to the 'political'. Having 'a room of one's own and five hundred pounds a year'[2] can be the difference between living a life exclusively in the private sphere, or the freedom to 'exist' in public. That said, '*can be*' is operative here—class privilege, capital, and family ties, all which 'a room of one's own' is code for, do not lift all structural barriers women face. Even in circumstances of immense privilege, such as an Oxbridge college,[3] or international treaty negotiations, women will face more or less overt attempts to put them back in their (private) place.

This essay looks at Joyce Gutteridge, CBE, first woman Legal Officer at the British Foreign Office (FO), to explore the tensions between the individual personal circumstances contributing to her ascent to the public sphere at the FO, whilst also highlighting the skills and personal resilience that allowed her to flourish in an often-inhospitable environment. This vignette draws on my previous work on obituaries and networks of international lawyers,[4] in which Gutteridge appears as one of only two women posthumously memorialized in the *British Yearbook of International Law*.[5] I have also used my own privileged networks to find out more about her life and work—this piece was written with the contribution of Lesley Dingle, International Law librarian at the

[1] Catharine A MacKinnon, *Toward a Feminist Theory of the State* (Harvard University Press 1989) ch 191.

[2] Virginia Woolf, *A Room of One's Own* (Random House 1929).

[3] Woolf uses the juxtaposition between two fictional male and female-only Cambridge colleges and the luxuries of the former over the latter to illustrate the struggles women of all classes must (to different degrees) overcome in their professional lives. ibid.

[4] Luiza Leão Soares Pereira with Niccolò Ridi, 'Mapping the "Invisible College of International Lawyers" through Obituaries' Leiden Journal of International Law (forthcoming).

[5] A friend of Gutteridge's, Iain Scobbie, Jean D'Aspremont, and Yenkong Ngangjoh Hodu, 'Professor Gillian White (1936–2016)' (2017) 86 British Yearbook of International Law 1.

Luiza Leão Soares Pereira, *Working from 'Rooms of Their Own'* In: *Portraits of Women in International Law.*
Edited by: Immi Tallgren, Oxford University Press.
DOI: 10.1093/oso/9780198868453.003.0039

Figure 39.1 Joyce Gutteridge representing the United Kingdom, and Ambassador Francis T.P. Plimpton (U.S.); Mr. El Sayed Raouf El Reedy (U.A.R.); and Ambassador Platon Morozov (U.S.S.R) at the UN Committee on Peaceful Uses of Outer Space, 1961.
Source: UN Photo/MH.

University of Cambridge and person behind the Eminent Scholars Archive, who contacted Phillip Allott, Maureen MacGlashan, Cherry Hopkins, and Michael Prichard on my behalf to find out more about Gutteridge. I contacted Sir Franklin Berman and Eileen Denza, junior colleagues of Gutteridge at the Foreign Office (FO), then Foreign and Commonwealth Office (FCO), who very helpfully shared their memories of her. Sir Franklin wrote of his friendship with Joyce as her junior at the FO, making himself available for a fruitful telephone conversation.[6] He put me in contact with Eileen Denza, junior to Joyce at the FO. Denza, who is another woman international law exponent in her own right, shared many recollections of Joyce and her experiences as woman at the FO during that time online on 18 November 2020.[7]

In piecing together the ebb and flow between privilege and struggle, in the lives of Joyce Gutteridge and of many other women in this volume, we can attempt to have a more nuanced intersectional[8] appreciation of their trailblazing legacies. Using the metaphor of the portrait, I sought to exhibit not a posed oil painting of Joyce Gutteridge alone, surrounded by books in an oak-pannelled 'room of her own', but a

[6] On file with the author.
[7] On file with the author.
[8] Kimberle Crenshaw, 'Demarginalizing the Intersection of Race and Sex: A Black Feminist Critique of Antidiscrimination Doctrine, Feminist Theory and Antiracist Politics' (1989) 1989 University of Chicago Legal Forum 271. See also Rosemary Auchmuty and Erika Rackley, 'Feminist Legal Biography: A Model for All Legal Life Stories' (2020) 41 Journal of Legal History 186.

realistic—and no less impressive—still photograph of her in action, hard at work at an international conference, surrounded by her mostly male counterparts.[9]

The Political—Joyce Gutteridge's Biography

Joyce Ada Cooke Gutteridge was born in 10 July 1906 in Bromley, Kent. She went to school at Roedean, a school for girls founded in 1885 to prepare women for the newly created Cambridge and Oxford women's colleges. She later read History at Oxford in one of these colleges, Sommerville, in 1925. The 'Sex Disqualification (Removal) Act 1919', which allowed women to be called to the bar, had recently been passed. Joyce was called to the Bar relatively later in life, in 1938, at Middle Temple.[10] There is no information as to Joyce's professional life between her graduation and her call. In 1939, during the outbreak of the Second World War, she joined the Auxiliary Territorial Service (ATS), which was the women's branch of the British Army, where she became an army lawyer. For her legal duties at the ATS she was recruited into the Foreign Office, as it then was, in 1947 by Sir Gerald Fitzmaurice, in what was initially a temporary role of legal researcher. In 1950 she was appointed 'Assistant Legal Adviser' to the FO, the first woman to have ever held that position. In 1960 she was promoted to 'Legal Counsellor'. In 1962, she was made Commander of the Order of the British Empire (CBE). She continued to perform her legal duties as a Legal Counsellor, until her retirement in 1966, retaining advisory capacity for a further year after that. She was then the highest-ranking woman in the British Diplomatic Service.

During her time at the Foreign Office, Joyce Gutteridge was exposed to a variety of subject-matters. As expounded upon by both Berman and Denza in their interviews, this is natural to the Legal Adviser role: they are exposed to what comes their way, according to where they are posted, and what is in the roster of requests by government at that time. Much of this is led by conferences as well as incidents, but more on that later. Early in her career, Joyce represented the UK in the conferences leading up to the Geneva Conventions, in 1949, specifically in the area of Prisoners of War. Another one of her areas of practice was Law of the Sea, which was developing rapidly during her time at the FO. She represented the UK government in the 1958 Convention on the Continental Shelf, and spent time in Iceland dealing with fisheries disputes between the UK and Iceland known as the Cod Wars. During her time as a Legal Counsellor to the UK in the UN Permanent Mission in New York (1961–1964), the height of space exploration, she specialized in the Law of Outer Space, being one of the pioneers in the field, and representing the UK in the UN Outer Space Committee (1966). She retired in 1966, but remained attached to the FO for a further year in an advisory capacity. In 1967, she was part of the legal team advising the government on the *SS Torrey Canyon* incident, the notorious oil spill off the coast of Cornwall, one of the first incidents of

[9] The portrait in question documents Gutteridge's participation in the UN Committee on Outer Space. There was another woman in the Committee, Ambassador Agda Rossell, Sweden's UN Permanent Representative.

[10] Although that does not seem to be an unusual path, especially for women at the bar. Patrick Polden, 'Portia's Progress: Women at the Bar in England, 1919–1939' (2005) 12 International Journal of the Legal Profession 1919.

its kind. That incident was a prominent part of the recollections of both Berman and Denza on Joyce, who was 'on call' at the time, and had to quickly articulate the UK's legal position on the subject.

Joyce Gutteridge also published academic works on international law, and was involved in editing the *International and Comparative Law Quarterly* as well as the British Yearbook of International Law.[11] Her contributions include pieces on the Geneva Conventions,[12] immunities of diplomatic staff,[13] the Supplementary Anti-Slavery Convention,[14] the role of the UN in codification and progressive development,[15] the Law of the Sea,[16] nationalization laws in parts of the Soviet Union,[17] and, most famously, her Melland Schill lectures on the United Nations.[18] She also published a short piece on the role of the government legal adviser.[19]

The Personal

The Strictly Personal

After handing in the first draft of this paper, I was encouraged to find fragments that made Joyce Gutteridge's portrait more colourful. Why was my portrait so focused on exploring the structures that enabled and oppressed Joyce and other women in law, or women in the Foreign Office? There are two reasons for that. The first is political. My increasingly intersectional personal politics nudged me towards telling a story that recognized the merit in Joyce's individual journey, but also explored how structure was a pivotal part of enabling her career, similarly to other trailblazing women's.[20] I hope readers do not take this as dismissal of Joyce's work on my part, and that this portrait still does her rich life justice.

A more practical reason for the absence of Joyce's voice from my portrait is that little information was available about her that shed light on her project for international law, or her politics. Beyond recognition of her kindness, and her soft demeanor—gendered descriptions in their own right—there was little information about her life. She did not have a partner, or children whom to contact. This led me to spend time on the lives of people that orbited around her about whom more information is available. It 'so happens' that some of these people were 'great men'. The irony does not bypass me, and is indicative of the difficulty in doing research on women and gender-diverse

[11] Cherry Hopkins, on file with the author. Sir Franklin Berman, on file with the author.

[12] 'The Geneva Conventions of 1949' (1949) 26 British Yearbook of International Law 294.

[13] 'Immunities of the Subordinate Diplomatic Staff' (1947) 24 British Yearbook of International Law 148.

[14] 'Supplementary Slavery Convention' (1956) 6 International & Comparative Law Quarterly 449.

[15] 'Selected Problems of the United Nations Program for the Codification and Progressive Development of International Law', American Society of International Law. Proceedings of the Annual Meeting (1962).

[16] 'Beyond the Three Mile Limit: Recent Developments Affecting the Law of the Sea' (1974) 14 Virginia Journal of International Law 195.

[17] 'Expropriation and Nationalisation in Hungary, Bulgaria, and Roumania' (1952) 1 'Supplementary Slavery Convention' (1956) 6 International & Comparative Law Quarterly 14.

[18] *Melland Schill Lectures: The United Nations in a Changing World* (Manchester University Press 1969).

[19] 'Foreign Policy and the Government Legal Adviser' (1972) 2 Georgia Journal of International and Comparative Law.

[20] Auchmuty and Rackley (n 8).

individuals from the past. I did, however, accumulate anecdotes about her. She kept a large collection of dolls from the countries she visited.[21] She generously invited her junior female colleague to lunch, Mrs Denza, at the Oxford and Cambridge Club in Pall Mall, making Denza feel welcome in a male-dominated environment.[22] She 'got on with it' as one of the few women in her position at the time, indicating minimal engagement with gender politics in her public life.[23]

Gutteridge's scholarship reveals little about her, maybe due to the style of legal scholarship produced in Britain at the time, or her position as a government official. She used her practice as inspiration, making for a varied portfolio exploring humanitarian law, law of the sea, the interaction between domestic and international law, outer space.[24] Her writing style was analytical and precise, and her pieces were dedicated to clarifying the law in a grey area, rather than reimagining institutions. A piece on the work of government advisers illuminates her approach to the discipline and her practice.[25] She was pragmatic: problems she had to solve were not 'academic', but 'arise from factual situations... more often than not [not falling] neatly into any of the textbook categories' that require knowledge of the political situation on the ground.[26] She knew the importance of understanding the personality of her interlocutors when framing the advice.[27] She believed advisers must reach a balance between giving the appropriate legal advice, and 'offering constructive solutions' so they are not sidelined by policymakers.[28] She saw the role of the legal adviser as not 'passive', but 'active and creative',[29] allowing room of 'progressive development'.[30] Being a legal adviser in particular, according to Gutteridge, required patience—legal developments are often hindered or stifled by politics.[31]

Networks

Joyce Gutteridge was one of *two* women memorialized in one of over sixty obituaries in the British Yearbook of International law.[32] A snippet of Joyce's network[33] excerpted from my previous work on the subject[34] reveals her connections to other four key

[21] Sir Frank Berman, on file with the author.
[22] Eileen Denza, on file with the author.
[23] Eileen Denza, on file with the author.
[24] 'Expropriation and Nationalisation in Hungary, Bulgaria, and Roumania' (n 17); 'Immunities of the Subordinate Diplomatic Staff' (n 13); 'Supplementary Slavery Convention' (n 14); 'The Geneva Conventions of 1949' (n 12); *Melland Schill Lectures: The United Nations in a Changing World* (n 18); 'Selected Problems of the United Nations Program for the Codification and Progressive Development of International Law' (n 15).
[25] 'Foreign Policy and the Government Legal Adviser' (n 19).
[26] ibid 72.
[27] ibid.
[28] ibid.
[29] ibid.
[30] ibid 74.
[31] ibid 75.
[32] Pereira and Ridi (n 4).
[33] Interactive version available at https://nridi.000webhostapp.com/OBTS/index.html#Joyce%20Gutteridge accessed 6 October 2022.
[34] Pereira and Ridi (n 4).

figures—HC Gutteridge, Sir Gerald Fitzmaurice, Sir Francis Vallat, and Gillian White. In addition, her friendship with Eileen Denza, 'the' other woman in the FO at the time whom I had the privilege of talking to inform this piece, was revealed in interviews about Joyce and has been included.

The Father—HC Gutteridge

The first person in Joyce's network is Harold Cooke Gutteridge (1876–1953), first Professor of Comparative Law at Cambridge, and Joyce's father. He was memorialized not once, but six times in law journals in both English and French after his death.[35] The act of memorialization is telling of his standing in the legal community, and the content of his obituaries demonstrate the esteem he enjoyed by colleagues and former pupils such as Rene David, Kurt Lipstein, Alfred Thompson Denning, and Arnold McNair, the latter an international lawyer and friend from Cambridge. HC Gutteridge was described as someone who 'was perhaps better known throughout the world than any other English lawyer'. He wrote the first English language book on Comparative Law,[36] and 'possessed a charming personality which enabled him to exercise a wide influence', something particularly important when promoting a then sub-discipline.[37] In a study about the first women called to the bar, Joyce is mentioned as 'daughter of an academic lawyer, became a well known figure in international law by her role as a legal adviser to the Foreign Office and her publications'.[38]

Recollections of Joyce often came intertwined with her father. Michael Prichard,[39] legal historian and one of the longest standing members of the Cambridge Law community, stated that he thought of Harold Gutteridge 'a most genial person. He only came into the Squire and the Law Faculty tea-room very occasionally by then, but the older members of the Faculty always spoke of him warmly and clearly had a great respect for him as an outstanding comparative lawyer who was also a master of the common law.'[40] Cherry Hopkins and Philip Allott also mention HC Gutteridge in their recollections of Joyce.[41]

HC Gutteridge was connected to many other British international lawyers—Arnold McNair, with whom he maintained a close friendship,[42] Hersch Lauterpacht,[43]

[35] Marc Ancel, 'Harold Cooke Gutteridge' (1954) 3 International and Comparative Law Quarterly 373; CJ Hamson, 'Note on the Bibliography of H. C. Gutteridge' (2020) 3 International and Comparative Law Quarterly; AT Denning, 'Professor H. C. Gutteridge, QC' (1954) 3 International and Comparative Law Quarterly 230; CJ Hamson and Kurt Lipstein, 'H. C. Gutteridge at Cambridge' (1954) 3 International and Comparative Law Quarterly 377; Arnold McNair, 'In Memoriam Professor Harold Cooke Gutteridge' (1954) 1 American Journal of Comparative Law 1; Rene David, 'Harold Cooke Gutteridge (1876–1953)' (1954) 6 Revue internationale de droit comparé 77.

[36] McNair (n 35) 473.

[37] ibid 476.

[38] Polden (n 10).

[39] Lesley Dingle and Daniel Bates, 'Mr Michael J Prichard' (Eminent Scholars Archive 2012) <https://www.squire.law.cam.ac.uk/eminent-scholars-archive/mr-michael-j-prichard> accessed 30 October 2020.

[40] On file with the author.

[41] On file with the author.

[42] McNair (n 35).

[43] Martti Koskenniemi, 'Lauterpacht: The Victorian Tradition in International Law' (1997) 8 EJIL 215.

recommended by Gutteridge to a London School of Economics professorship, and Sir Robert Jennings, who was taught by both McNair and Gutteridge.[44]

Supportive, or at Least Non-Obtrusive, Mentors—Fitzmaurice and Vallat

Joyce Gutteridge's career is reported to have been championed by two men in particular—Sir Gerald Gray Fitzmaurice, and Sir Francis Vallat.[45]

Fitzmaurice was 'one of the greatest public international lawyers of his generation'.[46] He worked as a Legal Adviser at the FO (1929–1960), and then judge at the International Court of Justice (1960–1973), and the European Court of Human Rights (1974–1980), and often arbitrator.[47] During the start of the Second World War, seconded as Principal Legal Adviser to the Ministry of Economic Warfare (1939–1943), he is reported to have come across Joyce's work in ATS, and creating a legal researcher spot for her when he resumed his work at the FO in 1947.[48] Although it is unclear how exactly Fitzmaurice became acquainted with Joyce's work, one can speculate whether connections to Cambridge had something to do with it. Fitzmaurice was educated under Arnold McNair,[49] who was a good friend of HC Gutteridge,[50] Joyce's father. Two years later, still under Fitzmaurice, her post was made permanent, and Joyce Gutteridge became the first woman Legal Adviser to the Foreign Office.[51]

Fitzmaurice was replaced by Sir Francis Vallat. Vallat, like Joyce, had been a member of the FO after the war.[52] Like Fitzmaurice, he studied in Cambridge under McNair, who was close to H.C Gutteridge. Albeit 'hands off' in his handling of the department, he was 'forward looking' enough to champion the careers of Joyce Gutteridge and her junior colleague, legal researcher, and later Legal Adviser Eileen Denza.[53]

A Network of Women?—Gillian White, Eileen Denza

Aside from Joyce Gutteridge's connections to her father and two Foreign Office Legal Advisers, above, obituaries and interviews demonstrate her connections to two other women who were her contemporaries in British international law circles—Gillian White[54] and Eileen Denza.[55]

44 Sir Robert Yewdall Jennings, 'Hersch Lauterpacht: A Personal Recollection' (1997) 8 EJIL 301, 301.
45 Francis Vallat, 'Miss Joyce Gutteridge, CBE (1906–1992)' [1992] British Yearbook of International La xiv; Maurice Mendelson, 'Sir Francis Vallat GBE, KCMG, QC (1912–2008)' (2009) 79 BYIL 3.
46 Sir Robert Yewdall Jennings, 'Gerald Gray Fitzmaurice' (1985) 55(1) British Yearbook of International Law 1.
47 ibid.
48 Vallat (n 45).
49 Sir Robert Yewdall Jennings (n 46).
50 McNair (n 35).
51 Vallat (n 45) xiv–xv.
52 Mendelson (n 45).
53 ibid 4.
54 Scobbie, D'Aspremont, and Ngangjoh Hodu (n 5).
55 On file with the author.

Gillian White was alongside Joyce one of only two women memorialized in the British Yearbook. She was the first woman law professor in mainland Britain in Manchester.[56] She undertook her LLB at King's College London in 1957, for which she received a First Class degree, 'attending classes as an evening student while she worked as an Assistant Examiner in the Estate Duty Office'.[57] She received her Doctorate at the University of London shortly after in 1960, after which she moved to Cambridge where she assisted Sir Elihu Lauterpacht, and was college lecturer in New Hall, now Murray Edwards, before taking up a permanent position in Manchester, where she succeeded Ben Wortley as the International Law chair. She maintained a close friendship with Gutteridge: 'there are countless examples of her kindness—for example, she regularly made the long and indirect journey from Manchester to Cambridge to visit an ailing and elderly Joyce Gutteridge during her final and protracted illness'.[58] Joyce's Melland Schill lectures of 1969, 'The United Nations in a Changing World',[59] were probably given at White's invitation.

Eileen Denza was a more junior Legal Adviser at the FO, and appears as one of the women championed by Vallatt alongside Joyce during his time as head FO Legal Adviser. Denza generously spoke to me on 18 November 2020,[60] and presented a recollection of Gutteridge and her experience as pioneer women at the FCO. She mentions Gutteridge's invitation, at the start of Denza's time at the FCO, for lunch at the Oxford and Cambridge Club in Pall Mall, in London. Gutteridge had just returned from her posting at the UN in New York. The invitation stood out to Denza as one of the first she had received from a co-worker, and helped her feel more welcome at her post. According to Denza, though collegiate, all her male colleagues were married, and thus unavailable for such activities. As outdated as one going home for lunch on a workday, were some other customs, such as the inappropriateness of paying for a round of drinks when entertaining male colleagues on duty, one of the difficulties Denza and Gutteridge bonded over in relation to being women in a male-dominated profession. Otherwise, Denza states one just needed 'to get on with it', as 'it did no good to complain about' their status as women.[61] Unlike Gutteridge, Denza married, which required permission from her superior, Vallatt. He also granted her permission to continue working at the FCO after her pregnancies. Denza's postings accounted for her condition—she was posted to missions such as the European Union, close to home so she could be home in time for dinner, after a train ride from Brussels.[62] Denza's strenuous routine and passion for her work is awe-inspiring.

[56] Scobbie, D'Aspremont, and Ngangjoh Hodu (n 5).
[57] ibid.
[58] ibid.
[59] *Melland Schill Lectures: The United Nations in a Changing World* (n 18).
[60] On file with the author.
[61] On file with the author.
[62] On file with the author.

Not a Smooth Ride—Women at Work

As indicated by Denza's account of balancing family and work at the FCO, it is clear the life of the women who managed to join the English Bar or the Foreign Office was not easy. Attaining an undergraduate degree was difficult for women at the time—Oxford started granting women undergraduate diplomas in 1921, only four years before Gutteridge's admission.[63] The Bar lifted its ban on women joining in 1919, through the Sex Disqualification (Removal) Act, less than twenty years before Joyce qualified. A study of the first thirty years of women at the English Bar showed that women made up on average 4 per cent of its total intake of 300, out of which only around thirty women actually practiced after their call.[64] The difficulties of women at the Bar included the prohibition of earning a living outside practice, and the difficulty in women receiving briefs in the first place;[65] the inhospitability of convivial activities such as dining in Hall;[66] the difficulty in obtaining pupillage which was important for building a relationship with solicitors and clerks responsible for procuring clients;[67] and the hurdles to obtaining tenancy.[68] From dress codes to the absence of lavatories,[69] from overt discrimination to patronizing treatment by colleagues and news outlets,[70] the bar was not a friendly place for women in Joyce Gutteridge's time.[71]

Both Berman and Denza asserted the FO was not inhospitable for women, and how well-liked and regarded Gutteridge was during her time there. However true at the individual level, reports show that women in general did not have it easy at the FO. Although many successfully served in temporary capacity during the War years, the Foreign Office only first officially admitted women in 1946, a year before Joyce joined its ranks.[72] As revealed by Denza's experience of having to rely on the patronage of a male superior to pursue her desired family life, the marriage bar and the bar on motherhood were still literal bars to the full access of women to the public sphere in general and Foreign Office work in particular. Promotions were difficult, women were paid around 20 per cent less than their male counterparts for the same job, and outright prejudice was still part of their realities even after they were allowed to enter the institution.[73] Women's entry into the UK Foreign Service was consequently more a 'trickle than a flood' in Joyce's time—the door to Whitehall was open to them, but only just.

Leaving aside structural bars to women's access, Denza and Berman provided no evidence of outright prejudice against Gutteridge in particular and other women FO lawyers. However, as put by Dame Margaret Anstee (recruited by the FO 1948): 'In day-to-day relations, negative reactions ranged from openly hostile to (sometimes

63 Cambridge only officially granted degrees to women in 1948.
64 Polden (n 10) 295, 314.
65 ibid 321.
66 ibid 322.
67 ibid.
68 ibid 323.
69 ibid 327, 329.
70 ibid.
71 ibid.
72 FCO, 'Women and the Foreign Office' (2018) History Notes 1, 19.
73 ibid.

involuntarily) patronising.'[74] There is no reason to believe Joyce Gutteridge was immune to hostility or patronizing behaviour. Gutteridge's obituary written by Vallat starts by contrasting her father's 'enthusiasm, vigour, and precision', to say she managed to 'succeed in a man's world' despite possessing a comparably 'outwardly less forceful disposition'. Rather than 'formidable', 'genial', and 'impressive', Joyce has 'zeal' for her work, and 'proved' to be 'determined, persistent, and most effective'.[75] She 'was not well-adapted to a soldier's life', but 'acquired a natural and genuine interest in her work'[76] at the FO. She received the Commander of the Order of the British Empire for her services, although it surely 'would have been [the more prestigious CMG] if she had been a man'.[77] It is for the reader to decide whether that sounds like 'involuntary patronising'.

Boyd Van Dyke[78] unearthed one particular instance of outward gender-based prejudice in Gutteridge's career. In correspondence between UK representatives during the drafting of the Geneva Conventions in 1949, an excerpt read:

> On the legal side the present intention is, I understand, that the delegation should rely on Miss Gutteridge for legal advice. She has been most helpful and assiduous in the discussions which have hireto taken place and has much knowledge of the subject, but I venture to suggest that you should consider whether Conventions of such importance in the International humanitarian field, and in which the terms to be used in the difficult Articles may well have implications far outside the Conventions, do not require a background of wider experience than Miss Gutteridge can have had (sic.) the opportunity to acquire up till now.[79]

The picture was more bleak for people of colour, and people of diverse sexual orientations and gender identities. Systems created to weed out communists from the FO ranks such as a Positive Vetting, introduced in 1951, was used to exclude queer people from the diplomatic service on account of their propensity for receiving blackmail.[80] People of colour were not outwardly excluded from the FO, although a control on their intake was cogitated in the 1950s,[81] but had the burden to demonstrate their Englishness as representatives of Britain abroad.[82] Beyond outright discrimination and exclusion of marginalized groups the effect of structural racism, sexism, and homophobia on recruitment, retention, and promotion of members of these groups, cannot be overstated.

[74] ibid.
[75] Vallat (n 45).
[76] ibid.
[77] ibid.
[78] 'Typical Gender Discrimination against Female Drafters—UK Officials Questioning the "experience" of Joyce Gutteridge as Legal Adviser of the UK Delegation Revising the Geneva Conventions (1940s)',<https://twitter.com/boyd_vandijk/status/1037262674911027201> accessed 2 November 2020.
[79] ibid.
[80] James Southern, 'Black Skin, Whitehall: Race and the Foreign Office 1945–2018' (2018) History Notes 5.
[81] ibid 7.
[82] ibid 6.

Conclusions: A Realistic Photo of Women in Action

Interviews and correspondence from Joyce Gutteridge's colleagues and contemporaries reveal she was a kind collegiate person. Her academic work was pragmatic, informed by her varied practice at the FO. This piece seeks to paint a realistic portrait of Joyce Gutteridge in particular but 'trailblazing' women in general memorialized in this volume. It accounts for the enormous difficulties and prejudices they faced due to their gender, but also teases out some of the personal reasons they were 'allowed' to ascend in the profession in the first place. Famous fathers, such as HC Gutteridge, networks of prominent male mentors, such as Sir Francis Vallat and Sir Gerald Fitzmaurice, and support from female colleagues, such as Eileen Denza and Gillian White, all must be taken into account when painting a more realistic picture of their career paths. Similarly their access to elite institutions, such as in Gutteridge's case Oxford and the English Bar, must be borne in mind. These were not spaces open to all women.

It is in the intersections of oppression and privilege between different identities that include race, class, sexual orientation, and gender identities, and the personal connections enabled by some of these identities, that a more realistic picture emerges—one that honours the trailblazing legacies of these women hard at work, but that avoid purely meritocratic narratives that ignore why such few women occupied these spaces. This picture demonstrated how Joyce's and other women's professional ascent into the public sphere was enabled by sheer determination, personal resilience, and technical ability, but also by having 'a room of *their own*', which was not available to everyone.

PART XI

PORTRAITS OF ARTISTS, JOURNALISTS, AND VISIONARIES OF INTERNATIONAL LAW

40
'If only they listened to Simone Weil'
From Rights to Roots

Outi Korhonen

Prologue

For those who think of Simon/e Weil[1] as an eccentric philosopher, mystic and ascetic, it may come as a surprise that we would have much stronger human rights today if René Cassin would have taken the 'Red Virgin's manuscripts as the basis for the drafting of the Universal Declaration of Human Rights (UDHR), for which he later received the Nobel Peace Prize (1968).[2] In fact, Weil's second grand ouevre (*L'Enracinement*) was a counter-proposal to the vision supported by General de Gaulle and his legal right-hand man Cassin, who had welcomed Weil to the French Resistance's London team.[3] Weil was adamant that the human rights based post-war international order should not be built on the fundamentally flawed rights tradition.[4] Weil argued that the European liberal paradigm carries a legacy that leads to a self-deconstructive social program and human rights for the post-war world. It produces states in which the Janus-faces of humanism/terror keep alternating and causing ever increasing alienation and violent oppression. Despite Cassin's sympathy for the maverick thinker, who was feverishly writing in the office next door to his at the *Commissariat National de l'Intérieur Section de réforme de l'État* (at 19 Hill Street, London), he could not endorse the proposals of someone dismissed by his boss as '*une folle*'.[5] In their drafts,

[1] Simon/e Weil's gender position was non-binary and non-personalized. However, this chapter has too limited space to elaborate on it and many other sides to Weil. I find it appropriate to refer to Simone Weil with the singular 'they/them' rather than a gendered pronoun. This is because a combination of things such as Simon/e alternately signed letters by either Simone or Simon, refused any customary 'feminities' in life, apologized to their mother for not being a son, made an identity-based suicide attempt at fourteen-years of age, and advocated the destruction of self as one of their main philosophical positions. Yet, Weil's thought is thus intricate and complex that they have served as inspiration for many feminists among various genres, which, to me, does by no means contradict my approach to the pronoun question.

[2] See, eg, Christophe Barret, 'René Cassin et la Guerre des 'Droits de L'Homme' No 61 *Revue de la Fondation de la France Libre* (Septembre 2016) 21–23, at http://www.france-libre.net/site/wp-content/uploads/2014/01/Fondation_FranceLibre_61.pdfaccessed 15 January 2019.

[3] See, eg, Guy Basset, 'Albert Camus, Simone Weil et le travail' (2010) 1 Présence d'Albert Camus 104–08.

[4] See Robert Zaretsky, What We Owe to Others: Simone Weil's Radical Reminder, *New York Times*, Opinion (20 February 2018), at https://www.nytimes.com/2018/02/20/opinion/simone-weil-human-rights-obligations.htmlaccessed 5 February 2019.

[5] De Gaulle's depiction of Weil as 'a crazy' came as a reaction to Weil's proposal as they arrived to work at the French Resistance in London (1942–1943) and proposed to stage a mythological spectacle of good (*grace*) versus evil (*pesanteur*), the proposal was to parachute white-dressed nurses (including or led by Weil themselves) to the frontlines of the raging war to descend from the heavens snow-like to treat the wounded and martyr themselves in contrast to cruelties performed simultaneously by the black-uniformed SS troops.

Outi Korhonen, *'If only they listened to Simone Weil'* In: *Portraits of Women in International Law*. Edited by: Immi Tallgren, Oxford University Press. © Outi Korhonen 2023. DOI: 10.1093/oso/9780198868453.003.0040

the French Resistance laid the foundation for the 'fathering' of the UDHR by Cassin.[6] Looking at the ineffectiveness and failings of post-war human rights through Weil's lens, we could say that the post-war human rights founders were well forewarned of the moulding defects in the liberal rights paradigm.

Introduction

To paraphrase Albert Camus, it was impossible to conceive of the rebirth of humanity without heeding Simone Weil's insight.[7] Weil was a free spirit[8] who denounced democracy, physical relationships, gendered womanness,[9] rights, who pestered acquaintances for dangerous jobs, who was constantly dismissed, who read the Bhagavad-Gita and the Upanishads in Sanskrit, Plato, Sophocles and Heraclitus in Classic Greek, Cicero in Latin, and managed to write several thousands of pages on matters ranging from justice and quantum physics to theatre plays. Weil's posthumously published notebooks are filled with mathematical equations, geometric drawings, translations of ancient texts, social and political remarks, reflections on Zen *koan*, religion, spirit, humanity, labour, and records of experiences, discussions and debates.[10] Weil perished prematurely at the age of thirty-four (1943).

In life, Weil was an unrelenting critic of well-nigh every contemporary political and philosophical celebrity not to mention every non-contemporary from Aristotle onwards. Weil even snubbed schoolmate Simone de Bouvoir's concerns by saying: 'One can see that you have never experienced hunger.'[11] Whether it was due to their *École normale supérieure* brand, martyr-esque behaviour, or the appreciation of Weil's famous comrades including Camus, Sartre, Trotsky, and Merleu-Ponty, Weil is an unforgettable thinker on whose work treatises and seminars keep piling over a century after their birth.[12] Weil opposed personalized[13] esteem, called everyone out without any political correctness, zigzagged between disciplines, joined anarchists, worked at minimum wage assembly lines in addition to lecturing, fought against Franco in Spain, defended absolutes such as Truth, joined and critiqued the French Resistance, planned sabotage, and extolled anonymity:

> When science, art, literature, and philosophy are simply the manifestation of personality they are on a level where glorious and dazzling achievements are possible, which

[6] See, eg, Patrick James Flood, *The Effectiveness of Human Rights Institutions* (Praeger 1998), 31–49; Philippe Etchecopar in Florence Piron and others (eds), *Simone Weil Philosophe (1909–1934), Femmes savantes, femmes de science* Tome 2, 2015, at https://scienceetbiencommun.pressbooks.pub/femmessavantes2/chapter/simone-weil-philosophe-1909-1943/accessed 6 February 2019.

[7] Sian Miles (ed), *Simone Weil, An Anthology* (Penguin 1986), Introduction 1–68, 57.

[8] See, eg, Sophie Bourgault, 'Beyond the Saint and the Red Virgin. Simone Weil as Feminist Theory of Care' (2014) 35(2) Frontiers 1–27.

[9] See (n 1) on Simon/e. Weil emphasized the importance of embracing humanity as a non-individuated matter and promoted destruction of the self (one's individuated personhood) towards this goal.

[10] Simone Weil, *Cahiers I & II* (Plon 1968).

[11] Etchecopar (n 6).

[12] See Barret (n 2), Flood (n 6), and Etchecopar (n 6).

[13] For a discussion, see Joke Hermsen, 'The Impersonal and the Other, On Simone Weil (1909–43)' (1999) 6(2) European Journal of Women's Studies 183–200.

> can make a man's name live for thousands of years. But above this level, far above, separated by an abyss, is the level where the highest things are achieved. These things are essentially anonymous.[14]

Although Weil had many constructive and pragmatic proposals, such as the abolition of yellow press, Weil could easily be one of the later critical theory scholars while they disavow association to any labels, approaches, ideologies, and disciplines. Weil is an epistemological and ideological nonconformist, picking, choosing, criticizing, and turning inside out everything from a Renault factory to Marxism, liberalism, and Zen. Weil's contribution to sciences, humanities, and art achieves the level of 'essential anonymity'—the highest category—what could also be called the Otherwise. Weil would attack this *portrait* for doing exactly what they considered to be a debasement of thought: personalizing it. Weil demanded de-creation of personality as a condition to encountering the Other[15] as party to naked humanity. Therefore, human rights, for instance, went the wrong way in building up the personal thus running immediately to paradox and paralysis. To respect this position, rather than explain and personalize Weil's message, this paper situates Weil's human rights critique *dans le projet de l'enracinement*. True to the project of laying roots, this paper also seeks to root Weil's messages in our situation beyond any pretenses of historical realism.[16] Although seen as peripheral to international law at best by many, Weil is at the core of the critique of the liberal international, which is yet far from spent.

Simone Weil's Background

Simone Adolphine Weil was born in Paris in 1909 to an agnostic and well-off family. Weil's parents were of Alsacian Jewish descent and later fled France in the eve of the German invasion of 1940. Weil's education enabled the finding of academic positions as a lecturer yet Weil felt, on the one hand, the need to teach fervently against dogma and to talk politics to the extent that the students failed examinations and Weil was laid off. Weil declared that the purpose of education was to 'train the attention, to teach the attitude of intellectual waiting (*l'attente*) and to develop the capacity of the self to disappear. Thinking personally (was) to commit the sin of pride in forgetting one is God.'[17]

Weil did not mind dismissals from privileged employment because they felt the need to share the risks and hardships of the life of the afflicted poor to be able to study

[14] Weil, Human Personality, in Miles (n 7) 69–98, 75.

[15] See, eg, Steven Burns, 'Justice and Impersonality: Simone Weil on Rights and Obligations' (1993) 49(3) Laval théologique et philosophique 477–86.

[16] For situationality theory in international law, see Outi Korhonen, *International Law Situated, An Analysis of the Lawyer's Stance Towards Culture, History, and Community* (Kluwer 2000); also note that Weil discourages the fantasy that there is a higher level intellectual endeavour that can be attributed to a 'we' but, without going into the detailed philosophical explanation on which conditions the pronoun may be utilized at this point, suffice it to say that the author recognizes that, strictly speaking, she refers primarily to her own individual situation and only secondarily or indirectly to the community context.

[17] Miles (n 7), Introduction 50; see Christopher Thomas, 'Simone Weil: The Ethics of Affliction and the Aesthetics of Attention' (2020) 28(2) International Journal of Philosophical Studies 145–67.

social injustice and develop the rooting project (*l'enracinement*)[18] as a comprehensive pragmatic response. Weil wrote to Maurice Schumann:

> The suffering all over the world obsesses and overwhelms me to the point of annihilating my faculties and the only way I can revive them and release myself from the obsession is by getting for myself a large share of danger and hardship. That is a necessary condition before I can exert my capacity for work. I beseech you to get for me, if you can, the amount of hardship and danger which can save me from being wasted by sterile chagrin.[19]

Weil perished little over a year after writing thus to Schumann. Weil's *declaration des devoirs envers l'etre humain* (declaration of 'duties'[20] towards the human being) is here set against the legacy of the Universal Declaration of Human Rights (UDHR). The Allied governments and resistance movements had started envisioning the future world organization and its socio-philosophical basis of human rights in the early years of the war and even before since the collapse of the League of Nations. Weil's is a critical intervention to those projects, especially on the ideas pushed by de Gaulle and his circle.[21] Weil saw the liberal concept of rights as a harmful inheritance of Roman Law and even likened it to Hitler's order:

> (i)t is singularly monstrous that ancient Rome should be praised for having bequeathed to us the notion of rights. If we examine Roman law in its cradle, to see what species it belongs to, we discover that property was defined by the *jus utendi et abutendi*. And in fact the things which the property owner had the right to use or abuse at will were for the most part human beings. The Greeks had no conception of rights. They had no words to express it. They were content with the name of justice.[22]

Weil's ideas transgress the familiar semantics. As Weil often urged, the meaning—other than the one fed to us from without—can only be encountered in the silence and emptiness beyond words,[23] noise of discourse, beyond the 'we', and even the 'I'. Attacking the idolization of the French revolution by de Gaulle's circle Weil said: 'The notion of rights (…) has proved unable, because of its intrinsic inadequacy, to fulfil

[18] Simone Weil, *The Need for Roots: Prelude to a Declaration of Duties Towards Mankind* (AF Wills tr, Routledge and Kegan Paul 1952). Originally published as *L'Enracinement: Prelude a une declaration des devoirs envers l'etre humain* (Gallimard1949); see also *Weil*, Human Personality, in Miles (n 7) 81.

[19] ibid 44.

[20] On Weil's position vis-a-vis duties and rights: Weil only later titled their writing with the concept 'duties' and this was in order to relate it to the terms used in the debates of the Resistance sub-commission that discussed the various human rights proposals and eg whether any duties should be included to complement rights. Thus, Weil attempted to 'popularize' their proposal at the cost of the philosophical accuracy of what was meant.

[21] See A Rozelle-Stone, Rebecca and Benjamin P Davis in Edward N Zalta (ed), *Simone Weil, The Stanford Encyclopedia of Philosophy* (Autumn 2020 edn), at https://plato.stanford.edu/archives/fall2020/entries/simone-weil/ accessed 15 January 2019, also *Miles*, Introduction (ibid) 57.

[22] Weil, Human Personality, in Miles (n 7) 73.

[23] See Alessia Ricciardi, 'From Decreation to Bare Life, Weil, Agamben, and the Impolitical' (2009) 39(2) Diacritics 75–93.

the role assigned to it. To combine two inadequate notions, by talking about the rights of human person(ality), will not bring us any further.'[24]

Declaration of Roots Instead of Rights

The roots of human existence in the world are of two main kinds: physical and mental (intellectual, spiritual, rational). The innate humaneness connotes that every subject is obligated to respond to the needs of the Other. To be human is to be *response-able*[25] which is predicated on waiting (*attendre*), reaching toward the other (*tendre*), and attending to them. To not focus attention on the one who bears the responsibility and has the power to provide for the needs makes the project ineffective. Those in need clearly have no power to satisfy their needs, and rights do not give them any more power to do so; even worse, they force the afflicted to claim abstract rights without any guarantee that they would ever be backed by sufficient force. In truth, rights are a paradoxical concept that separates rather than unites human beings with each other.[26] This, to Weil, adds to the indignity of the wretched. In their version of subaltern theory,[27] Weil held that those who suffer from injustice most are the least able to articulate that suffering[28] because of the epistemic and discursive violence at work. The logical interdependence of need, power/force, duty, responsibility, and right has been misconceived in the human rights tradition that is complicit in 'planned miseries', such as hunger and poverty.[29]

In Weil's declaration physical and mental needs and responsibilities coincide since the dignity of human existence necessitates both. The material side of the former is crucial but does not save a human being from uprootedness if there is no *nourriture de l'ame*. Weil's perhaps best known critique is the deracinated indignity produced by the fragmented pandemonium of labour and its devastating effect depriving meaning from one's toil. It cannot be won back through salary bargain alone. Weil was both a critic and a participant in labour unions—*un/e syndicalist/e*.[30]

Weil's essay *un prélude à une déclaration des devoirs envers l'être humain*, the draft declaration of human 'duties', bears the concept of rooting (*l'enracinement*) as its main title. Weil used the concept of 'duty' only reluctantly to get the draft into the debate. All of Weil's 'duties' must be understood as cluster concepts *embedding the interplay of human responsibilities, rights, needs and trust* (as subordinate species of the genus

[24] Weil, Human Personality, in Miles (n 7) 70.

[25] See Korhonen Outi and Toni Selkala, 'Theorizing Responsibility' in A Orford and F Hoffmann (eds), *The Oxford Handbook of the Theory of International Law* (OUP 2016), DOI:10.1093/law/9780198701958.003.0042.

[26] Weil, *Cahiers II* (n 10) 105.

[27] Weil delves into it in their commentary on the Iliad dealing with force, see eg Dean Hammer and Michael Kicey, 'Simone Weil's Iliad: The Power of Words' (2010) 72 The Review of Politics 79–96; also Weil, The Iliad or the Poem of Force, in *Anthology* (n 7) 182–215.

[28] Miles, Foreword, in *Anthology* (n 7) xi–xii.

[29] Susan Marks, 'Human Tights and Root Causes' (2011) 74(1) Modern Law Review 57–78.

[30] See, eg, Robert Sparling, 'Theory and Praxis: Simone Weil and Marx on the Dignity of Labor' (2012) 74(1) Review of Politics 87–107; and see Inese Radzins, 'Simone Weil on Labor and Spirit' (2007) 45(2) Journal of Religious Ethics 291–308.

concept).[31] They have meaning only as parts of the project of rooting human being, life, and existence. Just before their death Weil published a shortened version of the 'duties' in the press of the Free French movement.[32] It is written as a model pledge that every official i.e. anyone with power over others should consent and declare.

Weil's list starts with order continuing with liberty, obedience, responsibility, equality, hierarchy, honour, punishment, freedom of opinion, security, risk, private and collective property, roots, and truth. As such the concepts seem commonplace; some even repulsive, e.g. the 'need of hierarchy' or 'punishment'.

The Order–Hierarchy–Security–Equality Complex

Weil finds that the dignity of a human life is structurally conditioned. These conditions either do or do not satisfy fundamental needs. Everyone exercising any power over others should commit to combating structural violence. For Weil, the needs of order and hierarchy mean that the structure and texture of social relationships must be free from terror and correspond to the innate order of Being and beings.[33] Weil uses the metaphor of beautiful works of art, thus, to say that a supportive social structure corresponds to aesthetic harmony, the fitting together of 'the complexity of individual factors'. Weil's order is a structure where external circumstances have no power to inflict violence.[34] The concept of hierarchy, and the human need for it, evokes the same notion: an ordered social structure, the dialectical check of which is the 'duty' of equality.[35]

The Second Complex: Responsibility–Punishment–Honour–Property–Expression

What is described as the 'duty' of responsibility in Weil's bill and pledge, in the modern academic discourse would be called belonging. Weil talks about the need to feel needed, be useful for common purposes, have a role, experience indispensability, locally and regionally.[36] The need of private and common property and the positive claim to them arises from feeling at home in one's immediate surroundings.[37] The tools of one's profession, a home and a piece of land are akin to physical extensions of the body in terms of belonging and trust. They are parts of one's immediate physical security. Thus, there is the 'duty' to provide for everyone to have a home. In the surrounding of the home, there should be commons—collective property regardless of

[31] See also Ferenc Mújdrizca, 'The Roots of Trust' (2019) 14(1) European Journal of Mental Health 109–42.

[32] Simone Weil, Draft Statement of Human Obligations (4 August 1943) in Miles (n 7) 221–30, 222.

[33] See Jukka Hankamäki, 'Muistammeko Simone Weilin: Filosofia vastaan politiikka' in Juha Varto, (ed), *Silleen jättäminen ja politiikka* (FITTY Tampere 1992) 77.

[34] Weil, The Needs of the Soul, in Miles (n 7) 112.

[35] Weil, Draft Statement (n 32) 224.

[36] ibid 117–18.

[37] Weil, The Needs of the Soul, in Miles (n 7) 135.

title. Weil says: '(A)ny possession which does not satisfy someone's need of private or collective property is useless', and adds that there is no necessary connection of property and money.[38] The emphasis on the latter has led to increased insecurity, homelessness, and deracination.

Weil pairs punishment with honour.[39] Their dialectics are about community ethics, the necessity of the community to give a wake-up call for someone if rehabilitating measures fail or would be 'too exhausting' of resources.[40] If an individual receives a wake-up call they are reminded of their role in the community and the duty to stop behaving (anti-socially) against it. Weil's punishment is the consequence for anti-community action or abuse of power, ie anti-human action;[41] its purpose is to allow atonement, reconciliation, closure, and re-education. It restores belonging. For Weil, it is a paradox to suggest that a homeless, uprooted, anti-social subaltern could benefit from a rights claim in any matters.[42]

For Weil, freedom of opinion is crucial, but, again, contrary to the UDHR's approach, only as integral part of the rooting paradigm—not as a stand-alone wild card. The longest passages in both the essay and the pledge are about the conditions of the freedom of opinion. They imply simultaneously responsibilities to improve community, participate in culture, take a role in striving together for truth, beauty, and good, as in, eg, Weil's concept of science.[43]

The Third Complex: Liberty–Obedience–Risk

The third complex of Weil's rights-alternatives calls for an order in which people can enjoy liberty checked by obedience, and risk-taking checked by a social safety net that secures them against fears that stifle civil courage. The dialectic between liberty and consented obedience is Weil's critique of Western liberalism. Dissecting the Greek roots of 'obedience', Weil sees it as the other side of resistance.[44] With a massive background in Indian, Ancient Greek, Persian, Jewish, Marxist, Zen, and various *folk* philosophies, Weil cannot conceive of liberty as separate from obedience—which we can understand, for example, as obeying a cause, truth, oneself. Obedience is consent to a sensible order, rule (of law), and one's moral conscience. Weil makes a difference between service and servility;[45] the dictates of 'duties' and belonging. Liberty is the right to challenge rules and leadership. For Weil, Liberty is Critique.

Weil's idea of hierarchies of responsibility means that there are leaders and subjects, who share a project and discuss its aims. The 'duty' to recognize human liberty is to

[38] ibid 136–37.
[39] Weil, Statement (n 32) 229.
[40] Weil, The Needs of the Soul, in Miles (n 7) 123.
[41] See Christopher Hamilton, 'Power, Punishment and Reconciliation in the Political and Social Thought of Simone Weil' (2008) 11(3) European Journal of Social Theory 315–30.
[42] Weil, Human Personality in Miles (n 7) 91.
[43] Hankamäki (n 33) 60–61.
[44] See, eg, Simone Fresse, 'Révolte et obéissance chez Simone Weil' (1975) 10 Nouvelle Serie No 450, 530–43; Martin Steffens, 'Resisting with Simone Weil' (2015) 29(2) Inflexions 65–73.
[45] Steffens (n 44) 116.

Figure 40.1 Simone Weil by Ona Aurélia (2020).
Source: Courtesy of the artist Ona Aurélia.

allow for moral choice every day.[46] Weil's own life is an example of the moral choice that is more often than not disobedience, critique, and resistance to e.g. dogmatic teaching rules, supervisors, parents, social customs, gender roles, intellectual or political authorities. Risk is civil courage; it should not incite the kind of fear that 'crushes the soul' but emboldens.[47]

Conclusion: Truth and Rooting

Weil envisioned a European and international council for the reorganization of the post-war political life. Although Weil pushed the paradigm change from 'human rights to human roots' at the cradle of UDHR, we hardly find a trace of Weil in the Western human rights project.[48]

To Weil, the duty to Other makes up an order without structural violence in which education and science enable knowledge, culture, and love that point towards Truth in a constant state of growing roots and transcending them.[49] To travel to such a situation one would have to surpass both the Great Beast and the limits of personalism.[50]

[46] Weil, The Needs of the Soul, in Miles (n 7) 115–16.
[47] ibid.
[48] See also Oche Onazi, '(Disability) Justice Dictated by Surfeit of Love: Simone Weil in Nigeria' (2017) 28(1) Law and Critique 1–22.
[49] *Weil*, Love, in Miles (n 7) 290–96.
[50] cf Hankamäki (n 33) 85.

41
Helene Halperin-Ginsburg
The Social Function of International Law

*Ksenia Shestakova**

Introduction

Recent centenaries of equal women's rights to practice law,[1] equal voting rights, and the 1917 Russian Revolutions revived scholars' interest in the early twentieth century. Helene Halperin-Ginsburg, crowned the first woman international legal scholar in Imperial Russia, has recently been introduced to Russian and Ukrainian law textbooks in efforts to recognize female figures in the history of law.[2] However, they depict her mostly as a woman 'of dashing courage'[3] who studied law abroad. According to critics, Halperin-Ginsburg showed either a great reading of the European legal scholarship, but added 'nothing new', or was 'more successful' in 'critically assessing the revolutionary moments from the international law perspective'.[4] Nonetheless, Russian[5] and Ukrainian[6] feminist history barely mentions her. Though Helene's sister, Frida

* The author would like to thank the editor of the volume Immi Tallgren for her invitation, kind help during the hard pandemic times, insightful comments, and valuable inputs; my research assistant Maria Naumenko for her help with finding archival information; Laura Kraft for photographing the gravestone in the Berlin suburb cemetery, and Kateriina Flinck for her comments and suggestions to the final text.

[1] Постановление временного правительства от 1 июня 1917 года 'О допущении женщин к ведению чужих дел в судебных установлениях' (1917) 132 Собрание узаконений и распоряжений Правительства, издаваемое при Правительствующем сенате. Ст. 706. [Decree of the Provisional Government of 1 June 1917 'On the admission of women to prepresent clients in courts' (1917) 132 Collection of decrees and orders of the Government, published under the Governing Senate, art 706].

[2] Олена Самойленко, 'Олена Гальперіна-Гінзбург—доля жінки-юриста в контексті епохи' (2020) 31 Правова держава 152. [Olena Samoilenko, 'Olena Galperina-Ginzburg—The Fate of the Female Lawyer in the Context of the Epoch' (2020) 31 Pravova Derzhava 152.]

[3] Виктор Кумок и Семён Воловник, *Евреи Мелитополя*. Т.1. (изд. дом МГТ 2012) 105 [Viktor Kumok and Semyon Volovnik, *Jews of Melitopol* vol 1 (MGT Publishing House 2012) 105.

[4] Людмила Ануфриева, Дамир Бекяшев, Камиль Бекяшев и др., *Международное публичное право: учебник* (отв. ред. Камиль Бекяше, 4-е изд., Изд-во Проспект 2005) 73–74. [Lyudmila Anufrieva, Damir Bekyashev, Kamil Bekyashev, and others in Kamil Bekyashev (ed), *Textbook on Public International Law* (4th edn, Prospect Publishing House 2005) 73–74] Григорий Стародубцев, *Международно-правовая наука российской эмиграции* (Книга и бизнес 2000) 32–33. [Grigory Starodubtsev, *International Legal Scholarship of Russian Emigration* (Kniga i Bisness 2000) 32–33].

[5] Ирина Юкина, *Русский феминизм как вызов современности* (Алетейя 2007) [Irina Yukina, *Russian Feminism as a Challenge to Modernity* (Aletheya 2007)]; Richard Stites, *The Women's Liberation Movement in Russia: Feminism, Nihilism, And Bolshevism*, 1860–1930 (Princeton University Press 1991).

[6] Людмила Смоляр, *Минуле заради майбутнього. Жіночий рух Наддніпрянської України II пол. XIX—поч. XX ст. Сторінки історії* (Астропринт 1998) [Ludmila Smolyar, *The Past for the Sake of the Future. Women's Movement of Dnieper Ukraine II Half XIX—Beginning XX Century. Pages of History* (Astroprint 1998)]; Martha Bohachevsky-Chomiak, *Feminists Despite Themselves: Women in Ukrainian Community Life, 1884–1939* (CIUS Press 1988).

Ksenia Shestakova, *Helene Halperin-Ginsburg* In: *Portraits of Women in International Law*. Edited by: Immi Tallgren, Oxford University Press. © Ksenia Shestakova 2023. DOI: 10.1093/oso/9780198868453.003.0041

Figure 41.1 Grave of Halperin-Ginsburg accompanied by a sculpture by William Wauer.
Source: Photograph courtesy of Laura Kraft.

Grigorovich-Barsky,[7] left a biographical sketch, according to the twentieth-century biographical traditions she skipped most of Helene's private life and focused on her public achievements. Historian Alexander Kiesewetter[8] briefly analysed her journalistic and academic work, and lawyer Boris Mirkin-Getzevich[9] wrote an *in-memoriam* notice. This portrait re-introduces[10] Halperin-Ginsburg to the historical narrative of international law and revisits her legal scholarship.

[7] Her own name as the author is missing frim the sketch [Фрида Григорович-Барская,] 'Короткая жизнь (биографический очерк)' в Елена Гальперин-Гинзбург, *Под знаменем права: Сборник статей* (тип. Куммер и К° 1923) 7–53 [Frida Grigorovich-Barskaya, 'A Short Life (Biographical Sketch)' in Helene Halperin-Ginsburg, *Under the Banner of Law: Collection of Essays* (Kummer & Co 1923) 7–53].

[8] Александр Кизеветтер, Елена Гальперин-Гинзбург и ее публицистическая деятельность в Елена Гальперин-Гинзбург, *Под знаменем права*: Сборник статей (тип. Куммер и К° 1923) 55–73. [Alexander Kiesewetter, 'EA Galperin-Ginsburg and her Scholarly Writings' in Helene Halperin-Ginsburg, *Under the Banner of Law: Collection of Essays* (Kummer & Co 1923) 55–73].

[9] Борис Миркин-Гецевич, 'Елена Абрамовна Гальперина-Гинзбург (некролог)' *Еврейская трибуна* (Париж, 19 мая 1922) 969 5–6. [Boris Mirkine-Guetzévitch, 'Elena Abramovna Galperina-Ginzburg (*in-memoriam*)' *Evreiskaia tribuna* (Paris, 19 May 1922) 969 5–6].

[10] Halperin-Ginsburg gradually enters European scholarship as well. See Philippa Hetherington, 'From Sex and Security to Sovereignty and Self-Determination: Elena Gal'perin-Ginzburg between Transnational and International Law' (2020) ASEEES (cited with the permission of the author).

General Historical Context and Halperin-Ginsburg's Early Years

As Helene Halperin-Ginsburg was a socially active Jewish woman in Imperial Russia, prior to looking into her personal history, I answer two preliminary questions. First, who were socially active women in Imperial Russia prior to the 1917 Russian Revolution? Second, what did being a Jewish woman from a Ukrainian region add to the picture?

At the turn of the twentieth century, though women in Imperial Russia enjoyed economic and limited civil rights,[11] their social roles were reduced to running the family. The Alexander II Great Reforms abolished serfdom, led to the nobility's decline, the slow democratization of society, and a mental ferment of a radical political character among educated people. 'The transformation of the social system did not mean to ... introduce political representation. A granting of new institutions did not follow the political reform.'[12] 'The economic conditions of Russian life and the social upheaval took place on 19 February 1861, forced women to fight for their existence, and made labour indispensable. Compelled by the need, and not by fashion—as it seemed then to many—they declared readiness to acquire the same rights to knowledge and work as men, their claim to higher education.'[13] Many women wanted to participate in public life instead of family matters and find fulfillment in publically valuable fields. The abolition of serfdom did not bring similar changes to Jewish communities leaving under the Pale of Settlement Regulation where women have always played active, albeit subordinate roles.[14]

[11] Яков Канторович, *Женщина в праве: с приложением всех постановлений действующего законодательства, относящихся до лиц женского пола.*(Тип.-лит. М. Я. Минкова 1895) 87–88. [Yakov Kantorovich, *Woman in the Law: with the Appendix of All Resolutions of the Current Legislation Regarding the Persons of the Female Sex* (Typography of M Minkov 1895) 87–88].

[12] Сергей Платонов, *Лекции по русской истории* (10-е изд, Ив. Блинов 1917). [Sergei Platonov, *Lectures on Russian History* (10th edn, Ivan Blinov 1917)].

[13] Екатерина Некрасова, 'Студентка на войне: Письма из Румынии (1877)' (1898) 7 Русская мысль 808 [Ekaterina Nekrasova, 'A Female Student at War: Letters from Romania (1877)' (1898) 7 Russkaya Mysl 808].

[14] Martha Bohachevsky-Chomiak, 'Jewish and Ukrainian Women: A Double Minority' in Howard Aster and Peter J Potichnyj (eds), *Ukrainian-Jewish Relations in Historical Perspective* (Canadian Institute of Ukrainian Studies, University of Alberta 1990) 356. At the end of the nineteenth century, nearly half of the world Jewry was placed under the sceptre of the Russian tsar. When in 1791, after the first partitioning of Poland, Jews first became subjects of Imperial Russia, they were forced to reside only within the Pale of Settlement (*cherta osedlosti*) , which included among others parts of modern Ukraine, Belarus, and Lithuania. The Pale was introduced in response to the question about how to treat 'others', who did not fit into Imperial Russia's traditional lifestyle. Because of the expansion of Russia's borders and changing political interests, the Government regularly reviewed the Pale's contours, ordering Jews to re-settle. It also revised the list of the occupations available to Jews and exceptions to it, allowing 'useful' categories to reside outside the Pale. See: Abramson Henry, *A Prayer for the Government: Ukrainians and Jews in Revolutionary Times, 1917–1920* (Harvard University Press 1999) 3. Eli Lederhendler, 'Classless: On the Social Status of Jews in Russia and Eastern Europe in the Late Nineteenth Century' 50(2) Comparative Studies in Society and History 509–34. Павел Полян, '17-й год: Жизнь за чертой' (24.03.2017) 4287 Ведомости [Pavel Polyan, 'The Year 17: The Life Behind the Pale' (24.03.2017) 4287 Vedomosti]. Павел Полян, 'Сто лет без черты оседлости: к юбилею еврейской эманс ипации в России' (2017) 3 (113) Неприкосновенный запас. Дебаты о политике и культуре 11–30 [Pavel Polyan, 'One Hundred Years without the Pale of Settlement: On the Anniversary of Jewish Emancipation in Russia' (2017) 3 (113) Neprikosnovennyi zapas. Debaty o politike i kulture 11–30].

State policies towards 'new' women were labelled the 'women's question' and attempted to respond to the needs of the new group of 'others' in the traditional Imperial Russian society. The Imperial Russian Government's attitude towards the women's question fluctuated with its general approach towards liberal reforms.

Between 1861 and 1905, the women's movement in Imperial Russia was an elitist urban social campaign and lacked any protest character. Before 1905, women avoided labelling themselves feminists, preferring the Russian term collocated from 'equal rights'—'ravnopravki'.[15]

Initially, the rights to education and work were central for the movement. Due to Russia's slow transition from an absolute monarchy to a democracy, women pushed for rights for all social classes and nationalities. Jewish women did not define the rights to education and labour, and later voting rights, equally along with some type of national rights, as only women's goals as these were the goals of their entire community. As Martha Bohachevsky-Chomiak observes, Ukrainian and Jewish women—and I would add Russian women too —developed a 'pragmatic' or 'community' feminism that 'demonstrated a remarkable ability to adapt to existing institutions' and promote 'economic, social, and cultural change phrased in terms acceptable by their social groups'.[16] Being community-oriented, women relied on self-help and worked within the accepted social structures; most of them chose their professions motivated by community welfare and not by individual gain.

Much has been written about the 'pioneering trio', Maria Trubnikova, Nadezhda Stasova, and Anna Filosofova,[17] who successfully advanced women's right to education through private preparatory schools, higher medical education, and the first women's universities. In the 1870s, the government amended gender-neutral legislation allowing women to attend lectures as non credit students, forcing them to study abroad. Soon, frightened by general revolutionary sentiments among young educated people and believing that it flourished in emigration, the Government in particular, required female students to return to Russia, threatening them with sanctions[18]. Against that background, the 'trio' smartly lobbied the first private courses preparing women for universities opened in St Petersburg, Moscow, and Kyiv and Higher Courses for Women at St Petersburg (Bestuzhev Courses), and later in Kyiv, Kazan, and Moscow Universities with full students rights.[19] However, they had succeeded in the very limited fields that were a 'natural extension' of the women's private life and a lot of occupations, including law, remained closed for women.

[15] Yukina (n 5) 65.

[16] Martha Bohachevsky-Chomiak (n 14) 356.

[17] Francisca de Haan, Krassimira Daskalova, and Anna Loutfi (eds), *A Biographical Dictionary of Women's Movements and Feminisms. Central, Eastern, and South Eastern Europe; 19th and 20th Centuries* (1st edn, CEU Press 2006).

[18] 'О мерах прекращения прилива русских женщин в Цюрихские университет и политехникум' (1873) Российский государственный исторический архив. Фонд 733. Опись 191. Дело 268. ['On measures to stop the influx of Russian women in the Zurich University and Polytechnic' (1873) Russian State Historical Archive. Fund 733. Inventory 191. File 268].

[19] Yukina (n 5) 65; Татьяна Иванова, 'У истоков высшего женского образования в России: организационная деятельность В. И. Герье в свидетельствах современников' (2009) 37(175) Вестник Челябинского государственного университета. История 169 [Tatiana Ivanova, 'At the Origins of Women's Higher Education in Russia: Organizational Activities of Vladivir Ivanivich Guerrier in Evidence of Contemporaries' (2009) 37(175) Bulletin of Chelyabinsk University History 169].

By the early 1900s, the aspiration to become politicians and lawyers had become popular among women. However, it became evident that even liberal men saw no reason for women's political rights. Educated women started wording their ideas in terms of rights, the archaic and discriminatory character of the existing laws, and the need for women in the seats of power and decision-making processes.[20] They pushed for legal education for women. Between 1905 and 1917, the Russian women's movement gradually transformed into an all-Russian political feminist movement.[21] It set the stage for the formal recognition of women's equal rights to education, labour, and voting rights that the 1917 Revolutionary Governments had only to put on paper.[22]

Against that background, Halperin-Ginsburg's mother, Ekaterina Korenblit[23], had no economic reasons and did not dare for emancipation in the 1870s. She was born to a Jewish family in Mikhailovka, Melitopol Uezd, Ukrainian Taudride Province. Her father, Elyukim Korenblit, was a learned Talmudist[24] keen on modern philosophy, *the haskala*, a staunch constitutionalist, and supporter of women's equal rights. Ekaterina married Abram Ginsburg from a wealthy town family.[25] They had six children: four girls and two boys. The Ginsburg daughters aspired for independent life as society gradually recognized women's rights to education and employment.

Two of Halperin-Ginsburg's sisters became doctors, as medicine was among the few fields enabling women's professional fulfillment. They married members of wealthy Kyiv families: Grigorivich-Barsky[26] and Halperin.[27] Halperin-Ginsburg's[28] way to her profession was less straightforward. From early on, she developed the habit of systemic reading and critical thinking and showed an acute sense of justice, empathy, and interest in social problems.[29] After being home-schooled, Halperin-Ginsburg graduated from Nikolaev Girls' High School. At the time, the government toughened educational laws by introducing *numerus clausus* for Jews, reforming women's universities,

[20] Yukina (n 5) 65.

[21] Галина Крижановская, 'Деятельность общественных организаций российской империи по защите права женщин на получение высшего юридического образования на рубеже XIX–XX веков' (2021) 6 Юридическая наука: история и современность 101 [Galina Krizhanovskaya, 'Non-Governmental Organizations of the Imperial Russia in the Protection of the Women's Right to Higher Legal Education at the Turn of the XIX–XX Centuries' (2021) 6 Legal Science: History and the Presence 101].

[22] Yukina (n 5) 66.

[23] Born 1853, died in the United States in the1940s. See Arriving Passenger and Crew Lists (including Castle Garden and Ellis Island) (New York 1820–1957).

[24] Kumok (n 3) 28.

[25] Grigorovich-Barskaya (n 7) 9–11.

[26] Frida Ginsburg married Dmitry Grigorovich-Barsky from one of the oldest Kyiv families, a lawyer, known as the defendant in the *Beilis affair*. Елена Г-г, 'Процессы ведьм и ритуальные процессы' Киевская мысль (Киев, 23 октября 1913) [Elena G-g, 'Witch Hunting and Ritual Processes' *Kyiv Mysl* (Kiev, 23 October 1913)].

[27] Arnold's Halperin father Wolf was the first guild merchant, and a brother of Moses Halperin, a major sugar manufacturer in Imperial Russia and a philanthropist from Kyiv. Nowadays, the permanent committees of the Ukrainan *Verkhovna Rada* occupy historical Moses Halperin's family mansion. See: Аркадий Третьяков, *Купцы города Киева* (Сучасний письменник 2017) 115 [Arkady Tretyakov, *Merchants of the City of Kyiv* (Suchaniy Pismennik 2017) 115]).

[28] She was born between 1883 and 1885: the author was unable to locate the exact date. Frida Grigorovich-Barsky writes that she died in 1922 in the age of thirty-eight; 1883 is the year written on Helene Halperin-Ginsburg's gravestone. However, historical events and biographical facts discussed in Grigorovich-Barskaya (n 7) may suggest otherwise.

[29] Grigorovich-Barskaya (n 7) 17–19.

shortening women's school curricula, and strengthening disciplinary measures. She stayed in Mikhailovka, giving private lessons and reading Marxist literature in the local library.

Halperin-Ginsburg's upbringing in an educated family—her grandfather's liberal cosmopolitan ideas, respect for equal and minorities rights, the importance of the right to education, absolute opposition to violence, established Jewish self-help tradition, and life in a multinational and multireligious community—influenced her worldviews. Inclined to humanities, Halperin-Ginsburg experienced injustices of the Pale policies, witnessed the impoverishment of the village after the abolition of serfdom, and established self-help tradition capable of dealing with some social problems. It was therefore not surprising that her personal experience coupled with Marxist literature moved her towards law.

In 1901, the Ginsburgs moved to Kyiv. Halperin-Ginsburg's interests grew into a penchant for the history of revolutions. Eventually, she became determined to advance into the legal profession. Because of the Pale, she travelled abroad to attend the Law Faculty of Brussels University in 1903 and Paris Ecole de Droit in 1904. She, together with only five other female students, was reluctantly welcomed in Paris as male students would reportedly 'noisily scratched the parquet with their boots' as women entered the lecture hall.[30] In parallel with her studies, she organized a student circle on the history of revolutions. The same year, her future husband, Arnold Halperin, attended Paris Ecole de Droit as a non-credit student.

Marxist Influence

Halperin-Ginsburg, as with many young people at the turn of the twentieth century, believed in Marxists ideas. She was particularly adherent to Georgi Plekhanov's social democratic adaptions of Marxist theory to Russian realities, his general opposition to violence, and an understanding of historical materialism. As the founder of Russian Marxism, Plekhanov's works, such as *On the Development of the Monist View of History* (1895), shaped Halperin-Ginsburg's political beliefs.[31]

The 1905 Russian Revolution introduced the State Duma and Elections Regulations and had two immediate consequences. Firstly, the new laws changed the gender balance in society and excluded women from voting. Thus, bitter disappointment permeated the Women's Mutual Philanthropic Society's petition to the State Duma: 'the Government has deprived half the population of the right to vote in a cause common for all citizens, labeled it legally incompetent and placed in the category of minors and disenfranchised creatures'.[32] Secondly, with the electoral law, different groups, circles,

[30] ibid 28. Most likely, Ekaterina Fleischitz, who graduated from Sorbonne University law school the same year, was one of her classmates. See Fleischitz (n 39).

[31] ibid 30.

[32] Анна Шабанова, 'Текст обращения Российского Женского Взаимно-Благотворительного Общества в Государственную Думу' *Первый женский календарь на 1907 год* (Сакнт-Петербург 1907) 372 [Anna Shabanova, 'Petition of the Russian Women's Mutual Philantropic Society to the State Duma' First Women's Calendar for the Year 1907 (St Petersburg 1907) 372].

and associations sprang up like mushrooms representing the whole political spectrum from the extreme right to the extreme left.

As nobody officially voiced the women's question, a women's movement opposing the legal amendments organized itself politically to successfully lobby for equal education and labour rights including same curricula, equal admission rights to state universities, equal right to practice law and public service, and equal employment rights including fabric inspectress.[33] Helperin-Ginsburg later covered these topics in newspaper articles. Turning more political, the movement lobbied with political parties and executives, engaged in the legislative process, filed court cases, and raised public attention in media and literature.

The movement mobilized Russian women, who started to choose between women's organizations and left-wing parties, prioritizing women's right to vote over all people's equality and vice versa. In their rallies, women always demanded voting rights without prejudice to gender, religion, and nationality. The Russian Social Democratic Labour Party had added 'the women's question' on its agenda already in 1903. However, in practice, equal voting and labour rights were just a tribute to socialist theory.[34]. They reduced 'the women's question' to sporadic agitation among proletariat women; Alexandra Kollontai confronted the mainstream movement.[35] After the split, the Bolsheviks refused to enact real change, while the Mensheviks co-operated with women's organizations. Feminists, despite widespread pro-socialist sentiments, criticized Social Democrats the most as they 'had high hopes from them'.[36] Under feminist pressure, the Constitutional Democrats added equal voting rights to their programme in 1906. In 1905, spirited by the Manifesto and outraged by violent Jewish pogroms she evidenced that year, Halperin-Ginsburg joined the socialist movement. She engaged in its agitation work but soon dropped it as boring and ineffective and briefly turned to lecturing in typographists' circles.

Legal Profession and Feminism

Twice, in 1902 and 1907, Halperin-Ginsburg relatives were arrested for keeping socialist literature. In 1902, she visited the prison overcrowded with detainees and arranged messages and parcels. In 1907, Halperin-Ginsburg passed her diploma examinations in Paris. Having swiftly returned to Kyiv, she managed to see the governor and persuade him to discharge her family members on parole until their trial. Improvement of the Russian penitentiary system became her passion project both academically and politically.

[33] Yukina (n 5) 221.

[34] ibid 28.

[35] See Sergey Vasiliev, 'Aleksandra Kollontai: New Woman' in this volume.

[36] Анна Кальманович, 'Женское движение и отношение партий к нему. Речь на Первом Всероссийском женском съезде' Труды Первого Всероссийского женского съезда (Санкт-Петербург, 1909) 748 [Anna Kalmanovich, 'The Women's Movement and the Parties' attitude to it. Speech at the First All-Russian Women's Congress' Proceedings of the First All-Russian Women's Congress (St Petersburg 1909) 748].

To practice law in imperial Russia, Halperin-Ginsburg required an external degree from a Russian University. She applied to Moscow University but was refused because, as a Jew, she had no right to reside in Moscow. With no residence permit, Halperin-Ginsburg moved to Kyiv under a false identity to access the university library. In 1909, she passed exams at Kharkiv University[37] and became one of its few female law graduates. Notwithstanding the gender-neutral legislation, the choice of legal occupations was minimal for women. Thus, women initiated a campaign on equal rights in practicing law. Having received her diploma, Halperin-Ginsburg applied for an attorney's assistant (*prisiazhnyi poverennyi)* position in the Kyiv District Court. Famed Russian legal professional, Ekaterina Fleischitz did the same in St Petersburg. The Kyiv Court rejected Halperin-Ginsburg, but the St Petersburg Court accepted Fleischitz.

In the following years, several newspapers simultaneously reported two cases involving female lawyers.[38] The first of 'Dr. Ginsburg', who appealed to the Governing Senate to make her case. The second of 'Dr. Fleischitz', who took her first case to court as a defence attorney. The prosecutor refused to plead against a woman and left the courtroom. The Minister of Justice addressed the matter to the Governing Senate, which clarified that under the Russian law, only men were eligible for attorney status; it further prohibited women from pleading in courts as client's advocates. Fleischitz's status was revoked.

Both Halperin-Ginsburg and Fleischitz turned to women's organizations and academic writing instead. Fleischitz joined the League for Women's Equal Rights. Together with other women lawyers, she drafted legal opinions and laws that the League lobbied with the State Duma on, for instance, divorce, spouses' separate domicile, and abolishing prostitution regulations.[39] In 1913, to focus the women attorney campaign, the League created the St Petersburg Women Lawyers Society.

Halperin-Ginsburg supported the campaign with articles in *Kyiv Mysl*. According to her, the prohibition to practice law made women's legal diplomas nonsense; the absence of a ban in the regulation's original gender-neutral language meant permission. Moreover, when the law was adopted, the women's higher education social movement already existed. Thus, the prudent legislator who always bears in mind possible social changes could not deliberately exclude women from that rule's scope.[40]

Having settled in Kyiv, Halperin-Ginsburg worked with NGOs: she lectured criminal law at the Public University and reported to the Kyiv Law Society about French judicial reform.

[37] Grigorovich-Barskaya (n 7) 39.

[38] 'Скарга д-ки Гинзбург' *Киевская Рада* 5 (Киев, 5 ноября 1909); *Киевская Рада* 277 (Киев, 8 декабря 1909); *Право* 286 (18 декабря 1909); 'Хроника' *Право* 44 (Санкт-Петербруг, 1 ноября 1909) 2392–93; *Право* 46 (Санкт-Петербруг, 15 ноября 1909) 2513–16; *Право* 47 (Санкт-Петербруг, 21 ноября 1909) 2573–76. ['Complaint of Doctor Ginsburg' *Kyiv Rada* 5 (Kyiv, 5 November 1909); *Kyiv Rada* 277 (Kyiv, 8 December 1909); *Pravo* 286 (18 December 1909); 'Chronicle' *Pravo* 44 (St Petersburg, 1 November 1909) 2392–2393; *Pravo* 46 (St Petersburg, 15 November 1909) 2513–16; *Pravo* 47 (St Petersburg, 21 November 1909) 2573–76].

[39] Екатерина Флейшиц, 'О женской адвокатуре' *Право* 2 (Санкт-Петербург, 10 января 1910) 66–73; *Право* 3 (Санкт-Петербург, 17 января 1910) 143–51. [Catherine Fleischitz, 'On Women Attorneys' *Pravo* 2 (St Petersburg 10 January 1910) 66–73; *Pravo* 3 (St Petersburg 17 January 1910) 143–51].

[40] Елена Г-г, 'Женщина-адвокат' *Киевская мысль* (Киев, 24 сентября 1909, 11 ноября 1909) [Elena G-g, 'Woman Attorney' *Kyiv Mysl* (Kyiv, 24 September 1909 and 11 November 1909)].

Elaborating on Russia's penitentiary system, she studied prison patronage in other countries. Her articles[41] raised professional and broad interest in public control over prisons. As Halperin-Ginsburg saw the primary petitionary system goal in correctional rehabilitation and crime prevention, she argued for local public patronage at every prison. The patronage's principal rights should be the ability to apply for early release and unhindered meetings with prisoners. Funds should come from membership fees and donations. In her opinion, the feeling of care would be mutually beneficial for the local society and the prisoner. With the Kyiv Governor's and District Court's Chairman's consent, she established the Kyiv Prison Patronage Society.[42]

Expanding the idea of criminals' re-integration into society, Halperin-Ginsburg advocated for separate juvenile courts.[43] The hearings should be closed, less formal and in the presence of parents or custodians appointed by the judge from the list of reputable local community members who cared and could positively influence the child's upbringing; and minors should not be imprisoned with adults. Largely thanks to Halperin-Ginsburg's efforts, juvenile courts began to function in 1911.

In 1912, Halperin-Ginsburg became the only women-member of the Russian group of the International Union of Penal Law and reported about functioning of Kyiv Prison Patronage.[44] She wrote for the official journal of the Russian group in 1912–1913,[45] and reported about the meetings of the Russian group in 1912 and 1914 in *Kyiv Mysl*.[46]

In 1912 and 1913, Halperin-Ginsburg wrote two *in-memoriams* of pioneer women's movement activist and philanthropist Anna Filosofova.[47] Firstly, in the socialist tradition, she dismissed feminism as detached from working class problems and praised Filosofova for seeing women's issues in a broader socio-economic context. A year

[41] Елена Г-г, 'О тюремном патронате' *Киевская мысль* (Киев, 8 октября 1909, 23 октября1909, 2 ноября 1909, 1 февраля 1910, 9 апреля 1910) [Elena G-g, 'On Prison Patronage' *Kyiv Mysl* (Kyiv, 8 October 1909, 23 October1909, 2 November 1909, 1 February 1910, and 9 April 1910)].

[42] Елена Г-г, 'Тюремный патронат' *Киевская Рада* 256 (Киев, 12 ноября 1909) [Elena G-g, 'Prison Patronage' *Kyiv Rada* 256 (Kyiv, 12 November 1909)].

[43] Елена Г-г, 'Суд для малолетних в Киеве' *Киевская мысль* (Киев, 2 февряля 1914). [Elena G-g, 'The Court for Minors in Kyiv' *Kyiv Misl* (Kiev, 2 February 1914)].

[44] Елена Г-г, 'Из жизни и опыта Киевского патроната' (1912) 1 Журнал уголовного права и процесса, издаваемый при Русской группе Международного союза криминалистов 217–22 [Elena G-g, 'From the Life and Experience of the Kiev Patronage' (1912) 1 Journal of Criminal Law and Procedure, published by the Russian Group of the International Union of Penal Law 217–22].

[45] Елена Г-г, 'Реформа французского уголовного процесса' (1912) 4 Журнал уголовного права и процесса, издаваемый при Русской группе Международного союза криминалистов 59–69 [Elena G-g, 'Reform of the French Criminal Procedure' (1912) 4 Journal of Criminal Law and Procedure, published by the Russian Group of the International Union of Penal Law 59–69]; Елена Г-г, 'Борьба с порнографией'(1913) 1 Журнал уголовного права и процесса, издаваемый при Русской группе Международного союза криминалистов 102–09 [Elena G-g, 'The Fight Against Pornography'(1913) 1 Journal of Criminal Law and Procedure, published by the Russian Group of the International Union of Penal Law 102–09]; Елена Г-г, 'Влияние прессы на преступность' (1913) 4 Журнал уголовного права и процесса, издаваемый при Русской группе Международного союза криминалистов 62–70 [Elena G-g, 'The Media Influence on Crime' (1913) 4 Journal of Criminal Law and Procedure, published by the Russian Group of the International Union of Criminalists 62–70].

[46] Елена Г-г, 'К съезду Русской группы криминалистов' *Киевская мысль* (Киев, 18 марта 1912, 15 февраля 1914) [Elena G-g, 'On the Congress of the Russian Group of Criminalists' *Kyiv Mysl* (Kyiv, 18 March 1912, and 15 February1914)].

[47] Елена Г-г, 'Памяти А.П. Философовой' *Киевская мысль* (Киев, 20 март 1912, 17 март 1913) [Elena G-g, 'In Memory of Anna Filosofova' *Kyiv Mysl* (Kyiv, 20 March 1912, 17 March 1913)].

later, Halperin-Ginsburg reversed her opinion and spoke about young women's gratitude for Filosofova's educational and charity projects. She became a feminist as the women's question hindered her legal career. Together with her sister Grigorovich-Barsky, Halperin-Ginsburg joined the Kyiv Women's Assembly.[48] In her articles in *Kyiv Mysl*, Halperin-Ginsburg covered all traditional feminist topics of her time: married women's rights,[49] women's suffrage,[50] and fabric inspectresses.[51] In 1916, the Kyiv Women's Assembly sent Halperin-Ginsburg as a delegate to the All-Russian Women Congress.[52] The text of her report was forwarded to the State Duma.

In 1914, Helene Halperin-Ginsburg married Arnold Halperin in Italy, changing her maiden surname Ginsburg to the hyphenated surname Halperin-Ginsburg. The couple returned to Russia two weeks before the First World War. As in other countries, Russian feminists overwhelmed with patriotism supported their government. The women's organizations refocused on assisting the front. With the influx of refugees to the Kyiv region, Halperin-Ginsburg established the League for Childhood's Defence under the auspice of the Kyiv Women's Assembly, introducing 'several children's institutions for different ages; an information office on refugee children; attendants on duty at the train station, and a library'.[53]

International Legal Scholarship

Famously, the choice to support their governments or to take the pacifist stance was a turning point for the international socialist movement. In Russia, most of socialists condemned the war, demanding immediate peace. However, Plekhanov's group *Edinstvo* believed to the contrary that Russia's loss in the war would be a national tragedy and a blow to the Russian labour movement.[54]

The First World War deeply moved Halperin-Ginsburg as a 'violation of international guarantee'.[55] Already in 1914, in *Kyiv Mysl*, she raised acute *jus in bello* topics

[48] Елена Г-г, 'В женском клубе' *Киевская Рада* 94 (Киев, 26 апрель 1914) [Elena G-g, 'In the Women's Club' *Kyiv Rada* 94 (Kyiv 26 April 1914)].

[49] Елена Г-г, 'Права замужней женщины' *Киевская мысль* (Киев, 10 февраль 1914) [Elena G-g, 'The Rights of a Married Woman' *Kyiv Mysl* (Kyiv, 10 February 1914)].

[50] Елена Г-г, 'Избирательные права женщин' *Киевская мысль* (Киев, 2 май 1916) [Elena G-g, 'Women's Suffrage' *Kyiv Mysl* (Kyiv, 2 May 1916)].

[51] Елена Г-г, 'Фабричные инспектриссы' *Киевская мысль* (Киев, 22 июнь1916) [Elena G-g, 'Factory Inspectoress' *Kyiv Mysl* (Kyiv, 22 June 1916)].

[52] Елена Гальперина-Гинзбург, *Женщина-крестьянка в нынешней войне и реформа волостного самоуправления: Доклад, читанный на совещании делегаток женских организаций в г. Москве 23-24 апреля 1916 г.* (МО Лиги равноправия женщин, Москва, 1916) [Helene Halperin-Ginsburg, *A Peasant Woman in the Current War and the Reform of Volost Self-Government: A Report Read at a Meeting of Delegates of Women's Organizations in Moscow on April 23–24* (MO League of Equal Rights for Women, Moscow, 1916)].

[53] Елена Г-г, 'Лига защиты детства' *Киевская Рада* 105 (Киев, 10 мая 1914) [Elena G-g, 'Childhood Defense League' *Kyiv Rada* 105 (Kyiv, 10 May 1914)].

[54] Георгий Плеханов, 'Интернаціоналисты, да только съ другой стороны' в О войне: статьи (Петроград, изд-во 'ОГНИ' 1917) 52. [Georgy Plekhanov, 'The Internationalists, Only from the Other Side', in *On War: Essays* (OGNI Publishing House 1917) 52].

[55] Grigorovich-Barskaya (n 7) 43. I would disagree that Halperin-Ginsburg became 'a hearty advocate for the specificity of the Russian voice in international legal discussions and International Union of Penal Law'. For her, Russian voice was both the tool and the result. This is equally true for her wartime articles in Kyiv Mysl. See: Hetherington (n 10).

and explained them in terms of international law.[56] In 1915, she attempted to organize the International Lawyers Society in Moscow and Petrograd but dropped the idea.[57] The lawyers specializing in international law were a rather small, but very diverse group at the second half of the nineteenth century and the beginning of twentieth century: most of them shared progressive liberal views of their time (eg Leonid Kamarovsky, Feodor Martens), some sympathized as socialists (eg, Nikolai Golubev, Alexander Yaschenko), others shared socialist views and remained working in Russia after the Revolution (eg Mikhail Reisner, Vladimir Hrabar). Although this period is generally regarded as Russian doctrine's 'golden epoch' and scholarly writings on international law were plentiful, most of them tackled narrow issues, and only a few general courses were published.[58]

Halperin-Ginsburg's views of international law were formed by the positivist approach to it as well as by the Marxist theory of history and its potential to drive social change. She firmly believed in liberal democracy and the possibility of what would now be called the constitutionalization of international law. Halperin-Ginsburg did not tolerate violence; she understood both the necessity and the power of collective action in the common good. She adopted the basic principle of economic determinism and believed that the inevitable transition from the pre-capitalist to the capitalist stage should proceed gradually and peacefully. Understood in this way, Marxism gave her scientific grounds to believe that democratic social states would naturally replace autocratic regimes. She projected this idea on international relations: the single international power (court and legislature) should govern the international community in the universal human interests based on the rule of law.[59]

In 1916, she finished her first book on international law, *The World War and the Fate of International Law*,[60] in which she answered two questions: 'why international law is law?', and 'what will international law gain from the First World War?'. The first question explained why she dropped the untimely idea of the International Lawyers Society: sadly, the Russian academic community and the broader public displayed scepticism about international law.

According to Halperin-Ginsburg, nobody would deny the existence of an expanded international community capturing ever more spheres of life.[61] Famously, every social communication generates its own kind of rules and celebrates different achievements at every stage of its development: international law would be no exception.[62] With

[56] Елена Г-г, 'Недозволенные средства войны' *Киевская мысль* (Киев, 15 сентября 1914) [Elena G-g, 'Prohibited Methods of War' *Kyiv Mysl* (Kyiv, 15 September 1914)]; Елена Г-г, 'Морская война' *Киевская мысль* (Киев, 24 октября 1914) [Elena G-g, 'Naval Wafare' (Kyiv, 25 October 1914)]; Елена Г-г, 'Блокада' *Киевская мысль* (Киев, 23 января 1917) [Elena G-g, 'Blockade', *Kyiv Mysl* (Kyiv, 23 January 1917)]; Елена Г-г, 'Доктрина Монро' *Киевская мысль* (Киев 25 января 1917) [Elena G-g, 'Monroe Doctrine' *Kyiv Mysl* (Kyiv 25 January 1917)].

[57] Grigorovich-Barskaya (n 7) 44.

[58] Камиль Бекяшев, Григорий Стародубцев 'История науки международного права' в *История юр идических наук в России* (под ред Олег Кутафина, Виктор Блажеев и др. Москва, 2009) 208–51 [Kamil Bekyashev, Grigory Starodubtsev 'History of the Scholarship of International Law' in Oleg Kutafin, Victor Blazheev, and others (eds), *History of Legal Scholarship in Russia* (Moscow 2009) 208–51].

[59] Елена Гинзбург-Гальперина, *Мировая война и судьбы международного права* (тип. т-ва АС Суворина 'Новое время' 1916) [Helene Ginsburg-Halperin, *The World War and the Fate of International Law* (AS Suvorin's Publishing House 'Novoe Vremya' 1916) 14].

[60] Ginsburg-Halperin (n 59).

[61] ibid 9.

[62] ibid 15.

historical examples from international humanitarian law, she traced how states gradually changed their attitude to certain military practices and codified them into international conventions as social requirements evolved.

Answering to the lack-of-enforcement critique, she argued that people respect law not only threatened by sanctions, but also because of advanced legal consciousness. While people violated national laws with severe sanctions, they observed the Geneva Convention on the Wounded and Sick. She wrote that the democratization of international relations and the rise of international legal consciousness would remedy the lack of enforcement for three reasons.[63] First, by its nature, international law is based on a joint will and agreement in common interests. Halperin-Ginsburg criticized Germany for its misuse of international law, justifying aggression: its 'liberation of oppressed peoples'[64] threatened freedom, democracy, and law. Thus, the development of international law is impossible when one state 'enslaves it'[65] by force.

Second, people are estranged from international law and thus frustrated. In contrast to national law that gradually involves people in its formation, they participate in international relations through their governments. Thus, people must strengthen parliamentary control over international relations as governmental power rests on popular sovereignty and not the ruler's will.

Finally, although international communication exceeded national borders and penetrated gradually national life as states increasingly faced tasks requiring joint efforts—epidemics, postal, telegraph, and railway communication—the media, sadly, did not cover international law wide enough. Halperin-Ginsburg did it herself and called on the Russian press to react actively to breaches of international law, as 'law is . . . a readiness to take up arms against its violation'.[66]

Halperin-Ginsburg's response to the second question, 'what will international law gain from the First World War?', was twofold. First, no state could isolate from the international community regardless of its military power.[67] Second, the First World War boosted international cooperation, thus more peoples and states would engage with international law leading to its democratization. 'We cannot downgrade the progress [of law] to a purely mechanical process. . . .; law cannot be detached from historical processes, but . . . the most important for the formation of law is the living participation of people'.[68] The war has become 'a school of social and state organization' and the adaptation to a crisis created new forms of social and political relations: the 'principle of the independence of private production' changed as 'voice of the masses merged with the interest of the general welfare of the state, and the revolution, bloodless, occurred'.[69] She concluded that Russia must enter the peace conference well-prepared to voice its stance on the new world order: 'to win a war means both military superiority and readiness to use victory for the future peace'.[70]

[63] ibid 11 and 61.
[64] ibid 28.
[65] ibid 29.
[66] ibid 21.
[67] ibid 56.
[68] ibid 22.
[69] ibid 55.
[70] ibid 64.

After the February 1917 Revolution, Halperin-Ginsburg joined Plekhanov's political group *Edinstvo* and actively engaged in the Constituent Assembly pre-election campaign. From 1917 to 1920, Kyiv was an epicentre of armed conflicts, and in 1919, the Bolsheviks ordered Halperin-Ginsburg's apartment requisition; she escaped saving her valuables, her library, and folk artworks. She hid in Kyiv and without access to libraries finished her second book, *The World of Russian Revolution or Woodrow Wilson's World? On the Guarantees of the Lasting Peace.*[71] The book's title could be read as a play on words as the Russian word '*мир*' means both 'world' and 'peace'. She dedicated it to Georgi Plekhanov who died in 1918; stylistically its first part reads as a tribute to his *Our Disagreements.*[72]

The book could be logically divided in three parts. In the first part, Halperin-Ginsburg criticized Zimmerwaldists' foreign policy ideas as utopian, leading post-revolutionary Russia to a dead end. In the second part, comparing the lasting peace formulas by Revolutionary Russia and the United States, Halperin-Ginsburg explained why the former failed. In conclusion, she presented her own theory of international law.

According to Halperin-Ginsburg, Revolutionary Russia, obsessed with internal power struggles, missed an excellent opportunity to participate *on par* with other states in the peace conference and transform international relations after the First World War. Her criticism of the Zimmervaldists and Bolsheviks revolved around the utopian nature of their project and ignorance of international law.[73] They took foreign policy ideas—a focus on domestic transformation, the unrestricted right of people to self-determination, the ban on annexations, and secret diplomacy—from the French Revolution but never tested them against political reality.[74] Socialists have always fought on the domestic battlefield and paid no attention to international law. Disinterested in the prerequisites for the change and the proletariat's capability of the mission, Bolsheviks did not know how to treat the First World War in their political program.[75] Regrettably, their efforts hindered a worldwide discussion on the Peace Treaty. Halperin-Ginsburg saw the Bolsheviks' peace formula as contradictory: they denied co-operation; and their understanding of people's right to self-determination conflicted with the prohibition of annexations. She saw the key problem in the Russian revolutionary movement's organization. Narrow circles and isolation from political life made its adherents feel less responsible to the people than to their doctrine. Instead of consolidating to win the war and agreeing on the future international relations organization, the Bolsheviks fought against the phantom Russian bourgeoisie, spread artificial hatred, misoriented the army, and eroded the credibility of the Russian Government to seize its reins. Thus, Bolshevik foreign policy supported their domestic power struggle. She further criticized them for dropping the principle

[71] Елена Гинзбург-Гальперин, *Мир русской революции или мир Вильсона? Гарантии прочного мира* (Тип. 'Культура и знание' 1919). [Helene Ginsburg-Halperin, *The World of Russian Revolution or Woodrow Wilson's World? On the Guarantees of the Lasting Peace* (Kultura i Znanie Publishing House 1919).

[72] This is the only direct reference to any socialist theoretician in her legal scholarship.

[73] While the emigrant Russian doctrine of international law was formed in the 1920s, the Soviet theorists would generally fill this gap only in the 1940s. Eugeny Korovin published his first book in the 1920s and emigrant colleagues criticized it. See: Starodubtsev (n 4) 32–33.

[74] Ginsburg-Halperin (n 71) 14–27.

[75] ibid 28–40.

of the rule of law: a flawed court system and deficient law are always better than their absence she argued.[76]

In comparison, she further turned to Woodrow Wilson's democratic peace formula. Briefly looking at the American history of international relations, she praised the United States for promoting a peaceful settlement of disputes to the rule of regional customary international law and endeavouring to codify regional international law on the Pan-American Conferences. As war is the greatest of all evils, international law must absorb the practical historical experience of the United States. Sadly, Russian and European scholars neglected American practice because of the Monroe Doctrine. However, the United States already had democracy; their Congress played a more active role in foreign policy than European Parliaments. Halperin-Ginsburg conceded to United States interventions in the affairs of smaller states under the Olney Doctrine. Still, she called such interventions 'enlightened' and named only instances that were social or infrastructural in their nature.[77]

For Halperin-Ginsburg, a permanent international court and international organizations were indispensable for the just and peaceful world order. While international organizations would act in the international community's interests, the court would resolve disputes, making resorting to force unnecessary. International law codification would be further essential for the international relations democratization and rise of international legal consciousness. As only democratic states could truly ensure the lasting peace, international rules must become both national and international law. Contrary to the position of many states and scholars, this would not violate state sovereignty and impermissibly intervene into states' internal affairs.

To understand the function of sovereignty in international relations, Halperin-Ginsburg traced its history: it has always been a flexible tool that became absolute only in response to concrete threats to states.[78] As the First World War threatened *all* states, it would be in the common interests to limit sovereignty by international law for the lasting democratic peace as the common value. She saw the notion of absolute sovereignty as not living, an *a priori* concept, and unable to evolve. For her, international law must enact the real change, as states have already delegated *some* decision-making and enforcement powers to administrative unions, restricting their sovereignty.

The non-interference, as the practical manifestation of sovereignty, prohibits to intervene into domestic affairs, including state's constitution, political custom, domestic legislation. Absolute sovereignty would have led to the 'squaring the circle' problem: how to establish an international legal order on the model of a single state without violating the least of every existing state's sovereignty?[79] For her, as non-interference evolved together with sovereignty, the proper question should be: how to normalize the instances of intervention? Adherents to absolute sovereignty already put the question this way. For example, Feodor Martens called the principle of non-intervention 'the greatest conquest of international law', and any exceptions to it

[76] Елена Г-г, 'Революция и суд' *Призыв* (Париж, 9 января 1918) [Elena G-g, 'Revolution and Courts' *Prizyv* (Париж, 9 January 1918)].

[77] Ginsburg-Halperin (n 71) 42–59.

[78] ibid 28–40.

[79] ibid 80.

extremely dangerous. However, he justified exceptions necessitated by the interests of international communication.[80] According to Halperin-Ginsburg, an international legal order should tolerate absolute sovereignty as little as states—unrestricted will of individuals. With reference to Lassalle, she argued that the unhindered enjoyment of individual rights would be insufficient *per se*, as moral social life in addition required solidarity of interest, commonality, and reciprocity in development. Individual states must recognize the higher order above them and submit to it, raising international law above the arbitrariness of individual states.[81]

She criticized the inviolability of states' constitutions: it should matter if a state entering international communication is liberal, absolutist, or despotic. Otherwise, international law would be compelled to serve the absolutism of a national law. She made a twofold conclusion: first, states must change their laws and, if necessary, constitutions to comply with international law; second, states must not invoke domestic law, including constitutions, to disobey international law.

Turning to people's right to self-determination, she conceded that the notion of 'people/nationality' required meticulous study. Criticizing Bolsheviks, she wrote 'to claim that international motives negate national ones is to repeat the old fallacy that the state negates the human personality'.[82] In democratic states, all peoples would enjoy their right to self-determination internally, making secession necessary only under stringent conditions. The unrestricted right, to the contrary, would bring chaos in international relations.[83]

In conclusion, Halperin-Ginsburg elaborated on the nature of international law and its role in international relations. No progress of human culture and law occurred only by the wisdom of individuals; it depended on the intellectual growth of peoples and the objective course of social development.[84] For the success of law, theoretical projects meant less than partial reforms.[85]

The gradual democratization of international and national relations would guarantee the lasting peace: democratic states waged wars less easily.[86] Referring to von Jhering, she recalled that law was a public good , which history did not give any people as a gift, but they acquired it through difficult struggles and often bloody feats. The conquest of democracy was such a feat in the people's turn to international law.[87] International legal solidarity would only be possible with civil legal solidarity within states. In order for persons to feel themselves members of a state, they must overcome the sense of alienation as humans. This is only possible when the rights of every person become a secured fortress. To imbue with the interests of a citizen one must first imbue with the interests of a person: the same should apply to states.[88]

[80] ibid 81.
[81] ibid 94.
[82] ibid 102.
[83] ibid 109
[84] ibid 120.
[85] ibid 122.
[86] ibid 129.
[87] ibid 122.
[88] ibid 130.

In 1919, Halperin-Ginsburg moved with her husband to Odessa and then back to Kyiv. Cut off from her studies, she took care of the people ruined by the Revolution and dreamt of moving abroad. In 1921, the couple moved to Berlin and later brought their family there. Grieving over the educated Russians' fate, she organized help: together with a group of Swedish women teachers and the New York Committee for Aid to Hungry, she sent aid to Russian educators, writers, scholars, and public figures. Simultaneously, Halperin-Ginsburg started her third book on the League of Nations' first years and an essay on the Pan-American Conferences. She was invited to lecture on international law at Paris Public University,[89] shortly before her death on 18 May 1922 at the age of thirty-eight.

Conclusion

Halperin-Ginsburg was an exponent of her epoch. As a socialist and later feminist, she joined the feminist movement resulting from an intense academic interest in social issues, international law, and equal rights. Halperin-Ginsburg became a feminist when the women's question hindered her own legal career. She was acutely concerned about the archaism of law that was lagging behind social development. Her personal struggles and encounters with unjust legal practices and social problems, including criminal justice procedures and women's lack of opportunity to pursue the legal profession, led to her activism. She genuinely believed in local communities' potential in solving social problems and the progressive forces of equal education, media, and, of course, law. She picked up social issues and turned them into her legal projects, including the 'woman attorney' campaign and international relations transformation after the First World War, despite the many setbacks she faced as a woman in law and international law.

[89] Most likely, by Boris Mirkine-Guetzévitch. See Mirkine-Guetzévitch (n 9).

42

Human Rights and Communist Internationalism

On Inji Aflatoun and the Surrealists

Mai Taha[*]

Perhaps not the most likely candidate for a *Portrait on Women in International Law* of *New Names* and *Forgotten Faces*, for Inji Aflatoun (1924–1989) was neither *an international lawyer*, nor *a new name*, nor *a forgotten face*. Today, she is remembered as a famous Egyptian communist painter, a feminist, a human rights activist, and a former political prisoner. In an attempt to open a fresh archive of international law beyond that of the League of Nations, the United Nations (UN), and national state archives, I look into the barracks of activism, specifically radical activism that invoked some notion of international human rights. Through Inji Aflatoun and the surrealists, I want to think about how radical movements have used human rights when they were rooted in socialist internationalism, anti-imperialism, and feminist solidarity. I look at how they assembled a different vision of internationalism and solidarity from the one dreamed up by international lawyers at the *Palais Nationale* in Geneva that so comfortably embodied a civilizational hierarchy founded upon liberal internationalism and free trade. I am interested in writing a profile of the activist–thinker in action, in her socio-political milieu and in her historical context with its contradictions and conflicts. As if to recall some remnants of radical uses of human rights from history, this portrait engages with the past to disrupt and unsettle the present state of international human rights that is mired in the politics of neoliberalism, neocolonialism, and white feminism. To that end, this is a profile with a political agenda. This agenda is neither about rescuing human rights nor about letting the 'subaltern speak',[1] for she was certainly speaking. It is about how Inji Aflatoun was able to invoke human rights as one fragment within a constellation of intersecting struggles. More specifically, the radicality of her uses and disuses of law and rights cannot be fully articulated without understanding that it was part of this constellation of struggles that spanned from armed resistance to communist agitation and political art.

[*] I am thankful to Immi Tallgren for her feedback and for curating a series of brilliant workshops in the midst of the pandemic. I am particularly grateful to Chris Gevers for his close reading of an earlier version of this text and for his characteristically insightful comments.

[1] Gayatri Spivak, 'Can the Subaltern Speak?' in *Marxism and the Interpretation of Culture* (MacMillan Education 1988) 272.

Mai Taha, *Human Rights and Communist Internationalism* In: *Portraits of Women in International Law*.
Edited by: Immi Tallgren, Oxford University Press. © Mai Taha 2023. DOI: 10.1093/oso/9780198868453.003.0042

Figure 42.1 Inji Aflatoun in her studio in Cairo, Egypt.
Source: Courtesy of Safarkhan Art Gallery Est. 1968.

Long Live Degenerate Art!

Aflatoun came from a well-connected bourgeois family, studied at elite French schools, and grew up in a sheltered and comfortable life. As a high school student, she was introduced to the ideas of surrealism and socialism initially through her art teacher Kamel Telmisany, and later through her participation in exhibitions organized by the surrealist Art and Freedom Group or *Jama'at al-Fann wa al-Hurriya* (JFH for the Arabic acronym) in Cairo of which Telmisany was a founding member.[2] The group's objectives were, to put it simply, 'to tear down and remake the world'.[3] JFH was the Egypt chapter of the International Federation of Independent Revolutionary Art

[2] Don LaCoss, 'Art and Liberty: Surrealism in Egypt' (Fall–Winter 2009–2010) Communicating Vessels 21, 28–33. The group's name is sometimes translated as 'Art and Liberty' and at others 'Art and Freedom'. I choose to use 'Art and Freedom' because liberty has different connotations in the English language than the Arabic *Hurriyya*.

[3] Kaelen Wilson-Goldie, 'Public/Private: The Many Lives of "Rebel Painter" Inji Efflatoun' (2016) Afterall 73–85, 76.

(FIARI in French), which was established in the summer of 1938 in Coyoacán, Mexico City at Frida Kahlo's and Diego Rivera's iconic blue house by surrealist poet André Breton and the exiled Leon Trotsky.[4]

The Egyptian surrealists, following the broader surrealist movement around the world, understood the real and material conditions of life under capitalism but imagined the surreal, where the founding entails the dissolving and opens up the possibilities for improvization and revolution.[5] But in the Egyptian context, these new possibilities needed to grapple with the realities of racial hierarchy manifested in the British colonial occupation of Egypt (1882–1954). Their internationalism rejected fascism, colonialism, and the monarchy that supported the British presence in the country. Writing against traditional and state sanctioned art, the group authored their famous manifesto 'Long Live Degenerate Art!' (*Yahya al-Fann al-Munhatt*) which called for embracing distorted imagery to 'capture social truths (and ultimately precipitate social renewal)'.[6] This manifesto was a response to the Degenerate 'Art' (*Entartete 'Kunst'*) exhibition that opened in Munich 1937, which was a Nazi propaganda exhibition that denigrated the works of artists such as Otto Dix, Marc Chagall, Max Beckmann, and many others, by establishing links between modernism, mental illness, and biological imperfection.[7] By adopting this manifesto as one of its early texts, the JFH professed their anti-fascist and internationalist politics at the height of the rise of fascism in Europe, and only a few years after Fascist Italy's colonial occupation of neighbouring Libya.

The JFH became the first socialist art organization to be led by Arabic-speaking Egyptians. They organized a series of what they called *Ma'arid al-Fann al-Hurr* (The Exhibitions of the Free Art) between the years of 1940 and 1945. One of them, held in the famous Immobilia building in downtown Cairo, was designed as a labyrinth with 'handshaped cutouts upside-down posters hanging along the way in an attempt to confuse rather than guide'.[8] These exhibitions were not simply spaces for display, but performances that attempted to disrupt its visitors' daily logics of 'bourgeois imagery'.[9] These performances were also directly responding to nationalist and institutionalized art by improvizing new, internationalist, and imaginative

[4] Alexandra Dika Seggerman, 'Al-Tatawwur (Evolution): An Enhanced Timeline of Egyptian Surrealism' (2013) 19 Dada/Surrealism 1–26, 1.

[5] When Walter Benjamin spoke of the surrealists, he remembered Rimbaud's book *Saison en enfer*, where in the margins of his personal copy next to the passage 'on the silk of the seas and the arctic flowers', Rimbaud writes: 'there's no such thing', announcing and perhaps celebrating the negation and fictionality of his own work. The surrealists in Egypt were interested in a similar project in their own artwork and political activism. See Walter Benjamin, *Surrealism: The Last Snapshot of the European Intelligentsia* (Routledge 1989) 49. Special thanks to the Cairo-New-York Walter Benjamin Reading Group. See also, Robin Kelley, 'Internationale Blues: Revolutionary Pessimism and the Politics of Solidarity' (2019) Annual Lecture of the Internationalism, Cosmopolitanism and the Politics of Solidarity research group at LSE.

[6] Anneka Lenssen, Sarah Rogers, and Nada Shabout (eds), *Modern Art in the Arab World: Primary Documents* (The Museum of Modern Art 2018) 87.

[7] Don LaCoss, 'Egyptian Surrealism and "Degenerate Art" in 1939' (2010) 18(1) Arab Studies Journal 78–117, 86.

[8] Laura Galián Hernández and Costantino Paonessa, 'Caught between Internationalism, Transnationalism and Immigration: A Brief Account of the History of Anarchism in Egypt until 1945' (2018) 26(1) Anarchist Studies 29–54, 45, citing Patrick Kane.

[9] ibid, citing Maria Cavadia.

futures.[10] Through the art, thought, and activism of Inji Aflatoun, I engage with how this improvization toward new internationalist futures sometimes took the form of a demand for human rights.

International Human Rights and Praxis

Critical international law scholarship has, by now, put forward a strong critique of liberal internationalism.[11] Scholars have rightly pointed out that the professed internationalism of international law and its institutions came with a gradation of sovereignty along the lines of the now familiar spectrum of civilization. Similarly, the universality of human rights has been criticized by post-colonial, post-modern, and feminist thinkers.[12] On a philosophical level, a claim of universality is a claim of abstraction, where the individual protected somehow always ends up being a mannequin of a white, heterosexual, middle class, and able-bodied male. It is therefore unsurprising that the discourse of universal human rights has been mobilized in defense of wealth and power, as Jessica Whyte has brilliantly argued.[13] This discourse has also denigrated revolutionary politics as 'totalitarian', promoting instead an individualist and neoliberal 'belief that a functioning competitive market required an adequate moral and legal foundation'.[14] Radha D'Souza also shows how social movements have not been able to let go of rights even when they recognize that those rights 'have always been an essential precondition for capitalism and colonialism, for displacement and dispossession throughout capitalism's history'.[15] Even the radical indigenous critique of individual property rights, D'Souza argues, has been diluted by the reification of the dualism of property and human rights through their call for a human right to land.[16] Afterall, property rights are the fulcrum of all rights, as Karl Marx has argued.[17] Marx's words in his famous essay, 'On the Jewish Question', still echo in today's leftist critique of human rights. Ultimately, rights would never drive human emancipation. At its best, rights can push for political emancipation within the chains of class society under capitalism.[18]

While many leftist activists understood the critique of human rights on both the philosophical and practical levels, they sometimes still chose to deploy this language in litigation and organizing. Here, I am interested in probing this idea through Inji Aflatoun's activism. For her, it was not about the invocation of law and rights per se,

[10] ibid.

[11] See eg Susan Marks, *The Riddle of All Constitutions: International Law, Democracy, and the Critique of Ideology* (OUP 2000).

[12] Makau Mutua, *Human Rights: A Political and Cultural Critique* (University of Pennsylvania Press 2002); David Kennedy, 'The International Human Rights of Movement: Part of the Problem?' (2002) 15 Harvard Human Rights Journal 101; Wendy Brown and Janet Halley (eds), *Left Legalism/Left Critique* (Duke University Press 2002).

[13] Jessica Whyte, *The Morals of the Market: Human Rights and the Rise of Neoliberalism* (Verso 2019) 3.

[14] ibid 4, 8.

[15] Rahda D'Souza, *What's Wrong with Rights?* (Pluto Press 2017) 9.

[16] ibid 7.

[17] Karl Marx, 'On the Jewish Question' (1843) in Karl Marx, *Early Writings*, Rodney Livingstone and Gregor Benton trs, (Penguin 1990) 211, 221.

[18] ibid.

but about how international human rights fit within a broader vision of a just society. Far from being a child of the 1970's United Nations, international human rights were invoked by many movements around the world.[19] Most importantly, however, human rights were never enough. For Inji Aflatoun, illegality was a perfectly ethical and revolutionary choice. In fact, she was a member of an illegal and underground communist movement for many years. The invocation of international human rights was only one tactic of agitation and organization among many that sought to transform global society.[20] In one police report, the surrealists' journal, *al-Tatawwur* was described as a publication aimed at spreading anarchy, destroying morals and religion, and bringing about 'the collapse of the pillars of the social and legal establishment necessary for running the country'.[21] In fact, the surrealist JFH was put under surveillance in 1945, and forty-five of its members were arrested, after publishing a pamphlet calling for a classless society.[22] It was precisely the consciousness of the relationship between law and violence that helped Aflatoun formulate a more radical conception of international human rights through praxis.

'Eighty Million Women with Us': Another Internationalism

In 1944, communist women formed the League of Women Students and Graduates from University and Egyptian Institutes. As a leading member of the League, Inji Aflatoun traveled to Paris in 1945 to participate in the Women's International Democratic Federation (WIDF) congress. Established in Paris, November 1945, and known as a space that cultivated leftist, feminist, and anti-colonial solidarity, the WIDF attracted women from all over the Global South. Many of its founding members were active in the armed resistance against Nazism and fascism in Europe, while some survived prisons and concentration camps.[23] It became the largest post-Second World War international women's organization in terms of its membership. It was founded on four basic principles: 'anti-fascism, lasting peace, women's rights, and better conditions for children'.[24] Later the WIDF would help initiate the famous 1975 United National International Women's Year, which kickstarted the movement toward the creation of a binding international treaty for the protection of women's rights.

[19] Most famously, Samuel Moyn wrote a new historiography of human rights that locates its birth in the 1970s in Europe and America. See Samuel Moyn, *The Last Utopia: Human Rights in History* (Harvard University Press 2010). Joseph Slaughter writes an alternative history of human rights that changes the locus of the story from the West to the Global South. Unlike Moyn, he argues that the 1970s marked, not a rebirth, but a neoliberal hijacking of human rights. See Joseph Slaughter, 'Hijacking Human Rights: Neoliberalism, the New Historiography, and the End of the Third World' (2018) 40 Human Rights Quarterly 735–75. See also, Upendra Baxi, *The Future of Human Rights* (OUP 2007).

[20] On strategy and tactics, see Robert Knox, 'Marxism, International Law and Political Strategy' (2009) 22(3) Leiden Journal of International Law 413–36.

[21] LaCoss, 'Art and Liberty' (n 2).

[22] Hernández and Paonessa (n 8) 47. Kamel later formed the Bread and Freedom group, which drew membership from the workers of Cairo's Shubra al-Khaima and Matariyya suburbs.

[23] Francisca de Haan, 'Continuing Cold War Paradigms in Western Historiography of Transnational Women's Organizations: The Case of the Women's International Democratic Federation (WIDF)' (2010) 4 Women's History Review 547–73, 550

[24] ibid 548.

Specifically, the Federation pushed for the adoption of the legally binding convention instead of the 1967 Declaration on the Elimination of Discrimination against Women, which was not legally binding.[25]

After speaking at the founding congress of the Federation in 1945 on behalf of Egyptian women, Aflatoun published her important book, *Eighty Million Women with Us*, recounting her experience at the Paris congress, whose participants represented eighty million women around the world. In her book, she connects the anti-fascist movement to the anti-colonial one, explaining that Fascism could be understood as a 'despicable and monstrous' form of colonialism that eviscerates rights and freedoms. It is the dictatorship of a small minority from the bourgeoisie over the rest of the population.[26] Recalling the speech of Marie-Claude Vaillant-Couturier, the notable member of the French Resistance and the French representative at the congress, Aflatoun states that no capitalist country is safe from regressing into fascism, which also lends itself to patriarchy, thus making a theoretical and historical connection between the logics of different structures of oppression.[27]

Aflatoun's book is a manifesto for another internationalism than the one imagined by international institutions. International women's rights in the book are conceptualized differently. Any notion of women's rights, she argues, would have to account for the working woman, both in the factory and at home, the colonized woman, and the woman living under fascist regimes. As a factory worker, the working woman doesn't earn equal pay for equal work, and as a worker at home, she bears the burden of child-rearing, or what the autonomist feminists have called 'reproductive labour',[28] without any return or wage.[29] As a colonized woman, she is subjected to the injustice and exploitation of colonialism and capitalism.[30] As a woman living under fascism, she is stripped of her rights and reduced to a mere tool of reproduction for the strength of the fascist state.[31] Aflatoun's vision of international human rights would embody all of those women at the same time. Citing interventions made by the Soviet, Chinese, French, Spanish, Austrian, and other representatives, she addresses Egyptian women, making the claim that all of the struggles of these women are part of their own struggles in Egypt.

Aflatoun recounts how women's rights were imagined at the Congress: rights were conceived as complex and multi-layered entitlements that are informed by radical democratic principles and that embody the different experiences of women across the world.[32] Rather than speak to the abstract individual, human rights would embody difference. Rather than serve as 'morals of the market', human rights would become part of the tactics of the oppressed, neither as an end in itself, nor as a sufficient

[25] ibid.
[26] Inji Aflatoun, *Thamanoun 'Imra'a Ma'na: Al-Mu'tamar Al-Nisa'i Al-Dawli Al-Dimoqrati* [Eighty-million Women with Us: The International Women's Congress] *(Paris November 1945)* (Dar Al-Fajr Publishers 1948) 14.
[27] ibid 15.
[28] Silvia Federici, 'Social Reproduction Theory: History, Issues and Present Challenges' (2019) 2 Radical Philosophy 4.
[29] Aflatoun, *Thamanoun 'Imra'a Ma'na* (n 26) 11.
[30] ibid.
[31] ibid 15.
[32] ibid 35, 36.

one. In the congress, their vision of women's rights entailed a re-writing of curricula where principles of equality and radical democracy would replace imperialist and fascist education.[33] Their vision of human rights also entailed rethinking women's labour through demanding new public institutional structures that recognized the specificity of women's work at home and in the factory. Their idea of maternity leave included at least a two months' paid vacation during pregnancy. They demanded the establishment of a global centre for children impacted by the violence of war and colonialism.[34] These ideas seem like a far cry from what later became the Universal Declaration of Human Rights (UDHR), after which the work done by the feminists of the WIDF was effaced from the history of international human rights.

For Inji Aflatoun, the WIDF represented a global feminist solidarity organization that, as was proven only a few hours after delivering her speech, would threaten those in power and build an internationalist movement against all systems of oppression and exploitation. As she was celebrating with her comrades the success of the congress, Aflatoun was called to Quai d'Orsay for questioning at the Ministry of Foreign Affairs.[35] While she attempted to go to the scheduled meeting, she lost her way and couldn't make an appearance, but on arriving at the Alexandria port back from Paris, she was arrested along with Safiyya Fadel and Souad Kamel who were also attending the congress.[36] Her bag—full of socialist books, reports, and pamphlets from the congress—was confiscated. Since that moment after attending the WIDF congress, a file at the state security was opened under her name, and she was added to the blacklist.[37] This would not be her last confinement. Three years later, she would be called to the police station and accused of 'membership in an international organization [WIDF] without the [colonial] government's permission'.[38] She would later be banned from entering France partly as a result of her activism for the release of the Algerian revolutionary and member of the FLN, Jamila Bouhired.[39] After independence, Aflatoun would be also targeted by the Nasser regime, and would spend four and a half years in prison for her communist organizing.

Intersectionality in Art and Thought

The WIDF was actively involved in the United Nations from the beginning, but as a result of Cold War politics at the UN, its consultative status in category B was withdrawn from 1954 to 1967.[40] Indeed, many members of the WIDF self-identified as communists, yet others who had important leadership positions in the Federation never did.[41] Still, the WIDF was known as an organization that attracted socialists

[33] ibid 36.
[34] ibid 35, 36.
[35] Inji Aflatoun, *Mudthakarat Inji Aflatoun* [The Autobiography of Inji Aflatoun] (Dar Souad Al-Sabbah 1993) 61.
[36] ibid 62, 63.
[37] ibid.
[38] ibid 100.
[39] ibid 141.
[40] de Haan (n 23) 550.
[41] In fact, Ceza Nabaraouy, the Egyptian vice-President of WIDF and long-time collaborator with Inji Aflatoun, was not a communist. Others, such as Dr Andrea Andreen who represented the WIDF before the

and was often viewed with suspicion. Other organizations, such as the International Alliance of Women (IAW), competed with what they called 'the communist women who would organize the Near East', referring to the WIDF.[42] In fact, many feminists 'on the "right" side of the Curtain, assumed that communists ... could not possibly be feminist'.[43] This stigma was primarily as a result of a general fear of communism as morally dubious and dangerous to the principles of European democracy. But on a more critical level, orthodox versions of communism have sometimes imposed class reductionist worldviews where gender and race play only secondary roles, if any. Inji Aflatoun rejected the position that feminism was incompatible with communism,[44] a position taken by both liberal feminists and orthodox communists. As the Egyptian delegate in the WIDF Congress in Paris, she shared the experiences of 'the colonial dimension of gender inequalities' with other attending members.[45] Her intervention was about how 'the liberation of the masses and end of imperialism had to be linked to women's liberation'.[46] Most importantly, her feminism was intersectional even if this term was not yet part of the global activist vocabulary, and even if, by now, it has lost some of its radical potentialities.[47]

This intersectional analysis grew from her involvement, not only with the underground communist movement in Egypt, but also from her work with the surrealists, who did not fall into the same trap that many communist parties fell for around the world. They were interested in human emancipation and were critical of orthodox versions of communism. In her autobiography, Aflatoun recounts her experience of reading Marxist literature for the first time after being exposed to the ideas of the surrealist Art and Freedom Group (JFH). 'I was impressed by how this literature presented a total analysis of the problems facing society—poverty, class exploitation, and the double exploitation of women in capitalist societies, as well as imperialism and national liberation', she remembers.[48]

Her human rights work was informed by both the eclectic politics of the surrealists, as well as the traditional Marxist analysis of the communist movement in Egypt. But this human rights work was only one part of her story. Key to understanding her activism on international human rights is to recognize that it was one tactic among many, again, a fragment within a constellation of struggles.

At the height of the anti-colonial moment, she co-founded a new women's council to support the armed resistance against the British occupation in 1951.[49] The women's

UN in 1954, the Australian Jessie Street, who was the only woman on the Australian delegation in the 1945 founding conference of the United Nations, also did not identify as communists. ibid 555.

[42] ibid 552.

[43] Jadwiga E Pieper Mooney, 'Fighting Fascism and Forging New Political Activism: The Women's International Democratic Federation (WIDF) in the Cold War' in Jadwiga E Pieper Mooney and Fabio Lanza (eds), *Decentering Cold War History: Local and Global Change* (Routledge 2012) 54.

[44] ibid.

[45] ibid 61.

[46] ibid.

[47] Sara Salem, 'Intersectionality and its Discontents: Intersectionality as "Traveling Theory"' (2016) 25(4) European Journal of Women's Studies 403–18.

[48] Aflatoun, *Mudthakarat Inji Aflatoun*, (n 35) 32. (translation is mine).

[49] ibid 128, 129.

popular council called for a complete economic boycott of all British goods. They established support networks to help workers who withheld their labour from British camps, and they formed nursing and medical units to support those wounded in struggle.[50] While working on the ground in the anti-colonial resistance, she held an art exhibition of her most recent artworks in March 1952, showing paintings on the crimes of colonialism, as well as the injustices facing Egyptian women. As if stretching time, the exhibition was held only two months after the Cairo Fire and a few months before the *coup-d'etat* that would topple British rule in the country. The exhibition embodied the complexity of her activism and thought, from international human rights, to communist internationalism, feminism, and the radical role of art in society. One of the pieces exhibited, *We will not forget*, was gifted by Aflatoun to Cairo University and was displayed in the student housing. It would later become a central image in anti-colonial print activism on campus. It was copied by university students and used widely in their pamphlets and posters to organize within the anti-colonial movement, until the painting was removed from the building by the administration for 'causing trouble'.[51]

Aflatoun would continue her activism after independence from Britain, despite being targeted by the Nasser regime for her involvement in the underground communist movement. After the 1956 Tripartite aggression of England, France, and Israel on Egypt (known as the Suez crisis), she joined the women's committee of the people's resistance, and led the branch in the working-class neighborhood of el-Gammaliyya in Cairo. In those branches women were trained on the use of weapons, and were provided a space to discuss the political and social threats facing the country as a result of the aggression.

For the WIDF, the Suez crisis was taken seriously. Aflatoun reports that the Federation formed a commission of inquiry on the violence committed during the aggression, comprised of four women from India, Finland, Romania, and Lebanon, and chaired by the Secretary General of the WIDF, the Italian Angiola Minella.[52] As the Harold Macmillan government placed a ban on any 'lessons learnt' from the Suez crisis let alone form a public inquiry,[53] the WIDF commission arrived in Port-Said in 1957 to investigate the impact of the aggression on the population. They also attended a conference organized by Aflatoun under the auspices of the women's committee of the people's resistance. The WIDF's final report denounced the aggression and called for women around the world to stand in solidarity with the Egyptian people against this aggression.[54] As if by mimicry and mockery,[55] the WIDF chose a mechanism that was quite commonly used by both the League of Nations and later the United Nations. The WIDF's commission of inquiry, however, reimagined its role to solidify relationships of solidarity and internationalism. Almost mocking the poverty of other

[50] ibid.

[51] ibid 138.

[52] ibid 166.

[53] Charlotte Peevers, *The Politics of Justifying Force: The Suez Crisis, the Iraq War and International Law* (OUP 2013) 124.

[54] Aflatoun, *Mudthakarat Inji Aflatoun* (n 35) 167.

[55] I borrow this expression from Zeina Ghandour. See Zeina Ghandour, *A Discourse on Domination in Mandate Palestine: Imperialism, Property and Insurgency* (Routledge 2010).

League/UN commissions of inquiry, the WIDF commission read the Suez crisis as also a women's question.

In the same year and during the Algerian war for independence, Jamila Bouhired would be sentenced to death by a French court, despite the efforts put in her defence submissions by Jacques Vérges.[56] Considering this a show trial, Aflatoun organized a women's march to the UN building in Cairo demanding an intervention by Dag Hammarskjold to free Bouhired from the guillotine sentence. Aflatoun recalls that they were attacked by the police and beaten inside the UN building, as they screamed 'Save Jamila, Hammarskjold! Damn you, France.'[57] Hammarskjold, of course, did not intervene, but the WIDF would invite Inji Aflatoun to draw a portrait of Jamila, which was distributed to all member organizations around the world as part of a global campaign to free Jamila Bouhired that was launched on 9 March 1959, coinciding with international women's day.[58]

Conclusion

Inji Aflatoun lived her life struggling with contradictions—between her communist politics and her upper-class subject position, her French education and her attachment to Arabic as the language of struggle, and between the legality and illegality of her tactics. This portrait was an attempt to think about the life around human rights demands: the spaces of activism, and the daily life of organizing, from the moments of solidarity, triumphs and elations to, as Jill Richards put it, moments of 'impasse, boredom, and failure'.[59] While rights often depoliticize and abstract, the life around human rights demands does not, especially if this life is informed by anti-colonial, feminist, and internationalist thought. International human rights were neither an end nor a sufficient tactic of resistance. Aflatoun's invocation of human rights was simply one fragment in a constellation of struggles that also included armed resistance, political art activism, as well as her commitment to the illegal communist movement. This constellation of struggles conditioned her understanding of international human rights, away from abstraction and liberal internationalism and towards embodying difference, radical democracy, and socialist internationalism. Today, the state commemorates her only as an artist, but not as a communist and international human rights activist. There is a street named after her father, Hassan Aflatoun, who was apparently an important entomologist, but not after her. And through the mysterious works of serendipity, I lived on that street in Cairo for more than twenty years.

[56] Jaques Vérges, 'The Defense of Djamila Bouhired' (1990) available at <https://www.marxists.org/archive/verges/1990/djamila-bouhired.htm>.

[57] Aflatoun, *Mudthakarat Inji Aflatoun* (n 35) 193.

[58] ibid 195.

[59] Jill Richards, *The Fury Archives: Female Citizenship, Human Rights, and the International Avant-Gardes* (Columbia University Press 2020) 2.

43
Fearless Speech
A Portrait of UN Typist Shirley Hazzard

Dianne Otto

> I was 20 and I was part of that feeling of hope that came into the world with the end of the [second world] war. I went, like many other people then, to apply to the United Nations in a spirit of idealism, little dreaming that idealism was the last thing that was wanted there.[1]

In this portrait taken in 2003, many years after leaving her United Nations (UN) job, Shirley Hazzard 'demurely' conveys some of the hopefulness that she speaks of. Her unswerving determination to revive that idealism is less obvious. Like many young women of her time, Hazzard, Australian expatriate, was eager to take advantage of the opportunities promised by the UN Charter's commitment to women's equal participation in its work.[2] She hoped that her employment would enable her to take part in shaping a new world order committed to promoting peace and human rights. Like Frank Moorhouse's fictional Edith Campbell Berry,[3] who was drawn by similar ideals to work for the League of Nations three decades earlier, her hopes were dashed. Unlike Campbell Berry who held a diplomatic post in Geneva, Hazzard worked for the UN Secretariat in a clerical position between 1952 and 1961, with no power to influence organizational policy or practice. As she said, 'I typed' and 'I was still typing when I had the exalted title of administrative assistant in development programs'.[4] The atmosphere was one of 'grim occasion' rather than hopefulness.[5]

Most of the Secretariat's female employees were employed in clerical positions, despite the promise of equal opportunity. From there, Hazzard had an insider's view of the new organization—one that fell short of her expectations. Propelled by this experience, in the three decades after leaving her UN position she built a passionate and unique archive of the UN's misfeasance. She showed how it was not fulfilling

[1] Jan Garrett, 'The Transits of Hazzard (Interview)' (1984) 96 Look and Listen 36, 38, hereafter Garrett, 'Transits'.

[2] *Charter of the United Nations* (1945) 1 UNTS XVI art 8, hereafter *UN Charter*.

[3] The fictitious Edith Campbell Berry is the main protagonist in Frank Moorhouse's trilogy on the League of Nations: *Grand Days* (Pan Macmillan 1993); *Dark Palace* (Random House 2000); and *Cold Light* (Random House 2011).

[4] Nan Robertson, 'Lonely Crusader Battles Sexism She Sees in U.N.' *New York Times* (3 February 1976), hereafter Robertson, 'Lonely Crusader'.

[5] Shirley Hazzard, 'Reflections I: Breaking the Faith' *New Yorker* (29 September 1989) 63, 72, hereafter Hazzard, 'Reflections I'.

Dianne Otto, *Fearless Speech* In: *Portraits of Women in International Law.* Edited by: Immi Tallgren, Oxford University Press.
 DOI: 10.1093/oso/9780198868453.003.0043

Figure 43.1 Shirley Hazzard at her apartment in New York 2003.E2.
Source: © Nancy Crampton.

its responsibilities under the UN Charter and the Universal Declaration of Human Rights. She sought to expose the UN's lack of impartiality from parochial state interests, its commitment to Western supremacy and the resulting failure to act in the face of widespread human rights abuses and Cold War armed conflicts.

Hazzard lived in New York from 1951 and her writing on the UN was published by iconic New York mastheads, including the *New Republic*, *New Yorker*, and *New York Times*.[6] Her depiction of the UN's demise begins with the secret agreement in 1949, between the United States Administration and the UN's first Secretary-General, Trygve Lie. As she argues, this agreement compromised the independence of UN staff and, almost from the start, meant the organization would never be able to live up to its ideals. A collection of her satirical short stories about 'the Organization' (patently modelled on the UN Secretariat) was published in 1967.[7] This collection was followed in 1973 by her first monograph on the UN, *Defeat of an Ideal: A Study of the Self-Destruction*

[6] Many of these articles can be found in Brigitta Olubas (ed), *We Need Silence to Find Out What We Think: Selected Essays by Shirley Hazzard* (Columbia University Press 2016).

[7] Shirley Hazzard, *People in Glass Houses* (Macmillan 1967), hereafter Hazzard, *Glass Houses*.

of the United Nations.[8] Hazzard's harshest and most sustained criticism is reserved for the appointment (and later reappointment) of Kurt Waldheim as the fourth Secretary-General. She was one of the first to break news of his Nazi past in 1980.[9] A decade later, she published a damning monograph on the affair, *Countenance of Truth: The United Nations and the Waldheim Case*.[10] Hazzard's final UN writing appeared in the *New Republic* in 1992. She was still calling for reform, or rather, for starting all over again.[11] She passed away in 2016 in New York, the city that tested, but never defeated, her fiery critical optimism.

Hazzard is most well-known for her novels, notably *The Transit of Venus*[12] and *The Great Fire*.[13] Yet, I focus here on her critique of the UN and how it was received by international legal scholars, UN officials, and the general public at the time. As she explained in one interview, she felt she had an obligation to speak out in order to see that the public became informed and engaged.[14] Her writing is about the UN during the Cold War years, and her 'cosmopolitan humanism'[15] needs to be read and understood in this context. Nonetheless, I suggest that her fearless assessment of the UN's failures laid some of the groundwork for feminist and other critiques of international law that emerged in the post-Cold War era: first, by insisting that the 'private' UN institutional culture and practices helped to shape its 'public' politics and engagements and, second, by refusing to be silenced by the charge that publicly exposing the organization's failings would play into the hands of its naysayers and opponents. Even so, international legal scholars have rarely referred to her work, not even those concerned with the legal histories and geographies of international organizations.

'The Transit of Shirley Hazzard'

The Second World War presented new opportunities for Hazzard's father. In turn, these opened the world of international politics, as well as the vicissitudes of love, for Hazzard herself.[16] After the war, Reginald Hazzard was appointed Australia's Trade Commissioner in Hong Kong,[17] where he relocated with Hazzard, her mother and her older sister in 1947. At this point, the nearly sixteen-year-old Hazzard left school. *En route* the ship stopped at the port of Hiroshima, Kure, where she witnessed the

[8] Shirley Hazzard, *Defeat of an Ideal: A Study of the Self-Destruction of the United Nations* (Macmillan 1973), hereafter Hazzard, *Defeat of an Ideal*.

[9] Shirley Hazzard, 'The League of Frightened Men: Why the UN Is So Useless' *New Republic* (19 January 1980) 17, hereafter Hazzard, 'Frightened Men'.

[10] Shirley Hazzard, *Countenance of Truth: The United Nations and the Waldheim Case* (Viking 1990), hereafter Hazzard, *Countenance of Truth*.

[11] Shirley Hazzard, 'System Failure: The Trouble with the UN' *New Republic* (21 September 1992).

[12] Shirley Hazzard, *The Transit of Venus* (Macmillan 1980).

[13] Shirley Hazzard, *The Great Fire* (Farrar, Straus and Giroux 2003).

[14] Robertson, 'Lonely Crusader' (n 5).

[15] Brigitta Olubas, *Shirley Hazzard: Literary Expatriate and Cosmopolitan Humanist* (Cambria Press 2012), hereafter Olubas, 'Shirley Hazzard'.

[16] Jan McGuinness, 'The Transit of Shirley Hazzard' in Brigitta Olubas (ed), *Shirley Hazzard: New Critical Essays* (Sydney University Press 2014) 123, hereafter McGuinness, 'Transit'.

[17] ibid 126.

devastation of the atomic bomb. Many years later, Hazzard set *The Great Fire* in the occupied Kure of 1947. In 1951, Hazzard's father was relocated to New York, which really set the course for her future. Through her father's connections, she got a job at the UN Secretariat in 1952. Jan McGuinness, who interviewed Hazzard many years later, writes: '[t]he secretarial job was "in the dungeons", according to Shirley, unimportant and dull, and the new and inspiring organisation appeared to be anything but for those who toiled within'.[18] Further, Hazzard told the *Australian Women's Weekly* in 1975 that this was 'where she learned about male chauvinism first-hand'.[19]

Thankfully for Hazzard, the Suez crisis in 1956 led to the establishment of a UN peacekeeping supply base in Naples where she was posted as a typist for twelve months. While she continued her Secretariat service in all its monotony and tedium, she fell in love with Naples and its surrounds, as she recounts in her novel *The Bay of Noon*.[20] After returning to New York Hazzard sent a short story to the *New Yorker*, 'not expecting to succeed'.[21] Yet her writing was warmly received and the first of many of her short stories was published in 1961.[22] This led to an agreement giving the magazine the first option on her output and secured her a resident's visa. The agreement enabled her to resign from her UN job where she felt she was 'steadily dying'.[23]

In 1963 Hazzard married American Francis Steegmuller, a member of New York's liberal intellectual and arts community and well-known author and French translator. Hazzard's marriage considerably widened her circle of friends and acquaintances, including people from higher ranks of the UN Secretariat which she said made her 'even more disillusioned'.[24] Her closest friends included Muriel Spark, Graham Greene, WH Auden, and Igor Stravinsky. Martin Stannard observes that the '"Steegs" [...] knew everyone'.[25] This milieu, and her growing international reputation as a literary figure, enabled Hazzard to reflect on her years at the UN from a position of relative power, although her views were always shaped by her experience as a poorly paid and undervalued typist. These 'two faces' of Hazzard can be traced through all of her UN-related writing.

'The League of Frightened Men'

Hazzard vividly conveys the substance of her critique of the UN in the title of the article in which she exposes Waldheim's Nazi affiliations, published in the New Republic in 1980.[26] She excoriates a succession of UN Secretaries-General, their advisers and assistants, for remaining silent in the face of a long list of catastrophic wars and human rights abuses. On her list were silences about the brutalities of the Shah's regime in Iran; 'about American ravages in Asia, and about Pol Pot; about genocide in Biafra

18 ibid 129.
19 ibid.
20 Shirley Hazzard, *The Bay of Noon* (Little, Brown and Co 1970).
21 McGuinness, 'Transit' (n) 131.
22 Shirley Hazzard, 'Woollahra Road' *New Yorker* (8 April 1961) 58.
23 Garrett, 'Transits' (n 1) 39.
24 Robertson, 'Lonely Crusader' (n 5).
25 Martin Stannard, 'Meeting Shirley Hazzard' in Brigitta Olubas (ed), *Shirley Hazzard: New Critical Essays* (Sydney University Press 2014) 137, 143.
26 Hazzard, 'Frightened Men' (n 9).

and Indonesia, starvation in Ethiopia, torture in Greece, Chile, Argentina, Guatemala, the Philippines, and Uganda; about punitive mutilation in Saudi Arabia, and about the vast prison network of the Soviet Union'.[27] Hazzard attributes these silences to the 1949 secret agreement. Other states had also installed their nominees in 'virtually all significant, and in many insignificant, U.N. posts [. .] some of whom, devoid of qualifications, were unwanted in their homelands for political motives, while still others arrived trailing rumours of incompetence or scandal'.[28] As she did not find herself subject to these vetting procedures, it can be surmised that the 'men' did not expect to be 'frightened' by a gritty Australian typist.

In the thirty years since leaving her UN job in 1961, Hazzard wrote frequently of the continuing lack of impartiality, deploring the failure to remedy the situation and condemning the absence of press interest. For Hazzard, this was a disastrous capitulation to state interests, especially those of the US, which occurred despite the UN Charter containing stronger provisions on the independence of international civil servants than those in the Covenant of the League of Nations.[29] Like other employees, Hazzard would have sworn to work 'with the interests of the United Nations only in view' and not take instructions 'from any government or other authority external to the Organization'.[30]

No doubt, the hollowness of this pledge quickly became apparent as the upheavals and injustices of the McCarthy anti-communist purges which, facilitated by the secret agreement, were extended to UN staff. Hazzard later recounted that this meant that 'virtually every free-thinking employee in [the Secretariat's] senior and intermediate grades' was 'expelled, repelled, persecuted, intimidated, or alienated'.[31] At least forty United States nationals were dismissed between 1951 and 1953,[32] eleven of whom were eventually awarded substantial compensation by the (independent) UN Administrative Tribunal, chaired by the French public international law expert Suzanne Bastid.[33] American fury at this decision led to the General Assembly requesting an Advisory Opinion from the International Court of Justice (ICJ) as to whether the UN had any grounds to refuse to pay the compensation awarded. The ICJ's Opinion, delivered in 1954, upheld the ruling of the Tribunal[34] and the payments were made in 1955. Yet, this important acknowledgment of the unjust treatment of staff was not the end of the matter for Hazzard. The secret agreement was confirmed by second Secretary-General Dag Hammarskjöld 'with superficial adjustments',[35] and had continuing corrosive effects on the employment practices of the UN. Scathingly, Hazzard observes that it was only rescinded in 1986 because private United States citizens challenged these practices in domestic courts.[36]

[27] ibid 20.
[28] Hazzard, *Countenance of Truth* (n 10) 27.
[29] UN Charter, arts 100(1) and 101(3).
[30] Philip C Jessup, 'The International Civil Servant and His Loyalties' (1955) 9(2) Journal of International Affairs 55, 57.
[31] ibid 18.
[32] Hazzard, 'Reflections I' (n 5) 66.
[33] See Immi Tallgren and Antoine Buchet, 'Suzanne Bastid: The First of the "Firsts"', in this volume.
[34] Effects of Awards of Compensation Made by the United Nations Administrative Tribunal (Advisory Opinion) [1954] ICJ Rep 47.
[35] Hazzard, 'Reflections I' (n 5) 74.
[36] ibid.

Hazzard's conviction was that the UN's governmental or 'public' sphere was intimately connected to its institutional or 'private' life. This insight would later be reflected in feminist critiques of the public/private distinction structurally embedded in international law.[37] As she explains in *Defeat of an Ideal*, her purpose was 'to trace a more intricate relation between the two [spheres] than has yet been suggested, and to depict a set of reciprocal, and mutually destructive, repercussions'.[38] Consequently, in Hazzard's analysis, it was the compromised and enfeebled state of the Secretariat that enabled the election of Waldheim as Secretary-General over stronger candidates in late 1971. She argues that by then UN senior officers, with the Secretary-General at the pinnacle, were 'chosen for their very lack of moral courage and independent mind'—a method that reached its 'consummate expression' in the selection of Waldheim.[39] Hazzard makes a compelling case that Western governments knew of Waldheim's Nazi past, including his criminal war record in the Balkans, but kept it to themselves, most probably to ensure his compliance.[40] It was her 1980 article in the *New Republic* that prompted the first of Waldheim's many dishonest denials.[41] She described his UN tenure as 'dense with irreproachable statements on global peril, and punctuated by referrals of critical questions to governmental bodies whose inaction was assured'.[42] It was not until after Waldheim had left the UN that the press began to seriously investigate and expose his past. In 1987, he was finally placed on the United States Watch List of undesirable aliens prevented from entering the country.[43] Though vindicating Hazzard's long campaign of exposure, it was too little too late.

In addition to her determination to draw attention to the UN's public betrayal of its aims and purposes, the other 'face' of Hazzard set about exposing the compounding internal issues of low pay, bureaucratic devaluing, and lack of advancement opportunities for Secretariat clerical staff. Her advocacy never wavered. Indeed, in 1976, Hazzard described the UN's treatment of its female employees as the '"domestics" of the place […] frozen in menial jobs'.[44] She told *New York Times* reporter Nan Robertson that the just-ended International Women's Year was 'the prefect expression of the unauthenticity of the U.N. Secretariat, the supposed custodian of world standards while it discriminates appallingly [against its own female employees]'.[45] In 1977, she joined a panel of speakers, including Bella Abzug and Margaret Meade, to address a packed UN meeting room to mark International Women's Day. She received enthusiastic applause when she deplored the relegation of women in the UN to the 'lower' jobs and called the organization a 'temple of discrimination'.[46]

Hazzard's satirical short stories about 'the Organization' bear a resemblance to Kafka's illusory promise of 'justice'. Her characters struggle to breathe in the stifling

[37] See Hilary Charlesworth and Christine Chinkin, *The Boundaries of International Law: A Feminist Analysis* (Manchester University Press 2000).
[38] Hazzard, *Defeat of an Ideal* (n 8) xii.
[39] Hazzard, 'Frightened Men' (n 9) 18.
[40] Hazzard, *Countenance of Truth* (n 10) 58–65.
[41] Olubas, *Shirley Hazzard* (n 15) 39.
[42] Hazzard, *Countenance of Truth* (n 10) 78.
[43] Hazzard, 'Reflections I' (n 5) 92.
[44] Robertson, 'Lonely Crusader' (n 5).
[45] ibid.
[46] Kathleen Teltsch, 'U.N. Aides Use Women's Day to Protest on Jobs' *The New York Times* (9 March 1977).

bureaucratic culture that smothers all talent and initiative, and methodically defeats idealism. Like Swoboda, for example, who as a stateless person in Europe after the Second World War had initially felt himself fortunate to be employed by the Organization as a clerk, but more than twenty years later, still employed at the same rank and still treated condescendingly by his supervisor, finds himself doubting his luck.[47] Another story refers to the work of the Department of Aid to the Less Technically Oriented (DALTO) which conditions aid to countries that have admitted their 'backwardness' on the acceptance, for example, of an atomic reactor: 'Progress was a draught that must be drained to the last bitter drop'.[48] As international legal scholar Guy Fiti Sinclair has said, it is worth considering assigning one of these stories for courses on international institutions.[49]

Friend or Foe of the UN? Responses to Hazzard's Critique

Hazzard's writings on the UN drew the attention of UN officials seeking to defend the UN, and international relations scholars largely dismissive of her 'idealism' and her polemical style. Her hope that her writings would inform the public and foster pressure to revive the UN's public interest goals was sadly never realized. In Robertson's view, *Defeat of an Ideal* 'did not sell very well' because 'the subject bores many people'.[50] The conclusion offered by Hazzard's biographer, Brigitta Olubas, is that while Hazzard's UN commentary was welcomed by some UN employees at the time, it 'had scant effect on the institution itself or on public debate around it'.[51] That Hazzard continued her quest, despite these attacks, speaks loudly of her courage and determination to expose the many abuses of power that threatened internationalism and its post-War institutions.

Among the UN officials who responded to Hazzard's work was Brian Urquhart, former Undersecretary-General for Political Affairs (1971–1985). In 1990, in the *New York Review of Books*, he accused her of being 'remarkably careless with facts' and of writing 'with a rage and a self-righteousness that efface historical accuracy and any sense of proportion', referencing the impending publication of *Countenance of Truth*.[52] He decried her lack of understanding of the 'extraordinary atmosphere of panic' of the McCarthy period and defended Waldheim by listing some of his positive contributions. He reproached Hazzard for wanting to 'sink' the UN while he had 'tried to make it work better'. Urquhart thus adopted an attitude that was familiar to Hazzard, which she described as 'a form of moral blackmail' whereby critics are routinely 'discredited

[47] Shirley Hazzard, 'Nothing in Excess' in Hazzard, *Glass Houses* (n 7) 9.

[48] Shirley Hazzard, 'The Story of Miss Sadie Graine' in ibid 84, 103.

[49] Guy Fiti Sinclair, 'Favourite Readings 2018: The Passage of Time' EJIL: TALK! 19 December 2018 <https://www.ejiltalk.org/favourite-readings-2018-guy/> accessed 17 February 2021, many thanks to Jan Klabbers for this reference.

[50] Robertson, 'Lonely Crusader' (n 5).

[51] Brigitta Olubas, 'What Would Shirley Hazzard Do? Paris Review (30 September 2020) <https://www.theparisreview.org/blog/2020/09/30/what-would-shirley-hazzard-do/> accessed 17 February 2021.

[52] Brian Urquhart, 'The United Nations and Its Discontents' 27(5) *New York Review of Books* (15 March 1990); Shirley Hazzard and Brian Urquhart, '"The UN and its Discontents": An Exchange' 37(7) *New York Review of Books* (26 April 1990).

as an enemy of world peace'.[53] It is testament to her steely determination, fostered perhaps in the 'dungeons' of the Secretariat, that she defended herself against such attacks.

Other UN officials responded to Hazzard's opinion pieces in a similar vein. They include Genichi Akatani (Assistant Secretary-General, Office of Public Information) who dismissed her UN criticisms as reliant on 'a series of false assumptions and basic errors of fact',[54] and Andre Lewin (Spokesman of the UN Secretary-General) who accused her of starting 'a new round of her unfounded offensive' against Waldheim.[55] Hazzard's rejoinders always defended the 'truth' of her accounts.[56] In some academic circles, critics have responded similarly. One reviewer described *Defeat of an Ideal* as lacking 'the organization, care in analysis, or weighing of possible reforms that would make its stark conclusion—i.e. to start all over again-persuasive'.[57] Reviewers also dismissed *Countenance of Truth* as 'a diatribe so shrill that it loses credibility even if many of its observations may be fundamentally correct',[58] and a 'vitriolic and perhaps exaggerated account of the problems of the Secretariat'.[59] The misogyny that seeps into some of these reviews is reminiscent of the treatment Hazzard experienced as a UN employee.

Yet others were more positive. Jean Siotis' 1975 review of several books about the UN included *Defeat of an Ideal*, which he described as a 'well written polemical piece of a kind that is seriously lacking in the literature on the UN'.[60] He observed that the book 'may be judged by some as too passionate, but in the face of the hypocrisy which characterizes so many pronouncements about the international civil service, such passion is not altogether unjustified'.[61] In 1974, a reviewer for the *Harvard Journal of International Law* cited *Defeat of an Ideal* approvingly, as an example of the 'recent emergence of voices which urge a complete restructuring of the United Nations, or its replacement by a truly effective world government organization'.[62] Why such positive responses to Hazzard's work were in the minority raises many questions—about transparency, accountability, equality, power, and who is authorized to speak. These questions remain central to the work of international lawyers today.

Among the very few international lawyers mentioned in Hazzard's work is Oscar Schachter, who held a succession of key UN legal posts for two decades from 1946. Hazzard is critical of Schachter's acquiescent approach to the McCarthy investigations of UN staff, quoting him thanking the McCarran Committee (Senate Internal Security Subcommittee) for its 'spirit of complete fairness'.[63] I am not aware of any direct communications between Schachter and Hazzard. Still, he explained over three decades later, in a UN Oral History Project interview, that 'one hoped that by

53 Shirley Hazzard, 'A Call for U.N. Reform' *The New York Times* (24 October 1970).
54 Genichi Akatani, 'Facts About the U.N.' in Letters to the Editor *The New York Times* (5 March 1974).
55 Andre Lewin, 'Hazzard Again' in Letters to the Editor *The New York Times* (6 October 1974).
56 See eg Hazzard's reply to Lewin in Letters to the Editor *The New York Times* (6 October 1974).
57 'Recent Books on International Relations' (1973) 51(3) Foreign Affairs (April 1973) 629.
58 Andrew J Pierre, 'Recent Books on International Relations' (1990) 69(3) Foreign Affairs 170.
59 Harold K Jacobson, 'The United Nations System in the Nineties: Opportunities and Challenges' (1989) 45 International Journal 765 fn 16.
60 Jean Siotis, 'Insights into International Service' (1975) 27(2) World Politics 298, 301.
61 ibid 302.
62 'Book Reviews' (1974) 15(1) Harvard International Law Journal 182, 199.
63 Hazzard, 'Reflections: I' (n 5) 72.

bending, one would save people and save the institution.'[64] Schachter also expressed his frustration with Lie, describing his conduct at the time of the United States investigations of personnel as 'duplicitous'.[65] While making it clear that he was an admirer of Hammarskjöld, Schachter criticized his treatment of staff as well. He stated that 'Hammarskjöld was not a great defender of the staff and he went after people and in some cases, in my judgment quite unfairly.'[66] These recollections confirm Hazzard's 'truth'.

In the post-Cold War period, attention has slowly turned to examining international organizations more closely. Jan Klabbers observes that they 'started to lose some of their glamour' from the mid-1980s whereas earlier generations had considered them to be 'inherently good and benign'[67] (despite Hazzard's labours). Attention has also turned to the responsibility of the UN for its internal human rights violations. One of the few contemporary international legal scholars who has cited Hazzard is Guglielmo Verdirame. He points to Hazzard's reference to Lie's warning that 'Everything you say will be used against this organization by the enemies of the United Nations.'[68] This silencing strategy continues to linger in the post-Cold War era. Examples thereof can be found in the denial of sexual abuse by UN peacekeeping personnel to avoid 'bringing the UN into disrepute', and the deflection of criticism of international criminal tribunals by accusing critics of 'protecting perpetrators of genocide'.

Hazzard's Legacy

While Hazzard's polemical style goes against the grain of more dispassionate scholarly tradition, her purpose was to draw public attention to the institutional or 'private life' of the UN, which, unlike the 'much chronicled political developments', was not widely known about.[69] Her hope was that the 'peoples of the world' would insist on change once they were informed. Many contemporary international legal scholars share Hazzard's concern about the dominance of states and her belief in the importance of public engagement and accountability. Hazzard's dismay at the UN's allegiance to powerful and wealthy states rather than to the international public interest continues to resonate. The progeny of the 'active humanitarianism'[70] that Hazzard saw emerging from the vacuum created by UN inaction on human rights abuses and the use of force has flourished. Further, the lack of accountability fostered by the public/private distinction has been thoroughly exposed by feminist international lawyers.

[64] United Nations Oral History Project, 'Interview with Oscar Schachter by William Powell' (11 October 1985) ST/DPI/ORAL HISTORY(02)/S23, 29 <https://digitallibrary.un.org/record/477016?ln=e> (accessed 17 February 2021).
[65] ibid 23.
[66] ibid 30–31.
[67] Jan Klabbers, 'Theorising International Organizations' in Anne Orford and Florian Hoffman (eds), *The Oxford Handbook of the Theory of International Law* (OUP 2016) 618, 624.
[68] Guglielmo Verdirame, *The United Nations and Human Rights: Who Guards the Guardians?* (Cambridge University Press 2011) 63.
[69] Hazzard, *Defeat of an Ideal* (n 8) xii–xiii.
[70] Hazzard, 'Frightened Men' (n 9) 19.

Hazzard's discontent remained for the rest of her life which is preferable to the exile of Moorhouse's imagined Edith Campbell Berry, who returns to Canberra after the demise of the League of Nations, far away from anyone interested in building a better world. Hazzard's fearless idealism has bequeathed us ardent insights into the institutional failings of the UN during the Cold War years. She also teaches us to be attentive to the everyday operations of power—both private and public—and their interconnectedness. Paradoxically, the UN's mistreatment of one of its 'domestics' has given us a unique archive of its Cold War 'self-destruction', which should today be compulsory reading for all who remain hopeful about achieving international peace and universal enjoyment of human rights.

Epilogue

Exit through the Gift Shop

Hilary Charlesworth

A common instinct on leaving a gallery or museum is to head for the gift shop; indeed, such businesses are often located at the exit precisely to exploit this tendency. Here we hope to find images, catalogues, or objects that capture some of the pleasures and colours of the exhibition—to send to others or to retain on desks or in cupboards for later reliving the experience. I am always a little abashed by my own penchant for commercializing an encounter with a gallery so soon after experiencing it, although I treasure the items from gallery gift shops that recall the visits.

What gifts feature as the viewer leaves this gallery of portraits of women in international law? First, the gallery offers a panoply of stories about the lives of women from all over the globe. The names of a few of the women represented here may be familiar to international lawyers, but most are not. I found in these pages many extraordinary characters who I had never encountered before. The authors do not sugar-coat the portraits, acknowledging the contradictions and tensions in the positions their subjects took, on occasion their authoritarian politics or racist views. The group portraits are particularly moving, full of unsung visionaries and tireless workers otherwise submerged in a collective.

What emerges is the profound contribution of these women to shaping ideas about international law as well as the radical nature of their thought. Consider Olympe de Gouges's Declaration on the Rights of Women and the Female Citizen in 1793, Anna Julia Cooper's articulation of the idea of intersectional discrimination and racial capitalism over a century ago, Thomas Baty's dedication to the abolition of distinctions based on gender in all fields, including international law, Rosa Luxemburg's identification of the impact of capitalism and imperialism on the environment in the early twentieth century, Paulina Luisi's claim that international organizations should control the distribution of resources and arms production, Simone Weil's critique of the European rights tradition, Felice Morgenstern's development of the principle of legality in international organizations, Avabai Wadia's commitment to women's reproductive rights, Ester Boserup's analysis of the links between productive and reproductive labour, Elizabeth Mann Borghese's ecological relational thinking, Yayori Matsui's insistence on the recognition of sexual violence by the Japanese Imperial Army during the Second World War. Many of these women's portraits manifest their concern with poverty and social justice long before these issues emerged as relevant to international law. At the same time, the collection chronicles the lack of recognition of their contributions by their contemporaries and later historians of ideas.

Hilary Charlesworth, *Epilogue* In: *Portraits of Women in International Law.* Edited by: Immi Tallgren, Oxford University Press.
 DOI: 10.1093/oso/9780198868453.003.0044

In some cases, women's contributions have been viewed through a gendered lens. Bertha von Suttner, for example, was celebrated more for her social skills and capacities for diplomacy and mediation than for her legal capacities. Other examples of gendered assessment include a contemporary's reference to Rosa Luxemburg's 'wretched female's squirt of poison', de Gaulle's dismissal of Simone Weil as '*une folle*', a dislike of Marguerite Frick-Cramer within the International Committee of the Red Cross on the basis of her outspoken nature, and the dismissal of Shirley Hazzard's criticism of Kurt Waldheim's war record on the basis that it was emotional and intemperate.

Second, the chapters give us detail, particularly personal, about even the well-known names. Many came from prosperous backgrounds; a number were deeply religious; some published novels as well as international legal writings. We learn that they were noted for their kindness (Joyce Gutteridge, Paula Escarameia), or a shy and sometimes spiky nature (Felice Morgenstern) or for disregard for conventional sexual mores (Aleksandra Kollontai, Lea Meriggi). Optimism about the possibilities of international law to achieve social and economic justice also marks the contributions of many of the subjects of these portraits.

Many women seem to have accepted the skewed distribution of professional advantage in the field of international law and simply worked harder and longer than their male contemporaries. Some were interested in women's rights in their professional work, and became activists on this issue, such as Helena Halperin-Ginsburg. Many, however, were immersed in mainstream fields of international law. Indeed, we learn about the diffidence of a number of these women towards the feminist movement, perhaps because it was seen as leftist or militant. On the other hand, Aleksandra Kollontai rejected feminism as too timid, ignoring the significance of class and accommodating women in a system of fundamentally unequal economic and social structures. Inji Aflatoun raised parallel concerns in a colonial context, insisting that invocation of women's human rights was useful only a tactic of the oppressed, rather than constituting a goal in itself.

Relationships with men are a critical part of these stories. This is most obvious in the case of Maria van Reigersberch who seems to have devoted all her considerable acumen and energy to sustaining Hugo Grotius and ensuring his legacy after his death. Jawaharlal Nehru overshadowed the significant contributions of his sister, Vijayalakshmi Pandit, in galvanizing the Third World as a force in international institutions. Occasionally men supported the portrayed women financially, allowing them to work on questions relating to international law. In some cases, the status of grandfathers, fathers, brothers, or husbands gave the women international lawyers depicted here admission to international legal circles, although only ever at the margins. In other cases, such as that of Alva Myrdal, husbands were credited with the fruits of a woman's intellectual vitality and originality, while also relying on the domestic labour of the woman in caring for children and the household. Despite her brilliance, Suzanne Bastid was sometimes overshadowed as 'only' a daughter of a famous international lawyer and the wife of a notable politician of the resistance.

A third gift of this volume is as a showcase of a variety of feminist methodologies. The most discernible is that of locating women and their stories in the interstices of the international legal system, responding to the question 'where are the women?'. As Immi Tallgren has pointed out, women have not been absent from the international order, but they have been invisible.[1] This may be the result of being relegated to unpaid or anonymous work, or to the lack of access to patrons who can smooth the path to powerful networks or fragmentary archival resources. The portraits also highlight other feminist methods. For example, Kate Grady and Gina Heathcote warn of the risk that feminist involvement with international law may be confined to areas that do not threaten the current order. They contrast Jane Addams's attention to plural subjectivities through her work with Black and immigrant communities in the United States and her challenges to heteronormativity a century ago. Addams's ability to envision the international sphere as unbounded by sovereign states remains radical. Another feminist method, described in the portrait of Inji Aflatoun, is the use of art and imagery as an activist technique.

Finally, a major gift of this exhibition of portraits is to model an approach to the absence of women in international legal histories. Immi Tallgren's curation of an exhibition of portraits to sit alongside the traditional male gallery of 'greats', along with Karen Knop's meditation on the metaphor's potential and ironies, emphasizes the significance of who commissions portraits, who frames them, and who hangs them. This recalls Linda Nochlin's famous essay, written in 1971, 'Why Have There Been No Great Women Artists?'[2] Nochlin challenged the standard account of 'great artists' as based on the achievements of extraordinarily gifted individuals, 'bearing within his person since birth a mysterious essence, rather like the golden nugget in Mrs. Grass's chicken soup, called Genius or Talent'. She insisted that attention rather be paid to the 'total situation' of generating and assessing the quality of art. This includes the social context, institutional structure, and systems of patronage that make up the art world: 'The fault ... lies not in our [women's] stars, our hormones, our menstrual cycles, or our empty internal spaces, but in our institutions and our education—education understood to include everything that happens to us from the moment we enter this world of meaningful symbols, signs and signals'. Nochlin observed that '[t]hose who have privileges invariably hold on to them, and hold tight'.

> Thus the question of women's equality—in art as in any other realm—devolves not upon the relative benevolence or ill-will of individual men, nor the self-confidence or abjectness of individual women, but rather on the very nature of our institutional structures themselves and the view of reality which they impose on the human beings that are part of them. As John Stuart Mill pointed out more than a century ago: 'Everything which is usual appears natural'.... Most men, despite lip-service to equality, are reluctant to give up this 'natural' order of things in which their advantages are so great.

This rich collection effectively illustrates Nochlin's observations in the field of international law. The portrait gallery displays some of the structures and systems of the

[1] Immi Tallgren, 'Absent or Invisible? "Women" Intellectuals and Professionals at the Dawn of a Discipline' in Frédéric Mégret and Immi Tallgren (eds), *The Dawn of a Discipline: International Criminal Justice and its Early Exponents* (Cambridge University Press 2020) 381.

[2] Originally published in *ArtNews* January 1971. A later version appeared in *ArtNews* 30 May 2015, available at <https://www.artnews.com/art-news/retrospective/why-have-there-been-no-great-women-artists-4201/>.

world of international law and the processes by which value is conferred. 'Great' international lawyers are not born with a burning talent but emerge from a highly specific context. They are clever students who are able to focus on their studies, then on their professional work, almost invariably with the support of a parent or a partner who takes on all domestic responsibilities. They quickly find encouraging male mentors who smooth their paths, introducing them to influential communities and inducting them into prestigious organizations that reinforce the aura of success. The lives of the 'greats' cast a wide shadow over other types of lives. But we can see in these portraits that the careers of women whose qualifications and experience equal, or exceed, those of successful male contemporaries, always attract much less recognition. Examples here include Sarah Wambaugh, Felice Morgenstern, Marjorie Whiteman, Joyce Gutteridge, Suzanne Bastid, and Marie Theres Fögen. This temporary exhibition highlights some of the structures of the world of international law that restrict women's progress within it.

The array of stories in this volume expands the idea of being an international lawyer and of the measures of 'greatness'. A number of the women portrayed here have no formal qualifications in international law but have contributed to its fabric in significant ways. The portraits also extend the elements of the world of international law to include community organizing, activism, as well as the production of art and fiction, offering an intriguing account of the everyday life of international law. Their gift is the courage to question the content and quality of the ubiquitous galleries of great male international lawyers.

Index

For the benefit of digital users, indexed terms that span two pages (e.g., 52–53) may, on occasion, appear on only one of those pages.